THE ANNALS OF SAN FRANCISCO

THE
ANNALS OF SAN FRANCISCO

by

FRANK SOULÉ,
JOHN H. GIHON, M.D.,
and JAMES NISBET

**THE FIRST PAPERBACK EDITION
OF THE WORK ORIGINALLY PUBLISHED IN 1855**

---

with Introduction
by **RICHARD H. DILLON**

and Index
by **CHARLES H. GOEHRING**

BERKELEY HILLS BOOKS
BERKELEY, CALIFORNIA
1999

The Annals of San Francisco
By Frank Soulé, John H. Gihon, and James Nisbet
with Introduction by Richard Dillon
and index by Charles Goehring

Published by
Berkeley Hills Books
P.O. Box 9877
Berkeley California 94709

ISBN 1-893163-08-3

Library of Congress Cataloging-in-Publication Data
available upon request.

INTRODUCTION

FRANKLIN WALKER POINTED OUT in his classic study, *San Francisco's Literary Frontier*, that *The Annals of San Francisco* has been the sourcebook for so many writers of Californiana that modern concepts of early San Francisco life—from gargantuan Norwegian rats to petite Cantonese prostitutes—are based almost entirely on the work of the three compilers of the volume, Frank Soulé, James Nisbet, and John Gihon.

Thus, *The Annals of San Francisco* is not only the best single book ever written on the City, as Walker avers, but has also proved itself to be the most influential book ever set in type to concern itself with San Francisco. In short, the book, over the long haul, has been as important to the student of San Franciscana as the staggering array of sheepskin-bound volumes of H. H. Bancroft has been to the amateur of Californiana in general.

The knowledgeable Los Angeleños who in 1945 totted up the *Zamorano 80* bibliography—a list of what they supposed to be the 80 most significant books on California history to that date—considered the *Annals* "a necessary reference book" on the city up to the mid-1850s and pointed out its iconographic value as well. But whereas the *Zamorano 80* was guilty of understatement, Gary Kurutz in his exemplary bibliography, *The California Gold Rush* (1997), cited its broader, "extra-municipal" value. He noted that the *Annals* not only offered an outstanding narrative history, but also supplied much information on mining and its importance to the instant city. Remarkably, the *Annals* was not superseded as an account of the city's adolescence till A. L. Bancroft published John S. Hittell's (1878) *A History of the City of San Francisco*... Some might argue that the *Annals* was the most important book to issue from San Francisco before Henry George's *Progress and Poverty* of 1879.

None of the three writers who compiled the *Annals* was a professional historian, which is not surprising, in that a Herodotus was hard to find in 'Frisco, circa 1855. Soulé, preeminent in the editorial triumvirate, was a journalist and sometime politician; Nisbet was a Scots lawyer turned newspaperman, the protégé of Soulé; Gihon was a doctor with a consuming literary avocation.

Between 1849 and 1869, the year in which the closing of the gap between the roadbeds of the Central Pacific and Union Pacific Railroads put an end to San Francisco's splendid solitude, the City enjoyed a precocious and impressive literary growth, rendered all the more surprising by its isolation from all other cultural centers of the world. During the two decades, San Francisco rudely wrenched away from Cincinnati its slogan—"The Athens of the West"—and gave it real meaning. From its renaissance in 1848 San Francisco was peculiarly receptive to literature, art, and music and it has never lost that propensity. But a true historical phenomenon was the overnight sophistication of squalid Yerba Buena into metropolitan San Francisco, although the existence of wealth, population, opportunity, and leisure do much to explain it.

In the High Plains and the Southwest, the frontier crept slowly westward. But in California, the Gold Rush brought tens of thousands of rootless young men, rolling in like tumbleweeds in the path of a norther. Among such a large and heterogeneous mass of migrants, few of them the plodding agrarians of Appalachia or the Great Plains, there was bound to be a goodly number of educated and intellectually curious men. From this cultural cadre came such well-known writers as Mark Twain, Bret Harte, Ambrose Bierce, and Joaquin Miller, not to forget Ina Coolbrith, Charles Warren Stoddard, J. Ross Browne, Prentice Mulford, George H. Derby, and Henry George. But the literary circle of antebellum days in San Francisco was far wider; doctors dabbled in prose and lawyers scribbled poems betwixt torts. Perhaps the brothers Hittell—John S. and Theodore H.—personify best this literary life of the professional man in San Francisco, but Soulé, Nisbet, and Gihon are not far behind. A city living on champagne and oysters could well afford books, libraries, and writers, but it was incredible, still, that an urban upstart in California could brag in the mid-1850s that its newspapers rivaled those of London in both quantity and quality. This bit of Victorian brag is important, for most of San Francisco's earliest creative writers came from the ranks of the Fourth Estate.

If most of the writing of the 1850s was rather narrow-gauge literature, much of it was wide-gauge journalism. The *magnum opus* of this production was the *Annals*, destined to survive a century after the most ambitious column of the *Daily Alta California*, *Golden Era* or *Wide West* was dead and forgotten. Franklin Walker, rightly, stressed the 1860s over the prior decade because more of the writers' output transcended journalism and became true literature. This is to be expected: the Argonauts were young men, writers or not, and it took time for them to mature. But not only did they reach their creative peak in the Civil War decade but so, too, did the City, itself, mature to a point where the climate or ambience was most favorable for creativity and the background rich and colorful enough to encourage local history and literature.

All the more reason, then, to applaud the quality of the *Annals*, which was published in 1855, just seven years after San Francisco was a woebegone and somnolent village of forty score souls dozing on the shores of the bay. With Los Angeles a dusty cowtown beside an even dustier river (most of the year) and Portland and Seattle hardly hamlets as yet, San Francisco was the sole focus of economic, political and social life on the Coast as well as the unique literary and cultural center of post-Coloman California. The biography of San Francisco is, in fact, a reflection of life in the whole frontier that lay along the Pacific littoral. Hence, the importance of this book, a collector's item for a century and a decade and an historian's *vade mecum.* Yet the book, strangely, was neglected until 1966 saw its first reprinting, although the California Historical Society published Dorothy H. Huggins's "Continuation of the Annals of San Francisco, June 1, 1854 to December 31, 1855", in the *Quarterly* in 1936–38 and as a book in 1939. The "Continuation" was a sequel, of sorts, to the Society's Special Publication Number 10 of 1935. This was Charles Francis Griffin's *Index to the Annals of San Francisco*, prepared for the press of Lawton Kennedy by Douglas S. Watson, Chairman of the Publications Committee of the Society, and enriched by Joseph Gaer's SERA (i.e. WPA) Project index of the *Annals*.

The most interesting section of the *Annals* has proven to be the chronological survey of the years 1846–1854. This story, anecdotal and detailed, is a colorful social history of one of the most amazing cities of the world in its time of exuberant youth. Contemporaries of Soulé, Nisbet, and Gihon sometimes expressed disappointment in the *Annals*, expecting the newsmen to be Gibbon, Macaulay, and Motley reincarnate. But the quality of the book to which these critics were blind, and which has made it a favorite for almost three and a half generations of readers lucky enough to find a copy in bookshop or library, is its intimate acquaintance with the local scene and its sprightly style of narrative.

When the long-awaited *Annals* of San Francisco arrived at the desk of the *Daily Alta California* editor, he reported, on June 11, 1855, that it was a splendid-looking book. He did not try to review it on such short acquaintance but ventured that some of the woodcuts were correct and lifelike while others were somewhat rough. He also commented, "The book is written in a pleasant style and affords very agreeable reading. Of its historical accuracy we cannot express an opinion as yet but it must be a valuable book and one that every Californian ought to have." Predicting an immense sale, he congratulated the authors for writing a book "so creditable to themselves and to California".

A full review appeared in the *Daily Alta California* on June 21. The reviewer, who signed no name and left us no initial, thought that the book's statistics were meager and, thus, "as a book of history it amounts to little". He described the volume as more of a panorama of early San Francisco than a history *per se.* "It gives a glowing and vivid idea of the trials, disappointments, excitements and dangers of the California pioneers... It is an interesting book. It is pleasantly written and running over with incident and humor." In general, the reviewer gave the *Annals* a very good grade. "The authors of this work undertook if not a difficult, at least a dangerous, work. To write a correct and acceptable history of the times in which the chief actors are yet alive is next to an impossibility... [But] after reading it, a person is led to exclaim, 'O, for those rare old times again!' It is a book that every Californian ought to have for it will always be a pleasant thing to refer to and will be convenient for reference in regard to many important subjects."

Robert E. Cowan, the bibliographer, considered the *Annals* to be authoritative. Phil Townsend Hanna, Lawrence Clark Powell, and the other compilers of *Libros Californios* described it as extremely readable and informative on almost any fact of San Francisco life at mid-19th century and growing scarce as its merits became better-known to readers. Carl Wheat, in his *Books of the California Gold Rush*, found it to be one of ten titles appearing on four or more of sixteen lists of "most important" books which he studied. Nor did he mince words in describing it as the most important contemporary work on San Francisco of the post-gold discovery decade, and "a classic".

Soulé, Nisbet, and Gihon found a major publisher for their study in D. Appleton & Company of New York, probably because the firm maintained an office on Montgomery Street in San Francisco. The firm had done some books with which the three were undoubtedly familiar, too, such as *The Gold Seeker's Manual* of 1849. Appleton had just moved when they took the *Annals*. Their new headquarters was at 346–348 Broadway and editing and publishing chores were carried on in the deluxe upper stories while the ground floor served as a handsome retail bookshop. A reporter from *Gleason's Pictorial and Drawing Room*

Companion, who toured the new quarters on June 24, 1854 described them with awe: "You will find no such brilliant establishment for books among the famous houses in Oxford Street, Regent Street, or the Boulevards. The ceilings are supported by fourteen Corinthian columns and the ceiling and walls are painted in fresco... The book cases are of oak, and artistic effect has been studied in the interior decorations throughout."

From time to time, warnings have been sounded to alert readers to weaknesses of the book as a source. Critics are suspicious of the statistics in the book, the accuracy of certain breezy passages, and the history of events occurring long before the arrival of the compilers in California. Frank Soulé arrived on May 29, 1849, John Gihon on November 25th of that year. James Nisbet did not land in San Francisco until November 1852. But most collectors, librarians, and writers would echo Phil Townsend Hanna's opinion that the *Annals*, whatever its flaws, is not badly in error.

Partly responsible for the slight taint of unreliability which has attached itself to the *Annals* over the years was William Francis White, a writer who was rather unimaginative when he chose an alias, or *nom de plume*, taking "William Grey". He wrote *A Picture of Pioneer Times in California. Illustrated with Anecdotes and Stories Taken from Real Life*, printed for him by W. M. Hinton of 536 Clay Street, San Francisco, in 1881. Moralizing, chauvinistic, and pedantic in the best Victorian manner, it was slanted at California's younger readers and was, in fact, "respectfully dedicated to the boys and girls born on the Pacific Slope of pioneer parents".

The book is poorly written and virtually unreadable in its section devoted to three stories supposedly based on true incidents. They are "Ellen Haney, or the Wife's Disappointment", "Ada Allen, or, the Husband's Surprise", and "Minnie Wagner, or the Forged Note", all pure Victorian kitsch. But the initial part of the book has its interest: it is a curious diatribe against the *Annals* and its three compilers. White arrived in California on June 30, 1849 with his wife, on the *South Carolina*, and was one of only two witnesses to the marriage of Paul Geddes, alias Talbot H. Green, to the Widow Montgomery by Assistant Alcalde Frank Turk, that fall. Gratifyingly, White appears to have been a one-book man although at least one of his speeches ("An Address to the Workingmen of California") was printed in 1884 and is to be found in the clutches of Gary Kurutz in the California Section of the State Library in Sacramento.

In his first paragraph, without mentioning Soulé, Nisbet, and Gihon by name, White drew a bead on them, explaining that the object of his book was to expose and correct the misstatements of such itinerant lecturers and thoughtless or vicious writers, who delighted in misrepresenting the habits and characters of California's founders. White took up the crusade because, he said, the pioneers of '49 were passing away and he was afraid that soon none would be left to defend themselves against the slanderous charges of Soulé, Nisbet, and Gihon. And, he insisted of his own work, "In the picture I have drawn, I have sought to avoid claiming for the pioneers one virtue not fairly theirs; nor have I attempted to conceal their errors."

The critic, bewildered by the popularity of the *Annals*, tried to explain it away by saying that it appeared during a time of rush and excitement when no one had the time to attack it or expose it for what it was. White himself, after all, did not find time for twenty-five years to write a rebuttal of it. It did not occur to him that the particular charm of the book was its narrative style, which he denounced as "a style of bold, immoral, bravado, that was disgusting to all true Californians". Perhaps White's plans for a similar book in the 1850s had been thwarted by the appearance of the *Annals*. He certainly pouted in 1881 that "its publication...prevented any attempt by others to write a more faithful history of the times..." He tried to say that almost no one ever read the book, at the same time that he denounced it for its bad (and wide) influence. Lamely, he told his young readers that it was found in few collections but, unfortunately, writers and lecturers insisted on referring to it as authentic history.

Grudgingly, White admitted that the *Annals'* account of the discovery of gold at Sutter's Mill was accurate—because it followed Captain Sutter's own story. But he argued that its consequences were misrepresented in the volume, and the Argonauts vilely slandered. He denied that the men of '49 were wild, worthless, drunken rascals, for the most part, and that there were no decent women or families on the Coast. He denied that the years 1848–1852 constituted one great debauch. White was particularly (and puritanically) outraged by the *Annals'* claim (still true today), that San Franciscans admire the "style" of the City's wickedness and folly. White, alias Grey, insisted that most American emigrants during the Gold Rush, for all their wild hair and beards, were refined and educated men. He also insisted that, by New Year's Day, 1851, not one woman in twenty was of "the abandoned class".

A true picture of San Francisco's early years lies somewhere between the *Annals'* version and White's angry diatribes and whitewashes. The *Annals* must be criticized for its annoying and unfair jingoism and bigotry (all typically Victorian) which led it to state, flatly, that the California Indians were no better than beasts and that the state owed nothing to the Franciscan missionaries. Or witness its ruthless philosophy: "Apart from sickly sentimentalism and Rousseau-like theories, the sooner the aborigines of California are altogether weeded away quietly, the better for humanity. Yet the Fathers would retain them; then sweep away the Fathers, too." But the compilers did not always let prejudices get in the way of facts. Nisbet and friends drew heavily from the files of the *Californian*, *California Star*, *Herald*, *Alta*, and *Chronicle* whereas whitewasher White preferred to draw as much upon his spleen as his head or heart for inspiration.

An *Annals'* critic of larger caliber was Josiah Royce, distinguished University of California and Harvard professor and a major American philosopher of his day. He differed greatly from White in that he was more a moralizer than the latter, who was really an irrational, quarrelsome scold, jealous of the three coauthors at the same time that he felt superior to all of them as a local historian. Eight years after Hittell and thirty-one years after Soulé *et al.*, Josiah Royce contributed a volume to a series on the various states of the Union called *American Commonwealths*. The full and cumbersome title of Royce's work of 1886 was *California, From the Conquest of 1846 to the Second Vigilance Committee: a Study in Character.* Interestingly, its time frame was almost the same as that of the *Annals*; but its geographical scope, of course, was broader.

Probably, Royce saw the events of 1856 as a major, if ultimately ineffective, attempt to stop the civic excesses documented so distressingly in the *Annals*. His subtitle, *A Study in Character*, was important to him. He was interested in the city's psyche.

Royce was, himself, a product of California's frontier and, even in "exile" in Cambridge, always considered himself 100% Californian. But he was the opposite of most pragmatic Californians. He was an idealist who deplored—no, despised—the state's pervading mythology, a romanticized, sentimental nostalgia that passed for bona fide history. He considered it to be as false as Bret Harte's Dickensian tales of rough miners with hearts of solid gold. So he lumped the *Annals* with fiction because of all the wrong emphases (as he saw it) in the book, the dwelling on the colorful, the unruly and the illegal. The theme of his own book was the struggle of good to overcome evil in California.

Bibliographer Robert A. Cowan described Royce's book as one of the best authorities on the events of a single decade. Librarian Leslie Bliss of the Huntington Library, in a *Zamorano 80* entry, saw the professor's goal as not just to demonstrate the development of national character in the first years of American occupation of the Coast but to convey the process by which "a new and great community first came to a true consciousness of itself". But Bliss did not warn us of the judgmental Royce's hostility to the *Annals* and its description of San Francisco's rites-of-passage from adolescence to quick maturity.

Sounding more like a Back Bay Brahmin than an émigré Californian, the Harvard professor was even more critical of the philosophy of the *Annals* writers than of their facts. Royce was aghast at the uninhibited, reckless conduct of people in San Francisco in the 1850s, and very disappointed at the attitude of the journalists-turned-historians of 1855. He appeared to discern, between the lines, a sort of co-conspiratorial sympathizing with the wild behavior of early "S. F". It was more than just a pole apart from Philadelphia or staid Boston. Not even boisterous New York subscribed to the runaway revels of the Western city, seemingly so badly misnamed for a Catholic saint.

In condemning early San Francisco's morals, the critic virtually ignored the fact that elements of society had soon organized churches, schools, libraries, Christian newspapers, and a YMCA (1853) in direct reaction to the prevailing low moral tone of the community at large. But as an uphill fight for reformers, it was alpine. In 1853 the young city maintained 537 saloons, forty-six gambling houses, and uncounted brothels. It had grown up overnight from a nearly all-male, youthful and rowdy Gold Rush encampment of rude shelters made of old sails from abandoned brigs and barks aground in Yerba Buena Cove, their looted canvas jerry-built as tents.

William Tecumseh Sherman of Civil War fame and notoriety was a peaceful San Francisco banker at the time the *Annals* appeared. He sized up the local scene very well. To him, the very nature of the place begat speculation, extravagance, failures, and rascality. "Nobody feels a fixed interest here; all are ready to bolt as soon as a good chance offers. Everything is chance, everything is gambling." To which the popular writer, Prentice Mulford, added: "Five years was the longest period anyone expected to stay. Five years, at most, was to be given to rifling California of her treasures, and then that country was to be thrown aside like a used-up newspaper."

The gambling, hedonism, and lawlessness of the Gold Rush, as J. S. Holliday has pointed out, had long-lasting effects. Indeed, it created a libertarian culture that has dominated the city ever since, as a hangover from the days of the *Annals*. When San Francisco had to re-invent itself after the great seismic shocks and firestorm of 1906, it did not choose to become another Des

Moines or a second Boston, but a fair copy of the frolicking 'Frisco of 1855.

The professor could not accept the truism of Alice D. Wiley, writing in the *Golden Era*, that "Newspapers mirror the civilization of the communities of their time." He disbelieved much of the social history of the journalism-based account, such as the story of a church turned into a jail; of gamblers being treated like an aristocracy; and the (one) preacher said to have become a professional gambler. "Little dependence can be placed on such gossip," he wrote.

Royce then hit upon a syndrome to explain the source of much of what he saw as misinformation in the *Annals*. It had to be that real pioneers of yesteryear, who had not made fools of themselves, always (for some reason not given by Royce) yielded the literary floor to boastful, swaggering old windbags who, incoherently, bragged with equal earnestness of the piety and viciousness, the seriousness and gaiety, the brutality and peaceableness of early times. Like a practicing, if unlicensed, psychologist, the Harvard philosopher now coined a catchall term to explain definite facts detailed in the pages of the *Annals*. "Overexcitement" led to extravagant consequences, like nervous strain and dissipation.

As for the extent of the demoralization of local society, surely that was too extreme—something that the authors dreamed. "No such thing took place." Royce, to use a modern phrase, was deeply "in denial". Lamely and ludicrously, he continued on the slippery slope leading to downright foolishness. He grudgingly admitted that dissipation took place; but it was nocturnal, and occurred in an area of few police and even fewer street lamps!

In the case of the rare preacher, merchant or lawyer who actually "went to the devil" in gambling dens, he said that they simply stood out from run-of-the-(roulette)-wheel fools. No wonder that they were preserved in memory and exaggerated in number. But he still believed that when a few respectable men elbowed their way to a faro or monte table, the worse crime was that the decent public was silent before such misbehavior; that there was no (proper) condemnation from the better elements in an irreligious, *laissez faire* society. To him, evil was evil. Royce found more absurd than shocking the Annalists' treatment of whores as if they were leaders of society, although he knew how scarce were feminine '49ers, and that even "soiled doves" gave an almost completely masculine society much of its grace and gaiety.

Actually, the *Annals'* compilers were just being good reporters and pretty objective avocational historians. They were not editors or pamphleteers. They rationed their polemic and, instead, simply "told it as it was", vulgar warts and all. They were unwilling to become sundial-like historians, recording only the bright hours. And, in any case, they argued that no city ten times the size of theirs could print a list of men and institutions that had accomplished so much real good—and with so little cant and hypocrisy.

In sum, the authors of the *Annals* come off better than the renowned *philosophe* who, in lashing out at San Francisco and its trio of early historians, performed more like a censorious Victorian than a keen interpreter of the American scene. Much of the critical comment of the eminent academic in regard to the *Annals* was just silly. One wonders if a copy of William F. White's self-published diatribe of 1881 somehow fell into his hands and poisoned his mind toward the *Annals of San Francisco*.

The Honorable Frank Soulé, as he was addressed formally in letters to the State Capitol at Sacramento, if not always so grandly in letters to the editor in San Francisco, was a Down Easter, born in Freeport, Cumberland County, Maine, on January 17, 1810. Although he was intellectually inclined, it was said that he gravitated toward college and pedagogy not because he felt the "call" of arts and letters as much as because he was in too frail health to consider pursuing more vigorous careers. In any case, he received a good education and graduated in 1838 from Wesleyan College, Middletown, Connecticut, enjoying the honor of being chosen Class Poet.

After graduation the Maine-man went to the Deep South

and a position as instructor at Halsey Academy, Woodville, Mississippi. There he married a New Yorker, Mary Pierson Hand, and a son was born to them, Frank, Jr., in 1845. A few years of teaching persuaded Soulé that the classroom was not meant to be the proper arena of life for him. By the time his son was born, he had exchanged the schoolroom for the desk of editor-publisher of the *Woodville Republican*. In 1848, however, Soulé's wife died and, grief-stricken, he decided to abandon the scene of so many painful memories. Leaving the boy with his maternal grandmother, he set out for New Orleans and a new life. In the Crescent City Soulé obtained the post of editor of the *New Orleans Mercury*. However, the news of Jim Marshall's discovery of gold in Sutter's tailrace soon reached him and he chucked everything to make a weary five-month horseback trip to California via the Gila Trail.

Frank Soulé reached the Mother Lode at Sullivan's Diggins on or around Bastille Day, 1849. The camp, on Tuolumne County's Sullivan Creek, was named for its Irish founder, John Sullivan. The Irishman had discovered one of the richest gold deposits in the Sonora District there in 1848. Daniel B. Woods, in his *Sixteen Months at the Gold Diggings*, suggested the richness of the diggins about the time of Soulé's arrival. "A Dutchman followed a vein of gold down to a large rock, which continually became richer as he progressed. Aided by some friends, he succeeded in removing the rock and, in two hours time, took out forty pounds of the precious ore."

About a year after his arrival, Soulé decided that mining was not for him. He went to San Francisco to rejoin the Fourth Estate. He, or Nisbet, was really describing himself when he wrote in the *Annals*, "Newly-arriving men...brought with them from the East some knowledge of printing, of journalism, and of publication and...when tired of mining...turned to the newspapers in search of opportunities for swift returns on small investments." Soulé was fortunate enough to secure the post of Associate Editor of the *Daily Alta California*. Editor Edward Cleveland Kemble had to leave for the East with publisher and senior editor Edward Gilbert, just elected to the House of Representatives. Kemble and John E. Durivage, Assistant Editor, introduced their new associate to their readers in the September 27, 1850 *Alta*, and Soulé published a card. In this he said that he hoped to prove worthy of the trust and confidence of friends and the demands of the public. He assured his future readers that he had no interests other than those linked to the progress and prosperity of the young state of California and a willingness to contribute to the state's interests.

Kemble and Durivage demonstrated their satisfaction with the high degree of integrity and assiduity which Soulé brought to the free press. They should have mentioned his poesy. Some of the Victorian's flowery poeticness crept into his newspaper copy, including his introductory "card" which he cast, tastefully, into the third person: "He can only hope that his pen may answer readily to the call of his heart which, it is but simple truth to say, is devoted to her [i.e., California's] best good..." He was well aware, he said, of the *Alta*'s independence of parties, cliques, and sects, and he promised to be governed by his principles. "A perfect freedom to praise what is thought worthy, [to] withhold approbation when truth and conscience cannot approve, is the position he occupies and one which he will not knowingly disgrace. With a high estimation of the Press, and, he hopes, a correct one of human nature and society, he trusts that neither may suffer by his connection with them."

Soulé was afforded a fine welcome by the editor of the *Placer Times* in Sacramento, Joseph E. Lawrence: "It was our fortune to meet Mr. Soulé on his start for California and we were favored to enjoy his company during a part of the journey hither... Possessing a cultivated intellect, in expression ever refined and elegant, he is a valuable acquisition among our contemporaries. Experience in the pursuit in which he again engages renders him at home in all his requisitions. We know how well he will fill the position which he now assumes."

The *Alta* was the West's leading paper in terms of prestige and, possibly, in terms of prosperity, too. Edward C. Kemble claimed that monthly receipts ran to $15,000 and that it paid its assistant editor $6,000 a year. He suggested that some of the paper's staff were able to grow comparatively rich by reason of their association with the *Alta*. Since all the newspapers were politically conscious, it was only natural that politics should attract Soulé. He was civic-minded and popular. His political baptism came with the state convention of the Whig Party in Sacramento on June 8, 1852. Soulé was defeated for nomination as a member of Congress. However, the *Alta* picked up and boosted the rumor that he was really more interested in the State Senate. The editors said that they were pleased that good men were hoping to fill state offices. They knew of no man more competent to discharge such duties than Soulé, they added. "As his best wishes are centered in the success of California, we refer his nomination to the citizens of this district with pleasure."

Soulé was elected and sat for San Francisco County in the State Senate during the Third Regular Session, 1852. He was elected Chairman of the Senate's Education Committee and prepared a bill to bolster California's feeble schools. While his political convictions were Whiggish, he was not a hard-line partisan. Like so many politicians of the day he was "anti-coolie" and his actions suggest a more general tendency to xenophobia by being anti-Mexican, too. In an 1853 letter to the *Alta* describing transcontinental railroad enthusiasm in the East, he was glad to report that it would not run across the Isthmus of Tehuantepec because negotiations with "the effete, emasculated, chaos called Mexico…(they deserve not the name of nation)…" would degrade the U.S.

Soulé was not hard-boiled enough for success in politics. In 1853 he was one of six Whig nominees for lieutenant governor and he lost. The next year, although he was State Chairman and called the Convention to order, he withdrew his candidacy for congressional nomination. In 1862 Soulé was a member of the Civil War-born Union Administration Convention. This time, he was nominated for Superintendent of Public Instruction but lost again. John Swett won, of course. In 1867 Soulé's name was placed in nomination for Congressman by the Union Party but, for a second time, he withdrew it. The following year, the Republican Party's First District Convention met in San Francisco and Frank M. Pixley was nominated for Congress on the first ballot, over Soulé, by a vote of 72 to 18. It was the same story in 1875 when the Republicans nominated Ira P. Rankin for Congressman, again on the first ballot and over Soulé, by a 59 to 4 vote.

The newspaperman finally tired of being a perennial bridesmaid and withdrew from politics, contenting himself with poetry as an avocation. As early as February, 1863, after a political squabble with a man named T. W. Park, he made clear his growing disillusionment with politicking: "What little I have had to do with politics has invariably been done upon the square… I have never yet had anything to do with any dishonorable political act and I have no inducement to commence at this late day. Politics have ever been to me a loss and vexation and, each day, I wish more and more that I never had been dragged into the whirlpool."

After his term at Sacramento, Soulé went East in 1853. He sent political news to the *Alta* by a "Letter From Washington" reporting that there were forty political gladiators for each office made available by the spoils system of the new Pierce administration. He thought that only A. A. Selover, the gallant Mexican War veteran—"and as insinuating and active as ever"—was assured, of all the California job seekers, of a post. If he wanted it, the San Francisco postmastership was his. But Soulé predicted that San Francisco would not get its U. S. Mint for three or four years. He reported sadly, "It is astounding to perceive the utter ignorance which prevails here even among Members of Congress—aye, with learned gentlemen in the U. S. Senate—in regard to many of the most important questions touching the interest of our young Pacific state." Strangely, Soulé displayed the most heat in his letter, printed by the *Alta* on March 9, when he wrote of the anti-liquor crusade in the capital. It was tearing the political parties apart, he said. He personally felt that prohibition was unconstitutional, an abuse of private rights and personal dignity. He lambasted the "self-constituted clubs of hypocritical loafers, momentary reformed drunkards and ex-keepers of tippling shops."

On Friday, April 15, 1853, Soulé arrived back in San Francisco on the Pacific Mail steamer *Golden Gate,* after an almost-record run of 24 days from New York. With plans for the *Annals* well under way, he also began publishing an evening paper, the *California Chronicle.* The *Alta* editors thought it to be a mere copy of the *Alta* in format and style (which it was) but greeted Soulé as "a gentleman universally known and esteemed and to whom is cheerfully accorded an honorable position socially, practically and in all the various accomplishments of literature". The *Chronicle*'s staff, in large part, was composed of ex-*Alta* men and its type had been intended for the *Alta* but William L. Newell had sold it to Soulé for $3,000 when the *Alta* proved to be a poor credit risk.

The *Chronicle* started out in life beautifully and by 1855, with James Nisbet and John S. Hittell as Soulé's associate editors, it enjoyed the largest circulation in the City. But Soulé's refusal to jump on the Vigilante bandwagon after the murder of James King of William (who had attacked him and the *Chronicle* along with criminals and everyone else who differed with the *Evening Bulletin*) sent its circulation tumbling. When it became the organ of the Republican Party, Soulé gave up the editorship. Its value declined from $50,000 to $5,000 despite all the skill of Soulé, Edward Kemble, and J. H. Purdy. Soulé relinquished control of the paper in 1856; in just two years it was dead.

Soulé almost joined his paper in the tomb during 1854. An article of his in the *Chronicle*, "Stop, Thief!" (June 30) so angered Hezekiah L. Bateman, because of slights against his wife's reputation, he said, that he paraded the streets, armed, "looking for Soulé". The editor, after arming himself, made himself easy to find. He deliberately walked past Zeke three times. On the third time, Bateman bumped into him and Soulé went for his gun. With his revolver drawn, he felt his arms pinioned by a bystander or friend of Bateman's. His friend and associate, William L. Newell, drew his own revolver to protect Soulé and fired. Bateman returned the fire and when a man named Wilson rushed him, Bateman shot at him, too. Luckily, no one was killed or even wounded, although Bateman fired from three to five shots and Newell either two or three.

Judge Bager of the Recorder's Court, after considering the provocation of Soulé's article, declined to refer Bateman to trial but simply fined him $300 for assault. Soulé accused the Judge of being a "Dogberry" (i.e., a blundering official—from the absurd, talkative, constable in Shakespeare's *Much Ado About Nothing*), and took the case to the Grand Jury. Bateman was indicted and tried before the Court of Sessions and promptly acquitted. The *Chronicle* labeled the trial a farce but sympathy was shifting more and more to Bateman. He published a letter to the public on September 2, 1854 in which he offered to undergo a third trial and asked, rhetorically, just what system of trial and justice might satisfy the editor of the *Chronicle*.

Taking a long sea voyage vacation to Australia, Soulé was back in San Francisco in time to fill the post of editor of the *San Francisco Times*. In 1861 he accepted an appointment to a position in the Customs House and in 1864 became the chief editor of the *San Francisco Call*. He resigned this post to accept appointment by President Lincoln as Collector of Internal Revenue in San Francisco. During the Civil War Soulé was a Unionist tower of strength. After a visit to Maine in 1872, he accepted the editorship of the *Alta* and, finally, a position in the U. S. Mint. During the 1870s particularly, he wrote many poems. The most popular of all was titled *Labor*, and a number were published in the *Alta*.

Frank Soulé died on July 3, 1882, survived by his second wife, Eunice, and two children, Charles Z. and Kathleen. The obituaries made no mention of his son, Frank, Jr. The day after his death, the *Examiner* paid him tribute: "Frank Soulé proved himself to be a man of the highest integrity and, in spite of his political labors, the breath of suspicion never attached itself to his name. He was an easy, graceful, talented writer and has written many charming verses. The dull, grinding routine work of a daily paper never drove the poetry out of the honest, earnest labors of his life. His aim was to make men and women wiser and better and, though his best labors were engulfed in the yawning abyss of impersonal journalism and his talent but little known outside of a small circle of readers, their effects will live although he never reaped any adequate reward... Frank Soulé died a poor man, in spite of years of toil and a lifetime's practice of self-denial."

If Soulé was always in the news, Dr. John Hancock Gihon almost never "made the papers". He was born on April 21, 1811 in Philadelphia and taught school at Milford, near Hightstown, New Jersey. Although a graduate in medicine of the Philadelphia College of Medicine and Surgery in the 1840s, he did not practice during his early adulthood. He preferred printer's ink to plasma and established a printing office on the northeast corner of Sixth and Chestnut Streets in Philadelphia. Bitten by the gold bug, he shipped the entire plant to California on the *Grey Eagle,* via Cape Horn, in January 1849. He made the mistake of not escorting his fonts to San Francisco but followed on another vessel. When he arrived, he found the remains of his printery pied all over the beach at Yerba Buena Cove. Gihon pitched his tent where the United States Marine Hospital would later stand, thereby becoming one of the first settlers of Rincon Hill.

Gihon was—or became—a close friend of John W. Geary, destined to be a Civil War hero but, long before that, first postmaster and mayor of San Francisco and last alcalde of the town. The doctor was soon the proprietor of the *Evening Picayune*, San Francisco's first afternoon paper. Like Soulé, he also tried his hand at mining but after losing a small fortune in the seaside *borrasca* of Gold Bluffs, in Humboldt County, he returned to the world of type and paper. He opened a luxurious ("extravagant" is the word his son used to describe it) bookstore underneath the San Francisco Masonic Hall and made considerable money before losing it again.

Gihon was a dedicated Mason. He received his degrees in the Eastern Star Lodge of Philadelphia and visited the California Lodge during its third meeting (December 20, 1849). He petitioned for affiliation and was elected a member on the 27th of December, 1849, and, the next day was elected Secretary of the California Lodge. He held the post until December 27, 1850 when he declined reelection because he planned to leave the state. On April 17, 1850 he was one of three representatives from the California Lodge who met in Sacramento to organize the Grand Lodge of California and was elected Grand Secretary of it on the 19th. He remained in office until the end of the Masonic year, May 8, 1851. On April 15th, 1851 he told his lodge brothers that he was going back to Philadelphia.

Gihon went east and served as private secretary to John Geary as Governor of, first, Kansas Territory and, later, Pennsylvania. In 1857 be wrote a 348-page book, published by Charles C. Rhodes of Philadelphia, titled *Geary and Kansas.* Drawn largely from the Governor's reports and correspondence, it is an interesting picture of Bleeding Kansas.

According to the *Pacific Medical and Surgical Journal*, Gihon next became the Physician in charge of the Lazaretto of Philadelphia. Finally, he went to Louisiana to practice. The editors of the *Journal* reported that "he maintained a good reputation through a chequered and eventful life."

The doctor's son, Albert, himself President of the Military Surgeons of the United States and Medical Director of the United States Navy, stated that his father went to Louisiana during the Civil War and died there, "the fact not reaching us till long after and then with no positive information as to date or place". This is incorrect. The *Sacramento Union* on page one, column four, of its February 12, 1875 edition reported, via the Overland Express, the recent death of Gihon. The co-author of the *Annals* had died January 11, 1875 at Shreveport, where he was a physician. His passing was recorded in the Caddo County–Shreveport Health Unit Ledger of Deaths, Book A, page 7, but the exact circumstances of his demise are still shrouded in mystery.

Soulé's death was a quiet one; Gihon's passing was mysterious. But James Nisbet's life was doomed to end violently and tragically.

Nisbet, a life-long bachelor, was born in Glasgow, Scotland, on November 1, 1816. He chose law as a profession after traveling in Europe but did not like the courtroom and, according to the *San Francisco Evening Bulletin*, was "more inclined to seek literary pursuits than to contend for the rights of clients in the legal tribunals". He became a notary public and broker and, about 1852, lost most of his wealth in an unfortunate railroad stock investment.

The Scot decided to start fresh, and as far from home as possible. He sailed to Australia but did not like it Down Under and returned to England. But, shortly, he sailed again, this time to California. He arrived in San Francisco in November 1852 and there met Soulé.

Soulé hired Nisbet to help with the compiling of the *Annals*, and the *Evening Bulletin* was correct when it stated, "His industry, discriminating judgment and power to thoroughly perform great intellectual labor at once surprised and delighted his colleagues." Documents which Warren Howell (San Francisco bookseller) turned up in 1966 show that Nisbet, at first, was lumped with daguerreotypes, woodcuts, books, rent, and writing desks as one of many miscellaneous expenses of partners Soulé and Gihon. An account dated Philadelphia, January 1, 1855, for example, listed payments of $50, $50 and $75 to Nisbet between November, 1853 and December 6, 1854, plus the sum of $1,200 on December 6th for "one year's services devoted exclusively to publication of 'Annals' at $100 per month".

So pleased were Soulé and Gihon with Nisbet who, in truth, seems to have shouldered the burden of writing the *Annals*, that they made him a partner in the enterprise on February 16, 1855. They so notified D. Appleton & Company, with whom they had contracted on April 3, 1854 for publication of the work. (Appleton was to handle all expenses of publication in return for one-half of the book's earnings.) Soulé and Gihon asked

Appleton to pay, in future, one-fourth of their profits to Nisbet "...in consideration of the said Nisbet's literary and other services in assisting in the preparation and completion of the 'Annals of San Francisco'". The document sent to Appleton was signed by Soulé and Nisbet in San Francisco on March 8, 1855 and by Gihon in Philadelphia on April 11.

While still working on the *Annals*, Nisbet was given a desk at the *Chronicle* by Soulé but James King of William lured the diligent Scotsman to the *Evening Bulletin* with a better position. For eight years Nisbet was Supervising Editor for the firebrand. He demonstrated almost unparalleled industry. He was so absorbed in his work that the later editors of the paper wrote that "it seemed as if the very type, by spontaneous action, were all obedience to his will whenever he came near them." King of William found Nisbet a great asset to his newspaper, with his well-balanced intellect, his love of justice, and his strong physical constitution. He handled both news and literary departments and his finishing touches were seen in almost every column of the *Bulletin*.

Although he had nothing to do with the paper's controversial editorial positions, and personally assailed no one, he was, ironically, attacked by King of William's enemies and, in the words of the *Bulletin*, "No journalist of this country was ever so continuously reviled for the faults or pretended faults of others." He was said by the editors to be responsible for more of the newspaper's excellence and less of its faults than any of his colleagues. Nisbet had his weaknesses, particularly his oversensitivity to personal criticism, but the paper was probably not far off when, in an obituary, it said of him, "Nisbet possessed the best elements of character to wield power as a journalist, his devotion to his friends not [being] counterbalanced by a hatred of enemies. He preferred to forget them."

When James King of William was shot down by James Casey on May 15, 1856, Nisbet was named Acting Editor until the crusader should recover. But King of William died and after thirteen days as Editor-in-Chief Nisbet stepped aside for the dead man's brother, Thomas S. King. The latter sold out his interest in January 1858 to C. O. Gerberding. In January 1861 the C. O. Gerberding Company was dissolved and the paper was published by the San Francisco Bulletin Company, a partnership of five men including Nisbet.

On July 28, 1865, Nisbet sailed from San Francisco on the California Steam Navigation Company steamer *Brother Jonathan*, commanded by Captain S. J. DeWolf. He planned to spend a four- or five-week vacation in Oregon, Washington Territory, and Victoria, British Columbia. At 1:30 p.m. on July 30, in a light fog, the steamship struck a submerged rock of St. George Reef off Crescent City, on California's Redwood Coast. The life-saving equipment of the steamer included four iron lifeboats, two surfboats and 397 cork-filled life jackets. But two of the boats swamped alongside and three were left on their davits. The *Brother Jonathan* sank in forty-five minutes with only the lifeboat of Third Officer James Patterson getting away. Saved by Patterson were only seventeen adults and two children, of all the passengers.

Boats hurried out from Crescent City but returned at 8 o'clock having found nothing but empty sea at the site of the disaster. The *Daily Alta California* reported, August 3rd, on the shock of the news which reached the City by telegraph from Jacksonville, Oregon. "The terrible catastrophe has thrown the whole community into mourning. Anxiety, sorrow and horror are depicted on every countenance. Every flag in the city and on the shipping in the bay is at half-mast and the grief is general."

The next morning's *Alta* hit the streets with heavy mourning rules framing the front-page lead columns. The story was broken into three parts, focussing on the loss of Brigadier General George Wright, Nisbet, and Captain John Chaddock of the U. S. Revenue Service. Lamented the *Alta*, "By the loss of James Nisbet, San Francisco loses one of her best men." The paper reminded readers that the Scot had occupied a position of great influence over the community and that he had used it with the strictest regard for the rights of the public and for his duty toward them.

In 1862, Frank Soulé had written the "poetry" (i.e. lyrics) of a lachrymose piece of sheet music by P. R. Nichols entitled *I Do Not Want To Be Drowned.* This tearjerker was suggested by the fiery shipwreck of the paddlewheeler *Golden Gate* off Manzanillo on July 27 of that year. Soulé's words of 1862—"On deck there is terror and agony wild"—came true again in 1865 on St. George Reef. But James Nisbet did not fall victim to panic. He met a brave death. As the deck canted steeply, he was seen, bracing himself, writing his last will and testament on a scrap of paper.

George W. Russell of Crescent City found Nisbet's body. In a pocket was the holograph document. Russell dried the will on his stove, made a copy and put the original in his safe until he could get it to Nisbet's brother, Thomas, in San Francisco, designated by the newspaperman as his sole executor (although he had sisters in Scotland).

James Nisbet was buried in Lone Mountain Cemetery in San Francisco on August 27, 1865, next to the tomb of his martyred chief, James King of William. Dr. Gihon lived until 1875, Soulé until 1882.

But the proper place to end the story of the writing of the *Annals of San Francisco* is on the steep-pitched deck of the *Brother Jonathan* off the rugged Del Norte coast. What better obituary could a man ask than that tendered Nisbet by the *San Francisco Evening Bulletin* and reprinted by the *Sacramento Union*:

"With the horror of sudden death staring him in the face, Nisbet was calm and thoughtful enough to write out a will in pencil... The act was eminently characteristic of his unselfish and courageous nature. Instead of being concerned for his own safety, he appears to have employed his last moments as he had employed his life, in doing good to others. We never met an instance of greater self-possession and thoughtfulness in the midst of deadly peril."

— RICHARD H. DILLON
MILL VALLEY, AUGUST 1999

NOTE TO THE READER:

This paperback edition of *The Annals* includes the complete chronological survey of the years 1846–1854, which, as noted in the Introduction, has proven to be "the most interesting section" of the book. Part III, consisting mostly of biographical sketches of local worthies of the day, has been mainly omitted (as indeed, one of the first reviews of the book, in the *Daily Alta California*, said it ought to be). Because of their inherent interest, however, this edition does retain two chapters from the final part: one on the Hounds, and a related one on the Vigilance Committee.

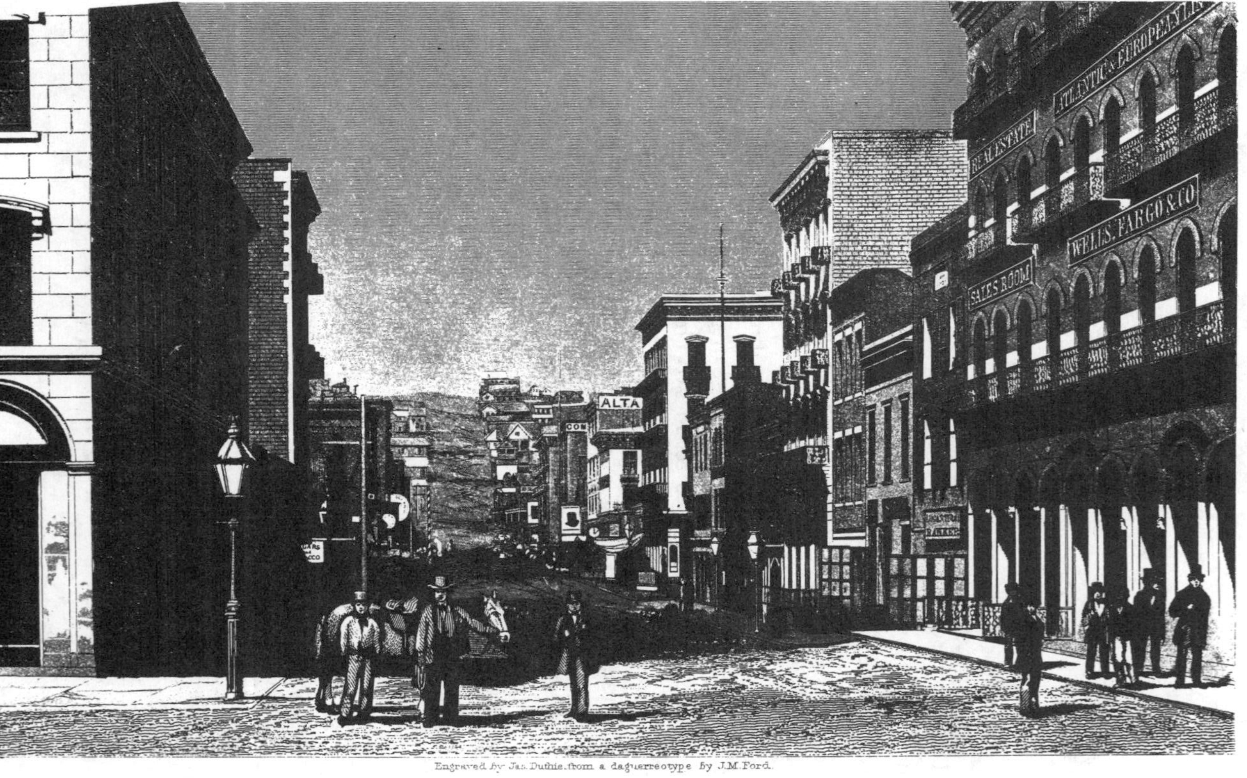

Engraved by Jas. Duthie, from a daguerreotype by J.M. Ford.

Montgomery Street, northward from California Street, June 1854.

THE

ANNALS OF SAN FRANCISCO;

CONTAINING

A SUMMARY OF THE HISTORY OF THE FIRST DISCOVERY, SETTLEMENT, PROGRESS, AND PRESENT CONDITION OF

CALIFORNIA,

AND A COMPLETE HISTORY OF ALL THE IMPORTANT EVENTS CONNECTED WITH

ITS GREAT CITY:

TO WHICH ARE ADDED,

BIOGRAPHICAL MEMOIRS OF SOME PROMINENT CITIZENS.

BY

FRANK SOULÉ, JOHN H. GIHON, M. D.,

AND

JAMES NISBET.

ILLUSTRATED WITH ONE HUNDRED AND FIFTY FINE ENGRAVINGS.

"Go to, let us build us a city, and a tower,
Whose top may reach unto heaven;
And let us make us a name."

NEW YORK:

D. APPLETON & COMPANY, 346 & 348 BROADWAY.

SAN FRANCISCO: MONTGOMERY STREET.

LONDON: 16 LITTLE BRITAIN.

M.DCCC.LV.

TO THE

"SOCIETY OF CALIFORNIA PIONEERS,"

THIS WORK

IS

RESPECTFULLY DEDICATED

BY

THE AUTHORS.

PREFACE.

Were not the plan, scope and purpose of the present volume sufficiently explained in the text of the work itself, we should despair of adequately initiating the reader in these subjects in the limited space necessarily assigned to a Preface. It is not necessary to offer a reason for the appearance of these "Annals." To read and to know something of the history of this new Tadmor which has grown up so suddenly in the midst of what was but recently merely a desert, the centre of that vast trade which the golden smile of California opened at once to the world, is so natural and inevitable a desire, that it may be taken for granted, and dismissed as a foregone conclusion. The plan of the work is such as its nature seemed to require, and the style and manner of treatment must rest for approval and criticism with the Public, for whom it was written and to whom it is now submitted.

To avoid the necessity of frequent references in the body of the work to authorities, and to those who have generously extended to the authors facilities for its production, the Preface has been selected as the most fitting place for expressing our obligations. For unrestricted access to the "Californian," the "California Star," and the "Alta California" newspaper files, we are indebted to the courtesy of Mr. Edward Conner, one of the proprietors of the last named journal. Much valuable statistical and other information has been derived from the "San Francisco Herald," full files of which were kindly placed at our disposal by its editor and proprietor, Mr. John Nugent. The "California Chronicle," from its commencement to the date of publication of this volume, was also placed by the proprietors at our service. We are likewise indebted to Messrs. T. J. Nevins and Wm. H. O'Grady for information respecting the public schools; to Mr. J. L. Van Bokkelin, for important facts concerning the fire department; to Mr. A. G. Randall, for particulars in regard to military organizations; to Rev's T. Dwight Hunt, Albert Williams, J. L. Ver Mehr, S. H. Willey and O. C. Wheeler, for matter relating to the early state of religion and churches in San Francisco; to Messrs. Thomas O. Larkin, William A. Richardson, Jacob P. Leese, Jacob R. Snyder, James Caldwell Low, Hiram Pierson, J. D. Stevenson, Samuel Brannan, R. H. Perry, David Jobson, Samuel J. Bayard, Nathaniel Gray and James King of William, for much useful and interesting information regarding the early and present history of the city; to Mr. J. M. Ford, daguerreian artist, for gratuitous services in taking portraits of many of the gentlemen whose memoirs are given; and to our citizens generally who have freely responded to our call for information, whenever they have been appealed to for that purpose. Many biographical sketches designed for this work have been omitted for want of room, the volume having extended to nearly double the size originally intended and promised. These, however, with other interesting matters connected with the progress of San Francisco, and a history of all the important cities and towns of California, will be published at an early day, in another volume, a great portion of the material for which is already prepared.

The necessity of condensing within the reasonable space of a single volume, the history of a city which has occupied for the five or six years of its existence so much of the attention of the world, and the unavoidable collateral history of California, has prevented, to some extent, a natural impulse and inclination to indulge more at length in many interesting details. But it is believed that the gist of the whole matter is embraced in the history as written, and that no important event has been omitted, which would have been of interest to the general reader.

CONTENTS.

PART I.

PART II.

PART III.

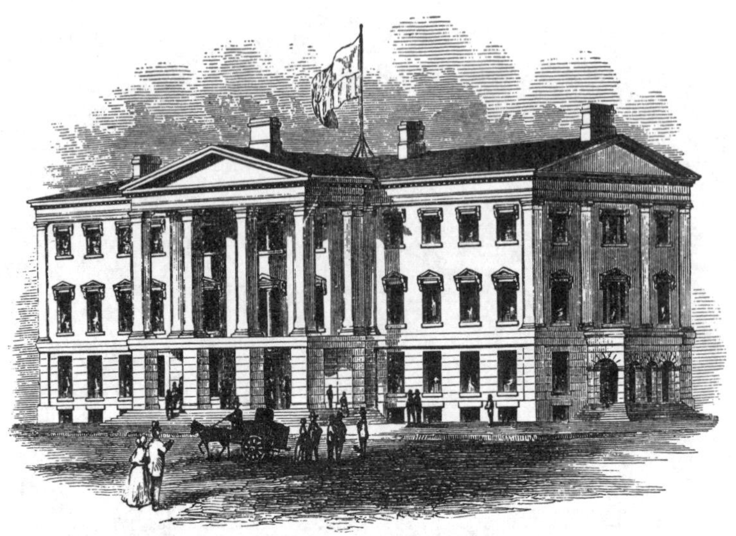

Custom-house, now (1854) being erected on Battery street.

ILLUSTRATIONS.

OFFICERS OF THE SOCIETY OF CALIFORNIA PIONEERS, ELECTED JULY 7TH, 1854.

JACOB R. SNYDER, *President.*

Vice-Presidents.

G. B. Post, San Francisco.	H. W. Theall, Tuolumne.	W. A. Richardson, Marin.
J. C. L. Wadsworth, do.	P. C. Carillo, Santa Barbara.	G. Yount, Napa.
B. S. Lippincott, do.	J. A. Sutter, Sutter.	H. L. Ford, Colusi.
J. P. Leese, Monterey.	J. Bidwell, Butte.	C. R. Johnson, Los Angeles.
J. Belden, Santa Clara.	P. B. Cornwall, Sacramento.	S. Purdy, San Joaquin.

J. Caldwell Low, *Secretary.* W. T. Sherman, *Treasurer.*

Board of Directors.

W. Van Voorhies, O. P. Sutton, J. Shew, T. A. Warbass,
J. M. Huxley, G. F. Lemon, S. W. Haight.

Corresponding Members.

D. S. Turner, S. R. Harris, F. Soule, W. B. Farwell,
A. G. Abell.

MAP
OF
SAN FRANCISCO
BAY OF SAN FRANCISCO
MISSION BAY
CHANNEL
RINCON POINT
NORTH POINT
CLARK'S POINT
LAGOON
ADDITION OF MISSION
YERBA BUENA CEMETERY
PUBLIC SQUARE
SPRING VALLEY
RUSSIAN HILL
BELLEVUE
PLEASANT VALLEY
HAPPY VALLEY
MISSION
HOWARD
FOLSOM
BRYANT
CHANNEL
TOWNSEND
KING
BERRY
SECOND
DOLORES ST.
VALENCIA ST.
SCALE.
0 1 2 3 4 5 6 7 8 9 10

ANNALS OF SAN FRANCISCO.

PART FIRST.

CHAPTER I.

Proposed Treatment of the Work—Etymology of the name California—Lower or Old California—Grixalva and Mendoza—First Discovery—Expeditions of Cortez—Cabrillo—Ferrelo—Drake—Drake's Description of the Natives—Bodega and San Francisco Bays—Sir Francis Drake's Bay—Cavendish—Captain Woodes Rogers—His Description of the Natives—The English Buccaneering Expeditions along the West Coasts of the Americas—Political Reasons why the Spanish Government strenuously prosecuted the Discovery and Settlement of the Californias.

It appears expedient, before entering upon the annals of *San Francisco* proper, to give a short review of the first discovery, settlement, and progress of California itself, including an account of the aboriginal inhabitants, and of the first establishment, rise, and decline of the priest class, their sovereigns, whose domination forms a most peculiar and interesting phase in the general history of the country. The subject indeed comprehends, or naturally demands, some notice of these points; for, up to a recent period, San Francisco, from its being the "golden gate" to the wealth of the State, and from its many physical advantages, its population, the rapidity and grandeur of its wondrous rise and progress, the energy of its citizens, the extent of its home and foreign commerce, its universal fame, arising chiefly from its being associated in the minds of men,

Americans as well as foreigners, with the first discovery and subsequent astonishing produce of gold—San Francisco, from these and other causes, has been in a great measure identified with California itself. No history, therefore, of the city, could be complete, unless it included some account of the circumstances which preceded and immediately accompanied its rise, and which have made it what it almost already is, but which it will more plainly soon become, the greatest and most magnificent, wealthy and powerful maritime city in the Pacific—a city which is destined, one day, to be, in riches, grandeur and influence, like Tyre or Carthage of the olden time, or like Liverpool or New York of modern days.

We propose to embody in a succinct and continuous narrative, the subjects already particularly noticed—a general account of the causes, progress, and consequences of the war of 1846, between the Mexican and American States—the cession of California to the latter—the first discovery of gold, and the immediate results of that discovery upon the prosperity and population of the country—its admission as a *State* into the American Union—and a description of its physical geography, and of its commercial, agricultural, pastoral, and mineral wealth, and capabilities to receive and satisfy millions of additional inhabitants. These matters will form Part First of the work.

We shall afterwards, at somewhat greater length, describe, in a similar continuous narrative, the progress and the various incidents which happened, year by year, and month by month, in San Francisco itself, from the period when California was ceded by the Mexicans, and State and town became American, up to the present time, and which, properly speaking, alone constitute the "Annals" of the city. This subject will constitute Part Second.

In the subsequent portion of the volume, we shall devote special chapters, in no particular order, to the more minute details of whatever things were most peculiar and interesting—physical and intellectual, social and moral, and their causes and consequences—which marked the progress of the city, and gave it a world-wide reputation for good or for evil. In this division of the work will be included biographical and personal sketches, and anecdotes of the more prominent and distinguished actors in the bustling scenes of the time, and whose names are closely associated either with the general history of California, or with the particular rise and progress of San Francisco itself. These topics will be comprehended in and constitute PART THIRD.

The remembrance of these matters is still fresh in the minds of our people ; but, in the silent lapse of years, many of them must gradually fade away. It would then be well, that after the present generation disappears, our posterity should know something of the early history and triumphant progress of their glorious city, and of its worthiest or most noted sons, and the exciting, troublous scenes of the last seven or eight years, all drawn from the fullest and most accurate sources that are still to be had. We propose then to make this book an original record of the subjects alluded to.

The etymology of the name CALIFORNIA is uncertain. Some writers have pretended that it is derived from the two Latin words *calida fornax*, or, in the Spanish language, *caliente fornalla* —a hot furnace. This, however, is doubted by Michael Venegas, a Mexican Jesuit, in his " Natural and Civil History of California" (2 vols. Madrid, 1758), a work of much research and high authority. In his opinion, the early Spanish discoverers did not name their new-found lands in this pedantic fashion. " I am therefore inclined to think," he says, "that this name owed its origin to some accident ; possibly to some words spoken by the Indians, and misunderstood by the Spaniards," as happened in several other cases.

The name *California* is first found in Bernal Diaz del Castillo, an officer who served under Hernando Cortez, in the conquest of Mexico, and who published a history of that extraordinary expedition ; and is by him limited to a single bay on the coast. On the other hand, Jean Bleau, the celebrated geographer (Amsterdam, 1662), includes under the term all those immense tracks of country lying west of New Spain and New Galicia, comprehending the whole coast line from the northern parts of South America to the Straits of Anian (Behring's Straits). In this larger sense of the word, Jean Bleau is followed by several other geographers.

However, whatever be the limits of the country, the name has occasionally changed. In some English maps it is called New Albion, because Sir Francis Drake, the well known English admiral, who touched on the coast in 1579, so styled it. About a century later, it is denominated Islas Carolinas (the peninsula of California being then supposed to be an island), in honor of Charles II. of Spain; and this designation was adopted by several writers and geographers of repute. After a time, the original name of California was revived, and soon silently and universally adopted.

California—meaning the existing Lower, or Old California, was known to be a peninsula so early as 1541, when a map drawn up at Madrid, by Castillo, already mentioned, represents the direction of the coasts nearly as they are known at present. Yet this fact was unaccountably forgotten for one hundred and sixty years, when Father Kühn (Kino, of the Spaniards) seemed, for the first time, to prove that California was not an island, but a peninsula. In the early part of the sixteenth century, dreams of a direct western opening to the Indias filled men's minds, as later did those of a north-west passage. This was the first idea of Columbus, which led to his great discoveries, and which he held till death. In 1523, Charles V., in a letter, dated from Valladolid, recommended to Cortez to seek on the eastern and western coasts of New Spain, for such a passage. Cortez, in his answer to the emperor, speaks with the greatest enthusiasm of the probability of such a discovery, "which," he adds, "will render your majesty master of so many kingdoms that you will be considered as the monarch of the world;" and seems to have undertaken several voyages for the purpose of ascertaining the fact.

In 1534, Cortez fitted out two ships under the command of Hernando Grixalva and Diego Becerra de Mendoza, a relation of his own, partly to learn the fate of a missing vessel of a previous expedition, but chiefly to continue the coast discoveries. These two ships happened to separate the first night following their departure from Tehuantepec, and did not meet again. Grixalva, after sailing three hundred leagues, came to a desert island, which he called *Santa Thome*, believed to lie near the point of California. This is supposed to be one of the group of islands now called the *Revillagigedo Islands.* He proceeded no farther north, and made no fresh discoveries ; but shortly afterwards returned to New Spain. Becerra, the commander of the other ship of this expedition, was of a choleric, haughty disposition ; and, having shown that offensively to his people, was murdered by a malcontent crew, led on by his pilot Ortun, or Fortuño Zimenes, a native of Biscay.

Zimenes afterwards continued the voyage of discovery, and appears to have sailed westward across the gulf, and to have touched the peninsula of California. This was in the year 1534. He therefore was the first discoverer of the country. " But," says Venegas, " he could not fly from the hand of Omnipotence ; for coming to that part which has since been called *Santa Cruz Bay,* and seems to be part of the inward coast of California, he went ashore, and was there killed by the Indians, with twenty other Spaniards." Upon this disaster, the remaining crew got frightened, and returned to New Spain. This Bay of Santa Cruz, so named by Cortez the following year, seems to be the same as that now called *La Paz,* lying on the western side of the Gulf of California, about a hundred miles north of Cape St. Lucas. Some writers, however, suppose it to have been situated much nearer the southern extremity of the peninsula.

Humboldt, in his " Political Essay on the Kingdom of New Spain," in stating these circumstances, mentions in a note, that he found in a manuscript preserved in the archives of the viceroyalty of Mexico, that California was discovered in 1526, though he knew not, he says, on what authority this assertion was founded. From an examination which he seems to have made of other manuscripts of the period, preserved in the Academy of History at Madrid, Humboldt seems satisfied that this alleged discovery of California in 1526 was unfounded, and that the country had not even been seen in the expedition of Diego Hurtado de Mendoza, who was a near relation of Cortez, so late as 1532.

In 1535, Cortez himself coasted both sides of the Gulf of California, which was first called the *Sea of Cortez,* but was more generally known as the *Mar Roxo, ó Vermejo,* (the Red, or Vermillion Sea), probably from its resembling the Red Sea between Arabia and Egypt in shape, or from the discoloration of its waters at the northern extremity by the *Rio Colorado*, or Red River. Gomara, the Spanish historian, in 1557, likened it more judiciously to the Adriatic. In the English maps, it is generally marked as the *Gulf of California*. Francisco de Ulloa, at command and likewise at the personal expense of Cortez, prosecuted farther discoveries along the coast, and during the subsequent two years, succeeded in exploring the gulf nearly to the mouth of the Colorado. Neither Cortez, however, nor Ulloa seems to have discovered the coast of New or Upper California.

That honor was reserved to Juan Rodriguez Cabrillo, one of the pilots of Cortez. Cabrillo was a Portuguese by birth, and a man of great courage and honor. On the 27th June, 1542, under instructions from the then viceroy of Spain, Antonio de Mendoza, he sailed from the port of Navidad in Mexico, on an expedition of discovery of the coast towards the north. He touched at various places on the voyage. The large cape between the fortieth and forty-first degrees of latitude he named *Cape Mendoza*, or *Mendocino*, in honor of the viceroy. Cabrillo reached 44° lat. N., where he found the cold (10th March) intense. This, the want of provisions, and the bad condition of his ships, compelled him to return to Navidad, the harbor of which place he re-entered on 14th April, 1543. This is according to the authority of Venegas. Other accounts say that Cabrillo, who had been long sick, and was overcome at last by the fatigues of the voyage, died at Port Possession, in the Island of San Bernardo, one of the Santa Barbara group, about the thirty-fourth parallel, upon the 3d January, 1543, leaving the subsequent guidance of the expedition farther northwards to Bartolomé Ferrelo, his pilot. Ferrelo is said to have named a promontory about the forty-first degree of latitude, *Cabo de Fortunas* (Cape of Perils, or Stormy Cape), from the rough weather and dangers encountered in its vicinity. This promontory is supposed to be the same, already noticed, which was called Cape Mendocino. There is therefore some discrepancy between the accounts of the voyage under the command of Cabrillo, or successively of him and his pilot Ferrelo. Neither of these navigators, however, while they noticed and named various prominent points of the coast, seem to have discovered the entrance to the great Bay of San Francisco.

SIR FRANCIS DRAKE.—From an old English Painting.

In 1577, Sir Francis, then only Captain Drake, already distinguished as an experienced navigator, fitted out, with the pecuniary aid of some friends, a buccaneering expedition against the

Spaniards, which ultimately led him round the globe. In those days, and for a long time afterwards, the rich Spanish ships, which bore over so many seas the wealth of their new-found world, were the natural prey of the English buccaneers—or, to give them a more honorable title, since they generally sailed under formal license from the government, of the English *privateers.* Drake, Cavendish, Dampier, and many other famous early navigators, were all of that class. The wealth of the Philippines was generally conveyed by a single annual galleon from Manilla to Acapulco, on its way to Europe. To intercept this particular ship was one great aim of these privateers. Drake, in his expedition of 1577, after safely threading the Straits of Magellan, reached, at length, the Pacific, north of the equator, and appears, in 1579, to have sailed along the shores of California. All along the west coast of the Americas he had been capturing and plundering the newly settled Spanish towns, and such ships as came in his way. Wishing at length to return home, and afraid lest the Spaniards might be waiting to catch him off the Straits of Magellan, he tried to sail westward, and so reach England by the Cape of Good Hope. This was in the autumn of 1579. Contrary winds preventing that course, "he was obliged," to use the language of an old chronicler of the voyage, "to sail towards the north; in which course, having continued at least six hundred leagues, and being got into forty-three degrees north latitude, they found it intolerably cold; upon which they steered southwards, till they got into thirty-eight degrees north latitude, *where they discovered a country, which, from its white cliffs they called* NOVA ALBION, *though it is now known by the name of California.*

"They here discovered a *bay*, which entering with a favorable gale, they found several huts by the water side, well defended from the severity of the weather. Going on shore, they found a fire in the middle of each house, and the people lying round it upon rushes. The men go quite naked, but the women have a deer skin over their shoulders, and round their waist a covering of bulrushes after the manner of hemp.

"These people bringing the admiral (Drake) a present of feathers and cauls of network, he entertained them so kindly and generously, that they were extremely pleased, and soon afterwards they sent him a present of feathers and bags of tobacco. A number of them coming to deliver it, gathered themselves together at the top of a small hill, from the highest point of which one of them harangued the admiral, whose tent was placed at the bottom. When the speech was ended, they laid down their arms and came down, offering their presents; at the same time returning what the admiral had given them. The women remaining on the hill, tearing their hair and making dreadful howlings, the admiral supposed them engaged in making sacrifices, and thereupon ordered divine service to be performed at his tent, at which these people attended with astonishment.

Sir Francis Drake and the California Indians.

"The arrival of the English in California being soon known through the country, two persons in the character of ambassadors came to the admiral, and informed him, in the best manner they were able, that the king would visit him, if he might be assured of coming in safety. Being satisfied on this point, a numerous company soon appeared, in front of which was a very comely person, bearing a kind of sceptre, on which hung two crowns, and three chains of great length. The chains were of bones, and the crowns of net work, curiously wrought with feathers of many colors.

"Next to the sceptre-bearer came the king, a handsome majestic person, surrounded by a number of tall men, dressed in skins, who were followed by the common people, who, to make the grander appearance, had painted their faces of various colors, and all of them, even the children, being loaded with presents.

"The men being drawn up in line of battle, the admiral stood ready to receive the king within the fences of his tent. The company having halted at a distance, the sceptre-bearer made a speech, half an hour long, at the end of which he began singing and dancing, in which he was followed by the king and all the people; who, continuing to sing and dance, came quite up to the tent; when sitting down, the king took off his crown of feathers, placed it on the admiral's head, and put on him the other ensigns of royalty; and it is said that *he made him a solemn tender of his whole kingdom; all which the admiral accepted in the name of the queen his sovereign*, in hopes that these proceedings might, one time or other, contribute to the advantage of England.

"The common people, dispersing themselves among the admiral's tents, professed the utmost admiration and esteem for the English, whom they considered as more than mortal; and accordingly prepared to offer sacrifices to them, which the English rejected with abhorrence, directing them, by signs, that their religious worship was alone due to the Supreme Maker and Preserver of all things.

"The admiral and some of his people, *travelling to a distance in the country*, saw such a quantity of rabbits, that it appeared an entire warren; they also saw deer in such plenty as to run a thousand in a herd. THE EARTH OF THE COUNTRY SEEMED TO PROMISE RICH VEINS OF GOLD AND SILVER, SOME OF THE ORE BEING CONSTANTLY FOUND ON DIGGING.

"The admiral, at his departure, set up a pillar with a large plate on it, on which was engraved her majesty's name, picture, arms, and title to the country; together with the admiral's name, and the time of his arrival there."

This is a curious and interesting picture of the aborigines of California. From the description of their naked bodies and painted faces, their howlings, singing and dancing, the girdles of bulrushes of the women, and the "kind of sceptre, on which hung" the chains of bone and the crowns of network "curiously wrought with feathers of many colors," of the king, it may be presumed that the people were in the rudest state of barbarism. Though the earth seemed streaked with gold, or, as Pinkerton says in his description of Drake's voyage, "the land is so rich in gold and silver, that upon the slightest turning it up with a spade or pick-axe, these rich metals plainly appear mixed with the mould," yet the natives do not appear to have worn any ornaments made of these metals, which has usually been the case with other savages when they had access to them. The beauty and purity of the metals named, especially of gold, and the ease of working in them, naturally render them precious in the eyes of the most barbarous tribes. Unless, therefore, we suppose the Indians to have been the most stupid and helpless people existing, it may be reasonably doubted whether so extensive indications of gold and silver were found as the broad statements of the chroniclers seem to imply. Certainly, however, the traces of the precious metals discovered by Drake were the first authentic intimation of the mineral wealth of the country.

There is no reason to suppose that Drake knew of the previous discovery of the country by the Spaniards; and accordingly long afterwards, and even with people to this day, it has been believed that he was the first discoverer of California. Queen Elizabeth afterwards knighted him for his services in this and previous expeditions, "telling him, at the same time," in the words of the writer of his voyages already quoted, "that his actions did him more honor than his title." The queen, however, took no steps to secure the country which her admiral had discovered: and the "pillar, with a large plate on it," and all its rusted engravings, may peradventure be yet some day discovered by the antiquary.

In popular estimation the *bay* which Drake entered is believed to be that of San Francisco; while many who might have had opportunities to examine into the subject have hastily concluded

Sir Francis Drake's Bay, or Jack's Harbor

that it must have been Bodega Bay. There is, however, another bay not far from these, and lying between them, known formerly under the very name of *Sir Francis Drake's Bay,* though better now as *Jack's Harbor.* This, on a careful examination of the subject, seems to have been the true and only bay which Drake ever visited on the coast. There is a sad confusion, even among recent writers and geographers, as to the names and relative positions of these bays. Most of them seem to think that Bodega and Drake's Bays are the same. Thus Humboldt says, "This port (San Francisco) is frequently confounded by geographers with the *Port of Drake* farther north, under the 38° 10′ of latitude, *called by the Spaniards the Puerto de Bodega.*" The latitude of Jack's Harbor, or Drake's Bay, is 37° 59′ 5″ (longitude 122° 57½′), thus corresponding exactly with the statement of the chronicler; while San Francisco and Bodega Bays are a good many miles to the south and north respectively of the parallel named by him. If Drake had really entered San Francisco Bay, it is more than likely that he, or his chronicler, would have said something more of its peculiarities—its unusual excellence, and the great arms which it stretches both to south and north. In the English maps, constructed after Drake's voyage, there is a bay laid down bearing his name; although, owing to the general ignorance of the coast and the confusion in regard to particular bays alluded to, this bay has been often held to be the same as that of Bodega. There is, therefore, every probability that the Bay of San Francisco had never been seen at all by either the Spanish or the English navigators (for there were others of the latter nation after Drake along the California coast), but that, in reality, it was discovered by travellers on land, and most probably first by the missionaries in 1769. It may also be remarked in corroboration of these opinions, that the white cliffs and the abundance of rabbits seen by Drake, closely correspond to the present description of *Punta de los Reyes* (Cape of Kings), and the country around Jack's Harbor. The cliffs about this part of the coast, for a space of nearly forty miles, resemble in height and color, those of Great Britain in the English Channel, at Brighton and Dover. Hence the propriety of the old designation of the country, *New Albion.* We give an illustration of these cliffs and of Drake's Bay. This bay has somehow grown out of most people's remembrance, or at least their appreciation, since it is a very safe and most important port of refuge along a foggy and dangerous coast. A number of fishing vessels have made use of it during the last few years, and it was their crews who dubbed it Jack's Harbor, in ignorance of its previous name. It is likely that public attention will be called to its peculiar advantages before long. We think, however, that no new name should be allowed to supersede the historical one of "Sir Francis Drake's

3

Bay." It would be a pity not to preserve some such remembrance of one of the greatest and earliest navigators along our coasts.

On the 14th of October, 1587, Captain Thomas Cavendish, afterwards knighted by Queen Elizabeth, when in a privateering expedition against the Spaniards, fell in with Cape St. Lucas, at the extremity of California. A fine bay, named by the Spaniards *Aguada Segura*, is within this cape, and there Cavendish lay in wait for the Acapulco galleon, laden with the wealth of the Philippines. At length she appeared, and after a severe fight, was taken possession of by the English admiral. "This prize," says the relator of the voyage, "contained one hundred and twenty-two thousand pezoes of gold, besides great quantities of rich silks, satins, damask and musk, and a good stock of provisions." Pretty fair all that for an English adventurer! In those days, piracy was honorable, and legalized by formal license, though the spoil was only gold and silver and light moveable goods—booty of the common robber. After all, the old buccaneers were poor grovelling souls. In our own times, pirates—called "filibusters," whose business is notoriously unlawful, have much grander views of glory and profit. Cuba and Sonora, which are countries equal to Italy of the old world in beauty, fertility and real wealth, are certainly prizes worth stealing and fighting for—the rewards of Alexanders, Cæsars and Bonapartes. But then, principles of action being nearly the same, "Young America" is very much *smarter* than "Old England."

The next Englishman who is specially recorded to have touched the California coast is Captain Woodes Rogers, who was in command of the usual filibustering or privateering expeditions. This was in November, 1709. He describes the aborigines of the peninsula as being "quite naked, and strangers to the European manner of trafficking. They lived in huts made of boughs and leaves, erected in the form of bowers, with a fire before the door, round which they lay and slept. The men were quite naked, and the women had only a short petticoat reaching scarcely to the knee, made of silk grass, or the skins of pelicans or deers. Some of them wore *pearls* about their necks, which they fastened with a string of silk grass, having first notched them round: and Captain Rogers imagined that they did not know how to bore them. These pearls were mixed with sticks, bits of shells and little red berries, which they thought so great an ornament that they would not accept of glass beads of various colors, which the English would have given them. The men are straight and well built, having long black hair, and are of a dark brown complexion. They live by hunting and fishing. They use bows and arrows,

Landing of Captain Woodes Rogers,—from an old English engraving.

and are excellent marksmen. The women, whose features are rather disagreeable, are employed in making fishing lines, or in gathering grain (doubtless what grew spontaneously), which they grind upon a stone. The people were willing to assist the English in filling water, and would supply them with whatever they could get; they were a very honest people, and would not take the least thing without permission." This description, and that already given from Drake's voyage, make up a pretty complete picture of the aborigines of the Californias. They appear to have been a simple, honest, good-natured, stupid race of people, and, in most respects, resemble the savages which we find in other newly discovered countries.

Captain Rogers was, of course, lying in ambush for the "great Manilla ship;" and, in due course of time, she appeared and was captured. "The prize was called *Nuestra Señora de la Incarnacion*, commanded by Sir John Pichberty, a gallant Frenchman; and the prisoners said that the cargo in India amounted to two millions of dollars. She carried one hundred and ninety-three men, and mounted twenty guns."

As illustrating the career of these English buccaneers, and the state of terror in which the Spaniards were constantly kept by their depredations, and which was one of the chief causes that induced the Spanish Government, as we shall afterwards see, strenuously to prosecute farther discoveries and settlements along the coast of California, we shall give a copy of a deed, or instrument, executed between the said Captain Rogers and the town of Guiaquil. The exploits of Rogers and his men are indeed much later in date than some of the expeditions yet to be noticed, of the Spanish navigators along the California coast; still, as they forcibly explain one reason, at least, *why* such expeditions were undertaken on the part of the Spaniards, it appears better to notice them here than in mere chronological order. The notices of the voyages of Drake, Cavendish and Rogers, are taken from accounts contained in an old folio volume of voyages and travels kindly placed at our disposal by the "Society of California Pioneers."

The "high contracting parties" entered into the following agreement:

"CONTRACT FOR THE RANSOM OF THE TOWN OF GUIAQUIL:

"*Whereas* the City of Guiaquil, lately in subjection to Philip V., King of Spain, is now taken by storm, and in possession of the Captains Thomas Dover, Woodes Rogers, and Stephen Courtney,"—[the expedition, fitted out at the cost of some "British gentlemen," consisted of the *Duke*, a ship of three hundred tons burthen, thirty guns and one hundred and seventy men, commanded by Rogers, and the *Duchess*, of two hundred and seventy tons, twenty-six guns, and one hundred and fifty-one men, under the command of Courtney]— "commanding a body of her Majesty of Great Britain's subjects; we, the underwritten, are content to become hostages for the said city, and to continue in the custody of the said Captains Thomas Dover, Woodes Rogers and Stephen Courtney, till thirty thousand pieces of gold should be paid to them for the ransom of the said city, two new ships, and six barks; during which time no hostility is to be committed on either side, between this and Puna: the said sum to be paid at Puna, within six days from the date hereof; and then the hostages to be discharged, and all the prisoners to be delivered immediately; otherwise the said hostages do agree to remain prisoners till the said sum is discharged in any other part of the world.

In Witness Whereof, We have voluntarily set our hands, this twenty-seventh day of April, old stile, in the year of our Lord, 1709."

This ransom seems to have been punctually paid, and the hostages faithfully liberated. However, Captains Thomas Dover, Woodes Rogers and Stephen Courtney appear, in addition, to have plundered the town pretty thoroughly.

CHAPTER II.

Expeditions of Viscaino.—Admiral Otondo and Father Kino.—First settlement, and introduction of the priest rule in the Californias.—Failure and withdrawal of the first missions.—Renewed attempts to make settlements.—Father Salva-Tierra and his coadjutors.—Final establishment of the Jesuits in the country.—Geographical discoveries of Father Kino.—Jesuits expelled and superseded by Franciscan Friars; these, in turn, by the Dominican Monks.—Population and physical character of Old or Lower California.

We shall now return to the progress of the Spaniards in discovering and settling the coast of California:—In 1596 Gaspar de Zuniga, Count de Monte-rey, then viceroy of Mexico, received an order from Philip II. to make farther discoveries and settlements on the coast of California. The visit of Drake, and his naming and claiming the country as first discoverer, for Queen Elizabeth, had struck the inhabitants of the coast lower down with consternation; and already Englishmen, particularly the famous Thomas Cavendish, and others, had fortified themselves on the coast, and molested the rich Spanish ships which yearly sailed between the Philippine Islands and New Spain, and which generally made the coast of California about Cape Mendocino. At that period, there was much talk of a north-east passage from the Pacific to the old world by the Straits of Anian (Behring's Straits), and the Spanish Government in Europe was considerably alarmed lest the English should, by that probable route, strike a deadly blow at their unprotected colonies on the west coast of the Americas. An expedition to make fresh discoveries was accordingly undertaken, and put under the command of General Sebastian Viscaino, a man of great and tried abilities.

Viscaino accordingly sailed from Acapulco, but does not appear to have proceeded far northwards; for, in the same year (1596), we find him returned to New Spain. Want of provisions and unfortunate disputes with the Indians, produced this speedy result. The Spanish Government, however, was keeping the matter in view. In 1599 another order was dispatched from Europe to Count Monte-rey to fit out a new expedition for the purposes already mentioned. This again was placed under the command of General Viscaino. In May, 1602, Viscaino, in pursuance of his instructions, sailed from Acapulco, and proceeded

View in the Interior of California.

northwards till he reached the forty-second degree of latitude. Up to the twenty-sixth parallel, he appears to have surveyed the coast minutely ; but between that degree and the most northern limits of his voyage, he seems to have been satisfied with merely keeping the land in sight. He discovered the ports of San Diego and Monterey, which latter was so named in honor of the viceroy. Still not a word of San Francisco Bay. Indeed it is quite evident that up to this period that great harbor had escaped the observation of all the navigators who had attempted to explore the coast. Viscaino, excited by his imperfect discoveries, and full of hope of making more important ones on a fresh expedition, solicited the viceroy for permission to pursue it at his own expense ; but the viceroy referred him to the

Court at Madrid, who seemed to have taken the business into their own hands. Viscaino therefore visited Spain, and pressed his suit, but in vain. At last, in 1606, after Viscaino, wearied and sick at heart with "hope deferred," had retired, moody and discontented, to Mexico, another ordinance was issued by Philip, commanding a fresh expedition of discovery and settlement to be undertaken. The conduct of this was bestowed upon Viscaino, who accepted the charge with alacrity; but before any progress was made in the matter, he was seized with a fatal distemper. After his death nothing was done or said about the expedition.

Various attempts on a moderate scale, partly by adventurers at their own cost, and partly under royal ordinances, were subsequently made to prosecute the survey and settlement of the coast. In 1615, in 1633 and 1634, in 1640, 1642, 1648, 1665, and 1668, several fruitless efforts were made for these purposes. In the interval, the public mind was filled with magnificent views of the wealth of the scarcely discovered country. It was known that pearls, of great beauty and value, were found at various places in the gulf and along the coast. Perhaps also the glowing statements made by Sir Francis Drake of the golden sands and other mineral riches which he saw there, helped to fire the imaginations of the Spaniards. *Omne ignotum pro magnifico.* California was long viewed as the *Dorado* of New Spain; and was believed not merely to be abounding in pearls and gold and silver, but also in diamonds, and all manner of other precious metals and gems. Our own days have justified these sparkling fancies, though scarcely perhaps in the exact manner and localities of which the old Spaniards dreamed.

In 1677, instructions were, after long and mature deliberation, sent by the Court at Madrid to Don Francis Payo Enriquez de Rivera, archbishop of Mexico, and viceroy of New Spain, to undertake afresh the survey, conquest and settlement of California; and that Admiral Pinadero, who had previously carried on some private expeditions for the same end, at his own cost, should be employed in the affair;—that, if he declined, the business should be offered to, and managed by others, also at their expense, under certain specified conditions;—but that, if no volunteer came forward, the undertaking should be conducted at the cost of the Crown. The enterprise fell to Admiral Don Isidro Otondo and Antillion, who signed an instrument for that purpose, in December, 1678, which was approved of at Madrid on 29th December, 1679. By this deed, the spiritual government was conferred on the Jesuits and Father Eusebio Francisco Kühn, —a German by birth, called by the Spaniards Kino, and who was a distinguished member of the Society of Jesus. This seems the origin of the connection of the Jesuits and priest class with California. Otondo and his Jesuits put to sea from Chacala, in May, 1683, and sailed up the gulf. During two years the admiral and his missionary priests, who had meanwhile learned the native languages, met with various success among the Indians of the peninsula, many of whom they succeeded in converting to Christianity. However, they occasionally found rebellious tribes ; and on the whole, were unable to make any serious impression on their minds, or to establish any permanent settlement of importance. This was caused indeed more by the natural barrenness of the country, and the difficulty and expense of supporting existence there, than by the vicious habits of the natives, who are described as a simple, inoffensive and feeble race, more prone to consider their white visitors as absolute deities on earth than as invaders of their territorial rights.

The Spanish Court, which appears to have been drawn into a large expenditure by this expedition, and by another, which immediately followed, conducted by the same parties, soon got tired of the subject, and judged the conquest and settlement of the country to be impracticable. They declined, therefore, to prosecute the undertaking farther; but knowing the political importance of having it somehow accomplished, they recommended the Society of Jesus to finish it, and offered that body large annual subsidies from the royal treasury in aid. The Society, after discussing the "estimates" of Admiral Otondo and Father Kino, and their own "ways and means," respectfully rejected the royal proposal ; and thus a measure which had been agitated for nearly two hundred years, and of which all admitted the political importance, while the personal and pecuniary reward of success was believed to be immense, was abruptly brought to a close. So doubtful, expensive and dangerous did the undertaking appear, that the Crown refused the petition of Captain Francisco Luzenilla to attempt it at his own expense. In the year 1694, indeed, a royal license was granted to Captain Francisco Itamarra for making a descent at his own risk and charges ; but he had no better success than his predecessors.

Spanish ship of the seventeenth century, and coast of California.

The missionaries, who had accompanied the expeditions of Admiral Otondo, were now drafted to different places elsewhere, although many of them deeply regretted that the rich harvest of heathenism should be so suddenly and unexpectedly abandoned, just when the sickle was sharpened and the laborers were in the field. They had labored with great industry to accomplish an object toward which they looked forward with anxious hopes, which they now saw would never be realized. They thought that their Indian conversions would, sooner or later, have extended over the whole tribes in California, had they been enabled to retain settlements there ; while it was more than probable that their new converts would relapse into their old idolatry on the departure of their spiritual teachers. Without detailing, therefore, the various steps taken by the

Fathers to preserve and advance their spiritual ascendency in California, it may be sufficient to say, that Father Kino, who had these conversions much at heart, met with Father Salva-Tierra, a man, like himself, of great enthusiasm for the Catholic faith, and of untiring courage, and much benevolence and sweetness of disposition. These two men,—particularly the latter, who had chosen St. Francis Xavier as his model,—were the true apostles of California. Somewhat later, Fathers Francisco Maria Piccolo and Juan Ugarte associated themselves with these pioneers of Christianity and civilization. Their biographies would make an indispensable and most interesting chapter in the early history of Lower California, but are out of place in this short summary of the progress of discovery and gradual settlement of the general country. It is sufficient to observe that their pious zeal urged them on against every obstacle—the unwillingness of their own Society of Jesus—the indifference of the Court, when it had to advance the whole funds—the delays of officials—the poverty of their own means, and the fewness of their coadjutors. At last, the eloquence and pertinacity of Father Salva-Tierra kindled some life among the superiors of their order and in a few wealthy laymen. The last assisted the Society by large donations; and soon subscriptions began to pour in from the general public, to promote the pious work of conquering California to Christianity. A crusade—peaceful, if the devil got frightened and retired from the contest; but warlike, if need were—was proclaimed; and all were invited to support the scheme by pecuniary means, while the Spanish Government supplied the necessary soldiers to protect the Fathers, and execute their decrees and those of heaven. It was all, in terms of the motto and ruling spirit of the Society, *ad majorem Dei gloriam;* and great indeed would be the reward in heaven of the patrons of the business. After many hardships, and a slow, painful progress, the Jesuit missionaries succeeded in planting various missions over the whole peninsula. Aided by subscriptions from the pious, and donations from the Crown, they were enabled to give the simple Indians daily food and a scanty raiment, and soon, with unwearied patience, converted them into excellent and faithful servants and devout Christians. They had no more sense than mere children, and they were accordingly treated as such. Like children, they were always believing and obedient. Ignorant and helpless, they were slaves both in body and mind, and knew no will but that of their spiritual and temporal lords.

Father Salva-Tierra, in 1705, was chosen provincial of his Order in Mexico, and thus absolutely governed the country both in spiritual and temporal things. It was in 1700 and 1701, by some accounts, and in 1709 by others, that, in the course of several journeys undertaken for the purpose, Father Kino discovered that California was united with the main land. We have seen that this fact was known as early as 1541, where it appears a peninsula in the map of Castillo; but somehow the circumstance had been unaccountably forgotten, and the contrary was almost universally believed.

In 1767, the Fathers lost the missions, in consequence of an ordinance issued by Charles III. for the instant and general expulsion of the Jesuits from all the Spanish dominions. This stringent decree was immediately obeyed in the Mexican provinces, where the Jesuits were arrested without delay, and hundreds of them shipped off to Europe. They were succeeded in California by a body of Franciscan Friars from Mexico; but these in turn were soon superseded by the Dominican Monks, who still retain possession of the country.

The population of Lower California was never great, and towards the end of last century was rapidly diminishing. Humboldt, in his "Political Essay on New Spain," estimates that the population, in 1803, did not exceed nine thousand of all races,—somewhat more than the half of which number consisting of the domesticated converts of the Fathers. The missions had then been reduced to sixteen. Mr. Alexander Forbes, in his "History of Upper and Lower California" (London, 1839), estimates the total population, in 1835, not to exceed fourteen or fifteen thousand. Compared with New California, the old country of that name is a dry and barren land—with a serene and beautiful sky, indeed, but with a rocky, or sandy and arid soil, where rains seldom fall, and vegetation is consequently of little account. Such a country could never become very populous, either in a savage or a civilized state.

CHAPTER III.

First settlement of New or Upper California by Franciscan Monks.—Supposed earliest discovery of San Francisco Bay.—Origin of the name.—Establishment of a Mission and Presidio there, and ceremonies on the occasion.—Gradual establishment of Missions and Presidios over the country.—List of these, and population of same at various dates.—The *gente de razon* and the *bestias*, or the rational creatures and beasts of the country.—Causes why free white settlers few in number.—Character of the natives as given by Venegas, and other writers.—Progress and apparent destiny of the Anglo-Saxons in the Pacific.

STILL later than Old California, and upwards of two hundred years after its first discovery, New or Upper California, was first settled. The Spanish Court, afraid, as of old, lest some of the other maritime nations of Europe should settle on the north-west coasts of America, and induced by other political reasons, alluded to in the previous chapters, sent instructions to the Marquis de Croix, then viceroy of New Spain, to found missions, and *presidios* for their military protection, in the ports of San Diego and Monterey, and at various other parts of the country. This was accordingly done, with the aid of the church, in 1769, and following years ; and immediately, in gratitude or in terms of special agreement, both the spiritual and temporal government of the country were put under the control of certain monks of the Order of St. Francis, two being placed at the head of each mission established. Presidios, in addition to those at San Diego and Monterey, were subsequently formed at Santa Barbara and San Francisco. Father Junipero Serra,—a man of the Salva-Tierra and Kino stamp,—was the first presiding missionary ; and under his immediate auspices the mission of San Diego was founded in 1769, being the earliest.

Without dwelling on the successive establishment of the other missions, let us say a few words upon that of San Francisco. The missionaries, in proceeding northwards, with the intention of reaching Monterey, happened to take the eastern side of the range of mountains which borders the coast north of San Diego, which place they had just left, after establishing its mission. They undesignedly passed by Monterey, and journeyed on till they reached the magnificent bay and harbor which are now called San Francisco; and which are said to be so named from the following circumstance:—Father Junipero, on leaving Lower California, had received instructions from the *visitador*, or inspector-general of the Spanish Government, respecting the names of the proposed missions, and the saints carefully selected from the calendar, to whose special patronage they should be entrusted; but among them the name of St. Francis did not happen to occur. "What!" exclaimed the good missionary, surprised and shocked at such an insulting neglect, "is not our own dear Father, St. Francis, to have a mission assigned to him?" To this remonstrance, the visitador calmly replied, "If Saint Francis wish a mission, let him show you a good port, and then it will bear his name." When accordingly the missionaries, in their progress northwards, discovered the spacious bay mentioned, they cried out, "This then is the port to which the visitador referred, and to which the saint has led us—blessed be his name!" And forthwith they named it San Francisco Bay, in compliment to their patron and guide. They next set up the usual cross, took formal possession, and returned to San Diego, where they arrived on the 24th January, 1770. From any thing that can be certainly learned of the proceedings of previous travellers and voyagers, this seems the true and first discovery of that great bay—nearly two hundred years after Sir Francis Drake was *reputed* to have visited it.

The mission itself of San Francisco was only founded in 1776, though it had been projected ever since the discovery of the bay, about the end of October, 1769. On the 27th June of the first mentioned year, an expedition which had started by land from Monterey, arrived on the borders of a small lake,—the same which is now called "*Washerwoman's Lagoon*,"—near the sea-shore, from which it is separated by a low sand-hill. This is situated towards the northern extremity of the Peninsula of San Francisco, and the surplus waters of which discharge themselves into the strait that connects the bay with the ocean, and which was afterwards called the "*Golden Gate.*" The neighborhood of this lake promised to be the best spot for establishing the mission; though it was subsequently planted about two miles to the south. A store-ship had previously left Monterey with the necessary supplies for the wants of the missionary band. Some soldiers, and a few families from Sonora, as intending settlers, had accompanied the expedition. They carried with them a number of black cattle and sheep, horses, mules, field and garden seeds, and other necessary means of stocking and making the settlements a profitable investment. While waiting the arrival of the store-ship from Monterey, which, owing to foul winds, did not take place till the 18th August following, the expedition began to make preparations for their permanent abode by cutting down timber, and selecting what appeared to be the most eligible site for a settlement. On the 17th day of September, solemn possession was taken of the presidio—"the day," according to Father Palou, the historian of the achievements of Father Junipero, "being the festival of the impression of the sores of Saint Francis, the patron of the port. After blessing, adoring, and planting the holy cross, the first mass was chaunted, and the ceremony concluded by a *Te Deum*; the act of possession in the name of our sovereign being accompanied with many discharges of artillery and musketry by sea and land."

After these ceremonies, the harbor was surveyed, both from the shore and by means of a launch, from the water; when it was ascertained that there was only one outlet to the sea, that by which the store-ship had entered. On the 9th day of November—being the day of Saint Francis—a similar ceremony was performed on taking possession of the mission; when, as Father Palou remarks of the establishment and consecration of the mission and church of San Fernando, "the want of an organ and other musical instruments was supplied by the continual discharge of the fire-arms during the ceremony, and the want of incense, of which they had none, by the smoke of the muskets." No doubt the pious priests thought this was a pretty way of pleasing the Omnipotent. Certainly it was one admirably suited to enchain the minds of the scared natives. The white "sorcerers" were clearly more clever than the brown ones. This mission subsequently bore the name *Dolores*, in commemoration of the sufferings of the Virgin.

Mission of San Francisco.

The Fathers showed much good taste in selecting the site of the mission buildings, which was a small fertile plain, embosomed among gentle, green-clad hills, little more than a mile from the shore and about two miles from the centre of the present city of San Francisco. Several tiny rivulets of clear, sweet water, met about the spot, whose united streams were conducted to the bay by one larger creek, known by the name of Mission Creek. Farther north the land was one continued succession of bleak sand-hills, among which the present city is situated. An exception, however, must be made of the spot where the presidio was established, which indeed was very prettily and agreeably situated A small cove lay to the eastward of the presidio, within the narrow entrance to the bay, where good anchorage ground and shelter could be had. This was the original port of the mission, though latterly the cove of Yerba Buena, a few miles distant, and within the bay itself, was more frequently adopted as a harbor.

On the arrival of this expedition at the bay, many of the natives had affectionately approached the missionaries with demonstrations of peace, and all the signs of extreme pleasure at their appearance; but before the ceremonies alluded to—the imposing chanted masses and *Te Deums*, and still more wonderful salvos of artillery and musketry—had been played, the whole of the natives who had inhabited the place, having been surprised by an unfriendly tribe, suddenly disappeared. This untoward circumstance somewhat delayed the conversions, the first baptism having taken place only on Saint John's Day, December 27th, of the same year.

The names and foundations of the various missions, up to 1803, according to the authority of Humboldt, taking them in their order from south to north, with their respective Indian populations at the close of 1802, are as follows:—

Foundations.	Missions.	Males.	Females.	Total.
1769	San Diego,....................	737	822	1559
1798	San Luis Rey de Francia,........	256	276	532
1776	San Juan Capistrano,............	502	511	1013
1771	San Gabriel,....................	532	515	1047
1797	San Fernando,...................	317	297	614
1782	San Buenaventura,...............	436	502	938
1786	Santa Barbara,..................	521	572	1093
1787	La Purissima Concepcion,........	457	571	1028
1772	San Luis Obispo,................	374	325	699
1797	San Miguel,.....................	309	305	614
1791	Soledad,........................	296	267	563
1771	San Antonio de Padua,.........	568	484	1052
1770	San Carlos de Monterey,.........	376	312	688
1797	San Juan Bautista,..............	530	428	958
1794	Santa Cruz,.....................	238	199	437
1777	Santa Clara,....................	736	555	1291
1797	San José,.......................	327	295	622
1776	San Francisco,..................	433	381	814
	Total, ...	7945	7617	15562

NOTE.—Forbes gives this table as taken from *Humboldt;* but there is a slight discrepancy in the two sets of figures. It is possible that the English translation is incorrect. Forbes' table distinguishes the males and females which Humboldt's does not. Forbes' table is therefore adopted with some verbal corrections from Humboldt direct. This translation, or the original work itself, has various discrepancies in its figures. For instance, it talks of the population being 15,562, at one place, while in its table, for the same year, the figures summed up, make 15,630.

These populations include only the converted Indians, who were attached to the missions. There are no statistics which can be relied upon as to the numbers of wild Indians,—or *gentiles*, as they were called by the Spaniards. Indeed as these gentiles were naturally of an emigratory habit, roaming from place to place in search of game, or in pursuit of hostile tribes, they could scarcely be classed as among the permanent inhabitants of any particular district of country. It was estimated by Humboldt that, in 1802, the number of whites, mestizoes and mulattoes, and who lived either in the presidios or in the service of the monks, was only about thirteen hundred. These were the *gente de razon*, or rational creatures of the country, in contradistinction to the natives, who were considered only as *bestias*, or beasts.

In 1802, the total Indian population connected with the missions, when they were eighteen in number, as shown by the above table, amounted to 15,562. In 1801, Humboldt says, that the Indian population was 13,668, and in 1790, when the missions were eleven in number, it was 7748. La Pérouse, in 1786, when there were only ten missions, estimates the converted or domesticated Indians at 5143. These figures show a very rapid increase of population, or rather of conversions, in so few years. The real increase of population, however, would have been considerable among the *gente de razon* had not the traditionary customs or laws, which regulated the Spanish presidios for ages, stood in the way of the settling of the white population. The governing priests were jealous of their white subjects (*the people of reason*), and wished only a tame Indian population, who were supposed unable to reason. Therefore the soldiers of the presidios were not allowed to establish themselves as colonists, nor was any building permitted to be erected in the neighborhood of these fortresses. Indeed no marriages were tolerated among the soldiers, without the consent of the Spanish Crown, and such consent the Fathers hindered as much as lay in their power. Notwithstanding these impolitic restrictions, the fertility and pleasantness of the land were so great as gradually to draw a small number of white settlers from other provinces of New Spain; and although grants of land could only flow from the Fathers themselves, yet, either through favor or direct interest, such grants were occasionally obtained, though generally the land thus given lay at a considerable distance from the missions and presidios.

The Indian population attached to the missions were meanwhile becoming an industrious, contented and numerous class, though indeed, in intelligence and manly spirit, they were little better than *bestias*—beasts, after all. Generally speaking, the Indians along the whole north-west coast of America were a very inferior order of beings to the great tribes who inhabited the Atlantic border; and, in particular, the different races who dwelt in California were but poor wandering clans who subsisted on what they could procure by hunting and fishing, and on the fruits and grains which grew spontaneously; but they knew nothing of the arts of agriculture, or even of a pastoral life. They might properly enough be compared to the aborigines of Australia or to the Hottentots, or, perhaps, even the Bosjesmans of Southern Africa, who have been considered the most barbarous and brute-like people on the earth. On this subject, Humboldt remarks that "the Indians of the Bay of San Francisco were equally wretched at that time (the establishment of the missions), with the inhabitants of Van Diemen's Land." Venegas has said of the aborigines of the peninsula, who closely resembled their brethren in Upper California, that "it is not easy for Europeans who were never out of their own country to conceive an adequate idea of these people. For even in the least frequented corners of the globe there is not a nation so stupid, of such contracted ideas, and weak both in body and mind, as the unhappy Californians. Their characteristics are stupidity and insensibility, want of knowledge and reflection, inconstancy, impetuosity and blindness of appetite, an excessive sloth, and abhorrence of all fatigues of every kind, however trifling or brutal; in fine, a most wretched want of every thing which constitutes the real man and renders him rational, inventive, tractable, and useful to himself and society."

The worthy Father Michael certainly paints, in dull enough colors, his *protégés* and converts. It may be farther remarked, that the Indians appear to have had little or no notion of religion, although they seem to have had a kind of *sorcerers* among them, who amused or terrified themselves and their patients with sundry superstitious observances. Some writers, such as La Pérouse, say, that they had no knowledge of a God or a future state;

others simply call them idolaters. The natives around San Francisco Bay appear to have burned the corpses of their people, while other tribes, more to the south, always buried theirs. Occasionally, they appear to have eaten pieces of the bodies of their more distinguished adversaries killed in battle, although this was pro-

1. *Wahla*, chief of the Yuba tribe,—civilized and employed by Mr. S. Brannan. 2. A partly civilized Indian. 3. A wild Indian.—From daguerreotypes by Mr. W. Shew.

bably only to insure, as they imagined, that a portion of the brave spirit and good qualities of the slain should enter into and be incorporated with their own systems along with the literal flesh of their antagonists.

These notices and the extracts previously given from the voyages of Drake and Cavendish, abundantly establish the fact of the wretched state of humanity in California. And so it might have been till doomsday, had not a new people appeared on the scene. The Spanish population, and the Fathers, could not, or would not, as truly they did not, as we may afterwards see, do any thing to promote the happiness of the human race in the country. Men feed the ox and the sheep for their milk and fleece, the hog for his flesh, the ass for the strength of his back, and all for their increase ; so did the Fathers feed their Indian converts, and find abundant profit in their labor and personal services, whom they left, as they perhaps found, if they did not transform them into moral beasts, just as tame, dull and silly, dirty, diseased and stupidly obstinate as the other brutes named. Meanwhile, the little independence, natural intelligence and superiority of mind and character which even the rudest savages possess over the lower creatures were gradually sapped and brushed away, and the Christian converts left ignorant, superstitious and besotted, having neither thoughts nor passions, strength nor will, but at the command and beck of their spiritual and temporal teachers and masters. Better, a thousand times, that the missions and all their two-legged and four-legged *beasts* should be ruthlessly swept away, than that so fine a country, one so favored and framed by bountiful nature for the support, comfort and elevation of her worthier children, should longer lie a physical and moral waste—a blotch on the fair face of creation.

But another race was destined soon to blow aside the old mists of ignorance and stupidity, and to develope the exceeding riches of the land, which had lain, undisturbed and concealed, during so many ages. The Spaniards had scarcely proceeded any way in the great work,—if they had not rather retarded it,—when the Anglo-Saxons, the true and perhaps only type of modern *progress*, hastily stepped in, and unscrupulously swept away both their immediate forerunners as effete workers, and the aborigines of the land, all as lumberers and nuisances in the great western highway of civilization. This highway is fated to girdle the globe, and probably, in the course of a few centuries, will join the original starting-point in the natal home of the "Pilgrim Fathers" in old England. The "*pioneers*" of California are *our* "Pilgrim Fathers," and there need be not the slightest doubt but that the empire, or rather the great *union* of peoples and nations in the Pacific will soon—perhaps in fifty years, perhaps in a century—rival, if not surpass the magnificent States of the Atlantic. Indians, Spaniards of many provinces, Hawaiians, Japanese, Chinese, Malays, Tartars and Russians, must all give place to the resistless flood of Anglo-Saxon or American progress. These peoples need not, and most of them probably cannot be swept from the face of the earth ; but undoubtedly their national characteristics and opposing qualities and customs must be materially modified, and closely assimilated to those of the civilizing and dominant race. The English in India have already shown how a *beginning* may be made ; the Americans, on the California coasts, and *farther west,* will still more develope the modern system of progress. People may differ in opinion as to the equity of the particular steps attending the process, and many honest folk may even doubt its ultimate benefit to mankind ; yet that some such grand result will hereafter be evolved from the energy and ebullition of the American character, and from the peculiar circumstances of American position in the world, must be evident to all who take a dispassionate and unprejudiced view of the matter.

Not only are Japan and China much nearer to the Californian coast than India is to England ; but with the aid of steam the time for accomplishing the distance is immensely reduced. In the palmy days of the English conquests in India, her ships took several years to make the voyage out and home. Now, the ocean steamship may traverse the whole northern Pacific from California to China, and back again, within two months ! Indian sepoys fought the battles of England against their own countrymen. Chinese sepoys may do the same for Americans. China, like India, has been long used to, and its national spirit broken by the usurping governments of foreign races. And even while we write, its extensive dominions are being separated by a wide-spread and hitherto successful rebellion, into detached kingdoms under the sway of military chiefs. These, standing alone, and mutually jealous of their conquering neighbors, may be easily played off, one against another, by a white people skilled enough to take advantage of circumstances and direct the moves of the political chess-board. So it was with the English in India ; and so it may be with the Americans in China. Only give us *time.* England has not been very scrupulous in her stealthy progress over Hindostan, Ceylon and Birmah. Then neither need America fear her reproaches, if she, in like manner, acquire, conquer, or *annex* the Sandwich Islands, the Islands of Japan, those of the great Malayan Archipelago, or the mighty "Flowery Empire" itself. A few more years, and a few millions of Americans on the Pacific may realize the gigantic scheme, which even our fathers, on the Atlantic border, would have laughed at as impossible and ridiculous. The railway across, or *through* the Snowy and Rocky Mountains, which will bind all North America with its iron arm into one mighty empire, will facilitate the operation. And then SAN FRANCISCO—in the execution and triumph of that scheme, will assuredly become what Liverpool, or even London is to England, and what New York is to the Middle and Eastern States of America—a grand depot for numberless manufactures and produce, and a harbor for the fleets of every nation. Long before that time, the English and American peoples will have finished the last great struggle which must some day take place between them for the commercial and political supremacy of the world. It is more than probable that the hosts of English from India, and Americans from California, will meet on the rich and densely peopled plains of China, and *there* decide their rival pretensions to universal dominion. Whatever may, in 1854, be thought of the relative strength of the two nations, it appears very evident to the people of America, that the natural increase of their population must necessarily make them victors in the end.

CHAPTER IV.

Conduct of the Fathers towards the natives.—Their mode of instructing, employing and subsisting the converts.—The Fathers do not appear to have promoted the true welfare of the aborigines, or done any good to humanity.—Pictures, if gaudily colored and horrible in subject, great aids to conversion.—Missions and population of the country at recent dates.—Table on this subject.—Tables of the farm produce and domestic cattle of the country.—Table of prices.

It may now be necessary to explain shortly in what manner the Fathers conducted their missions, and the state of their property and finances down to the decline of their prosperity and ultimate fall. Their mode of conversion, if not very ingenious, was easy enough. It was like the teaching of a monkey, or a dog, by means of food and caresses, or sometimes by kicks, to perform a few simple tricks. The Indian—like the hare in Meg Dodds', or it may be Mrs. Glass's Cookery Book, being first *caught*, was dressed in the following fashion, as described by Captain Beechy, in his second voyage:—"I happened to visit the mission about this time and saw these unfortunate beings under tuition. They were clothed in blankets, and arrayed in a row before a blind Indian who understood their dialect, and was assisted by an *alcalde* to keep order. Their tutor began by desiring them to kneel, informing them that he was going to teach them the names of the persons composing the Trinity, and that they were to repeat in Spanish what he dictated. The neophytes being thus arranged, the speaker began:—*Santissima Trinidad, Dios, Jesu Christo, Espiritu Santo*—pausing between each name to listen if the simple Indians, who had never spoken a Spanish word before, pronounced it correctly, or any thing near the mark. After they had repeated these names satisfactorily, their blind tutor, after a pause, added, *Santos*—and recapitulated the names of a great many saints, which finished the morning's tuition."

The pay and inducement to the Indians to submit to what

would doubtless appear even to them a farrago of nonsense, were a daily allowance of *Atole* and *Pozzoli*, which were two kinds of pottages, the first composed of barley flour and the second of the same, varied by the addition of peas, beans and maize. The for-

Indians under instruction

mer was the usual breakfast and supper dish, the latter was chiefly taken for dinner. Then huts, of which the Fathers kept the keys, were provided for the nightly lodgings of the faithful; while a simple kind of clothing was furnished to them at intervals. Soldiers took care meanwhile that order, decency and obedience were strictly observed at work and play, at devotion and rest. In return for these benefits, the Indians rose early, and attended mass every morning, for an hour; and during the day, in the intervals between a second mass and meals and pretty constant prayers, cultivated the gardens and fields of the missions, gathered, preserved and arranged for sale the farm produce, herded and attended to the wants of their cattle, built their houses, spun, wove and cooked, and in all respects drudged patiently, though they do not appear to have taken the work very laboriously, as the born slaves of the Fathers, whose absolute will was all that they could comprehend or obey. With the instinct of a dog, they fawned on and loved their owners, and perhaps would have readily died to do them service. How different all this from the free, intelligent and bold spirit of the present community! To sharpen the intellects of the converts, sticks, whips, long goads and the like were unhesitatingly employed by the beadles of the churches, during mass and prayers, to silence the unruly and make the refractory attentive and dutiful. Starvation and stripes indeed attended the perverse Indian wherever he went; and it was his interest,—he could be made to understand that at all events,—to comply with the wishes of his kind priestly persecutors, as far as his animal nature would permit.

The conversion produced by such means could scarcely be intellectual or very sincere. It seemed sufficient, however, that the Indian duly attended mass (which he was obliged to do under penalty of a sound, edifying whipping), knelt and muttered his incomprehensible Spanish words, made the sign of the cross often and properly enough, and could correctly repeat to his spiritual tutors, when called upon, the few cabalistic phrases which they had taught him. Whether he understood the meaning of these things was quite another question, as to which it was not necessary for the Fathers to be impertinently curious. What were these brown things, after all, but *beasts*—irrational beings, who might have a soul truly to be saved, but whom it was absurd to consider as having a mind! Individually, the Fathers seem to have been pious and philanthropic men; but certainly humanity and California owe them nothing. Every thing, even happiness, is comparative; and to the mind, undarkened by the gloomy theology which considers the formal act of baptism without the understanding soul to be sufficient for salvation, it must surely be evident that the aboriginal savage, "lord of all he surveyed," was a more dignified and happy creature than the sleek, lazy, stall-fed beast of burden into which the Fathers had entrapped, or converted him.

In the churches, which were, of course, the leading and most substantial buildings of the country, the walls were hung with glaringly painted pictures—the more gaudy, the more valuable and effectual—of the saints, and especially of heaven and hell, to astonish and fix the faith of the converts. La Pérouse observes that a horrible representation of hell in the church of San Carlos has thus had a wonderful effect in promoting conversion ; while

Father Garzes and the Indians.

he considers that the picture of paradise in the same church, by reason of its subdued coloring and treatment, had comparatively little effect. In 1775, when Father Garzes was travelling, on a crusading or proselyting expedition, from Sonora to California, he carried with him a painted banner, on one side of which was represented the Blessed Virgin Mary, and on the other the devil in the flames of hell. On arriving at an Indian settlement, the missionary took his first step of conversion. Just as the travelling mountebank blows his horn and flutters his flag on approaching a village of likely gulls, so did our good Father hoist his standard, and cry aloud; when, as he naively observes, the fascinated Indians, on seeing the Virgin, usually exclaimed, *good!*—but when they observed the devil, they as often said, *bad!* Probably this was faith enough to entitle them to immediate baptism, absolution and salvation. Food, lodging and raiment, and freedom from the cares of family and the future, naturally followed.

By such means the Fathers speedily converted the whole Indian tribes within their reach; while, year by year, as the missions, and their servants and cattle increased in number, they took possession of the most fertile and desirable lands in the country. Much judgment and discretion were exhibited, as well in selecting the localities of the missions, as in subsequently managing them for a time to the best possible advantage. The means adopted for converting, training, and employing the natives, were admirably devised, and were more successful and satisfactory than could have been anticipated. The Fathers eagerly desired to make Indian converts; for every convert, besides becoming a partaker of immortal glory, was a valuable slave; but they dreaded, and never invited the approach of free white settlers.

The first mission, San Diego, was founded in 1769; in 1776, others had been established to the number of eight; there were eleven in 1790; and, in 1802, they had increased to eighteen. In subsequent years, three more were added, viz., those of San Francisco Solano, San Rafael and Santa Ines. In 1831, according to the authority of Mr. Forbes in his excellent work, already mentioned, on the "History of Lower and Upper California," the population of all classes for the whole latter country was 23,025—the Indians constituting 18,683 of this number, and the garrisons, missions and free settlements comprehending 4342. That author supposes that as the population, for some years afterwards, was nearly stationary, the same enumeration would nearly hold good for 1835, when he wrote, although his statements were not published till 1839. We extract a valuable table from Mr. Forbes' volume, showing the localities peopled, with the amounts of their population respectively:—

NAMES OF THE JURISDICTIONS, MISSIONS AND TOWNS.	PEOPLE OF ALL CLASSES AND AGES.				
	Men.	Women.	Boys.	Girls.	Total.
Jurisdiction of San Francisco.					
PRESIDIO OF SAN FRANCISCO..............	124	85	89	73	371
Town of San José de Guadalupe........	166	145	103	110	524
Mission of San Francisco Solano.........	285	242	88	90	705
" of San Rafael....................	406	410	105	106	1027
" of San Francisco..................	146	65	13	13	237
" of Santa Clara....................	752	491	68	60	1371
" of San José......................	823	659	100	145	1727
" of Santa Cruz....................	222	94	30	20	366
Jurisdiction of Monterey.					
PRESIDIO OF MONTEREY..................	311	190	110	97	708
Village of Branciforte......................	52	34	27	17	130
Mission of San Juan Bautista...........	480	351	85	71	987
" of San Carlos....................	102	79	34	21	236
" of Na. Sa. de la Soledad........	210	81	23	20	334
" of San Antonio	394	209	51	17	671
" of San Miguel	349	292	46	61	748
" of San Luis Obispo.............	211	103	8	7	329
Jurisdiction of Santa Barbara.					
PRESIDIO OF SANTA BARBARA............	167	120	162	164	613
Mission of La Purissima................	151	218	47	34	450
" of Santa Ines....................	142	136	82	96	456
" of Santa Barbara................	374	267	51	70	762
" of Buenaventura.................	383	283	66	59	791
" of San Fernando................	249	226	177	181	833
Town of La Reyna de los Angeles........	552	421	213	202	1388
Jurisdiction of San Diego.					
PRESIDIO OF SAN DIEGO..................	295				
Mission of San Gabriel	574				
" of San Juan Capistrano.........	464	1911	683	621	* 5686
" of San Luis Rey..................	1138				
" of San Diego.....................	750	520	162	143	1575
Totals........	10272	7632	2623	2498	23025

From the pages also of Mr. Forbes, who seems to have made minute researches on the subject, we extract the two following tables,—the first of which shows the whole produce, in grain, of the country, in 1831, calculated according to localities, and in *fanegas*. The second table, calculated also by localities, gives the total number of cattle, of all descriptions, in the same year. It may be mentioned, however, that in addition to the number of domestic cattle in the table, there were great numbers, particularly mares, running wild ; and which were occasionally hunted

* "We are unable," says Mr. Forbes, "to give these latter details accurately, the copy having accidentally caught fire when in the hands of the printer."

and killed to prevent them eating the pasture of the tamer species.

GRAIN.

NAMES OF THE JURISDICTIONS, MISSIONS AND TOWNS.	Wheat.	Maize or Indian Corn.	Frijoles or Small Beans.	Barley.	Beans, Garvanzas and Peas.	Total Fanegas.
Jurisdiction of San Francisco.						
PRESIDIO OF SAN FRANCISCO	233	70	40			343
Town of San José de Guadalupe	1657	1560	191			3408
Mission of San Francisco Solano	1171	200	24	241	24	1660
" of San Rafael	774	130	15	388	20	1327
" of San Francisco	670	15	9	340	58	1092
" of Santa Clara	2400	60	25		200	2685
" of San José	4000	1000	123	1100	418	6641
" of Santa Cruz	160	300	10	386	20	876
Jurisdiction of Monterey.						
PRESIDIO OF MONTEREY	490	332	131			953
Village of Branciforte	103	160	80			343
Mission of San Juan Bautista	840	170	40	256	6	1311
" of San Carlos	200			215	62	477
" of Na. Sa. de la Soledad	538	50		243	62	893
" of San Antonio	955	115	40	568	23	1701
" of San Miguel	599	36	9	57	33	734
" of San Luis Obispo	350	60	20	20		450
Jurisdiction of Santa Barbara.						
PRESIDIO OF SANTA BARBARA		300	90			390
Mission of La Purissima	700	100	20	56	17	893
" of Santa Ines	800	400	20			1220
" of Santa Barbara	730	90	50	336	30	1236
" of Buenaventura	700	200	160	800		1860
" of San Fernando	200	250	40		65	555
Town of La Reyna de los Angeles	138	1758	179			2075
Jurisdiction of San Diego.						
PRESIDIO OF SAN DIEGO	140	125	5			270
Mission of San Gabriel	1400	400	13		25	1838
" of San Juan Capistrano	450	625	30		5	1110
" of San Luis Rey	1800	2000	200	1200	15	5215
" of San Diego	2946	420	80	1200		4646
Total fanegas	25144	10926	1644	7405	1083	46202

Taking the fanega at two and a half English bushels, the harvest in 1831 would be as follows :—Wheat, 7857½ quarters ; maize, 3414½ quarters ; frijoles, 514 quarters ; barley, 2314 quarters ; beans, garvanzos and peas, 338 quarters ; total, 14,438 quarters. Reckoning the average price of grain in California at the same period to be, wheat and barley two dollars the fanega, or one pound five shillings the English quarter, and maize at one and a half dollars, or one pound per quarter, the following will be the value of the produce, viz. : wheat, $49,114 25, or £9,822 17s. sterling ; maize, $21,340, or £4,268 ; barley, $11,570, or £2,314 ;

peas and beans, reckoned as barley, $4,260, or £852; total, $86,284 25, or £17,256 17s. The quantity of wheat produced it will be perceived, is much greater than any of the other sorts of grain, which is the reverse of what takes place in the Mexican States, where the produce of wheat is small in proportion to that of maize, the latter being the staple bread corn.

DOMESTIC CATTLE.

NAMES OF THE JURISDICTIONS, MISSIONS AND TOWNS.	Black Cattle.	Horses.	Mules.	Asses.	Sheep.	Goats.	Swine.
Jurisdiction of San Francisco.							
PRESIDIO OF SAN FRANCISCO ...	5610	470	40				
Town of San José de Guadalupe..	4443	2386	134				
Mission of San Francisco Solano.	2500	725	4		5000		50
" of San Rafael..........	1200	450	1		2000		17
" of San Francisco........	4200	1239	18		3000		
" of Santa Clara..........	9000	780	38		7000		
" of San José............	12000	1300	40		13000		40
" of Santa Cruz..........	3500	940	82		5403		
Jurisdiction of Monterey.							
PRESIDIO OF MONTEREY..........	5641	3310	70				
Village of Branciforte...........	1000	1000	8				
Mission of San Juan Bautista....	7070	401	6	1	7017		17
" of San Carlos...........	2050	470	8		4400	55	
" of Na. Sa. de la Soledad..	6599	1070	50	1	6358		
" of San Antonio.........	5000	1060	80	2	10000	55	60
" of San Miguel..........	3762	950	106	28	8999	15	60
" of San Luis Obispo......	2000	800	200	50	1200		24
Jurisdiction of Santa Barbara.							
PRESIDIO OF SANTA BARBARA.....	7900	1300	220				
Mission of La Purissima........	10500	1000	160	4	7000	30	62
" of Santa Ines...........	7300	820	112		2200		50
" of Santa Barbara........	2600	511	150	2	3300	37	63
" of Buenaventura........	4000	300	60		3100	30	8
" of San Fernando........	6000	300	60	3	3000		
Town of La Reyna de los Angeles	38624	5208	520				
Jurisdiction of San Diego.							
PRESIDIO OF SAN DIEGO..........	608	625	150	58			
Mission of San Gabriel..........	20500	1700	120	4	13554	76	98
" of San Juan Capistrano..	10900	290	30	5	4800	50	40
" of San Luis Rey........	26000	2100	250	5	25500	1200	250
" of San Diego............	6220	1196	132	14	17624	325	
Total........	216727	32201	2844	177	153455	1873	839

The average prices of cattle, about the same period, were, for a mule or saddle horse, ten dollars, or two pounds sterling; a mare, cow or fat ox, five dollars, or one pound; a sheep, two dollars, or eight shillings.

In regard to the preceding tables, it may be remarked that, in 1831, the missions had already lost much of their former splendor and greatness. Ever since 1824, their progress had been of a downward character. Most of them had so wilfully mismanaged their estates, or so dissipated their means, or been plundered of them by the Mexican authorities, that their wealth in cattle, farm produce, &c., had dwindled down to less than one-fourth, while the pecuniary affairs of many of their number showed a still more ruinous appearance. We have given at length the tables of Mr. Forbes, because he appears to have paid much careful attention to the subject ; and we would now add some statistics as to the riches of the missions, during the period of their reputed greatest prosperity, extracted from the Rev. Walter Colton's "Three Years in California" (New York, 1850), whose statements, however, are somewhat more sweeping and less detailed than those of Mr. Forbes.

The Mission of *San Francisco Dolores*, in 1825, is said to have possessed 76,000 head of cattle, 950 tame horses, 2,000 breeding mares, 84 stud of choice breed, 820 mules, 79,000 sheep, 2,000 hogs, 456 yoke of working oxen, 18,000 bushels of wheat and barley, $35,000 in merchandise, and $25,000 in specie :—*Santa Clara*, in 1823, branded, as the increase of one year, 22,400 calves. It owned 74,280 head of full-grown cattle, 407 yoke of working oxen, 82,540 sheep, 1,890 trained horses, 4,235 mares, 725 mules, 1,000 hogs, and $120,000 in goods :—*San José*, in 1825, had 3,000 Indians, 62,000 head of cattle, 840 tame horses, 1,500 mares, 420 mules, 310 yoke of oxen, and 62,000 sheep :—*San Juan Bautista*, in 1820, owned 43,870 head of cattle, 1,360 tame horses, 4,870 mares, colts, and fillies. It had also seven sheep farms, containing 69,530 sheep ; while the Indians attached to the mission drove 321 yoke of working oxen. Its storehouse contained $75,000 in goods, and $20,000 in specie :—*San Carlos*, in 1825, branded 2,300 calves, and had 87,600 head of cattle, 1,800 horses and mares, 365 yoke of oxen, nine sheep farms, with an average of about 600 sheep on each, a large assortment of merchandise, and $40,000 in specie :—*Santa Cruz*, so lately as 1830, had 42,800 head of cattle, 3,200 horses and mares, 72,500 sheep, 200 mules, large herds of swine, and $25,000 worth of silver plate :—*Soledad*, in 1826, owned about 36,000 head of cattle, and a greater number of horses and mares than any other mission in the country. The increase of these animals was said to be so great, that they were given away to preserve the pasturage for cattle and sheep. This mission had about 70,000 sheep and 300 yoke of tame oxen :—*San Antonio*, in 1822, owned 52,800 head of cattle, 1,800 tame horses, 3,000 mares, 500 yoke of working oxen, 600 mules, 48,000 sheep, and 1,000 swine :—*San Miguel*, in 1821, owned 91,000 head of cattle, 1,100 tame horses, 3,000 mares, 2,000 mules, 170 yoke of

Mission of Santa Barbara.

working oxen, and 47,000 sheep :—*San Luis Obispo* was reputed to have been one of the richest of the missions. At one time, it owned 87,000 head of grown cattle, 2,000 tame horses, 3,500 mares, 3,700 mules, and eight sheep farms, averaging 9,000 sheep to each farm. When its presiding priest, Luis Martinez, returned to Spain, he took with him $100,000 of mission property :—*La Purissima*, so lately as 1830, had over 40,000 head of cattle, 300 yoke of working oxen, 2,600 tame horses, 4,000 mares, 30,000 sheep, and 5,000 swine :—*Santa Inez*, in 1820, possessed property valued at $800,000 :—*Santa Barbara*, in 1828, had 40,000 head of cattle, 1,000 horses, 2,000 mares, 80 yoke of oxen, 600 mules, and 20,000 sheep :—*San Buenaventura*, in 1825, owned 37,000 head of cattle, 600 riding horses, 1,300 mares, 200 yoke of working oxen, 500 mules, 30,000 sheep, 200 goats, 2,000 swine, a thrifty orchard, two rich vineyards, $35,000 in foreign goods, $27,000 in specie, with church ornaments and clothing valued at $61,000 :—*San Fernando*, in 1826, owned 56,000 head of cattle, 1,500 horses and mares, 200 mules, 400 yoke of working oxen, 64,000 sheep, and 2,000 swine. It had also in its stores about $50,000 in merchandise, and $90,000 in specie. Its vineyards yielded annually about 2,000 gallons of brandy, and as many of wine :—*San Gabriel*, in 1829, had 70,000 head of cattle, 1,200 horses, 3,000 mares, 400 mules, 120 yoke of working oxen, and 54,000 sheep. It made annually from four to six hundred barrels of wine, the sale of which produced an income of upwards of $12,000 :—*San Luis Rey*, in 1826, had 70,000 head of cattle, 2,000 horses, 140 yoke of tame oxen, 300 mules, and 68,000 sheep :—*San Juan Capistrano* and *San Diego* were reputed to be among the most opulent of the missions, and their possessions were not inferior to those of the others named.

Let the reader contrast these statements with those of Mr. Forbes, and consider what havoc must have been produced among the missions in the short space of six or seven years. It was the impending secularization, or, in other words, the confiscation of their property, which seems to have produced this lamentable state of affairs, and made the Fathers quite careless in the management of their property. The large occasional grants, also, out of which the laity either wheedled or bullied the Fathers, mightily helped the disastrous result. The ravens had been long gathering round the carcass of the still breathing creature. In its last spasms, it recklessly threw aside all decorum, and thinking nothing of the future only endeavored to share in and for the moment enjoy its own spoils, along with the grasping and sacrilegious Mexican officials and their Californian favorites. Soon lands and stocks were all swept from the reach of the Fathers, the very Indian converts disappeared, and nothing was left but their huge empty churches, stripped of most of their valuable and gaudy ornaments, and fast crumbling into ruins. With the general disappearance of the stock of domestic cattle, those laymen who had acquired grants to the different parts of the mission possessions now turned their attention more to tillage.

CHAPTER V.

Pious Fund of California—General description of the Missions—Patriarchal kind of life of the Fathers—Reflections on the subject—General description of the Presidios, Castillos, and their garrisons, and of the free Pueblos and Ranchos.

THE missions of Upper California were indebted for their beginning and chief success to the subscriptions which, as in the case of the missionary settlements of the lower province, were largely bestowed by the pious to promote so grand a work as turning a great country to the worship of the true God. Such subscriptions continued for a long period, both in Old and New Spain, and were regularly remitted to the City of Mexico, where they were formed into what was called "*The Pious Fund of California.*" This fund was managed by the convent of San Fernando and other trustees in Mexico, and the proceeds, together with the annual salaries allowed by the Crown to the missionaries were transmitted to California. Meanwhile, the Spanish Court scarcely interfered with the temporal government of the country. It was true that some of the ordinary civil offices and establishments were kept up; but this was only in name, and on too small a scale to be of any practical importance. A commandante-general was appointed by the Crown to command the garrisons of the presidios, but as these were originally established solely to protect the missions from the dreaded violence of hostile Indians, and to lend them, when necessary, the carnal arm of offence, he was not allowed to interfere in the temporal rule of the Fathers. He resided at Monterey, and his annual salary was four thousand dollars.

In every sense of the word, then, these monks were practically the sovereign rulers of California—passing laws affecting not only property, but even life and death—declaring peace and war against their Indian neighbors—regulating, receiving, and spending the finances at discretion—and, in addition, drawing large annual subsidies not only from the pious among the faithful over all Christendom, but even from the Spanish monarchy itself, almost as a tribute to their being a superior state. This surely was the golden age of the missions—a contented, peaceful, believing people, abundant wealth for all their wants, despotic will, and no responsibility but to their own consciences and heaven! Their horn was filled to overflowing; but soon an invisible and merciless hand seized it, and slowly and lingeringly, as if in malicious sport, turned it over, and spilled the nectar of their life upon the wastes of mankind, from whence it can never again be collected. The golden age of another race has now dawned, and with it the real prosperity of the country.

The missions were originally formed on the same general plan, and they were planted at such distances from each other as to allow abundant room for subsequent development. They were either established on the sea-coast, or a few miles inland. Twenty or thirty miles indeed seems all the distance the missionaries had proceeded into the interior; beyond which narrow belt the country was unexplored and unknown. Each mission had a considerable piece of the best land in the neighborhood set aside for its agricultural and pastoral purposes, which was commonly about fifteen miles square. But besides this selected territory, there was generally much more vacant land lying between the boundaries of the missions, and which, as the increase of their stocks required more space for grazing, was gradually occupied by the flocks and herds of the Fathers, nearest to whose mission lay the previously unoccupied district. Over these bounds the Fathers conducted all the operations of a gigantic farm. Their cattle generally numbered from ten thousand to twenty thousand, and their sheep were nearly as numerous—though some missions had upwards of thrice these numbers—which fed over perhaps a hundred thousand acres of fertile land.

Near the centre of such farms were placed the mission buildings. These consisted of the church—which was either built of stone, if that material could be procured in the vicinity, or of *adobes*, which are bricks dried in the sun, and was as substantial, large, and richly decorated an erection as the means of the mission would permit, or the skill and strength of their servants could construct. In the interior, pictures and hangings decorated the

Mission of San Carlos.

walls; while the altars were ornamented with marble pillars of various colors, and upon and near them stood various articles of massy gold and silver plate. A profusion of gilding and tawdry sparkling objects caught and pleased the eye of the simple congregations. Around, or beside the church, and often in the form of a square, were grouped the habitations of the Fathers and their household servants, and the various granaries and workshops of the people; while, at the distance of one or two hundred yards, stood the huts of the Indians. The former buildings were constructed of *adobes*, and covered with brick tiles, frail and miserable materials at the best. The huts of the Indians were occasionally made of the same materials, but more commonly were formed only of a few rough poles, stuck in the ground with the points bending towards the centre like a cone, and were covered with reeds and grass. An *adobe* wall of considerable height sometimes inclosed the whole village. The direction of the affairs of the settlement was in the hands of one of the Fathers, originally called a president, but afterwards a *prefect;* and each prefect was independent in his own mission, and practically supreme in all its temporal, and nearly in all its spiritual matters, to any human authority.

Thus the Fathers might be considered to have lived something in the style of the patriarchs of the days of Job and Abraham. They indeed were generally ignorant and unlettered men, knowing little more than the mechanical rites of their church, and what else their manuals of devotion and the treasuries of the lives of the saints taught them; but they seem to have been personally devout, self-denying, and beneficent in their own simple way. They thought they did God service, and perhaps much more the Indians themselves, in catching, taming, and converting them to Christianity. That was their vocation in the world, and they faithfully obeyed its calls of duty. If ever stern necessity, or sometimes a forgetfulness of the value of life to the wild Indians prompted them, or their military guards and executioners, to the slaughter of a tribe, now and then, of the more fierce, thievish, and untractable natives, they were scrupulously careful first of all to baptize the doomed; and, therefore, though the hapless aborigines lost earthly life and the freedom of a savage state, their souls were saved, and they entered into and enjoyed paradise for ever. Towards the converts and actually domesticated servants, they always showed such an affectionate kindness as a father pays to the youngest and most helpless of his family. The herds and flocks of the Fathers roamed undisturbed over numberless hills and valleys. Their servants or slaves were true born children of the house, who labored lightly and pleasantly, and had no sense of freedom nor desire for change. A rude but bounteous hospitality marked the master's reception of the solitary wayfarer, as he travelled from mission to mission, perhaps bearing some scanty news from the outer world, all the more welcome that the Fathers knew little of the subject and could not be affected by the events and dangers of distant societies. All these things have now passed away. The churches have fallen into decay, deserted by the old worshippers, and poverty-stricken—the *adobe* houses of the Fathers are in ruins—and there is scarcely any trace left of the slightly erected huts of the Indians, who themselves have deserted their old hearths and altars, and are silently though rapidly disappearing from the land. But the memory of the patriarchal times, for they were only as of yesterday, still remains fresh in the minds of the early white settlers.

The quiet beauty and peacefulness of such a life make a delightful subject of contemplation to the wearied spirits who labor through the turmoils, anxieties, and vexations of the great world. But the Indian neophytes had no such contrasts to show them the inherent charm of their contented life. They grew and flourished as the cabbage on the rich soil of their own land ; but they also were as dull and earthly as the same cabbage. It may be very true, the more knowledge, the more sorrow ; yet we cannot avoid thinking that the more sources of intellectual enjoyment a man has, the keener and more numerous also his moments of pleasure. Even in many of the natural anxieties of civilized society, there is a sense of power and heroic endurance which softens the blow. The mere memory of past pains has almost always something cheerful in it ; while the remembrance of intellectual and refined enjoyments gilds the last and setting hour of our existence. On the other hand, the hopes of the intelligent being are infinitely more agreeable and ennobling than those of the untutored, brutal savage. Therefore it may be concluded that, apart from sickly sentimentalism and Rousseau-like theories, the sooner the aborigines of California are altogether quietly weeded away, the better for humanity. Yet the Fathers would retain them : then sweep away the Fathers too.

Like the missions, the presidios were established on one general plan. They were originally formed, as we have seen, to give military protection and the aid of the carnal arm to the Fathers in their conquest and civilization of the country, and in capturing and taming the wild Indians. These presidios were four in number, viz. : those of San Diego, Santa Barbara, Monterey, and San Francisco. They were built in the form of a square of about three hundred feet on each side, surrounded by a wall twelve feet high, made of *adobes,* and most of them are now little better than a confused heap of dried mud, rapidly crumbling into dust. Within these bounds were included the commandante's house, barracks for the troops, a church, store-houses, and various other buildings. At some distance from the presidio was the *castillo*, or fort, which might be sufficient to overawe the simple Indians, but was too defenceless a structure to prevent a superior force of white men taking easy possession of it. A few guns of small calibre were mounted on the ramparts, which, however, seemed more for show than use, since they were never attended to. Soon, therefore, from the ravages of time and the weather, their carriages fell to pieces, and the guns themselves became honey-combed by rust and rot.

The soldiers assigned to each presidio were cavalry, and seem always to have been of the worst kind of troops. As soldiers, they were of little account; as men and settlers, absolutely worthless. There were supposed to be two hundred and fifty attached to each presidio, but their complement was never complete, and generally they were ridiculously short of that number. Undisciplined, wretchedly clothed, and irregularly paid, they were indolent, riotous, and good for nothing but to hunt, and shoot, or capture for new converts and servants, the wild Indians, and to act as policemen over the converts already made. Yet even in these capacities, they generally gave more trouble to the meek Fathers to manage and keep in decent order, than the wild or disobedient natives themselves. These were the soldiers of California in the days of the Spanish monarchy, and they were no better under the Mexican republic. They are represented to have been commonly the refuse of the Mexican army, and were generally either deserters, mutineers, or men guilty of military offences, who were sent to California as to a place of penal banishment. To these presidios also the convicted felons of Mexico were often transported. Such was a considerable portion of the white population of California. We have already seen of what nature the Indian inhabitants were.

Occasionally, the old soldiers of the presidios, upon their retirement, after a certain number of years, from active service, received grants of land from the Fathers, upon which they settled, married, and left descendants. These formed the *nuclei* of a few free towns (*pueblos*), which were not under the control of the missions, but under the immediate government, first of the Spanish and afterwards of the Mexican authorities. As they were established in the most fertile places of the country, they began gradually to attract other white settlers to their neighborhood, and soon exceeded in population and importance most of the original mission villages themselves. These pueblos, however, were only three in number, viz.: that of *Nuestra Señora de los Angeles* (the principal one, and indeed the chief town in California), and those of *San José*, near the mission of Santa Clara, and *Branciforte*, close to the mission of Santa Cruz.

Mission Rancho.

Besides the missions, presidios, castillos, and pueblos, it may be remarked that there were certain public farms, called *ranchos*, set apart for the use of the soldiers. They were generally four or five leagues distant from the presidios, and were under the control of the different commandantes Little use, however, seems to have been made of these farms, and they commonly were left in a state of nature, or afforded only grazing to the few cattle and horses belonging to the presidios.

CHAPTER VI.

Independence of Mexico in 1822, and gradual changes in the character and constitution of the Missions. —Manumission of the Indians in 1826; but plan found unworkable, and return to the old state of things.—Gradual disappearance of the Pious Fund.—Increasing riches of the Fathers.—Changes of 1833 and 1834 in the Missions, and attempts by the Mexican Congress to secularize their property.—Santa Anna.—Attempted Centralization of the Mexican Government.—Overthrow of the old Federal Constitution in 1836.—Revolt and Declaration of Independence of the Californians. —Continual sinking of the Fathers, and final fall of the missions in 1845.—Indian converts sent adrift, and Mission property sold or rented.—Cost of the support of the Missions to the Spanish and Mexican Governments.

THE state of things described under the missions continued without alteration until the overthrow of the Spanish power in Mexico in 1822, and the establishment of a republican constitution in 1824. At that time, as population formed the basis of the Federal States, New California was only admitted into the Union as a *territory*, it not having the necessary population to constitute a State. Under this character, it had a representative in the Mexican Congress, who sat in the assembly and shared in debates, but who was not entitled to vote on any question. The republic was represented in the territory, as the Spanish monarchy had previously been, by a commandante-general, who was nominal governor of the country. However, the practical legislative powers and virtual government remained in the hands of the missons as before. The commandante-general indeed had a kind of advising or privy council given him by law, called a *deputation*, and which was chosen by the people ; but their functions, although appearing to take the form of a local and free government, were very limited, and their meetings accordingly seldom took place.

In 1826, the federal government first began to tamper with the ancient state of affairs. In that year, the Mexican authorities proclaimed the manumission of the Indians, and sent instructions to California that all those should be liberated "who had good characters, and were supposed able to maintain themselves from having been taught the art of agriculture or some trade." Certain portions of land were allotted to them, and the whole country was divided into parishes, under the superintendence of curates. The old salary of the missionaries (four hundred dollars *per annum*) out of the national exchequer was also suspended, as the country was expected to maintain its own local establishments.

This plan, however, was quickly found to be unworkable. The simple Indians were quite incapable of standing alone, and rapidly gambled away, or otherwise squandered the little property assigned to them. Beggary or plunder was only left them to subsist upon. Such a state of things soon restored the Fathers to their former position. The most respectable white settlers entreated them to receive the *beastly* Indians back into the old fold ; and this, in the following year, the Fathers did. But they first took occasion to make the circumstances the ground of petition and complaint to Congress, who subsequently, and in consequence of their remonstrances, ordered not only the old salaries to be continued, but the arrears then due to be paid in full. Thus the reign of the Fathers was prolonged for a few years.

Meanwhile, the old *Pious Fund of California* was become only a name. After the separation of the Mexican provinces from Spain, the ancient subscribers got lukewarm in their payments, and new ones were not easily to be had. In the disturbed state of the country, and in the change of ideas arising from political circumstances, there were more tempting channels for the application of loose money than in riveting the chains of Christianity on poor heathens, or securing the Fathers in their comfortable domicils. But, to compensate for the loss of these subscriptions, the real and personal estate of the missions was rapidly rising in value. Traders had come on the coast, who purchased the hides and tallow of their cattle, and the produce of their fields. The Fathers were becoming excellent men of business, and began to drive a thriving trade. They were now *independent*, in the fullest sense of the word ; so much so, that, whereas formerly they were indebted to foreign contributions and royal or republican assistance to support their missions, they now not only could manage to subsist without these aids, but were enabled, and in truth obliged, to support the Mexican forces and civil establishments in their territory at a vast annual expense.

Portrait of one of the Fathers—Antonio Peyri (aged 67 years), Missionary at San Luis Rey, from 1799 to 1832.

Up to this time, and so late as 1833, the Mexican government had not sought, or rather was unable, to interfere materially with the management of the Fathers. In that year indeed a body of eleven Franciscan friars was ordered by Congress to be sent to the missions to strengthen their establishments. At this time, General Don José Figueroa was appointed military governor, or commandante-general. Some time later, in the same year, the democratic party being then in power, the Mexican Congress passed a law for entirely removing the missionaries, and dividing the lands among the Indians and settlers, and appropriating the funds of the Fathers in Mexico to state purposes. Commissioners were appointed to see this act carried into effect, and free emigrants were engaged to proceed from Mexico to settle in the country. This was the most serious blow the missions had ever received, and would have been a deadly one, but for one of those revolutions or party triumphs which so frequently occur in Mexico. Santa Anna, who was opposed to the democratic party, happened to come into power before the provisions of the act could be carried into execution. He immediately overturned all that had been arranged on the subject, and forwarded, by express, counteracting instructions to California. When subsequently the emigrants from Mexico arrived in the country, General Figueroa received them so coldly, and gave them so little encouragement, that soon the greater number of them returned to Mexico. The missions therefore continued as before ; and so ended this attempt on the part of the Mexican Government to secularize the property of the Fathers, and augment the population and resources of the country.

In 1835, the party at whose head was Santa Anna determined to remodel the Mexican republic, and *centralize* the government, thereby destroying, in a great measure, the federal constitution of 1824. But no time was allowed him to make the necessary changes and their exact nature therefore was never known ; for, in the following year, 1836, by one of the usual *coups d'état*, and while he himself had been defeated and taken prisoner by the Texans, another party opposed to his general views of policy came into power. This party, however, agreed with the previous administration on the necessity or propriety of remodelling the federal system. The old constitution was therefore abolished, and a new one adopted. By this change, the separate states were deprived of many of their former prerogatives, and nearly the whole rights and duties of government were confined to the general Congress and executive. This sweeping alteration of the federal constitution was opposed in many parts of the republic, and in no quarter more vigorously than in California. The people of Monterey rose *en masse*, and at once declared themselves independent until the federal constitution was re-adopted, and passed formal resolutions to that effect. Their example was quickly followed by the inhabitants of the other towns and villages. But while the people of the southern parts of the country were inclined to adhere to Mexico, upon certain conditions, those of the nothern districts were determined henceforward, and for ever, to sever the connection with the other States, and to stand alone, free and independent of Mexican domination.

Mexico, meanwhile, was not exactly idle, for it answered the Californian proclamations, addresses, and long inflammatory speeches, by epistles and speeches of a similar nature on the opposite side. California and Mexico—the local and general governments—each party appealed to the *patriotism* of the people in support of their cause. Señor Don Mariano Guadalupe Vallejo, whose name will again occur in our pages, was appointed commandante-general on the part of the Californians, and forthwith the whole train of congressional officials was forcibly expelled from office and the government troops disbanded, and before long transported to the Mexican territories. The Mexicans threatened an expedition to chastise the rebels, and recall them to repentance and duty ; while the Californians defied their menaces, and resolved to abide the consequences of their first steps to freedom. However, General Urrea, who had been charged by the Mexican Government with the conduct of this expedition, soon afterwards joined the federalist party, and wilfully delayed the execution of his orders. At the same time, as the rebels were so far away, and the opposite factions in Mexico had so many more pressing matters to settle among themselves at home, somehow all about California appeared to be forgotten, and it was left, for a time, to any constitution, or none at all, and anarchy, just as its people pleased. About the end of July, 1837, the excitement among the Californians had subsided so far, that they then quietly accepted the new Mexican constitution without a murmur, and voluntarily swore allegiance to it.

It is probably unnecessary to dwell upon the successive and rapid changes of administration in Mexico, each of them differing widely from each other in their general views of home and foreign policy. In one thing indeed they pretty cordially agreed, and that was the destruction of the missions as a ruling body in

California, and the secularization of their property for state and other purposes. Accordingly, administration after administration adopted the extreme democratic views on this matter, and soon the Fathers were legally, if not equitably, stripped of their possessions, and of all their former dignity and influence.

Foreseeing and dreading the results of the long threatened proceedings, the Fathers lost courage, and neglected the missions. If they themselves were not to enjoy their great estates nobody else should. Their cattle, therefore, were recklessly slaughtered, their fields and crops were neglected, and their property was granted away or sold for trifling sums. Long before their final fall, most of the missions had become but a wreck of what they had been but a few years before. Perhaps the period of their greatest prosperity was immediately previous to 1824, when the Mexican constitution was declared. After that time they all gradually fell into decay. In successive years from the date mentioned, and particularly from 1834 downwards, specially marking the disastrous years 1840 and 1845, various acts were passed in the Mexican Congress, which completely denuded the Fathers of both power and property.

This, however, was a work of considerable time, and occasionally, as rival administrations, differing in this matter a slight shade from each other, came into office, a gleam of their setting and cloud-shrouded sun would appear to cheer the hearts of the Fathers. But that sun finally sunk in 1845, never again to rise in California. In the year named, a considerable number of the missions were sold by public auction. The Indian converts attached to certain others, and who now were wandering idle and wretched over the country, were ordered to return to and cultivate the portions of land, which had been assigned them by government. If that return and cultivation were delayed more than a month, then these portions of land and the missions to which they were attached would also be sold ; and this was subsequently done. The remaining missions were to be rented. The price and rents of all these missions were then divided into three parts : one was bestowed upon the missionaries themselves, and another upon the converted Indians, for their respective maintenance, while the last was converted into a new *Pious*

Fund of California, for the support and extension of education and general charitable purposes.

Before closing this account of the former state of the missions, we may mention what was the cost of the country to the Mexican Government, independent of the salaries allowed to the Fathers, which, however, seldom seem to have been paid. Take the year 1831 :—In that year, the expense of the presidial companies, according to the estimates, was $91,000. To this must be added the pay of the commandante-general and sub-inspector, the expense of maintaining auxiliary troops and convicts, and various other charges, $40,000. Together, these sums make $131,000. But, as the net amount of the public revenue, which was principally derived from exorbitant and often prohibitory tariff duties, which necessarily encouraged smuggling, was only $32,000, a short-coming of $109,000 was left to be provided by the general government. Other years showed an equally unprofitable state of public affairs. However, as the general government wanted the means, and perhaps the credit, elsewhere, they *borrowed* the deficiency from their nominal subjects, the wealthy Fathers ; and, accordingly, we find that the Mexican Congress, in 1831, owed the missions the large sum of $450,000. This circumstance, it might be thought, should have held back the destroying hand ; but perhaps it only nerved it to greater and more speedy destruction. The ungrateful are always the most cruel.

CHAPTER VII.

California distinct in physical character and national feeling from the other Mexican provinces.—Beginning and progress of immigration into the country.—The Russians at Bodega Bay.—Later great increase of foreign white settlers; Americans largely preponderating.—Outrage committed upon the settlers by Mexican authorities.—Commodore Jones takes possession of Monterey.—Foreign settlers scatter themselves over the whole country, and silently, but rapidly, revolutionize or Americanize it.—Origin of the war of 1846 between the Mexican and American States.

NEW CALIFORNIA has always been a distinct country from the rest of the Mexican provinces, having nothing in common but that its few early white settlers were descended from the same race. Locally it was separated by vast deserts from the peopled parts of the same empire—in its constitution and government it was *sui generis*—in its productions, climate and general character of country there was no resemblance to any other portion of Mexico. In the very feelings of the inhabitants there was little sympathy with those of the Mexicans. Mexico never could become a naval power: its mineral, pastoral and agricultural wealth were very great, but it wanted the ports and the facilities for procuring ship-building timber and other marine stores which California has within a comparatively small space of territory. California possesses an equable, mild and healthy climate—excellent harbors—(one of which is equal, in capacity, safety, and ease of entrance and departure to any other on the globe)—a soil extremely fertile, capable of producing every kind of grain and vegetables, except a few tropical varieties—and extensive forests and other tracks of land which yield most kinds of marine stores, such as timber, resin, &c. These things—if it only had population, would necessarily, at all times, have rendered it independent of Mexico, which is deficient in many of them. Accordingly, the free white settlers early began to show that they cared little about the Mexican Government, and that,

6

sooner or later, they were determined to be independent. This consideration was always present in the minds of the Mexican people, and a secret jealousy of the consequences generally prevented them from heartily encouraging the immigration into California of new white settlers.

We have seen that so early as 1836, and when the *gente de razon* did not exceed, if they amounted to five thousand, the people of Monterey declared themselves independent of Mexico, and that their example was followed by the other inhabitants of the country. This desire for independence was soon much increased by the continual inroad of immigrants which now began to come from the United States of America, and from many of the islands and ports of the Pacific.

In 1812, the Russians, without asking leave of the Spanish authorities, had formed a small settlement at Bodega Bay, between fifty and sixty miles to the north of San Francisco. Some years afterwards, they established another small station, called Ross, about thirty miles farther north than Bodega. These settlements were founded chiefly in order to supply the Russian-American Fur Company with agricultural supplies, but also as fishing stations for procuring the skins of seals and otters, which animals abounded on the coast and on the adjacent rocky islands. The Russians, however, were very jealously eyed by the Spanish and Mexican authorities, and were compelled to maintain strong forts and a large number of military to protect their settlers. In 1841, therefore, they judged it expedient to relinquish their possessions. They accordingly disposed of their stations and property to Captain John A. Sutter, an adventurous Swiss gentleman, whose name is closely connected with the later history of California and will again occur in our pages. The Russians then altogether retired from the country.

But previous to 1826 there were comparatively few other foreign settlers in California than the Russians. When, however, in that year, the Columbia and North American Fur Companies had united their interests, several hundred trappers and fur traders were always wandering about the borders of the country, and occasionally even penetrated as far as San Francisco Bay and Monterey. Their visits were in general coldly received by the Californians; and much suspicion of their ulterior views being raised in the Mexican Government, laws were occasionally passed by Congress for the removal of all foreigners from California. Notwithstanding, the flow of immigration gradually increased, and trappers, fur traders, whalers, and adventurers of all nations, but particularly from the American States, began to throng the harbors, and to settle down in the more fertile parts of the country. Soon the majority of merchants in the ports were of American, or else of English or French extraction; while many of the land squatters, and the shop and tavern-keepers and artisans in towns were adventurous immigrants from every country on earth. They had perhaps roamed over the wide Pacific for years, and now, tired of their vagabond career, had chosen California as a pleasant resting place, and a home for the remainder of life. Runaway seamen and stragglers from Columbia and Missouri swelled the number of white settlers. The indolent Spaniards stupidly looked on, while the prestige of their name, their wealth and influence were quietly passing into other and stronger hands.

Occasionally indeed they seemed to make a desperate struggle against their fate; but it was like the useless splash of the unwieldy whale when the harpoon has struck his vital parts. In 1840, a violent outrage was committed, under the instructions of Don Juan B. Alvarado, then governor of the Californias, upon many of the most respectable settlers of foreign extraction. In April of that year, nearly one hundred individuals, American and British subjects, of every rank and profession in life, were seized, and carried to Monterey, where they were imprisoned, some of them in irons, for a short time. No charge was made against these people, yet they were treated as vilely as if they had been condemned felons. A few were released, without explanation, at Monterey, and the remainder carried as prisoners to Santa Barbara. There a few more were released, again without explanation, while the rest proceeded, still prisoners, to San Blas. There several others were discharged, and left to find their way back to Monterey, without money, passports or any assistance whatever. Those who were still left were imprisoned for an indefinite time at San Blas, or sent to other Mexican towns.

A considerable number died from the severe treatment they experienced; while it was fifteen months before the last of them was set at liberty. And still no reason was alleged for this worse than Turkish or Russian despotism. Nor has it ever been fairly known why such outrageous proceedings had been adopted by the Mexican authorities, although it was suspected that they considered the foreign settlers in California were engaged in some revolutionary movement. This, however, was a most unlikely thing. The prisoners in conversation all denied, while the Mexicans ridiculously failed, or perhaps never seriously attempted to establish it. Probably a better reason might be found in the fact that the Mexicans had got so fretfully jealous and alarmed at the progress of foreign immigration, that they were determined to disgust the present settlers with the country, and to frighten all others from entering into it. Besides the people mentioned, there were many other foreign settlers of large property who were arrested, though Governor Alvarado thought it prudent not to imprison them. No redress seems ever to have been obtained from the Mexican Government for this daring attack on the liberty of American subjects, and for all the losses, pecuniary and otherwise, sustained by the victims of these violent, arbitrary and unlawful proceedings. At that period, there was no regular United States ship-of-war stationed on the coast, nor any consul appointed, to whom the injured could appeal, and who, in his official capacity, could have enforced some compensation for such manifold wrongs. As it was, indeed, Mr. Thomas O. Larkin, afterwards our respected consul at Monterey, in his private character as a merchant of the place and an American subject, exerted himself strenuously to preserve the honor of the United States flag and the lives and properties of his fellow subjects; but without effect. Several commanding officers of United States ships in the Pacific likewise interested themselves in the matter, when they happened to approach the coast; but as they were but transient visitors, having no proper commission effectually to interfere, the few steps they took led to no settlement of the business.

In 1842, a premature attempt was made by an American officer forcibly to take possession of the country. In that year,

Commodore Jones, then in the Pacific, having fancied that the Mexican and American States were at war on the Atlantic side of the continent, sailed with his frigate, the United States, and the sloop-of-war Cyane, to Monterey, where he arrived on the 19th of October. He immediately took possession of the town and hoisted the American flag, publishing proclamations over

Sutter's Fort,—New Helvetia.

the whole country, declaring it a portion of the United States. After only twenty-four hours possession, the commodore received intelligence which altered his views of matters. He therefore revoked all his recent orders, hauled down the "stripes and stars," and restored the place to its former owners, with as handsome an apology as he could make for his extraordinary proceedings.

So early as 1837, several societies were formed in the American States to promote emigration to Oregon and California. In the following years, and particularly in 1843, 1844, 1845 and 1846, many thousand emigrants journeyed across the Rocky and

Snowy Mountains, enduring much suffering by the way, to settle in California and the adjacent territory of Oregon. Other large numbers proceeded thither through Mexico, across the Isthmus, or by way of Cape Horn. The Valley of the Sacramento, where Captain Sutter, already mentioned, possessed, under a grant from the Mexican government, an extensive tract of country, called by him New Helvetia, was the general resort of the larger number of those immigrants whose wishes were directed towards an agricultural life. Many, however, distributed themselves over other parts of the country, and those whose views were turned more to trade and commerce flocked to the towns on the coast, where they soon became the most influential part of the community, and in some instances formed even the numerical strength of the white population.

Meanwhile the Mexican Congress, alarmed at an immigration so steadily increasing and so powerful, fulminated proclamation after proclamation against the intruders, and instructed the governor of the province to take steps for their immediate expulsion. Such a measure, however, was now too bold an undertaking for the whole Mexican power to execute. There the stubborn settlers were, and would remain; the squatter on his land, the merchant in his office, the artisan, shopkeeper and trader at the posts they had severally selected. Accordingly, the commandante-general of California contented himself merely with publishing, in their order, the impotent ordinances of Congress as they reached himself, without daring or taking the least trouble to enforce them. It was felt by all parties that a silent revolution was rapidly going on, the effect of which was thoroughly to Americanize the whole province. It was barely possible that England might have delayed this movement somewhat, if she had received, as was at one time seriously proposed by many influential personages, the territory of California from the Mexican Congress, in lieu of the large public debt which her subjects held against the insolvent republic. But even such a political cession of the country to England would scarcely have stopped the onward progress of American settlements, or removed the profound feeling that California was destined, one day very soon now, to pass under the protection of the "star-spangled banner."

The pear was ripening, and, if not plucked a little earlier by impatient hands, would certainly soon fall at the feet of the watcher. Matters were in this condition, when the war of 1846 broke out between the United States of America and the Mexican States, which brought matters to a crisis, and finally settled the destiny of California. The origin of the war was shortly this :—

In 1835, Texas, like California and many other provinces of the Mexican republic, dissatisfied with the overthrow of the federal constitution, revolted and declared itself independent. War was accordingly proclaimed by the general government, and an army, under the command of Santa Anna, was forthwith sent to the rebellious province to compel obedience. But the Texans, who were now chiefly of American descent, and who had no sympathies with the Mexicans, having flown to arms, defeated and captured Santa Anna himself, on the 21st April, 1836. In the power of the enemy, and fearing the machinations of political foes in the capital, Santa Anna was glad to sign a treaty with the Texans, in which he acknowledged the independence of the province. Meanwhile, another party had come into power in Mexico who refused to confirm the proceedings of Santa Anna, and still claimed Texas as an integral part of the republic. The disordered state, however, of the general country prevented active measures being taken to establish this claim ; and Texas governed itself, and was acknowledged as an independent power, by several European and other nations.

In the interval, the Texans applied to the American Congress for permission to be received into the Union. This, for various reasons, was refused on the part of Congress ; and similar applications made during the next eight or nine years were likewise declined. At last, in 1845, the American Congress saw reason to change its opinion, and on the 1st of March of that year, passed resolutions sanctioning the annexation of Texas, upon certain preliminary conditions, with which, as it happened, Texas was ultimately found ready to comply. Five days after the passing of these resolutions, the Mexican ambassador, at Washington, protested against them, and demanded his passports. Generally such a course is only adopted where there is good reason to suppose that war is shortly about to follow. In the present instance, war was not immediately declared, nor did any hostilities take place. However, the Mexican people were much embittered against the American States when they reflected on the course of these events, and every where a popular feeling was produced inimical to America, and which insisted on immediate war.

To complicate matters, the Mexican Government had acknowledged itself indebted to American subjects in a large sum, (some millions of dollars), which it never could or would pay ; and the mere consideration and fixing the amount of which had occupied some tedious years. This sum was the amount of damage (assessed under the formal arbitration of mutual commissioners), done to Americans, by reason of various seizures of and outrages upon their ships and goods, which the Mexicans had made during many previous years, partly, perhaps, through malicious wantonness, and partly to replenish their impoverished exchequer. Successive weak and poor governments among the Mexicans pretended to acknowledge the justice of this debt, and faithfully promised payment, though always at some future day ; until the injured Americans got tired of remonstrating on the subject, and indignantly clamored for warlike measures being adopted against Mexico, to compel redress of their own and the national grievances. Thus the popular mind in both countries was ripe for war ; while both governments secretly began preparations to carry it to extremities. The Mexicans made great levies and collected numerous forces around their capital and on the Texan border. On the other hand, the American Congress dispatched a considerable fleet to the gulf of Mexico to be at hand when wanted, and likewise ordered large forces to be assembled and to quarter themselves on the Rio Nueces in Texas. That river was held by the Mexicans to be the south-western boundary of the province, while the Texans themselves, and the United States taking up their cause, claimed the Rio Grande, some one hundred and thirty miles farther to the south-west, as the true and proper limits of their territory. Thus the murderous train was laid which a spark was to fire.

It is not our province further to develope the causes of the war which ultimately broke out between the contending powers.

Suffice it to say, that, in April, 1846, war was formally declared between the two countries ; and that, after a brilliant series of battles and victories upon the Rio Grande, under General Zachary Taylor, and a still more triumphant progress, bloody but decisive, from Vera Cruz to Mexico, under General Winfield Scott, the modern Cortez, the Americans were enabled, in the capital itself, to dictate their own terms of peace to the Mexicans—one of which was the cession of Upper California by the latter. Previous to this time, however, American subjects had conquered and held in possession the last named country itself ; and to a short summary of their proceedings in that quarter we will now direct the reader.

CHAPTER VIII.

Col. John C. Fremont.—General José Castro.—Fremont declares war against California.—Capture of Sonoma.—Proclamation of William B. Ide.—Letter of Pio Pico, Governor of the Californias, to Thomas O. Larkin, Consul of the United States.—Thomas O. Larkin's reply to Pio Pico.—California declared independent.—California desired by the American Government.—Col. Stevenson's regiment.—Movements of General Kearney.—Seizure of Monterey.—Proclamation of Com. Sloat.—Commander Montgomery takes possession of Yerba Buena and Fremont of San Juan.

Colonel John C. Fremont is generally considered the conqueror of California; where his exploits, undertaken with so small a force and against such superior numbers, place him on a par with the famous heroes of the days of chivalry. Yet to the bold, daring and energetic measures adopted and prosecuted by Commodore Robert F. Stockton, as we shall hereafter see, may justly be ascribed the final reduction of the country. Holding a commission in the topographical corps of engineers, a great part of Fremont's duties had hitherto consisted in exploring the districts of country around the base of the Rocky Mountains, and the best lines of communication from the Missouri to Oregon and California. In 1845, Fremont was instructed by the War Department to ascertain a shorter and more southerly and convenient route to the Columbia River. In the execution of this duty, he reached Monterey in California, in the month of January, 1846. Allusion has already been made to the jealousy with which the successive immigration of American settlers was viewed by the Californians, or rather the Mexican authorities. Accordingly, when Fremont appeared with his small force near Monterey, General José Castro, the commandant at that town, had his suspicions aroused as to their ulterior intentions, and prepared to dispute their farther progress. To allay these suspicions, Fremont, leaving his little army, hastened to Monterey and made such personal explanations to Castro as seemed to satisfy the latter that he had no reason to be alarmed at the appearance of the Americans. Castro having

Colonel J. C. Fremont.

confessed himself satisfied on the subject, Fremont returned to his people ; but, shortly afterwards being informed by the American consul at Monterey that the Mexican general secretly intended to attack him, he at once occupied a strong position in the neighborhood, and displayed the American flag. Castro meanwhile having thought better on the subject, especially after reconnoitering the American position, determined to leave those foolish, obstinate people alone.

Fremont, thus freed from molestation, proceeded on his proposed route to Oregon. He had gone but a little way when he found that hostile Indians (supposed to have been urged on by the Mexican authorities), barred his farther progress; and learned with extreme surprise and indignation, that Castro intended to attack the American settlers, and expel them from the country. Upon ascertaining this fact, Fremont took the bold resolution of declaring war against California, and of carrying it too into the very camp of the enemy. His force, at this time consisted of only sixty-two men. On the 15th of June, in pursuance of this determination, he, or others acting under his advice, surprised and took possession of the military post of Sonoma, part of the spoils of which place were nine cannon and two hundred and fifty stand of arms. Four days previously they had also cut off an important convoy from Castro's camp. It is true that various contradictory accounts have been given of Fremont's personal connection with these events; and it is difficult to ascertain the real state of the facts. If he had no active share in them, which is probably the true state of the case, it is certain that he formed the resolution mentioned above, just when the noted "bear-flag" party had actually surprised Sonoma, and that he immediately cordially joined them.

After the capture of Sonoma, Mr. William B. Ide, a native of one of the New England States, who had immigrated to California the previous year, and a man of courage and intelligence, was intrusted with the command of the small garrison. At the same time he issued a proclamation explaining the views of the American party, the reasons for their present act, and the principle on which they proposed to conduct their future proceedings. This proclamation is as follows:—

"*A proclamation to all persons and citizens of the District of Sonoma, requesting them to remain at peace, and follow their rightful occupations without fear of molestation.*

"The Commander-in-chief of the troops assembled at the fortress of Sonoma, gives his inviolable pledge to all persons in California, not found under arms, that they shall not be disturbed in their persons, their property, or social relations, one with another, by men under his command.

"He also solemnly declares his object to be: first, to defend himself and companions in arms, who were invited to this country by a promise of lands on which to settle themselves and families; who were also promised a Republican Government; when having arrived in California they were denied the privilege of buying or renting lands of their friends; who, instead of being allowed to participate in or being protected by a Republican Government, were oppressed by a military despotism; who were even threatened by proclamation, by the chief officers of the aforesaid despotism, with extermination, if they should not depart out of the country, leaving all their property, arms, and beasts of burden; and thus deprived of their means of flight or defence, were to be driven through deserts inhabited by hostile Indians to certain destruction.

"To overthrow a government which has seized upon the property of the missions for its individual aggrandizement; which has ruined and shamefully oppressed the laboring people of California, by enormous exactions on goods imported into the country, is the determined purpose of the brave men who are associated under my command.

"I also solemnly declare my object, in the second place, to be to invite all peaceable and good citizens of California, who are friendly to the maintenance of good order and equal rights, and I do hereby invite them to repair to my camp at Sonoma, without delay, to assist us in establishing and perpetuating a Republican Government, which shall secure to all civil and religious liberty; which shall encourage virtue and literature; which shall leave unshackled by fetters, agriculture, commerce, and manufactures.

"I further declare, that I rely upon the rectitude of our intentions, the favor of heaven, and the bravery of those who are bound and associated with me, by the principles of self-preservation, by the love of truth, and the hatred of tyranny, for my hopes of success.

"I furthermore declare, that I believe that a government to be prosperous and happy, must originate with the people, who are friendly to its existence; that the citizens are its guardians, the officers its servants, its glory its reward.

"WILLIAM B. IDE.

"*Head Quarters, Sonoma, June 18th*, 1846."

These sudden, bold, and unexpected proceedings produced much alarm and excitement among the Mexican authorities, as we may learn from the following copy of the translation of a long epistle—too interesting to be omitted, and now published for the first time—addressed by his Excellency, Don Pio Pico, the governor of California, to Thomas O. Larkin, Esq., the United States consul at Monterey :—

"The undersigned, Constitutional Governor of the Department of the Californias, has the deep mortification to make known to Mr. Thomas O. Larkin, Consul of the United States of North America, that he has been greatly surprised in being notified by official communications of the General Commandancia of this Department and the Prefecture of the Second District, that a multitude of foreigners of the United States of America have invaded that frontier, taken possession of the fortified town of Sonoma, treacherously making prisoners of the military Commandante, Don Mariano G. Vallejo,

Lieut. Colonel Victor Pruden, Captain Salvador Vallejo, and Mr. Jacob P. Leese, and likewise have stolen the property of these individuals.

"The undersigned can do no less than make known to the Consul of the United States, that acts so extraordinary and alarming have caused very great grief.

"Until the present the Departmental Governor is wanting the least positive information that would give him to understand of a declaration of war between Mexico and the United States, and without such information he judges the course pursued at Sonoma the most atrocious and infamous that can be imagined, so much so that the like is not seen among barbarians.

"They have attacked the rights of the people, breaking the established social compacts; profaning the sacred soil of another nation; indeed scandalously usurping an integral part of the Mexican Republic, and what is more provoking still, as an ignominious libel, is the folly of the principal of this multitude of foreigners, William B. Ide, the separation of the Mexican Union. This act tends to excite the mind of the undersigned, and causes him to suspect that the Government of the United States are concerned in this matter, which certainly should increase his regrets.

Mr. Thomas O. Larkin will permit the undersigned to say to him frankly that he has witnessed with extraordinary coolness the invasion of the Department, and that he has failed to note the general movement of all the inhabitants, in defence of their country and liberty; he has not been known to make any arrangement that might make the invaders recede from their abominable designs, and prevent the misfortunes which they can cause by means of hostile provocation: misfortunes that the Departmental Government will place to the responsibility of the chief authors before God and the entire world. So base management as observed on this occasion highly compromises the honor of the United States, and if it shall have such a stain upon itself, there is no doubt that it will be graven eternally in the remembrance of all nations, and will cause it to be despised.

"The undersigned believes that the Consul of the United States will agree with him, that the acts committed by the party of foreigners, Americans, have the appearance of actual and downright robbery; also that the Consul will agree with him, that his indifference to prevent such fatal results, seeing that they were subjects of his own nation who were violating this part of the Mexican Republic, compromises more and more both nations.

"The undersigned in fulfilment of his duties sees himself obliged to recommend to the Consul, Thomas O. Larkin, that he make declarations of the occurrence which has happened at Sonoma, to exact full satisfaction from him, hoping that he will use all the means in his power to escape in time such terrible consequences, and finally to protest solemnly, in the name of the Departmental and Supreme Government of the Nation, that it is decidedly opposed to all aggressions, defending to extremity its independence, liberty, inalienable rights; repeating that the principal authors are responsible to the Representative of the United States near this Department for those abuses and results of corrupt designs from which they are not deterred.

"The undersigned hopes, from the prudence and judgment of the Consul of the United States at Monterey, that, admitting the justice that assists him, the answer to this letter (and imploring that it may soon come), may be in accordance with (*veneboles*) desire.

"God and Liberty!

"Pio Pico.

Santa Barbara, 29*th June*, 1846."

Thomas O. Larkin, Esq.

To this indignant and piteous missive, Mr. Larkin returned the following answer:—

"*Consulate of the United States of America,*
Monterey, Cal. July, 5*th*, 1846.

"To His Excellency, Don Pio Pico,
Governor of California.

"Sir:—The undersigned, Consul of the United States of America for California, has the honor to acknowledge the reception of His Excellency's letter of the 29th of last month, which was received yesterday afternoon.

His Excellency may be well assured that the undersigned is duly sensible of the great importance of the subject brought before him, and is compelled to say that he cannot alone enter into any mode for the expulsion of the foreigners who have taken possession of Sonoma. He is bound not only to protect his countrymen in California from any unjust oppression, and settle in an amicable manner any disputes in which they may be concerned; but firmly to refuse them support when they have been wilfully guilty of any infractions of the laws of this Department, giving aid to the Authorities in such cases, which aid has been refused by the Governor and Prefect.

The undersigned must assure His Excellency was wrongly informed when told he made no exertions to aid the proper Authorities, and His Excellency can learn that the undersigned has used the only means in his power as a Consul, and that the Consular service had not been accepted.

His Excellency is pleased to say that the Americans engaged in this affair are responsible to this Consulate. The undersigned must observe that he knows not where this responsibility exists, and will not underrate the good sense of his being in the idea that he believes Consular letters would have effect on the persons in question, or that the Authorities would have given him soldiers to bring into Monterey an equal number of Americans, when General Castro, with three times their force, did not see proper to expel those who took Sonoma.

The reasons brought forward by His Excellency as proofs that the Government of the United States is concerned in this matter, not being sustained, will, being by the undersigned proved to be erroneous, require no farther assertion on his part to convince His Excellency on the subject.

The undersigned has the honor to renew to His Excellency the Governor of California, assurance of his deepest respect and consideration.

THOMAS O. LARKIN."

While these epistles were being interchanged, Fremont was proceeding to the valley of the Sacramento, where the chief settlements of the American population were, with the intention of enlisting recruits for the farther prosecution of the war. A garrison of only fourteen men had been left at Sonoma, which was shortly afterwards increased to about forty. Scarcely had Fremont departed, when General Castro prepared to attack the feebly manned post. News of that general's movements speedily followed Fremont, who instantly, with only a troop of ninety riflemen, hurried, night and day, to the relief of the garrison. He arrived just in time to frustrate the designs of Castro. To follow up his original scheme, Fremont next called a meeting of the Americans at Sonoma, on July 4th, 1846; when, acting on his advice, the assembly proclaimed the independence of the country, appointed Fremont governor, and declared war against Mexico.

Meantime, nothing was known of the condition of affairs in the United States, nor that actual hostilities had taken place between them and Mexico. While this ignorance existed in California, there was equal want of knowledge in the United States respecting the proceedings on the opposite side of the continent. Very comprehensive measures to conduct the war on all sides had been formed by the American government. Not only were American generals advancing on the Rio Grande and on Mexico itself, by way of Vera Cruz and Jalapa, but an expedition under General Stephen W. Kearny, was formed to proceed across the whole continent, from the Missouri, first to Santa Fé, and after the expected reduction of New Mexico, farther west to California. This latter province had long been desired by the Americans, and the government was now determined, since circumstances rightfully permitted the attempt, to secure the country. To further this undertaking, Congress ordered a corps of mounted riflemen to be raised, the command of which was given to Captain, then first created Lieutenant-Colonel, Fremont, and who, from his knowledge of the country, and his being there at the very time, seemed the most proper person on whom the honor of the command could be bestowed.

A regiment of volunteers, a thousand strong, to serve during the war in California, was likewise raised in New York, and placed under the command of Colonel Jonathan D. Stevenson, to whose energy and ability the formation and organization of the corps was chiefly owing. This regiment, though it arrived in California too late to take any part in the actual hostilities of the war, was subsequently of great service in preserving the peace of the subjugated country. Col. Stevenson reached San Francisco March 7th, 1847, and immediately afterwards his regiment was divided into companies, which were severally stationed at Sonoma, San Francisco, Santa Barbara, and Monterey, which last place, first was head-quarters, afterwards removed to Los Angeles. So desirous was the United States Government to preserve California at all hazards, that particular care had been taken, in the raising of this regiment, that the men composing it should be of good habits, and as far as practicable, of various pursuits, and such as would be likely to desire to remain in the country at the end of the war.

While these measures were being carried out by Congress, General Kearny, having left Fort Leavenworth, on the Missouri, in June, 1846, was marching, at the head of sixteen hundred men, across the deserts which lie between that place and Santa Fé. After the capture of Santa Fé, and the proclamation of New Mexico being now a portion of the American republic, and after making the necessary arrangements for strengthening his power there, Kearny, at the close of September, 1846, proceeded farther west to California, to carry out the instructions given him by Congress. He had gone but eleven days' march from Santa Fé, when he met an express from Commodore Stockton and Colonel Fremont, bearing despatches to Congress announcing the conquest of California. Kearny, then dismissing two hundred of his dragoons, to assist in the reduction of New Mexico, continued his progress westward, accompanied by a troop of only one hundred men, and two howitzers. His course lay across the wild and untrodden country east of the Gila, down which river he next proceeded, until he approached the frontier of California. Meanwhile, Americans there were completing what we have seen they had begun, the reduction of that country.

At the time when Fremont was forcing the Mexicans out of California north of the Bay of San Francisco, Commodore Sloat, who was then in command of the American squadron in the Pacific, being apprised of the actual commencement of hostilities between the American and Mexican states, had seized upon Monterey. This was done on the 7th of July, when the American flag was hoisted, and the following proclamation read. It is not our intention to give a detailed history of the war in California; but since this proclamation was the first formal announcement of the intentions of the American Government, while the documents previously quoted were very important in themselves, we have been induced to give them all at length, though they perhaps swell this branch of our subject more than was at first contemplated.

"TO THE INHABITANTS OF CALIFORNIA.

"The central government of Mexico having commenced hostilities against the United States of America, by invading its territory, and attacking the troops of the United States stationed on the north side of the Rio Grande, and with a force of seven thousand men under the command of General Arista, which army was totally destroyed, and all their artillery, baggage, &c., captured on the 8th and 9th of May last, by a force of two thousand and three hundred men, under the command of General Taylor, and the City of Matamoras taken and occupied by the forces of the United States, and the two nations being actually at war by this transaction, I shall hoist the standard of the United States at Monterey immediately, and shall carry it throughout California.

"I declare to the inhabitants of California, that, although I come in arms with a powerful force, I do not come among them as an enemy to California: on the contrary, I come as their best friend, as henceforth California will be a portion of the United States, and its peaceable inhabitants will enjoy the same rights and principles they now enjoy, together with the privilege of choosing their own magistrates, and other officers for the administration of justice among themselves, and the same protection will be extended to them as to any other State in the Union. They will also enjoy a permanent government, under which life, property and the constitutional right and lawful security to worship the Creator in the way the most congenial to each other's sense of duty, will be secured, which, unfortunately, the central government of Mexico cannot afford them, destroyed as her resources are by internal factions and corrupt officers, who create constant revolutions to promote their own interests and oppress the people. Under the flag of the United States, California will be free from all such troubles and expenses; consequently, the country will rapidly advance and improve both in agriculture and commerce, as, of course, the revenue laws will be the same in California as in all parts of the United States, affording them all manufactures and produce of the United States, free of any duty, and all foreign goods at one quarter of the duty they now pay. A great increase in the value of real estate and the products of California may also be anticipated.

"With the great interest and kind feeling I know the government and people of the United States possess towards the citizens of California, the country cannot but improve more rapidly than any other on the continent of America.

"Such of the inhabitants of California, whether native or foreigners, as may not be disposed to accept the high privileges of citizenship, and to live peaceably under the Government of the United States, will be allowed time to dispose of their property and to remove out of the country, if they choose, without any restriction; or remain in it, observing strict neutrality.

"With full confidence in the honor and integrity of the inhabitants of the country, I invite the judges, alcaldes, and other civil officers to execute their functions as heretofore, that the public tranquillity may not be disturbed; at least until the government of the territory can be more definitely arranged.

"All persons holding titles to real estate, or in quiet possession of land under color of right, shall have those titles guaranteed to them.

"All churches and the property they contain in possession of the clergy of California, shall continue in the same rights and possessions they now enjoy.

"All provisions and supplies of every kind furnished by the inhabitants for the use of the United States ships and soldiers, will be paid for at fair rates; and no private property will be taken for public use without just compensation at the moment.

"JOHN D. SLOAT,

"*Commander-in-chief of the U. S. force in the Pacific Ocean.*"

A despatch was immediately forwarded by land to Commander Montgomery, who landed at Yerba Buena without opposition, took possession of the place, hoisted the American standard on the public square, and posted the proclamation of his commanding officer. Fremont, hearing of these proceedings, took possession of the mission of San Juan.

CHAPTER IX.

Commodore Stockton takes charge of the American forces in California.—Hostility of the Californians.—Proclamation of Com. Stockton.—Landing at San Pedro, and manœuvres of the sailor army.—Castro's commissioners.—March on Los Angeles, and flight of General Castro.—Triumphant entry into Los Angeles.—Provisional government formed.—The difficulties of Stockton's march, and the complete success of his plans.—Reported hostility of the Walla-Walla Indians.—Enthusiastic reception of Stockton at San Francisco and other places.—Satisfaction of the people of California with the new government.—Stockton designs to cross Mexico and unite with the forces of General Taylor.

COMMODORE ROBERT F. STOCKTON arrived at Monterey in the Frigate Congress, on the 15th of July, 1846, and on the 23d of that month assumed command of the squadron, Com. Sloat having left on that day to return to the United States. The bold and comprehensive mind of Stockton perceived at once the circumstances by which he was surrounded. He was deeply impressed with the grave and important trust that devolved upon him. But he was neither dismayed nor perplexed with the importance of his position nor the difficulties he was compelled to confront. With a decision of character, promptitude and sagacity worthy of commendation, he adopted the plan of a campaign, which the most complete success vindicated, and which, if judged by its results, is unsurpassed in the most brilliant records of military achievement.

For a correct appreciation of the motives which governed Com. Stockton, as well as of the ability with which his plans were conceived and executed, we must briefly advert to the condition of California at that time, and the circumstances that influenced his course. The country was sparsely inhabited; its population chiefly clustering around isolated settlements at great distances apart, or in the neighborhood of *ranches,* scattered with wide intervals, over its vast surface. Large bodies of Indians occupied much of the territory. To defend themselves from these and the predatory incursions of more warlike tribes in the interior of the continent, the Californians were necessarily familiar with arms. They were hardy and expert horsemen, and excelled in all equestrian performances. Possessed of a fleet and admirable race of horses, they had all the elements of the best cavalry force, in which indeed consisted their chief military strength. At this period the Californians were greatly incensed against the United States. They were ignorant of the declaration of war with Mexico, and considered the demonstration of Fremont and the immigrating parties reported to be approaching, as unprovoked aggressions. They were disposed to treat all Americans as lawless adventurers or freebooters, whose designs were hostile to the peace and authority of Mexico. The colonization of California by citizens of the United States for the purpose of ultimate annexation (as in the case of Texas), they determined to defeat by the most decisive measures. Accordingly, Andreas Pico issued a proclamation intended to stimulate the most sanguinary treatment of all Americans. The occupation of Monterey and some other ports on the coast by Com. Sloat, was viewed by the Californians as parts of the same aggressive scheme, indicated by the elevation of the "Bear Flag" by Fremont, and the approaching immigration. Com. Stockton, aware of these hostile feelings, was painfully solicitous for the safety of the enterprising companies of immigrants which he knew were crossing the Rocky and Snowy Mountains. He concluded that unless a diversion was produced of the Californian forces—unless they were kept fully employed in their own defence, or absolutely dispersed, that the fate of the immigrants would be inevitable. They would be slaughtered in detail as they arrived, jaded, exhausted and enfeebled by their long and arduous journey. Besides, it was quite evident, that if left at liberty to concentrate their troops, the Californians would overwhelm and repossess themselves of Monterey and other ports, at which the flag of the United States had already been elevated by Com. Sloat on the eve of his departure.

The Provincial Congress of California were in session at this time, and under the influence of British agents, the most lavish grants to them of vast tracts of territory were in progress of consummation. There was reason to believe, that in contemplation of the ultimate cession of California to the United States, the Provincial Congress intended to render the acquisition of the territory as valueless as possible. Com. Stockton, aware of these proceedings and designs, was determined to frustrate them. He was well informed of the strength of the enemy, while, he was aware, they were totally unacquainted with his available force. He had really but three hundred and fifty men who could be spared for active service on land, with which to oppose the Californians, about fifteen hundred strong, and composed, for the most part, of the finest cavalry in the world. But the commodore knew that these people were not familiar with the enemy they were to meet, and that to magnify the efficiency of his own strength, it was only necessary to excite the fears of his adversary. The boldest, most decided and adventurous measures, only, could therefore be relied on for success. To disperse the military organization of the enemy, crush all resistance, occupy the prominent positions in the interior around which the population was collected, and thus to acquire and hold possession of the country, he foresaw would afford security to the approaching immigration, and baffle the cupidity of British agents and the crafty malevolence of Mexican animosity ; while it would effectually facilitate, at the close of the war, any negotiations for the cession of California which our Government might institute. The quiet possession of the country, after its subjugation, would be likely to render Mexico better disposed to relinquish the sovereignty which her people were so incapable of defending. Thus informed, and with these views, Com. Stockton, on the 28th July, issued the following proclamation :—

"On assuming the command of the forces of the United States, on the coast of California, both by sea and land, I find myself in possession of the ports of Monterey and San Francisco, with daily reports from the interior of scenes of rapine, blood and murder. Three inoffensive American residents of the country, have within a few days been murdered in the most brutal manner; and there are no Californian officers who will arrest and bring the murderers to justice, although it is well known who they are and where they are. I must therefore, and will, as soon as I can, adopt such measures as may seem best calculated to bring these criminals to justice, and to bestow peace and good order on the country.

In the first place, however, I am constrained by every principle of national honor, as well as a due regard for the safety and best interests of the people of California, to put an end, at once and by force, to the lawless depredations daily committed by General Castro's men upon the persons and property of peaceful and unoffending inhabitants.

"I cannot, therefore, confine my operations to the quiet and undisturbed possession of the defenceless ports of Monterey and San Francisco, whilst the people elsewhere are suffering from lawless violence; but will immediately march against these boasting and abusive chiefs, who have not only violated every principle of national hospitality and good faith towards Captain Fremont and his surveying party, (but who, unless driven out, will, with the aid of the hostile Indians, keep this beautiful country in a constant state of revolution and bloodshed,) as well as against all others who may be found in arms aiding and abetting General Castro.

"The present general of the forces of California is an ursurper—has been guilty of great offences—has impoverished and drained the country of almost its last dollar, and has deserted his post now when most needed. He has deluded and deceived the inhabitants of California, and they wish his expulsion from the country. He came into power by rebellion and force, and by force he must be expelled. Mexico appears to have been compelled, from time to time, to abandon California to the mercies of any wicked man who could muster one hundred men in arms. The distances from the Capital are so great, that she cannot, even in times of great distress, send timely aid to the inhabitants: and the lawless depredations upon their persons and property go invariably unpunished. She cannot or will not punish or control the chieftains who, one after the other, have defied her power and kept California in a constant state of revolt and misery.

"The inhabitants are tired and disgusted with this constant succession of military usurpers and this insecurity of life and property. They invoke my protection. Therefore upon them I will not make war. I require, however, all officers, civil and military, and all other persons to remain quiet at their respective homes and stations, and to obey the orders they may receive from me or by my authority, and if they do no injury or violence to my authority, none will be done to them."

In twenty-four hours after assuming the command, Commodore Stockton organized a battalion of mounted riflemen, which had previously been raised by Capt. Fremont, and Lieut. Gillespie of the marine corps, and which consisted of about one hundred and sixty men. These officers and their men volunteered to serve under Stockton so long as he should require their services in California. Fremont was appointed major, and Gillespie captain of the battalion. On the evening of the 23d, it was embarked on the sloop-of-war Cyane and despatched to San Diego, with orders to co-operate with the commodore in his proposed movement on

Ciudad de los Angeles. On the 1st of August, Stockton sailed in the Congress, and on the way to San Pedro, landed at Santa Barbara, of which he took possession, and leaving a small detachment for its defence, proceeded to his destination, where he arrived on the 6th of August. Here he immediately learned, that the enemy, headed by Generals Castro and Andreas Pico were strongly posted near *Los Angeles* with a force estimated at fifteen hundred strong. He was also informed that Major Fremont had safely landed at San Diego, but found great difficulty in obtaining the needful supply of horses. In the absence of Fremont's battalion, Stockton was destitute of cavalry. Yet impressed with the importance of celerity of movement, he determined not to delay on that account striking a decisive blow as soon as possible. His whole disposable force of sailors and marines was immediately disembarked, a camp formed, and efforts made to discipline for shore service his aquatic troops, to which novel duty they submitted with cheerfulness and alacrity. The anchorage at San Pedro is insecure and unprotected, and it was apparent to all that when they left the coast there was no certainty of finding their ships on their return. Rough weather would compel them to put to sea, or seek a better harbor. Victory or death must, therefore, be the result of their enterprise. But confident in the resources and gallantry of their leader, the hopelessness of retreat only inspired the men with the prophetic certainty of success. Six small guns, obtained from merchant vessels, constituted their artillery. These were rudely mounted and dragged by hand. The sailors were, of course, ignorant of the drill of soldiers, and it was impracticable to subject them to the army discipline. Each man was simply instructed to observe the movements of his right hand comrade, and always to keep to his left. With this single order they soon became expert in forming in line, square or column as required. Though in forming they would appear in inextricable confusion, yet in a few moments all was in order, and every man in his proper place.

A few days after landing, a flag of truce was discovered approaching at a distance over the hills, borne by commissioners from Castro. Acting upon his preconceived views of the enemy's ignorance of his strength, Stockton at once determined to impress

Castro's messengers with most exaggerated ideas of the number of his forces and their formidable equipment. His little army was accordingly ordered to march directly on the line of vision of the approaching commissioners, at intervals of twenty or thirty paces apart, to a position where they were sheltered from observation. Thus seen at a distance, their numbers, judging from the time occupied in defiling, would appear very considerable. The commissioners, coming more as spies than negotiators, as was subsequently ascertained, were completely deceived. On their arrival, they were led up by order of the commodore, to the mouth of a tremendous mortar, which, excepting its huge aperture, was entirely enveloped in skins. Such an engine of war Stockton knew had never before met their gaze, and could not fail to inspire apprehensions of its unknown and terrific qualities. Thus posted he received the emissaries in a stern and repulsive manner, and in an imperious tone demanded the object of their visit. This they delivered with so much confusion as to disclose the serious impressions they felt. They were bearers of a letter from Castro, proposing a truce, upon condition that all active operations should cease, and each party hold its own possessions until a general pacification. The commodore had fully considered the whole matter, and believed that action, not negotiation, was his true policy—that no terms would be kept by the enemy longer than fear dictated—and that if time were allowed him to ascertain the comparative strength of the opposing forces, the worst consequences might be anticipated. He therefore contemptuously rejected the proposition of Castro as insolent and insulting; and dismissed the commissioners with instructions to assure their master, that, unless he immediately broke up his command and disbanded his troops, he would be most severely punished, and that no other terms than an unconditional submission, should shield him from the just vengeance of an incensed foe. The messengers hastened to place the mountains between them and the commodore, and no doubt returned to Castro with an appalling account of the numbers, strength and sanguinary spirit of the great invading army, preparing for his utter destruction. The subsequent conduct of Castro and his superior forces, shows well the sagacity and wisdom with which Stockton had operated on his imagination and fears.

Two days afterwards other messengers arrived from Castro, bringing a bombastic letter, rejecting the terms of Stockton, and concluding with the declaration,—"I will not withhold any sacrifice to oppose your intentions: and if through misfortune the flag of the United States waves in California, it will not be by my acquiescence, nor by that of the last of my compatriots!" These commissioners were treated much the same as were their predecessors—impressed with the formidable character of the American force, and intimidated with the ferocity and implacable purpose of conquest which seemed to animate the invaders.

Having now completed his arrangements, Stockton resolved on pushing forward with expedition before the paucity of his troops could be ascertained, and striking a blow while the apprehensions he had excited were still fresh and undiminished. He dispatched a courier to Fremont with orders to join him on the Plains of the Mesa, and on the 11th of August commenced his march to meet Castro. The most constant vigilance was now necessary to prevent surprise. The enemy's skirmishers were almost daily in sight, and it was impossible to estimate their numbers. The only provisions with which the commodore was supplied were those afforded by the cattle, which were driven along in hollow squares. The artillery was dragged over hill and plain, and through rugged valleys, slowly and painfully, yet with the utmost alacrity. A cheerful and courageous spirit animated the little host, inspired by a leader in whom they felt the most unbounded confidence. The distance between San Pedro and Los Angeles was thirty miles, and was traversed in a single day by Stockton and his little army. But before they could come up, Castro, advised by his spies of their march, despite his previous gasconade and boastful threats, and no doubt mindful of the terrible engine of destruction seen by his commissioners, broke up his camp, disbanded his forces, and fled with all possible expedition to Sonora. Between seven hundred and a thousand mounted troops strongly posted, with seven pieces of artillery, dissolved and disappeared before the daring demonstration of the American commander, at the head of only about three hundred seamen and marines, as poorly equipped, and as motley and as curious a specimen of military organization as ever before took the field, to meet in an unknown country any civilized foe. Colton, in his "*Three years in California*," says: "Gen. Castro had taken up his position just outside the pueblo, on an elevation which commands the town and adjacent country. He was well supplied with field pieces, and had a force of seven hundred men. Com. Stockton landed at San Pedro with three hundred seamen and marines from the Congress, and marched against him. His route, which extended some thirty miles, lay through several narrow passes, which Gen. Castro might easily have defended against a much superior force. But the general kept in his entrenched camp; and informed the commodore by a courier, 'that if he marched upon the town he would find it the grave of his men.' 'Then,' said the commodore, 'tell the general to have the bells ready to toll in the morning at eight o'clock, as I shall be there at that time.' He was there; but Castro in the mean time had broken up his camp, mounted with an armed band and fled."

Stockton, who was subsequently joined by Fremont, took possession of Los Angeles on the 13th of August. A number of Mexicans of high rank surrendered themselves prisoners of war, among whom were Don José Maria Flores and Don Andreas Pico, who were permitted to go at large on their *parole* of honor not to bear arms against the United States; a clemency which they abused afterwards by violating their parole. Commodore Stockton now by proclamation declared California a Territory of the United States; and as all resistance had ceased, proceeded to organize a civil and military government, appointing various civil functionaries and establishing provisional rules of administration, himself retaining for the present the positions of commander-in-chief and governor. The people were invited to assemble on the 15th September to choose officers under the existing form of government. A tariff of duties on imports was prescribed, and the inhabitants were encouraged to resume their usual occupations. Thus, in less than one month from the time when Stockton commenced his operations, California was conquered, in the face of a superior hostile army; that army vanquished and dispersed, and the government of the conquerors quietly imposed on the country. In establishing a local government for California, Com. Stockton displayed the discretion, abilities, discrimination, and judgment of the skilful statesman, as conspicuously as he had exhibited on the field the prudence, enterprise, and valor of the soldier.

This march of Stockton upon the capital of California, though it was accomplished without a battle, or the loss of a single man, was nevertheless performed under circumstances of great difficulty as well as danger. A less enterprising officer would have contented himself with protecting those places on the coast already occupied ; and a less penetrating and comprehensive mind would not have appreciated the importance of suppressing all demonstrations of hostility in every part of this extensive territory. The moral effect of Stockton's march on *Ciudad de los Angeles* upon the minds of the Californians was equivalent to a triumphant victory, and the effusion of streams of blood. It broke down the spirit of resistance, destroyed all confidence in the courage or capacity of the Californian generals, and inspired the inhabitants with terror of an enemy who moved with such celerity and boldness, while his humane conduct reconciled the people to the change of government. The conception of such an expedition, into the heart of an enemy's unknown country, with a force composed principally of sailors, unaccustomed to the fatigues and obstacles of a long march ; to encounter an opposing army of vastly superior numbers, upon their own soil, in defence of their own country, well armed, the best horsemen, and mounted on the finest horses in the world, required the most intrepid courage, indomitable energy, fertility of resource, and self-reliance, such as we find only combined in minds of the highest order, and characters cast in a heroic mould. Yet despite all the difficulties with which he had to contend, in the modest language of his despatch to the government, in less than one month from the time he assumed command, he had "chased the Mexican army more than three hundred miles along the coast, pursued them into the interior of their own country,—routed and dispersed them, and secured the territory to the United States,—ended the war, restored peace and harmony among the people, and put a civil government into successful operation."

While these events were occurring, official intelligence was received by Stockton of war between Mexico and the United States. On hearing which, he left fifty men to garrison Los Angeles, and a still smaller force at Santa Barbara and San Diego, and proceeded north to look after the condition of affairs in that quarter. At Monterey he was informed that Sutter's settlement was threatened by one thousand Walla-Walla Indians. He at once sailed for San Francisco with the intention of making a demonstration against this new enemy. But on his arrival there, he found that the reports of Indian aggressions were unfounded ; and after an interview with some of the Indian chiefs he ascertained their friendly disposition, and confirmed their amicable opinions by such assurance as secured their subsequent neutrality.

Everywhere on his progress through the country, the commodore was greeted with an enthusiastic welcome, and hailed as the conqueror and deliverer of the territory. At San Francisco, the entire population of that place and the adjacent country gave him a formal reception—men, women and children marching in procession to low-water mark to meet him—and addressing him in terms of the most exalted praise and ardent devotion. His triumphant advent was celebrated with a banquet and ball, and the wildest demonstrations of joy and satisfaction. The industrious, sober, and peacefully disposed part of the inhabitants were glad to be relieved from the domination of the cruel and plundering chiefs and governors, who alternately ravaged the country, contended with each other, and oppressed the people. They soon perceived the advantages of security to life and property, which they never had enjoyed until the flag of the United States was floating ŏn their soil.

The disposition of the inhabitants of the northern part of California in favor of the new government was particularly manifested at this time, on the occasion of a rumor that a large force was being collected in Sonora for the purpose of re-conquering the country. They exhibited the utmost repugnance to any such event, offering the commodore all needed assistance in their power to contribute, and displaying their fears with the earnestness of perfect sincerity. Having called on Stockton to express their apprehensions, he assured them, in a characteristic harangue, of his protection, and confirmed their confidence in his determination to preserve his conquest : "You tell me," he said, " that a thousand Sonorians are on their way to encounter my men. Be not alarmed. Ten thousand Sonorians could not excite our fears or arrest our progress. The sons of liberty are on their way, and God alone can stay their march." They returned with this assurance, satisfied that under such a leader no reverse could happen which would endanger their present security. In this state of flattering tranquillity and general acquiescence with the new order of things, prevailing over the greater part of California, but more particularly at the north, Stockton was justified in believing, so far as appearances went, that the conquest of California was complete. The civil government was in successful operation, and seemed fully adequate to the exigencies of the country.

Such being the condition and aspect of affairs, the active mind and patriotic impulses of Stockton induced him to seek another field of useful service. He conceived the vast, magnificent and bold design of recruiting a force of volunteers in California from among the American population then about settling in the territory, sailing with them to Acapulco, and then striking across the continent to unite with the forces of General Taylor, then, as he supposed, approaching the City of Mexico.

The following is a copy of one of his confidential despatches revealing his purpose :—

[" CONFIDENTIAL.]

" *U. S. Frigate Congress, Bay of Monterey,*
September 19*th*, 1846.

"DEAR SIR :—I have sent Major Fremont to the North to see how many men he could recruit with a view to embark them for Mazatlan or Acapulco, where, if possible, I intend to land and fight our way as far on to the City of Mexico as I can.

" With this object in view, your orders of this date in relation to having the squadron in such places as may enable me to get them together as soon as possible, are given.

"You will on your arrival on the coast get all the information you can in reference to this matter.

"I would that we might shake hands with General Taylor at the gates of Mexico.

"Faithfully,

"Your obedient servant,

"R. F. Stockton, *Commodore, &c.*

"*To* Capt. Wm. Mervine, *U. S. Frigate Savannah.*"

Certainly a more daring, brilliant, and master-stroke of military sagacity, has seldom ever been conceived. It reminds us of the famous exploits of the most renowned heroes of ancient and modern times. Instructions were given Col. Fremont, who had previously been appointed military commandant of California, to raise the necessary force to execute this bold design. But while he was engaged in the performance of these orders, intelligence from the south arrived which compelled the abandonment of the proposed expedition, and concentrated all the attention of Stockton upon the theatre of his recent success.

Engraved by H.B. Hall from a Painting on Ivory by Newton London 184[illegible]

Yours truly
R. F. Stockton

New York. D. Appleton & Co. 346 & 348. Broadway.

CHAPTER X.

Insurrection of the Californians.—Proclamation of General Flores.—Defeat and surrender of Talbot and Gillespie.—Captain Mervine defeated, with the crew of the Savannah.—Com. Stockton defeats the Californians at San Diego.—Defeat of General Kearny at San Pasqual.—The official relations of Com. Stockton and Gen. Kearny.—Movement against Los Angeles.—Battles of the Rio San Gabriel, and the Plains of the Mesa.—Fremont negotiates with General Flores and Andreas Pico.—Fremont appointed Governor, and subsequently tried by Court Martial.—Arrival of Commodore Shubrick, and the confirmation of General Kearny as Governor.—Mexican Governors of California.—Foreign Consuls in the Territory.

No sooner had Stockton left Los Angeles for the north, than the Mexican chiefs, indignant and chafed with the knowledge of the smallness of the force before which they had fled so ingloriously, sought to retrieve their tarnished honor. Gen. Flores secretly rallied the fragments of his scattered troops, and suddenly, on the 23d of September, invested Los Angeles with a force overwhelmingly superior to that of the garrison. Capt. Gillespie, who was in command, was obliged to capitulate on the 30th, and was allowed to retire to Monterey. Lieut. Talbot, who had charge of Santa Barbara, was also compelled to evacuate that place, but without surrendering his arms. Intelligence of these successes, greatly exaggerated, was soon spread over the whole country, and almost the entire Mexican population of the southern portion of California rose in arms, to drive the invaders from their soil. Flores, who was chiefly instrumental in fomenting the insurrecrection, issued the following proclamation :—

"*Mexican Army*, *Section of Operations*,
Angeles, *October* 1*st*, 1846.

"Fellow-Citizens :—It is a month and a half that, by lamentable fatality, fruit of the cowardice and inability of the first authorities of the department, we behold ourselves subjugated and oppressed by an insignificant force of adventurers of the United States of America, and placing us in a worse condition than that of slaves.

"They are dictating to us despotic and arbitrary laws, and loading us with contributions and onerous burdens, which have for an object the ruin of our industry and agriculture, and to force us to abandon our property, to be possessed and divided among themselves.

"And shall we be capable to allow ourselves to be subjugated, and to accept, by our silence, the weighty chains of slavery? Shall we permit to be lost the soil inherited from our fathers, which cost them so much blood and so many sacrifices? Shall we make our families victims of the most barbarous slavery? Shall we wait to see our wives violated—our innocent children punished by the American whips—our property sacked—our temples profaned—and, lastly, to drag through an existence full of insult and shame? No! a thousand times no! Countrymen, first death!

"Who of you does not feel his heart beat with violence; who does not feel his blood boil, to contemplate our situation; and who will be the Mexican who will not feel indignant, and who will not rise to take up arms to destroy our oppressors? We believe there is not one so vile and cowardly. With such a motive the majority of the inhabitants of the districts, justly indignant against our tyrants, raise the cry of war, with arms in their hands, and of one accord swear to sustain the following articles:—

"1st. We, the inhabitants of the department of California, as members of the great Mexican nation, declare that it is, and has been, our wish to belong to her alone, free and independent.

"2d. Consequently the authorities intended and named by the invading forces of the United States are held null and void.

"3d. All the North Americans, being enemies of Mexico, we swear not to lay down our arms till they are expelled from the Mexican territory.

"4th. All Mexican citizens, from the age of fifteen to sixty, who do not take up arms to forward the present plan, are declared traitors, and under pain of death.

"5th. Every Mexican or foreigner who may directly or indirectly aid the enemies of Mexico will be punished in the same manner.

"6th. The property of the North Americans in the department, who may directly or indirectly have taken part with, or aided the enemies, shall be confiscated and used for the expenses of the war; and their persons shall be taken to the interior of the republic.

"7th. All those who may oppose the present plan will be punished with arms.

"8th. All the inhabitants of Santa Barbara, and the district of the north, will be invited immediately to adhere to the present plan.

"José Ma. Flores.

"*Camp in Angeles, September 24th*, 1846."

[Signed by more than 300 persons.]

This proclamation, thus numerously signed, indicated a spirit of the most decisive hostility, and a consciousness of strength, which, considering the small force of the American commander-in-chief, was calculated to alarm him, with the insufficiency of his means to cope with an enemy so superior in numbers. It was now apparent that the work of conquest would have to be repeated, and the most prompt and energetic measures were adopted for that purpose. Stockton proceeded at once to San Francisco, and despatched the frigate Savannah for San Pedro, to reinforce the American garrison at that place. Fremont, then at Sacramento, was ordered to San Francisco, with what force could be collected, and about the 12th of October sailed, with one hundred and sixty volunteers, for Santa Barbara, where he was directed to procure horses, and subsequently to move simultaneously with Stockton upon the enemy at Los Angeles. The Savannah did not arrive at San Pedro till after the defeat and surrender of Talbot and Gillespie. Her crew, however, about three hundred and twenty, though poorly armed, were landed, and under Captain Mervine, attacked a large body of mounted Californians about twelve miles from San Pedro. After a severe engagement, they were repulsed, and retreated with the loss of five killed and six wounded. Several subsequent skirmishes took place, but with no material results.

As soon as Com. Stockton had completed his arrangements for the security of the north, he proceeded in the frigate Congress to the seat of war. Upon his arrival at San Pedro, about the 23d of October, he landed his crew in the face of the enemy, who were in force to the number of eight hundred men. They seemed, however, indisposed for an encounter, and retired into the interior. And in order to give time to Fremont to mount his men and co-operate in the contemplated campaign, as well as on account of the greater security of the anchorage and protection from the storms which prevailed at this season on the coast, and from the impossibility of procuring animals either for food or transportation, (the enemy having driven them all into the interior,) Stockton re-embarked his men and sailed for San Diego. In attempting to enter that harbor, the Congress grounded after crossing the bar, and in such a way that it was necessary to support her with spars. While thus engaged, the Californians attacked the town; but in despite of the necessity of employing a part of his force about the frigate, the commodore landed with the remainder, and after a short encounter, defeated the enemy. The condition of San Diego was miserable in the extreme, and neither horses nor cattle could be obtained in the neighborhood. The enemy were in great force at San Bernardo, thirty miles distant, from whence detachments repeatedly visited San Diego, keeping up for many days their desultory attacks. A party of Americans were despatched down the coast in pursuit of cattle, a supply of which they fortunately met and drove into camp.

Immediately after landing at San Diego, Stockton commenced energetic preparations for a march on Los Angeles. His men were daily disciplined according to the tactics adopted, and whatever time could be spared was employed in building a fort, and making saddles, shoes, and other equipments. Information was received from Fremont that he could not procure horses at Santa Barbara, and that he had gone to Monterey for that purpose. Capt. Gibson had obtained a few horses, but they were poor and worn down with severe marches, requiring rest before they could be fit for service. Capt. Hensley, however, who had been sent on an expedition to the south, after much arduous service, returned with five hundred head of cattle and one hundred and forty horses. While preparations were progressing for the march on Los Angeles, a messenger arrived about the 3d of December, with a letter from General Kearny, apprising Com. Stockton of his approach, and expressing a desire to open a communication, but without disclosing his actual situation. On the same evening, Captain Gillespie was despatched with a force of thirty-five men to meet Kearny. On the 6th of December, another messenger arrived, bringing information of the defeat and perilous situation of General Kearny at San Pasqual. On his way from New Mexico, with a considerable force, while a few days from Santa Fé, Kearny met Carson, the courier sent by Com. Stockton, with despatches to the Government, giving information of the conquest of California, and the establishment there of a civil government. Considering, therefore, the work of subjugation of that territory completed, Kearny turned back the greater part of his troops, and proceeded on his way toward California, taking Carson as his guide. At, or near San Pasqual, he was intercepted by the Californians, and defeated, with the loss of eighteen men killed and as many wounded, and one of his two howitzers. He took refuge on a rocky eminence, closely invested by the enemy. All his ammunition and nearly all his provisions were exhausted. Under cover of night he despatched couriers, who with much difficulty eluded the vigilance of the foe and reached San Diego. On learning these facts, Stockton was about to proceed in person with all his force to the relief of Kearny; but subsequent messengers brought intelligence that the strength of the enemy was much less than had been represented. He therefore despatched Lieut. Gray, with two hundred and fifty men, upon whose approach toward San Pasqual, the besiegers abandoned the field, and left the relief party to return unmolested with Kearny and his dragoons.

As the official relations of Com. Stockton and Gen. Kearny have been the subject of much discussion, it is proper we should say in what light we consider them. Gen. Kearny was directed by instructions from the Secretary of War to invade California with a prescribed force, and "should he conquer it," to establish a civil government there. On his way, learning that the objects of the expedition had been accomplished by Com. Stockton, as above related, he turned back his troops, proceeded with a small party, was attacked and defeated by the enemy, and relieved from imminent danger by the detachment sent by Stockton. Arrived at San Diego, he consented, according to the testimony of all then present, to act under Stockton, then on the eve of a movement against Los Angeles. The following lucid statement of the reception of Kearny by Stockton, and of their relative positions in that movement, we extract from the official letter of the commodore to the Secretary of the Navy, made subsequent to the court martial which tried Col. Fremont, and dated February 18th, 1848:—

"On their arrival, General Kearny, his officers, and men, were received by all the garrison in the kindest and most respectful manner. So far as my observation extended, no civility or attention was omitted. Having sent with Captain Gillespie every horse that was fit for use to General Kearny, I was without one for my own accommodation. I was therefore compelled on foot to advance and receive the general, whom I conducted to my own quarters, until others more agreeable to him could be prepared. The arrival of General Kearny was to me a source of gratification: although it was my decided opinion, which as yet I have seen no reason to change, that under the circumstances that existed I was entitled to retain the position in which I was placed, of commander-in-chief: yet in consideration of his high standing in the army, his long experience as a soldier, the importance of military science and skill in the movements that were to be made in the interior of the country, I immediately determined to yield all personal feelings of ambition, and tc place in his hands the supreme authority. In accordance with this determination I tendered to General Kearny the position of commander-in-chief, and offered to accompany him as his aid.

"This proposition was on more than one occasion renewed, and with all sincerity and singleness of purpose. The responsibility of moving from San Diego, and leaving the safety of the ships deprived of so large and efficient a portion of their crews, was of itself a momentous one. This, however, in the discharge of duty I felt no inclination to shrink from. But the fate of the territory itself might depend upon the issue of a battle to be fought on shore against an army organized to encounter us. The nature of the service, and the importance of the stake, it seemed to me appertained rather to a general in the army than a captain in the navy. Whatever ambition I might feel for distinction, either on my own account, or on that of the gallant officers and men under my command, was voluntarily and deliberately offered as a sacrifice to a paramount sense of duty. The offers thus made were, however, on every occasion positively and distinctly declined by General Kearny, who on his side offered to accompany me in the capacity of my aid, and tendered to afford me the aid of his head and hand. A few days before I expected to take up the line of march, I addressed a note to the general, expressing a wish that he would accompany me. In his reply, he repeated the language which he had before employed—that he would so accompany me, and afford me the aid of his head and hand. Accordingly, on the morning of our departure he appeared upon the ground. *After the troops had been paraded, and were nearly ready to commence the march*, as I was about to mount my horse, General Kearny approached me, and inquired, who was to command the troops. I replied, Lieutenant Rowan was to have command. On his expressing a wish that he should himself command them, I replied that he should have the command. The different officers were at once convened, and informed that General Kearny had volunteered to command the troops, and that I had given him the appointment, reserving my own position as commander-in-chief. This arrangement having been made, we proceeded on the march."

Gen. Kearny himself, on examination before the court martial, testified on the fourteenth day of the trial, in relation to the expedition to Los Angeles,—"Under Commodore Stockton's directions every arrangement for the expedition was made. I had nothing whatever to do with it." Col. Fremont, in his defence, says,—"Both Gen. Kearny and the officers under him received and obeyed the orders of Com. Stockton, in some instances in opposition to those first given by Gen. Kearny, both on the march and in the battles." Lieutenants Gray, Minor and Emory testified to the same effect. From this, and much other corroborating evidence, it is historically true that whatever of responsibility or credit belongs to the movement upon Los Angeles, at this time, must be attributed to Com. Stockton. He originated the expedition, provided the means for its prosecution, conducted it as commander-in-chief, and is fairly entitled to the praise due for its success.

On the 23d of December, general orders were issued, as follows:—

"GENERAL ORDERS.—The forces composed of Capt. Tilghman's Company of Artillery, a detachment of the 1st Regiment of Dragoons, Companies A and B of California Battalion of Mounted Riflemen, and a detachment of sailors and marines from the frigates Congress and Savannah, and the ship Portsmouth, will take up the line of march for the *Ciudad de los Angeles* on Monday morning, the 28th inst., at 10 A. M.

"By order of the Commander-in-Chief,

"J. ZEILAN,

"*Brevet Captain and Adjutant.*

"*San Diego, 23d December*, 1846."

On the 29th the march commenced. The distance to be travelled between San Diego and Los Angeles was one hundred and forty-five miles, the track lying through deep sands and over steep and rugged ascents. The entire force consisted of five hundred and forty sailors and marines, and sixty of Kearny's dragoons, and six pieces of artillery. The men, for the most part, were poorly clothed, their shoes generally being made by themselves of canvas. Stockton, in his despatch of February 5th, 1847, to the Secretary of the Navy, says,—"We came to San Diego with the Congress alone—her resources being almost exhausted in a previous campaign. The town was besieged by the insurgents, and there were no stores or provisions of any kind in it, and we were reduced to one fourth allowance of bread. We had to build a fort—to mount our artillery,—to make saddles, bridles, and harness: we had, in truth, to make an army, with all its necessary appendages, out of the mechanics and sailors of this ship, and to take our horses and beef cattle from the enemy." Captain Turner, of the dragoons, declined using the horses, in their feeble condition, preferring to proceed without them, and those taken along for purposes of draught were so miserable that they daily became disabled, which devolved much hard work on the men, in dragging the guns and the carts heavily laden with provisions and ammunition. "Their route," says a writer already quoted, "lay through a rugged country, drenched with the winter rains, and bristling with the lances of the enemy. Through this the commodore led his seamen and marines, sharing himself, with the general at his side, all the hardships of the common sailors. The stern engagements with the enemy derive their heroic features from the contrast existing in the condition of the two. The Californians were well mounted, and whirled their flying artillery to the most convenient positions. Our troops were on foot, mired to the ankle, and with no resources except in their own indomitable resolution and courage. Their exploits may be cast in the shadow by the clouds which roll up from the plains of Mexico, but they are realities *here*, which impress themselves with a force which reaches the very foundations of social order."

The enemy were frequently seen during the march, and the utmost vigilance was constantly necessary, to prevent a surprise. The celebrated Kit Carson had been selected to command a small corps of scouts, and to act as spies and skirmishers, which duty was performed in a most efficient manner. On the 3d of January, at San Luís del Rey, Stockton despatched a messenger to apprise Fremont of his advance, and to caution him against the hazard of an action until a junction of their forces had taken place. This messenger, however, did not reach Fremont until the 9th January. Lieut. Selden, of the navy, was also sent with a small vessel to the maritime defile of Rincon, to protect that pass through which Fremont was expected to march. While advancing, propositions were received from Flores to negotiate, which were rejected in the most peremptory terms. The bearers were informed that no communication would be held with Flores, he having forfeited his honor as a soldier, by breaking his parole. They were likewise assured that Flores and every Mexican who had broken his parole, if caught, would immediately be shot.

On the evening of January 7th, the whole force of the enemy

being not far distant, the commodore despatched a confidential emissary to ascertain, under cover of night, their exact position and strength. They were formed between the invading army and the *Rio San Gabriel*, apparently waiting to give battle, and were estimated at from one thousand to twelve hundred men, composed almost wholly of cavalry. On the morning of the 8th, Stockton ordered all the guns of his men to be fired and re-loaded, and passing through their ranks, reminded them that it was the anniversary of the battle of New Orleans. They were then formed in a square, with the baggage and cattle in the centre. On approaching the river, the enemy were observed prepared for their reception, and strongly posted on the opposite heights. The banks commanding the ford (which was occupied by the artillery of the Californians), were about fifty yards from the river, quite steep, and about fifty feet high. When within a quarter of a mile of the ford, the men were formed in line, and orders given that not a gun should be fired until the crossing was effected. The enemy, however, kept up a perpetual and brisk fire, though with little effect. In the act of crossing, the water being about four feet deep, word was sent by Kearny to the commander-in-chief that the bed of the river consisted of quicksand and could not be passed with the guns. Stockton instantly repaired to the head of the column, seized the ropes, and with his own hands assisted to drag over the artillery. The passage effected, the troops were again formed for battle. The commodore took charge of the artillery, and pointed his guns with such precision that the enemy were soon compelled to abandon theirs; when he sent Lieut. Gray with orders to Kearny to charge up the bank and seize them, while he prepared to receive a charge which was about being made on his flank. Before Kearny could reach the summit of the ascent, the Californians returning, withdrew their guns, making but a feeble stand against the general. The greater part of their force, after making a circuit of some hundred yards, descending to the level of the river, attacked Stockton on his left flank; but they were so warmly received that they retreated upon the hill, the commodore following, charging up the declivity with his artillery, in the very face of the enemy. On his reaching the heights, the latter were seen at a short distance, drawn up in battle array, with their artillery in front. The Americans were now ordered to lie down, while their leader ran out his guns, and poured upon the adversary a well-directed fire, he himself aiming each piece as fast as it was loaded, with such fatal effect, that the enemy were repeatedly driven from their guns. Several ineffectual attempts were made by them to charge ; but the steady front, cool courage, and well aimed rifles of the assailants repelled their attacks. Dispersed in every direction on the heights, a portion of their right wing wheeled upon the rear of the American forces, and attacked Capt. Gillespie, encumbered with his baggage and cattle, who received them so warmly that they fled across the river. Their main body retreated before the assailants, until reaching a ravine, they renewed a brisk fire, when Stockton again took charge of the guns, and by his well-directed shots, drove them from their position. They then rapidly fled, carrying off their killed and wounded, the numbers of which could not be ascertained. The Americans lost two killed and nine wounded.

On the 9th, Stockton pursued the retiring foe in the direction of Los Angeles, and after a march of six miles came up with them on the *Plains of the Mesa.* They were well posted, with a ravine to the left of their line, which masked their artillery. When about six hundred yards distant they opened a fire on the advancing column. Preparations for a charge were visible in their ranks, and they were observed to be joined by a strong reinforcement. Stockton formed his whole force in square, with the baggage, horses and oxen in the centre, and gave imperative commands to his men not to fire a shot until he gave the signal, which he said would not be until he could see the eyes of the enemy. The Californians made a gallant charge. It is said by those who witnessed it, to have been a brilliant spectacle. Gayly caparisoned, with banners flying, mounted on fleet and splendid horses, they bounded on, spurring to the top of their speed, on the small but compact square into which the American force was compressed. The very earth appeared to tremble beneath their thundering hoofs—and nothing seemed capable of resisting such cavalry. But inspired with the cool courage and dauntless heroism of their leader, his men patiently awaited the result. The signal was at length given, and a deadly fire, directed according to orders at the horses, was poured into the ranks of the advancing foe, which emptied many saddles and threw them into complete confusion. Retreating a few hundred yards, they again formed, and despatching a part of their force to the rear, they attacked simultaneously three sides of the square. Orders were renewed to reserve fire until the enemy's near approach, and with the same decisive results,—their ranks breaking up and retreating in disorder. A third time, having rallied, they returned to the charge, but once more their ranks were thinned by the deadly aim of the assailed; and despairing of their ability to cope with men so cool, unflinching and resolute, confused and discomfited, they scattered and fled in every direction.

On the 10th of January, at the head of his advanced guard, on the broadest and principal road leading into Los Angeles, the Commodore, with banners waving, marched into the city. He directed Captain Gillespie to raise the same flag which he was compelled to strike on the previous September.

A few days after these events, Fremont, without knowledge of Stockton's movements and success, encountered Gen. Flores and Andreas Pico and their disheartened remnant of followers, who in humble terms sued for peace. Not knowing that the commander-in-chief had refused to treat with them, Fremont entered into negotiations, and finally agreed upon articles by which they stipulated to surrender their arms, including the gun captured at San Pasqual from Gen. Kearny, and cease from all further resistance. These articles it was thought desirable to approve, as they were considered a final pacification in the territory between the contending parties, and as clemency on the part of the conqueror was more likely to insure that result than the sanguinary exercise of inexorable justice.

The following *general order* must close our narrative of the military operations of Com. Stockton in California. We have extended it far beyond the limits originally contemplated; but as the history of these events is closely connected with the subsequent prosperity of the country, and the present condition of San Francisco, we have thought best to give it in all its interesting details.

"*Head-quarters, Ciudad de los Angeles,*
January 11*th*, 1847.

"The COMMANDER-IN-CHIEF congratulates the officers and men of the southern division of the United States forces in California on the brilliant victories obtained by them over the enemy on the 8th and 9th instants, and on once more taking possession of *Ciudad de los Angeles*.

"He takes the earliest moment to commend their gallantry and good conduct, both in the battle fought on the 8th, on the banks of the *Rio San Gabriel*, and on the 9th inst., on the *Plains of the Mesa*.

"The steady courage of the troops in forcing their passage across the *Rio San Gabriel*, where officers and men were alike employed in dragging the guns through the water, against the galling fire of the enemy, without exchanging a shot, and their gallant charge up the banks against the enemy's cavalry, has perhaps never been surpassed; and the cool determination with which in the battle of the 9th they repulsed the charge of cavalry made by the enemy at the same time on their front and rear, has extorted the admiration of the enemy, and deserves the best thanks of their countrymen.

"R. F. STOCKTON,
"*Governor and Commander-in-Chief of the Territory of California.*"

Commodore Stockton, in pursuance of instructions which he had communicated to the Government in September, now appointed Col. Fremont governor of the territory, and Wm. H. Russell, secretary. It is painful to relate that unfortunate disputes arose as to the right of Fremont to the high dignity of governor. General Kearny produced a commission appointing himself to the office. His pretensions, however, were opposed both by Stockton and Fremont, who contended that a new train of circumstances had arisen since the produced commission had been granted. The instructions to General Kearny from the war department, ("should he conquer the country,") Com. Stockton considered as anticipated by himself; and of course the resulting action prescribed by those instructions contingently, ("to form a civil government,") as devolving on himself, the real conqueror of the territory. In these views of Stockton, the Government entirely acquiesced,—so far as respected the approval in mass of his whole conduct,—the secretary of the navy specially thanking him for anticipating the wishes of the Government. It is not a little singular, that although the validity of Stockton's acts was thus sanctioned, yet Col. Fremont, for obedience to his orders, was tried by court martial, and convicted of disobedience to the orders of Gen. Kearny. His sentence was suspension from the service; but the President, in consideration of his many services and mitigating circumstances, was pleased to remit the punishment, and ordered him to be restored to his former rank. But Fremont, being of opinion that he had done no wrong, refused to accept this clemency, and accordingly resigned his commission, and retired from the American military service. Whatever may have been the merits of this case, it is certain that Fremont showed himself a true hero, in his efforts to overthrow the Mexican power in California, and is deserving of the gratitude of American settlers in that territory. As an adventurous, persevering and talented explorer, who has laid open practicable and easy paths to a great country that had long been closed against the boldest pioneers, he deserves the approbation of the civilized world.

In the mean time, General Kearny applied to Commodore Shubrick (who arrived in California on the 22d of January, 1847, and as senior in commission, superseded Commodore Stockton in command of the squadron,) to place him in the chief command. But under the instructions to Com. Sloat of 12th July, 1846, which devolved on the naval commander the conquest and civil government of California, Shubrick did not consider himself authorized to accede to his wishes. Soon after, however, other instructions, dated 9th November, 1846, having been received by Com. Shubrick, Kearny was recognized as governor, and acted as such until he relinquished the command to Colonel Mason, upon his departure for Washington. These instructions Kearny did not communicate to Fremont. Thus there were two acting governors at the same time in California, and Fremont, without any knowledge of his authority being annulled by the instructions of the 9th November, subjected himself, in the performance of what he considered his duties, to charges of disobedience to his superior officer. He was ordered to surrender the howitzer lost by Kearny at San Pasqual, at this time in possession of the California battalion, to the Mormon regiment under Col. Cooke. This could not have been done without the hazard of a revolt, and therefore was declined by Fremont.

Before narrating the further steps adopted by the Americans, when they had thus taken military possession of the country, we may give a brief notice of the various governors and other public officers who were connected with California, subsequently to the Mexican declaration of independence. The list is somewhat a long one for so short a period; and illustrates the feeble hold which Mexico had upon the political affections of so remote and neglected a province:—

Sola was the last Californian governor under the Spanish flag and the first under the Mexican. In 1823 he was ordered to Mexico, and *Don Luis Antonio Argüello* was named governor, with all the powers of his predecessor, and remained so until the arrival of *Echeandia,* in the beginning of 1825. Echeandia had command until the arrival of *Victoria,* in 1830. Victoria continued in power until the winter of 1832, when the Californians revolted, and sent him away. At that time *Pio Pico* was the senior member of the territorial department, and by law became governor *pro tempore.* Echeandia, meanwhile, had remained among his friends at San Diego, probably expecting some speedy change in political affairs; and, when Victoria was about to leave, he took the military command. Both he and Pico continued in office till the arrival of *Figueroa* in 1833. Figueroa died in 1835; and, during his last illness, delivered over the civil command to *Don José Castro,* and the military to *Don Nicolas Gutierrez,* Castro being at that time senior member of the department. These remained in office until the arrival of *Chico,* in 1836. The same year Chico was sent away by the Junta department. Previous to his departure he left the military and civil command with Gutierrez, he having been formerly his second.

On the 6th of November, 1836, the Californians, assisted by foreigners under Captain Graham, an American, and Captain Coppinger, an Englishman, revolted against Gutierrez; and the latter was forced to leave the country, with all his officers, except those who took part in favor of the natives, and wished to remain. *Don Mariano Guadalupe Vallejo* played an important *rôle* in this revolution, and became commander of the forces; while his nephew, *Don Juan Bautista Alvarado,* was made civil governor. These positions they held until the arrival of *Micheltorena,* in 1842. Early in 1845, Micheltorena was sent away by the Californians, after forming a sort of treaty with them (he being desirous to proceed to Mexico), leaving José Castro with the military command. Pio Pico, who was again the senior member of the Junta department, then became governor. These two continued in power, as military and civil heads respectively, until the Americans took possession of the country. Sola, Argüello, Echeandria, Victoria, Figueroa, Chico and Micheltorena, all had the united civil and military authority.

In 1843, *Mr. Thomas O. Larkin* was appointed the first, as he happened to be the last *American* consul in California. That gentleman also held various other official and important appointments from the United States Government up to the year 1848, when peace was declared, and the country became American. In 1845, Mr. Larkin, who resided at Monterey, the nominal Mexican capital of the province, named *Mr. William A. Leidesdorff* the United States vice-consul, at the port of San Francisco. *Mr. James A. Forbes* received the appointment of the first *British* consul in 1844, or 1845. The first *French* consul, *Don Luis Gasquet*, arrived in California, *via* Mexico, about the 10th of May, 1845, and left some time in 1847. He remained a considerable time in the country after he delivered the consulate over to *M. Movenhaut.*

CHAPTER XI.

Peace concluded between the Mexican and American States.—Terms of the Treaty.—California ceded to the United States.—The country ruled provisionally by American Governors.—Rapid increase of population by immigration.—Discovery of gold on the American River by Mr. James W. Marshall.—Great excitement in consequence of the discovery, and rush of people to the gold placers.—Mixed character of the population.—Necessity for the establishment of a proper form of Government.—Independent sectional legislation inadequate and unsatisfactory.—Meetings held to effect a general civil organization.—General Riley issues a proclamation for a meeting to be held at Monterey to adopt a State Constitution.—Names of delegates appointed.—Meeting at Monterey.—Constitution of California adopted, and rejoicings on the occasion.

The general war continued for about a year after the reduction of California. At last, in the month of February, 1848, an armistice was entered into between the hostile parties, which endured till a formal treaty of peace was concluded. This was ratified by the Senate of the United States in March, and by the Mexican Congress in May following of the year just named. By this treaty a considerable territory was ceded by Mexico. The boundary line between it and the United States was declared to be the Rio Grande, up mid-channel of which it ran till about the thirty-second parallel; from whence, turning westward, along the southern limit of New Mexico till it cut the Gila, down the middle of which river it proceeded till its junction with the Rio Colorado; from whence it ran westward till it reached the Pacific, at a point about one league south of San Diego, nearly on latitude thirty-two and a half. Thus Texas, to its full extent, New Mexico and Upper California were altogether contained within the boundary line on the American side. The free navigation of the Rio Colorado, from the mouth of the Gila to the Gulf of California, as well as of the gulf itself, were likewise secured to the United States. To compensate, in some measure, for the cession of such a vast territory, the American Government agreed to pay to Mexico the sum of $15,000,000; and, moreover, took upon itself all liability for the damages due by Mexico to American subjects, which, as before stated, was one of the original causes of the war. Each nation was to defray its own expenses in conducting hostilities. There were several minor stipulations in the treaty; but with these we have nothing here to do. It is sufficient merely to say, that California was now, wholly and legally, a portion of the American Union; and her people of Spanish or of other origin, were henceforward American citizens.

Meanwhile the country was ruled, provisionally, by successive American governors, until a constitution could be granted by Congress, when it would be formally assumed as a *Territory* of the Union. Events, however, were about to happen which superseded the necessity of such a constitution, and hastened the development of California into a *State*, without passing through the intermediate stage of a territory. Like the Minerva on its public seal, it started into life a full grown being, ripe in all its faculties and powers, and at once fitted to contend with whoever and whatever should oppose its wonderful progress. This was owing to the discovery of gold in the country and consequent rush of immigration thither, with all its attendant effects.

But before this discovery took place, a vast immigration from all sides had begun to flow towards California. The previous advantages which the country had offered to the intending immigrant, were on a sudden immensely increased by the circumstance of its being now a portion of the American Union. Accordingly, large bodies of people were beginning to flock to the land; and agriculture, trade and commerce were greatly benefited by the accession of such numbers of active, intelligent and industrious settlers. In 1845, it was estimated that the white population had increased to about 8,000; while the domesticated Indians, who but a dozen years before had numbered nearly 30,000, now scarcely amounted to one-third of that number. As for the wild or "gentile" Indians, it was impossible to form any reasonable conjecture as to their numbers. They were, however, generally supposed, by different parties, to number from one to three hundred thousand. As they inhabited districts hitherto scarcely visited by the white man, their presence and numbers were considered as of no account in the progress of the country. The years 1846 and 1847 brought a very large accession to the white population. Colonel Stevenson's regiment of New York volunteers alone gave a body of a thousand hardy settlers, as nearly the whole number, officers as well as men, remained in the country upon being disbanded, which indeed had been anticipated. But beside these, great numbers of Americans had journeyed from the Atlantic States across the Rocky and Snowy Mountains, and settled in California. Numerous companies of Mormons likewise either came direct from the Eastern States, or from their settlements beside the Great Salt Lake. A portion of these had formed the noted "Mormon Battalion" of the war. At the same time, far more than the usual proportion of stragglers, runaway seamen, and adventurers from all nations continued to pour into the country, so soon as the war and its first results were known. At the close of hostilities, it was estimated that the white population, of all nations, numbered between 12,000 and 15,000, which was not merely annually but daily increasing. Such was the beneficent influence and magic power of the American flag! People knew that they were safe under its folds, and free to run the race of a prosperous career.

But immeasurably exceeding all other causes in raising the swelling tide of immigration was the discovery of gold. This happened at Coloma, a valley and town situated between fifty and sixty miles east of Sacramento City, in the month of January, 1848; curiously enough, just when the land was ceasing to be Mexican. Many strange and improbable stories have been told as to the alleged earliest discoveries; but we believe that the only reliable account is that given by Captain Sutter, upon whose ground the precious metal was first found, and which we shall therefore adopt, without noticing the various fabulous statements alluded to.

It appears that Captain Sutter, during the winter of 1847–48, was erecting a saw-mill for producing lumber, on the south fork of the American River, a feeder of the Sacramento. Mr. James W. Marshall contracted with Sutter for the building of this mill; and, in the course of his operations, had occasion to admit the river water into the tail-race, for the purpose of widening and deepening it by the strength of the current. In doing this, a considerable quantity of mud, sand and gravel was carried along with the stream, and deposited in a heap at the foot of the tail-race. Marshall, when one day examining the state of his works, noticed a few glittering particles lying near the edge of the heap. His curiosity being aroused, he gathered some of the sparkling objects; and at once became satisfied of their nature and the

Sutter's Mill.

value of his discovery. All trembling with excitement, he hurried to his employer, and told his story. Captain Sutter at first thought it was a fiction, and the teller only a mad fool. Indeed, he confesses, that he kept a sharp eye upon his loaded rifle, when he, whom he was tempted to consider a maniac, was eagerly disclosing the miraculous tale. However, his doubts were all at once dispelled when Marshall tossed on the table before him an ounce or so of the shining dust. The two agreed to keep the matter secret, and quietly share the golden harvest between them. But, as they afterwards searched more narrowly together, and gloated upon the rich deposits, their eager gestures and looks, and muttered, broken words, happened to be closely watched by a Mormon laborer employed about the neighborhood. He followed their movements, and speedily became as wise as themselves. As secrecy was of little importance to him, he forthwith divulged the extraordinary intelligence, and in confirmation of the story, exhibited some scales of gold which he had himself gathered. Immediately, every body in the neighborhood left his regular employment, and began to search for the precious metal. A large body of Mormon immigrants about this time was approaching California by the south pass of the Rocky Mountains; and, on hearing news of the discovery, hastened at once to the spot. Rumors of these circumstances speedily flew across the length and breadth of the land, variously modified by the warmth or coolness of fancy of the successive narrators, but all agreeing in this, that gold was to be had in large quantities, for the mere trouble of picking it up, at Sutter's Mill, on the south fork of the *Rio de los Americanos.* To that quarter, then, all the loose population around instantly directed their steps. Soon the neighborhood swarmed with diggers; and, within a few days after the first discovery, upwards of twelve hundred people were busily at work, with spades, shovels, knives, sticks, wooden bowls, cradles, and all manner of implements, many of them of the rudest and most primitive fashion, excavating, riddling and washing earth for the precious particles it contained. Over all California the excitement was prodigious. Spaniard, American and foreigner were all alike affected. The husband left his wife; the father, his family; people tore themselves from the most pressing duties at home; men deserted their masters, and these followed their servants—all hurried to Sutter's Mill. Some withstood the temptation for a short time; but, very soon, nearly the whole male population of the country, unable to resist the evidence of their senses when specimens of the newly found gold were exhibited before their dilated eyes, became suddenly infected with the maddened whirl of the "yellow fever,"—the *auri sacra fames*, and rushed off at a tangent, helter-skelter, to gather riches, as Aladdin had plucked fruits of priceless value in his fairy garden, in the bowels of the earth, among the valleys of the Snowy

Mountains. Towns were dispeopled, ships in harbor deserted, all kinds of business sent to the dogs; the whole settled parts of the country were suddenly deprived of their inhabitants, or women and children alone formed the population, though even of these many flocked to the *placers* and the *diggings*, to see and be seen, to make money somehow, and as surely to spend it.

Meanwhile, other streams and other valleys were found to contain the auriferous sands. Not only the whole strip of country west of the Sierra Nevada, which was drained by feeders of the Sacramento, but that other strip, locally in connection with the former, and lying to the south, which was watered by the streams which fell into the San Joaquin, was ascertained also to possess auriferous deposits in large quantities. In fact it was believed that the gold regions could not be exhausted of their treasures during countless generations. There was enough, therefore, and to spare, for all comers, though their name should be "legion." Individuals were daily making considerable fortunes, while all who chose to work steadily at the business, were sure to earn much larger wages than they could do at any other kind of labor in the country.

All this while, the few ships that were enabled to get away from the coast, and travellers and expresses by land, were spreading the news far and wide over remote seas and through foreign climes. The circles of excitement grew wider and wider, and scarcely lost strength as they spread farther distant. First, the Mexicans from the nearest, and then those from the remotest provinces, flocked to California. The indolent, yet adventurous, half-wild population of Sonora poured in its many thousands from the south; while Oregon from the north sent its sturdy settlers in almost equal numbers. The Sandwich Islands followed, with their strange medley of white and colored races. Peru and Chili then hurried an innumerable crowd, as fast as ships could be obtained to carry them to the fields of gold. Before long, China sent forward her thousands of thrifty wandering children, feeble, indeed, both in body and mind, but persevering, and from their union into laboring companies, capable of great feats. Australia likewise contributed her proportion of clever rascals, and perhaps as many clever adventurers who had not been convicted felons. The United States, which at all times contain a vast roving and excitable population, next were affected to their very centres ; and armies—to use a moderate term, were on a sudden organized instantly to proceed to California and share in the golden spoil. The year 1848 was lost for the land passage ; but by the early summer of 1849, great and numerous caravans were in full march, by various routes, across the Rocky Mountains. Many hardships were endured by these immigrants, and numbers died on the road. But their unburied bodies and bleaching skeletons were unheeded by the succeeding throng, or only pointed out to the weary yet restless travellers the paths where others had gone before, and which perhaps the new-comers should only avoid. On—on ! to the land of gold ! There, fortune smiled on all, while her worshippers revelled among riches. On—on ! Round Cape Horn fleets were bearing additional thousands ; while through Mexico to all her eastern ports, and especially across the Isthmus of Panama, still other thousands were hurrying, by new ships on the Pacific, to the "Golden Gate." Later in the year, and somewhat diminished in intensity, the excitement produced in Europe similar results. Many of the young, strong and adventurous, the idle, dissipated, reckless, sanguine youths of Great Britain, France and Germany, broke through the ties of home, friends and country, and perhaps of civilization itself, and embarked for California, to seize fortune in a bound, and with one eager clutch, or to perish in the attempt.

These astonishing circumstances soon gathered into California a mixed population of nearly a quarter of a million of the wildest, bravest, most intelligent, yet most reckless and perhaps dangerous beings ever before collected into one small district of country. Gold, and the pleasures that gold could buy, had allured them to the scene. They were flushed with hope and excitement. Chiefly young men, they were naturally boisterous and riotous. When their "blood was up" they would dare all things, heedless of consequences. Rich or poor—fortunate, or the reverse in their search for gold, they were almost equally dangerous members of the community. If unsuccessful, they were moody and discontented, fit and ready for any new and desperate enterprise : if fortunate, the excesses of warm youthful constitutions, the gaming table, women and drink, were certain to produce a prolific crop of vice, crime and all social disorders. Without family ties, without the restraining and softening charms of home and modest female society, the strange mixed population of California at this time was like the dormant volcano, which at some unexpected moment may break forth and devastate all within its influence. Or it may be compared to the swelling flood of a mighty river which threatens every instant to overleap or burst its banks, and overwhelm the great country through which it rolls, and which, when the stream is confined within proper limits, it only fertilizes and enriches. The good sense of the community, and the speedy establishment of a legal constitution could alone save California from the threatened manifold evils of its heterogeneous population, and direct its immense and wavering energies into the best and most profitable channels for their reception.

The cooler and more intelligent settlers in California early foresaw the urgent necessity of a regular constitution being adopted. The provisional government subsisting since the conquest of 1847 was but a make-shift at the best; fit perhaps to regulate the concerns of such a limited community as then inhabited California, but by no means able to satisfy the wants of the great, growing and dangerous population which now so strangely and suddenly had arisen. Probably, Congress, at a distance, was not sufficiently alive to the pressing need of adequate measures being instantly taken to remedy the alarming state of things described, by means of a formal territorial government. At any rate, the most honest, intelligent and influential inhabitants of California believed that they could wait no longer the slow movements of Congress, and conceived that their own social safety would be best consulted by at once improvising governments of their own. Accordingly, attempts were soon severally made, by the people of San Francisco, Sonoma and Sacramento, to form legislatures for themselves, which they invested with supreme authority. Other portions of the country prepared to follow the example of the places named. It was quickly found, however, that these independent legislatures threatened occasionally to come into collision with each other, while the existence in a limited country of so many different supreme courts, each governed by its own maxims and principles of procedure, betrayed an anomalous state of things too uncertain and unsatisfactory to be longer patiently borne. A general feeling therefore became evident that the sooner such partial legislation was put a stop to the better for the country; and that nothing less than a general constitution and complete civil government would be held satisfactory by the people.

Great meetings for these purposes were held at San José, San Francisco, Monterey, Sonoma, and other places, in the months of December and January, 1848-49. It was there resolved that such a civil organization was expedient, and that delegates should be chosen by popular election, from each district of the country, who should afterwards assemble at San José, though the place of meeting was subsequently changed to Monterey. The period of meeting was first fixed for the 8th of January, then extended to the 5th of March, next to the 1st of May, and finally, in order to give ample time to every district to make the necessary arrangements, to the first Monday in August. The delegates to meet at this convention were to frame the constitution desired. The resolutions adopted at these primary meetings were forwarded to and exchanged between the principal districts and towns of the country for their consideration and approval; by which places they were unanimously approved of. These initiatory movements were not dictated by political faction; but were the true and honest result of popular feeling on the subject. There were no partisans in the matter, where there was only one great party, and that included the whole thinking population.

While the people of California were thus working out for themselves the great problem of a State constitution, the military governor, General Riley, thought fit to interfere. On the 3d of June, 1849, he issued a proclamation, in which was fairly enough stated the anomalous and unsatisfactory position of the country, both in its local and general governments; and he thereupon ordained the inhabitants in certain specified districts to return delegates to a convention, which would meet at Monterey on the 1st of September, to frame a State Constitution, and which should afterwards be submitted to the people for their approval. In the same proclamation he likewise made provision for the election of certain district officials to complete the temporary local organization. The people in many parts of the country considered the interference of the military authority to be unnecessary as it was uncalled for. As, however, matters could not be improved, the different districts were content to adopt the provisions of General Riley's proclamation, and chose their delegates accordingly.

These delegates were forty-eight in number, and while they nominally represented only different parts of California, they might have been taken as a fair representation of every State in the Union. They likewise included natives of various European countries. They were chiefly men of comparatively youthful years, many of them not much accustomed, at least of late, to the study of those abstract questions which might have been anticipated in devising the constitution of a State. But they were all fully impressed with the importance of their trust, and determined to do their duty in the best manner possible. Among the number were individuals of high talents, whose wisdom, despatch and aptitude for legislation were eminently displayed. As these delegates cannot be too well known, we give the following list of their names, and the districts they represented :—

San Diego.

Miguel de Pedrorena,
Henry Hill.

Los Angeles.

Stephen C. Foster,
José Antonio Carillo,
Hugo Reid,
Manuel Dominguez,
Abel Stearns.

Santa Barbara.

Pablo de la Guerra,
Jacinto Rodriguez.

San Luis Obispo.

Henry A Tefft,
José M. Covarrubias.

Monterey.

Henry W. Halleck,
Thomas O. Larkin,
Charles T. Botts,
Pacificus Ord,
Lewis T. Dent.

San José.

Joseph Aram,
Kimball H. Dimmick,
J. D. Hoppe,
Antonio M. Pico,
Elam Brown,
Julian Hanks,
Pedro Sansevani.

Sonoma.

Joel P. Walker,
Robert Semple,
Mariano G. Vallejo.

San Francisco.

Edward Gilbert,
Myron Norton,
William M. Gwin,
Joseph Hobson,
William M. Stewart,
Francis J. Lippitt,
A. J. Ellis,
Rodman M. Price.

San Joaquin.

Thomas Lloyd Vermeule,
O. M. Wozencroft,
B. F. Moore,
J. M. H. Hollingsworth,
J. M. Jones,
Benjamin S. Lippincott.

Sacramento.

Jacob R. Snyder,
Winfield S. Sherwood,
L. W. Hastings,
John McDougal,
William E. Shannon,
John A. Sutter,
Elisha O. Crosby,
M. M. McCarver.

Monterey.

The delegates, at their first regular meeting on the 4th of September, chose, by a large majority of votes, Dr. Robert Semple as president of the convention; Captain William G. Marcy was then appointed secretary, and the other necessary offices were properly filled up. The house in which the delegates met was a large handsome two-story stone erection, called "Colton Hall," and was perhaps the best fitted for their purposes of any building in the country.

Without narrating the particular incidents and debates that occurred among the delegates, it may be sufficient to say, that, after rather more than a month's constant labor and discussion, the existing constitution of California was drafted and finally adopted by the convention. This noble document was formed after the model of the most approved State constitutions of the Union, and was framed in strict accordance with the most liberal and independent opinions of the age. Some indeed of its provisions may be open to cavil, as for instance, whether the judges —supreme ones particularly—should be chosen by direct election of the people, and for only a limited period, and whether the free descendants of the black and red races should be excluded from the rights of suffrage and election. But, taking it as a whole, the constitution, which is essentially democratic in its nature, must certainly be pronounced, in its declaration of rights and the various divisions regulating the election, powers and duties of the legislative, executive and judicial departments, as well as the portion respecting education, a wonderful advance and improvement in the modern art of government. Among other things, it expressly rejected slavery and "involuntary servitude," and declared the right of women to hold as their own separate property after marriage, the estates, both real and personal, which they possessed before it, or which they might afterwards acquire by gift, devise or descent. But it is unnecessary in our narrow limits to dwell on the peculiar features of this celebrated constitution. We refer our readers to the document itself, which should be in the hands of every Californian. It will bear keen criticism, and merits the close study of statesmen of every country.

On the 13th of October, the delegates signed the precious instrument; and so finished the labors they were appointed to perform. While the signatures were being affixed, shot after shot slowly boomed from the guns of the fort in honor of the Union, and as the *thirty-first and last* was heard, which was a little louder, the listeners thought, than those that had gone before, the suppressed feelings of the people broke forth, and all joyously exclaimed—"*That's for California!*"—and so it was.

Thus was completed the great duty of 1849. From this time forward, the history of the State demands a separate volume. In this, we have only aimed at giving a mere sketch of its previous history, as a proper introduction to the "Annals of San Francisco." Our next chapter will contain a short account of the physical geography, and of the commercial, agricultural, pastoral and mineral capabilities of the country, which will conclude Part First of the present work.

CHAPTER XII.

Geographical limits of Upper California.—General description of the country.—Two great divisions of the northern part of the State.—Fertility of the soil.—Peculiarities of the climate.—Two seasons: wet and dry.—Products of the country.—Fogs and winds on the coast.—The harbors.—Country west of the Sierra Nevada.—The Sacramento and San Joaquin rivers, and their valleys.—This region of country abounds in timber.—Excessive heat in the dry season.—Localities of the chief gold placers.—Immense size of trees.—Silver, lead, copper and coal mines.—Advantages to the immigrant.

In the "Constitution," the boundary of the State of California is declared to be as follows :—

"Commencing at the point of intersection of the 42d degree of north latitude with the 120th degree of longitude west from Greenwich, and running south on the line of said 120th degree of west longitude, until it intersects the 39th degree of north latitude; thence running in a straight line in a south-easterly direction to the River Colorado, at a point where it intersects the 35th degree of north latitude; thence down the middle of the channel of said river, to the boundary line between the United States and Mexico, as established by the treaty of May 30th, 1848; thence running west, and along said boundary line to the Pacific Ocean, and extending thereon three English miles; thence running in a north-westerly direction, and following the direction of the Pacific coast to the 42d degree of north latitude; thence on the line of said 42d degree of north latitude to the place of beginning. Also, all the islands, harbors and bays, along and adjacent to the Pacific coast."

Within the above limits, California extends, from south-east to north-west, nearly seven hundred and fifty English miles in length, and, in average breadth, from east to west, about two hundred and fifty. Its superficies, therefore, may be estimated at about 187,500 square miles, or nearly twice the size of Great Britain. The south-eastern part of the country, excepting a narrow belt along the coast, has not yet been explored, and little is known of its character. A great chain of mountains, called by the Spaniards the *Sierra Nevada*, or Snowy Range, runs nearly through the centre of the southern district. Farther north, this mountain range, which has a probable average height of from eight to ten thousand feet above the sea level, though many of its parts rise much higher, and are covered with perpetual snow, becomes the eastern boundary of the State, and at the extreme northern limit, by various cross ranges, separates it from the territory of Oregon. Eastward of the Sierra Nevada, and between it and the territory of Utah, lies the curious and extensive district called the Great Basin, which has no outlet to the ocean for its waters. This is a wild country that has been hitherto traversed only in one or two great lines, but never thoroughly explored, and which does not seem to have been intended by nature for the abode of any large human population. To the south of the boundary line is situated the Mexican province of Old or Lower California. The Pacific Ocean forms the western limit of the State.

The northern portion of California, to the extent of three fourths of the whole country, naturally falls into two great divisions. One lies on the east, and stretches over the whole of the space mentioned from south to north, comprehending the valleys of the San Joaquin in the south and the Sacramento in the north, together with all the lateral valleys and foothills from the summit elevation of the Sierra Nevada, and extending westward to the watershed that separates the streams which flow into the San Joaquin and Sacramento from those which either flow directly into the Pacific, or into the Bay of San Francisco. The other great division includes the whole country drained by the last named streams; and may also be allowed to embrace the country farther to the south, likewise drained by streams which disembogue directly into the Pacific. As already stated, the extreme south-eastern part of the country supposed to be watered by streams which empty themselves into the *Rio Colorado*, has not been fully explored, and no proper description can therefore be given of it.

The missions, of which a particular account has been given in preceding chapters, were located in the second mentioned division of country, and excepting only two lying on the northern side of the Bay of San Francisco, were all situated to the south of the entrance to that inlet. A multitude of pleasant, fertile valleys extend from the coast inland a length of from twenty to forty miles; and every main valley, of any extent, had its mission. The hills in this division seldom exceed two thousand feet in height. The whole country is exceedingly diversified and beautiful, and has hitherto been almost wholly devoted to the grazing of innumerable herds of cattle and horses, and also of large flocks of sheep. The tables and statements already given of the possessions of the Fathers in domestic cattle and farm produce, may serve in some measure to show the astonishing fertility of the soil, and its capabilities to support a large population, as well as the comparative value of different districts. These tables and statements, however, by no means exhibit the extent of cultivated land. Very far from that. Much of the mission property was neglected, and most of it never turned to the best use of which it was capable. The fertility of the soil indeed is so great, and the genial warmth and general climate so propitious to agriculture, that corn crops and all kinds of grasses, fruits and vegetables show such an increase as if they had been planted in a hot-bed, and manured and watered by rule to the best advantage.

The climate of this division of the country varies considerably, as it might be expected to do when it is considered that the land extends over nearly ten degrees of latitude; but still more it varies from the circumstance of the various districts being more or less subject to particular fogs and winds which prevail along the coast. Towards the extreme south, the fogs and winds alluded to are not felt; but north of Point Conception, about latitude 34° 30′, all the coast, extending from half a dozen to a dozen miles inland, is peculiarly exposed to cold, penetrating winds, blowing from the north, north-west and west, and thick wet fogs, which, especially in the summer season, are remarkably disagreeable. These fogs, however, serve one good purpose, as they supply abundant moisture to the crops and herbage, which might otherwise fail for the want of occasional rains in the summer. Properly speaking, there is neither winter nor summer; but the months comprehended under these terms are here called the rainy and the dry seasons. This is the case over the whole country. The rains usually begin about the middle of November, and continue with short occasional dry intervals, (the most charming periods indeed of the year, when the air is balmy. the surface of the earth green and fresh, and all nature, animate and inanimate, rejoices in a holiday,) till the month of May. During the remainder of the year, commonly no rain falls; but its place is supplied along the coast by copious dews and the wet fogs we have alluded to.

The heat in the division of country now before us is never excessive. Below Point Conception, it may be said that eternal summer reigns; and the same high character may be given to all north of that point, which is situated a few miles inland, and not immediately exposed to the piercing winds and fogs of the coast. The atmosphere in these regions is ever mild and agreeable. The temperature is never too high to prevent active exercise out of doors, nor too low to need fires in the houses. There is not much great timber, nor indeed wood of any kind, but the undulating fields teem with rich natural grasses and an exuberance of wild flowers and flowering shrubs. Whole districts are covered with natural oats, which supply provender to innumerable tame and wild creatures, when the herbage is dry, or has partially disappeared in the heat of summer. The climate is also remarkably salubrious; while as if to heap upon this happy land all natural blessings, the fecundity of its living creatures,—human beings as well as the lower animals,—far exceeds what generally occurs elsewhere. The grape, the fig, the orange and the olive grow luxuriantly in these regions, and so too do all other sorts of semi-tropical produce. All varieties of European fruits thrive in great plenty: plums, cherries, peaches, apricots, melons, pomegranates, pears, apples, &c. In the more southern parts, the plantain and banana likewise ripen. Wheat, barley and maize, potatoes, cabbages, turnips and every other kind of vegetable for the table, grow to the utmost perfection, and yield a return the like of which can scarcely be paralleled in any other country. It is believed also that the climate, in particular districts, is admirably adapted for the profitable culture of tobacco, cotton and sugar. In short, there is no vegetable production of any value raised in the temperate zone, and very few peculiar to the torrid, which may not be cultivated to perfection in these finer parts of California.

We have alluded to the prevailing winds and fogs of the coast. These render navigation near the shore dangerous at times, and are themselves very unpleasant to the new comer. It must be admitted that they are some drawback to the otherwise unmingled beauty and agreeableness of the climate. However, in the summer season, when these fogs generally prevail, they usually clear off by noon, leaving the rest of the day with a bright and warm sky. The settler soon gets used to them; while, knowing the important part which the fogs play in dropping fatness on the dry earth, he readily learns even to welcome their presence.

There are several excellent harbors along the coast, the chief of which is, of course, the incomparable Bay of San Francisco. San Diego, however, at the extreme south, has likewise an admirable port; while the havens, or roadsteads of Monterey and Santa Barbara, sheltered from all but certain unusual winds, are by no means despicable, but may match with good reputed harbors of many another country. Besides these, there are several other fair anchorage grounds and partially sheltered roadsteads along the coast, of less note; while north of the Bay of San Francisco there are some bays which form excellent occasional harbors of refuge, if not first-rate ports. The Bay of San Francisco itself is so extensive, while the country surrounding it is so fertile, and will one day become so populous, that many more harbors than the one at the city of that name, will hereafter be formed in this moderate sized inland sea. There is ample depth of water around its shores, and sheltered coves enough for the formation of several other harbors, which may almost rival that of the City of San Francisco itself.

The other great division of the country, that lying east of the one just dwelt upon, and west of the *Sierra Nevada*, has been less thoroughly examined than the coast district, and not so often described; yet enough of it is known to show that it is capable of supporting a vast immigrating population in comfort and plenty. This division comprehends the great valleys of the Sacramento and San Joaquin, with all the smaller side valleys running into them. The Sacramento takes its rise near the extreme northern limit of the State, in the neighborhood of Mount Shasta, which is 14,400 feet in height above the sea level. From thence it flows, in a southerly direction, for nearly three hundred miles, carrying off the waters of numerous streams on both sides till it receives those of the San Joaquin, which have come to meet it from the south-east, for nearly two hundred miles. The united streams then run westward a further distance of sixty or seventy miles, through various arms of the Bay of San Francisco, till they rush through the "Golden Gate," to bury themselves in the Pacific. The Sacramento has already been navigated by steamers for one hundred miles above its junction with the San Joaquin, while the latter has been navigated by the same class of vessels, above the point mentioned for seventy miles.

The great longitudinal valley of these rivers contains an exceedingly fertile soil, fitted to grow any kind of grain, fruits and edible roots. There is much timber in various parts of this great region. Many varieties of the pine tribe are common, most of which grow to an enormous size. But besides pines, the oak especially abounds, as also elm, ash, beech, birch, plane and other kinds of trees. The native fruit trees are not numerous. The number and variety of indigenous herbs are very great. As besides the pines which yield tar and resin, and every size of spar and good timber for ship-building, it is found that hemp and flax grow wild, and thrive exceedingly well in the country, it will be seen that this region contains most of the material elements to make California a great maritime nation. It was in the valley of the Sacramento that a large number of American immigrants had settled previous to the discovery of gold. Portions of the lower districts of both it and the San Joaquin valley are liable to be overflowed by floods which sometimes swell the rivers to a great depth, when storms and meltings of the snow on the Sierra Nevada suddenly gorge all the mountain torrents. At other times, after a long track of dry weather, irrigation would almost seem to be indispensable for profitable farming in several districts ; although this, as yet, is considered to be by no means certain. The cold winds and moist fogs of the coast are sometimes wanted in this division, as well to water the parched earth, as to temper the excessive heat of the solar rays, reflected from the sides of the hills in the narrower valleys, and concentrated every where to a high degree. In the great longitudinal valley, and still more in the smaller cross valleys which lie between the former and the Sierra Nevada, the heat in summer is sometimes very dreadful—rising frequently, and that too, day after day, for months together, to 100° and 110° of Fahrenheit. Still, notwithstanding these drawbacks, the soil is so rich and productive, and the climate so extremely dry and healthy, that there is every reason to believe these districts will soon be largely inhabited by an agricultural population. In some parts of the valley of the San Joaquin which are liable to be overflowed by the river floods, it is believed that rice may be profitably cultivated. Meanwhile, there is abundance of deer and smaller game in the forests and plains ; the streams and lakes absolutely swarm with the most delicious fish ; while geese, ducks, and other wild fowl are exceedingly plentiful.

It is in the cross valleys running up to the summit elevation of the Sierra Nevada that the chief gold *placers* are situated. The whole country in this quarter, for a length of at least five hundred miles, and an average breadth of perhaps thirty or forty, is highly auriferous. The loose bed of every stream particularly, but also the dry sandy soil of most of the intervening plains, uplands and hills, contains particles of gold ; while even the deep seated rocks in many parts are impregnated with the precious metal, and are beginning to be wrought in a scientific manner for its extraction. If some small portion of the auriferous district may already seem to be almost exhausted, yet its whole extent is so great, and so many parts are yet untouched, while all, by the aid of proper scientific appliances, can be made still to render a bountiful reward to the miner, that it may be truly said, generations must pass before the Californian gold regions can be emptied of their treasures, or cease to be profitably wrought. This may be more particularly said of the gold-bearing quartz rocks and veins, which in many places are exceedingly numerous and rich.

Nature, as if content to scatter her bounties in this quarter beneath the surface, has not also gifted the soil with exceeding fertility, although there are many beautiful and fertile small spots to be found in the district. In the months of April and May, these places bloom and smell like a well tended garden, from the variety, beauty and perfume of their wild flowers. The mineral riches make it less desirable that these districts should also possess a rich and prolific soil. Still it is in this quarter that those enormous trees chiefly grow which amaze and almost terrify by their prodigious height and bulk, those who have been only used to the puny forests of less favored climes. A common enough height for these trees is three hundred feet, while an equally common diameter may range from fifteen to twenty feet. Many, however, have been found of much larger dimensions. The forests on the western slopes of the Sierra Nevada will give an inexhaustible supply of timber for household and most other purposes to which wood is applied in the country.

Besides the gold mines on the west skirts of the Snowy Mountains, there are several others scattered over California ; while many other mineral treasures are to be found. There is a valuable mine of quicksilver near San José, and many silver, and silver and lead mines, as well as others of copper and lead are already known in various parts of the country. However, the population up to the time of the rush to the gold regions was too small, and the capital and energy of the owners too limited, to permit these and similar mines to be wrought to advantage. Coal has been discovered in some parts as well as iron. There is excellent stone for building purposes to be had in various places. Sulphur, asphalte and many other valuable mineral substances are also ascertained to exist in different localities. The mineral wealth of the country indeed, though not fully examined, is believed to be far more extensive than what has hitherto appeared, however great it may seem in these times.

To the immigrant from an old settled land, where competition exists in severity, and the means of a bare subsistence are not easily to be had, California offers every inducement to draw him to her country. *Here* is political and social freedom—a beautiful, pleasant, and healthy climate—a soil rich, and fertile, producing every necessary, and most of the luxuries of life—rivers and bays, abounding with delicious fish; forests and fields, with game of every species—mineral regions, where fortunes may be made on a sudden, and, at all events, where the industrious laborer is sure to provide a moderate competency for himself, in a wonderfully short space of time. *Here* are towns starting yearly, nay, almost weekly, into existence, whose inhabitants are full of life, energy and hope, determined and certain to prosper; great cities and ports, swelling into magnificence before one's eyes, destined ere long to bear sway over the broad Pacific, by reason of their natural position, their wealth, energy and power. *Here* labor is honorable, and meets an ample reward; and, *here*, while the most unbounded ambition, in mining and agricultural, commercial and political pursuits, may gratify its most daring inner wishes, and the patriotic enthusiast foresee a glorious future to this, his adopted country, the peaceful, retiring and contented settler may select a quiet, sunny, cheerful spot for his abode, and beneath unclouded skies and through perpetual summer, among vines, and fig-trees, and flowers, and all bright and pleasant things, pass life happily away.

PART SECOND.

CHAPTER I.

Description of the Golden Gate.—Origin of the name.—The Bays of San Francisco, San Pablo, and Suisun.—Rivers emptying into Suisun Bay.—Description of the adjacent country.—Indian tradition.—Remarkable fertility of the soil.—Farm produce and mode of farming.—Location of the City of San Francisco.—The name Yerba Buena.—The first house built.—Disadvantages of the locality.—No provision made for desirable public squares or parks.

The mid-entrance to the Bay of San Francisco lies in latitude 37° 48′ N., and longitude 122° 30′ W., from Greenwich. This is a strait, running nearly north-east, call.d *Chrysopalæ*, or the Golden Gate, about five miles long, and of an average breadth of one and a half or two miles. The name "Golden Gate" first appears in the "Geographical Memoir of California," and relative map, published by Col. Fremont in the spring of 1848. The term was descriptive, not of the literal golden regions within, then as yet undiscovered, but merely of the rich and fertile country which surrounded the shores of the bay, and of the wealth which the commerce of the Pacific, passing through the strait, would certainly give to the future great city of the place. The name was probably suggested by the Golden Horn of Constantinople. Since the discovery of the auriferous character of the country, the title has become of a still more happy nature; and its bestower must surely have had a prophetic soul, though he himself knew it not. At the narrowest point of the strait, where it is little more than a mile wide, the Spaniards had erected a small fort for the protection of the neighboring mission. This building is now in course of removal, to be speedily replaced (let us hope) by a larger and stronger fortress for the adequate defence of the bay. The southern point of land, on the side of the ocean, is called in the Spanish language, *Punta de los Lobos* (Wolves' Point), and the northern, *Punta Bonita* (Pretty Point). A few small rocks, at all times quite visible, lie about the entrance, and along the coast of the strait ; but the channel otherwise is very deep and free from obstruction. About twenty or thirty miles off the coast, and in a westerly direction from the Golden Gate, lie certain small rocky islands, called the *Farralones,* once favorite places for hunting seals and sea-otters by the Russians, and upon which that people had a small permanent settlement. Upon these islands the creatures mentioned are still to be found. A bar lies nearly across the mouth of the strait, upon which occasionally there is a heavy swell. Formerly this bar ran right across and within the actual limits of the strait, but during the last thirty years it has gradually shifted two miles farther to seaward, so that it now forms a kind of arch, altogether outside of the entrance, spanning from point to point of the strait. In the same period, a bank has likewise advanced from the south shore. By these natural operations the entrance channel to the bay has been much improved. On this subject it may be stated that all the shores in the mouth of the bay are liable to be washed off every year, by the combined strength of the wind, tides, local currents, and floods. In the great freshets of the spring of 1825 more than fifty yards of land were swept away to the westward of the fort.

The depth of water on the bar at low tide is considerable enough to permit the largest ship of war to safely cross it. The strait itself has a depth varying from five or six to sixteen fathoms and upwards. The shores are bold and rocky, and in some parts precipitous, swelling on the north side into mountains of upwards of two thousand feet in height. The hills on the southern side are more of a sandy nature, and may be only three hundred or four hundred feet high. On both sides they are quite bare and barren. The strong winds and heavy fogs which constantly assail them, and their own sandy or rocky nature, have effectually prevented trees or luxuriant vegetation of any kind from growing. On the very summit, however, of the mountains on the northern side of the strait, there happens to be a solitary group of red-wood trees, whose tall forms make a striking landmark to the mariner at sea. As he approaches the strait from the south, the voyager has seldom perhaps seen so dismal a looking place. A multitude of low, bleak sand hills on the sea shore, often swept over by flying clouds of dense mist, first greet

Entrance to the Golden Gate.

his eyes. On passing gradually through the Golden Gate, however, the interior coasts begin sensibly to improve upon him. The hills assume a more even character, which, as well as the beautiful islands that stud the bay, are at certain seasons of the year covered with vegetation, presenting a truly pleasing appearance.

The tidal stream rushes through the gate in mid-channel generally about six knots an hour. Along the projecting portions of the strait there are numerous eddies. By taking advantage of this great tidal speed, and of particular winds, which can almost daily be depended upon, blowing either in or out of the channel at certain periods of the day, ships may always safely enter or depart from the bay at all times of the year. An occasional wreck, where ships may have been driven by the strength of the tide or local currents upon the rocky shores, has indeed taken place; but this has generally been traceable to the ignorance or carelessness of the pilot. Hitherto that class of men, as might have been anticipated, have not been all picked individuals; and some of them may not have had sufficient time to study the peculiarities of the channel. It may, however, be confidently asserted, that there are very few harbors in the world where the entrance and departure are so easy and safe as those of the one of San Francisco. To talk of it in the same breath with such difficult and dangerous ocean ports as those of Liverpool and New York, or the river ones of London and New Orleans, is simply ridiculous.

After passing the strait, the great Bay of San Francisco suddenly opens up. This bay lies almost at right angles to the entrance just described; and extends from north to south nearly seventy miles, with an average breadth of about ten or twelve. The southern division, comprehending about two-thirds of the entire length, chiefly lies south of the entrance, and is more properly styled the *Bay of San Francisco;* although the whole body of inland waters, when spoken of in a general sense, is commonly understood by that phrase. The northern division, which is in some degree topographically separated from the other by narrows and several small islands about the eastern end of the strait, is known by the name of the *Bay of San Pablo.* At the eastern extremity of the last named bay, the waters contract into the *Strait of Carquinez.* Still more to the east, they again widen into *Suisun Bay,* into which, through various channels, called the *Slough,* a sort of delta much overrun with large trees and jungle, the mingled streams of the Sacramento and San Joaquin, enter and lose themselves. From the ocean to the north-east corner of Suisun Bay, following the line of mid-channel, there may be a distance of between fifty and sixty miles. The largest ships may sail as far as the city of Benicia, originally called Francisca, situated on the north side of the Strait of Carquinez, where the channel is little more than a mile wide, and at which place are a government dock-yard and naval stores. Above that point, the water is at parts scarcely deep enough to allow vessels of great burden to proceed, while the channels of the Sacramento, through the delta, or slough, are intricate, and encumbered with shifting shoals and sand-banks.

The Golden Gate.

Around the northern shores of the Bays of San Pablo and Suisun lies a very fertile and beautiful country, watered by streams, severally called the Suisun River, Napa, Sonoma, and Petaluma Creeks. The valleys of these rivers will in a few years be the residence of a great number of agricultural settlers, while already numerous small towns are beginning to be established among them. But the Sacramento and its greater tributaries, the Puta Creek, and the American, Feather and Butte Rivers, and the San Joaquin, with its leading feeders, the Mokelumne, Calaveras, Stanislaus, and Tuolumne Rivers, are the great highways of communication between the interior country and the ocean ; and in the extensive, beautiful, and most fertile districts drained by them will be located hereafter the abodes of many millions of human beings. In the valley of the Sacramento and its offshoots are situated the great city of that name, and the thriving towns of Marysville and Nevada. In the valley of the San Joaquin, or in the connecting valley, are the considerable and growing towns of Stockton and Sonora. Besides these places, there are numerous other towns beginning to be established in this great district.

South of San Pablo and Suisun Bays, and east of the Bay of San Francisco proper, lies the district of country called *Contra Costa.* This quarter is very mountainous, some of the summits being upwards of three thousand feet high. One of them, *Monte Diablo,* is three thousand seven hundred and seventy feet in height. On the west, however, between the mountains and the Bay of San Francisco, is a considerable tract of level land which, like nearly all of a similar description in the country, is exceedingly rich and productive.

On the opposite side of the bay, and between it and the ocean, lies the long peninsula called the District of San Francisco. This strip of land is upwards of thirty miles long, with an average breadth of perhaps twelve or sixteen. The side immediately next the ocean is cold and barren. In the interior, and towards the bay, it possesses a mild climate, and is of great fertility. The surface is irregular and hilly ; but the many small glens are green to the top, covered with luxuriant herbage, on which feed many thousands of sheep and cattle. The northern portion of this district is generally bare of trees and the larger shrubs ; but much heavy timber grows in the middle and southern parts. At the southern extremity of the bay lies an extensive tract of land, which may be considered the choicest portion of all the country we have been describing. Here, near the mouth of the valley, watered by the River Guadalupe, are situated the towns of San José and Santa Clara. The beauty and salubrity of this district, its mild and agreeable climate, and exceeding productiveness, make it especially the granary, orchard and garden of the City of San Francisco and surrounding parts.

We may observe here, that there is a tradition among the Indians of California, that San Francisco Bay originally formed a fresh water lake. An earthquake, however, suddenly opened the line of mountains along the coast, when the sea rushed in, and changed the region to what it now is. The surplus fresh waters of the old lake were supposed to have been discharged into the Bay of Monterey, by a great river flowing through the valley of San José and Santa Clara. This river was believed to pass near the Mission of San Juan, and to fall into the present stream of the Pajaro.

City of Stockton.

In the fertile districts of country all around the shores of the bay the average productiveness of the soil is exceedingly great, far beyond the usual return from tillage lands in most other countries of the temperate zone, and rivalling, in fact, those of the torrid zone itself. A common yield from sown wheat is from seventy to eighty fold, though it is said to run often as high as one hundred and upwards. A moderate average may be taken at fifty fold. Maize occasionally gives a return of one hundred and fifty fold; while if it produces less than one hundred, it is scarcely considered worthy of notice. It may be remarked that the seed in general is much less thickly sown than in most other countries; and, naturally, therefore, having space to spread and fructify, there is a greater corresponding increase. Potatoes have been found of the enormous weight of seven and eight pounds, while those of two and three pounds are quite common. The usual yield of potatoes is from two to three hundred sacks an acre. And such potatoes! In no part of the world are there larger, finer, firmer and healthier roots grown. Newly-come immigrants and casual visitors are invariably full of raptures at the sight of such magnificent earth apples. The cabbages, again, are absolute monsters in size, often from fifteen to twenty inches in diameter; and as good in quality as enormous in bulk. Carrots often grow nearly a yard in length, and are of corresponding girth. Turnips, beets, radishes, onions, and indeed every kind of edible root and table vegetable grows equally large, and of the best and most wholesome description. California is indeed celebrated for its garden and field productions. The berries and fruits of the vineyard and orchard show a corresponding increase, and are of the most excellent kind. Long ago it had been imagined by hasty travellers and writers, that California had only an arid, sterile soil, never adapted to the successful pursuit of agriculture. On the contrary, the country is exceedingly well watered, the soil is naturally rich, and the diffused warmth and geniality of the climate is such as to force to safe maturity an abundant harvest of all kinds. Of course, manure in the present stage of California, is out of the question. The teeming fields will not require it for a generation or two, if ever. The present practice is simply to break fresh ground every year; and until the agricultural settlers become much more numerous, there will be abundance of land for such a mode of farming. There is no need of farm buildings to house and stock the grain for shelter. The climate is so dry in the harvest season that the crops are never spoiled by wet; but the ears are just threshed out on the fields where they grow. Farming operations formerly were of a very rude nature, as they still generally are, though the soil shows so large a return. When an improved method of husbandry is adopted, the yield will be correspondingly great. A slight wooden shed, open upon one side to the weather, and merely covered with canvas or scantling, affords quite a sufficient shelter, summer and winter, to milch cows and the most delicate trained horses.

From the previous description of the districts surrounding the inland waters known by the general name of the Bay of San Francisco, it will be noticed that their respective productions, seen to be so great, can best be interchanged across that bay; and that their only communication with the ocean is through the Golden Gate. Conveniently placed as nearly as possible to this gate lies the city of San Francisco, in latitude 37° 48′ N. and longitude 122° 25′ W. from Greenwich. It is situated on the north-east corner of the peninsula already mentioned, about a mile south of the eastern end of the general entrance to the bay, and is distant about six miles from the ocean. The situation happens to be about the most barren part of the district; and the immediate vicinity consists chiefly of low sand-hills, covered with coarse shrubs and scattered patches of grass. The name of the Spanish village which originally stood on a portion of the site of the present city was *Yerba Buena*—good herb. In some maps of the country it was designated as San Francisco; but locally it was only known by the name we have mentioned. Yerba Buena signifies also the herb *mint*, great quantities of which grew about the spot, and from that circumstance no doubt the name of the place is derived.

An island, lying in the bay about two miles east of the city likewise bears the name of Yerba Buena, where the herb mentioned grows abundantly. Probably this island first bore the name which later was given to the cove lying between it and the main land; and subsequently it was extended to the plain and village surrounding the beach. But the name mentioned was descriptive both of the island and the shore itself, since on both grew the *yerba buena*. This herb grows through the underwood in form of a vine, some feet long. The leaves are six inches apart, each directly opposite another. It is very fragrant, and is used to make a tea or alterative medicinal drink, though its frequent use is said to debilitate the system. The name of so insignificant an herb for the rising city being perhaps judged not sufficiently imposing, it was changed into SAN FRANCISCO in January, 1847, by an ordinance of the then alcalde of the place, and under this last designation it has been alone known to the world at large.

The village of Yerba Buena was situated in the small cove of that name, which extended little more than half a mile between *Clark's Point* (so named by Captain J. F. Hutton, in 1849), on the north-west, and the *Rincon*, or *Rincon Point*, on the south-east. The first tenement was constructed in the year 1835, by Captain W. A. Richardson, and up to the year 1846, there might not be more than twenty or thirty houses of all descriptions in the place. The only practicable landing spot for small boats at low tide was at Clark's Point, where there were a few rocks. In the inside of the cove where the water was shallow, there was an

Island and Cove of Yerba Buena.

extensive flat of mud, laid bare at low water. The rise and fall of ordinary tides was about eight feet. About a quarter of a mile from the beach, the water deepened to five and six fathoms, and continued of the same or of little greater depth the whole distance to the Island of Yerba Buena opposite. This space now forms the present harbor and centre of the anchorage ground of San Francisco. As Yerba Buena began to increase in size and importance, the beach and water lots were seen to be of the utmost value; and measures accordingly were taken, in 1847, and following years, to extend the village, or town as it might now be called, over a great portion of the cove. About the same time the present character of the place began to be formed, which subsequent years developed into the existing grand plan of the City of San Francisco.

Rising up from Clark's Point, and between Yerba Buena Cove and the cove farther to the north-west, now called the *North Beach*, is the high ground named the *Telegraph Hill.* West and south of this hill, in a semicircular direction, lie other connecting high grounds, bearing the names of *Russian Hill*, *Fern Hill*, &c. These hills are about three hundred feet high. From the Rincon likewise rises a high ground of about from one hundred to one hundred and fifty feet in height, which runs a short distance in a westerly direction towards the Mission Dolores. Beyond and south of the ridge alluded to lies Mission Bay, and the low ground bordering Mission Creek. The distance between Telegraph Hill and the last mentioned ridge, may be about three quarters of a mile; while that between the semicircular line of hills on the west and the advanced line of streets built much within the limit of ebb tide in Yerba Buena Cove, may be nearly the same.

Upon this limited space stands the most valuable and business portion of San Francisco, and its most substantial and magnificent buildings. However, over all the hills, and much of the country on every side beyond them, the ground has been regularly laid out into building lots, lying upon long straight streets, crossing each other at right angles; and many excellent houses, together with a scattered multitude of an inferior description, have been erected on them. Indeed the nominal limits of the city and the building stances, as actually surveyed and mapped out, at this time, extend from the west side of North Beach to the south side of Mission Creek, a distance of nearly four miles, in a straight line; and from Rincon Point to the Mission Church, a distance, likewise, in a direct line, of upwards of three miles. Over all this space, some eight or nine square miles, on height and in hollow, and upon every degree of elevated site, are spread a variety of detached buildings, built partly of stone and brick, though principally of wood. But, as we have already stated, the heart and strength and wealth of the city is contained within the little level space lying between the hills or rising grounds particularly mentioned, and the narrow waters of Yerba Buena Cove. These waters are yearly continuing to be encroached upon as the cove gets filled up with sand and rubbish, excavated from the sand-hills and the foundations of the limits behind, and as new streets and houses, formed on piles, are pushed further out into the bay. By these operations the old character of the cove has been completely changed, and at present, instead of the former semicircle of beach there is almost a straight line of building extending across the middle of the cove from the Rincon to Clark's Point. In many places of what is now the very centre of the business portion of the city lie large vessels, which in the disastrous years of shipping, 1848 and 1849, got stranded or were used as store-ships or lodging-houses on the beach. When the extension of the city towards the waters of the cove took place, these ships remained where they lay, fast imbedded in mud, while long streets, hollow beneath, and numerous solid houses arose on every side, effectually to hem them in for ever.

The deepening water will prevent the city from moving much farther into the bay, while the steep rising grounds in the rear will equally prevent it from climbing and spreading over the sandy, irregular country beyond them. The city will probably therefore be forced to proceed northward towards the North Beach, where there is already a long pier formed, but where there is remaining but limited building room at best. It will also spread, as it is beginning to do, over the extensive and comparatively level tract of ground lying to the south-west, on the banks of Mission Creek, and in the direction of the Mission Dolores. Perhaps not many years hence the whole shores at North Beach and South Beach (Mission Bay), and the bay itself to a considerable distance from the present high-water mark, will be covered with streets and houses, quays and long piercing piers, just as now is the cove of Yerba Buena. The existing surveys and plans of the city, anticipating futurity, already exhibit these places, both on land and sea, divided and fairly mapped out into streets and wharves.

Over all these square miles of contemplated thoroughfares, there seems no provision made by the projectors for a public park —the true "lungs" of a large city. The existing *plaza*, or Portsmouth Square, and other two or three diminutive squares, delineated on the plan, seem the only breathing-holes intended for the future population of hundreds of thousands. This is a strange mistake, and can only be attributed to the jealous avarice of the city projectors in turning every square vara of the site to an available building lot. Indeed the eye is wearied, and the imagination quite stupefied, in looking over the numberless square—all *square*—building blocks, and mathematically straight lines of streets, miles long, and every one crossing a host of others at right angles, stretching over sandy hill, chasm and plain, without the least regard to the natural inequalities of the ground. Not only is there no public park or garden, but there is not even a circus, oval, open terrace, broad avenue, or any ornamental line of street or building, or verdant space of any kind, other than the three or four small squares alluded to ; and which every resident knows are by no means verdant, except in patches where stagnant water collects and ditch weeds grow.

While the position of San Francisco on the shores of the bay was undoubtedly the best that could have been selected for maritime purposes, there certainly have been sad drawbacks to the extension of the place on the land side. The want of sufficient level space on which to found so great and growing a city, has been partially rectified, at an enormous expense, by taking building ground from the waters, and by lowering, and in many cases absolutely removing bodily the multitude of sand hills, by which the place is immediately surrounded. What with digging out and filling up, piling, capping and planking, grading and regrading the streets, and shifting, and rebuilding, and again rebuilding the houses, to suit the altered levels, millions upon millions of dollars have been spent. This has not been recklessly or foolishly done, and the present magnificence and business capabilities of the city are the consequence ; while future years will still more exhibit the grand result of all the money that has been sunk in municipal improvements. It would be out of place to say more of the present appearance of the city at this portion of the work ; but a more particular account of it will be given towards the conclusion of "Part Second."

CHAPTER II.

The Mission and Presidio of San Francisco.—Formation and survey of the village of Yerba Buena.—Disputes and litigation in regard to Yerba Buena being a Pueblo.—Captain Richardson the first Harbor Master.—Visits of national and other vessels to Yerba Buena Cove.—Reasons why the whale ships ceased to enter the harbor for supplies.—Traffic between Yerba Buena and foreign ports.—Hides and tallow the chief exports.—Prices obtained for these.—Heavy rains and their effects.—Earthquakes.—Unusual drought.—Mr. Jacob P. Leese establishes himself at Yerba Buena.—Celebration of the Fourth of July at Leese's house.—First child born.—Limits of the original survey.

The Mission of San Francisco, as mentioned in the first part of this work, was founded in the year 1776. It was situated about two and a half miles to the south-west of the Cove of Yerba Buena. Besides the mission buildings, there were erected, at the same time, a presidio and fort, along the margin of the Golden Gate, the former being distant from the mission about four miles, and from the cove nearly the same space. The latter was situated about a mile nearer the ocean than the presidio, close upon the sea-beach, and on a rocky height at the narrowest point of the strait.

Before 1835, the village of Yerba Buena had neither name nor existence. The Mexican Government had some time before resolved to found a town upon the cove of that name, which was reputed the best site on the shores of the Bay of San Francisco for establishing a port. Much discussion and litigation, involving immense pecuniary interests, have occurred as to the date and precise character of the foundation of Yerba Buena. It has long been matter of keen dispute whether the place was what is called a Spanish or Mexican "*pueblo;*" and although, after previous contrary decisions, it was assumed (not being exactly decided upon evidence) by the Supreme Court to be a "pueblo," the subject seems to be still open to challenge. It is unnecessary in this work to do more than merely allude to the question. In the year last above mentioned, General Figueroa, then governor of the Californias, passed an ordinance, forbidding the commandant of the presidio of San Francisco to make any grants of land around the Yerba Buena Cove nearer than two hundred varas (about one hundred and eighty-five yards) from the beach, without a special order from the governor, the excluded portion being intended to be reserved for government uses. Before any steps could be taken for the survey and laying out of the proposed town, General Figueroa died; and the place was neglected for some years, and left to proceed as chance and individuals would have it. There had been previous applications for grants of the whole land around the cove for professedly farming purposes, which circumstance led to the governor's passing the temporary ordinance, lest, some time or another, the portion of ground intended to be reserved should, through accident or neglect, be granted away.

Captain W. A. Richardson was appointed the first harbor-master, in the year 1835, and, the same year, he erected the *first house, or description of dwelling*, in the place. It was simply a large tent, supported on four red-wood posts, and covered with a ship's foresail. The captain's occupation in those days seems to have been the management of two schooners, one belonging to the Mission of San Francisco, and the other to the Mission of Santa Clara. These schooners were employed in bringing produce from the various missions and farms around the bay to the sea-going vessels which lay in Yerba Buena Cove. The amount of freight which the captain received was twelve cents a hide, and one dollar for each bag of tallow. The tallow was melted down and run into hide-bags, which averaged five hundred pounds each. For grain, the freight was twenty-five cents a fanega (two and a half English bushels).

Some years before this period, Yerba Buena Cove had been occasionally approached by various ships of war and other vessels. For many years, the Russians had continued to pay it annual visits for supplies of meat and small quantities of grain. One of their vessels took away annually about one hundred and eighty or two hundred tons of such provisions. In 1816, the English sloop of war "Racoon" entered the port; also, in 1827, the

"Blossom," of the same nation, on a surveying cruise. In the last named year, the French frigate "Artemesia," of sixty guns, arrived. In 1839, there appeared the English surveying ships, the "Sulphur" and the "Starling." In 1841, the first American war vessel, the "San Luis," sloop, arrived; and, later in the same year, the "Vincennes," also American, on a surveying expedition. In 1842, came the "Yorktown," the "Cyane," and the "Dale," all of the American navy; and in the same year, the "Brillante," a French sloop-of-war. From this last named year downwards both ships of war and merchantmen of all nations occasionally entered the port. Whale ships first began to make their appearance for supplies in the fall of the year 1822, increasing in number, year by year, since that period. However, some impolitic port restrictions by the authorities had the effect latterly of sending off a considerable number of this class of ships to the Sandwich Islands, a place much less convenient for obtaining supplies than San Francisco Bay. Since likewise the discovery of gold in the country, and the consequent temptation of seamen to desert, as well as the enhanced price of most supplies, whale ships have not found it their interest to visit San Francisco, but prefer victualling and refitting at the Sandwich Islands.

Previous to 1822, a small traffic was carried on between the coast of Mexico and the California ports; the latter exporting principally tallow and a little soap. Some small vessels from the Sandwich Islands also visited occasionally San Francisco and the other harbors in California. It was in the last year named that the trade began between California and the United States and England. The country then sent its tallow chiefly to Callao and Peru, and its hides to the States and to England. The price of a hide in 1822, was fifty cents, and of tallow, six dollars per hundred weight. These prices had the effect of soon decreasing the number of cattle; and, in the following year, hides rose to one and a half dollars apiece, payable in cash, or two dollars, if the amount was taken in merchandise. The trade value of hides continued at nearly this rate until the war between the United States and Mexico.

Some few natural occurrences during these early years of the place are worth recording. In December 1824 and in the spring of the following year, very heavy rains fell over all this part of the country. The Sacramento and tributaries rose to a great height, and their valleys were flooded in many places to a depth of fourteen feet. It was partly owing to the great volumes of fresh water brought down through the bay, in 1825, that a portion of the land at the southern side of the entrance, was washed away as stated in a previous chapter. In September, 1829, several very severe shocks of an earthquake were experienced in San Francisco, which forced open lock-fast doors and windows. In 1839, an equally severe earthquake took place. In 1812, however, a much more serious convulsion had been felt over all California, which shook down houses and some churches in several parts of the country, and killed a considerable number of human beings. The Church of San Juan Capistrano was completely destroyed, and forty-one persons, chiefly Indians, were killed by its fall. We have already said that an Indian tradition attributes the formation of the present entrance to the Bay of San Francisco to an earthquake, which forced open a great passage through the coast range of hills for the interior waters. It may be mentioned, when on this subject, that since these dates, no serious occurrences of this nature have happened at San Francisco. though almost every year slight shocks, and occasionally smarter ones have been felt. God help the city if any great catastrophe of this nature should ever take place! Her huge granite and brick palaces, of four, five and six stories in height, would indeed make a prodigious crash, more ruinous both to life and property than even the dreadful fires of 1849, 1850 and 1851. This is the greatest, if not the only possible obstacle of consequence to the growing prosperity of the city, though even such a lamentable event as the total destruction of half the place, like another Quito or Caraccas, would speedily be remedied by the indomitable energy and persevering industry of the American character. Such a terrible calamity, however, as the one imagined, may never take place. So "sufficient for the day is the evil thereof." This maxim abundantly satisfies the excitement-craving, money-seeking, luxurious-living, reckless, heaven-earth-and-hell-daring citizens of San Francisco.

We have elsewhere explained the nature of the climate in respect that the winter and summer months are simply the rainy and dry seasons of the year. We have seen above, the effects of excessive rains; and we may also mark the result of unusual drought. In the personal recollections of Captain Richardson, who is our authority on this subject, there have been several such seasons in the country around the Bay of San Francisco since 1822, when that gentleman came to California. The grass on such occasions was completely dried up, and cattle perished in consequence. The missionaries were under the necessity of sending out all their Indian servants to cut down branches of oak trees for the herds to subsist upon. In these dryer seasons, too, the crops suffered greatly from grasshoppers; which insects, about the month of July, when the corn was still green, would sweep all before them. It may be remarked generally, that while the year is divided into two seasons—wet and dry—there is great irregularity, in the case of the former, as to the average quantity of rain falling annually. During some winters heavy rains pour down, without intermission, for months together; while, on other and often alternate winters, the sky is clear for weeks—then for only a few days slight showers will descend—and again there occurs a long period of the most delightful and dry weather imaginable. Slight frosts are occasionally felt during the winter months; and ice, from the thickness of a cent to that of an inch is seen for a day or two, nearly every season. Generally, however, the winter climate is mild and open, and the winter months are the most pleasant of the year.

The excessively and injuriously wet and dry seasons are exceptional cases, and do not impugn the accuracy of the statements, made elsewhere, of the general mildness of the climate, productiveness of the soil, and safety of the harvest. A fertile field or a fruitful tree will not lose its character, because occasionally there happens to be a short crop. The Pacific is still reputed a serene ocean, though sometimes a gale or tempest sweeps over it. Even in the case of possible earthquakes, nobody would hold France, or Spain, or even Italy—the *bella Italia* of the old world, as California is of the new one—to be dangerous countries to live in, although historical records show that much damage has been done in them, at long intervals, by volcanic eruptions and subterranean movements.

In May, 1836, Mr. Jacob Primer Leese arrived in the Cove of Yerba Buena, with the intention of establishing a mercantile business at San Francisco, in partnership with Mr. Nathan Spear and Mr. W. S. Hinckley, who were to remain at Monterey, and

Jacob Primer Leese.

manage the business of the firm there. Mr. Leese brought letters from the then governor of California, Don Mariano Chico, to the alcalde and commandante of San Francisco, desiring them to render him all assistance in their power in arranging a location and otherwise. Mr. Leese at once fixed on the beach of Yerba Buena Cove for his establishment, but as the ordinance of General Figueroa, concerning the government reserve, was still in force, he could not procure an allotment nearer the beach than at the distance of two hundred varas. The alcalde and commandante were much pleased that Mr. Leese should come to settle among their people, and at once offered him a choice of two locations, one being at the mouth of Mission Creek, and the other at the entrance to the bay near the presidio. Mr. Leese, however, had made up his mind on the subject; and, partly for his own business convenience, and probably, in part, foreseeing the increased future value of sites around Yerba Buena Cove, would accept no grant but one in that quarter. In this the local authorities could not legally aid him; so Mr. Leese returned forthwith to Monterey with his story and complaint to Governor Chico. On explanations there, the governor informed Mr. Leese that he would instruct the alcalde of San Francisco to grant an allotment within the limits of the government reserve, and in the mean time authorized Mr. Leese to select for himself the most convenient place he could find elsewhere.

Back to Yerba Buena Cove hastened Mr. Leese, and on the first of July presented to the alcalde his new letters. On the following day he landed boards and other materials for building, and immediately took possession of a one-hundred vara lot, adjoining on the south side that on which Captain Richardson's tent was already erected. Mr. Leese's lot was situated about two hundred or two hundred and fifty yards from the beach, and is the spot where the St. Francis Hotel was subsequently erected, at the corner of Clay and Dupont streets. Mr. Leese was indefatigable in hastening the erection of his dwelling, which was finished by ten o'clock on the morning of the 4th of July—the *first* glorious fourth—when the independence of America was commemorated in style in California. These two houses, belonging to Capt. Richardson and Mr. Leese, were the earliest houses erected in Yerba Buena, and formed the beginning of the City of San Francisco. It is but eighteen years since their erection, and now there is a population of over fifty thousand around the spot!

While Mr. Leese was erecting his mansion, which seems to have been rather a grand structure, being made of frame, sixty feet long and twenty-five feet broad, Captain Richardson was kindly proceeding across the bay to Sonoma, where he invited all the principal folks of the quarter to a banquet in the new building. Two events—each great in their way—were to be celebrated:

first, Independence Day, and next, the arrival of Mr. Leese in the country, his welcome and house-warming. The two worthy souls, cordially fraternizing, were determined to make a great affair of it; and so indeed it happened. As it was the first grand scene in the future San Francisco, where there have since been so many, we are tempted to dwell a little on the eventful occasion. Future generations will pleasantly reflect on this auspicious commencement to the pride of the Pacific, then like a new-born infant cradled by its tender parents, Capt. Richardson and Mr. Leese, and tricked out in all the magnificence of an heir's baby clothes.

At this time there was lying in the cove the American barque "Don Quixote," commanded by Mr. Leese's partner, Capt. Hinckley, and on board of which were their goods. There were also at anchor in the port another American ship and a Mexican brig. These vessels supplied every bit of colored bunting they could furnish, with which was decorated Mr. Leese's hall. A splendid display was the result. Outside of the building floated amicably the Mexican and American flags—the first time the latter was displayed on the shore of Yerba Buena. Captain Hinckley seems to have been somewhat extravagant in his passion for sweet sounds, since he always travelled with a band of music in his train. Through this cause the most stylish orchestra, perhaps, ever before heard in California, was provided by him. This consisted of a clarionet, flute, violin, drum, fife and bugle; besides two small six pounders to form the bass, and to add their emphatic roar to the swelling din, when a toast of more than usual importance should be given. These last, however, were borrowed from the presidio.

The feast was prepared; the minstrels were met; and the guests began to assemble about three o'clock on the afternoon of the Fourth. They were about sixty in number, and included General M. G. Vallejo and all the principal families from the neighborhood of Sonoma, such as the Castro, Martinez, &c., as well as the chief inhabitants of San Francisco. Besides the banqueting hall, Mr. Leese had erected a number of small tents, in which to receive his numerous guests and provide for them comfortably. At five o'clock dinner was served, and immediately afterwards followed the toasts. First of all was given the union of the Mexican and American flags. (How little did the convivial parties then dream of the near advent of the sole and absolute sway of the Americans in the country !) General Vallejo next paid the honors to Washington. Then followed appropriate national and individual toasts in their order ; but which it is

Celebration of the Fourth of July at Leese's House.

needless to particularize. The guests were as happy as mortals could well be ; and, in short, "all went merry as a marriage bell." The abundance and variety of liquors at table seemed to tickle the Californians amazingly. One worthy gentleman took a prodigious fancy to lemon syrup, a tumbler full of which he would quaff to every toast. This soon made him sick, and sent him off with a colic ; which was all matter of mirth to his "jolly companions, every one." At ten o'clock our "city fathers" got the table cleared for further action, and dancing and other amusements then commenced. The ball was kept hot and rolling incessantly, all that night, and it appears, too, the following day; for, as Mr. Leese naively observes, in his interesting and amusing diary, "*our fourth ended on the evening of the fifth.*" Many of the simple-minded Indians and such lower class white people as were not invited, had gathered around while the festivities and sports were going on among the people of quality, and could not contain themselves for joy, but continually exclaimed, "*Que buenos son los Americanos!*"—What capital fellows these Americans are! And doubtless the white gentry thought, and often said the same.

But let a Yankee alone for knowing his own interest in spending money lavishly! In a few days afterwards, Mr. Leese had concluded the landing of his twelve thousand dollars worth of goods, when he opened his store for business. The grateful guests, and all the people around, at once flocked to purchase; and trade, he says, became quite brisk, at most satisfactory prices.

Shortly after this event, Mr. Leese, upon a hasty courtship—or rather, for he seems to have had no time to wait, and California was beginning to shake off her lethargy and be a go-ahead country; in fact, none beyond "popping the question," in smart business fashion, on the 1st of April, 1837 (ominous day for such a deed!)—was married to a sister of General Vallejo. On the 7th of the same month they were tied together, for life, by the "holy bands of matrimony;" and from this union, on the 15th of April, 1838, sprung their eldest child—ROSALIE LEESE—*being the first born in Yerba Buena.*

In this year, Mr. Leese erected a large frame building on the beach, with consent of the alcalde, the latter observing that the governor had informed him he was going to lay out a few town lots. He therefore permitted Mr. Leese, in order to forward his plans, to take a one-hundred vara lot provisionally where he wished. The present banking-house of Mr. James King of William, at the corner of Commercial and Montgomery streets, and which is situated in what may be called the centre of San Francisco, occupies the site of Mr. Leese's frame building on the beach of Yerba Buena Cove. In this year also, Captain Richardson erected an adobe building on the same lot he had always occupied, and which has been already noticed. This adobe building, one and a half stories high, was the old "*Casa Grande*" which stood on the west side of Dupont-street, between Washington and Clay streets, and was taken down in 1852. About this time, some native Californians and a few visitors of foreign extraction, chiefly American, began to settle in the rising town. The arrivals of ships likewise were gradually increasing.

In 1839, Don J. B. Alvarado, then constitutional governor of California, dispatched an order to the then alcalde of San Francisco, Francisco Haro, to get a survey taken of the plain and cove of Yerba Buena. This was accordingly made by Captain Juan Vioget in the fall of the same year, and was the first regular survey of the place. It included those portions of the present city which lie between Pacific street on the north, Sacramento street on the south, Dupont street on the west, and Montgomery street on the east. The original bounds of the new town were therefore very limited. The lot on which Mr. Leese built his second house was marked No. 1 on the plan, and its eastern front made the line of the present Montgomery street, which then formed the beach of the cove. Mr. Leese seems to have been pretty well treated by the authorities in the matter of the new town, since he appears to have received, besides the allotment already mentioned, farther grants of three one-hundred vara lots on the west side of Dupont street, and two on the south side of Sacramento street, as well as of other three lots, likewise outside of the survey. To conclude this notice of Mr. Leese's close connection with the rising fortunes of Yerba Buena, it may be mentioned, that, in the month of August, 1841, he sold his dwelling-house to the Hudson's Bay Company, and removed his property and family to Sonoma, with the intention of engaging in extensive cattle transactions in Oregon, which territory was then attracting much notice, and had begun to draw to it many agricultural settlers.

CHAPTER III.

Removal of the Hudson's Bay Company.—Rapid growth and increase of population of Yerba Buena. —First newspapers established in California.—Tables showing the number of inhabitants in 1847, with their places of birth, ages, sexes and occupations.—Ordinance of the alcalde changing the name of Yerba Buena to San Francisco.—W. A. Bartlett was the first alcalde under the American flag, who was succeeded by George Hyde, and he by Edwin Bryant.—Powers of an alcalde. —Great sale of beach and water lots, agreeably to a decree of General Kearny.—Price of grants of property, and subsequent increased value of city lots.—Width of the streets.—Municipal regulation restricting purchasers.

DURING the early years of the existence of Yerba Buena, little occurs worthy of notice. The place continued merely a village; and its history for some years subsequent to 1841, would be simply a record of the private business transactions of the Hudson's Bay Company, whose agents and people formed nearly the entire settlement. Even so lately as 1844, Yerba Buena contained only about a dozen houses, and its permanent population did not exceed fifty persons. In 1846 the Hudson's Bay Company disposed of their property, and removed from the place. After that period it began gradually to increase in importance and population. The progress of political events during which the country passed into American hands, was, as might have been anticipated, the chief cause of the rapid strides onward which the place now began to take.

By mid-summer of 1846, the population numbered upwards of two hundred, and the buildings of all kinds had increased to nearly fifty. From this date the place advanced with wonderful rapidity. On the first April of the following year, it contained seventy-nine buildings, viz.:—twenty-two shanties, thirty-one frame-houses, and twenty-six adobe buildings. In the course of the subsequent five months, seventy-eight new tenements were erected, viz.:—forty-seven of frame, eleven of adobe, and twenty shanties. About this time the permanent population had increased to nearly five hundred. By the end of April, 1848, about the time when the "*rush*" to the "*diggings*" commenced, the town contained nearly two hundred buildings, viz. :—one hundred and thirty-five finished dwelling-houses, ten unfinished houses of the same class, twelve stores and warehouses, and thirty-five shanties. At this last date the population numbered about a thousand individuals, composed almost entirely of people from the United States or from European countries. Every day was bringing new immigrants, and every week additional houses were erected.

Three kinds of buildings generally appear early in the progress of American settlements :—the church, tavern and printing-office. The last was established so early as January, 1847, when the population was little more than three hundred ; and, on the 7th of that month the first number of the "*California Star*" appeared. This paper was published by Mr. Samuel Brannan, and edited by Dr. E. P. Jones. It was a small sheet of four pages, about fifteen inches by twelve of type, and appeared every Saturday. It was a neat production—type, matter and arrangement being of excellent quality. A passage in the prospectus gave notice that "it will eschew with the greatest caution every thing that tends to the propagation of sectarian dogmas." This clause may have been inserted in consequence of the publisher having but recently been prominently connected with a certain religious sect, and with a view to assure the public that it was no part of his intention to make the "Star" the medium of promulgating its peculiar sectarian tenets.

"*The Californian,*" also a weekly newspaper, of still smaller dimensions, and of much inferior typographical pretension, had previously appeared at Monterey, where its first number was issued on the 15th August, 1846, by Messrs. Colton & Semple, by whom also it was edited. Commodore R. F. Stockton, however, was the originator of this publication. This was the first newspaper in the English, or indeed, in any language, which was published in California. For the sake of the natives, the editors gave a portion of the contents in Spanish ; but the greater part from the beginning, and soon the whole of it, was printed in English. The publishers seem to have been reduced to considerable difficulty in getting out their paper. In one of the impressions they give this explanatory and apologetic note for its rude appearance. We copy literally :—

"OUR ALPHABET.—Our type is a spanish font picked up here in a cloister, and has no VV's [W's] in it, as there is none in the spanish alphabet. I have sent to the sandvvich Islands for this letter, in the mean time vve must use tvvo V's. Our paper at present is that used for vvrapping segars ; in due time vve vvill have something better: our object is to establise a press in California, and this vve shall in all probability be able to accomplish. The absence of my partner for the last three months and my buties as Alcaldd here have dedrived our little paper of some of those attentions vvhich I hope it vvill hereafter receive.

"VVALTER COLTON."

The printer is responsible for a few errors in the above extract ; but the editor seems also blameable for the rapid changes from singular to plural and back again. It will be noticed from the date of the first number of the "Californian," that it was issued immediately after the capture of Sonoma and the first hoisting of the American flag in the northern towns of California ; and no doubt these events hastened its appearance. In the prospectus the editor says : "We shall maintain an entire and utter severance of all political connection with Mexico. We renounce at once and forever all fealty to her laws, all obedience to her mandates. * * * We shall advocate a territorial relation of California to the United States, till the number of her inhabitants is such that she can be admitted a member of that glorious confederacy. * * * We shall support the present measures of the commander-in-chief of the American squadron on the coast, so far as they conduce to the public tranquillity, the organization of a free representative government, and our alliance with the United States. * * * We shall go for California—*for all her interests, social, civil, and religious* —encouraging every thing that promotes these ; resisting every thing that can do them harm." Thus, every thing was showing that the Americans were resolved, at whatever cost, to keep the country, and make it their own. Meanwhile, San Francisco was rising into such importance as to make it a much superior place for publication to Monterey ; and accordingly on the 22d day of May, 1847, Mr. Robert Semple, who seems now to have been the sole publisher of the "Californian," issued the first number of the second volume of that paper at the former town, much enlarged and every way improved. This therefore was the second newspaper established in our city, at a time when the permanent population did not exceed four hundred.

From the columns of these early papers we extract much curious information regarding the number and elements of the population of San Francisco in the latter part of June, 1847. The following table shows the total number of inhabitants, the sex and age of the whites, and the sex of the Indians, Sandwich Islanders, and negroes; excluding the officers and soldiers of the detachment of New York volunteers stationed there at the time:—

Whites.	Males.	Females.	Total.
Under 5 years of age	28	23	51
Over 5 and under 10 years	18	14	32
" 10 " 15 "	10	14	24
" 15 " 20 "	11	11	22
" 20 " 25 "	29	15	44
" 25 " 30 "	54	19	73
" 30 " 40 "	61	19	80
" 40 " 50 "	20	10	30
" 50 " 60 "	12	3	15
" 60 " 70 "	2	—	2
" 70 " 80 "	2	—	2
Total whites	247	128	375
Indians (of different ages)	26	8	34
Sandwich Islanders (of different ages)	39	1	40
Negroes (of different ages)	9	1	10
Total	321	138	459

From this table it will be seen that upwards of four-fifths of the whole population were under forty years of age; while more than one-half were between twenty and forty—the prime of life. Under twenty, the sexes were nearly equal in number; but above that age, the vast majority were males. These circumstances must be borne in mind when the reader considers the restless enterprise, energy and capability exhibited by the comparatively small population of the town. We have already alluded to the mixture of foreigners who settled in San Francisco. We now give the birth-places of the above white population :—

Born in the United States, 228 ; in California, 38 ; other Mexican departments, 2 ; Canada, 5 ; Chili, 2 ; England, 22 ; France, 3 ; Germany, 27 ; Ireland, 14 ; Scotland, 14; Switzerland, 6 ; at sea, 4 ; Denmark, Malta, New Holland, New Zea-

San Francisco, from the Bay, in 1847.

land, Peru, Poland, Russia, Sandwich Islands, Sweden and West Indies, *one* each.

As of the number stated to have been born in California, eight were children of immigrant parents, it will be seen that the total population of Spanish or Mexican descent was only thirty-two. Three-fifths of the total inhabitants were of direct American origin ; and perhaps one-fifth more was composed of people who had previously settled or lived in the United States. The Americans, however, as may be supposed, were from every

State in the Union, and were often as different from each other in personal characteristics, as if they had been so many foreigners of separate countries.

The number who could read and write was two hundred and seventy-three ; those who could read, but not write, were thirteen ; while those who could neither read nor write, were eighty-nine.

From these statements it appears that the number who could neither read nor write bore a near relation to the number of inhabitants under ten years of age. At that period, it may be mentioned, there was only one school in the place, and no proper facilities were as yet given for bestowing a suitable education upon the young.

The occupations or professions of the white males were as follows :—1 minister ; 3 doctors ; 3 lawyers ; 2 surveyors ; 1 school-teacher ; 11 agriculturalists ; 7 bakers ; 6 blacksmiths ; 1 brewer ; 6 brick-makers ; 7 butchers ; 2 cabinet makers ; 26 carpenters ; 1 cigar-maker ; 13 clerks ; 3 coopers ; 1 gardener ; 5 grocers ; 2 gunsmiths ; 3 hotel-keepers ; 20 laborers ; 4 masons ; 11 merchants ; 1 miner ; 1 morocco-case maker ; 6 inland navigators ; 1 ocean navigator ; 1 painter ; 6 printers ; 1 saddler ; 4 shoemakers ; 1 silversmith ; 4 tailors ; 2 tanners ; 1 watchmaker ; 1 weaver.

The places in which the inhabitants conducted their business, were as follows, viz. :—shops, 1 apothecary, 2 blacksmith, 3 butcher, 1 cabinet maker, 2 carpenter, 1 cigar-maker, 2 cooper, 1 gun-smith, 1 shoemaker, 2 tailor, and 1 watchmaker ; 8 stores ; 7 groceries ; 2 hotels ; 1 wind-mill ; 1 horse-mill ; 2 printing-offices ; and 3 bakeries.

The Indians, Sandwich Islanders, and negroes, who formed nearly one-fifth of the population, were mostly employed as servants and porters. Many of the Sandwich Islanders were engaged in navigating the bay, and were very expert boatmen.

On the 30th of January, 1847, the following important "ordinance" appeared in the "California Star."

"AN ORDINANCE.

"WHEREAS, the local name of Yerba Buena, as applied to the settlement or town of San Francisco, is unknown beyond the district ; and has been applied from the local name of the cove, on which the town is built: *Therefore*, to prevent confusion and mistakes in public documents, and that the town may have the advantage of the name given on the public map,

"IT IS HEREBY ORDAINED, that the name of SAN FRANCISCO shall hereafter be used in all official communications and public documents, or records appertaining to the town.

"WASH'N A. BARTLETT,
" *Chief Magistrate.*

"Published by order,
"J. G. T. DUNLEAVY, *Municipal Clerk.*"

Mr. Bartlett was the first alcalde of San Francisco under the American flag. He was a lieutenant in the United States navy; and on being subsequently ordered to his ship, Mr. Edwin Bryant was appointed in his place, and sworn into office on the 22d day of February, 1847. This gentleman had travelled the previous year across the country from Independence, Mo., to the Pacific, and had subsequently joined Col. Fremont as a volunteer in the reduction of California. Shortly afterwards, he published in New York an interesting account of his travels under the title, "What I saw in California." Before Mr. Bryant's appointment to the chief-magistracy, Mr. George Hyde had acted for a short time as temporary alcalde.

Under the laws of Mexico, an alcalde had the entire control of municipal affairs, and administered justice pretty much according to his own ideas of the subject; without being tied down to precedents and formal principles of law. He could make grants of building-lots within the town boundaries to intending settlers; and really in general, his right of administration (except in cases of importance, either civil or criminal), seems to have been only limited by his power to carry his decrees into effect. When the Americans seized the country, and until peace should be declared or a formal constitution adopted, they were obliged to make use of the existing machinery of local government and the customary laws that regulated it. They accordingly every where appointed alcaldes, or chief-magistrates of towns and districts (it was of little consequence that they were not *lawyers*, but only ministers, doctors, adventurers, men of business, or of pleasure, and the like), and instructed them to dispense justice in the best manner they could, paying always as much regard as possible to the national laws of Mexico and the provincial customs of California.

The laws of Mexico reserved to the governor of a province the disposal of lands in towns within a certain number of feet below high-water mark. By this time, from the number of ships arriving in the Bay of San Francisco, it was becoming absolutely necessary that proper facilities should be given for the discharge and the reception of cargoes, and that wharves and other landing-places should be built across the great mud flat close upon the beach at the town, and extended to deep water, so that vessels could lie alongside. Upon the application therefore of the alcalde, Mr. Bryant, the then governor of California, General Kearny, in anticipation that the country was ultimately to become American, formerly renounced, on the 10th of March, 1847, in favor of the municipal authorities, the beach and water property lying between the points known as the Rincon and Fort Montgomery, upon the conditions stated in his decree. An extended survey and plan of the town had been previously commenced by Mr. Jasper O'Farrell, under the instructions of the former alcalde, Mr. Bartlett, and were now continued so as to embrace the beach and water property. When this survey was completed, the shore lots, as distinguished from those on the beach, were disposed of by private sale to applicants at a fixed price put on them by the alcalde, agreeably to the Mexican customs. The plan of the city, as surveyed and mapped out by Mr. O'Farrell, fronted the cove, and included the Telegraph Hill and the Rincon. It extended about three quarters of a mile from north to south, and two miles from east to west, and embraced about one and a half square miles. As the disposal of the beach and water lots was a great event in the history of San Francisco, we give a copy of the advertisement announcing the sale, and which was published in the "California Star," of the town, and in the "Californian," of Monterey, in conformity with the governor's decree :—

"GREAT SALE OF VALUABLE REAL ESTATE IN THE TOWN OF SAN FRANCISCO, UPPER CALIFORNIA.

"By the following decree of His Excellency, General S. W. Kearny, Governor of California, all the right, title and interest, of the United States, and of the Territory of California, to the BEACH AND WATER lots on the east front of the town of San Francisco, have been granted, conveyed, and released, to the people or corporate authorities of said town:—

'DECREE OF GENERAL KEARNY.

'I, Brigadier-General S. W. Kearny, Governor of California, by virtue of authority in me vested by the President of the United States of America, do hereby grant, convey, and release unto the town of San Francisco, the people, or corporate authorities thereof, all the right, title, and interest of the Government of the United States, and of the Territory of California, in and to the beach and water lots on the east front of said town of San Francisco, included between the points known as the Rincon and Fort Montgomery, except such lots as may be selected for the use of the United States Government by the senior officers of the army and navy now there: PROVIDED, the said ground hereby ceded shall be divided into lots, and sold by public auction to the highest bidder, after three months notice previously given; the proceeds of said sale to be for the benefit of the town of San Francisco.

'Given at Monterey, capital of California, this 10th day of March, 1847, and the 71st year of the independence of the United States.

'S. W. KEARNY.

'*Brigadier-General and Governor of California.*'

"In pursuance of and in compliance with the conditions of the foregoing decree, all the ungranted tract of ground on the east front of the town of San Francisco, lying and situated between Fort Montgomery and the Rincon, and known as the water and beach lots (the reservations by the general and town governments excepted), will be surveyed, and divided into convenient building lots for warehouses and stores, and offered at public sale to the highest bidder on Tuesday, the 29th day of June next, at ten o'clock, A. M. A plan of lots in connection with a general map of the town will be made out and exhibited on or before the day of sale.

"Terms of sale, one fourth cash,—one fourth in six months,—one fourth in twelve months,—and one fourth in eighteen months, the purchaser giving approved security bearing an interest of *ten per cent. per annum* from the day of sale.

"Other conditions will be made known on or before the day of sale.

"The site of the town of San Francisco is known to all navigators and mercantile men acquainted with the subject, to be the most commanding commercial position on the entire eastern coast of the Pacific Ocean, and the town itself is, no doubt, destined to become the commercial EMPORIUM of the western side of the American continent. The property offered for sale is the most valuable in, or belonging to the town, and the acquisition of it is an object of deep interest to all mercantile houses in California and elsewhere engaged in the commerce of the Pacific.

"EDWIN BRYANT,

"*Alcalde, or Chief Magistrate, Town and District of San Francisco.*

"*San Francisco, Upper California, March* 16*th*, 1847."

This great sale was subsequently postponed to Tuesday, the 20th of July following, by order of Mr. George Hyde, who was then alcalde of the town. On the day last named the sale took place, and lasted for three successive days. The lots were all contained between the limits of low and high-water mark; and four-fifths of them were entirely covered with water at flood tide. The size of the lots was sixteen and a half varas in width of front, and fifty varas deep. A *vara* is a Spanish yard, and is equal to about *thirty-three and one-third inches* of English measure. There were about four hundred and fifty of these lots in all, of which number two hundred were disposed of at the public sale above mentioned. The attendance of buyers was pretty fair; and the prices given were very considerable (ranging from fifty to one hundred dollars), considering the population and circumstances at the time. The price of some of the same lots *now* would somewhat astonish the projectors of the town extension of those days.

Curiously enough, we were in the act of finishing the last sentence, when we were informed of the prices obtained by the municipal authorities for other water lots which they were at this time (26th December, 1853) disposing of likewise at public auction. These last lots were situated much farther out in the bay, at places always covered with many feet of water, and measured less than one-half the size of the old ones, being only twenty-five feet in front by fifty-nine feet nine inches back. Yet they brought prices varying from *eight to sixteen thousand dollars!* Four small sized building blocks alone produced, in all, the enormous sum of $1,200,000; thereby restoring the injured credit of the city. Such is one contrast between 1847 and 1853 at San Francisco!

But the principal part of the town was laid out in lots of fifty varas square; six of them making a building block, bounded on the four sides by streets. In August, 1847, there had been about seven hundred of this description of lots surveyed, of which number nearly four hundred and fifty had been applied for and disposed of by the alcalde at a fixed price, which now seems to have been merely nominal. This price was *twelve dollars per lot,* and when the office fees for deed and recording (three dollars and sixty-two and a half cents) were added, the total cost was less than *sixteen dollars.* The conditions of sale were that the buyer should fence in the ground, and build a house upon it within one year; failing which, the lot and improvements were to revert to the town.

The south-eastern portion of the town was laid out in lots of one hundred varas square, six of which also formed a building block, bounded by regular streets at the four sides. The part of the town formed by these last lots was supposed to be the least valuable, and the lots themselves were expected to be the last taken up and improved by purchasers. The price established by law for these lots, which were four times the size of the fifty vara ones, was only *twenty-five dollars* each, and when the deed and recording fees were added (three dollars and sixty-two and a half cents), the total cost was under *twenty-nine dollars.* In August, 1847, about one hundred and thirty lots of this description were surveyed and laid out, of which number about seventy had been sold. The conditions of the sale were similar to those applicable to the fifty vara lots.

The proceeds of all these sales made up a considerable sum, and saved the necessity of levying municipal taxes for a short time. Real estate has advanced so rapidly in value since those days, that it would only be ridiculous to compare the prices obtainable now with those fixed by the alcalde in 1847. In many cases, however, an immense sum has been actually expended in first bringing the ground into building condition.

In Mr. O'Farrell's plan, the streets are all regularly laid out at right angles with each other, and are seventy-five and eighty feet wide. One, however, is one hundred and ten feet in width. The streets in the oldest part of the town—that portion surveyed by Capt. Juan Vioget, as stated in the previous chapter—are only about sixty feet broad.

There was at one time a municipal regulation, by which individuals were prevented from purchasing and holding more than a single fifty or one hundred vara lot. The object of this appears to have been to exclude speculators from jobbing in the lots, and to insure their speedy improvement by the real owner. By procuring lots, however, in the names of third parties, speculators soon contrived to evade this regulation, and thus a few individuals became possessed of a large portion of the extension of the town. The alcalde and town council therefore, shortly afterwards, did away with this restriction upon purchasers.

CHAPTER IV.

1846–1847.

Captain Montgomery hoists the American flag on Portsmouth Square.—Arrival of the ship Brooklyn from New York, with a large company of Mormon and other immigrants.—Disputes among her passengers, leading to the first jury trial in San Francisco.—Grand ball at the residence of Wm. A. Leidesdorff.—Nautical fête given by Capt. Simmons.—Public reception of Com. Stockton.—Attempts to establish a public school.—Name of town changed to San Francisco.—Number of buildings and inhabitants.—Suffering immigrants in the Sierra Nevada.—Trustees of the proposed school chosen.—Delegates to represent the District of San Francisco in the new legislative council.—Arrival of Col. Stevenson and New York Volunteers.—Vessels in the harbor, 18th March, 1847.—"The California Star" adopts the name of San Francisco.—Mails established between San Francisco and San Diego.—Proposed erection of a church.—Grand illumination in honor of Gen. Taylor's victory at Buena Vista.—Celebrations of Anniversaries.—Public meeting to consider the claims of Col. Fremont to the office of Governor of the Territory.—Sale of beach and water lots.—Election of the first town council.—The first public school.—Gales in San Francisco Bay.—The first steamboat.—Thanksgiving Day.—Commercial Statistics.

Having got the new town of San Francisco fairly planned, and given some general notion to the reader of the elementary composition of its inhabitants, shortly before the time when the discovery of gold was altogether to change its appearance and character, we shall now turn back a little in the order of time, and detail such few scattered notices of previous events as may seem to us worthy of being recorded among the "Annals" of the place.

1846.

July 8th.—The American flag was, on the morning of this day, hoisted in the *plaza*, or public square of Yerba Buena, by Capt. Montgomery, of the United States sloop-of-war *Portsmouth*, then lying in the bay. Two days before Commodore Sloat had despatched a messenger to Capt. Montgomery, informing him of his intention to raise the American flag at Monterey, and commanding him to do the same in the northern parts of the province around the Bay of San Francisco. This Montgomery did at the above date, accompanied by a party of seventy sailors and marines, and under a salute of twenty-one guns from the Portsmouth. The plaza at this time received the name of *Portsmouth Square*, and the street lying on the beach was called *Montgomery Street.* It may be mentioned that the American flag was raised at Sonoma on the 10th of this month; and soon afterwards at every principal place in the northern portion of California, where it was generally beheld with tranquillity, if not with applause.

July 31st.—The ship "Brooklyn" arrived in San Francisco Bay with a company of Mormon and other immigrants from New York. On landing at Yerba Buena, they immediately set up their tents among the sand-hills close to the beach. Very soon disputes began to arise between the Mormon people and their leaders, which ended in an open rupture, and a secession from their body of several of the principal men. Mr. Samuel Brannan, one of the most prominent of the party, was bitterly reviled, and accused of sundry malversations in his office as president of the association and as one of the managers of their funds. A jury trial—the first ever seen in California—was the consequence; in which Mr. Brannan was successful. These proceedings had the effect of preventing the Mormons at this time from selecting lands together and establishing themselves as a distinct community. Soon afterwards many of them volunteered to serve in the war in California, and joined Colonel Fremont's battalion.

September 8th.—The people of Yerba Buena, though still few in number, and particularly deficient in the fair sex, seemed determined to enjoy life while they might. A grand ball was given on the evening of this day at the residence of Mr. William A. Leidesdorff, by the officers in the service of the United States, and by the citizens of the town; when upwards of one hundred Californian and American ladies were present, with a large number of gentlemen. The dancing was very spirited, and kept up till daylight. This was the first gathering of ladies and gentlemen since the hoisting of the American flag. It was not long allowed to be the only one; for on the 18th of the same month, we find Capt. Simmons, of the American whale-ship "Magnolia," giving a nautical *fête* on board his ship on the evening of that day. One hundred and fifty family invitations were issued in

Yerba Buena and around the bay. From repeated traces which we find, of subsequent balls, grand dinners and suppers, and other festive entertainments, it may be presumed that the people of Yerba Buena were an exceedingly gay set. Business was brisk, and the town thriving; while the majority of the population being unmarried and without proper homes, it seemed that some such kind of continual public diversion was the only way in which they could unbend their minds from the contemplation of the "almighty dollar," and enjoy themselves.

October 5th.—This day, His Excellency, Commodore Robert F. Stockton, the governor and commander-in-chief of California, was honored with a public reception on the occasion of a visit to San Francisco. At a preliminary meeting to make the necessary arrangements, nearly every male adult of the place had been present; and on this day again all turned out in procession, to welcome the commodore. After the magistracy of the district and foreign consuls, there came the committee of management and the masters of the ships in port, concluding with a long line of citizens. A military escort and band of music attended on the occasion. General M. G. Vallejo, with several other native gentlemen who had held office under the last government, also appeared in the procession. We may mention that the general (many of whose relations were American or English), and some other leading Californians, had been early of opinion that the best hopes for their country lay in immediate annexation to the United States; and, accordingly, on all occasions, when duty permitted, they had been firm friends to the Americans. After an appropriate address to Commodore Stockton, in which he was complimented upon his efforts and success in reducing California, and a suitable reply by him, the ceremonies of the day, after a long procession to the mission and back again, concluded by an excellent collation, followed by a ball in the evening.

1847.

January.—Various attempts have been made of late to establish a public school. The "California Star" has weekly been calling attention to this important subject. At last a committee was appointed to ascertain the amount of subscriptions that might be expected from the inhabitants, the cost of the building and the salary of the teacher. Very unlike the usual proceedings of the citizens, much time and talk seem to have been lost on this subject ; nor was the object wished for obtained till upwards of twelve months after this date.

It was in this month that the term Yerba Buena was changed into San Francisco, by an ordinance of the alcalde, as stated in the preceding chapter. There were only about fifty houses at this period in the whole place, most of which were small single story buildings, constructed chiefly of *adobes.* They were scattered irregularly over the space lying between the foot of Telegraph Hill and Happy Valley. In April, of this year, the population numbered three hundred and seventy-five, without reckoning the Indians, who were by this time few in number.

February 3d.—A public meeting was held on the evening of this day to consider the alarming situation of a party of immigrants, who the previous year had attempted to reach California by a new route through the Great Basin ; but who, in ignorance of the country and other causes, had been so long delayed on the journey, that they were caught among the winter snows of the Sierra Nevada, where some of them had already perished, and the remainder were in imminent peril. Not content, however, with a mere expression of feeling, the meeting subscribed nearly fifteen hundred dollars, and immediately fitted out an expedition of twenty men, with an old mountaineer as guide, to proceed to the mountains with supplies to the sufferers, and to assist in extricating them from danger. Other expeditions, from various parts of the country, one of which was organized and altogether maintained at the personal charges of the benevolent Capt. Sutter of New Helvetia, likewise made the attempt to penetrate the mountains, and carry glad tidings and safety to the unfortunates. By these means those still alive were all rescued by the middle of spring. The descriptions given by the survivors, and by such members of the expeditions as were able to reach them, show a state of things of the most painful and horrible character. Many indeed had perished, through excessive cold and exposure to the weather, bodily fatigue and sheer hunger. When the provisions of the party were exhausted, and there was no strength nor opportunities left to kill game for food, necessity forced them to feed upon the dead bodies of their companions, two of whom (Indian guides), a small detached party of the white people killed for their support. Some even began to relish this kind of food, and sought it in preference when other provisions might have been obtained. One man, particularly, named Kiesburg, was suspected

Suffering Immigrants.

of foul murders to enable him to gratify this new and unnatural propensity. Before the time of trial, however, was over, all were glad enough of opportunities to partake of the horrid messes of human blood and uncooked entrails.

Packed closely together to preserve animal heat, in miserably small tents, with masses of snow beneath and around them, while piercing winds and snow blasts penetrated through all their defences, and the temperature was much below the freezing point, these unhappy beings for months saw only ultimate destruction from cold and hunger before them. There were husbands and wives, parents and children, all bearing the same physical suffering, and the elders likewise the mental anguish of thinking upon the sad fate of their little ones and the females dependent on them. Snow had begun to fall earlier than usual among the mountains, and when the party had arrived at the eastern side of the great pass across the Sierra Nevada, it lay too soft and deep for them to proceed. To retrace their steps was impossible; and, accordingly, they were forced to encamp where they were, with all the gloomy months of winter before them, unprepared, in every respect, in clothing, food, and lodging. Soon despair filled every heart; while the stealthy approaches of starvation and the daily sight of their misery brought insanity in their train. Many died raving mad; while the minds of all were in some sense affected by the horror of their situation. By great efforts and much physical exertion some few scattered members of the company managed to struggle through the snowy barrier, and slowly and painfully, reached the nearest settlements on the western slope of the mountains. The warm hearts of the settlers beat with generous emotion on hearing the sad tidings from the few who had thus escaped, and soon the whole country around San Francisco Bay was aroused to carry relief to the people still among the snows.

The following notice of the appearance of the suffering immigrants when the relief party reached them, is taken from the "California Star" of the 10th April, 1847:—

"The bones of those who had died and been devoured by the miserable ones that still survived, were lying around their tents and cabins. Bodies of men, women and children, with half the flesh torn from them, lay on every side. A woman sat by the side of the body of her husband, who had just died, cutting out his tongue; the heart she had already taken out, broiled and eat! The daughter was seen eating the flesh of the father—the mother that of her children—children that of father and mother. The emaciated, wild and ghastly appearance of the survivors added horror to the scene. Language cannot describe the awful change that a few weeks of dire suffering had wrought in the minds of the wretched and piteous beings. Those who but one month before would have shuddered at the thought of eating human flesh, or of killing their companions and relatives to preserve their own lives, now looked upon the opportunity by these acts afforded them of escaping the most dreadful of deaths, as a providential interference in their behalf. Calculations were coldly made, as they sat gloomily around their camp fires, for the next and succeeding meals. Various expedients were devised to prevent the dreadful crime of murder; but they finally resolved to kill those who had the least claims to longer existence. Just at this moment, however, as if by divine interposition, some of them died, which afforded the rest temporary relief. Some sunk into the arms of death cursing God for their miserable fate, while the last whisperings of others were prayers and songs of praise to the Almighty.

"After the first few deaths, but the one all-absorbing thought of individual self-preservation prevailed. The fountains of natural affection were dried up. The chords that once vibrated with connubial, parental and filial affection were rent asunder, and each one seemed resolved, without regard to the fate of others, to escape from the impending calamity. Even the wild hostile mountain Indians, who once visited their camps, pitied them; and instead of pursuing the natural impulse of their hostile feelings to the whites, and destroying them, as they easily could have done, divided their own scanty supply of food with them.

"So changed had the immigrants become, that when the party sent out arrived with food, some of them cast it aside, and seemed to prefer the putrid human flesh that still remained. The day before the party arrived, one of the immigrants took a child of about four years of age in bed with him, and devoured the whole before morning, and the next day eat another about the same age before noon.

"It is thought that several more of these unfortunate people might have been saved, but for their determination not to leave their property. Some of them who started, loaded themselves with their money and other effects to such an extent that they sunk under them, and died on the road."

It was expected that this calamity would have had a serious influence in deterring future immigration into California from the United States. But the discovery of gold immediately afterwards destroyed all calculations on the subject, and sent headlong tens of thousands across the plains and over the Rocky and Snowy Mountains where the above party had suffered so much, to encounter in some cases nearly the same amount of misery as they. We have seen that the town of San Francisco nobly did its duty on the lamentable occasion. Of the eighty individuals who composed the party, of whom forty-eight were males and thirty-two females, thirty-six perished. Of these, twenty-eight were males, and only eight females. The story of their sufferings and end make a striking incident in the history of California, and is worthy of being recorded in the "Annals of San Francisco," if it were only to mark the liberal exertions made by its citizens in their behalf.

FEBRUARY 21st.—Dr. F. Forgeaud, C. L. Ross, Dr. J. Townsend, J. Serrine and W. H. Davis, were appointed trustees of the proposed school.

MARCH 4th.—A meeting of citizens was held this day to consider the propriety of resolving, that the District of San Francisco should be fitly represented by one member in the new legislative council, convened by the governor, until a proper constitution should be obtained for the Territory ; when it was resolved to that effect, and Mr. J. G. T. Dunleavy was chosen by a majority of votes, to be representative accordingly. It appeared that the legislative council, recently organized by Com. Stockton, consisted of seven individuals, four of whom were Californians, one Englishman and two Americans ; while it was an undoubted fact that the majority of the white population was from the United States, and the constant immigration was daily increasing this majority. Similar meetings complaining of the insufficient American representation in the council were held at Sonoma, Santa Clara, and other places, at which American delegates were chosen to represent their interests, the governor being entreated by these meetings to accept of their choice, and formally to re-appoint their nominees as members of the legislative council. It does not appear that any notice was taken of these proceedings, or that the "people's choice" became also His Excellency's. The latter alone had the complete control of the Government—which, so long as war with Mexico lasted, was necessarily a military one—and appointed only such officers to assist him in the same as suited his personal views of the subject.

MARCH 6th.—The ship Thomas H. Perkins arrived from New York, bringing Col. Stevenson of the New York volunteers, and the first detachment of his regiment. With few exceptions, the volunteers were mechanics and single men; and as they were enlisted to serve during the war, and when peace came, to be disbanded only in California, it was expected that they would nearly all remain as permanent settlers in the country. The colonel himself and all his officers, had likewise expressed their wish and determination to make California their home after the termination of hostilities.

MARCH 13th.—There were in the harbor at this date six square-rigged vessels, viz. : the United States ship Cyane, the ships Moscow, Vandalia, Barnstable, Thomas H. Perkins, and the brig Euphemia.

MARCH 20th.—The local newspaper, the "California Star," is pleased, at last, to acquiesce, very unwillingly, in the change of name from Yerba Buena to San Francisco; and to-day, for the first time, dates its leader from the latter. This change seems not to have gratified every party. Mr. Semple, of the Monterey "Californian," and Mr. T. O. Larkin, who had jointly founded the new city of Francisca, on the Strait of Carquinez, afraid lest their rising town should be confounded and lost in the name and fame of San Francisco, were forced to change the appellation of the former to *Benicia*. In those days, Benicia was anticipated by many to be the great future rival of San Francisco. Later times have shown how unnecessary fear was on the subject.

APRIL.—Semi-monthly mails established between San Francisco and San Diego and intermediate places.

MAY 6th.—A public meeting was held to consider the propriety of erecting a church in the town; when a committee was appointed for the purpose of taking steps to procure the erection.

MAY 28th.—First grand illumination in San Francisco. This was in honor of General Taylor's great victory over the Mexicans at Buena Vista. Every building in the town, of frame or adobe, and shanty itself, shone with as much lustre as an unlimited allowance of oil and tallow could bestow. Fire-arms cracked, and bonfires blazed on all sides.

JULY.—Two great anniversaries were held this month, in a becoming manner, at San Francisco, viz.: the independence-day of the United States, on the 4th,—and the independence or conquest-day of California, on the 7th; on which latter day, in the previous year, the American flag had been hoisted at Monterey by Com. Sloat. We have already had occasion to notice the celebration of a "glorious fourth," just eleven years before, when Mr. Leese had erected the first solid building (his house being of frame, while Capt. Richardson's, erected the preceding year, was only a canvas-covered tent), that was seen in Yerba Buena. Then the country was Mexican, and while the guests were chiefly of that nation, the flags of both Mexico and the United States floated amicably together. Now—only eleven years later—the country was American, and her flag alone was displayed, while the vast majority of those who shared in the festival was of that nation. What a wonderful change these few years had made in the character and prospects of the country! As before we had occasion to chronicle Mr. Leese's musicians, his six pounders, his dinner, drinks, dancing and general festivities; so we may here say, that the day of 1847 was celebrated in a similar manner, under salutes from men of war in the bay, and the presidio, when people on shore processed to musical strains, and when flags waved, and much powder was burned, and the citizens speechified and hurrahed, toasted, drank, danced and made merry as is usual on such occasions. The 7th was observed in a similar fashion.

July 14th.—On this day was held a public meeting of a large number of citizens to consider the conduct of Col. Fremont in California, and his claims to be chosen by the President of the United States as Governor of the Territory. It appears that after the colonel's volunteer regiment of "mounted riflemen" was disbanded, there had been no money forthcoming for the arrears of pay, or even to reimburse the heavy pecuniary loss and outlay which many of the officers and men had incurred. Governor Kearny, and his successor, Governor Mason, would not, or could not, make such payments from the territorial exchequer, or rather grant available warrants upon the national treasury without the previous sanction of Congress. They had accepted a country conquered partly by these very volunteers, and had entered upon possession of its revenues, and yet would not, or cruelly delayed to pay the necessary cost. Col. Fremont therefore appeared, in the mean time, the only debtor; but as it was impossible that he could pretend to be able to make payment of the very large sums disbursed on account of the war in California, and for the benefit solely of the United States, much personal dissatisfaction was expressed against him by all who had suffered in this way, and by many sympathizing friends, especially in the northern districts of the country. In the southern quarters, from whence he had drawn few or no volunteers, and owed therefore neither pay nor supplies, the colonel had become exceedingly popular; and this although he had been a successful invader. In these parts of the country a petition had been got up and was numerously signed, praying Congress to appoint him Governor of California. The same petition being taken northwards for the approval and signatures of the Americans around San Francisco Bay, excited much angry feeling on the subject. Col. Fremont was in danger of losing all his recent popularity, and in the rage and injustice of the moment, was even denied many of the claims, formerly advanced and elsewhere allowed, to the heroic part he had taken in the conquest of the country. At the meeting above mentioned, a committee of eight gentlemen was formed to investigate and publish all reliable instances of his misconduct; and meantime, the meeting protested against his being chosen as their governor by Congress. It may just farther be stated on this subject, that Congress, a considerable time afterwards, allotted a large sum to satisfy all claims against Fremont on account of the war in California, and which naturally fell upon the United States as accepting the country reduced to their hands.

July 20th.—Beginning of the great sale of beach and water lots in San Francisco, as detailed in a preceding chapter.

July 28th.—The alcalde, Mr. George Hyde, selected six gentlemen to assist him in disposing of the great and daily accumulation of municipal business. These were the *ayuntamiento*, or "town council," as they were called, and were to remain in office until the governor should think fit formally to cause an election to take place among the citizens to fill their places. Accordingly, on

August 15th, Governor Mason issued an ordinance addressed to Mr. Hyde, in regard to such an election. As it explains the manner in which the municipal government was carried on in those days, we quote the principal portion of it:—

"There is wanted in San Francisco an efficient town government, more so than is in the power of an alcalde to put in force. There may be soon expected a large number of whalers in your bay, and a large increase of your population by the arrival of immigrants. It is therefore highly necessary that you should at an early day have an efficient town police, proper town laws, town officers, &c., for enforcement of the laws, for the preservation of order, and for the proper protection of persons and property.

"I therefore desire that you call a town meeting for the election of six persons, who when elected shall constitute the town council, and who in conjunction with the alcalde shall constitute the town authorities until the end of the year 1848.

"All the municipal laws and regulations will be framed by the council, but executed by the alcalde in his judicial capacity as at present.

"The first alcalde will preside at all meetings of the council, but shall have no vote, except in cases where the votes are equally divided.

"The town council (not less than four of whom shall constitute a quorum for the transaction of business), to appoint all the town officers, such as treasurer, constables, watchmen, &c., and to determine their pay, fees, &c.

"The treasurer to enter into ample and sufficient bonds, conditioned for the faithful performance of his duties: the bonds to be fully executed to the satisfaction of the council before the treasurer enters upon his duties.

"The second alcalde shall, in case of the absence of the first alcalde, take his place and preside at the council, and there perform all the proper functions of the first alcalde.

"No soldier, sailor or marine, nor any person who is not a *bona fide* resident of the town shall be allowed to vote for a member of the town council."

In pursuance of the foregoing order, Mr. Hyde fixed the election for six members for a town council, upon

SEPTEMBER 13th.—We give the names of the gentlemen elected, along with the names of those who had previously been appointed by the alcalde, as an interim council:—

Councillors elected.	No. of votes.	Councillors chosen by Alcalde.
William Glover,	126	William A. Leidesdorff.
William D. M. Howard,	114	Robert A. Parker.
William A. Leidesdorff,	109	José P. Thompson.
E. P. Jones,	88	Pedro T. Sherreback.
Robert A. Parker,	74	John Rose.
William S. Clark,	72	Benjamin R. Buckelew.

The town council chose Mr. Leidesdorff their treasurer. The first alcalde was Mr. George Hyde; and the second, Dr. T. M. Leavenworth. Immediately after the formation of the town council, its members entered with spirit upon the duties of their office. They passed a multitude of laws affecting the general interests of the town, regulating the streets and buildings, the licensing and character of business allowed, appointed constables, &c. Soon, therefore, the place became to assume a steady progressive appearance, and some fair sort of order was every where established. This council may be said to have had every thing to do to found the city. Our work would swell beyond all reasonable limits, should we attempt to name every public act of importance—when nearly all they did was new and of vital consequence to the well-being of San Francisco—performed by this council. We can only, therefore, give an occasional notice in future of their proceedings. One, however, of their earliest resolutions may just be glanced at, viz.: the rescinding of those conditions in the sale of town lands, which made it imperative on the buyer to fence in and erect a building upon his lot within a year after the purchase. One effect of this was certainly to encourage speculation, since jobbers in lots could now safely hold an indefinite number, when not obliged to erect buildings upon them within a limited time.

SEPTEMBER 24th.—Messrs. Leidesdorff, Glover and Clark were appointed by the town council a committee to take measures for the establishment of a public school. Various resolutions were subsequently passed by the council on this subject, and after much public agitation, at length, on 17th March, 1848, a teacher was appointed, with a salary of one thousand dollars ; and on the 3d of April following, Mr. Thomas Douglas formally opened the long delayed and much needed school, for the instruction of the youth of both sexes. This was the first public seminary established in San Francisco.

OCTOBER 20th.—A severe *Norther* visited the harbor which did considerable damage to the shipping. Similar furious gales have since been experienced every year, when more or less loss has been occasioned to the shipping and to the wharves themselves. The exposure to excessive winds from the north and southeast is one of the most serious drawbacks to the safety and convenience of the port. The extension of the city, in late years, over the waters of Yerba Buena Cove, has increased the liability of vessels to damage during the prevalence of these winds.

NOVEMBER 15th.—"The Steamboat,"—being the only one it had no distinct name,—performed an experimental trip round "Wood Island." This was but a small concern which had been brought by Mr. Leidesdorff from Sitka. It was the first vessel of the kind in San Francisco Bay, and was quite a pet or plaything in its way. Two days afterwards "the steamboat" sailed for Santa Clara. In February following it was lost in a *Norther*.

NOVEMBER 18th.—The *first* "Thanksgiving Day" celebrated in New England style. Public worship was performed at the house of Mr. Lincoln. The "Sons of New England" afterwards had a public dinner.

DECEMBER 31st.—The following statistics show the extent of the commerce of San Francisco for the *three months* ending this day :—

Total value of exports, $49,597.53 ; imports, $53,589.73. Of the amount of exports, $30,353.85, represent the native produce of California, and were shipped as follows :—To the Sandwich Islands, $320 ; Peru, $21,448.35 ; Mazatlan, $560 ; Sitka, $7,285.50 ; Tahiti, $700. The other exports, amounting to $19,343.68, were the produce of foreign countries, and were shipped as follows :—$2,060 to the United States ; $12,442.18 (of which $11,340 were coined gold and silver), to the Sandwich Islands ; and $4,831.50 to Mazatlan. The imports came from the following countries :—United States, $6,790.54 ; Oregon, $7,701.59 ; Chili, $3,676.44 ; Sandwich Islands, $31,740.73 ; Sitka, $2,471.32 ; Bremen, $550.54 ; and Mexico, $160.

CHAPTER V.

1848.

Resolutions concerning gambling.—Public sale of City Property.—Price Current published.—Condition and population of the town.—Overland express to Independence, Mo.—George Hyde, alcalde, resigned, and succeeded by Dr. J. Townsend.—Death of Wm. A. Leidesdorff.—Discovery of gold, and immediate effects.—Illumination in celebration of the peace between Mexico and the United States.—Dr. T. M. Leavenworth elected alcalde.—First brick house.—Public meeting to regulate the price of gold dust.—First square-rigged vessel discharged at Broadway wharf.—Judicial limits of the town.—Rev. T. D. Hunt chosen chaplain.—First issue of the "Star and Californian."—State of the markets.—Public meeting to organize a Provisional Government.—New town council elected.—Election declared invalid.—Duties collected at the Custom-House

January 11th.—Stringent resolutions were passed by the council regarding gambling. This vice had been growing in popular favor, and at this period and for years afterwards, became one of the leading characteristics of the inhabitants. Besides heavily fining parties engaged in gambling, one of the resolutions authorized the authorities "to seize for the benefit of the town all the money *found* on a gambling table where cards are played." If this had been in force a short time afterwards, when the gold discoveries had enriched thousands, and the reckless miners hurried to San Francisco to spend their gains in the great public gaming saloons of the period, the town in a single night would have become wealthy. But at the next meeting of the council these resolutions were all repealed.

March 5th.—A great public sale took place by the town of some of its real estate. The preferable lots had already been secured by speculators, under the old regulations, at a nominal price, by private arrangement with the alcalde. The prices obtained at this sale do not show much advance in the value of town property, since the lots only brought from sixteen to fifty dollars, averaging about twenty-two dollars and fifty cents each for fifty-two lots. It is certain, however, that the value of desirable locations was immensely higher than this ; and the citizens, from their eagerness in getting up houses, and the high prices of labor and building materials, seem to have been satisfied on this subject. The population of the town was fast improving.

March 15th.—As a sign of the times, a weekly wholesale price-current was first published in San Francisco in the columns of the "Californian" of this date. In the "California Star," of the 18th instant, likewise appeared a similar document, and remarks on the state of the market, for the first time.

About this period the population of the town was ascertained by the Board of School Trustees, in canvassing the place for educational purposes, to be, 575 male and 177 female adults, and 60 children of ages to attend school, making a total of 812. Adding the number of infants and children still too young to attend school, the whole number of inhabitants amounted to about 850. The buildings of all kinds numbered 200. There were two large hotels in the place, besides boarding and public houses, and houses attached to ten-pin alleys, billiard saloons, &c. ; so that the town was becoming one of some consequence, and was assuming the pretensions and attractions of older, wealthier and more populous communities. Two wharves were in the course of construction, and extensive stores and warehouses had been erected. There were twelve mercantile houses established, consisting of agencies for large firms in the East and in the Sandwich Islands, auction and commission houses, and importers from the United States direct. The facilities for discharging ships and filling them anew with cargo, were rapidly increasing. There was much bustle, and even enthusiasm among the inhabitants, which promised a flattering future to the town. Current expenses were too high to prevent immediate fortunes being made ; still most persons in business believed they were laying the firm foundations of early wealth.

April 1st.—The "California Star Express" left San Francisco, to proceed overland to Independence, Mo. The passage was guaranteed to be accomplished in sixty days. Fifty cents was charged as the postage on single letters.

April 3d.—The first public school was opened. Dr. J. Townsend was also sworn in before the council, as first alcalde, *vice* George Hyde, resigned. Serious complaints had been made in regard to Mr. Hyde's conduct in office, which, being reported to Governor Mason, led to a formal inquiry on the subject. Some nine or ten charges of a criminal nature were made against the former alcalde, only two of which were ultimately held to be established by proof. These, in the whole circumstances of the case, seemed insufficient to warrant His Excellency to remove Mr. Hyde from office. But as popular clamor was somewhat loud and vexatious on the matter, that gentleman thought fit to resign his trust.

MAY 18th.—Mr. Wm. A. Leidesdorff died of the brain fever. This gentleman was the United States vice-consul at San Francisco, and was closely connected with all the interests of the place. His decease was much regretted by the town's people, a large number of whom attended in his funeral procession. All places of business and entertainment were closed on the occasion, the flags at the barracks and of the vessels in port hung at half-mast during the day; while minute guns were fired as the burial train moved on towards the Mission Dolores, in the church-yard of which place the body was interred. Mr. Leidesdorff was of Danish extraction, and of the Roman Catholic religion. He had been nearly nine years in business in San Francisco, and was about thirty-six years old. The property he left was of considerable value at the time of his death, (though heavily burdened with debts;) while, as much of it consisted of real estate, on which the growing city afterwards spread, its value at this date is immense. The deceased left no legal heirs on the spot, and his estate was administered by Mr. Wm. D. M. Howard, under authority of the alcalde, for behoof of all concerned. Much litigation, among parties claiming to be administrators, or heirs or assignees of heirs of the deceased, afterwards resulted, which it is believed is not yet fairly ended. The law proceedings and history of the estate generally form quite an *event* in the annals of the town, and deserve a more particular notice, which will be given in a subsequent chapter.

The promising state of things in San Francisco shortly before described was now to be suddenly checked by means which, unpromising at first, ultimately led to the most extraordinary prosperity in the city. Early in the spring of this year, occasional intelligence had been received of the finding of gold in large quantities among the foot hills of the Sierra Nevada, the particulars of which discovery we have already given. Small parcels of the precious metal had also been forwarded to San Francisco, while visitors from the mines, and some actual diggers arrived, to tell the wonders of the region and the golden gains of those engaged in exploring and working it. In consequence of such representations, the inhabitants began gradually, in bands and singly, to desert their previous occupations, and betake themselves to the American River and other auriferous parts of the great Sacramento valley. Labor, from the deficiency of hands, rose rapidly in value, and soon all business and work, except the most urgent, was forced to be stopped. Seamen deserted from their ships in the bay and soldiers from the barracks. Over all the country the excitement was the same. Neither threats, punishment nor money could keep men to their most solemn engagements. Gold was the irresistible magnet that drew human souls to the place where it lay, rudely snapping asunder the feebler ties of affection and duty. Avarice and the overweening desire to be suddenly rich, from whence sprang the hope and moral certainty of being so, grew into a disease, and the infection spread on all sides, and led to a general migration of every class of the community to the golden quarters. The daily laborer, who had worked for the good and at the command of another, for one or two dollars a day, could not be restrained from flying to the happy spot where he could earn six or ten times the amount, and might possibly gain a hundred or even a thousand times the sum in one lucky day's chance. Then the life, at worst, promised to be one of continual adventure and excitement, and the miner was his own master. While this was the case with the common laborer, his employer, wanting his services, suddenly found his occupation at an end; while shopkeepers and the like, dependent on both, discovered themselves in the same predicament. The glowing tales of the successful miners all the while reached their ears, and threw their own steady and large gains comparatively in the shade. They therefore could do no better, in a pecuniary sense even, for themselves, than to hasten after their old servants, and share in their new labor and its extraordinary gains, or pack up their former business stock, and travelling with it to the mines, open their new stores and shops and stalls, and dispose of their old articles to the fortunate diggers, at a rise of five hundred or a thousand per cent.

Rush for the gold regions.

In the month of May it was computed that, at least one hundred and fifty people had left San Francisco, and every day since was adding to their number. Some were occasionally returning from the auriferous quarter; but they had little time to stop and expatiate upon what they had seen. They had hastily come back, as they had hastily gone away at first, leaving their household and business to waste and ruin, now to fasten more properly their houses, and remove goods, family and all, at once to the gold region. Their hurried movements, more even than the words they uttered, excited the curiosity and then the eager desire of others to accompany them. And so it was. Day after day the bay was covered with launches filled with the inhabitants and their goods, hastening up the Sacramento. This state of matters soon came to a head; and master and man alike hurried to the *placeres*, leaving San Francisco, like a place where the plague reigns, forsaken by its old inhabitants, a melancholy solitude.

On the 29th of May the "Californian" published a fly-sheet, apologizing for the future non-issue of the paper, until better days came, when they might expect to retain their servants for some amount of remuneration, which at present was impossible, as all, from the "*subs*" to the "*devil*," had indignantly rejected every offer, and gone off to the diggings. "The whole country," said the last editorial of the paper, "from San Francisco to Los Angeles, and from the sea shore to the base of the Sierra Nevada, resounds with the sordid cry of *gold!* GOLD!! GOLD!!! —while the field is left half planted, the house half built, and every thing neglected but the manufacture of shovels and pickaxes, and the means of transportation to the spot where one man obtained one hundred and twenty-eight dollars' worth of the *real stuff* in one day's washing, and the average for all concerned is *twenty dollars per diem!*"

On the 14th of June the "California Star" likewise ceased. In the explanatory fly-sheet, the editor simply and sadly said, that his paper "could not be made by magic, and the labor of mechanism was as essential to its existence as to all other arts." And as every body was deserting him, why, the press and the paper stopped together—that was all.

July 15th.—The "Californian" revives, and promises an occasional paper, if that can be managed. It gives this day the first intelligence of the French revolution, under the alarming head, "The whole world at war!" though little did the gold-diggers and the speculative traders in San Francisco care about that. It chronicles likewise the observance of another "glorious fourth" which was held in the town as spiritedly as the few remaining inhabitants could manage. The rest of the news, and many of the advertisements were about the mines and gold. The city itself afforded few items of intelligence, except the continued desertion of the place, and the high and increasing prices of labor. The council had not met for two months; and its members, with many officials of the town, had all "gone to the diggings."

July 25th.—Governor Mason issued a proclamation calling on the people to assist the authorities in apprehending deserters, who had now become very numerous from both the army and navy service.

July 31st.—His Excellency consents to receive gold dust in payment of duties at the custom-house at a low rate, with right of redemption of the whole by the payer, within one hundred and eighty days, or of the half within ninety days, upon giving the proper amount in gold or silver coin. Several public meetings have been held on this subject, in which the community was much interested.

August 11th.—A second grand illumination. This time it was in celebration of the peace between Mexico and the United States, the official news of which reached Monterey on the 6th instant. In the early part of the day guns were fired on all sides, from the presidio and barracks, ships in harbor, and by every youngster on shore who happily owned, or could buy, borrow, or steal a little gunpowder and a fire-arm, from a musket to a rusty key with a priming-hole filed across the barrel. A cavalcade of citizens proceeded through the streets. In the evening, the windows of every house remaining inhabited were illuminated, many of them brilliantly. Tar barrels and bonfires blazed on all sides. Squibs, crackers and pistols boomed off in harmony with the general rejoicing.

August 29th.—Dr. T. M. Leavenworth elected first alcalde.

September 6th.—The first brick house was erected by Mellus & Howard, at the corner of Montgomery and Clay streets. This was the second brick building erected in Upper California, one having been previously constructed at Monterey.

September 9th.—A great public meeting was held to consider how best to fix the price of gold dust at a certain reasonable amount, to pass as a currency in the country, during the scarcity of coin, and until a branch mint could be established. This was supposed to be the largest meeting that had ever assembled in San Francisco, most of the old inhabitants having returned for a season from the mines. Dr. T. M. Leavenworth was called to the chair, and Mr. J. D. Hoppe appointed secre-

San Francisco, Winter of 1848.

tary. The meeting unanimously decided and resolved that sixteen dollars an ounce was a fair price for gold dust, and that it ought to be taken in all business transactions at that rate. A committee was also appointed to urge upon Congress the immediate establishment of a branch mint at San Francisco.

This month a square-rigged vessel (the brig Belfast, from New York,) first discharged a cargo at Broadway wharf. The price of goods consequently fell twenty-five *per cent.*, while real estate rose from fifty to one hundred *per cent.* A vacant lot at the corner of Montgomery and Washington streets was offered the day previous to the opening of the wharf for five thousand dollars, but there were no buyers. The next day the same lot sold readily at ten thousand dollars. This shows how property was beginning to be affected by the improvement of the town.

October 3d.—At a second election, Dr. T. M. Leavenworth was again chosen first alcalde. B. R. Buckelew and Barton Mowrey were also elected town councillors. One hundred and fifty-eight votes were polled.

October 9th.—First meeting of the town council since May last. At an adjourned meeting held on the 11th, it was resolved that the limits of the town for the administration of justice should be as follows, viz.: "That the line shall commence at the mouth of Creek Guadalupe, where it empties into the Bay of San Francisco, following the course of said stream to its head waters; from thence a due west line to the Pacific Ocean; thence northwards along the coast to the inlet to the harbor of the bay; thence eastwardly, through the middle of the said inlet into the Bay of San Francisco, and embracing the entire anchorage ground from the inlet to the mouth of the Creek Guadalupe."

November 1st.—No regular church had hitherto been established; but nearly every Sunday, for a long period back, occasional religious services had been performed by clergymen of various denominations; or, in their absence, by some serious minded layman. This day, the Rev. T. D. Hunt, who had been invited from Honolulu, was chosen Protestant chaplain to the citizens, and an annual salary of two thousand five hundred dollars appropriated to him, to be defrayed out of the subscriptions of various town's people. Divine worship on Sundays to take place in the Public Institute, (school-house,) Portsmouth Square.

November 18th.—The "Californian," having been bought up by the proprietors of the "California Star," a new paper, similar in appearance to both these, and virtually a continuation of the latter, which had stopped five months before, was issued this day under the title, "The Star and Californian."

December.—The markets, as might be expected, were very high about this time, though prices fluctuated considerably. On the 1st of this month, flour was twenty-seven dollars a barrel, beef twenty, pork sixty; butter was ninety cents a pound, and cheese seventy. Two weeks later, flour sold at from twelve to fifteen dollars a barrel, while other articles had fallen in proportion. Brandy was in demand at eight dollars a gallon, and gold dust dull of sale at ten dollars and a half an ounce.

December 12th.—The public school, after having been closed for many months during the gold-mania, re-opened. Rates of tuition were announced to be eight dollars a term.

December 21st and 23d.—Great public meetings were held, (Dr. Townsend in the chair,) regarding the propriety, and growing necessity of immediately organizing a provisional government. For some time back, much public agitation had existed on this subject. The frequent murders and other daring outrages committed of late in different parts of the country, especially at the mines, while there was no proper legal protection for the lives and property of the citizens, had forced the people to conclude that Congress had been trifling with them in delaying the long proposed constitution—that there was no more time to wait—and therefore that instant steps should be taken to establish a form of government for themselves. At these meetings resolutions were passed to the above effect, and five delegates appointed to be chosen at a subsequent public meeting, to represent the town and district at a general convention to be held at San José, in March next, for the purpose of framing a form of constitution. A meeting to the same effect had been held at San José on the 11th instant, which had fixed the assembling of the convention so early as the 2d of January following, and similar meetings were beginning to be called all over the country.

December 27th.—The following gentlemen were elected as town council, or *ayuntamiento*, for 1849, viz.: Stephen C. Harris, Wm. D. M. Howard, George C. Hubbard, Robert A. Parker, Thomas J. Roach, John Sirrine, and John Townsend—the last of whom was chosen president. The number of votes polled was three hundred and forty-seven.

December 28th, 29th and 30th.—Various meetings were held of the *old* town council, which ended in its resolving that the election of the 27th instant was invalid, owing to the votes of a small number of unqualified parties having been received; and a new election was ordered for the 15th proximo.

The duties collected at the custom-house, during 1848, were as follows:—First quarter, $11,931; second quarter, $8,835; third quarter, $74,827; fourth quarter, $100,480. The value of imported goods during the year was about one million of dollars. Coin was also imported to about the same amount. Gold dust to the value of two millions of dollars was exported in the last six months of 1848. A few years later as great a quantity was exported by every semi-monthly mail.

CHAPTER VI.

1848–1849.

General Effects of the Gold Discoveries.

While San Francisco, like so many other parts of the country, was forsaken in the manner described in the foregoing chapter, the neighborhood of the American River was overflowing with people, all busily engaged in gold hunting. The miners by the middle of May were estimated to be about two thousand. In another month they had increased probably to three ; and, two months later, their number was supposed to be about six thousand. From that period the arrival of persons at the different auriferous districts, which were known to extend over a large space of territory, was constant ; but no sufficient materials existed to form a correct opinion of their total number. The vast majority of all the laboring classes in the country had certainly deserted their former pursuits, and had become miners, while a great many others—merchants and their clerks, shopkeepers and their assistants, lawyers, surgeons, officials in every department of the State, of the districts and in the towns, runaway seamen and soldiers, and a great variety of nondescript adventurers—likewise began the search for gold. The miners were by no means exclusively American. They consisted of every kindred and clan. There were already tame Indians, Mexicans from Sonora, Kanakas from the Sandwich Islands, settlers from Oregon, mixed with the usual dash of Spanish, British, German and French adventurers that had for a long time existed in California. Later months were to bring other Mexicans, Chinese, Peruvians, and Chilians, and all these before the great impending immigration of Americans and Europeans.

At first the general gains of the miners, though great, were little compared to what shortly afterwards were collected. But any positive statement on this matter is naturally subject to error, since none could personally know more than what was taking place around the scene of his own operations, or where he was immediately travelling. If, however, we compare different accounts, and endeavor to form from them something like a fair average, we might find that from ten to fifteen dollars worth of gold dust was about the usual proceeds of an ordinary day's hard work. But while that might have been the average, people listened more to the individual instances of extraordinary success. Well authenticated accounts described many known persons as averaging from one to two hundred dollars a day for a long period. Numerous others were said to be earning even from five to eight hundred dollars a day. A piece of four pounds in weight was early found. If, indeed, in many cases, a man with a pick and pan did not easily gather some thirty or forty dollars worth of dust in a single day, he just moved off to some other place which he supposed might be richer. When the miners knew a little better about the business and the mode of turning their labor to the most profitable account, the returns were correspondingly increased. At what were called the "dry diggings" particularly, the yield of gold was enormous. One piece of pure metal was found of thirteen pounds weight. The common instrument at first made use of was a simple butcher's knife; and as every thing was valuable in proportion to the demand and supply, butchers' knives suddenly went up to twenty and thirty dollars apiece. But afterwards the pick and shovel were employed. The auriferous earth, dug out of ravines and holes in the sides of the mountains, was packed on horses, and carried one, two, or three miles, to the nearest water, to be washed. An average price of this washing dirt was, at one period, so much as four hundred dollars a cart load. In one instance, five loads of such earth sold for seven hundred and fifty-two dollars, which yielded, after washing, sixteen thousand dollars. Cases occurred where men carried the earth in sacks on their backs to the watering places, and collected eight to fifteen hundred dollars in a day, as the proceeds of their labor. Individuals made their five thousand, ten thousand, and fifteen thousand dollars in the space of only a few weeks. One man dug out twelve thousand dollars in six days. Three others obtained eight thousand dollars in a single day. But these, of course, were extreme cases. Still it was undoubtedly true, that a large proportion of the miners were earning such sums as they had never even seen in their lives before, and which, six months earlier, would have appeared a downright fable. When the "Californian" newspaper resumed its issue in July, the editors said, that the publisher of the paper, "when on a tour alone to the mining district," (probably in June,) "collected, with the aid of a shovel, pick and tin pan, about twenty inches in diameter, from forty-four to one hundred and twenty-eight dollars a day, averaging one hundred dollars." This is a fair specimen of the moderately fortunate miner.

The story has a shady as well as a bright side, and would be incomplete unless both were shown. There happened to be a "sickly season" in the autumn at the mines; and many of the miners sank under fever and diseases of the bowels. A severe kind of labor, to which most had been unaccustomed, a complete change of diet and habits, insufficient shelter, continued mental excitement, and the excesses in personal amusement and dissipation which golden gains induced, added to the natural unhealthiness that might have existed in the district at different periods of the year, soon introduced sore bodily troubles upon many of the mining population. No gains could compensate a dying man for the fatal sickness engendered by his own avaricious exertions. In the wild race for riches, the invalid was neglected by old comrades still in rude health and the riotous enjoyment of all the pleasures that gold and the hope of continually adding to their store could bestow. When that was the case with old companions it could not be expected that strangers should care whether the sick man lived or died. Who forsooth among the busy throng would trouble himself with the feeble miner that had miscalculated his energies, and lay dying on the earthen floor of his tent or under the protecting branch of a tree? There were no kind eyes to gaze mournfully on him, hearts to feel, lips to speak softly, and hands to minister to his wants. His gains were swept away to buy a hasty and careless medical attendance; and too generally he died "unwept, unknelled, unknown." Selfishness that heeded not the dying might perchance bury the dead, if only the corrupting corpse stood in the way of working a rich claim—scarcely otherwise. Many, not so far reduced, were compelled to return to their old homes, the living spectres of their former selves, broken in constitution and wearied in spirit; thoroughly satisfied that the diggings were not fit abiding places for them.

The implements at first used in the process of gold seeking, were only the common pick and shovel, and a tin pan or wooden bowl. The auriferous earth when dug out was put into the last, and water being mixed with it, the contents were violently stirred. A peculiar shake of the hand or wrist, best understood and learned by practice, threw occasionally over the edge of the pan or bowl the muddy water and earthy particles, while the metal, being heavier, sunk to the bottom. Repeated washings of this nature, assisted by breaking the hard pieces of earth with the hand or a trowel, soon extricated the gold from its covering and carried away all the dirt. But if even these simple implements were not to be had, a sailor's or butcher's knife, or even a sharpened hard-pointed stick could pick out the larger specimens—the *pepitas, chunks,* or *nuggets,* of different miners—while the finer scales of gold could be washed from the covering earth in Indian willow-woven baskets, clay cups, old hats, or any rude apology for a dish; or the dried sand could be exposed on canvas to the wind, or diligently blown by the breath, until nothing was left but the particles of pure gold that were too heavy to be carried away by these operations. Afterwards the rocker or cradle and Long Tom were introduced, which required several hands to feed and work them; and the returns by which were correspondingly great. Every machine, however, was worked on the same principle, by rocking or washing, of separating by the mechanical means of gravitation, the heavier particles—the gold from stones, and the lighter ones of earth.

Provisions and necessaries, as might have been expected, soon rose in price enormously. At first the rise was moderate indeed, four hundred *per cent.* for flour, and five hundred for beef cattle, while other things were in proportion. But these were trifles. The time soon came when eggs were sold at one, two, and three dollars apiece ; inferior sugar, tea, and coffee, at four dollars a pound in small quantities, or, three or four hundred dollars a barrel ; medicines—say, for laudanum, a dollar a drop, (actually forty dollars were paid for a dose of that quantity,) and ten

A Mining Scene.

dollars a pill or purge, without advice, or with it, from thirty, up, aye, to one hundred dollars. Spirits were sold at various prices, from ten to forty dollars a quart ; and wines at about as much per bottle. Picks and shovels ranged from five to fifteen dollars each ; and common wooden or tin bowls about half as much. Clumsy rockers were sold at from fifty to eighty dollars, and small gold scales, from twenty to thirty. As for beef, little of it was to be had, and then only jerked, at correspondingly high prices. For luxuries—of which there were not many ; if a lucky miner set his heart on some trifle, it might be pickles, fruit, fresh pork, sweet butter, new vegetables, a box of seidlitz powders or of matches, he was prepared to give any quantity of the "dust" rather than be balked. We dare not trust ourselves to name some of the *fancy* prices thus given, lest we should be supposed to be only romancing. No man would give another a hand's turn for less than five dollars; while a day's constant labor of the commonest kind, if it could have been procured at all, would cost from twenty to thirty dollars, at least. When these things, and the risks of sickness, the discomforts of living, and the unusual and severe kind of labor are all balanced against the average gains, it may appear that, after all, the miners were only enough paid.

About the end of May we left San Francisco almost a desert place, and such it continued during the whole summer and autumn months. Many ships with valuable cargoes had meanwhile arrived in the bay, but the seamen deserted. The goods at great expense had been somehow got landed, but there was nobody to take care of them, or remove them from the wharves where they lay exposed to the weather, and blocking up the way. The merchants who remained were in a feverish bustle. They were selling goods actually arrived at high prices, and could get no hands to assist them in removing and delivering the articles. By and bye, some of the miners came back to their old homes; but most of them were emaciated, feeble and dispirited. Here, therefore, as at the mines, the prices of labor and all necessaries rose exceedingly. The common laborer, who had formerly been content with his dollar a day, now proudly refused ten; the mechanic, who had recently been glad to receive two dollars, now rejected twenty for his day's services. It was certainly a great country, this—there was no mistake about it; and every subject was as lofty, independent, and seemingly as rich as a king. No money indeed could now buy the servile labor of many persons who had lately been glad to receive the meanest employment; and thus many necessary acts, and much manual business had to be done by principals themselves, or not done at all. Real estate, meanwhile, had rapidly advanced in value, and generally was considered worth from five to ten times its former price.

Within the first eight weeks after the "diggings" had been

fairly known, two hundred and fifty thousand dollars had reached San Francisco in gold dust, and within the next eight weeks, six hundred thousand more. These sums were all to purchase, at any price, additional supplies for the mines. Coin grew scarce, and all that was in the country was insufficient to satisfy the increased wants of commerce in one town alone. Gold dust, therefore, soon became a circulating medium, and after some little demur at first, was readily received by all classes at sixteen dollars an ounce. The authorities, however, would only accept it in payment of customs duties at ten dollars per ounce, with the privilege of redemption, by payment of coin, within a limited time.

When subsequently immigrants began to arrive in numerous bands, any amount of labor could be obtained, provided always a most unusually high price was paid for it. Returned diggers, and those who cautiously had never went to the mines, were then also glad enough to work for rates varying from twelve to thirty dollars a day ; at which terms most capitalists were somewhat afraid to commence any heavy undertaking. The hesitation was only for an instant. Soon all the labor that could possibly be procured, was in ample request, at whatever rates were demanded. The population of a great State was suddenly flocking in upon them, and no preparations had hitherto been made for its reception. Building lots had to be surveyed, and streets graded and planked —hills levelled—hollows, lagoons, and the bay itself piled, capped, filled up and planked—lumber, bricks, and all other building materials, provided at most extraordinarily high prices—houses built, finished and furnished—great warehouses and stores erected—wharves run far out into the sea—numberless tons of goods removed from shipboard, and delivered and shipped anew every where—and ten thousand other things had all to be done without a moment's unnecessary delay. Long before these things were completed, the sand-hills and barren ground around the town were overspread with a multitude of canvas, blanket and bough-covered tents,—the bay was alive with shipping and small craft carrying passengers and goods backwards and forwards,—the unplanked, ungraded, unformed streets, (at one time moving heaps of dry sand and dust ; at another, miry abysses, whose treacherous depths sucked in horse and dray, and occasionally man himself,) were crowded with human beings from every corner of the universe and of every tongue—all excited and busy, plotting, speaking, working, buying and selling town lots, and beach and water lots, shiploads of every kind of assorted merchandise, the ships themselves, if they could,—though that was not often,—gold dust in hundred weights, ranches square leagues in extent, with their thousands of cattle—allotments in hundreds of contemplated towns, already prettily designed and laid out,—on paper,—and, in short, speculating and gambling in every branch of modern commerce, and in many strange things peculiar to the time and the place. *And every body made money, and was suddenly growing rich.*

The loud voices of the eager seller and as eager buyer—the laugh of reckless joy—the bold accents of successful speculation—the stir and hum of active hurried labor, as man and brute, horse and bullock, and their guides, struggled and managed through heaps of loose rubbish, over hills of sand, and among deceiving deep mud pools and swamps, filled the amazed newly arrived immigrant with an almost appalling sense of the exuberant life, energy and enterprise of the place. He breathed quick and faintly—his limbs grew weak as water—and his heart sunk within him as he thought of the dreadful conflict, when he approached and mingled among that confused and terrible business battle.

Gambling saloons, glittering like fairy palaces, like them suddenly sprang into existence, studding nearly all sides of the plaza, and every street in its neighborhood. As if intoxicating drinks from the well plenished and splendid bar they each contained were insufficient to gild the scene, music added its loudest, if not its sweetest charms ; and all was mad, feverish mirth, where fortunes were lost and won, upon the green cloth, in the twinkling of an eye. All classes gambled in those days, from the starched white neck-clothed professor of religion to the veriest black rascal that earned a dollar for blackening massa's boots. Nobody had leisure to think even for a moment of his occupation, and how it was viewed in Christian lands. The heated brain was never allowed to get cool while a bit of coin or dust was left. These saloons, therefore, were crowded, night and day, by impatient revellers who never could satiate themselves with excitement, nor get rid too soon of their golden heaps.

We are, however, anticipating and going ahead too fast. We cannot help it. The very thought of that wondrous time is an electric spark that fires into one great flame all our fancies, passions and experiences of the fall of the eventful year, 1849. The remembrance of those days comes across us like the delirium of fever; we are caught by it before we are aware, and forthwith begin to babble of things which to our sober Atlantic friends seem more the ravings of a madman, than plain, dull realities. The world had perhaps never before afforded such a spectacle; and probably nothing of the kind will be witnessed again for generations to come. Happy the man who can tell of those things which he saw and perhaps himself did, at San Francisco, at that time. He shall be an oracle to admiring neighbors. A city of twenty or thirty thousand inhabitants improvised—the people nearly all adult males, strong in person, clever, bold, sanguine, restless and reckless——But really we must stop now, and descend to our simple "annals."

CHAPTER VII.

1849.

The Alta California newspaper established.—Delegates elected to the proposed convention to be held at San José.—New town council elected.—Three town councils at one time.—Meeting of the convention to frame a civil government postponed.—Public meeting respecting the conflicting councils.—Public meeting concerning negro slavery.—Town councils resigned, and legislative assembly chosen.—Arrival of the steamship California.—Address of delegates to civil government convention.—Arrival of steamship Oregon, and Col. John W. Geary with the first United States mails.—General Riley announced territorial governor.—Acts of the legislative assembly and of the governor.—Meetings concerning municipal and State governments.—Growth, population and general prosperity of the city.—Gambling and other vices and crimes.

JANUARY 4th.—"The Star and Californian" is dropped, and the "Alta California," a weekly newspaper of the same character and appearance, and published by the same parties, is issued in its stead.

JANUARY 8th.—Election of delegates to the proposed convention at San José, in conformity with the resolutions of the public meeting of 23d ultimo, when Wm. M. Stewart, Francis J. Lippitt, Elbert P. Jones, Myron Norton and John A. Patterson were chosen.

JANUARY 15th.—New election of town council, which resulted in the choice of Stephen C. Harris, Lazarus Everhart, Stephen A. Wright, Daniel Starks, Isaac Montgomery, John Sirrine, and C. E. Wetmore. Mr. Sirrine was appointed president.

There were at this period *three* town councils in San Francisco, viz. :—the old one of 1848, not yet dissolved, and those elected on the 27th December and 15th January respectively. The former of the two last insisted that the council of the previous year had expired the very day of its own election on the 27th December, and therefore the members met and transacted business as if it alone represented the town. A majority of the old council, however, insisted on continuing in office till those whom they considered their proper successors were chosen, and accordingly, they supported the council elected on the 15th January, and resolved to transfer the municipal records into its hands. The citizens generally seemed adverse to the pretensions of the old council, as scarcely a fourth part of the numbers that voted on the 27th December voted on the second election of the 15th January. Strong party and personal feelings existed among the inhabitants at this time. The alcalde, T. M. Leavenworth, and his official acts, among other subjects of contention, were vigorously attacked by one party, and as strenuously defended by the other.

JANUARY 24th.—The corresponding committee for the District of San Francisco, on the suggestion of the delegates chosen at Monterey, recommend a postponement of the assembling of the convention for framing a civil government to the first day of May, in order to give the southern districts sufficient time to elect delegates and appear at the convention. The movement for the election of such delegates is general over the country, as the people are satisfied that the present state of civil disorganization cannot safely be longer permitted.

FEBRUARY.—It was estimated that the population was now about two thousand.

FEBRUARY 12th.—Public meeting of citizens to consider the anomalous position of *two* town councils existing and acting, independently of each other, at the same time. Myron Norton was called upon to preside, and T. W. Perkins to act as secretary. George Hyde submitted a plan of municipal organization and government, which was adopted by the meeting; and resolutions were passed requesting the members of both councils to resign, and appointing an election of fifteen town councillors and three justices of the peace, to take place on the 21st instant.

FEBRUARY 17th and 24th.—Public meetings to consider the propriety of instructing the delegates to the convention of the 1st of May to oppose any incipient act that might tend to the introduction of negro slavery into California. Capt. J. L. Folsom was chosen president, and B. R. Buckelew secretary. It was known that the whole delay of Congress in providing a territorial government had arisen from the disputes, and the apparent impossibility of agreement between the two great political parties on this subject. The inhabitants of the country itself might be said to be unanimous against slavery in all shapes among them; and they were justly indignant that the Atlantic politicians should pretend to dictate to them any thing on the matter. At these meetings, resolutions were passed, instructing the delegates of the San Francisco district, "by all honorable means to oppose any act, measure, provision or ordinance that is calculated to further the introduction of domestic slavery into the territory of California."

FEBRUARY 21st.—In compliance with the wishes of the meeting of the 12th instant, the members of both town councils resigned their office, and an election of fifteen members of a legislative assembly and three justices of the peace took place this day, which it was hoped would settle all disputes between the rival partisans. The parties elected were as follows:—

Justices of the Peace.

Myron Norton,	Theron R. Per Lee,	Wm. M. Stewart.

District Legislature.

Stephen A. Wright,	Isaac Montgomery,	Thomas J. Roach,
Alfred J. Ellis,	Wm. M. Smith,	Wm. F. Swasey,
Henry A. Harrison,	Andrew J. Grayson,	Francis J. Lippitt,
George C. Hubbard,	James Creighton,	George F. Lemon.
George Hyde,	Robert A. Parker,	

On the 5th proximo these gentlemen met, and chose various officials; but as the whole proceedings were afterwards set aside, it is unnecessary here to detail more of them.

FEBRUARY 28th.—The steamship "*California*," being the first of the line of mail steamers along the coast, arrived. The citizens hailed her appearance with many cheers and other demonstrations of joy. General Persifer F. Smith, a passenger on this vessel, came to take command of the Pacific division of the military department of the United States, which comprehends Oregon and California.

MARCH.—An address to the people of California was issued by several of the delegates for San Francisco, Monterey, Sonoma, Sacramento, and other parts of the country, recommending a postponement of the meeting of the convention to frame a civil government, to the first Monday of August, and that the place of meeting be Monterey, instead of San José.

MARCH 31st.—The Pacific mail steamship "*Oregon*" arrived with about three hundred and fifty passengers, among whom were Col. John W. Geary and family. Col. Geary had been appointed postmaster for San Francisco, with powers to create post-offices and appoint postmasters throughout the territory; also to establish mail routes and make contracts for carrying the mails. He was the bearer of despatches from the United States Government to the commanders of the military and naval forces on the Pacific, and brought with him the first regular mail from the Atlantic States that was opened in San Francisco.

APRIL 13th.—Order issued by Brigadier-General Bennet Riley, announcing that he had assumed command of the tenth military department of the United States, and the administration of civil affairs in California.

JUNE.—For the last six months, and particularly during the last two, the public events of most consequence to San Francisco resolve themselves into two divisions, viz.: the appointment of proper district and municipal authorities, and the formation of a State government. We have already chronicled several meetings on both these heads; but notwithstanding all that had been said or done, no common action could be obtained to promote the ends in view to the satisfaction of all parties.

As regarded the municipal question, the recently appointed legislative assembly abolished the office of alcalde, and substituted the senior justice of the peace in his place. Afterwards, the alcalde, Mr. Leavenworth, was ordered to give up the town documents and official papers in his hands; upon which he applied for advice to General Smith, who recommended him not to comply with the demands of the legislative assembly. That body next ordered the election of a sheriff, who, when appointed, proceeded to take what he considered legal steps against Mr. Leavenworth, who had meanwhile resuscitated the old council of 1848, to sanction and confirm his proceedings, which it readily did, appealing to Governor Riley for advice and protection. The governor, accordingly, on the 4th of June, issued a proclamation to the citizens, recognizing the office and power of the existing alcalde, declaring the legislative assembly an illegal body, and forbidding payment of taxes to them.

While that was the state of affairs regarding the municipality and District of San Francisco, the governor, on the 3d of June, issued a proclamation to the people of California, in which, after narrating the position of the country, and the necessity of both district and general governments, he appointed the first day of August for the election, *first*, of certain specified municipal and district provisional officials over the whole country, according to Mexican custom; and *second*, of thirty-seven delegates to be chosen from the specified districts, as delegates to a general convention to be held at Monterey, on the first day of September next, for the purpose of forming a State Constitution.

Following upon these proclamations, the people of San Francisco held a mass meeting in Portsmouth Square, on the 12th of June, when Wm. M. Stewart was chosen president, and E. Gould Buffum, secretary. This meeting was large and enthusiastic, and after being addressed by several eloquent speakers, *resolved* that the people of California had a *right* to organize a government for their own protection—that, therefore, delegates should be chosen to frame a constitution—and that a committee of five be immediately appointed by the president of the meeting to correspond with the other districts of the country, in order to carry out in a practical manner the said resolutions. The meeting refused to recognize Governor Riley's proclamations as binding on them. The committee chosen consisted of Peter H. Burnett, Wm. D. M. Howard, Myron Norton, E. Gould Buffum, and E. Gilbert. This committee, on the 18th of June, issued an address to the public, in which, without admitting the right or power in Governor Riley to "*appoint*" time or place for the election of delegates and assembling of the convention, yet considered it best, as a matter of expediency, to adopt the terms of the governor's proclamation in these respects.

These steps settled the plan and course of future proceedings so far as the State Government was concerned. In respect to the municipality the legislative assembly published a long address to their constituents, in answer to Governor Riley's proclamation of the 3d, and the very "uncourteous and disrespectful" one of the 4th June. In this document, they resolved that they were a legally constituted body, and declared their determination to hold office and to act in the same until formally deprived of their authority by the people from whom it was derived. Thus arose a sort of civil war on a small scale. The assembly afterwards having considered it expedient to appeal directly to the people, a ballot was taken on the subject on the 9th July, when one hundred and sixty-seven votes appeared for their continuance in office, and only seven against it. But as this result showed either the indifference of the citizens on the subject, since but a small portion of their number voted, or else their tacit desire that the legislative assembly should altogether cease, that body thought fit, at last, to dissolve itself. Thus the old alcalde, Mr. Leavenworth, was virtually reinstated in triumph, and no obstacle left to the several elections ordered by Governor Riley's proclamation of the 3d of June. These various meetings and other proceedings narrated may possess little interest for the present inhabitants of San Francisco; but they certainly much excited those who dwelt in the town at the time of their occurrence. The excesses of the "hounds," fully described in a subsequent chapter, were much encouraged by the dissensions and jealousies which existed among the rival politicians and local partisans of those days.

During the first half of this year, San Francisco was rapidly increasing the number of its houses and population. Every day added sensibly to both. The mines were continuing to yield large returns, most of which were immediately forwarded to San Francisco, in exchange for new supplies. The bay was filling with shipping from all the ports of the Pacific coast of both Americas, from the Sandwich Islands, and from China, Australia and other ports towards the west. Nearly two hundred square-rigged vessels lay at anchor about the end of July. Hosts of passengers by these vessels, after staying but a little while in the town, hurried off to the diggings. Meanwhile, others who had been fortunate were returning from the mines with bags of gold dust, to squander in gambling, in drinking and all manner of thoughtless extravagance and dissipation. Gambling, which previously had been carried on to so great an extent, was now beginning to be developed on a still larger scale. Saloons, at the public tables of which every variety of game was to be found, arose in all quarters of the town, where play was carried on during the whole twenty-four hours, and where the gross amount of money or gold dust staked was enormous. It might almost be said that the same spirit of gambling or speculation reigned in every department of business; and prices rose and fell, and for-

San Francisco, in 1849, from head of Clay Street.

tunes were made, and lost, and made again, according to the "play" of the parties engaged. New towns, all of course in splendid locations, were beginning to be projected, and the building lots in them sold for immense sums of money. Sacramento and Stockton were among the first and best needed of these places; and soon they took such positions as commanded success and insured future prosperity. But besides these two cities, a multitude of other and inferior places were projected, and while the future of the whole country was uncertain, but over which hung a certain vague grandeur, their pretensions were very respectably set forth, and speculation in their allotments was rife. Some of these schemes have since shared in the general advancement of the country; while of others probably nothing again will ever be heard.

A short experience of the mines had satisfied most of the

citizens of San Francisco that, in vulgar parlance, all was not gold that glittered, and that hard work was not easy,—sorry truisms for weak or lazy men. They returned very soon to their old quarters, and found that much greater profits, with far less labor, were to be found in supplying the necessities of the miners, and speculating in real estate. For a time every body made money, in spite of himself. The continued advance in the price of goods, and especially in the value of real estate, gave riches at once to the fortunate owner of a stock of the former or of a single advantageously situated lot of the latter. When trade was brisk, and profits so large, nobody grudged to pay any price, or any rent, for a proper place of business. Coin was scarce, but bags of gold dust furnished a circulating medium, which answered all purposes. The gamblers at the public saloons staked such bags, or were supplied with money upon them by the "banks," till the whole was exhausted. There were few regular houses erected, for neither building materials nor sufficient labor were to be had; but canvas tents, or houses of frame, served the immediate needs of the place. Great quantities of goods continued to pour in from the nearer ports, till there were no longer stores to receive and cover them. In addition to Broadway Wharf, Central Wharf was projected, subscribed for, and commenced. Several other small wharves at landing-places were constructed at the cost of private parties. All these, indeed, extended but a little way across the mud flat in the bay, and were of no use at low tide; yet they gave considerable facilities for landing passengers and goods in open boats. The different religious denominations were beginning to make movements as to creating churches and appointing clergymen; while the Freemasons and Odd-Fellows were likewise beginning to take their characteristic first steps. Seamen deserted their vessels, as a matter of course, so soon as they dropped anchor in the bay, and hastened to the mines. Society, not merely there, but in San Francisco, was in a state of utter disorganization, which became worse and more terrible as the autumn and winter months brought new thousands of immigrants upon the place. We have seen that there was neither a proper government for the State, nor recognized municipal authorities, who could have protected the citizens and established order, and made provision for the systematic extension of the town and reception of the coming crowds. There was a military governor, indeed, and martial law could have been adopted, but the governor had not sufficient force at his command to curb the wild elements of the population ; nor, at best, would his forcible interference have satisfied American ideas of civil independence and the national privilege of self-government. Thefts, robberies, murders, and other outrages of the most desperate and criminal nature were taking place, and there were no proper officials to take cognizance of them, and bring the offenders to justice. Every man was intent on merely making money, and provided an outrage did not, in a direct manner, personally or pecuniarily affect himself, he was content to shut his eyes to the ultimate consequences.

By the beginning of 1849, the population of San Francisco had increased to two thousand. Two months later it was probably about three thousand ; whilst in July, when the riots and outrages of the "hounds" came to a height, it might be nearly five thousand. This was what might be called the usual and permanent population of the time—if any thing could be supposed permanent in so frail and fluctuating a place, although every day new arrivals of immigrants added temporarily to the number, till they flocked off to Sacramento, Stockton, and the mines.

CHAPTER VIII.

1849.

The Hounds.—Election of Supreme Judge, delegates to convention, and municipal officers.—Alcalde's address to the Ayuntamiento.—Duties of prefects.—The prison brig Euphemia, and storeship Apollo.—Churches.—Regulations and appointments of the Ayuntamiento.—The "Pacific News" commenced.—Meeting of the Constitution Convention at Monterey.—Merchants' Exchange. — Steam Navigation. — Death of Nathan Spear. — First democratic meeting. — Circus opened.—Constitution approved and State officers elected.—First habitation on Rincon Point.—Thanksgiving Day.—Judge Almond's court.—The "Alta California."—First great fire.

JULY 15th, *et seq.*—The affair of the "*hounds*" came to an end. This was an association of young men for the declared purpose of assisting each other in sickness, or when peril of any kind threatened any of the members. It had been imperfectly organized in the beginning of the year, and was virtually a gang of public robbers. The members assumed a kind of military discipline, under the guidance of regular leaders, who wore a uniform, and occasionally, but only on Sundays, paraded the streets with flags displayed and drum and fife playing. They attacked the tents of inoffensive people, chiefly foreigners, and if they could not extort money from the owners or inmates by threats, tore them down to the ground, and stole or destroyed money, jewels, and every thing valuable on the premises. These outrages, perpetrated usually at night, when the more peaceable citizens had retired to rest, were so frequent that the "hounds" became a terror to all well-disposed people of the town. They invaded the stores, taverns, and houses of Americans themselves, and rudely demanded whatever they desired. They could not be refused, for their numbers were so great, while they were well armed, that nobody durst resist them. The town was paralyzed with terror, and the "hounds," who latterly adopted the name of "*regulators*," committed the most violent and cruel outrages in open defiance of the law and common humanity. A series of the most barbarous, destructive, and daring attacks, were perpetrated by those desperadoes on Sunday, the 15th of July, which at last effectually roused the community to a determined counteraction. They formed themselves into a police force, and proceeded to measure their strength against the rioters. They were successful, and immediately afterwards some twenty of the offenders were put upon trial. At this time San Francisco had no proper municipal organization, while neither was there an efficient State government to which the citizens could appeal for protection. They therefore had to do every thing for themselves. They accordingly appointed judges and counsel for both prosecution and defence, and at once proceeded with the trial of the rioters, or *conspirators*, as they were charged with being. A jury found them guilty of conspiracy, riot, robbery, and assault, with intent to kill. Nine were convicted and sentenced to various periods of imprisonment and considerable fines, and the town was purged for a while of the more violent ruffians that had infested it. A full account of these proceedings will be found in the *Third Part* of this work.

August 1st.—The elections ordered by Governor Riley took place in a spirited, though orderly manner. The candidates were numerous, and the following parties were elected :—

Judge of the Supreme Court.

Peter H. Burnett, who had 1298 votes in San Francisco, and 76 at San José.

Prefect.

Horace Hawes, 913 votes.

Sub-Prefects.

Francis Guerrero, 1503 votes.
Joseph R. Curtis, 1399 "

First Alcalde.

John W. Geary, 1516 votes.

Second Alcalde.

Frank Turk, 1055 votes.

Ayuntamiento, or Town Council.

Talbot H. Green, 1510 votes.	**Rodman M. Price, 840 votes.**
Henry A. Harrison, 1491 "	**Wm. H. Davis, 835 "**
Alfred J. Ellis, 1354 "	**Bezer Simmons, 825 "**
Stephen C. Harris, 1323 "	**Samuel Brannan, 823 "**
Thos. B. Winton, 1052 "	**Wm. M. Stewart, 815 "**
John Townsend, 1052 "	**Gabriel B. Post, 691 "**

Delegates to Convention.		*Supernumerary Delegates.*	
Edward Gilbert,	1512 votes.	Wm. D. M. Howard,	876 votes.
Myron Norton,	1436 "	Francis J. Lippitt,	874 "
Wm. M. Gwin,	1073 "	Alfred J. Ellis,	872 "
Joseph Hobson,	839 "	Francisco Sanchez,	872 "
Wm. M. Stewart,	833 "	Rodman M. Price,	871 "

There were some ten or a dozen different tickets at this election, upon all of which the name of Col. John W. Geary appeared for the office of First Alcalde. He consequently received the whole number of votes polled. This decided evidence of public confidence was deserved and appreciated. At the first meeting of the *ayuntamiento*, the newly elected *alcalde* presented the following address. It is a document worthy of preservation, being well written, and giving a faithful account of the gloomy aspect of public affairs in San Francisco at that period, and much useful advice to those having the interests of the city in charge :—

" *Gentlemen of the City Councils* :—Having been called by the unanimous voice of my fellow-citizens to the office of chief magistrate of the city of San Francisco, I find it impossible to convey to them by words the feelings excited by this decided manifestation of their confidence and approbation. Profoundly sensible that the honor and trust which have been conferred upon me far transcend my deserts, I can make no other return, than a heartfelt declaration of my gratitude, accompanied by the assurance, that to the extent of my power, I will with zeal and fidelity cause the observance of every law and ordinance made for the good of this city.

"The citizens of San Francisco, appreciating the importance of the present crisis in the territorial history of California, and particularly the high and important destiny of their city, have conferred upon you, gentlemen, the onerous duty, yet high honor, of legislating for their future welfare and prosperity.

"As your presiding officer, I deem it my duty to call your attention to the situation of the city, and to ask your co-operation in making it, in point of order and security, what it must shortly be in wealth and importance, the first city, and great commercial and moneyed emporium of the Pacific. To effect this, gentlemen, it will require of you great devotion to your duties, as well as great diligence and a liberal supply of funds for municipal purposes.

" Economy in the expenditure of the public money is at all times desirable and necessary; but situated as we are here, without any superior body to legislate for us, the people of the city will, of necessity, be called upon to assume a responsibility in the enactment of laws, and in the expenditure of money for public purposes, not usual under ordinary circumstances. Of this every citizen of San Francisco is fully aware, and all who desire the prosperity and good government of the city will stand ready to sustain you in whatever you may do for its permanent improvement and benefit.

"At this time we are without a dollar in the public treasury, and it is to be feared the city is greatly in debt. You have neither an office for your magistrate, nor any other public edifice. You are without a single police officer or watchman, and have not the means of confining a prisoner for an hour; neither have you a place to shelter, while living, sick and unfortunate strangers who may be cast upon our shores, or to bury them when dead. Public improvements are unknown in San Francisco. In short, you are without a single requisite necessary for the promotion of prosperity, for the protection of property, or for the maintenance of order.

"I therefore repeat, that the present exigency in public affairs requires the utmost diligence on your part, in the performance of all your duties, as well as a liberal supply of funds, to provide for the security of life and property in San Francisco.

"There is perhaps no city upon the earth where a tax for the support of its municipal government can be more justly imposed than here. Real estate, both improved and unimproved, within a short space of time, has increased in value in many instances a thousand-fold, and even at its present high rates, will produce in the shape of rents the largest average income upon record. Yet notwithstanding this unprecedented increased value of real estate, the burdens of government should not be borne by a tax upon that species of property alone; each and every kind of business carried on within the limits of the district should bear its just and proper share of taxation. Equal justice to all should be your guide, and if strictly followed, none will have just cause of complaint.

"The charters of most cities in the United States, granted by the Legislatures, give the corporation the right to levy and collect a tax, as well to defray the expenses of its municipal government as for public improvements; and it is usual to submit a tax bill to the Legislature for its confirmation. This is done to prevent abuses. Yet I do not know of an instance where the tax imposed has been reduced by the Legislature. In towns not incorporated there is no resort to be had to the Legislature for a confirmation of the tax laws. The town officers, chosen by the people, impose the taxes, and collect a sufficient revenue by common consent; and their right to do so is never questioned. That you have a right to levy and collect a reasonable and proper tax, for the support of your municipal government, cannot, in my judgment, for a moment be questioned. In the absence of State legislative authority, you, as the representatives of the people, are supreme in this district, and your acts, so long as you confine them strictly to the legitimate sphere of your duty, will not only be sanctioned and approved by the present worthy Executive of our government in California, but will be most promptly confirmed by the Legislature, whenever one shall be assembled either for the Territory or State.

"I would, therefore, recommend that with all convenient despatch you ascertain, as near as possible, the amount of funds deemed necessary for the support of a proper and efficient municipal government for one year; that when you shall have determined this, you shall proceed to collect a just equitable tax upon real estate and upon sales at auction; and that you require all merchants, traders, storekeepers, &c., to take out a license for the transaction of their business, paying therefor an amount proportionate to the quantity of merchandise vended by them. Also, that all drays, lighters, and boats, used in the transportation of merchandise, and of passengers, to or from vessels in the harbor, be licensed.

"There is also another class of business proper to be taxed, which although sometimes prohibited by law, yet in many countries is regulated by law. I recommend you to adopt the latter course. The passion for gaming is universal, even where the severest penalties are imposed to prevent its indulgence. And it is a fact well known and understood, whenever gaming tables are licensed and subject to proper police regulations, they are less injurious to the interests and morals of the community than when conducted in defiance of law. In the one case the proprietors are amenable to the law which authorizes them, and are subject to proper control; while on the other hand, if prohibited, the evasion of the law by such means as are usually resorted to, does but increase the evil, and the community is in no way benefited. I would, therefore, recommend, under present circumstances, and until State legislation can be had on the subject, that you license gaming and billiard tables.

"For the collection of each and every tax, the imposition of which I have recommended, you have the example of almost every city in the world. A revenue is necessary for the proper maintenance and support of the municipality, — and it is a maxim everywhere acknowledged, that every citizen should, for the privileges he enjoys, aid in the support of the government under which he lives, and which affords him protection of life, liberty, and property.

"The public documents containing all the muniments of title, &c., for real estate, are not to be found in possession of my predecessor, but in the private keeping of a portion of the citizens.

"As these documents have not been transferred to me in a legal manner by an officer of the law, and as there may be a probability of their being more or less mutilated, I particularly request you to grant me authority to appoint a committee of three respectable and intelligent citizens, who, under oath, shall make an inventory of the said documents, and a schedule of any *mutilations*, *erasures*, or *interlineations*, which may be found on their pages. I feel confident that the importance of this matter has already suggested to you such a measure, inasmuch as the value of titles to real estate might be greatly impaired by failing to adopt it. This course will not only relieve from unjust suspicion the officer to whose charge and safe-keeping those documents are intrusted by the law, but it will also render him responsible for his own acts, and not for those of his predecessor, or of any other person.

"The laws under which we act oblige each officer, without regard to his station, to advance, with his utmost zeal, the cause of education. I, therefore, strongly urge upon you the propriety of adopting measures by which the children of the high, the low, the rich and the poor of this district, can have equal advantages of drinking freely at the fountain of primary knowledge; and it is to be hoped that our territory, which is ere long to be erected into a State, and placed by the side of her elder sisters of the Union, will show to them that she fully appreciates education as the only safeguard of our republican institutions; that the liberties of the people are based upon their intelligence, and that in this respect, as well as in all others, California will present herself to the world a model Republic, without spot or blemish.

"John W. Geary,
"*First Alcalde of the District of San Francisco. Cal.*"

Prison-brig Euphemia, and Sto-e-ship Apollo.

Prefect Hawes also ably addressed the council, chiefly explaining the duties of *prefects*, which are, he says, "to take care of public order and tranquillity; to publish and circulate, without delay, observe, enforce, and cause to be observed and enforced, the laws, throughout their respective districts; and for the execution of these duties they are clothed with certain powers, which are clearly specified and defined. They are particularly enjoined to attend to the subject of public instruction, and see that common schools be not wanting in any of the towns of their respective districts. They are also required to propose measures for the encouragement of agriculture and all branches of industry, instruction, and public beneficence, and for the execution of new works of public utility and the repair of old ones. They constitute the ordinary channel of communication between the governor and the authorities of the district, and are to communicate all representations coming from the latter, accompanied with the necessary information."

The first money appropriated by the ayuntamiento was for the purchase of the brig *Euphemia,* which was converted into a *prison* for the confinement of criminals. This was the first jail established in the place where convicted rogues could be kept in custody. We give a correct representation of the Euphemia. The store-ship *Apollo,* which is seen on the illustration, was anchored in the cove, some distance from the beach. It was subsequently used for a lodging-house and drinking-saloon. As the city improvements progressed, lots were piled, capped, and filled in on the flat covered by the waters of the bay, far beyond where the Apollo lay ; and strangers visiting the city were astonished to see the hull of a large ship located in the very heart of the city, surrounded on all sides with large blocks of substantial stone and brick edifices.

August 5th.—The first Protestant Church in California was dedicated by the Baptists. At this time the Episcopalians, Presbyterians, Congregationalists, and Methodists, were taking steps to build places of worship for themselves, while most of these denominations had already established sabbath-schools. The Roman Catholics had also erected a church in Vallejo-street, at which divine service was regularly performed on Sundays. The Rev. T. D. Hunt, whose appointment was noticed before, officiated at the chaplaincy ; and Mr. Lyman, a Mormon preacher, was holding forth at the Institute, on Portsmouth Square.

August 6th, 8th, and 11th.—The ayuntamiento meet, take the oaths of office, and organize and distribute themselves into various committees, for the purpose of systematically conducting the affairs of the town. On the 13th, they appointed the following municipal officials :—

Frank Turk, *Secretary.*
William M. Eddy, *City Surveyor.*
P. C. Landers, *Collector of Taxes.*
And on the 20th of the month,
Dr. T. R. Palmer, *City Physician.*
Jonathan Cade, *Sergeant-at-Arms.*
Malachi Fallon, *Captain of Police.*
A. G. Peachy, *City Attorney.*
John E. Townes, *Sheriff.*
Benj. Burgoyne, *City Treasurer.*

View of San Francisco in 1849, from head of California street.

AUGUST 27th.—The "*Pacific News,*" a San Francisco tri-weekly newspaper, published by Messrs. Falkner and Leland, makes its first appearance. This paper was the second in San Francisco at this period, and continued until 1851, when, after having several times changed its proprietors and political complexion, it expired. The only other newspaper in California was the "*Placer Times,*" published weekly at Sacramento ; but which merged into a daily, and was afterwards issued in San Francisco

The ayuntamiento this day issue an ordinance (subsequently amended and re-issued) for raising a revenue for municipal purposes, chiefly by means of a *percentage* duty on the sale of merchandise and real estate, and heavy license duties imposed on those engaged in different kinds of business. This was the beginning of those steps by which a very great revenue was afterwards collected.

SEPTEMBER 1st.—The convention of delegates to frame a State Constitution met at Monterey; and on the 4th instant, chose Robert Semple president, and Capt. Wm. G. Marcy secretary. The Constitution was finished and signed by the delegates on the 13th of October.

SEPTEMBER 10th.—The first "Merchants' Exchange" was projected a short time before this date; and at a public meeting of citizens, held to-day, the scheme was approved of and subscribed to by a considerable number of merchants and others. The undertaking, however, after going on some time, seems to have been dropped; and in November we find Mr. E. E. Dunbar opening a subscription "Merchants' Exchange and Reading Room" in Washington street, which was patronized by most mercantile people in the town.

OCTOBER 26th.—Steam navigation is beginning to be adopted in the bay and its upper waters. Just two years before this time Wm. A. Leidesdorff had attempted to run a small steamboat, about the size of a ship's jolly-boat, which had been procured from the Russian settlement at Sitka. But this vessel, in February, 1848, was sunk in one of the severe *northers* that visit the bay; and no steps had been taken to renew the experiment until some time after the gold discoveries made its success certain. Then speculators sent out many proper vessels from the Atlantic States. The "*Pioneer*," a little iron steamer, brought out in pieces from Boston, sailed upon the waters of the Sacramento River about a month before this date; and, being the first that had penetrated so far into the interior, deserves the title she had assumed. On the 9th instant, the small iron steamer "*Mint*" had a trial trip, which was highly satisfactory. She was intended to ply between San Francisco and the towns on the upper waters. This day the steam-propeller "*McKim*" left for Sacramento. Before this time voyages across the bay and up the Sacramento and San Joaquin Rivers were made in schooners and launches. These vessels were often detained a week or ten days in sailing that distance, which a steamer now accomplishes in half a day. Both the steamers mentioned sailed every alternate day from San Francisco, and on the intervening days left Sacramento for the return passage. The fares at first were thirty dollars cabin, and twenty dollars deck. If berths were used, five dollars *extra*. Meals on board, two dollars each. The well known steamer "*Senator*" was shortly afterwards placed on the same station, and the little "*Mint*" withdrawn and placed on another. This was the beginning of a very great increase of the transit trade of the bay. Later years have sent numerous large, well appointed, and beautiful steam-vessels, which have still further developed the interior water traffic, and added immensely to the resources of the country.

OCTOBER 21st.—Mr. Nathan Spear died of a disease of the heart. He was forty-seven years of age, and one of the oldest inhabitants of the place. This gentleman was partner to Mr. Jacob P. Leese, who built the first house and formed the first mercantile establishment in Yerba Buena. The death of Mr. Spear was much regretted by the citizens, and the flags of the ships in the bay were hung at half mast when it was announced.

OCTOBER 25th.—The first *Democratic Meeting* ever held in California assembled this evening at Dennison's Exchange. The attendance was so large that the meeting was compelled to adjourn to the public square. The officers chosen were :—*President*, Col. John W. Geary ; *Vice-Presidents*, Dr. McMillan and Messrs. O. P. Sutton, E. V. Joyce, Thomas J. Agnew, John McVickar, Annis Merrill, and W. H. Jones ; *Secretaries*, Messrs. Joseph T. Downey, J. Ross Brown, Daniel Cronin, and John A. McGlynn. Hon. Wm. VanVorhies delivered a spirited address, and a long series of resolutions expressive of democratic principles were adopted. The chief object of the assembly was to effect a party organization previous to the approaching State elections.

OCTOBER 29th.—Rowe's *Olympic Circus*, which was in a large tent, opened to a numerous attendance of spectators. This was the first public announcement of the dramatic or spectacle kind in San Francisco. The "house" could hold from twelve to fifteen hundred ; and the prices of admission were, three dollars to the pit, five dollars to the boxes, and fifty-five dollars for a private box. Two theatres had some time previously been announced, and were at this time in course of formation.

NOVEMBER 13th.—Ballot taken on the Constitution, and

election for State officers. Party politics were beginning to influence voters in the choice of candidates. The election, however, was conducted in a quiet and orderly manner. In San Francisco two thousand and fifty-one voted *for* the Constitution, and five *against* it. Over the whole country the votes were twelve thousand and sixty-four *for*, and eight hundred and eleven *against*. These numbers were much below what had been anticipated, partly on account of a mistake in the voting tickets at San Francisco, and partly from the heavy rains over the country, which prevented many voters from attending the polling places. Perhaps, also, after the first excitement was over, when the convention closed, the people became indifferent on the subject, and neglected the duty of voting. The following is a list of the State officers, senators, and representatives in Congress, first elected under the Constitution; also, the members of the first Legislature of California (to meet at San José), elected by the citizens of San Francisco.

Governor.
Peter H. Burnett.

Lieutenant Governor.
John McDougal.

United States Senators.
John C. Fremont, Wm. M. Gwin.

Representatives in Congress.
George W. Wright, Edward Gilbert.

Secretary of State.
Wm. Van Vorhies.

Treasurer.
Richard Roman.

Comptroller.
J. S. Houston.

Attorney General.
Edward J. C. Kewen.

Surveyor General.
Charles J. Whiting.

Chief Justice.
S. C. Hastings.

Associate Justices.
J. A. Lyon, Nathaniel Bennett.

State Senators.
Gabriel B. Post, Nathaniel Bennett.

Assembly.
Wm. Van Vorhies, Edmund Randolph, Levi Stowell, J. H. Watson, J. A. Patterson.

NOVEMBER 26th.—The first habitation on Rincon Point, erected by Dr. John H. Gihon. It was an India-rubber tent, and occupied the site of the present U. S. Marine Hospital. The entire hill was covered with gnarled oaks and thick underbrush. There were at that time but several buildings between the Rincon and California street, while the waters of the bay washed the foot of precipitous sand-hills the greater portion of the distance, which rendered it necessary for the pedestrian, when the tide was in, to wade up to his waist in the water in passing from the city to the point, he being compelled to follow the line of the beach. Those hills have since been transplanted into the cove, and made substantial building lots, where large vessels were then anchored.

NOVEMBER 29th.—The governor had appointed this as a day of solemn thanksgiving and prayer for the new State of California, and as such it was very generally observed.

DECEMBER 12th.—Some time previous to this date, the business of the alcalde had so greatly increased, as to render necessary the establishment of another court; and upon application made to the governor, he authorized William B. Almond, Esq., to open and hold a Court of First Instance, with civil jurisdiction only, and that in cases involving sums exceeding one hundred dollars. Judge Almond accordingly organized his court in the old schoolhouse on the plaza; and the novel and summary manner in which he conducted his business and disposed of sometimes very important cases, was a source of as much merriment to some and mortification to others as any thing else then transpiring in the town. Many a wag who was fond of fun, and had nothing better to do, would spend an hour in the court-room to enjoy the satisfaction of observing the chagrin of upstart attorneys, toward whose oratorical eloquence and legal knowledge the judge was wont to exhibit the most mortifying indifference. His Honor, at whose expense many a good anecdote has been told, had a sovereign contempt for Buncombe speeches, legal technicalities, learned opinions, and triumphantly cited precedents. He was a man of quick discernment and clear judgment; and his opinion once formed, and that sometimes occurred before even the first witness was fully heard, his decision was made. Nothing further need be said. His mind was as unalterable as were the laws of the Medes and Persians. Jury trials were then of rare occurrence, and the judge decided the cases that came before him; and there can be no reason to doubt, that his decisions generally were far more just and equitable than those more recently given in courts claiming greater legal knowledge, where learned judges gravely occupy the bench, and tampered juries are influenced more by bribes than testimony. On this day a case was tried in which a physician had sued the captain of a ship for medical attendance upon sick sailors during a voyage around Cape Horn. The prosecutor claimed five hundred dollars. A number of witnesses were called on both sides. The judge sat upon a rickety old chair, with his feet perched higher than his head upon a small mantel over the fire-place, in which a few damp sticks of wood were keeping each other warm by the aid of a very limited supply of burning coals. His Honor employed himself in paring his corns, or scraping his nails, while the "learned counsel" briefly presented the case, and called the first witness, whom the judge instructed, without changing his position, to tell all he knew about the matter, in as few words and as quickly as possible,—at the same time charging the lawyers not to interrupt him with questions. This witness was no sooner done, and he had but little to say, when the counsel called another; but His Honor informed him that it was unnecessary to pursue the inquiry further—the witness had told a plain, straightforward story—the court understood the merits of the matter, and its mind was made up. "But," says a lawyer, "you will at least hear us speak to the points of law?" "That would be a great waste of time, which is very precious," replied the judge; "I award the plaintiff one hundred and fifty dollars. Mr. Clerk, what is the next case?" Thus in less than fifteen minutes a case was equitably disposed of, which in an ordinary court of law might have occupied at least as many days; and in the course of the day, as much business was despatched in the same summary manner, as would occupy most courts an ordinary quarterly term. In the instance related the counsel for the plaintiff pocketed seventy-five dollars of the award, giving his client the balance, who was thus well paid for all the services he had rendered. Young lawyers, however, were not pleased with this summary method of disposing of business. To these the opportunity of making a speech, the tendency of which is usually to render a clear case obscure, though it doubtless serves to display the extent of their wisdom and intelligence, is of quite as much consequence as meat and drink to other people. They could not live without it. Hence, Judge Almond, who deprived them of this exquisite enjoyment, was no favorite with them. On one occasion after a case had been decided, in the usual way, the defeated attorney commenced reading aloud from a book he held in his hand. The judge abruptly turned round, and reminded him that judgment had been rendered, and all further remarks were useless. "I am aware of that," said the sprightly lawyer; "but I thought I would simply read a passage or two to convince you what an old fool Blackstone was." The anecdote was not bad, whether well applied or not, and even though it lacked originality.

The greater part of the business of Judge Almond's court was of a similar character, viz., the settling of claims against owners and masters of ships, instituted by their passengers or crews; and as the decisions were generally against the defendants, it was often maliciously remarked that the judgments of the court were always given against those who were best able to pay the costs. This might have been true, though not in the sense intended; for in these cases, the parties most competent to pay were almost invariably the parties at fault. It was a well-known fact, that during the first great rush of emigration to California, the most shameless impositions were practised upon passengers by shipping merchants and their agents. Vessels that had long been considered unseaworthy were hastily fitted up, without proper accommodations or provisions, and sent on a most dangerous voyage, without even a reasonable expectation in some instances of their reaching their place of destination, with passengers who had been solemnly promised every needed comfort. And, when at sea, they first discovered how they had been deceived, and began to proclaim their grievances, they were merely laughed and scoffed at by the brutal officers appointed (because of their peculiar qualifications for that purpose) to carry out the designs of their employers. These men had practised similar impositions with impunity often before; for how or where could a poor sailor or emigrant passenger obtain satisfaction for wrongs suffered at sea, when the courts, even if appealed to, were so tardy in their movements that the witnesses disappeared before an investigation could take place, or the complainant was subjected to expenses which he had no possible means to defray? Owners and masters of vessels never supposed that in California, where every thing was in a rude and unsettled condition, they would be punished for offences which had been winked at, if not sanctioned, by the legal authorities in the oldest and best regulated communities; hence, they were more reckless, bold and insolent than ever in sending their almost worthless ships around Cape Horn. But they were mistaken. Suits, well founded, were constantly brought against them by the passengers and crews of vessels arriving at San Francisco, and heavy fines and costs imposed for the practice of mean impositions and tyrannical abuses; until at length, Judge Almond's court became such a terror to merchants and captains of ships, that they would sooner compromise, even at a sacrifice, a disputed point with a sailor or passenger, than submit the case to the judgment of His Honor.

DECEMBER 14th.—An edition of the "Alta California" is published tri-weekly; the old weekly issue being also continued.

DECEMBER 24th.—This morning, about six o'clock, the awful cry of *fire* was raised in the city, and in a few hours property valued at more than a million of dollars was totally destroyed. The fire began in *Dennison's Exchange*, about the middle of the eastern side of the plaza, and spreading both ways, consumed nearly all that side of the square, and the whole line of buildings on the south side of Washington street, between Montgomery and Kearny streets. This was the first of the great fires which devastated San Francisco; and it was speedily to be followed by still more extensive and disastrous occurrences of a similar character. Something of the kind had long been anticipated by those who considered the light, combustible materials of which the whole town was constructed. That the flames did not spread further was in a great measure owing to the judicious steps early taken by the municipal authorities in pulling down, or blowing up with gunpowder, the houses at the extremity of the conflagration. Scarcely were the ashes cold when preparations were made to erect new buildings on the old sites; and in several cases within a few days, and in all, within a few weeks, the place was covered as densely as before with houses of every kind. These, like those that had just been destroyed, and like nearly all around, were chiefly composed of wood and canvas, and presented fresh fuel to the great coming conflagrations.

Dennison's Exchange, and Parker House, before the fire, December, 1849.

The first fire of any consequence that had previously occurred in the place broke out in January of this year, when the "Shades Hotel" was destroyed. In June following, the ship "Philadelphia" was burned in the harbor, as preparations were being made for her sailing to the Sandwich Islands.

CHAPTER IX.

1849.

Increase of population.—No proper homes.—Character of the houses.—Condition of the streets.—Employments of the people.—Every thing in apparent confusion; still nobody idle, and much business accomplished.—How the inhabitants lived.—Money rapidly made and freely spent.—Gambling.—Shipping deserted.—Extravagantly high prices obtained for every thing.—Rents and wages.—The mines the source of all the wealth.—Destitution, sickness and death.—Increase of crime.—Aspect of the Plaza.—Mixed character of the inhabitants.—The Post-office.—A pleasant prospect.

THE population of the State, and of San Francisco in particular, had been largely increasing during the last six months. Between the 1st of January, 1849, and the 30th of June following, it was estimated that fifteen thousand had been added to the population of the country; of which number nearly ten thousand came by sea, and landed at San Francisco. Only about two hundred of these were females. The next half year gave an average of four thousand immigrants per month, by sea alone, about five hundred of whom, in all, were females; and the whole of which numbers landed at San Francisco. In the early part of 1849, the arrivals were principally from Chili, Mexico, and other countries on the Pacific coasts of America; but later in the year, an immense number of Americans came direct from the Atlantic States, around Cape Horn, or by way of Panama, while many foreigners also arrived from China and from various parts of Europe. Hitherto the departures were comparatively few. Altogether nearly forty thousand immigrants landed at San Francisco during 1849. Besides that great number, some three thousand or four thousand seamen deserted from the many hundred ships lying in the bay. Probably two-thirds of all these proceeded to the mines, or to various parts of the interior; but, on the other hand, numerous fortunate diggers, or those who had tried gold digging and been disappointed, visited town, to spend their gains, recruit their health, or follow out some new pursuit there. It will be remembered also that somewhere about thirty thousand American immigrants had reached California across the plains, many of whom ultimately settled in San Francisco. Therefore, it may be reasonably estimated, that, at the close of 1849, the population of the town numbered, at least, twenty, and probably nearer

Muddy Streets.

twenty-five thousand souls. A very small proportion of these were females—a still smaller one, children of either sex; while the vast majority of inhabitants were adult males, in the early prime of manhood. This circumstance naturally tended to give a peculiar character to the aspect of the place and habits of the people.

There was no such thing as a *home* to be found. Scarcely even a proper *house* could be seen. Both dwellings and places of business were either common canvas tents, or small rough board shanties, or frame buildings of one story. Only the great gambling saloons, the hotels, restaurants, and a few public buildings and stores had any pretensions to size, comfort or elegance. The site on which the town is built was then still covered with numberless sand-hills. The streets were therefore uneven and irregular. By the continued passage of men, and of horses and drays with building materials and goods, while the rainy season (which commenced earlier than usual, and was remarkably severe) was shedding torrents from the clouds, the different thoroughfares were soon so cut up as to become almost, if not quite impassable. Indeed both horse, or mule and dray were sometimes literally swallowed up in the mud, while their owner narrowly escaped a similar fate. The town authorities caused numberless cart loads of brushwood and limbs of trees to be cut from the surrounding hills, and thrown into the streets; but these only answered a limited and temporary purpose. The difficulty could not thus be remedied. Nobody troubled himself to remove any rubbish from the way; but inmates of tents and houses satisfied themselves with placing a few planks, tobacco-boxes, bags of coffee, barrels of spoiled provisions, or any other available object, across and along the worst parts of the roads, to enable them safely to reach their own dwellings. It was not for every body, however, to attempt to navigate these perilous places, or hope to keep on the narrow, slippery, unsteady, and often interrupted path which spanned the unfathomed abysses of mud and water which lay on all sides. Lanterns were indispensable to pedestrians at night, and even in daylight not a few would lose their footing, and find it difficult to extricate themselves from their unpleasant predicaments.

In those miserable apologies for houses, surrounded by heaps and patches of filth, mud and stagnant water, the strange mixed population carried on business, after a fashion. It is not to be supposed that people could or did manage matters in the strict orderly manner of older communities. Very few were following that particular business to which they had been bred, or for which they were best fitted by nature. Every immigrant on landing at San Francisco became a new man in his own estimation, and was prepared to undertake any thing or any piece of business whatsoever. And truly he did it; but it was with a deal of noise, bustle and unnecessary confusion. The great recognized orders of society were tumbled topsy-turvy. Doctors and dentists became draymen, or barbers, or shoe-blacks; lawyers, brokers and clerks, turned waiters, or auctioneers, or perhaps butchers; merchants tried laboring and lumping, while laborers and lumpers changed to merchants. The idlest might be tempted, and the weakest were able, to do something—to drive a nail in frame buildings, lead a burdened mule, keep a stall, ring a bell, or run a message. Adventurers, merchants, lawyers, clerks, tradesmen, mechanics, and every class in turn kept lodging-houses, eating and drinking houses, billiard rooms and gambling saloons, or single tables at these; they dabbled in "beach and water lots," fifty-vara blocks, and new town allotments over the whole country; speculated in flour, beef, pork and potatoes; in lumber and other building materials; in dry goods and soft, hard goods and wet; bought and sold, wholesale and retail, and were ready to change their occupation and embark in some new nondescript undertaking after two minutes' consideration. All things seemed in the utmost disorder. The streets and passages, such as they were, and the inside of tents and houses, were heaped with all sorts of goods and lumber. There seemed no method in any thing. People bustled and jostled against each other, bawled, railed and fought, cursed and swore, sweated and labored lustily, and somehow the work was done. A spectator would have imagined the confusion inextricable, but soon had reason to change his opinion. Every body was busy, and knew very well what he himself had to do. Heaps of goods disappeared, as if by magic, and new heaps appeared in their place. Where there was a vacant piece of ground one day, the next saw it covered with half a dozen tents or shanties. Horses, mules and oxen forced a way through, across, and over every obstruction in the streets; and men waded and toiled after them. Hundreds of rude houses and tents were daily in the course of erection; they nestled between the sand-hills, covered their tops, and climbed the heights to the north and west of the town.

As we have said, there were no *homes* at this period in San Francisco, and time was too precious for any one to stay within doors to cook victuals. Consequently an immense majority of the people took their meals at restaurants, boarding-houses and hotels —the number of which was naturally therefore very great; while many lodged as well as boarded at such places. Many of these were indeed miserable hovels, which showed only bad fare and worse attendance, dirt, discomfort and high prices. A few others again were of a superior class; but, of course, still higher

Lodging Room.

charges had to be made for the better accommodation. At best all were inconveniently crowded, heated and disagreeable. The whole population was constantly moving, and always visible, which added greatly to its apparent numbers. If only people did not sleep in public, they at least worked, eat, and amused themselves in crowds. But even at night, they lay from half a dozen to two score in a room, on the floor, in rows of cots, or contracted and filthy bunks fastened to the weather-boards from floor to ceiling, in which were immense swarms of fleas and other troublesome vermin. At some lodging-houses and hotels, every superficial inch—on floor, tables, benches, shelves, and beds, was covered with a portion of weary humanity.

While wages and profits were so high, and there was no comfort at their sleeping quarters, men spent money freely at different places of riotous excess, and were indeed forced to pass their hours of leisure or recreation at drinking bars, billiard rooms and gambling saloons. Such places were accordingly crowded with a motley crew, who drank, swore, and gamed to their hearts' content. *Every body did so;* and that circumstance was a sufficient excuse, if one were needed, to the neophyte in debauchery. To vary amusements, occasionally a fancy-dress ball or masquerade would be announced at high prices. There the most extraordinary scenes were exhibited, as might have been expected where the actors and dancers were chiefly hot-headed young men, flush of money and half frantic with excitement, and lewd girls freed from the necessity of all moral restraint. A concert or a lecture would at other times help to entertain the weary spirits of the town. But of all their haunts, the gambling saloons were the most notorious and best patronized.

Gambling was a peculiar feature of San Francisco at this time. It was *the* amusement—*the* grand occupation of many classes—apparently the life and soul of the place. There were hundreds of gambling saloons in the town. The bar-room of every hotel and public house presented its tables to attract the idle, the eager and covetous. Monté, faro, roulette, rondo, rouge et noir and vingt-un, were the games chiefly played. In the larger saloons, beautiful and well-dressed women dealt out the cards or turned the roulette wheel, while lascivious pictures hung on the walls. A band of music and numberless blazing lamps gave animation and a feeling of joyous rapture to the scene. No wonder the unwary visitor was tempted and fell, before he had time to awake from the pleasing delusion. To make a fortune in the turning of a card was delightful—the very mingled hope and fear of eventual success was a charming excitement. For the moment, men felt as great conquerors may be supposed sometimes to feel; they manœuvred on the green cloth,—the field of their operations,—thinking their own skill was playing the game, when chance alone gave the result. At the end of a long evening's campaign of mingled victories and defeats—petty skirmishes—they would either draw off their forces to renew the game next day, or hazard their all, thousands of dollars perhaps, on the issue of one great battle, and a moment afterwards leave the table richer or poorer by a moderate fortune. Again and again, were such campaigns fought, till the excitement and intense desire of playing became chronic. When great sums could no longer be had, small ones served the same purpose ; and were, in the end, lost like the others. Gambling became a regular business ; and those who followed it professionally were really among the richest, most talented and influential citizens of the town.

The sums staked were occasionally enormous. One evening sixteen thousand dollars' worth of gold dust was laid upon a faro table as a bet. This was lost by the keeper of the table, who counted out the money to the winner without a murmur, and continued his business with a cheerful countenance, and apparently with as good spirits as though he had incurred no more than an ordinary loss. As high as twenty thousand dollars, it is said, have been risked upon the turn of a card. Five thousand, three thousand, and one thousand dollars were repeatedly ventured. The ordinary stakes, however, were by no means so high as these sums—from fifty cents to five dollars being the usual amount ; and thus the common day laborer could lay his moderate stake as stylishly as a lord. It was only when the rich gamester was getting desperate, or a half tipsy miner had just come from the diggings with a handsome "pile," that the larger sums were put on the cloth. Generally speaking, the keepers of the tables, or "bankers," had no objection to these heavy stakes ; they knew the game better than the player, and were well aware of all the chances in their own favor. But it was scarcely necessary for the professional gambler to encourage particularly large stakes. The combined amount of all the usual small ones was very large ; while every two minutes there was a new game formed, and new stakes put down. The extensive saloons, in each of which ten or a dozen such tables might be placed, were continually crowded, and around the tables themselves the players often stood in lines three or four deep, every one vieing with his neighbors for the privilege of reaching the board, and staking his money as fast as the wheel and ball could be rolled or the card turned. The professional gamblers, who paid great rents for the right of placing their tables in these saloons, made large fortunes by the business. Their tables were piled with heaps of gold and silver coin, with bags of gold dust, and lumps of the pure metal, to tempt the gazer. The sight of such treasures, the occasional success of players, the music, the bustle, heat, drink, greed and deviltry, all combined to encourage play to an extent limited only by the great wealth of the community. Judges and clergymen, physicians and advocates, merchants and clerks, contractors, shopkeepers, tradesmen, mechanics and laborers, miners and farmers, all adventurers in their kind—every one elbowed his way to the gaming-table, and unblushingly threw down his golden or silver stake. The whole of the eastern side of Portsmouth Square, three-fourths of the northern, and a portion of the southern sides were occupied by buildings specially devoted to gambling. At these portions of the plaza were perhaps the greater saloons, but all around the neighborhood there were numberless other places, where the same system was carried on, and where the proceedings were exposed to the careless look of every passer-by.

While such scenes, in hundreds of distinct places, were night and day being acted in public, the better or richer classes, who at first had openly appeared and gambled among the crowds at the general saloons, began to separate and confine themselves to semi-private play in the rear of the Parker House, and at similar places. There, if the external excitement of moving crowds and music was wanting, the interest in the sport arising from larger stakes was correspondingly increased, if that were possible. The amounts ventured in such secluded circles were immense; and almost surpass belief. Men had come to California for gold; and, by hook or by crook, gold they would have. It was a fair and honest game, they thought, to hazard one's own money against that of another. Therefore, they staked and lost—staked and won—till in the end they were rich indeed, or penniless. But poor or rich, the speculative spirit continued—(there was surely something infectious in the air!)—and either in direct gambling, or in nearly similar operations in mercantile, land-jobbing, or general business, the inhabitants of San Francisco, at this period of its history, seemed to be one great horde of gamesters. There were exceptions indeed, and some men scorned to enter a gambling saloon or touch a card, but these were too few comparatively to be specially noticed in the general hubbub and speculative disposition of the place.

Parker House when first opened.

Who can tell the joy, the hope, the triumph, or the fear, misery and ruin of the busy gamester? It is not avarice alone that urges his course—for we often find the professed gambler careless of money, liberal and generous to excess. There is mental excitement—personal victory—riches, and consequent power, honor and happiness in the game. Other passions have their moments of excitement and ecstasy; but perhaps few have more blissful ones than the uncontrollable spirit of play. Let cold-blooded, lethargic people, who condemn the practice—for it is still a pernicious vice—consider the temptations and pleasure, as well as the evils and crimes it induces, and withhold their indiscriminating censures against those who have fallen victims to it. Some countries indulge in national vices—it may be intoxication or gambling, gross superstition or fanaticism. But no man can know all the peculiar circumstances and temptations that lead to wrong-doing; and no man is so personally and morally pure that he is entitled to throw a stone at the offender. We would not seek to excuse the San Franciscans of those days for indulging in gambling; but we think some palliation might be found for their conduct in the anomalous circumstances in which they were placed, and much allowance made for their temptation and fall. The same speculative spirit continues, although in a much less degree. There are still many public gaming tables, open every day of the week, at nearly all hours; but the stakes are much smaller than before, and the more respectable classes of the community do not attend such places. Private play is likewise still carried on, but to nothing like the extent of former years. The evil is dying away; though many years must pass before it be altogether extinct. So long as San Francisco is without proper homes, and its population is composed chiefly of adult males, while enormous profits and wages are usually made in every undertaking, so long will the only amusements be public ones, and chief among them, gambling. The richer and more respectable classes have now such homes and families to enjoy themselves among, and they no longer gamble. Give an agreeable domestic circle to the mechanic and the laborer, the general speculator, the tradesman and the clerk, and they likewise will forsake the public haunts of dissipation.

We have occasionally alluded to the desertion of seamen. At the time of which we write there were between three and four hundred large square-rigged vessels lying in the bay, unable to leave on account of want of hands. Many of these vessels never got away, but, in a few years afterwards, rotted and tumbled to pieces where they were moored. As stores and dwelling-houses were much needed, a considerable number of the deserted ships were drawn high on the beach, and fast imbedded in deep mud, where they were converted into warehouses and lodgings for the wants of the crowded population. When subsequently the town was extended over the mud flat of the bay, these ships were for ever closed in by numberless streets and regularly built houses both of brick and frame. When, by and by, the runaway seamen returned from the mines, crews could be more easily had, though still at a great increase of wages; and gradually the detained vessels were enabled to leave the port, to make room for new fleets.

The circulation of money,—partly coin, partly gold dust,—was very great. Men had a sublime indifference to the smaller pieces of coin, and talked as familiarly of dollars as people elsewhere would of dimes. A copper coin was a strange sight. There was nothing less received for any service, however slight, than half a dollar; for any article, however trifling, than a twenty-five cent piece. The price of admission to the pit of the circus was three dollars; while fifty-five dollars was the cost of a private box. Thirty dollars a week, or eight dollars a day, was the sum asked for good boarding; while the most indifferent could not be obtained for less than twenty dollars a week. Every mouthful at dinner might be valued at a dime; and to get a hearty meal would cost from two to five dollars, according to the quality of the viands. Other things were in proportion. Wheat flour and salt pork sold at forty dollars a barrel; potatoes and brown sugar at thirty-seven and a half cents a pound; a small loaf of bread, such as might cost four or six cents in the Atlantic States, brought fifty cents; and the same price was required for a pound of cheese; coarse boots, the only description for which there was any demand, could not be purchased for less than thirty to forty dollars a pair, while superior ones of the same class were sold for more than one hundred dollars. And truly, when one considered the horrible muddy holes and ragged streets of the place, boots were reasonable at these rates. It was about as economical to throw away certain soiled articles of clothing and buy new ones, as to get the old ones cleaned, when people had to pay from twelve to twenty dollars for the washing of each dozen of articles, large or small. Laborers' wages were a dollar an hour; skilled mechanics received from twelve to twenty dollars a day. The carpenters struck work because they were getting only twelve dollars a day, and insisted on being paid sixteen.

Their employers then offered fourteen dollars a day, for a limited time, and afterwards an increase. Every brick in a house was roughly estimated to cost a dollar, one way and another, before the building was finished. Lumber rose to five hundred dollars per thousand feet.

Rents were correspondingly enormous. Three thousand dollars *a month*, in advance, was charged for a single store, of limited dimensions, and rudely constructed of rough boards. A certain two story frame building, known as the "Parker House," and situated on Kearny street, facing the plaza, paid its owners one hundred and twenty thousand dollars a year in rents. Of this sum, somewhere about sixty thousand dollars was paid by gamblers, who occupied nearly the whole of the second floor. The "El Dorado," a gambling saloon, which adjoined the Parker House on the right, at the corner of Washington street, and which was only a canvas tent of moderate size, brought at the rate of forty thousand dollars *per annum*. At another corner of the plaza a small building, which might have made a stable for half-a-dozen horses, was possessed by Wright & Co., brokers, under the name of the Miners' Bank, at a rent of seventy-five thousand dollars. The United States Hotel paid thirty-six thousand dollars ; a mercantile establishment, for a one-story building, of twenty feet front, paid forty thousand dollars, and seven thousand dollars per month was paid for the Custom House. The interest of borrowed money was rated by the same scale. From eight to fifteen *per cent. per month*, with the addition of real security, was regularly given, *in advance*, for the use of money. And people paid these enormous wages, rents and interests ; and still made fortunes to themselves ! Real estate, that but a few years before was of little more worth than an old song, now brought amazing prices. From plain twelve dollars for fifty-vara lots, prices gradually rose to hundreds, thousands and tens of thousands of dollars ; so that large holders of such properties became on a sudden *millionnaires.* Shippers in foreign countries realized large fortunes at first by their ventures to California ; and if, ere long, the expenses were so heavy and the wholesale prices of goods, by excessive supply and competition, dwindled so low that sometimes they would not pay landing or storage charges, why, still the commission agents of San Francisco, and the host of interior merchants, shopkeepers and other retail dealers, were doing a thriving business, and accumulating large sums. The holder of every office in the State and municipality was paid generously. There was no niggardliness in such things. A religious body, whose clergymen are seldom in the habit of receiving extravagant salaries, took the

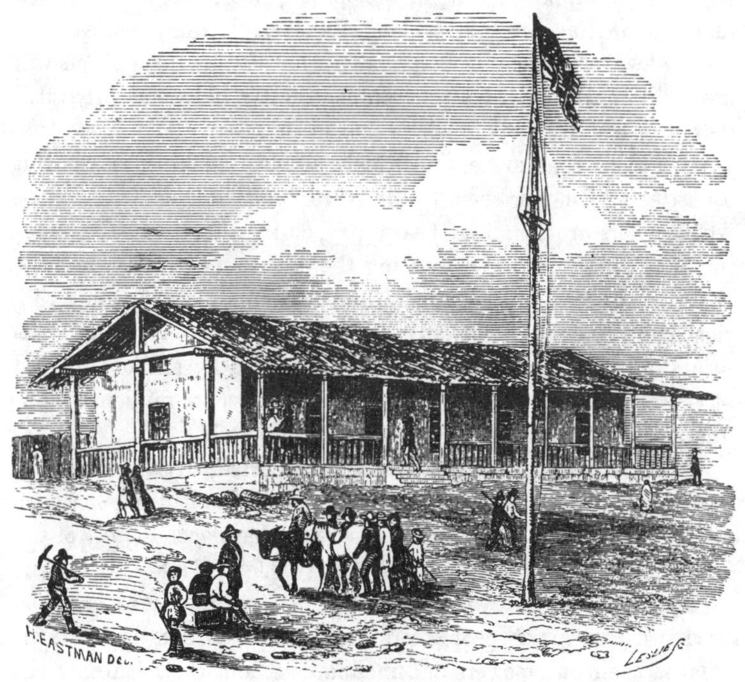

Custom House on the Plaza.

support of their minister on themselves, and voted him the princely allowance of *ten thousand dollars per annum!* Clerks and underlings were treated in the same handsome manner. The great sums, forming the total of such wages, salaries and profits, were always rapidly passing from hand to hand, and came and went, and finally disappeared in gambling-saloons and billiard rooms, at bars and in brothels, in land-jobbing, building and mercantile speculations, in every kind of personal profusion, extravagance and debauchery.

The main-spring of all this bustle and money-making trade

was the gold mining. Consider, therefore, the mightily enhanced prices of every article at the diggings! Gold dust paid for all foreign supplies, and filled the pockets of every active and shrewd man besides. Millions' worth of pure gold, in lumps and dust, reached San Francisco every month. The greater portion was forwarded to the Atlantic States and other distant quarters in payment of supplies; but, in the transit, much was appropriated and retained, as currency, among the ever plotting, restless and "wide-awake" people of San Francisco. Future generations will see California a rich and prosperous country independently altogether of her mineral wealth; but in those early days it was *the placers* alone that made, and which are still making it what it appears. All honor then to the sturdy and independent digger, whose labors are peopling the country, cultivating the fields, building cities, making roads, covering the ocean and the bays and the rivers of the land with steamers and great ships, and conferring riches and happiness not only on the growing population of California itself, that shall hereafter be numbered by millions instead of the present hundreds of thousands, but also on millions of industrious workmen in every quarter of the world!

While labor was so well paid at this period, in San Francisco, it is a melancholy fact that there was much destitution, sickness, and even death by want and exposure in the place. Many of the immigrants had landed in a sickly and emaciated state, ill of scurvy and other diseases which their long voyage and hardships had produced; and such people could not work. Others had miscalculated their own powers and inclinations, and the nature of the country they had come to, and were either ashamed or unable to perform honest labor; while perhaps they were too timid or upright to speculate in the variety of strange and often cunning ways by which other adventurers made a living and fortune. Disappointed diggers, returning from the mines with broken constitutions, swelled the destitute population. They probably lived in miserable habitations, sleeping often upon the bare earth. Around them were bustle and lucrative pursuits, while they alone seemed neglected. Then they lost heart, pined, took sick and died, cursing the country and its gold, and the foolish fancies, that had led them to it. Many committed suicide in the utter prostration of physical strength, in feebleness or disease of mind and absolute despair. Public meetings were held to consider the destitute situation of the poor—(strange word for such a country! yet San Francisco had its full share of the class),—and large sums were raised for their support. The Orders of Free Masons and Odd-Fellows, nobly did their part in the charitable work, and were the principal means by which now, and at a later period, hundreds of suffering beings were saved from a miserable end, or their remains decently interred after death.

San Francisco was like the scene of a great battle. There were victorious warriors braving and flaunting on all sides, while hope swelled the breast of every unwounded soldier. But, unheeded amid the crash and confusion of the strife, lay the wounded and dying, who had failed or been suddenly struck down in the *mêlée*. As in the case of other battles, there were likewise secret bands of unmanly ruffians, who attacked and plundered all sides alike. These were the thieves, burglars and murderers of the community, the "hounds" of recent times and their legitimate successors,—a large and fearful class indeed,—daily increasing in numbers, boldness and extent of depredation and crime. To their wickedness were afterwards ascribed, some of the extensive conflagrations which so repeatedly laid waste the most valuable portions of the growing town; and under cover of the alarm and confusion produced by which events, robberies could be carried on with impunity. What mattered it though millions' worth of property were consumed to enable the fire-raising villain to steal a few thousand dollars? He had still the few thousand dollars, and the universe might go to blazes for aught that he cared. In this manner, doubtless reasoned the "Sydney coves," and the other desperate and criminal adventurers with which the town was now infested. The "Vigilance Committee" had not yet arisen to terrify the wretches into good behavior.

The every-day aspect of the plaza and streets was of the most curious and interesting kind. Take the plaza, on a fine day, for a picture of the people. All races were represented. There were hordes of long pig-tailed, blear-eyed, rank-smelling Chinese, with their yellow faces and blue garbs; single dandy black fellows, of nearly as bad an odor, who strutted as only the negro can strut, in holiday clothes and clean white shirt; a few diminutive fiery-eyed Malays, from the western archipelago, and some handsome Kanakas from the Sandwich Islands; jet-black, straight featured, Abyssinians; hideously tattooed New Zealanders; Feejee sailors and even the secluded Japanese, short, thick, clumsy, ever-bowing, jacketed fellows; the people of the many races of Hindoo land; Russians with furs and sables; a stray, turbaned, stately Turk or two, and occasionally a half naked shivering Indian; multitudes of the Spanish race from every country of the Americas, partly pure, partly crossed with red blood,—Chilians, Peruvians and Mexicans, all with different shades of the same swarthy complexion, black-eyed and well-featured, proud of their beards and moustaches, their grease, dirt, and eternal gaudy serapes or darker cloaks; Spaniards from the mother country, more dignified, polite and pompous than even their old colonial brethren; "greasers," too, like them; great numbers of tall, goat-chinned, smooth-cheeked, oily-locked, lank-visaged, tobacco-chewing, large-limbed and featured, rough, care-worn, careless Americans from every State of the Union, dressed independently in every variety of garb, not caring a fig what people thought of them, but determined to "do the thing handsomely," and "go ahead;" fat, conceited, comfortable Englishmen, who pretended to compete in shrewdness with the subtle Yankee—as if it were not the "manifest destiny" of Jonathan, every where, but especially on his own ground, to outshine John! Then there were bands of gay, easy-principled, philosophical Germans, Italians and Frenchmen of every cut and figure, their faces covered with hair, and with strange habiliments on their persons, and among whom might be particularly remarked numbers of thick-lipped, hook-nosed, ox-eyed, cunning, oily Jews. Among this vast motley crowd scarcely could two hats be found alike in material, size and shape; scarcely could two men be found otherwise dressed alike. The long-legged boot, with every variety of colored top, the buckled-up trousers, serapes or cloaks, pea-jackets and broad-brimmed or slouched hats and glazed caps, were perhaps the commonest articles of dress. The fortunate miner with his dirty garments and hirsute face, could be readily distinguished from all others. He cared not to dress or cleanse himself properly, till the bars and gambling saloons had been duly visited, and his hard won gains were spent. Then did he shake, shave and wash himself, and start again for the golden placers.

The eye was delighted with the varieties of costume, and more readily distinguished the wearers ; while the ear was only confounded with the babble of unknown, and to it harsh, guttural and meaningless sounds which flowed from every mouth, and where all alike talked loudly, and many furiously gesticulated. Thus the people passed in pairs or in crowds—they loitered, stood still, and moved on again, while other parties jostled beside and around them. A horse or a bullock breaking loose would dash along the way, and make a momentary struggle and flight ; but soon again the scene resumed its old appearance. On two, if not three sides of the plaza, were the open doors of the "hells" of San Francisco, where gamblers, and others for amusement, passed out and in during the whole day. On the other portions stood hotels, stores and offices, the custom-house and courts of law, all thronged with numerous visitors. The little open space which was left by the crowds we have been describing, was occupied by a multitude of nondescript objects, by horses, mules and oxen dragging burdens along, by cars and carriages of various kinds, boys at play, stalls with sweetmeats, newspapers, prints, toys and other trifling articles of merchandise. At times a few Californians or some foreigners would appear on prancing steeds, the horses caparisoned with gaudy harness and brightly-colored saddle-cloths, while little bells jingled as they moved along. The riders wore strange leathern aprons before the legs, huge spurs on the heels, and perhaps had a cloak picturesquely thrown across their shoulders. Occasionally, too, even at this early period, the crowds would make way for the passage of a richly dressed woman, sweeping along, apparently proud of being recognized as one of frail character, or several together of the same class, mounted on spirited horses, and dashing furiously by, dressed in long riding skirts, or what was quite as common, in male attire.

We cannot leave this part of our subject without alluding to the scenes that daily occurred at the post-office, which was situated at the corner of Pike and Clay streets. Every body, of course, was anxiously expecting letters from *home ;* and every body hastened to look after them. The post-office was but a small building, and could neither accommodate many assistants and clerks inside, nor afford much standing-room to make inquiries without. When, therefore, soon after the arrival of the mail from the Atlantic States, which occurred but once a month, people came for their wished-for letters, exhibitions of an interesting character

The Post Office, corner of Pike and Clay streets.

were sure to transpire. To avoid riots and confusion, several regular lines were formed from the delivery windows, at the end of which applicants for letters took places as they arrived. So anxious were many to receive their epistles, that they posted themselves in the evening of one day to be early at the window on the morning of the next, standing all night in the mud, with a heavy rain pouring down upon their heads. The lines extended a great distance down Clay street to the plaza, and along Pike street, even across Sacramento street to the tents among the chapparel. Hours therefore, would elapse, before it came to one's turn to reach the window. To save such delay, sometimes people would employ and handsomely pay others to preserve places for them, which they would occupy, in room of their assistants, when they were approaching the loop-holes where the delivery clerks stood. Ten and twenty dollars were often paid for accommodation in this way. Indeed, many clever persons made large sums regularly by such work, by securing good places in the line early, never intending to seek letters for themselves, but only to sell their right of position to some richer man who was in haste, and regarded more his time than money. Some of these eager applicants had not heard from their far distant homes for many long months, and their anxious solicitude was even painful. It was therefore exceedingly distressing to mark the despondency with which many would turn away upon hearing from the delivery clerks the oft-repeated and much-dreaded sentence, "There is nothing here for you." On the other hand, it was equally pleasing to observe the cheerful and triumphant smile, not unfrequently accompanied with a loud exclamation of joy, that would light up the countenance of the successful applicant, who hastens from the window, and as soon as he can force a passage through the crowd, tears open and commences to read the more than welcome letter, every word of which awakens in his mind some tender reminiscence. He is now communing with the dearest idols of his heart. He knows no feelings but those of kindness and affection. The lines upon which his eyes are riveted, were written perhaps by an absent wife, and they have made him already a better man than he was an hour before. She is describing the sadness of the solitude his absence has occasioned, and urging him with all a true woman's fondness, to hasten back to the home which needs but his presence to be one of unmingled happiness. She tells him of their innocent children—of their improving loveliness—and how she has taught them in their daily prayers to lisp their absent father's name. Look close into the reader's face, and the nature of his emotions will not be mistaken. There is an unusual twitching of the muscles of the mouth, a growing dimness of the eyes, and tears are rapidly tracing down the furrows of his sunburnt cheeks. He is too much absorbed in his interesting occupation to know or care that he is an object of curious observation. What matters it to him what others think of his apparent weakness? It is a weakness of which he need not be ashamed. He at length carefully folds the paper and carries it to his comfortless abode, where he reads it over and over again, until by constant handling, and the tears that fall upon it, its characters become illegible. That night does not find him in the gambling-house, nor elsewhere in search of amusement; but in his own wretched chamber, he is silently communing in spirit with the loved ones at home. Such scenes were of hourly occurrence, and tended to exhibit the better portion of human nature, which neither the thirst for gold nor feverish excitement of the place could entirely destroy.

Turning from these busy scenes and ascending a neighboring height, the wearied spectator beheld one of the most peaceful prospects and pleasant sights of the world. It was winter by the calendar; but the winters of California are the springs and early summers of less favored lands in northern latitudes. Beneath was the little pandemonium he had left, where the devil-inspired worshippers of mammon burrowed in, and out, and about, holes and huts of canvas and wood; but the noise of whose never-ceasing labors reached not his ears. Beyond the narrow limits of the town were the calm waters of the bay, on which floated, swan-like, hundreds of trim and well-proportioned ships, all motionless, and deserted by their crews. Farther out was the high lying island of Yerba Buena, green to the summit. Beyond it lay the mountains of Contra Costa, likewise arrayed in verdant robes, on the very tops of which flourished groups of huge redwood trees; while far in the distance towered the gray head of Monte Diablo. The eye wandered to the northern and southern extremities of the bay, and still gazed on green hills, smooth waters and picturesque islands. It turned oceanward, and saw the Golden Gate studded with deep laden ships inward bound. The grand northern shores of the strait rose boldly and brokenly to the height of nearly three thousand feet, while the lower coast opposite was equally beautiful from the freshness of its fields and bushes, in the midst of which, and in the most beautiful spot embraced in the entire view, quietly nestles the presidio, now the solitary habitation of a small detachment of United States soldiery. The great Pacific might be dimly seen beneath the dense veil of mist that hung miles out at sea opposite the Gate. To the west and south-west the spectator next looked, and admired the Blue Mountain and the Pass that sheltered the quiet

The Presidio of San Francisco.

valley of the mission, and the long ridges of the Sierra San Bruno, their green color sinking into a faint blue as they were seen more distantly. Overhead was a sky as blue and as beautiful as imagination could picture ; the air was fresh and balmy ; the earth beneath one's feet, soft and fragrant with new herbage and flowering shrubs ; while the life-giving sun shed over all its own radiance and joy. All was clear and sharp-defined ; all was tranquil and motionless, except the flight of innumerable white and gray-winged gulls, that soared and fluttered among the deserted shipping in the cove before the town.

CHAPTER X.

1850.

Great sale of water lots.—An election day.—Newspapers.—Approval by the ayuntamiento of the city charter, and limits of San Francisco.—Squatter difficulty at Rincon Point.—Political meeting on Portsmouth Square.—The Colton grants.—First county election.—Col. John C. Hayes elected Sheriff.—City Charter adopted by the State Legislature.—First election under the City Charter.—Changes in the Common Council.

January 3d.—A great sale by the municipal authorities, of four hundred and thirty-four water lots, which brought $635,130. This sale had been ordered by the ayuntamiento by a resolution passed on the 3d of October, 1849, in accordance with a proclamation of General Kearny, directing three months' notice to have been previously given.

January 8th.—An election was held for members of the legislature, alcaldes and ayuntamiento. The interest on these occasions increased with the population, and the election of to-day was the most exciting that had yet been held. The weather was exceedingly unpleasant, the wind blowing a gale, and the rain pouring down in torrents. The streets were covered with mud and water so as to render them almost impassable. Still the neighborhood of the polls was crowded during the entire day with men and boys, zealous as they well could be in their endeavors to promote the public welfare. It is one of the glorious consequences of our republican institutions, that at such times, so many worthy people are always to be found, utterly regardless of their personal interests, and so entirely devoted to the general good. Although the excitement ran unusually high, the day passed off without disturbance, and much good humor was exhibited by the conflicting parties. The voters were numerous; every citizen of the United States being entitled to the elective franchise, and almost all who were here, from every part of the world, claimed to be American citizens. The way to the polls, for a considerable distance, on either side, was completely blocked up by roughly dressed men, who thrust their favorite tickets into the hands of every new comer, with loud exclamations in behalf of the parties for whom they were working. "Here's for Geary, and the old council!" cries one, "Geary and the old council for ever!" "For ever is a long day," says another; "rotation in office, is my doctrine. The old council has made money enough. Let's give a new one a chance at the public crib!" "The old ones are so fat they can't eat any more!" exclaims a third; "we had better keep them where they are!" "We have had the old council long enough!" vociferates a stout six-footer, wading up to his waist in the mud: "I go for a new council, *side-walks, and clean streets!*" "You do, do you?" replies a wag: "then I guess you will have to go an infernal long ways to find them!" "We want another yuntermenter," bawls out a youngster in a red shirt and tarpaulin hat, and resembling a drowned rat more than an independent voter:—"we want another yuntermenter, and here's the ticket for um!" "It's a gutterminty that ye want?" replies a brawny Irishman; "then take it, and good luck till ye!" giving the luckless wight a toss that sent him sprawling into the gutter overhead in water: "I am thinking ye won't want another gutterminty soon, any how!" With much difficulty the polling desk was reached, where other scenes no less amusing were transpiring. Around the judges and inspectors were an eager and excited crowd, some endeavoring to vote and others to prevent them. "I challenge that man's vote," cries a bystander, as a simple Sandwich Islander, almost as dark as an African, offered his ticket. "Then we must swear him!" says the judge, and the usual oath was administered. "Where were you born?" was the inquiry. "In New York!" whispered a prompter, and the answer was given accordingly. "Where did you come from last?" "New York," was again the reply. "Where was your father born?" "New York." "In what street did you live?" "New York." "Where is New York?" the judge next inquired. This was too much for the poor fellow. He knew as much of the locality and streets of the invisible world as he did of New York. His prompter, who had brought him there to vote, endeavored to instruct him, but without success. His impatient challenger at length exclaims: "Turn him out, he is a Kanaka!" and the vote was rejected. Another and another pressed forward, and similar questions and just as honest answers were given, and many a vote was polled, to the right of depositing which the elector was no more entitled than the poor Kanaka. Still the election proceeded, and notwithstanding the interest and excitement manifested, the best sort of feeling was preserved throughout. The polls were closed early in the evening, and the judges announced the following gentlemen elected to the offices named. The heaviest ballot cast was in favor of Col. John W. Geary, who received 3,425 votes:—

State Senator.—David C. Broderick.

Member of Assembly.—Samuel J. Clarke.

First Alcalde.—John W. Geary.

Second Alcalde.—Frank Turk.

Ayuntamiento.—A. J. Ellis, Talbot H. Green, Wm. M. Stewart, W. H. Davis, Samuel Brannan, James S. Graham, Frank Tilford, F. C. Gray, J. Hagan, M. Crooks, A. M. Van Nostrand, and Hugh C. Murray.

JANUARY 22d.—The "Alta California" is changed into a daily newspaper, being the first of the kind that has appeared in California. The weekly issue is likewise continued. The day following, the "Journal of Commerce" was started as a daily paper; and about six weeks later, the "Pacific News" took a similar form. The "San Francisco Daily Herald" came into existence on the first of June, and became a very popular journal. On the first of August following, the "Evening Picayune" also made its appearance. The latter was the fifth daily but the first evening paper. The "Courier" and the "Balance" followed soon after, and subsequently many other journals have been developed in San Francisco and other parts of the country. Some of these are still in existence, while others after a very brief and sickly career, perished for want of support. The "Placer Times," which was extensively circulated in the mining districts, had been commenced at Sacramento in April, 1849, and appeared weekly. This was also converted into [illegible]ly newspaper, and was subsequently removed to San Francisco. It is a political journal, devoted to the interests of the democratic cause.

FEBRUARY 13th.—A charter for the city, previously drafted and considered, was amended and approved of by the ayuntamiento, and Messrs. Hagan and Green were instructed to present it to the representatives of the city for adoption by the legislature. By the first section of the charter it was declared, that "the limits of the City of San Francisco shall be the same which bounded the pueblo lands and town of San Francisco; and its municipal jurisdiction shall extend to said limits, and over the waters of the Bay of San Francisco, for the space of one league from the shore, including the Islands of Yerba Buena, Los Angeles, and Alcantraz."

FEBRUARY 28th.—A squatter difficulty occurred at the Rincon. Most of the land here was held as United States government reserve, and as such was leased for a limited period to Mr. Theodore Shillaber. Upon attempting to take possession, this gentleman found the leased property mostly occupied by "squatters," the majority of whom were from Sydney. These refused either to pay rent or vacate the land. Captain Keyes, therefore, having charge of the presidio, marched to the Rincon with a company of twenty United States soldiers, and soon demolished all the tents and shanties that had been erected on the government grounds. A Mr. White, one of the leaders among the squatters, subsequently brought a civil action for damages against the captain; but the latter was sustained by the court, and the case was dismissed, the prosecutor being required to pay the costs.

MARCH 9th.—Party politics begins to embrace a good share of public attention, and among the seekers after fame and fortune, there is no scarcity of aspirants for political preferment. It is but lately, however, that party lines have been drawn, and whigs and democrats, as such, arrayed against each other in their patriotic efforts to promote the general welfare. But it was found less difficult to draw these lines than to rally the forces under their distinctive self-constituted leaders. There were as many officers as soldiers to enter the political campaign. At least, each party was divided into several factions, every faction having at its head, of course, men whose claims to public favor were superior to all others. Concerted action was therefore out of the question. The democrats had resolved to remedy this evil, so destructive of their party interests, by uniting or harmonizing all their conflicting elements. To this end a mass meeting was held this afternoon on Portsmouth Square. About one thousand persons assembled, a band of music played national airs, and a large and splendid ensign waved gracefully over the speakers' stand, upon which were stationed officers duly appointed to conduct the proceedings in proper form. The meeting was opened with great enthusiasm, and, for a time, every thing gave promise of the desired result. Several addresses were delivered with good effect, which were enthusiastically responded to by the admiring listeners. But a trying moment at length arrived. The committee chosen to draft resolutions expressive of the feelings and purposes of the democracy, presented their report, and the resolutions were submitted for passage. These called forth the factional prejudices of the assembly, which were exhibited in uproar and confusion. The chairman was unable to decide the votes, and hence, some of the most boisterous determined to decide them in a manner peculiar to themselves. What they failed to accomplish by the power of their lungs, they attempted to effect by "the force of arms." Blows were liberally bestowed and received, and broken heads and bleeding noses were the consequence. The fight commenced on the speakers' stand, and in a short time, the meeting was divided into a dozen squads, each taking an active part in the mêlée. Order was at length restored, and the mass once more gathered to adopt or reject the resolutions. The chairman again "put the question," and the "*ayes*" rang loudly through the air, which were followed no less loudly by the "*noes.*" It was impossible to decide whether the "ayes" or the "noes" were in the ascendency. The holding up of hands was next resorted to. The "ayes" were told to hold up their *right* hands, and after them the "noes;" but many of both parties seemed to imagine that in a matter of such importance, *all hands were right,* and consequently held up all the hands they had, doubtless regretting not having others for the purpose. It was then suggested that the "whigs" created all the difficulty, and they were requested to withdraw. The whigs accordingly fell back, leaving about one-half the assembly behind. Elated at the sight of their own numbers, they whirled their hats in triumph over their heads, which was accounted by their opponents as a signal for attack; and down they rushed upon the retiring force in a perfect torrent, sweeping before them all who were not levelled with the dust. It was now thought expedient to adjourn the meeting, which was effected with "three cheers" for the democracy, every aspirant for the honors, spoils and profits of which, internally resolving to support the party whenever its requirements did not conflict with his personal interests.

MARCH 26th.—For some time back there have been much agitation and discussion on the subject of the "*Colton Grants.*" It appears that Mr. Horace Hawes, prefect of the district of San Francisco, had chosen to consider that the duties and privileges of his office were more extensive than had been previously supposed. He had, in particular, instructed Mr G. Q. Colton, a justice of the peace in and for his district, to sell and convey away the municipal lands, accounting only to himself for the proceeds of the same. When, afterwards, the Court of First Instance, on the petition of the ayuntamiento, granted an injunction to restrain Mr. Colton from so acting, Mr. Hawes immediately issued a mandate annulling the said injunction. Mr. Colton meanwhile had sold or otherwise disposed of a great number of town allotments, some of them at nominal prices, to various parties. The ayuntamiento, holding that they alone were the proper parties to authorize such sales, thereupon determined this day to prefer against Mr. Hawes a number of charges, founded upon these and other facts, to the governor of the State; and passed a long string of resolutions on the subject. The governor subsequently suspended Mr. Hawes from performing the duties of his office; while the titles to the "Colton Grants," many of which had been signed in blank, and others were ante-dated, passed into the courts of law, and were for years afterwards a fertile source of litigation. In the end, it is believed that they were altogether found to be invalid.

APRIL 1st.—The first election for county officers. The principal office to be filled was that of sheriff, for which there were three candidates. Col. J. Townes was the regular whig nominee—Col. J. J. Bryant the nominee of the democratic party —and the celebrated "Texan Ranger," Col. John C. Hayes, was selected by the people as an independent candidate. It was soon apparent that the contest rested between the two last named. Col. Bryant was a man of fortune, and was determined to spare no exertions or expense to secure his election. He was proprietor of the most extensive and best conducted hotel in the place, known at that time as the "Bryant House," formerly the

San Francisco in April 1850, showing Clay street, opposite Portsmouth Square.

"Ward House," which was a great place of resort, for politicians, and where hundreds of the colonel's pretended friends and real supporters enjoyed, in no slight degree, the advantages of his generous hospitality. A band of music was daily stationed on the balcony of the Bryant House after the nomination of its proprietor, free lunches were served up in the spacious saloon, and on this day the building was literally covered with flags, signals, and banners of every form and beautiful color, while the finest liquors were gratuitously dispensed at the well-stocked bar to all who chose to drink. On Saturday afternoon, March 29th, the friends of Col. Hayes held a mass meeting on the plaza, which was a large and enthusiastic assembly. After several spirited addresses had been given, the meeting formed in procession, and headed by a band of music, paraded the principal streets, cheering and being cheered by multitudes of spectators as they passed along. In the evening the democrats also assembled in the square, making a truly splendid display. The whole plaza was covered with men, horses and wagons, and was illuminated with flaming torches and other lights, which blazed from the speakers' stand and hundreds of vehicles admirably arranged for effect. Numerous transparencies, banners and flags added greatly to the life and splendor of the pageant. Able speakers urged the claims of the democracy in general, and of Col. Bryant in particular, to the suffrages of the people, whilst, at regular intervals, cannons were fired to give effect and increase the excitement. This meeting also ended in a procession, which traversed the streets to a late hour of the night. Early this morning the different parties were in force about the polls, and in due time the judges, inspectors and clerks were chosen and installed in their respective offices. The election was conducted with more than usual spirit. At noon it was evident that Col. Hayes was the people's favorite, which incited to increased efforts the Bryant party. Accordingly they appeared with another grand display upon the plaza. A procession of mounted men, and carriages filled with musicians, with banners and flags waving and floating above them, occupied the square, and were in a measure, producing the desired effect. But in the midst of the excitement thus produced, Col. Hayes, mounted upon a fiery black charger, suddenly appeared, exhibiting some of the finest specimens of horsemanship ever witnessed. The sight of the hero, as he sat bare-headed and unattended upon his noble animal, took the people by surprise, and called forth the admiration and patriotism of the vast multitude of spectators, from every one of whom shout after shout rent the air, deadening the sounds of trumpets and drums, and being heard far and wide over land and sea. Men crowded around him on every hand, some seizing the bridle, others clinging to his clothing and stirrups, and each anxious to obtain a grasp of his hand. The noise and tumult terrified the spirited beast he strode, which reared and plunged among the enthusiastic crowd, though so admirably managed as to do injury to none; when, at length, his rider giving him the rein, he dashed into and along the adjoining street, followed and greeted by loud huzzas at every step. This settled the question. The cause of Col. Bryant was abandoned, and a vast majority of votes were given in favor of the "Texan Ranger." The following named parties were elected:—

Sheriff.—John C. Hayes.	*District Attorney.*—Calhoun Benham.
County Judge.—R. N. Morrison.	*County Clerk.*—John E. Addison.
County Recorder.—J. A. McGlynn.	*County Assessor.*—David M. Chauncey.
County Surveyor.—Wm. W. Eddy.	*County Coroner.*—Edward Gallagher.
County Treasurer.—G. W. Endicott.	*County Attorney.*—T. J. Smith.

Clerk of the Supreme Court.—E. H. Tharp.

April 15th.—The City Charter passed by the State Legislature. The limits of the city are now declared to be as follows: —"The southern boundary shall be a line two miles distant in a southerly direction from the centre of Portsmouth Square, and which line shall be a parallel to the street known as Clay street. The western boundary shall be a line one mile and a half distant in a westerly direction from the centre of Portsmouth Square, and which line shall be parallel to the street known as Kearny street. The northern and eastern boundaries shall be the same as the County of San Francisco." The city was to be divided into eight wards by the first council appointed by the charter; and for its government were to be elected a Mayor, and Recorder, a Board of Aldermen and a Board of Assistant Aldermen, which two boards should be styled the "Common Council," each consisting of one member from each ward. There was also to be elected by the city a Treasurer, Comptroller, Street Commissioner, Collector of City Taxes, City Marshal and City Attorney, and by each ward two Assessors. As at the time of the first election under the charter there were only four wards, it was provided that two chief and as many assistant Aldermen should be elected from each, while the same number of Assessors should be chosen. The municipal officers were to hold office only one year, and new elections to be made on the fourth Monday of April annually. The powers and duties of the Common Council and municipal officers are minutely laid down in the charter.

May 1st.—This day the City Charter was submitted to the inhabitants for approval, when it was adopted; and the first election under its provisions took place. The following candidates were returned as elected:—

Mayor.—John W. Geary.
Recorder.—Frank Tilford.
Marshal.—Malachi Fallon.
City Attorney.—Thos. H. Holt.
Treasurer.—Charles G. Scott.
Comptroller.—Benj. L. Berry.
Tax Collector.—Wm. M. Irwin.
Street Commissioner.—Dennis McCarthy.

Aldermen.

Charles Minturn, F. W. Macondray, D. Gillespie, A. A. Selover, Wm. Greene, C. W. Stuart, Wm. M. Burgoyne, M. L. Mott.

Assistant Aldermen.

A. Bartol, C. T. Botts, Wm. Sharron, John Maynard, John P. Van Ness, L. T. Wilson, A. Morris, Wm. Corbett.

Assessors.

Robert B. Hampton, Halsey Brower, John Garvey, John H. Gihon, Francis C. Bennett, John P. Haff, Beverly Miller, Lewis B. Coffin.

Before the term of election expired, several changes occurred in the Common Council. Mr. Burgoyne having made a visit to the Atlantic States immediately after the election, was never qualified, and his place was declared vacant; and Mr. Macondray resigned shortly afterwards. Their places were filled on the 27th June by the election of Moses G. Leonard and John Middleton. Mr. Maynard resigned June 24th, and soon afterwards the resignation of Mr. Botts was accepted; and a new election to fill the vacancies thus occasioned, on the 27th July, resulted in the choice of George W. Green and James Grant. Subsequently Messrs. Gillespie and Leonard retired from the Board of Aldermen, and Mr. Morris from the Board of Assistants. Their places were also supplied by election on the 20th January, 1851, by W. H. V. Cronise and D. G. Robinson to the first, and George W. Gibbs to the second Board. We are somewhat particular in mentioning these changes in the Boards of Aldermen, since the affairs of their salaries, and the famous medals, hereafter noticed, directed much attention to the individual members.

MAY 4th.—The *second* great fire in San Francisco, when property to the value of nearly four millions of dollars was supposed to be destroyed. It began about four o'clock in the morning, in the building on the east side of the place called the

Fire of May 4th, 1850.

United States Exchange; and before eleven of the forenoon, three immense blocks of buildings, with a few trifling exceptions, were totally destroyed. These were the blocks lying between Kearny, Clay, Montgomery and Washington streets; and the two blocks between Dupont, Montgomery, Washington and Jackson streets. A great many buildings were torn down or blown up by gunpowder to stay the progress of the flames; and, among others, nearly the whole erections in Dupont street were voluntarily destroyed to prevent the conflagration spreading on that side. While some of the populace readily and untiredly assisted in extinguishing the flames, others would lend no hand at the work without being first well paid for it. The police force was very efficient in preventing pillage, and preserving order among the real workers and the idlers at the fire. Circumstances occurred which led to the strong suspicion, if not moral certainty, that the fire arose through the agency of incendiaries, and a reward of five thousand dollars was offered by the mayor for their detection. Several parties were apprehended on suspicion, but no formal trial took place, and they were shortly afterwards liberated. As in the case of the former great fire, on the 24th December last, new buildings were begun to be erected while still the sites of the old were hot with smoking ashes. While even one extremity of the old tenement was still blazing, people were planning the nature of the new erection, and clearing away the embers and rubbish from the other scarcely extinguished end, to lay the foundation of the intended new pile. In a wonderfully short time the whole burned space was covered with new buildings, and looked as if no fire had ever been there; although it was generally remarked that these were even more unsubstantial and inflammable than those which had just been destroyed.

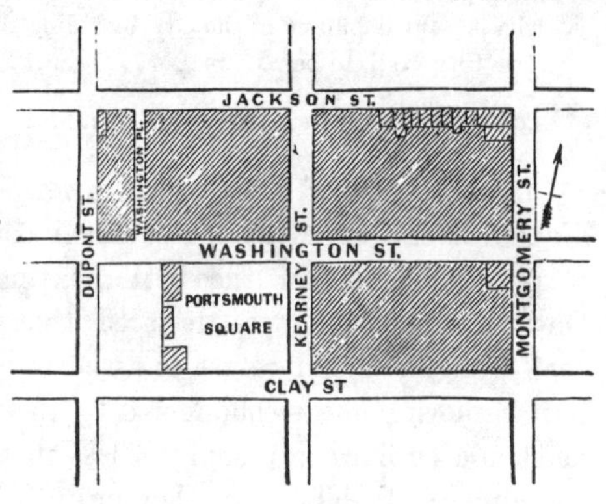

Diagram of the burnt district, May 4th, 1850.

May 9th.—The two boards of aldermen severally held meetings for the first time at the new City Hall, at the corner of Kearny and Pacific streets. The principal business of the meetings was to organize, appoint committees, and receive and read a message from the mayor. This latter was an able and interesting document, containing many truly excellent suggestions in regard to the interests of the corporation. Its great length precludes the propriety of its insertion. As the following extract, however, gives a correct statement of the financial condition of the city at this important period of its history, its omission would be inexcusable:—

"The Reports of the Treasurer and Comptroller are herewith submitted. The financial condition of the city is as follows:—

Amount on second instalment, of sales of water lots, due April 3d, 1850,	$23,049 00
Amount on third instalment, due July 3d, 1850	107,602 00
Amount on fourth instalment, due October 3d, 1850	107,602 00
	$238,253 00
The Report of the Comptroller, up to May 8, 1850, shows the present liabilities of the city, including the purchase of the City Hall, to be	$199,174 19
Excess over liabilities	$ 39,078 81"

In the course of this month, several stringent and useful ordinances were passed by the common council, which endeavored to provide means for the better extinguishing of future fires. One of these ordinances declared that if any person, during a conflagration, should refuse to assist in extinguishing the flames, or in removing goods endangered by the fire to a place of safety, he should be fined in a sum not less than five, and not exceeding one hundred dollars. Another ordinance authorized the mayor to enter into contracts for the digging of Artesian wells, and for the immediate construction of water reservoirs in various parts of the city. Another ordained every householder to furnish six water buckets, to be kept always in readiness for use during the occurrence of future fires. Such ordinances were all excellent in their way, though unfortunately they were somewhat late in being adopted.

CHAPTER XI.

1850.

Third great fire.—Aldermen's salaries.—Indignation meetings.—Veto message of the mayor.—Shipping in San Francisco Bay.—Celebration of the Fourth of July.—The Oregon Liberty Pole.—Custom-house at the corner of California and Montgomery streets.—Departure from California of General Riley.—Society of California Pioneers.—Squatter riots at Sacramento.—Suffering immigrants.—Presentation of Chinese Books.—Funeral ceremonies on occasion of the death of President Taylor.—A Chinese document.

JUNE 14th.—Scarcely had the citizens time to breathe after their recent exertions at the fire of the 4th of May, and the labors which followed in erecting new buildings in room of those destroyed, when again the terrible cry of *fire* rang in their ears. This was the *third* conflagration to which the city had been subjected, and its ravages exceeded even those of the two previous great fires united, being estimated at nearly five millions' worth of property. These successive losses would surely have broken the spirit of any people but Americans, and for a time indeed sank even theirs. But in proportion to the unusual depression was the almost immediate reaction, and the ruined citizens began forthwith to lay the foundations of new fortunes instead of those so cruelly destroyed. The fire, which arose from some defect in the chimney of the house where it broke out, began about eight o'clock in the morning, in a bakery, which was in a small wooden back building, between Sacramento and Clay streets, and in the rear of the Merchants' Hotel. The wind was high at the time, and the flames soon spread on all sides. In a few hours, the whole space situated between Clay, California and Kearny streets, down to the edge of the water, was one mass of flame; and, with few exceptions, all the buildings and goods lying within these extensive bounds, were totally consumed. The individual losses were very severe; and these occurring so shortly after the two preceding great fires, had the effect of reducing many citizens, previously wealthy, to poverty. But as the spider, whose web is again and again destroyed, will continue to spin new ones while an atom of material or a spark of life remains in its body, so did the inhabitants set themselves industriously to work to rear new houses and a new town. In the space of a few weeks the burned districts were covered over with other buildings, many of which were erected of far more substantial materials than before. Sad experience had taught the people that although the cost of fire-proof, brick structures was much greater at first than the old wooden ones, yet in the end, they were cheaper and better. From this time forward, we therefore begin to notice, that the street architecture gradually assumed a new and grander appearance. This was one good consequence of the repeated fires; while another was the immediate formation and organization of numerous hook and ladder, engine and hose companies. Many municipal ordinances regarding these companies and the establishment and completion of wells and reservoirs in various parts of the city, were likewise the result of these successive disasters.

During all this month, the community was kept in a state of excessive excitement, arising from certain extraordinary proceedings on the part of the Common Council. The members had not been long in office, when they nearly unanimously passed an ordinance providing for the payment of certain salaries to themselves and the chief municipal officers. The mayor, recorder, and some others, were to be paid annually the sum of ten thousand dollars, while the sixteen principal and assistant aldermen were each to receive six thousand. The salaries of the municipal officials were perhaps not more than were necessary at the period, since these gentlemen had really much work to do, while all their time was supposed to be passed in the service of the city; but it was considered by the citizens generally, that to bestow six thousand dollars a year upon sixteen private persons, for only two evening meetings in each week, was extravagant and ridiculous. As one of the speakers at a subsequent public meeting said, people in foreign countries, when they heard of such a thing, would be apt to call it "*a California lie.*" More especially the proposed aldermanic allowance seemed monstrous and unjust, from the fact that the city was then much embarrassed in pecuniary affairs, and that certain most obnoxious and heavy taxes were proposed to be laid upon the inhabitants.

Many public meetings of the citizens were held on the subject, at which resolutions strongly condemnatory of the council's proceedings were passed. One of these meetings took place on the plaza on the evening of the 5th of June, and was the largest that had ever assembled in San Francisco for any purpose. From three to four thousand people attended. General John Wilson was appointed president. After some introductory discussion, several resolutions were adopted by acclamation, the essence of which was this,—that we "instruct our mayor and common council to abandon the scheme of high salaries, and to remodel the schedule of oppressive taxation, as shadowed forth by their recent action; and unless they are willing to do so, to resign and give place to more patriotic and efficient men." A committee of twenty-five were then appointed to wait on the council and present a copy of the resolutions, and to request an answer to the same. The gentlemen composing the committee were Messrs. Wilson, Folsom, Crane, Post, Stoutenburg, Howard, Cooke, Kelly, Yale, Syme, Retan, Robinson, Courson, Robertson, Dunbar, Leonard, Minor, Parcells, Osborne, Wells, Duff, Parlon, Wakeman and Meacham.

The committee named, accordingly, through their chairman, Captain J. L. Folsom, presented the resolutions to the council. These the aldermen, who appeared determined to carry matters through with a high hand, received very coldly, and ordered them to lie indefinitely on the table. This not being deemed a sufficient answer by the committee, another "mass" and "indignation meeting" was called by them for the evening of 12th June; which was held on the plaza and was very numerously attended. Again General Wilson filled the chair. The report of the committee having been read, and the supposed "insolence of office" duly animadverted upon, the meeting, considering the "disrespect and insult" which their former representatives had met with, unanimously reappointed them as a committee, *with power to increase their number to five hundred*, and instructed them again to present the old resolutions to the council in such form as they should think fit. The committee thus fortified, afterwards chose the additional members, and fixed the evening of the 14th, when they should all march in procession to the place of meeting of the common council, and there again submit the "sovereign will" of the people to the aldermen, and require their prompt obedience to the same. On that day the great conflagration just noticed took place; and farther action on the subject of the high salaries and obnoxious taxation ordinances was indefinitely postponed. Popular excitement took a new direction in consequence of the fire; and, excepting in the columns of the *Herald* newspaper, and among a few testy individuals, little more was said on the matter till some months afterwards, when the question was revived. The previous meetings, however, had the effect of causing the obnoxious license ordinance to be withdrawn for a time. In the end, the salaries of both the municipal officers and the common council were reduced, the latter being ultimately fixed at four thousand dollars.

It is due to Col. Geary, mayor of the city, to observe, that from the beginning he opposed the payment of salaries to the members of the Boards of Aldermen, and at last vetoed the bill allowing them four thousand dollars each. His message, on returning the ordinance, unapproved, was a highly creditable document. After declaring that the ordinance in question was in direct opposition to the wishes of the people, whose will had been made known to the aldermen in the most emphatic manner, which he averred it was the duty of the latter to obey, he uses the following language:—

"Another view which presents itself with great force to my mind, in interpreting the executive right to arrest the ordinance in question, is that of expediency. With great unanimity a financial measure has been adopted to provide for the immediate payment of the city's indebtedness, by means of a loan of half a million of dollars. It is of the greatest importance to the interests of the city, that that measure should be made to succeed at the earliest possible moment. In my deliberate judgment its success would be injuriously impeded, if not entirely defeated, by associating with the proposition for a loan, an ordinance to appropriate so large a proportion of the amount demanded as sixty-four thousand dollars, to the payment of a class of officers whose services are usually rendered without any other remuneration than the honor conferred by their fellow-citizens, and their participation in the general good which it is their province and duty to promote. It could not fail to weaken our public credit to show a purpose to use it for the payment of salaries never contemplated by the people, especially in view of the admitted necessity for the practice of the most rigid economy, in order to complete by means of all the resources and credit we possess the public works in progress or in contemplation. With scarcely a dollar in the public treasury—without the means of discharging even the interest falling due for the scrip already issued—the city credit impaired, and general bankruptcy staring us in the face, retrenchment should be the order of the day, rather than the opening up of new modes of making enormous and heretofore unknown expenditures."

This act of the mayor was universally and heartily applauded by the people, and received the highest commendation of the entire press; while, on the other hand, it received the severest censures of the aldermen themselves, who not only passed the ordinance by a legal number of votes despite the mayor's veto, but for a long time refused to grant a salary to his honor. The sudden and angry burst of popular feeling on this subject led, the following year, to a provision in the new charter, then granted by the Legislature to the city, which declared that henceforward the members of the Common Council should not be entitled to any compensation for their services.

July 1st.—From the shipping lists published in the daily newspapers, it appears that about this time there were five hundred and twenty-six vessels lying in the port, the greater number of which were ships and barques, the remainder being brigs and schooners. Besides these, there were at least one hundred large square-rigged vessels lying at Benicia, Sacramento, and Stockton. Long before this time many of the old seamen who had deserted their ships had returned from the mines, and there was no difficulty in procuring crews for departing vessels, upon paying them the ordinary high wages of the time.

July 4th.—Another grand celebration of independence-day. This was particularly distinguished by the erection on the plaza of a magnificent flagstaff, or liberty-pole, which Messrs. S. Coffin and W. W. Chapman, on behalf of the citizens of Portland, Oregon, had presented to the citizens of San Francisco, and which was received by the mayor, Col. J. W. Geary. The length of this pole is one hundred and eleven feet. It is one foot in diameter at the bottom, tapering regularly to about three inches at the other end, and is as straight as an arrow. This is perhaps the longest and most faultlessly straight pole that is known, although the presenters apologized that no longer one had been sent, on account of the inconvenience of shipping a stick of larger dimensions. The old pole which used to stand on the plaza from Mexican days, and upon which the first American flag was hoisted, had been removed on the 7th of June preceding, and was erected in front of the custom-house, at the corner of Montgomery and California streets.

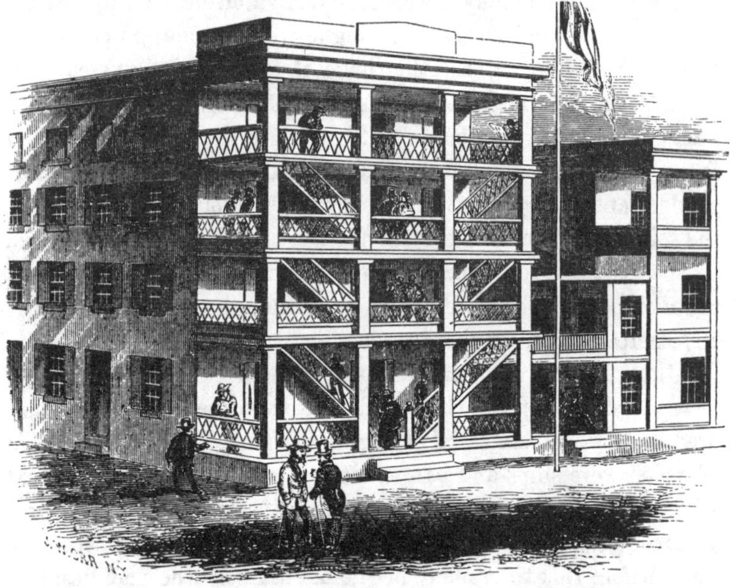

Cus om-house, at the corner of Montgomery and California streets.

The custom-house, occupied by Col. James Collier, then collector of the port, was a new four-story brick building, and the most imposing edifice in the city. It was destroyed by fire on the 4th of May, 1851, as was also the old liberty-pole.

July 15th.—General Bennet Riley, late military governor of the territory, left San Francisco for the Eastern States. Prior to his departure a letter was addressed him, signed by the mayor and numerous influential citizens, tendering him a public dinner, and complimenting him for the satisfactory manner in which he had performed his duties as governor of the country. Previous arrangements, however, prevented the general from accepting this invitation, in declining which he uses the following language:—"Both in my official and social relations with the people of California, I have ever been treated with the utmost indulgence and kindness. I can never cease to feel a lively interest in their happiness and prosperity, and I now leave them with feelings of deep regret. If California, by her mineral wealth, and the unexampled increase of her population and commerce, has attracted the attention of the world, her dignified course in the peculiar and trying position in which she has been placed, equally challenge universal admiration."

AUGUST.—Organization of the "*Society of California Pioneers.*" The objects of this society were declared, in the words of the constitution, to be "to cultivate the social virtues of its members, to collect and preserve information connected with the early settlement and conquest of the country, and to perpetuate the memory of those whose sagacity, enterprise, and love of independence, induced them to settle in the wilderness, and become the germ of a new State." The society "shall be composed of native Californians; foreigners residing in California previous to the conquest; and natives of other States and other countries, if citizens of the United States, resident here prior to January 1st, 1849, and their male descendants, who shall constitute the *first class;* and citizens of the old States of the Federal Government who shall have resided in California prior to January 1st, 1850, and their male descendants, who shall constitute the *second class;* and honorary members, who may be admitted in accordance with what may be prescribed in the by-laws." The admission fees, which are now (1854) ten dollars, and a monthly subscription of a dollar, payable half-yearly in advance, "and all funds arising therefrom or by donation, shall be safely invested, and the income arising therefrom shall be appropriated to charitable purposes, exclusively for the use and benefit of the widows and orphans of pioneer immigrants, members of this society." A list of the members in April, 1854, with the dates of their respective arrivals in California, their present residences, and the office-bearers of that year, appear in the Appendix. Here we may only name the first office-bearers of the society. They were as follows:—

President:—William D. M. Howard.

Vice-Presidents.

Jacob R. Snyder, Samuel Brannan, G. Frank Lemon.

Recording Secretary.
Joseph L. Folsom.

Assistant Recording Secretary.
J. C. L. Wadsworth.

Corresponding Secretary.
Edwin Bryant.

Treasurer.
Talbot H. Green.

Assistant Corresponding Secretaries.
W. C. Parker and A. J. Grayson.

Board of Directors.

James C. Ward,	H. W. Halleck,	J. Mead Huxley,
James C. Low,	J. D. Stevenson,	R. M. Sherman,
Samuel Kyburn,	James Hall,	Henry Gerke,
G. K. Winner,	Robert Wells,	G. W. Vincent,
H. A. Schoolcraft,	J. B. Frisbie,	R. A. Parker,
William Blackburn,	John Wilson,	W. H. Davis.

August 15th.—The city was thrown into a state of excitement by news of serious riots having occurred at Sacramento City on the preceding day. It seems that a great portion of the land covering that city and vicinity is held by grants from Capt. John A. Sutter, who claimed under an old Spanish title. Much of this land had been squatted upon by parties who denied the legality of Sutter's grants, and who claimed a right to the property as pre-emptionists or settlers. The holders of titles from Sutter appealed to the courts, and decisions were given in their favor; but upon attempting to possess themselves of their appropriated property they were forcibly resisted by the squatters. On the 13th instant, several of these latter were arrested for resisting the officers of the law and the process of the court, and in default of bail, two of them were held in custody on board the prison brig. On the day following an armed body of squatters repaired to the brig to release their companions, where they were met by the mayor, sheriff, and a posse, who drove them back a considerable distance into the city, when they turned and fired upon the legal authorities, who immediately returned the fire with guns and pistols. Of the latter, Mr. Woodland, city assessor, was killed, and Mayor Bigelow, Mr. Harper, assistant postmaster, and several others were wounded. Mahloney, the leader of the squatters, was shot dead from his horse. Several others of the same party were killed, and a number severely wounded. On the same day, other disturbances occurred at Brighton, six miles south of the city, when Sheriff Joseph McKinney was killed, and

Sacramento City

several of his posse were wounded; three of the squatters were also killed, and a number taken prisoners. Immediately upon receiving intelligence of these lamentable occurrences Mayor Geary issued a proclamation, calling upon "the citizens of San Francisco to meet at the earliest possible period, form companies, and hold themselves in readiness to answer such calls as may necessarily be made upon them." Soon the "California Guard," Captain Howard, numbering eighty men, and "Protection Fire Company, No. 2," Captain McCormick, between forty and fifty men, properly equipped and armed with muskets, reported themselves ready for service. This force, under the command of Col Geary, departed at 12 o'clock for the scene of the riots in the steamboat Senator, which, with characteristic decision, promptness, and public spirit, had been placed at their disposal by Mr. Charles Minturn. Their departure was witnessed and loudly cheered by a great multitude of citizens, who had hastily gathered upon the wharves. They arrived at Sacramento about 11 o'clock in the evening. In the mean time order was partially restored, and happily their actual services were not required. They were kindly received by the authorities and citizens, and hospitably entertained until the 17th instant, when they returned to their homes. Before leaving Sacramento they were presented with highly complimentary and laudatory resolutions and votes of thanks from the Boards of Aldermen and Military Department of the State for the tender of their ready and efficient aid. This prompt action on the part of the mayor and citizens of San Francisco, doubtless, had a tendency not only to assist in preserving the restored peace of their sister city, but to prevent the occurrence of similar disturbances in other portions of the State. Be this as it may, it was deserving of the praise it received, and was an example worthy of being followed.

August 21st.—Mayor Geary published a brief address to the citizens in all the morning papers, informing them that news had been received of the "destitution, distress, and extreme suffering of the immigrants to California by the overland route;" and that a committee had been selected for the purpose of calling upon them during the day for means of relief for the sufferers. The committee consisted of John W. Geary, E. E. Dunbar, E. C. Kemble, Talbot H. Green, Henry M. Naglee, W. H. Parker, Wm. Sharron, and David C. Broderick. It was also stated by J. Neely Johnson, Esq., Agent for the Sacramento Relief Association, who had recently returned from an expedidition of relief to the immigrants, that "it was supposed that 60,000 emigrants started across the plains by the Northern, or 'Southern Pass' route. On the 18th June, 39,000 had been registered at Fort Laramie. Of this entire number probably 20,000 had arrived. Of the remaining number, 10,000 would probably arrive this side of the Desert, without teams, money, or provisions; 10,000 more with their teams so much worn down as to require additional assistance to enable them to cross the mountains." Mr. Johnson described the condition of some whom he had met on his expedition as destitute, sick, and wretched in the extreme, and showed the necessity of speedy means being taken to save the immigrants from starving, or otherwise fearfully perishing before they could terminate their journey. These appeals were promptly responded to by the

Emigrant Train.

citizens. Before night the committee had collected an immense quantity of provisions, and about $6000 in cash, which was forwarded without delay to meet the wants of the sufferers.

AUGUST 28th.—A novel and interesting ceremony took place this afternoon in Portsmouth Square. Mayor Geary, Vice-Consul Frederick A. Woodworth, Rev. Albert Williams, and other members of a committee appointed for the purpose, assembled on the platform, to present the Chinese residents with certain religious tracts, papers, and books, printed in Chinese characters. The "China boys," as they are pleased to be called, having formed themselves in procession, marched to the square, and arranged themselves in a circle upon the platform. They were clothed richly in their native costume, and made a fine and pleasing appearance. Here the presentation took place, and addresses were made by each of the gentlemen above named, which were interpreted by As-sing, one of the Chinese. The mayor, on this occasion, extended to them an invitation to take part in the funeral ceremonies that were to occur on the following day.

August 29th.—The death of President Taylor was commemorated by a funeral procession. The military and fire companies, Masonic and Odd-Fellows' Lodges, a variety of benevolent and other associations, the clergy, officers of the army and navy, consuls and representatives of foreign governments, the councils and various municipal and State officers, a great number of private citizens, and a large company of Chinese residents, took part in the imposing ceremonies. Hon. John B. Weller acted as Grand Marshal. The procession moved through the streets to Portsmouth Square, where an appropriate prayer was made by Rev. Augustus Fitch, and an eloquent eulogy pronounced by Hon. Elcan Heydenfeldt. On the following day the Chinese, who henceforward took considerable interest in public affairs, where any ceremony of a festival or imposing nature was concerned, presented the mayor with the following document, written in Chinese characters :—

"*San Francisco, August 30th*, 1850.

"*To* Hon. John W. Geary, *Mayor of the City of San Francisco* :—

"Sir :—The "China Boys" wish to thank you for the kind mark of attention you bestowed upon them in extending to them an invitation to join with the citizens of San Francisco in doing honor to the memory of the late President of the United States, General Zachary Taylor. The China Boys feel proud of the distinction you have shown them, and will always endeavor to merit your good opinion and the good opinion of the citizens of their adopted country. The China Boys are fully sensible of the great loss this country has sustained in the death of its chieftain and ruler, and mourn with you in sorrow. Strangers as they are among you, they kindly appreciate the many kindnesses received at your hands, and again beg leave, with grateful hearts, to thank you.

"As-sing,
"A-he,
"*In behalf of the China Boys.*"

CHAPTER XII.

1850.

The first City Directory published.—Monetary crisis.—Fourth great fire.—Death of Captain Bezer Simmons.—The wharves.—Celebration on occasion of the admission of California into the Union of American States.—Explosion of the steamer Sagamore.—City Hospital burned.—Improvements in the city.—Plank road to the Mission Dolores.—Death of the mayor of Sacramento.—Thanksgiving Day.—Fire in Sacramento street.

SEPTEMBER.—The first "Directory" of the city was published this month by Charles P. Kimball. It was a duodecimo pamphlet of one hundred and thirty-six pages, and contained about twenty-five hundred names.

SEPTEMBER 7th.—There have been during the last few days a monetary crisis and great run upon the banks; when one of them, Mr. Henry M. Naglee's, suspended payment to-day. During the troublous and exciting winter of 1849–50, speculation had gone beyond all bounds both in every kind of merchandise and in real estate. When the reaction came, prices fell nearly as much below the prime cost of goods as previously they had been above it, and in many cases great quantities of valuable merchandise could be had at nominal rates. Real estate, when forced on the market, often did not fetch a tenth of its recent value. Added to this sudden collapse of prices, three great fires had helped to ruin many, and had affected indeed every inhabitant of the city in some measure prejudicially. Thus a general financial embarrassment ensued, and numerous bankruptcies of people previously reputed wealthy followed. Some of the most extensive firms of the city were compelled to assign their property for the benefit of their creditors. On a sudden a panic seized those who held deposits in the different banks, and an immediate "run" was made on these establishments. Messrs. Burgoyne & Co.,

James King of William, and Wells & Co., nobly met the unexpected demand, and kept their doors open during unusual and extra hours to accommodate the half frantic depositors.

SEPTEMBER 17th.—About four o'clock in the morning of this day, fire broke out in the "Philadelphia House," on the north side of Jackson street, near to the Washington market. It was the *fourth* great conflagration in the city. The principal portions of the different building squares lying between Dupont, Montgomery, Washington and Pacific streets were overrun by the flames. The buildings erected on these quarters were chiefly of wood, and generally one story only in height; so that, although the space over which the fire extended was very great, much less proportionate damage was sustained than on the occasions of the preceding great fires. The loss was estimated to be from a quarter to half a million of dollars. The newly organized fire companies were of much service in staying the progress of the conflagration, and would have been of still more had there not been a short supply of water. It was evident, however, that the want of a proper head or engineering chief sadly hindered the harmonious action not only of these and the hook and ladder companies, but of every person who volunteered help in extinguishing the flames. As usual, the burned space was so soon afterwards covered with buildings that in a few weeks all external traces of the disaster disappeared. It was remarked at this time that there were certain unlucky individuals whose properties had been consumed on each occasion of the four great fires—all within nine months! Many had suffered twice and thrice by these successive calamities. This surely was enough to try the patience of a modern Job, and drive the bravest to despair. But in a common calamity, however great, there is such sympathy and consolation, that the mind readily recovers its equanimity. People were almost beginning to consider that such conflagrations could not be avoided, but were surely sent either as a punishment for their wickedness or as a necessary drawback upon the otherwise great profits of general business. So those burned out just set themselves doggedly to work again, and soon reared up new and grander habitations for themselves. Happily indeed does the Phœnix appear on the corporation seal, since, like it, the city was continually reviving and springing from its own ashes a fairer and more substantial thing than before.

September 26th.—Captain Bezer Simmons, the senior partner of the well-known house of Simmons, Hutchinson & Co., died this day. He was among the most respected citizens of San Francisco, and the earliest business men of the place. His name appears on several occasions in these "Annals," in connection with subjects of public interest. Captain Simmons was a native of Woodstock, Vt. Some years previous to the cession of California to the American Government he was engaged in trading along the coast of Lower California, and in 1848, purchased property in San Francisco, where he settled, and soon afterwards engaged in extensive and successful business operations. In April, 1849, he was sorely afflicted by the death of his wife, (who was the sister of Frederick Billings, of the law firm of Halleck, Peachy & Billings,) and before the close of the year, he received intelligence of the death of his mother and a brother to whom he was strongly attached. In January, 1851, he repaired to Woodstock, with the remains of his wife, to bury them in her native town. On his return he learned that his business was in an alarming condition, and soon after the firm was declared insolvent. Being exceedingly sensitive, this rapid succession of misfortunes and afflictions were thought to aggravate an indisposition under which he had been for some time suffering, and which consequently terminated his life. His death was considered almost a public calamity, and his body was attended to the grave by an immense concourse of the best portion of the inhabitants of the city.

October 22d.—To show the rapid progress of the city in one direction, we shall give a short notice of the state of the wharves in the bay about this time.

Central Wharf.—So early as the autumn of 1848 the want of a good ship wharf was seriously felt, and different schemes were, in the following winter and spring months, projected to supply the deficiency. It was not, however, till May of 1849, that any active steps were taken in the matter. At that time a proper wharf association was formed, which raised considerable capital, and began operations. By December of the same year, eight hundred feet of the wharf was finished.

In the fire of June, 1850, a considerable portion was consumed, but the part destroyed was promptly repaired—even while the smoke of the ruins around continued to ascend. In August following, measures were taken to continue the work; and at the date of this notice, it extended so much as two thousand feet into the bay. This wharf had already cost $180,000; and was of the greatest service to the shipping of the port. Large vessels could lay alongside and discharge at any state of the tide.

MARKET STREET WHARF commenced at the foot of Market street, and had already run out six hundred feet into the bay.

CALIFORNIA STREET WHARF was four hundred feet long and thirty-two feet wide.

HOWISON'S PIER was eleven hundred feet in length, by forty feet in width—the depth of water, at full tide, being fourteen feet at the extremity.

SACRAMENTO STREET WHARF was eight hundred feet in length.

CLAY STREET WHARF was nine hundred feet in length, by forty feet in width; and in another month was extended to eighteen hundred feet.

WASHINGTON STREET WHARF was two hundred and seventy-five feet long.

JACKSON STREET WHARF was five hundred and fifty-two feet in length, with thirteen feet depth of water.

PACIFIC STREET WHARF was already five hundred and twenty-five feet long, and sixty feet wide.

BROADWAY WHARF was two hundred and fifty feet long, and forty feet wide.

CUNNINGHAM'S WHARF was three hundred and seventy-five feet long, and thirty-three feet wide, having a T at its end three hundred and thirty feet long, by thirty feet wide. It had twenty-five feet depth of water at the cross line.

LAW'S WHARF, at the foot of Green street, was likewise in the course of formation; and a wharf, to be seventeen hundred feet in length, was immediately about to be undertaken by the city, on the north beach.

The cost of these various wharves already amounted to nearly a million and a half of dollars; and they provided artificial thoroughfares to the extent of almost two miles. A few of them were the property of the corporation; but the greater number were owned by private companies or by individuals, who drew large returns from them. There is little trace left of these works, for the water space along their sides is now covered with houses, while the wharves themselves have become public streets, their future extensions forming the existing wharves and piers of the city. This gradual march across the deep waters of the bay is a peculiar feature in the progress of the city, and serves to liken it to those other queens of the sea, Venice and Amsterdam, and perhaps also to St. Petersburgh. But where the latter have canals for streets, and solid earth now beneath their first pile-founded buildings, San Francisco, over a great portion of its business and most valuable districts, has still only a vast body of tidal water, beneath both the plank-covered streets and the pile-founded houses themselves. Year by year, however, this strange watery abyss is being filled up by the removal of the sand hills behind, which may be said to be taken up and cast bodily into the deep. When the original wharves were erected they proved of the utmost benefit to the commerce and prosperity of the city; and their extent, as detailed above, shows in a striking manner the energy and enterprise of the people who had constructed them in so short a space of time.

October 29th.—This day was set apart to celebrate the admission of California into the Union. When, on the 18th instant, the mail steamer "Oregon" was entering the bay, she fired repeated preconcerted signal guns which warned the citizens of the glorious news. Immediately the whole of the inhabitants were afoot, and grew half wild with excitement until they heard definitely that the tidings were as they had expected. Business of almost every description was instantly suspended, the courts adjourned in the midst of their work, and men rushed from every house into the streets and towards the wharves, to hail the harbinger of the welcome news. When the steamer rounded Clark's Point and came in front of the city, her masts literally covered with flags and signals, a universal shout arose from ten thousand voices on the wharves, in the streets, upon the hills, house-tops, and the world of shipping in the bay. Again and again were huzzas repeated, adding more and more every moment to the intense excitement and unprecedented enthusiasm. Every public place was soon crowded with eager seekers after the particulars of the news, and the first papers issued an hour after the appearance of the Oregon were sold by the newsboys at from one to five dollars each. The enthusiasm increased as the day advanced. Flags of every nation were run up on a thousand masts and peaks and staffs, and a couple of large guns placed upon the plaza were constantly discharged. At night every public thoroughfare was crowded with the rejoicing populace. Almost every large building, all the public saloons and places of amusement were brilliantly illuminated—music from a hundred bands assisted the excitement—numerous balls and parties were hastily got up—bonfires blazed upon the hills, and rockets were incessantly thrown into the air, until the dawn of the following day. Many difficulties had occurred to delay this happy event, and the people had become sick at heart with the "hope deferred" of calling themselves, and of being in reality citizens of the great American Union. It is only necessary to state here, without going into particulars, that the delay had arisen from the jealousy of the proslavery party in Congress, at a time when they and the abolitionists were nicely balanced in number, to admit an additional free State into the Union, whereby so many more votes would be given against the peculiar and obnoxious "domestic institution" of the South. Several compromises had been occasionally attempted to be effected by statesmen of each great party, but without success. In the end, however, the bill for the admission of California passed through Congress by large majorities.

Such an occasion beyond all others demanded a proper celebration at San Francisco; and the citizens, accordingly, one and all, united to make the day memorable. On the 29th instant, a procession of the various public bodies and inhabitants of the city, with appropriate banners, devices, music and the like, marched through the principal streets to the plaza. The Chinese turned out in large numbers on this occasion, and formed a striking feature in the ceremonies of the day. The Honorable Nathaniel Bennett, of the Supreme Court, delivered a suitable oration to the people on the plaza, and an ode, composed for the occasion by Mrs. Wills, was sung by a full choir. During the day repeated discharges of fire-arms and a proper salute from great guns carried off some of the popular excitement, while the shipping displayed innumerable flags. In the evening, public bonfires and fireworks were exhibited from Telegraph Hill, Rincon Point, and the islands in the bay. The houses were likewise brilliantly illuminated, and the rejoicings were every where loudly continued during the night. Some five hundred gentlemen and three hundred ladies met at the grandest public ball that had yet been witnessed in the city, and danced and made merry, till daylight, in the pride and joy of their hearts that California was truly now the *thirty-first* State of the Union.

On this day (October 29th), the steamer "Sagamore" exploded, when about to leave the wharf for Stockton. Thirty or forty persons were killed.

OCTOBER 31st.—Destruction by fire of the City Hospital, which was situated at the head of Clay street, and owned by Dr. Peter Smith. This was supposed to have been the work of an incendiary. The fire broke out in an adjoining house, which was also consumed. Several of the patients were severely burned, and it was only by the most strenuous exertions of the firemen and citizens that they were saved at all.

NOVEMBER.—We have already noticed the progress that had been made in the erection of wharves, and we may now direct attention to the important steps that had been taken in grading, planking and otherwise improving the streets of the city. During the summer of this year, the care of the mayor and common council had been particularly turned towards the improvements of the communications through the town, and many ordinances had been passed with that view. Considerable hills had consequently been cut down and immense hollows filled up. Great quantities of rock and sand were removed, from places where they were only nuisances, to other quarters where they became of use in removing the natural irregularities of the ground, and making all smooth and level. Piles were driven deep in the earth where needed, the principal streets were substantially planked, and commodious sewers formed. The cost of these improvements was very great, it being estimated that nearly half a million of dollars would be required this year to complete those now in operation. The city paid about one-third of that amount, and raised the remainder by assessment upon the parties whose properties faced the streets which were altered. To show the extent of these improvements, we give the following lists of the streets in which they were now being executed. Those running north and south were as follows :—

Battery street	between	Market and California—		graded and planked.	
Sansome	“	Bush and Broadway,		“	
Montgomery	“	California	“	“	and sewer.
Kearny	“	“	“	“	“
Dupont	“	Sacramento	“	“	“
Stockton	“	Clay and Water,		“	
Ohio	“	Broadway and Pacific,		“	
Taylor	“	Lombard and Water,		“	

Those running east and west were as follows :

Bush street,	between	Battery and	Montgomery—	graded and planked.	
California	“	bulkhead	“	“	and sewer.
Sacramento	“	Sansome and	Dupont,	“	“
Clay	“	bulkhead and	Stockton,	“	“
Washington	“	“	Dupont,	“	“
Jackson	“	“	“	“	“
Pacific	“	Kearny	“	“	“
Broadway	“	Water and	Ohio,	“	
Francisco	“	“	Stockton,	“	

Thus the municipal authorities were taking precautions to remove, before the rainy season commenced, as many as possible of the obstacles, which, during the preceding winter, had rendered the streets nearly impassable.

November 18th.—This day an ordinance regarding the plank-road to the Mission Dolores, and which had previously been carried in the Board of Assistant Aldermen by a two-third vote, passed the Board of Aldermen by a constitutional majority, notwithstanding certain objections of the mayor and his consequent veto. The mission, which is situated two and a quarter miles from the plaza, was a place of common resort for the citizens, but the road to it being sandy, was difficult of travel, especially for vehicles. Owing to this cause, the cost of carriage was very great.

A load of hay, for instance, moved from the mission to the city, cost as much as fifteen or twenty dollars. The same way likewise led to San José, the capital of the State. It was therefore of considerable public importance that this road should be speedily improved. In the summer of this year, Colonel Charles L. Wilson conceived the plan of laying a plank-road from Kearny street to the mission, and presented a proposition to that effect to the Common Council. He offered to build the road, which, at that time, was considered a tremendous enterprise, in consequence of the high price of lumber and labor, on condition that he was allowed to collect certain rates of toll from those using it, and that he should have the exclusive right of the way for the term of ten years, at the expiring of which time the entire improvements were to revert to the city. An ordinance to grant Col. Wilson the privileges he asked, readily passed one of the boards of aldermen, but it was a long while before it obtained the concurrence of the other ; and not even then until it was so modified that seven years only were allowed the projector for the use of the road, and but five months granted him for completion of the work. The importance of the undertaking was admitted on all sides ; and the chief opposition to it was based upon the assumption that the city should rather make it at its own expense and reap the large profits which it was supposed would be the result. This, however, at that period, was impossible, the city being upwards of a million and a half of dollars in debt, and without the slightest prospect of being able for years to defray its unavoidable current expenses.

Having obtained the consent of the council, Col. Wilson next met with a formidable obstacle in rather an unexpected quarter. The mayor, after retaining the ordinance the full length of time allowed him, returned it unapproved. Notwithstanding, the council again adopted it with almost a unanimous vote. Still, the veto of the mayor affected the enterprise unfavorably to a considerable extent. Several parties, who had previously engaged to furnish funds for the work, now became alarmed as to the legality of the council's procedure, and withheld their promised aid. Col. Wilson was therefore left alone, to abandon altogether his weighty project, or to carry it on unassisted. He determined upon the latter course, and although without any definite idea of the source from whence the means were to be obtained, commenced the work. Having proceeded far enough to give a guarantee for the completion of the project, he visited the capital, and obtained from the

Beach of Yerba Buena Cove, Winter of 1849-50, from Central Wharf to Happy Valley.

legislature an act confirming the ordinance of the city council. This renewed confidence in the measure. A half interest in the undertaking was immediately sold, and funds were thus obtained for carrying it on. Upon the very last day allowed under the ordinance for completion of the work, loaded wagons passed on the road from the mission to the town.

This plank-road has proved of the greatest service to San Francisco, and the property through which it passes has increased immensely in value for building purposes. Formerly that property was at times nearly inaccessible, and on all occasions was very difficult and troublesome to reach; while it is now of comparatively easy access. Since the formation of this plank-way, another road of the same kind has likewise been formed to the mission, upon similar terms granted by the council to the projectors; and both are believed to have proved highly lucrative schemes to their spirited proprietors.

November 27th.—Hon. Harden Bigelow, Mayor of Sacramento City, died this morning at the Union Hotel. He had taken an active part in suppressing the squatter riots at Sacramento, when he received a gun-shot wound which required the amputation of an arm. The operation was performed by Dr. John Hastings, by whose advice Mr. Bigelow was removed to San Francisco, believing the climate of that city would conduce toward effecting a more rapid recovery from the effects of the injury. While here he was attacked with cholera, which caused his death. His body was conveyed to the steamboat New World, to be taken to Sacramento for burial, by an escort composed of the California Guard, the mayor, members of the Common Council, heads of departments of the city, and the Society of California Pioneers. Mayor Geary delivered a very appropriate address on the occasion, in which the many excellent traits in the character of the deceased were depicted in a most affecting manner.

November 30th.—A thanksgiving-day for the admission of California into the Union.

December 14th.—On the evening of this day a fire broke out in an iron building on Sacramento street, below Montgomery street. Several large stores and much valuable goods were destroyed. The total damage was estimated at about a million of dollars. Elsewhere such a fire might well be called a *great* one ; but it was not so reckoned in the "Annals of San Francisco."

CHAPTER XIII.

1850.

Population in 1850.—City improvements.—Grading and planking streets.—Wharves, steamers, manufactures.—Supply and demand for goods.—Mines yielding abundantly.—Expresses established.—Moral progress.—Better state of things.—Cholera.—California admitted to the Union.—City Charter granted.—First Common Council —The gold medals for Aldermen.—Corruption of officials.—Colton Grants.—Leidesdorff Estate.—City finances.—Outrages and fires.—The prisons and police.—Lynch Law agitated.

In the course of the year 1850, upwards of thirty-six thousand persons arrived by sea in San Francisco. Of these fully one-half came direct from foreign ports, while many of those that crossed the Isthmus of Panama were likewise from foreign countries. By far the greater number of immigrants were adult males, as might have been anticipated. The most of these persons hastened at once to the mines, only staying a few days, or at most a week or two, in town, to recruit their strength and make preparation for the digger's toil. Perhaps two thousand females, many of whom were of base character and loose practices, were also added this year to the permanent population, if that can be called permanent which dwelt at least a twelvemonth in the city. The immigration across the plains and by land generally into the State was also, as in the preceding year, very large. Great numbers of all these sea and land immigrants, after they had been some months at the mines, and made perhaps a few thousand dollars, returned by way of San Francisco, to their former homes. Many others, altogether disappointed with or unfit for the country, went hastily back to the places from whence they had come. Thus vessels leaving the bay, and especially the steamers, were nearly as well filled with passengers as when they had first arrived. This constant migration to and from the State gave a wonderful animation to the streets of the town. Many of the incomers remained in the place, and the regular population continued to increase. At the close of this year, the inhabitants probably numbered between twenty-five and thirty thousand. The Chinese had not yet arrived in any great numbers, but the Chilenos and other people of Spanish-American extraction continued very numerous.

The year 1850 saw a wonderful improvement in the aspect of San Francisco. Notwithstanding the conflagrations which had so often laid in ruins large portions of the city, or perhaps rather to some extent in consequence of them, the buildings in the business quarters were now remarkable for their size, beauty and solidity. The tents and shanties of last year had totally disappeared from the centre of the town, while many of the old frame buildings that had not been destroyed by fire were replaced by others of a larger and stronger kind, if not by extensive fire-proof brick structures. It is true that in the outskirts there were still numerous frail and unsubstantial habitations left, while, farther away many more of the same kind were being weekly and daily added ; but as population and the value of real estate and household property gradually increased, these temporary erections began to give place to more solid and comfortable buildings. Though labor still commanded high prices, during a great part of the year, most kinds of building materials could be obtained at comparatively low rates, probably at an average of one-fourth or one-sixth of the prices of the preceding season.

While houses were thus changing for the better, an equal improvement was taking place in the character of the streets. If nature had given to San Francisco magnificent water privileges, she had certainly been very chary in bestowing upon it land ones. The site, immediately available for building operations, was exceedingly small, and it was only by the expenditure of a vast amount of labor that additional space could be obtained for the necessary extension of the town. The land around was very hilly and irregular, which had all to be made smooth and plain before proper streets could be designed and convenient houses built. Fortunately the obstructing hills were composed chiefly of sand and easily removed. The original tents, shanties and houses had just been placed upon the old uneven surface, high up or low down as it happened; but it was soon found, that if the city was ever intended by its inhabitants to grow to greatness, some method must be observed in bringing them more upon a straight line, with ready access between all parts of the place. Very expensive works were therefore ordered by the town council, to establish a regular and convenient grade to the streets, while these were in many places substantially planked, and in some instances had sewers constructed along them. During the summer of 1850, such alterations had been proceeded with to a considerable extent, and now, when the winter and rainy season approached, their utility was seen and appreciated by all.

Other material improvements were keeping pace with those of the houses and streets. Numerous well appointed wharves were run out into the deep waters of the bay, at which the largest vessels could lay alongside and discharge. Better regulations were continually being adopted by the harbor masters to facilitate the shipping interests. In the year just passed six hundred and fifty-six sea-going vessels had arrived and discharged at the port. Of these five hundred and ninety-eight were American, and fifty-eight of different foreign countries. The public offices of the city and State were removed to more commodious and accessible buildings. The towns around the shores of the bay and those situated on the Sacramento and San Joaquin Rivers could now be easily, rapidly and cheaply reached, by means of numerous large, strong and beautiful steamboats. All along the outer coasts, magnificent steamships regularly carried the mails and passengers. In San Francisco itself, many workshops and manufactories began to be established; and, if few articles of trade were manufactured from the beginning out of raw materials, at least extensive repairs could always be now made upon them. The important suburb of "Happy Valley," on the southern side of the town, became quite a hive of manufacturing industry, where there were many large works for the building and repairing of steam and sailing vessels, foundries, lumber-yards, docks, flour-mills and workshops of various kinds. Labor of every description was highly paid, and generally all branches of the community had reason to be satisfied with their profits.

The enormous gains of the preceding year had tempted those

who partook of them to largely increase their shipments for 1850, while others, determined to share in the golden spoil, hastened to send additional goods to what was a limited market at best. The increased supply of merchandise soon affected the market, and prices in the spring of 1850 fell very considerably. There was a slight subsequent reaction in the course of the year, but towards the close, markets became more depressed than ever, and much embarrassment ensued to the mercantile class. This fall in prices, as well as the natural depreciation in the value of real estate from the former excessive rates, and the losses sustained by the many great fires, led to a monetary crisis, when a great number of merchants, real estate jobbers and others became bankrupt. One particular consequence of the excessive supply of goods was the sudden extraordinary increase of auctioneering business. When markets began to fall, and merchants found that their importations could not afford to pay storage and other charges, and still more, when commission agents desired to realize their advances, or were urged by foreign correspondents to sell at any price, then whole shiploads of merchandise were rattled off with a crack of the auctioneer's hammer. It seemed to be of little moment at what rate so that somehow the matter was fixed, accounts could be adjusted, and the distant sufferer made aware of the net amount of his loss. This was still farther the case during the succeeding year. The auction business was meanwhile becoming one of great importance, which it continued to be, and is now, in San Francisco. That system of disposing of goods possesses many advantages, among which are speedy returns, and in the case of brisk demand, perhaps also better prices than can be obtained otherwise, but, at a period of glut, it fearfully sacrifices the interests of the luckless absent proprietor of unsaleable merchandise. In 1850, and still more in 1851, these things could not well be helped by any party. Still, however great individual losses and sufferings might be, the general interests of the place were all this while steadily advancing ; and this was only one of the severe ordeals through which every great city in its unexpected origin and speedy progress might be expected to pass.

The mines were yielding larger returns than ever, the country was being rapidly peopled, agriculture was beginning to be followed to a considerable extent, towns were in course of erection, and magnificent structures built on all the land. San Francisco was the great centre from whence all these changes and improvements originated, and naturally kept to itself a large proportion of them. Steam and stage "expresses"—the invariable concomitants of American progress—were established over the whole country and to the Atlantic States, and letters, newspapers and packages were conveyed with speed and safety at moderate rates. A powerful press diffused general information, and from the pulpits of many able churches flowed religious and moral consolation. These are the marks of high civilization, and they were strikingly stamped upon San Francisco. Some of the first immigrants had sent for their wives and families, and a few of those who had come later brought them in their train. The "household gods" were set up in many a dwelling, and the inmates could now worship and enjoy their blessings together. Instead of the old scenes of terrible confusion which we have described as existing at the close of 1849, the city, only one twelvemonth later, presented an orderly, decent and busy aspect, with moderately clean and regular streets, houses of fair proportions, prices of provisions and goods reasonable, markets supplied with every luxury for the table, convenient wharves for shipping, "expresses" by sea and land, a dozen churches, half-a-dozen banking establishments, several theatres, well-filled book and music stores, six or seven daily newspapers, magnificent hotels and restaurants, handsome public carriages for the rich and ostentatious, and with almost every luxury, convenience and necessary, mental and corporeal, that old cities in long peopled and civilized countries could boast of. The earliest citizens formed themselves into the "Society of California Pioneers," and numerous associations were organized for municipal and defensive, literary, charitable, musical, social and similar purposes, just as we find in the old established communities. Most of the inhabitants certainly seemed to live purely to heap more dollars to their existing store; but it was not altogether so. Rays of refinement were shooting through the sordid mass, and gradually turning it towards a feeling that there was something higher, happier and better than mere money gathering. But while this ennobling leaven was silently and slowly at work among the busy multitudes, the great apparent characteristics of the place continued to be its material progress and the incessant stir and industry of the people. The town had been severely tried in the conflagrations which so repeatedly destroyed large portions of the most valuable districts ; but nothing could daunt the energy and enterprise of the inhabitants. These losses and all the natural obstacles of the site were successively overcome, and the city grew daily more grand and rich.

Cholera visited San Francisco in the fall of this year ; but its ravages were slight. The greatest number of deaths in any one day did not exceed ten or twelve. The epidemic began in October, was at its height in November, and disappeared by the close of the year. Notwithstanding the filth and rubbish which naturally collected around the scene of so many busy operations by a vast population which had hitherto adopted no proper means to preserve cleanliness and purity of atmosphere, the health of the place was wonderfully preserved ; and neither by cholera, which alights and is most deadly on the filthiest spots of a country, nor by other diseases, did a disproportionate or unusual number of deaths occur. This is high testimony to the extreme salubrity of the climate. The winter of 1850–51 was a remarkably dry and pleasant one, a striking contrast to the dreary winter of 1849–50.

In the course of 1850, two great political changes had taken place : California had been admitted into the Union, and a city charter, previously approved of by the inhabitants, had been granted to San Francisco by the State Legislature. The latter was much improved and re-granted in the following year. In the Appendix we give copies of the State Constitution and of the amended City Charter. By these events, the hands of both the general and local authorities were greatly strengthened, and the foundations of a firm government fairly laid.

The first common council of San Francisco, under the charter, had certainly a considerable deal to do, and perhaps did it well enough ; but their appropriation of a large portion of the city funds to themselves, by the name of salaries, met with much opposition from the citizens, which had at least the effect of reducing the amount one-third. At a later date of the year, the aldermen were said to have mysteriously voted to themselves a gold medal, of the value of one hundred and fifty dollars, supposed to be for those public and *extra* services which were not covered by the salaries of six or four thousand dollars, nor by the very many fine opportunities for corporation jobbery. But general curiosity being excited on the subject, and prying inquiries made as to the when and how, the why and the wherefore, these medals were earned, voted and paid for, the council boards suddenly found it convenient to pretend utter ignorance of the whole matter, and to quietly pay for the medals themselves, to put into the melting pot. The truth of the matter seems to have been that one of the sub-committees appointed to make arrangements for the public festival of the 29th October, to celebrate the admission of California into the Union, had wilfully or ignorantly overstepped their duties, and, assuming the glad consent of their brethren, had ordered these medals, on pretence of suitably decorating the aldermen for the occasion. But unluckily the medals were not, and could not have been procured in time for that celebration. The whole affair became an excellent joke, al-

Aldermen's Medal.

though a somewhat bitter one against the goaded council. To perpetuate the memory of those happy, or unhappy times for our "city fathers," we give illustrations of the wonderful medal. It will be noticed that a blank is left in the inscription for the name of the worthy recipient.

All human institutions are subject to abuse, and especially in the youth of a quickly growing community, where every member is heart and soul occupied in providing only for himself. Many charges have been made and more insinuated, as to the corrupt, careless, and extravagant behavior of most of the officials, since the fall of Mexican power, down even to 1854, in the administration of the revenues and properties, both of the State of California and of the City of San Francisco. In a country and place like these, where hitherto gold has been pretty generally the only thing supposed to be worth living for, one cannot avoid believing that many of these charges and insinuations were true; and yet the occupants of office might otherwise have been "indifferent honest" men, and, after all, perhaps quite as good as their clamant neighbors. When any transaction of a particularly glaring, base or improper nature was found out, public opinion was sure to rise in rebellion and shame the rogues to common decency at least. Much popular feeling was, at one period of 1850, expended at "mass" and "indignation" meetings against the municipal authorities; but, by and by, the community, who could not afford the pecuniary loss of such gratis excitement and attention, settled down into comparative calmness and indifference.

The "Colton Grants" and the "Leidesdorff Estate," proved the means of much litigation in the courts of law, and from the great extent of pecuniary interest involved, and the variety of parties interested, these legal matters became of exceeding public importance, and merit a passing allusion. We have already noticed the death of Mr. Leidesdorff on the 18th May, 1848. Circumstances had led that gentleman to become a Mexican citizen about the year 1844, whereby he was enabled to hold, as he afterwards acquired, real estate to a large extent in Yerba Buena and its neighborhood, now San Francisco. From the great immigration which subsequently took place, this property suddenly became of immense value. Mr. Leidesdorff was reputed to have died some fifty thousand dollars in debt, and yet within two years afterwards his estate was worth nearly a million. This indeed was a prize worth contending for. The very administration of its revenues, at San Francisco charges, was the means of making annual fortunes to lucky agents. Hence the legal strife, and perhaps the imputing and bandying of improper motives among the judges and parties chiefly interested. The Leidesdorff estate was subsequently claimed by the State of California, on the ground that Mr. Leidesdorff had died intestate, leaving only alien, though legitimate relatives, whereby his property escheated to the State. In the spring of 1854, measures were about to be taken by the Legislature to make that claim effectual.

The financial condition of the city continued in a very bad state. Large sums of money were raised on scrip and loan warrants, for the purposes of municipal improvements and to defray the ordinary expenses, which there seemed no apparent means of soon redeeming. It is true the city possessed considerable property, but it was not yet time to sell it to advantage, while the pressure of taxation was beginning to be heavily felt by the inhabitants. The interest payable for public loans, as likewise in the case of private accommodation of the kind, was exceedingly great, the ordinary rates varying from five to eight *per cent. per month*. When private parties borrowed, they had generally to give real security for the amount, and to pay these high rates of interest monthly in advance.

The social and moral state of general society had meanwhile improved but little. Gambling indeed was not pursued, at least openly, by the more respectable classes, and among all it was much diminished in intensity. The common council had likewise passed ordinances which effectually prevented the public following of the avocation on Sunday. But notwithstanding this tribute to religious decency, and check against one branch of profligacy, crime was increasing, and the boldness and number of the criminals became very alarming. All manner of burglaries, robberies and thefts were of daily occurrence. So were personal assaults of an aggravated nature ; while murders were repeatedly taking place. A great many attempts at incendiarism had been detected, although the charge seldom or never could be fairly brought home to individuals. If, however, there were some legal

San Francisco, Winter of 1849–50, showing Montgomery street North from California street. For same view in 1854, see Frontispiece.

uncertainty on the subject, which prevented convictions, no moral doubt existed but that there was an active and numerous band of desperadoes existing in the city, who added to many other crimes that of wilful fire-raising. They did not display banners and march in procession through the streets to the music of drum and fife, like the old "hounds," but nevertheless they seemed to be as thoroughly organized and to support each other when necessary, as that notorious gang of villains. Besides the numerous real cases, false alarms of fire were still more frequently raised; and during the attendant confusion many depredations were committed. Hundreds of the loafer and rowdy class haunted the town, who had no visible means of support, and whose lives showed only one continued scene of vice, crime and violence. There seemed a wide-spread combination among the rogues to divide systematically the different branches and gains of their unhallowed profession; and from petty theft and swindling up to highway robbery and murder, the actors seemed to be perfect adepts in their several parts. The prisons were full; but they could not hold a tithe of the offenders. The police were few and not very highly paid, and they could not pretend to cope with the more daring rascals, who defied all their efforts at capture and conviction. False swearing at trials, by trusty and unblushing comrades, confounded the few prosecutions and ensured ultimate escape to the most guilty.

People, at last, began to talk among themselves of the urgent necessity of again adopting Lynch law, since the tedious and uncertain measures of the authorities did not seem to have the effect of terrifying and putting down the disturbers of the public peace. Even a portion of the newspaper press boldly advocated such doctrines; considering that the present alarming juncture of events formed such an exceptional case as to require a departure from the ordinary course of administering justice. As the successive conflagrations had developed a large volunteer force to watch over the safety of the town from fire, so the continued increase of open and daring crime was certain in the end to induce the establishment of a great police that would not be trifled with, but would uproot, by some sure and terrible means, villainy and villains wherever they could be found. Already the necessity of such a police was recognized, and it only wanted a few more glaring cases of outrage, spoil and murder, to give it a sudden being and irresistible strength.

CHAPTER XIV.

1851.

The Gold Bluffs and Pacific Mining Company.—The excitement at the City Hall in February, 1851. —Attempt to Lynch Burdue and Windred.—Their subsequent escape.—Burning of the steamers Hartford and Santa Clara.

JANUARY.—San Francisco has been startled "from its propriety" by news from the celebrated "Gold Bluffs;" and during the greater part of this month has dreamed unutterable things of black sand, and gray sand, and cargoes of gold. A band of pioneers and prospecters had recently proceeded in the *Chesapeake* steamer northwards to the Klamath River, near which, on the sea shore, they fancied they had found the richest and most extraordinary gold field that had ever been known. The sands of the sea, for a broad space several miles in length, beneath cliffs some hundred feet high, appeared to be literally composed in one half, at least, of the pure metal. Millions of diggers for ages to come could not exhaust that grand deposit. Already a few miners had collected about the spot; but these were so amazed and lost in the midst of the surrounding treasure that they knew not what to do. Like the ass with its superabundance of hay, they could not resolve to begin any thing. No man could well carry more than seventy-five or a hundred pounds weight upon his back for any great distance, and with that quantity of pure gold it was ridiculous, so it was, to be content, when numberless tons lay about. So these men—there were just nineteen of them—(the tellers of the story were very particular in some facts),—had resolved to wait till the spring, when they would freight and fill a ship with the wealth which they were then jealously watching over. Let us not be misunderstood, or supposed altogether jesting. A brilliant reporter for the Alta California says—"The gold is mixed with the black sand in proportions of from ten cents to ten dollars the pound. At times, when the surf is high, the gold is not easily discovered, but in the spring of the year, after a succession of calms, the entire beach is covered with bright and yellow gold. Mr. Collins, the secretary of the Pacific Mining Company, measured a patch of gold and sand, and estimates it will yield to *each* member of the company the snug little sum of $43,000,000 [*say*, forty-three *millions* of dollars !] and the estimate is formed upon a calculation that the sand holds out to be one tenth as rich as observation warrants them in supposing." No digging even was required, since one had only to stoop a little and raise as much as he wished of the stuff—half gold, half sand, from the surface of the beach.

Back the adventurers hastened to San Francisco, where they had long been impatiently expected ; and the glorious news ran like wild-fire among the people. General John Wilson and Mr. John A. Collins, both of whom had been among the number of discoverers, frankly testified to the truth of these wonderful statements. The beach, they said, for a great distance, was literally strewed with pure gold. It was found in the greatest quantity in a certain kind of "black sand," although the "gray sand," which was rather more abundant, contained likewise a large proportion of the same black-colored stuff with its special share of gold. "Mr. Collins," says the poetic reporter, "saw a man [one of the nineteen, no doubt,] who had accumulated fifty thousand pounds, or fifty thousand tons—he did not recollect which—of the richest kind of black sand."

Such intelligence astounded the community. In a few days eight vessels were announced as about to sail for this extraordinary region. The magic phrase "GOLD BLUFFS !" "GOLD BLUFFS ! !" every where startled the most apathetic, and roused him as with a galvanic shock. "GOLD BLUFFS ! ! !" filled the columns of newspapers among the shipping advertisements ; they covered, on huge posters, the blank walls of houses at the corners of the streets ; they were in every man's mouth. A company was formed called the "Pacific Mining Company," the shares of which instantly rose to a handsome premium. There seemed no doubt of their incalculable gains, since they showed numerous samples of the wondrous "black sand," where the golden particles lay and shone mildly, as stars in the milky way, innumerable. The company had already, by the greatest good fortune, secured a considerable number of miners' claims, embracing indeed the entire beach beneath the "Bluffs," so that all was clear for immediate operations. We have seen the intelligent secretary's calculations on the subject. No wonder people raved, and either invested a few thousand dollars in shares of this company, or sold or forsook their all, and made sail for the *Gold Bluffs*. The ancient excitement of Mississippi and South Sea schemes was a bagatelle in comparison with that which now stirred San Francisco, used though it had been to all manner of rumors of placers, and gigantic "pockets" of gold. The skepticism of envious un-"progressive" people was happily ridiculed, and the press compared the ocean to a mighty cradle that had been rocking and washing up gold from the bottom of the sea for unknown ages, and had chanced to throw it in tons and shiploads beneath the hitherto undiscovered *Gold Bluffs*. It was truly great news for San Francisco.

The first damper to the hot blast that raged through the town, and from whence it spread and fired up distant countries, —until the arrival of the next mail,—was intelligence from the earliest miners, that they found it very difficult to separate first the black sand from the gray, and next the gold itself from the black sand, the particles of the precious metal being so remarkably fine. A little later, it was found that the innumerable "patches" of black sand began most unaccountably to disappear. Heavy seas came and swept them right away; and though it was hoped that heavier seas might soon bring them back again, the people got tired of waiting for that event, and hastily fled from the place, ashamed of their own hopes and credulity, and cursing the cruel wags that had exhibited in San Francisco sealed phials of dingy sand largely mixed with brass filings.

But we cannot pursue this pleasantry farther. Much serious loss was suffered by the *Gold Bluffs* piece of business. The unfortunate "Pacific Mining Company" had bought the *Chesapeake* at a cost for boat and repairs of *twenty thousand dollars*, had run her up the coast several trips at the loss of as many thousands more, and afterwards, when she had been injured in a storm, were glad to sell her for about two thousand dollars. If, however, the shareholders, or any single adventurer lost much money—why, they had at one time the most brilliant hopes imaginable of immense riches; and these were surely some compensation. For what, after all, is life without *hope?* There was considerable gold at the *Bluffs*, but it turned out in the end to cost more trouble to gather than it was worth. Hence the place was abandoned, except by a few still hopeful individuals, after a few months' trial. Since the whole affair formed a very striking, though latterly a ridiculous event in the progress of San Francisco, we could not refuse it a place in these "Annals."

FEBRUARY.—After the affair of the "Hounds," in 1849, the citizens left the execution of the laws against criminals in the hands of the constituted authorities. Either the laws, however, or the authorities, or something else soon went wrong, and crime fearfully increased. At length, not only were the people seriously inclined to believe that they must take the law back to themselves and issue it in a new form, but the public journals discussed the matter gravely and argumentatively, and urged the instant appointment of "volunteer police," or "regulators," who would supply the place of an inefficient executive and judicature. Hitherto there had been no organization for the purpose mentioned, although occasional mobs had ducked or whipped offenders caught in the act of crime.

On the 19th of this month, about eight o'clock in the evening, two men entered the store of C. J. Jansen & Co., and, professing to be purchasers, asked to see some blankets. Mr. Jansen, who was alone in the store, was in the act of producing the articles, when he was violently struck with a slung shot, and fell insensible on the floor. While in that state he seems to have been farther maltreated, and was probably considered by the ruffians as dead. These robbed the premises of two thousand dollars, and immediately fled. The whole circumstances of the outrage were of the most daring character, and the knowledge of them caused much excitement among the people. The next day a man was arrested, believed to be one James Stuart, but who gave his name as Thomas Burdue, on the charge of having murdered Mr. Moore, the Sheriff of Auburn, and of having robbed him of four thousand dollars. Stuart had been confined in the jail of Sacramento to await his trial, but had escaped two months before. Circumstances meanwhile had raised a suspicion that this man Stuart, *alias* Burdue, had had something to do with the attack on Mr. Jansen ; and accordingly he, and another

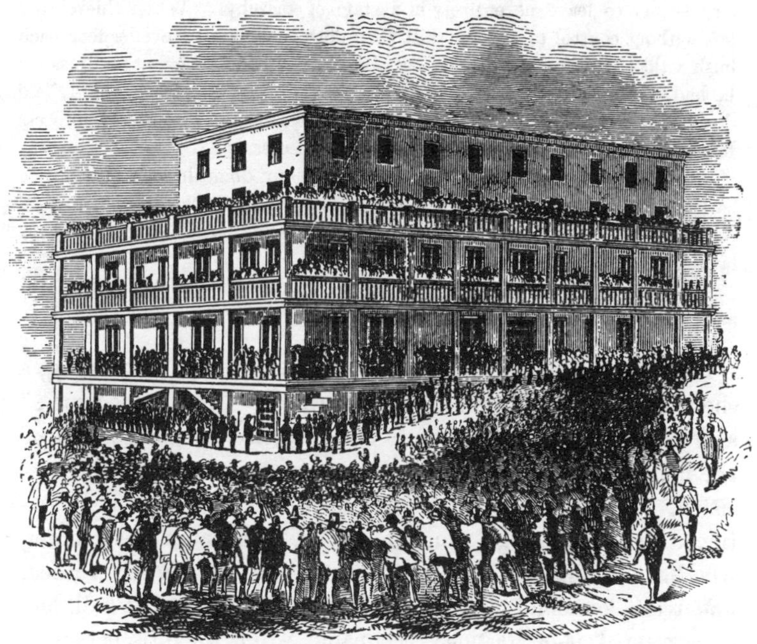

The City Hall, February 22d, 1851.

person of the name of Windred, who had been apprehended on suspicion of the same offence, were, on the 21st, confronted with the wounded man. Jansen at once recognized Stuart and also Windred, although with some faint doubt of the identity of the latter, as being the two persons who had committed the assault and the robbery. These circumstances being known, the citizens, in a state of the greatest excitement, gathered, on the following day (Saturday, 22d February), around the City Hall, where the examination of the prisoners was going on. Upwards of five thousand people thus collected. This was not a mob, but the *people,* in the highest sense of the term. They wanted only a leader to advise and guide them to any undertaking that promised relief from the awful state of social terror and danger to which they were reduced. Handbills were extensively circulated among the multitude, which were to the following effect:—

"CITIZENS OF SAN FRANCISCO.

"The series of murders and robberies that have been committed in this city, seems to leave us entirely in a state of anarchy. 'When thieves are left without control to rob and kill, then doth the honest traveller fear each bush a thief.' Law, it appears, is but a nonentity to be scoffed at; redress can be had for aggression but through the never failing remedy so admirably laid down in the code of Judge Lynch. Not that we should admire this process for redress, but that it seems to be inevitably necessary.

"Are we to be robbed and assassinated in our domiciles, and the law to let our aggressors perambulate the streets merely because they have furnished straw bail? If so, 'let each man be his own executioner.' 'Fie upon your laws!' They have no force.

"All those who would rid our city of its robbers and murderers, will assemble on Sunday at two o'clock on the plaza."

While the examination of the prisoners was progressing, a shout arose among the assembled multitude, "Now is the time;" and many rushed into the court room to seize the accused out of the hands of the authorities. This attempt was successfully resisted. The "Washington Guards," who had been secretly stationed in an adjoining room, through the foresight of the recorder, who had anticipated some outbreak of this nature, now rushed, under the command of Capt. A. Bartol, into the court-hall, and soon cleared it of its noisy occupants, while the prisoners were hurried through a back door into the cells beneath. During the whole day the excitement continued, and many of the spectators remained about the place, though the greater number gradually dispersed, chiefly through the persuasions of some parties who thought like themselves. Towards dusk the people again assembled around the City Hall in greater numbers than before, when, after some speeches, the following gentlemen were appointed a committee to consult with the authorities and guard the prisoners till the next day, viz.: Messrs. W. D. M. Howard, Samuel Brannan, A. J. Ellis, H. F. Teschemacker, W. H. Jones, B. Ray, G. A King, A. H. Sibley, J. L. Folsom, F. W. Macondray, Ralph Dorr, Theodore Payne, Talbot H. Green, and J. B. Huie.

This committee the same evening met in the recorder's room, and discussed the position of affairs, and what was next to be done. To show the temper, not of this committee, for they were moderate and cautious in their proceedings, but of the general public on the occasion, we may quote a short speech by Mr. Brannan, who seems to have been always for stringing up and hanging every rogue outright, on the shortest possible grace. His language was certainly to the point, and quite accorded with the sentiments of a great majority of the vast multitude that was anxiously waiting without. One of the committee having proposed that the citizens should choose a jury to try the prisoners, Mr. Brannan said:—

"I am very much surprised to hear people talk about grand juries, or recorders, or mayors. I'm tired of such talk. These men are murderers, I say, as well as thieves. I know it, and I will die or see them hung by the neck. I'm opposed to any farce in this business. We had enough of that eighteen months ago [alluding to the affair of the "hounds,"] when we allowed ourselves to be the tools of these judges, who sentenced convicts to be sent to the United States. We are the mayor and the recorder, the hangman and the laws. The law and the courts never yet hung a man in California; and every morning we are reading fresh accounts of murders and robberies. I want no technicalities. Such things are devised to shield the guilty."

The rest of the committee did not exactly think with Mr. Brannan, and after appointing a patrol of twenty citizens to watch over the prisoners, a majority of them adopted a resolution by Captain Howard, that they should adjourn to the following day, on the plaza, to report the proceedings to the people.

Next day (Sunday), about eight thousand people collected round the court-house. Mayor Geary, and others on the part of the authorities then addressed them, advising coolness and moderation, and suggesting that a committee of twelve of their number should be appointed to sit as a jury along with the presiding justice on the trial to take place the following day, the verdict of which jury should be final. Other counsels, however, prevailed; and on the motion of Mr. Wm. T. Coleman, a committee of twelve was appointed, to retire and consider the best course of action to be adopted. Almost immediately afterwards this committee returned and reported, that the trial should be conducted by and among themselves—that if the legal courts choose to assist in the business, they were welcome and invited to do so ; but if not, that counsel should be assigned to the prisoners, a public prosecutor appointed, and the trials immediately commenced. This was all accordingly done. The public authorities having declined to interfere farther in the matter, and being powerless before so numerous a body, retired from the contest.

At two o'clock of the same day, the committee and a great number of citizens assembled in the recorder's room, while outside, in Kearny and Pacific streets, an immense multitude had collected. The following parties were then empanneled as a jury, viz. :—R. S. Watson, S. J. L. Smiley, W. E. Stoutenburg, J. L. Riddle, George Endicott, D. K. Minor, George A. Hudson, David Page, Jas. H. Robinson, J. E. Schenck, S. J. Thompson and I. C. Pelton. J. R. Spence was appointed to preside on the bench, and H. R. Bowie and C. L. Ross were named associate judges. J. E. Townes was selected to officiate as sheriff, and W. A. Jones as judge's clerk. Mr. Coleman was chosen public prosecutor, and Judge Shattuck and Hall McAllister were appointed counsel for the prisoners. We are particular in giving the names of these gentlemen, since they show the high character and social standing of the parties who were concerned in this movement against the legal and municipal authorities. As we said before, the crowd was not a mob, but emphatically the *people*. After evidence was led for the prosecution, an impartial charge was given by Mr. Spence. The jury then retired, and were absent a considerable time, as they seemed unable to agree upon a verdict. Seeing there were no signs of being able to come to a speedy agreement, they returned to the court, and their foreman reported that *nine* were for conviction, and *three* had doubts. Much disappointment and agitation was now manifested by the people, who had considered the prisoners clearly guilty on the testimony. Loud cries burst from all quarters of "*Hang them, any how! A majority rules!*" After some time order was restored, and the jury were discharged. It was now midnight, and the numbers present were considerably diminished. The same excitement, however, prevailed, and it required all the efforts of the cooler and wiser portion of the assembly to preserve peace and decorum to the end. Addresses were spoken to this effect by Mr. Smyth Clarke, Dr. Rabe and Mr. Hutton. The latter gentleman was now chosen chairman, and the meeting adjourned to the outside of the building. At last—twenty minutes to one o'clock on Monday morning,—the question was put from the chair, that they should indefinitely adjourn, which being answered affirmatively, the crowd quietly dispersed.

During this excitement, it is proper to remark, that the mayor had collected together not only the regular police of the city, but an additional volunteer force of about two hundred and fifty citizens, and had determined that no injury should be done the prisoners until they were legally tried and found guilty of the alleged crime. In the mean time, parties were organized, who were resolved to seize the prisoners at all events, and hang them at the nearest convenient place, without regard either to decency or justice; and to carry out this object several attempts were made to break into the station-house where the prisoners were confined; but these were successfully resisted by the strong and determined force which the foresight of the mayor had gathered and with which the City Hall was surrounded.

The occasion of this outbreak was the greatest that hitherto ever agitated San Francisco, and the exciting scenes of Saturday and Sunday will be long remembered by the citizens of the period. For thirty-six hours the whole town had been in an uproar, and during a great part of that time many thousands of persons had been gathered in the court-room or in the streets outside. For months their patience had been severely tried by the knowledge that crimes of the most atrocious description—murders, burglaries, thefts, fire-raisings and violent assaults, had been of daily occurrence, and that few or no adequate punishments had been inflicted by the courts on the perpetrators. On this occasion the long suppressed ire against the supineness of the authorities burst forth, and the people were determined to make an example of those whom they believed guilty of the shocking assault upon Mr. Jansen and the robbery of his store.

They were indeed deceived in regard to the true criminals, and might have hanged innocent men. But the good sense of their temporary leaders, and a return to dispassionate reflection, hindered the execution of the sentence of death, which the general multitude wished to pronounce.

We may here shortly state the further incidents connected with the prisoners in relation to this matter. After being tried by the people, as above mentioned, when no unanimous verdict could be obtained, they were handed over to the proper authorities, by whom they were put a second time upon trial, for the same offence, according to the ordinary legal forms. On this occasion both prisoners were found guilty, and sentenced to fourteen years' imprisonment, being the highest penalty which the law could inflict for the imputed offence. Windred shortly afterwards escaped by cutting a hole through the floor of his prison. Stuart, *alias* Burdue, was sent to Marysville, to stand his trial for the murder of Mr. Moore, already noticed. He was found guilty for this crime also, and was sentenced to be hanged. This was in the course of the summer. Meanwhile, the Vigilance Committee, which had been recently organized, had contrived to lay hands on the *true* Stuart, who turned out not only to have been the murderer of Mr. Moore, but also one of those who had assaulted and robbed Mr. Jansen. Stuart was subsequently hanged by the people for these and other crimes, as detailed in our chapter on the Vigilance Committee. It was satisfactorily shown that neither Burdue nor Windred had ever had the slightest connection with any of the offences for which they were charged. The whole affair was a most curious case of mistaken identity. Burdue was at different places, and by different juries, twice convicted, and twice in the most imminent risk of death for the commission of offences of which he was perfectly innocent! The luckless man was sent back to San Francisco, where his sentence of imprisonment was annulled, and himself released. A handsome subscription was raised among the citizens to compensate in some measure for his repeated sufferings. What became of him ultimately we know not; but doubtless, in his cups, he will wax eloquent, and have strange stories to tell of his "hair-breadth 'scapes." Shortly after receiving the subscription from the citizens, he was seen on Long Wharf playing at "French Monte," and lustily bawling to the passers-by—" The ace ! the ace !—a hundred dollars to him who will tell the ace ! —The ace !—The ace !—who will name the ace of spades ? A hundred dollars to any man who will tell the ace !"

MARCH 3d.—The steamers Hartford and Santa Clara were burned this morning at Long Wharf.

CHAPTER XV.

1851.

Judge Parsons and the case of William Walker for contempt of Court.—Act of Legislature ceding Beach and Water Lots to the City of San Francisco.—Act to re-incorporate the city.—New city limits.—First election of municipal officers under revised charter.—Act passed to fund the State debt.—Act to establish State Marine Hospital.—Act to fund the floating debt.—Indebtedness of the city.—Municipal officers trafficking in city scrip.—Fifth great fire.

March 9th.—An "indignation" meeting, at which there were several thousand persons present, was held to-day on the plaza, to consider the conduct of Judge Levi Parsons, of the District Court, towards Mr. William Walker, one of the editors of the *Daily Herald.* It appears that for some time before this date the general public press had been endeavoring to rouse the community to a full knowledge of the increasing and alarming state of crime, and, in doing so, had taken repeated occasion to criticise severely the "masterly inactivity" of the judicature in trying and punishing criminals. This appears to have displeased Judge Parsons, and he thereupon, in an address to the grand jury, chose to style the press a "nuisance," and insinuated that the jury might offer some presentment on the subject. The grand jury, however, did not gratify his wishes. His honor's observations became a new text for the now offended press; and, among other unpleasant things, they began to take grave exceptions to his knowledge and application of the law as regarded grand and petit juries. The *Herald,* in an article headed "The Press a Nuisance," was especially severe in its strictures. A few members of the bar next began to make some feeble movement to soothe their brother on the bench; but their affected indignation only provoked laughter and made matters worse. Judge Parsons thereupon—some days after the obnoxious article had been published, issued an order from his own court to bring before him

Mr. Walker, the acknowledged or reputed author of the article in question. Mr. Walker accordingly appeared, and was duly convicted by his honor,—who was plaintiff, judge and jury in the case,—of contempt of court, fined five hundred dollars, and ordered to be kept in safe custody until the amount was paid. The offender having declined to pay the fine, refusing to recognize his honor's jurisdiction in and summary settlement of the matter, was forthwith imprisoned for an indefinite time.

These circumstances being extensively made known, produced great excitement in the city. One and all of the press were *down*—to use an expressive vulgarism—upon his honor; and as the people considered that the cause of the press was substantially their own, they resolved to make a "demonstration" on the subject. An "indignation" meeting accordingly was held, as above mentioned, at which resolutions were passed approving of Walker's conduct, and requesting Parsons to resign his judicial situation as no longer fit to hold it. A committee was then formed to transmit these resolutions to the latter. At the same time, the senators and representatives of the district were requested to propose articles of impeachment against the offending judge. The meeting next in a body,—some four thousand strong,—paid a personal visit of condolence and sympathy to Mr. Walker in prison.

Meanwhile, the matter was carried by a writ of *habeas corpus* into the Superior Court, by which Mr. Walker was discharged. It was held that Judge Parsons had abused his position, and that while the ordinary tribunals were open to him, if he considered that Mr. Walker had committed a libel, he had no right to cite and punish summarily that gentleman for any alleged contempt, that might be inferred from the published statements and remarks in a newspaper. The contrary doctrine would be destructive of the freedom of the press, and was opposed to the universally recognized principles of the constitution. This judgment was considered a great popular triumph. In the mean time, the question was farther discussed before the Legislature; and, on the 26th instant, a committee of the Assembly, upon the memorial of Walker, "convinced that Judge Parsons had been guilty of gross tyranny and oppression in the imprisonment of the memorialist," recommended the impeachment of the former. The majority of a select committee, however, afterwards appointed to inquire into the charges against Parsons, having reported that these, "and the testimony given in support of them, do not show sufficient grounds for impeachment," the matter was dropped.

At the period of which we write, the tribunals of justice were considered altogether insufficient for those dangerous times, and many of the individuals connected with them as both incapable and corrupt. The public looked chiefly to the press for advice and information as to their rights and duties, and had resolved that it should not be gagged and put down "by illegal orders, attachments, fines and imprisonments for imaginary contempts against courts *which cannot be reduced much lower than they have reduced themselves.*" So said the resolutions of the "indignation" meeting of the 9th instant; and this language was generally applauded.

MARCH 26th.—An act passed by the Legislature, ceding, for the period of ninety-nine years, all the right and interest which the State of California had in those parts of the city called the *Beach and Water Lots,* provided that twenty-five *per cent.* of all moneys thereafter arising in any way from the sale, or other disposition of the said property, should be paid over by the city to the State. The same act confirmed, also for ninety-nine years, all sales that had previously been made, in virtue of General Kearny's grant to the city, by the ayuntamiento, or town or city council, or by any alcalde of the city, the last having been confirmed by the said ayuntamiento, or town or city council, and the deeds of these sales having been duly registered in the proper books of records. This was a very important act, and tended, in some great degree, to ease the minds of legal possessors of city property. Owing to certain late conflicting decisions of different judges, in regard to real estate, considerable doubt had been cast upon the titles to almost every lot of vacant ground within the municipal bounds, and squatters had been thereby mightily encouraged to invade and secure for themselves the first and best unoccupied land they saw. This led to much confusion and even bloodshed among the contending claimants, and retarded for a considerable time the permanent improvement of the city. The "Colton grants," of recent notoriety, likewise increased the general uncertainty in regard to titles. The above-mentioned act of the Legislature was therefore considered a great benefit, coming when it did, in regard to at least the "Beach and Water Lots," about the titles to which there could be no dispute.

An act was passed by the Legislature on the 1st of May following, by which the right of the State to these lots was for ever relinquished to the city, provided only that the latter should confirm the grants of all lots within certain specified limits originally made by justices of the peace. As this provision was intended to sanction some of the obnoxious "Colton grants," the common council did not consider it for the interest of the city to accept the State's relinquishment upon such terms, and accordingly the last-mentioned act became inoperative. The boards of aldermen, however, who happened, it might be said, to be somewhat accidentally in office during 1852, attempted to force the provisions of this most obnoxious act upon the citizens, but were successfully opposed by the veto of Mayor Harris and the general cry of public indignation. The act itself was, on the 12th of March, 1852, repealed by the Legislature, just in time to prevent some of the usual jobbery.

April 15th.—Act passed by the Legislature to re-incorporate San Francisco. The limits were enlarged, and the city was thereafter to be bounded as follows:—"On the south, by a line parallel with Clay street, two and a half miles distant, in a southerly direction, from the centre of Portsmouth Square; on the west, by a line parallel with Kearny street, two miles distant, in a westerly direction, from the centre of Portsmouth Square. Its northern and eastern boundaries shall be co-incident with those of the county of San Francisco." As a copy of this act, which is the existing charter of the city, is given in the Appendix, it is unnecessary here to particularize its provisions. Nearly the same variety and number of municipal officers are appointed to be chosen annually under it as under the charter, already noticed, of 1850, and which latter act was declared to be now repealed.

April 28th.—The first election of municipal officers under

the amended city charter took place to-day. Considerable excitement had been manifested by the candidates and their friends, and several torch-light meetings and processions, with other popular demonstrations, had been going on for some time previous. The total number of votes polled was nearly six thousand. The parties elected were as follows :—

Mayor.—Charles J. Brenham.
Recorder.—R. H. Waller.
Comptroller.—George A. Hudson.
Treasurer.—R. H. Sinton.
Marshal.—Robert G. Crozier.
Tax Collector.—Thos. D. Greene.
City Attorney.—Frank M. Pixley.
Street Commissioner.—Wm. Divier.
Recorder's Clerk.—Jas. G. Pearson.
County Judge.—Wm. H. Clark.
Public Administrator.—David T. Bagley.
City Assessors.—W. C. Norris, George Frank Lemon.

Aldermen.

E. L. Morgan, C. L. Ross, A. C. Labatt, C. M. K. Paulison,
Ralph Dorr, James Grant, George Endicott, William Greene.

Assistant Aldermen.

Henry A. Meiggs, W. W. Parker, T. H. Selby, W. D. Connell,
Jos. Galloway, J. F. Atwill, Jas. Graves, Q. S. Sparks.

April 29th.—Act passed by the Legislature to fund the debt of the State. Bonds to the extent of $700,000 to be issued by the treasurer, in lieu of scrip or other obligations of indebtedness held by parties against the State. One-half of the sum mentioned is declared payable in New York upon the first day of March, 1855, and the other half, also in the city named, upon the first day of March, 1861. Interest (payable either in New York or at the office of the treasurer) to run upon the bonds at the rate of *seven per cent. per annum.* Henceforward all State taxes to be paid only in the legal currency of the United States, or in gold dust at the rate of sixteen dollars an ounce, excepting as mentioned in the act. Various declarations are also made for providing the interest, and as to the formation of a sinking fund to redeem the bonds, for payment of the principal and interest of which are pledged "the faith and credit of the State of California."

April 30th.—Act passed by the Legislature establishing a State Marine Hospital at San Francisco ; and, on 1st May, another act passed to provide a revenue for the same. As both of these acts were amended in the succeeding session, they will be noticed among the events of 1852.

May 1st.—Act passed by the Legislature, "to authorize the funding of the floating debt of the city of San Francisco, and to provide for the payment of the same." Peculiar circumstances, such as the necessity of grading and improving the public streets, building certain wharves, the purchase of expensive premises for corporate purposes, the monstrous salaries claimed by the boards of aldermen and other municipal authorities, the heavy outlay attending the hospital, fire and police departments, contingent expenses to a very large amount, printing, (—$41,905 20 for only nineteen months !—) surveying and numberless other charges, had involved the city in an enormous gross amount of indebtedness. By the Comptroller's Report, the total expenditure of the city from the 1st August, 1849, to the 30th November, 1850, was $1,450,122 57 ; and in the three following months a further expenditure was created of $562,617 53. In the space of nineteen months, therefore, the total expenditure was upwards of *two millions of dollars*. But as neither the property of the city, which had already been sold to a great extent, nor its ordinary revenues, were adequate to defray this immense sum, the municipal authorities had been for a considerable period obliged to issue *scrip*, in immediate satisfaction or acknowledgment of the corporation debts. This scrip, as the city got farther involved and could only make payment of its new obligations in the same kind of paper, soon became much depreciated, and was literally in common sale at from fifty to seventy *per cent.* discount. Meanwhile, nobody would do any business for the city on the same terms as they would for other parties, so long as they were to be paid in this depreciated scrip. The natural consequence was that the municipal officers had just virtually to pay, or rather give their promise to pay, twice or thrice the amounts they would have needed to lay out, if the city had been solvent, with cash in hand to meet all obligations. This circumstance therefore still farther added to the enormous weight of debt.

Truly the city seems to have been long considered fair game for every one who had spirit, skill, and corruption enough to prey upon its means. The officials complained that their salaries were paid in depreciated scrip. That was true, and hard enough upon many; but, on the other hand, certain leading office-holders made a fine thing of this same depreciation. They contrived to purchase vast quantities of corporation paper at one-third of its nominal value, which they turned over, in their several departments, to the city at *par*. In various ways they trafficked in this scrip, and always to their own great advantage. The tax-collector, for instance, refused to receive scrip in payment of license duties and other city taxes, on one ground or other, that it was not yet due, and the like, while instead of paying into the city treasurer the *cash* which was actually received, he only handed over his own comparatively worthless paper, purchased with the city's cash for that express purpose. The comptroller and treasurer were likewise parties concerned in this species of speculation. Considerable fortunes were thus gained by sundry officials, who could "*finesse*," and make money in any state of the corporation exchequer. Doubtless they quietly and gaily said to themselves, as the public thought, that "it was an ill-wind that blew *nobody* good." In those days—so recent, yet in the history of San Francisco so virtually remote—jobbing and peculation were rank, and seemed the rule in the city government. Public honesty and conscientious attention to the interests of the community were solitary exceptions. To such an extent did nefarious speculations in city paper prevail among people high in office, that the Legislature was at last compelled to interfere, and declare it a penal offence for any municipal officer to buy scrip or to traffic in it in any manner of way.

Meanwhile the scrip was bearing interest at the rate of three *per cent. per* month! On the 1st day of March, 1851, the total liabilities of the city were $1,099,557 56. At this time, the whole corporation property, if forced to a public sale, would not have brought one-third of that amount; while, if interest were to continue to run on the debt at the heavy rate just mentioned, the ordinary revenues would have fallen lamentably short of meeting it, after defraying the current expenses. In these circumstances, the act above mentioned was passed by the Legislature.

By this act certain commissioners were appointed to manage

the proposed "funded debt," who were empowered to issue stock, bearing interest at the rate of ten *per cent. per annum*, payable half-yearly, in lieu of scrip to a similar amount, which might be presented by holders of the same within a specified time. This funded debt was to be redeemed wholly within twenty years, and particular obligations were laid on the city that the sums necessary to be raised to pay the half-yearly interest, and ultimately the principal, should be solely applied to these purposes. Fifty thousand dollars, over and above the amount required to pay the interest on the stock, were to be levied annually, which sum was to be made use of by the commissioners, under certain restrictions, in buying up, and so gradually reducing the amount of the city liabilities. As the stock thus created was considered to be an undoubted security for the amounts it represented, which the old scrip was not, and as the former soon bore a higher market value than such scrip, the holders of the latter generally took occasion to convert their floating into the funded debt. The small amount of scrip never presented for conversion into stock within the specified time, and which was chiefly held by parties at a distance, was subsequently paid in full by the city. In 1852, a great financial operation of a similar nature took place, by which the then floating debt of the county of San Francisco was converted into a seven *per cent.* stock. This will be more particularly noticed in its chronological order.

May 4th.—The anniversary of the *second* great fire was signalized by the *fifth*, the ravages of which perhaps exceeded, in gross amount, those of all the fires together that had previously taken place in the city. For eight months the inhabitants had enjoyed comparative immunity from conflagration. Although single houses had caught fire, and been consumed, it was not believed that such a dreadful calamity could come as that which now happened. A considerable number of buildings, which were supposed fire-proof, had been erected in the course of the preceding year, the solid walls of which, it was thought, would afford protection from the indefinite spreading of the flames, when fire should unhappily break out in any particular building. But all calculations and hopes on this subject were mocked and broken. The brick walls that had been so confidently relied upon crumbled in pieces before the furious flames; the thick iron shutters grew red hot and warped, and only increased the danger and insured final destruction to every thing within them. Men went for shelter into these fancied fire-proof brick and iron-bound structures, and when they sought to come forth again, to escape the heated air that was destroying them as by a close fire, they

Fire of May 4th, 1851.

found, O horror! that the metal shutters and doors had expanded by the heat, and could not be opened! So, in these huge, sealed furnaces, several perished miserably. Many more persons lost their lives in other portions of the burned district, partly by the flames, and partly by the tottering walls falling on and crushing them.

The fire began a few minutes past eleven o'clock on the night of Saturday, the 3d of May, in a paint, or upholstery store, on the south side of the plaza. As particular care seems to have been observed in this establishment to extinguish all lights and fires, the sad work was likely commenced by an incendiary. The wind blowing strongly from the north-west, the conflagration proceeded in the direction of Kearny street, and soon swept before it all of the houses on some entire blocks. Then the breeze suddenly shifted, and blew from the south, carrying the fire backwards to the north and east. In a few hours the whole business part of the city was one entire mass of flame! The wind that would have been considered high, though no fire had existed, was now raised to a hurricane by the action of the flames, that greedily sucked in the fresh air. The hollows beneath the planked streets were like great blow-pipes, that stirred the fire to fearful activity. Through such strange channels, too, which themselves became as dry and inflammable as tinder, the flames were communicated from street to street, and in an amazingly short time the whole surface, over a wide region, glowed, crackled, and blazed, one immense fiery field. The reflection from the sky of this terrific conflagration was said to have been visible at Monterey, nearly a hundred miles off! where it filled the superstitious and timid with dismay and irrepressible terror. On all sides in the doomed city there was heard the fierce roar, as of many storms, that drowned the shouts of men and the shrieks of women. The firemen plied their engines vigorously, and sent showers of water on the wild flames, that only served to increase their fury. As the solid stream of some lofty cataract is scattered into spray and thin mist long before it reaches the earth in the chasm beneath, so were the jets from the fire-engines dissipated into clouds of mere steam which never fell upon or could not extinguish the hot centre of the resistless element. Houses were blown up, but the fire leaped lightly across the gaps, and pursued its terrible course. It ran along the planked streets, and from block to block, almost as if they were but a train of gunpowder. The short space of ten hours, from the commencement of the fire, saw from fifteen hundred to two thousand houses completely ruined. In the end, the absolute want of further fuel to consume was the chief cause of the conflagration ceasing. Eighteen entire squares, with portions of five or six others, were devastated, and, with fewer than twenty exceptions, all the houses and property of every description were totally destroyed. Only five of the brick buildings on Montgomery street escaped destruction, and ten or twelve in other localities. The burned district extended about three-fourths of a mile from north to south, and one-third of a mile from east to west. In this space was comprehended the most valuable part of the city, and where the most precious goods and merchandise were stored. All was destroyed ! The damage was moderately estimated at from ten to twelve millions of dollars.

San Francisco after the fire of May 4th, 1851.

In this conflagration some of the old store-ships that had been hauled high upon the beach, and gradually closed in by the streets growing over the bay, were consumed. Of these was the old "Niantic." This vessel had long lain fixed at the corner of Clay and Sansome streets, where the hotel, which bears its name, was afterwards erected. The "Apollo" and "General Harrison" were also burned. Among the incidents of the fire, it may be mentioned that Dewitt & Harrison saved their warehouse by using vinegar in the absence of water, eighty thousand gallons of the former fluid having been employed by them in protecting the building. By breaking up the wharves, and so cutting off the connection with the burning masses, the immense amount of valuable shipping in the harbor was saved, which at one time was in the most imminent peril.

San Francisco had never before suffered so severe a blow, and doubts were entertained by the ignorant that she could possibly recover from its effects. Such doubts were vain. The *bay* was still there, and the *people* were also there ; the *placers* of the State were not yet exhausted, and its soil was as fertile and inviting as ever. The frightful calamity, no doubt, would retard the triumphant progress of the city—but only for a time. Sour, pseudo-religious folk on the shores of the Atlantic, might mutter of Sodom and Gomorrah, and prate the idlest nonsense, while envious speculators in cities of California itself, that would fain rival the glories of its grand port, might preach till doomsday of the continual strong winds that prevailed in the latter place, and which were certain, so they said, among thousands of wooden houses, to fan the veriest spark into a conflagration, again and again. The citizens of San Francisco were content only to curse and vow vengeance on the incendiaries that kindled the fire, and resolved to be better prepared in future to resist its spreading ravages. After the first short burst of sorrow, the ruined inhabitants, many of whom had been burned out time after time by the successive fires, began again, like the often persecuted spider with its new web, to create still another town and another fortune. While the city lay one vast black and still smoking tract, preparations were made to erect new buildings. These were generally at first formed of wood, low in height, limited in extent, and slightly constructed ; but, before long, such rough, slim, temporary structures, began to give place to the present magnificent buildings that decorate our streets. But one other *great* fire was to come.

CHAPTER XVI.

1851.

T. Butler King removing the custom-house deposits.—Frank Ball's song, and custom-house appointment.—Dr. Robinson's rhymes.—Incendiarism.—The case of Lewis, charged with arson.—The facilities with which criminals escaped from punishment.—The Vigilance Committee.—Contracts of Mr. Merrifield and the Mountain Lake Water Company to supply the city with water.

MAY 28th.—The custom-house, at the corner of Montgomery and California streets, having been destroyed by the fire of the 4th instant, another building was speedily fitted up for the same purposes at the corner of Kearny and Washington streets. The treasure, amounting to upwards of a million of dollars, had been preserved in a large safe (which had escaped damage from the fire) in the old building. To-day the removal of this treasure to the new custom-house took place; and the manner of doing so created some little excitement and much laughter in the town, from the *excessive* care and military display which the collector thought fit to adopt on the occasion. Some thirty gigantic, thick-bearded fellows, who were armed with carbines, revolvers and sabres, surrounded the cars containing the specie, while the Honorable T. Butler King stood aloft on a pile of ruins with a huge "Colt" in one hand and a bludgeon in the other, marshalling his men and money "the way that they should go." The extraordinary procession proceeded slowly along Montgomery street to the new custom-house, Mr. King, marching, like a proud drum-major, at the head of his miniature grand army. The people, meanwhile, looked on with astonishment, and with some grief, that their city should be considered so lawless and wicked a place as to require so formidable a force even to guard millions of treasure in broad daylight, and along one or two of the principal streets, where there were continually present thousands of the most respectable inhabitants. But immediately the farcical nature of the whole exhibition struck the most phlegmatic, and peals of laughter and cries of ironical applause accompanied the brave defenders of "Uncle Sam's" interests to the end of their perilous march. It was felt that there was but one thing wanted to make the show complete—half-a-dozen great guns from the presidio.

In the absence of other matters of local importance, this bloodless achievement formed the subject of a humorous song, composed by a young man of the town, and which he sang in one or more of the public saloons, on many occasions, "with much applause." The thing had a run, and served to fill the clever author's purse. He had a large number of copies lithographed, on which was a caricature print of the procession, and these he disposed of at a dollar apiece. In a single night he sold five hundred copies at this rate. As the tune to which the song was set was a popular and easy one, soon the town rang with the story of "The King's Campaign." But besides this effusion, there immediately appeared innumerable paragraphs, squibs, jests, good sayings in social circles and the public journals. It is one of the penalties which people must pay for their superiority in place over their neighbors that their actions are pretty severely criticised, and, when occasion serves, ridiculed. It was so here "with a will," and to Collector King's great mortification. "Uneasy lies the head that wears a crown." But kings and collectors have potent remedies for the many evils that beset them. Frank Ball, the writer of the song in question, was shortly afterwards sent for by the collector, and favored with a private interview. Ordinary men might have "beat about the bush," or employed a friend in the little transaction which followed; but the Hon. T. Butler King, with the same dauntless face which he showed on occasion of the treasure removal, bluntly began conversation with the anxious poet, by asking whether he would not like to have a desirable post in the customs. Mr. Ball, gasping with surprise, mumbled, "*Yes, surely!*" "*Then, Sir, it is yours,*" said the collector, gravely. In gratitude Mr. Ball could do no less than stop singing his famous song, which was doubtless what his honorable and doughty chief expected. Cerberus was sopped. This anecdote would be incomplete unless we told that certain underlings attached to the custom-house, struck with a new light, began forthwith to chant the obnoxious stanzas. Unluckily they had mistaken the game, for the fact reaching the ears of the collector, one of them, caught in the act, was instantly, though quietly, dismissed from the service. It was a pretty illustration of the fable of "The Man, the Spaniel, and the Ass."

Caricature.

There are so many serious matters—murders, suicides, larcenies, grand and petty burglaries, assaults, fires, and the dismal-like in these "Annals," that we are glad, and so too may the reader be, to have an opportunity such as this of introducing a facetious subject, which once delighted the San Franciscans. We, therefore, give an illustration of the caricature above alluded to, and the song itself:—

"THE KING'S CAMPAIGN; OR, REMOVAL OF THE DEPOSITS.

"Come, listen a minute, a song I'll sing,
Which I rather calculate will bring
Much glory, and all that sort of thing,
On the head of our brave Collector King.
Ri tu di nu, Ri tu di nu,
Ri tu di nu di na.

"Our well-beloved President
This famous politician sent,
Though I guess we could our money have spent
Without aid from the general government.
Ri tu di nu, &c.

"In process of time this hero bold
Had collected lots of silver and gold,
Which he stuck away in a spacious hole,
Except what little his officers stole.
Ri tu di nu, &c.

"But there came a terrible fire one night,
Which put his place in an awful plight,
And 'twould have been a heart-rending sight,
If the money had not been all right.
Ri tu di nu, &c.

"Then he put his officers on the ground,
And told 'em the specie vault to surround,
And if any 'Sydney Cove' came round,
To pick up a cudgel and knock him down.
Ri tu di nu, &c.

"But the money had to be moved away,
So he summoned his fighting men one day,
And fixed 'em all in marching array,
Like a lot of mules hitched on to a dray.
Ri tu di nu, &c.

"Then he mounted a brick and made a speech,
And unto them this way did preach,—
'Oh, feller-sogers, I beseech
You to keep this cash from the people's reach.
Ri tu di nu, &c.

"'For,' said he, ''tis well convinced I am,
That the people's honesty's all a sham,

And that no one here is worth a d—n,
But the officers of Uncle Sam.'
Ri tu di nu, &c.

"Then he drew his revolver, and told 'em to start,
But be sure to keep their eyes on the cart,
And not to be at all faint of heart,
But to tread right up, and try to look smart.
Ri tu di nu, &c.

"Then each man grasped his sword and gun,
The babies squalled and the women run,
And all agreed that the King was one
Of the greatest warriors under the sun.
Ri tu di nu, Ri tu di nu,
Ri tu di nu di na."

They were a wild, perverse race, the San Franciscans in those days, taking much delight in whatever mortified the "city fathers." They are immoderately fond of fun and devilment still; and any thing of a peculiar spicy nature,—from a simple fall in the mud, or the kissing of a pretty girl, up to the five thousand dollar bribe of a senator, or a municipal papa, or grand-papa being caught lurking about the premises of a jealous married man, flies like lightning, or their own great fires over the whole city. The people live so much together in hotels and boarding-houses, they meet so frequently for talk and drink (*in vino veritas*) at bars and billiard-rooms, that every piece of scandal or matter of public interest is sure to ooze out and be discussed in all its bearings. A dozen daily papers by hint, inuendo, broad allusion, and description, considerably assist the promulgation and spreading of idle tales. Hence, they often assumed an importance which other communities may think they scarcely deserve. The year of which we write, 1851, had a full share of such local and temporary *facetiæ*, some of which may appear worthy of record, if it were only to illustrate the times. The affairs of the aldermen's salaries and the curious medal business were both prolific subjects for jesting and outrageous merriment. Dr. D. G. Robinson, a proprietor of the *Dramatic Museum*, gained considerable popularity by a series of doggerel, "random rhymes" which he gave on his own stage, in which almost every municipal man of mark was hit off, and sometimes pretty hardly too. So highly were these verses relished, and so much favor did the author gain thereby with the people, that Dr. Robinson was triumphantly returned as alderman to fill a vacancy which had occurred in the first board. He was afterwards seriously named as likely to be the most popular candidate for the mayoralty in 1852. Such rewards do the generous citizens bestow upon those who amuse them. Dr. Robinson's rhymes were subsequently collected into a small printed pamphlet, which will no doubt possess much interest to such as still relish the gossip and scandal of the day. It would be out of place to give here any characteristic quotations from the work. People look back already with surprise to the favorable notoriety which these songs gained for their author, and more especially to the elevated position to which they were the means of raising him. We have narrated the absurd affair of the removal of the treasure, and given the relative song, only because they were reckoned rather important *events* of the time, and concerning which there was much public merriment for a long period afterwards. The parties interested can now well afford to laugh heartily at the whole business. These things, also, form one illustration of the state of society and "life" in San Francisco at the date of their occurrence.

June 3d.—For some time back the attempts of incendiaries to fire the city seem to be increasing. Cases of this nature are occurring daily, where the suspicious circumstances are evident, but where unfortunately the really guilty party cannot be detected. It is extremely difficult to discover criminals in the very act of committing arson. Incendiaries do their deeds only in dark and secret corners, and if interrupted, they have always ready a dozen trifling excuses for their appearance and behavior. The train and the slow match can be laid almost any where unobserved, while the "foul fiend" quietly steals away in safety. The inhabitants had got nervously sensitive to the slightest alarm of fire, and were greatly enraged against the presumed incendiaries. This day one Benjamin Lewis underwent a primary examination on the charge of arson. As the evidence was being taken, the Recorder's Court began to fill, and much excitement to spread among the people. At this time, a cry of "*fire!*" was raised, and great confusion took place in the court-room, people rushing desperately out and in to learn particulars. This was a false alarm. It was believed to be only a *ruse* to enable the prisoner's friends to rescue him from the hands of justice. The latter was therefore removed for safety to another place. Meanwhile, some three or four thousand persons had collected outside of the building, who began to get furious, continually uttering loud cries of "*Lynch the villain! Hang the fire-raising wretch! Bring him out—no mercy—no law delays! Hang him—hang him!*" Colonel Stevenson harangued the crowd in strong language, encouraging the violent feelings that had been excited against the prisoner. Mayor Brenham endeavored to calm the enraged multitude. Loud calls were at length made for "Brannan," to which that gentleman quickly responded, and advised that the prisoner should be given in charge to the "volunteer police," which had been recently formed. A motion to this effect was put and unanimously carried. But when the prisoner was looked for, it was found that the regular police had meanwhile carried him out of the way—nobody knew, or would tell where. Perforce the crowd was obliged to be satisfied, and late in the afternoon it gradually dispersed.

This is one instance of the scenes of popular excitement which were now of frequent occurrence in the city. Repeated losses by fire, and the terrible array of unpunished, undetected, triumphant crime, were turning the inhabitants absolutely savage against the supposed criminals. Matters were coming fast to a head, which was immediately to ripen into the "Vigilance Committee." All these popular "demonstrations" were ineffectual in deterring the "Sydney coves," and those of a like character, from the commission of the most reckless, wanton, and flagrant outrages. Incendiary attempts were now remarked almost daily. Not only the desire for plunder, but malice against individuals, and an unnatural lust for general destruction, seemed to inspire the villains.

In regard to the particular case of Lewis, it may be mentioned that the grand jury found a true bill against him for arson. Twice shortly afterwards was he brought before the District Criminal Court for trial, and on each occasion his counsel found a "flaw" in the indictment, which quashed the proceedings. These delays and defects in the law were working the suffering people up to madness. This is only one case, but it may be taken as a fair specimen of the general inefficiency of the judicial officers and tribunals in punishing crime. The grand juries were continually making formal complaints that their presentments were disregarded, and that criminals were somehow never convicted and punished, while generally their trials were so long delayed that the prisoners either escaped from confinement, or the essential witnesses in the case had gone nobody knew whither; and so the prosecutions failed. San Francisco was truly in a desperate condition at this period of its history. Though few arrests were made in proportion to the number of offences actually committed, yet it may be mentioned, that, to take one instance, on Monday morning, the 9th June of this year, there were thirty-six cases before the Recorder's Criminal Court from one district alone (the second), out of the eight composing the city. "Of the whole," we quote from a journal of the time, "six were for drunkenness, six for fighting, six for larceny, three for stabbing, one for burglary, four for fast riding, four for assaulting officers, three for keeping disorderly houses, one for an attempt at robbery," &c. Yet the previous day, Sunday, on which these offences had been committed, had been remarked by the press as having been unusually quiet and decently observed—without any noise or crime worth noticing.

Of this date an ordinance was passed by the council boards, and approved of by the mayor, granting to Mr. Arzo D. Merrifield and his assigns, the privilege of introducing fresh water by pipes into the city. It had happened at the various fires that the numerous public water reservoirs were either wholly or partially empty; and great difficulty was at all times experienced in filling them. This reason, as well as the desire to have an abundant supply of pure, fresh water for household purposes, had long led parties to consider the best means of bringing it into the city by pipes from a distance. Various schemes were talked of among the public, and discussed in the journals. The plan of Mr. Merrifield to bring water from a small lagoon, called the "Mountain Lake," situated about four miles west of the plaza, and which was well supplied by springs, was at length approved of by the common council, and under the ordinance noticed the projector became entitled to certain privileges for the term of twenty-five years, upon condition of his plans being carried into effect. Mr. Merrifield, his associates and assigns, were authorized to break open the streets, and lay down water-pipes in the same, upon properly filling up and replacing the openings. The quantity of water to be provided in a general reservoir, and the amount of discharge by pipes, were both fixed; while provision was made for the amount of rates to be paid by the citizens using the water, which rates were to be adjusted by a board of commissioners to be chosen annually by the common council. At the end of twenty-five years, from and after the 1st day of January, 1853, the entire water-works were to be deeded to the city, in consideration of the privileges and benefits that might accrue to the projector and his assigns and associates during the said term of years. The corporate authorities were also to be entitled to the gratuitous use of the water for the purpose of extinguishing fires, and for hospital and other purposes. In terms of this act, Mr. Merrifield granted a bond for fifty thousand dollars that the works should be completed on or before the 1st of January, 1853.

The gentleman named having conveyed his privileges to a joint-stock company, called the "Mountain Lake Water Company," another ordinance was, of date 14th of July, 1852, passed and approved of, whereby the former one was amended to the following effect, viz.: That the new company should only be entitled to the privileges granted by the first ordinance for the term of twenty years:—that the board of commissioners to fix the rates payable by those who used the water should be chosen, three by the common council, and two by the Mountain Lake Water Company, under the regulations specified in the ordinance:—that the term within which the works should be completed should be extended to the 1st of January, 1854, provided the Water Company should expend fifty thousand dollars on the works within six months of the date of the ordinance, and at least a similar sum every six months thereafter until the said last mentioned date:—that the privileges granted to the said Water Company should be *exclusive* for the term of five years after 1st of January, 1853;—and, lastly, that the said ordinance should expire at such time after the 1st day of January, 1855, as the said Water Company should refuse, or be unable, to supply the city, at such elevation as the common council should fix, "one million of gallons of pure and wholesome fresh water during every twenty-four hours."

Hanging of Jenkins on the Plaza.

JUNE 11th.—The "Vigilance Committee" is at last formed, and in good working order. They hanged at two o'clock this morning upon the plaza one Jenkins, for stealing a safe. For the particulars of the trial and execution, we refer the reader to a subsequent chapter, where also will be found an account of the other doings of this celebrated association.

CHAPTER XVII.

1851.

The sixth great fire.—Destruction of old buildings.—Execution by the Vigilance Committee of Stuart, Whittaker and McKenzie.—County and city elections.—The Vigilance Committee suspend operations.—Wells & Co. suspend payment.—Opening of the Jenny Lind Theatre.—The American Theatre opened.—Shipping in San Francisco Bay.—Ball of the Monumental Fire Company.—Indian disturbances and volunteer military companies.—Severe storm.

June 22d.—The *sixth* great fire. It began a few minutes before eleven o'clock in the morning, in a frame house situated on the north side of Pacific street, close to Powell street. The high winds which usually set in about this hour from the ocean during the summer season, speedily fanned the flames, and drove them south and east. All day they spread from street to street, consuming one building-square after another. The water reservoirs happened to be nearly empty, and even where the firemen had water enough for the engines, their exertions were of little use in stopping the conflagration. Nor was it much better with the hook and ladder companies, whose useful operations were thwarted by the owners of the property they were seeking to pull down for the common good. Subsequent inquiries seemed to show that the fire must have been raised by incendiaries, while several attempts were detected during the day to kindle various distant quarters of the town, yet untouched by the flames. The fire extended from Powell nearly to Sansome street, and from Clay street to Broadway. Within these limits ten entire squares were destroyed, and large parts of six others. The total damage was estimated at three millions of dollars. Happily the chief business portion of the town escaped, and which had suffered so severely six or seven weeks before. In the fire of the 4th May, every newspaper establishment in the city, except that of the "Alta California," was totally destroyed. In the fire of the 22d instant, all escaped, *except* that of the journal named. These conflagrations made no distinctions of persons or properties; but with a wild justice, sooner or later, reduced all to the same level. The proprietors of the *Alta* now lost their building, presses, types, paper and office furniture, just as their brethren of the broad sheet were ruined before. The City Hall, located at the corner of Kearny and Pacific streets, which had been originally erected at an immense expense as a hotel, and was purchased more than a year before by the corporation for one hundred and fifty thousand dollars, and improved at a heavy cost, was totally consumed, although the principal office records were saved. Mr. Thomas Maguire, the proprietor of the "Jenny Lind Theatre," on the plaza, which was a most valuable building, now lost all again,—*a sixth time, by fire!* But it is needless to particularize losses, where every citizen may be said to have been burned out several times, and to have again and again lost *his all.* With a sigh or a laugh, according to the temperament of the sufferer, he just began once more to raise his house, stock it with new goods, and arrange his future plans. The indefatigable *spider* was at work again.

Many of the buildings erected since these last fires show a wonderful improvement in strength and grandeur. When the work was to be done it was now well done; and it is believed that if any buildings can possibly be made *fire proof* in the most trying circumstances, many have now been made so in San Francisco. Solid brick walls, two and three feet in thickness, double shutters and doors of malleable iron, with a space two feet wide between them, and huge tanks of water, that could flood the whole building from roof to cellar, seem to defy the ravages of the fiercest future conflagration. Of that substantial character are many of the banking establishments, the principal stores and merchants' offices, and the most important houses in the city. This improved style of building has chiefly been rendered necessary by the great conflagrations we have had occasion to notice. Of the different companies formed for extinguishing fires we treat in a subsequent chapter. It is believed that they form the most complete and efficient organization of their kind in the world.

The *six* great fires successively destroyed nearly all the old buildings and land-marks of *Yerba Buena*. We extract the following pleasantly written lamentation on this subject from the "Alta California" of 21st September, 1851 :—" The fires of May and June of the present year, swept away nearly all the relics of the olden time in the heart of the city. The old City Hotel

Old City Hotel.

[corner of Kearny and Clay streets], so well known and remembered by old Californians, after standing unscathed through three fatal fires, fell at the fourth. How many memories cling around that old building! It was the first hotel started in San Francisco, then the village of Yerba Buena, in the year 1846. When the mines were first discovered, and San Francisco was literally overflowing with gold, it was the great gaming head-quarters. Thousands and thousands of dollars were there staked on the turn of a single card, and scenes such as never were before, and never again will be witnessed, were exhibited in that old building during the years 1848 and 1849. In the spring of '49, the building was leased out at sixteen thousand dollars *per annum*, cut up into small stores and rooms, and underleased at an enormous profit. Newer and handsomer buildings were erected and opened as hotels, and the old 'City' became neglected, deserted, forgotten: then it burned down, and this relic of the olden time of San Francisco was among the things that were. Then the old adobe custom-house that had been first built for that purpose, and then used as a guard-house and military office by the Amer-

Residence of Samuel Brannan, Esq., in 1847.

icans, and then afterwards as the American custom-house, was also burned. The wooden building directly back of it, with the portico, was also one of the old buildings—erected and occupied by Samuel Brannan, Esq. in 1847. [In this house were exhibited the first specimens of gold brought from the *placeres.*] This also was burned, and all that remains of 1847, in the vicinity of the plaza, is the old adobe on Dupont street. This building, in the latter part of '47 and '48 was occupied by Robert A. Parker as a large trading establishment. This has stood through all the fires, and it is hoped that it may remain for years as a relic of the past." That hope was vain. In the following year the adobe on Dupont street was pulled down to make way for finer houses on its site. So has it been with all the relics of six or eight years' standing. What the fires left, the progress of improvement swept from the ground.

JULY 11th.—Trial and execution of James Stuart.

AUGUST 24th.—Recapture from the legal authorities of Whittaker and McKenzie, and their execution by the "Vigilance Committee."

SEPTEMBER 3d.—Annual election for the County of San Francisco. The following were the officials chosen :—

Senate.

Frank Soulé, Jacob R. Snyder.

Assembly.

B. Orrick, A. C. Peachy, A. J. Ellis, H. Wohler, G. W. Tenbroeck, R. N. Wood. Isaac N. Thorne.

Judge of the Superior Court.	*County Judge.*
John Satterlee.	Alexander Campbell.
Sheriff.	*County Clerk.*
John C. Hayes.	James E. Wainwright.
County Recorder.	*District Attorney.*
Thomas B. Russum.	H. H. Byrne.
County Treasurer.	*County Surveyor.*
Joseph Shannon.	C. Humphries.
Coroner.	*County Assessor.*
Nathaniel Gray.	Henry Vandeveer.

Harbor Master.—George Simpton.

The new city charter had provided that the first general election for municipal officers should be held on the fourth Monday of April, 1851, and "thereafter annually at the general election for State officers." Under this section of the charter it was understood by some that the *second* city election should take place in September of the year named, when the usual annual election of State officers occurred. Another construction was put upon the section in question by the parties already in office and by a large number of the inhabitants, to the effect that the *second* election under the charter could only take place in September, 1852. Thus one party would give the existing common council and municipal officers only half a year in power, while another party, including the present incumbents, claimed a year and a half.

So dignified, or so satisfied with the legal strength of their position, were the existing city officers, that they took no steps to order a new election in September, 1851. Their opponents, however, relying on their own interpretation of the words of the charter, proceeded to act without them, and, unopposed in any way, elected the whole parties on their ticket. The general public took little interest in the matter, and most people seemed to believe that the new election would end in nothing. So little did the citizens concern themselves, that some of those newly elected, polled but a very few votes. When the election was finished the new officers made a demand upon the old ones for a surrender of the public books and documents. This being refused, the new mayor elect, Stephen R. Harris, immediately raised the necessary legal action against the old mayor, C. J. Brenham, for a declaration of his own rights and the ejection of the latter from office. In the district court a judgment was given to the effect that the present incumbents should hold office till April, 1852, and that then those elected in September, 1851, should enter upon and remain in office for one year. The result of this decision would have been that six months would always intervene between the election and the entering upon office of the municipal authorities. This decision was unsatisfactory to most people. Mr. Harris next carried the case into the supreme court, where a majority of the judges (24th December), after able arguments were heard from the parties, reversed the judgment of the court below, and found Mr. Harris entitled to enter upon office as in September, 1851. Mr. Brenham promptly acknowledged the weakness of his position, and at once yielded to his legal successor. Party feeling prevented the other city officers from surrendering their seats so readily. Those already in power consisted of men of both of the great political parties—whig and democratic; and had been originally selected chiefly from among the independent candidates, as men who would earnestly work for the common good and the purification of the city from official corruption and wide-spread crime. On the other hand, those newly elected were altogether of the democratic party. The old council offered to resign, if the new one would do the same; when both could appeal a second time to the people. But the latter council refused to do this. Meanwhile, the legal courts had adjourned, and it would have cost much time and expense to drive out the old council from the places which they persisted in retaining; and their year of office would probably expire before this could be managed. In the end, however, the old council thought it best for their own honor and the interests of the city, to quietly retire from the unseemly contest, and make way for their unexpected successors. The names and offices of the latter were as follows:—

Mayor.—Stephen R. Harris.	*Recorder*—George W. Baker.
Marshal.—David W. Thompson.	*Street Commissioner.*—Theodore Payne.
Comptroller.—Jas. W. Stillman.	*Treasurer.*—Smyth Clarke.
Tax Collector.—D. S. Linell.	*City Attorney.*—Chas. M. Delaney.

Recorder's Clerk.—Thomas W. Harper.

City Assessors.—James C. Callaghan, David Hoag, Arthur Matthews.

Aldermen.

E. L. Morgan,	Wm. G. Wood,	Jos. H. Blood,	John Cotter,
Caleb Hyatt,	James Grant,	N. S. Pettit,	Wm. Moore.

Assistant Aldermen.

Henry Meiggs,	Jos. Galloway,	W. H. Crowell,	N. Holland,
D. W. Lockwood,	James Graves,	J. C. Piercy,	John W. Kessling.

SEPTEMBER 16th.—The "Vigilance Committee" agreed to suspend indefinitely farther operations regarding crime and criminals in the city. The old extensive chambers in Battery street were relinquished, and new rooms, "open at all times, day and night, to the members," were taken in Middleton and Smiley's buildings, corner of Sansome and Sacramento streets. During the three preceding months this association had been indefatigable in collecting evidence and bringing the guilty to justice. It had been formed not to supersede the legal authorities, but to strengthen them when weak; not to oppose the law, but to sanction and confirm it. The members were mostly respectable citizens, who had, and could have, only one object in view—the general good of the community. They exercised an unceasing *vigilance* over the hidden movements of the suspected and criminal population of the place, and unweariedly traced crime to its source, where they sought to stop it. They had hanged four men without observing ordinary legal forms, but the persons were fairly tried and found guilty, while three, at least, of the number, confessed to the most monstrous crimes, and admitted death to be only a due punishment. At this small cost of bloodshed, the "Vigilance Committee" freed the city and country of many reckless villains, who had been long a terror to society. When these had disappeared, outrages against person and property almost disappeared too, or were confined to petty cases. The legal and municipal authorities now acquired, what previously they lacked, sufficient power to master the remaining criminals; and the committee, having no longer a reason for continued action, gladly relinquished the powers they had formerly exercised. Grand juries, instead of offering presentments against them, only praised in the usual reports their useful exertions, while, like all good citizens, they lamented their necessity. Judges occasionally took offence at the terms of such reports, and sought to have them modified; but the grand juries were firm. Judge Levi Parsons applied to the Supreme Court to have certain obnoxious sentences in one of these reports struck out; but his petition was refused. People felt that there was much truth in the repeated declarations of the grand juries, and they hailed with delight their expressions of implied confidence in the Vigilance Committee. The weak, inefficient, and sometimes corrupt courts of law were denounced as strongly by the juries as by that association itself. In one report the grand jury said:—"The facilities with which the most notorious culprits are enabled to obtain bail, which, if not entirely worthless, is rarely enforced when forfeited, and the numerous cases in which by the potent influence of money, and the ingenious and unscrupulous appliance of legal technicalities, the most abandoned criminals have been enabled to escape a deserved punishment, meets with their unqualified disapprobation."

But the worst days were over, and comparative peace was restored to society. Therefore the Vigilance Committee ceased to act. The members, however, did not dissolve the association, but only appointed a special or executive committee of forty-five to exercise a general watchfulness, and to summon together the whole body when occasion should require. This was shortly afterwards done in one or two instances, when instead of being opposed to the authorities, the members now firmly supported them by active personal aid against commotions and threatened outrages among the populace. They had originally organized themselves to protect the city from arson, murder and rapine, when perpetrated as part of a general system of violence and plunder by hardened criminals. In ordinary crimes, and when these stood alone, and did not necessarily lead to general destruction, the Vigilance Committee did not interfere farther than as good citizens and to merely aid the ordinary officials whose duty it was to attend to all cases of crime. When, therefore, some six months later, a body of two thousand excited people sought to "lynch" the captain and mate of the ship *Challenge* for cruelty to the crew during the passage from New York to San Francisco, the Vigilance Committee, instead of taking the side of the enraged multitude, firmly supported the legal authorities. On many occasions, both before and after this time, the committee were of great service to the authorities. At their own cost, they collected evidence, apprehended criminals and delivered them into the hands of legal justice. When the city offered a reward of $2500 to any person who would give information which might lead to the apprehension and conviction of an incendiary, the committee offered a reward of $5000 for the same services. The members gave large contributions to hasten the completion of the public jail; and, in many ways, by money, counsel and moral aid, and active personal assistance, sought earnestly to raise the character of the judicial tribunals and strengthen their action. There could not be a greater calumny uttered against high-minded men than to represent, as was frequently done in other countries, and in the Atlantic States, the members of the Vigilance Committee as a lawless mob, who made passion their sole guide and their own absolute will the law of the land. Necessity formed the committee, and gave it both irresistible moral and physical force. One might as well blame a drowning wretch for clinging to a sinking brother, or to a straw, as say that the inhabitants of San Francisco did wrong—some in joining the association, and others in not resisting but applauding its proceedings. People out of California could know little at best of the peculiar state of society existing there; and such as condemned the action of the Vigilance

Committee positively either knew nothing on the subject, or they outraged the plainest principles of self-preservation. We all defend the *man* who, with his own hand, violently and unscrupulously slays the midnight robber and assassin, because he would otherwise lose his own life and property, and where the time and place make it ridiculous to call for legal protection. So also should we defend the *community* that acts in a similar manner under analogous circumstances. Their will and power form new *ex tempore* laws, and if the motives be good and the result good, it is not very material what the means are. This subject is treated at greater length in the chapter on the Vigilance Committee, and to it the reader is referred.

October 3d.—" Wells & Co." bankers, suspended payment. This and the bankruptcy of H. M. Naglee already noticed, are the only instances of failure among that class of the citizens of San Francisco. When the place and the speculative spirit of the people are borne in mind, it is high testimony to the general stability of the banking interest, that only two of their establishments have become bankrupt.

October 4th.—Opening of the new Jenny Lind Theatre on the Plaza. This was a large and handsome house. The interior was fitted up with exquisite taste ; and altogether in size, beauty and comfort, it rivalled the most noted theatres in the Atlantic States. It could seat comfortably upwards of two thousand persons. The opening night presented a brilliant display of beauty and fashion, and every part of the immense building was crowded to excess. A poetical address was delivered on the occasion by Mrs. E. Woodward. A new era in theatricals was now begun in San Francisco ; and since that period the city has never wanted one or two first class theatres and excellent stock companies, among which " stars " of the first magnitude annually make their appearance. Before this date there had been various dramatic companies in San Francisco, but not before had there been so magnificent a stage for their performances. The " Jenny Lind " did not long remain a theatre. The following year it was purchased by the town for a City Hall for the enormous sum of two hundred thousand dollars. The external stone walls were allowed to stand, but the whole interior was removed and fitted up anew for the special purposes to which it was meant to be applied.

Jenny Lind Theatre.

October 20th.—The "American" theatre opened. This was a large brick and wooden house in Sansome street, between California and Sacramento streets. It could contain nearly two thousand persons, and was very elegantly furnished inside. Mrs. Stark gave the opening address. The walls sank nearly two inches on the opening night, when the "house" was densely crowded. The site formed a portion of the bay, and the sand which made the artificial foundation had been deposited upon a bed of soft yielding mud. Considerable fears were entertained in such circumstances for the safety of the structure. Happily the sinking of the walls was regular, and after the first night no material change was perceptible.

October 31st.—To enable the distant reader to form an idea of the crowded state of the harbor, and which it may be mentioned was at all times about as well filled, we give the following accurate list of the number of vessels lying there at this date, viz :—

	Ships.	Barques.	Brigs.	Schooners.	Ocean Steamers.	Total.
American.........	42	64	67	50	9	232
British	5	23	5	3		36
French	9	1	1			11
Chilian	1	2		1	one sloop & one galliot	6
Bremen	1	4	4	1		10
Austrian	1 ship ; Swedish, 3 brigs,					4
German............	1 barque ; Italian, 1 brig ; Dutch, 2 barques,					4
Storeships,						148
					Total number of vessels........	451

The store-ships had originally belonged to all nations, though chiefly to America. In 1848 and 1849, most of the vessels that then arrived in the bay were deserted by their crews, while both in these years and in 1850, many old and unseaworthy vessels had been hurriedly pressed into the vast emigration service to California. A considerable number of all these vessels were not worth the expense of manning and removing, and so they were left to be used as stores and lodging-houses in the suddenly thronged town, or to rot and sink, dismantled and forsaken. We have had occasion at various places to mention that several of these ships are now lying on dry land, in the very centre of the city.

NOVEMBER 6th.—A grand ball was given in the evening of this day at the Parker House, by the Monumental Fire Company. It was one of the finest affairs of the kind held in the city. Upwards of five hundred ladies and gentlemen were present. Such balls were becoming too numerous to be all chronicled, while amidst the general brilliancy it is difficult to select any one as a specimen to show forth the times.

DECEMBER.—The southern portion of the State, having been recently in great danger from attacks of the confederated Indian tribes, applied for aid to Gen. Hitchcock, commanding U. S. forces in California. He accordingly sent as many of his troops as could be spared, and authorized the raising of two companies of mounted volunteers. Great excitement, in consequence of this permission and the previous alarming news, existed in the city, and numbers hastened to enroll themselves in the proposed companies. To the disappointment of many applicants, a selection only could be received. The two companies were placed under the respective commands of Col. John W. Geary and Capt. Daniel Aldrich, while Col. J. C. Hayes was appointed to the command in chief. Later intelligence from the south, to the effect that the Indian difficulties were being arranged, rendered it unnecessary for the volunteers to proceed thither.

December 21st.—This day was remarkable for an unusually severe storm of wind and rain, which continued during the night, and lasted several days without abatement. The tide was several feet higher than ordinary, and the swell from the bay rolled in so heavily as to wash away the sand from many of the newly-piled water lots. Several vessels dragged from their moorings and came in collision with others. Store-ships, that had long been imbedded in the sand, were set afloat and drifted to other quarters. The water at Jackson street rose so high as to cross Montgomery street, causing, at their junction, a lake of no inconsiderable dimensions. The cellars in the lower part of the city were inundated.

CHAPTER XVIII.

1851.

Immigration diminished.—Females comparatively few.—Great city improvements.—Productions of the country, game, &c., in the markets.—Character of the community changing for the better.—The circulating medium.—Extravagance in living, dress, &c.—Personal rencontres and other outrages common.—Titles to real estate uncertain.—Legal decisions.—Depreciated value of merchandise.—Amusements, dissipation and recreation.—The foreign population.—Great crimes less frequent.—The finances of the city.

THE arrivals by sea at San Francisco were not so numerous in 1851 as during the preceding year. The tide of immigration was slackening, only to roll in its much greater numbers the following season. During 1851, upwards of 27,000 persons arrived by sea. Of these rather more than one-half came by steamers from the ports on or near the Isthmus. The ordinary population of the city was increasing, though more slowly than before. At the close of this year the total number probably exceeded thirty thousand. Females were very few in proportion to the whole number of inhabitants, although they were beginning to increase more rapidly. A very large proportion of the female population continued to be of loose character. The Chinese now began to arrive in considerable bands, and occasionally a few of their females. Great numbers of French and Germans, of both sexes, as well as other foreigners, made their appearance. The immigrants generally were of the mining and agricultural classes, although a fair number of them ultimately settled in San Francisco. An extensive immigration continued among the various districts and towns of the country, and the population of all was constantly changing. Fewer fortunate miners now paid visits to the city for the sake of mere recreation, since the rising towns of the interior, particularly Sacramento and Stockton, the capitals of the northern and southern mines respectively, offered all the attractions of dissipation closer at hand. Yet in one way or another, at least one half of the entire population of the State passed through, or visited San Francisco. The ocean steamers carried away more people from the port than they brought. There was the usual large land immigration into the State, and, on the whole, the general population of the country was considerably increased.

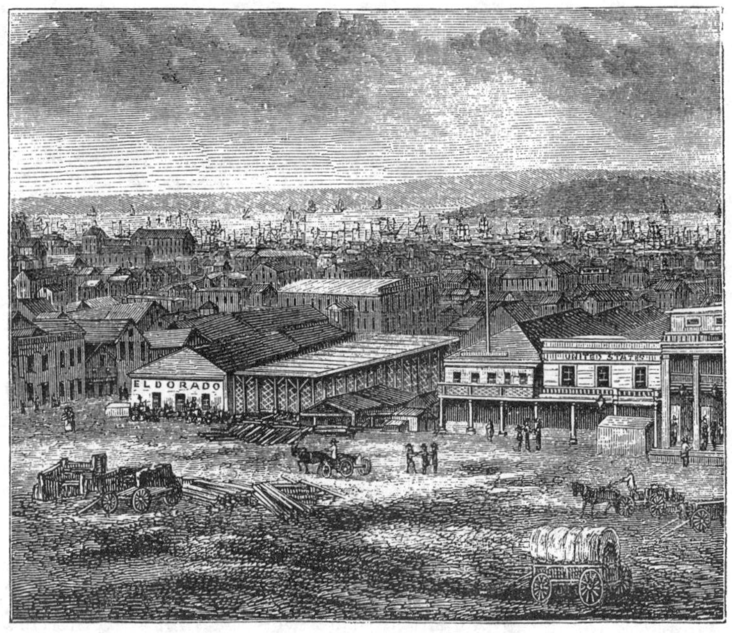

East side of Portsmouth Square, Spring of 1850.

In San Francisco material improvements were taking place. At Clark's Point, on the northern extremity of the city, huge precipitous rocks were quarried and removed, and the solid hill deeply excavated, whereby much new and valuable space was gained for building operations. New streets were graded, planked and built upon, and new and finer houses every where erected. In the southern districts, the "steam-paddy" had been set to work, and was rapidly cutting away the numerous sand hills that lay between the plaza and "Happy Valley." The rubbish was conveyed by temporary rails along the streets, and emptied into the bay at those parts where already roads were laid out and houses built on piles. Sansome and Battery, with the intersecting streets to a considerable distance, were gradually filled up, and firm foundations given for the substantial brick and stone houses that were beginning to be erected there. The town continued to move eastward, and new streets were formed upon piles farther out into the bay, across which the piers and wharves were shooting like the first slender lines of ice before the sheet of water hardens into a solid mass. Closer and thicker the lines ran, as house after house was reared on innumerable piles, while the steam-paddy and railway wagons, and horse-carts without number, were incessantly bearing hills of sand piecemeal to fill up the hollows, and drive the sea far away from the original beach. Where once ships of a thousand tons floated there now rose great tenements of brick and mortar securely founded in the solid earth. Portions of the loose sand were insensibly washed off by the tides from the first places where it was deposited, and the bay was slowly becoming shallower to a considerable distance from shore. As the wharves were pushed farther out, the shipping found less convenient anchorage, and were exposed to occasional strong tides and gales. The character of the port was perhaps changing somewhat for the worse, although the necessities of the town so far urgently required an extension across the bay.

The fires of 1850 and 1851, while they destroyed much valuable property, led in the end to a very superior kind of building, and may thus be said to have done some permanent good. They have stamped a wonderfully grand character upon the architecture of the place. What at first were called and believed to be *fire-proof* houses were becoming numerous, when successive conflagrations came and removed them all. Other houses were built of a still more substantial kind, and these were destroyed by fire in turn. At last, some buildings were erected that surely were *proof* against the most intense heat and flame; and upon their models all the later structures of pretension have been formed. While in certain respects these buildings assume the proportions and grandeur of palaces, in others they appear heavy and gloomy like the veriest prisons. The walls are enormously thick, and the windows deeply sunk in them, showing often at first sight only narrow, dark cavities. When the ponderous wrought iron shutters and doors are closed on the outside the resemblance to a jail is complete. It is believed that no fire from without can seriously affect such buildings, although they may be subject to internal conflagration. While improved houses were rising in the centre and business portion of the town, superior buildings of frame were replacing in the outskirts and suburbs the old habitations, or such as were destroyed by fire. The new plank road to the mission had opened up a large and valuable tract of building ground, and neat and substantial wooden houses were being erected along the whole way.

In the vicinity of the town, wherever a tiny fertilizing stream of water ran among the sand hills, at the mission and the presidio, numerous flower and kitchen gardens and small farms were laid out, which yielded large supplies of the more necessary or prized vegetables. In 1849, the announcement of a real cabbage at dinner would have set half the population frantic with strangely stirred appetites ; now, the many cultivated spots named, daily furnished numerous loaded carts of all kinds of fresh vegetables to the city markets. Potatoes were no longer a rarity ; turnips could be had for money—and at a moderate price, too. The markets made pleasant morning sights. Besides a profusion of vegetables and fruits, they were largely supplied with noble fish and game of all descriptions from the ocean, the bay and the interior. Salmon of huge dimensions, and vast quantities of like delicious fish, whole cart loads of geese, ducks, quails, and other wild fowl, innumerable quarters of bear, elk, antelope, deer, and smaller game, loaded the stalls of the dealers. Mutton was perhaps not so plentiful, but excellent beef was in abundance. Times had changed with San Francisco. The hardships and semi-starvation of 1849 were forgotten in these ample supplies of exquisite food. The epicure might traverse the globe, and have no finer living than what this city yielded ; the glutton would here find both eye and palate satiated. But two years had sufficed to this astonishing change.

The fires that cleared the ground and rendered necessary new building operations, and the improved style of house structures, gave constant employment to every body who could and would work. Wages therefore continued high, and the poorest of the laboring classes were enjoying the incomes of merchants and professional men of other countries. The general improvements in the aspect of the town and social character of the people, noticed

New World Market, corner of Commercial and Leidesdorff streets.

in the review of 1850, were still going on. New "Expresses" were hurrying to all points, stage coaches, mails and noble steamers communicated with the most distant quarters. Additional manufactories and stores, additional newspapers, theatres, public institutions, benevolent, useful and agreeable associations, were being constantly established. Schools and churches were springing up on all sides. A certain class largely patronized the last, though it must be admitted that very many, particularly foreigners, never entered them. The old life and bustle continued, though matters were now systematized, and offered less show and confusion. In 1849, San Francisco was like a great ant-hill, when its busy creatures happen to be disturbed, and when all were visible, hurrying to and fro, out and in, backwards and forwards, apparently in the most admirable confusion and cross purposes, as if every one were engaged in some life and death struggle. In 1851, the city was like the same ant-hill when the cause of fright had been removed and order restored. The old tenants were still as busy as ever, but there was method now in their actions. Some were closely engaged in the interior—the cells or houses of the place—and made no show. Outside lines of other eager workers ran here and there, without jostling or confusion, all filled with the thought of what they had to do, and doing it well and quickly. There was no sauntering, no idleness, no dreaming. All was practical and real; all energy, perseverance and success. In business and in pleasure, the San Franciscans were *fast* folk; none were faster in the world. Their rents, interest on money, doings and profits, were all calculated *monthly*. A month with them was considered equal to a year with other people. In the former short time, men did such deeds, and saw, felt, thought, suffered and enjoyed, as much as would have lasted over a twelvemonth in other lands. But then these were really *men*—giants rather, the very choice of the cleverest, most adventurous and hard-working people of America and Europe. California was a hot-bed that brought humanity to a rapid, monstrous maturity, like the mammoth vegetables for which it is so celebrated.

The city was settling fast into the condition in which it now is. The characteristics of a Spanish or Mexican town had nearly all disappeared. The barbarous magnificence of an old Californian rider was now seldom seen. The jingling, gaudy trappings of the horse, the clumsy stirrups and leathern aprons, the constant lasso and the reckless rider, had given place to the plain, useful harness of the American and his more moderate, though still dashing riding. Superb carriages now thronged the streets, and handsome omnibuses regularly plied between the plaza and the mission. People now, instead of being "every thing by turns and nothing long," more steadily confined themselves to one proper business. The old stores, where so recently all things "from a needle to an anchor" could be obtained, were nearly extinct; and separate classes of retail shops and wholesale warehouses were now the order of business. Gold dust as a currency had long given place to coin. Two years before, the buyer would carelessly tumble out a heap of "dust" in payment, while the seller would have his weights and scales ready for it as a matter of course. A little lump less or more to the quantity was of no consequence to either party. All that loose, stylish kind of thing was now changed. Coin was plentiful, and its fair worth was generally looked for. People found it somewhat more difficult to accumulate wealth, and were less foolishly lavish of their means, although they still always spent them most extravagantly. Specimens of nearly all the coinage of the civilized world were in constant circulation. Approximate values were bestowed upon the pieces, and if any thing like the mark, they readily passed current. The English shilling, the American quarter-dollar, the French franc, the Mexican double-real were all of the same value; so likewise were the English crown, the French five-franc piece, and the American or Mexican dollar. It did not matter although some were twenty-five *per cent.* more worth than others. Four single francs were quite as good as the English five-shilling piece. The smaller silver coins of whatever denomination and of every country were all alike *bits*, and passed for the same value. As for copper money, it was, of course, never seen. A *bit* was the lowest denomination of money, and very little of any thing would it buy. Besides the coins mentioned, there were Indian rupees, Dutch and German florins and guilders, the many coinages of South America, and in fact every known piece of money that circulated in Europe, and in many other parts of the world. The deficiency in the American proper coinage was thus amply made up, especially so far as silver money was concerned. In gold there was a less variety of foreign coin, although many European pieces of that metal were in circulation. The fifty dollar gold pieces called "slugs," and the twenty and ten dollar pieces, issued by the United States Assay Office, in San Francisco, served all the purposes of a regular standard coinage. Before, and shortly after the establishment of the assay office, large quantities of gold currency were supplied by about a dozen different private parties; but as these coinages were generally of less intrinsic worth, in purity and weight of metal, than their nominal value, they soon fell into disrepute and were gradually withdrawn from circulation. Some of them were very neatly executed, and stray specimens may still be occasionally found by the curious.

Formerly, that is, only two years before, the San Franciscans were careless in personal appearance, and rude in manners. Now, they dressed richly and extravagantly, and assumed the polished airs of gentlemen. A striking change was observable every where, and in every thing. The houses were growing magnificent, and their tenants fashionable. Perhaps this fashion was not quite *à la mode de Paris*, but rather *sui generis*. Balls and convivial parties of the most brilliant character were constantly taking place. The great number of flaunting women of pleasure, particularly the French, mightily encouraged this universal holiday, and gave ease, taste, and sprightly elegance to the manners of the town. There is perhaps no place in the world where money is so little regarded as in San Francisco. A man spends there like a prince, as he gains like one. The "almighty dollar" to him appears of less worth than a shilling does to people in England or in our Eastern States. At these balls, and at all public and private entertainments, immense sums were squandered. Trade might be dull, bad, ruinous—rents might rise or fall, and people be really insolvent—still they spent money on all sides. Business losses generally fell on distant correspondents, and the half-burned and supposed bankrupt and ruined city showed still the same brilliant bustle; and its inhabitants still pursued the same expensive round of amusements. Gold must come from the placers, and San Francisco never could in a certain sense be poor. The riches of the Californian mines on the one side, and the luxuries and conveniences of all countries in the world on the other, met in San Francisco. It would be hard indeed for its hot-blooded and venturous population if they did not make the treasures within their grasp minister to every enjoyment that youth and sanguine constitutions could crave.

Ever since the first great immigration many of the inhabitants carried some weapon of defence secretly about them. During the disturbed times in the early part of 1851, when nobody was safe from the assaults of desperadoes even in the public street or in his own dwelling, the practice of wearing deadly weapons became still more common. These were often used—

though not so much against the robber and assassin, as upon the old friend and acquaintance, or the stranger, when drink and scandal, time and circumstance had converted them into supposed enemies. The number of duels, and especially of sudden personal affrays, was fearfully great. The general population of San Francisco—with shame it must be confessed, in those days, as is still the case to a considerable extent—drank largely of intoxicating liquors. A great many tippled at times, and quite as many swore lustily. They are an adventurous people, and their enjoyments are all of an exciting kind. They are bold and reckless from the style of the place and the nature both of business and amusement. New-comers fall naturally into the same character. It may therefore be imagined that personal rencontres frequently occur among such a population. In 1851 these were constantly happening. One man perhaps called another a "liar," and straightway revolvers were produced on both sides. Repeated shots were hastily fired, with sometimes as much damage to the by-standers as to the half-drunken quarrellers themselves. Some scenes of a most savage and atrocious description, ending occasionally in death, took place between parties who were reputed to be of the first class of citizens. Among the lower American orders, and in all classes of foreigners, down to the vilest "greasers," the same violent spirit of personal revenge and deadly outrage was common. On the slightest occasion, at a look or touch, an oath, a single word of offence, the bowie-knife leaped from its sheath, and the loaded revolver from the breast pocket or the secret case, and death or severe wounds quickly closed the scene. The spectators often shared in the same wild feelings, and did not always seek to interfere. The law was powerless to prevent such personal conflicts. Men thought as little of their blood and lives as of their money, and to gratify high swelling passion would madly waste them all alike.

One considerable cause of personal disputes and bloodshed was the uncertainty of legal titles to property, which encouraged squatterism. Owing to recent conflicting decisions by the courts of law it almost appeared that the only, or the best title to real estate was actual possession. A great many people made a practice of settling down upon any vacant lot they fancied, and perhaps in the course of a night would fence it in and erect some small house on the ground. When daylight and the proprietor came, the intruder defied ejection. To seek redress from the tribunals whose judgments had led to these encroachments was only ridiculous ; so the parties generally fought it out among themselves, with the aid of friends and long purses to hire help, until both suffered considerably in the battle. The effect of these conflicting legal decisions on the titles to real estate had otherwise a very prejudicial effect. They hindered the immediate and permanent improvement of property, since no man would expend large sums in that way when his title to the ground was in jeopardy. Lenders, already alarmed at the foolish proposals of usury bills in the Legislature, became shy in advancing money on the security of many properties ; the value of real estate fell considerably ; in some instances no price whatever could be obtained where the title was disputed ; and all was painful doubt on the subject. In 1850, real estate in the city was assessed at the value of $16,849,024 ; while, in 1851, it was only $10,518,273 ; and this was notwithstanding the vast improvements that had taken place in the interval. In the end, certain acts passed by the State, which confirmed sales of the beach and water lots by the city and sanctioned its title to those lots still unsold, and also later and more satisfactory decisions of the Supreme Court in the matter of titles, helped to re-establish confidence on the subject, and secure the old owner in his property against the mere squatter.

The commerce and imports of San Francisco were very great during 1851—too great indeed for a profitable trade. The fall in the prices of nearly all kinds of merchandise which lasted over a great part of 1850, continued during the following year. Matters were perhaps not quite so bad as when, in the spring of 1850, chests of tobacco were used to pave the streets or make a solid foundation for houses, and when nearly every article of merchandise went a-begging for a buyer, and not finding one was cast aside to rot, or used to fill up mud-holes ; but still, in 1851, most kinds of goods were a dead loss to the owner. In the palmy days of '48 and '49, all were purchasers, at any price : now every body sought to sell, at no matter what sacrifice. In '49 a dollar was paid for a pill, and the same sum for an egg ; a hundred dollars for a pair of boots, and twice that sum for a decent suit of clothes ; a single rough brick cost a dime, and a plank some twenty feet long was cheap at ten dollars. At one period of that wondrous year, common iron tacks of the smallest size, sold for their weight in gold ; and for a long period were in request at from five to ten dollars *an ounce.* But in '51, bales of valuable goods were sometimes not worth their storage. There happened to be no plaster walls in '49, and small tacks,—of which there was only a very meagre quantity in the country,—were in extreme demand for fastening the usual muslin coverings to the wooden partitions of houses. Hence the apparently extravagant sum that was given. Every thing that was useful and really needed in those earlier days commanded the most astonishing prices. The supply was limited and the demand great, while money was suddenly plentiful. But in 1851, the stock of all kinds of goods was greatly over-proportioned to the natural demand of the place. The population of the city and country generally, although numbering only about a quarter of a million persons, yet being nearly all in the prime of life, rich and careless, and with large appetites, consumed and wasted the goods and provisions that would have satisfied an ordinary population of perhaps a million of people. Still the imports into San Francisco were far ahead of the most extravagant demands and consumption of the ravenous, wasteful people of California. For any article actually required, and of which there might be but a scanty stock in the market, noble rates were still given ; but as the supply of most goods was immense, prices fell accordingly. The auctioneers, whose business and importance daily increased, rattled away shiploads of merchandise at often nominal prices. Extravagance and waste did their best, but they could not destroy every thing. Enormous losses were sustained during 1850, and especially in 1851, by foreign shippers. The commercial people in San Francisco generally acted as agents on commission for others, and did not often import as merchants on their own account. The losses therefore on merchandise did not so very much affect individual citizens, while to the general public it was a positive gain to have an unlimited supply of goods at low prices.

In the ordinary recreations of the city a change was gradually taking place. The gambling-saloons, though still very many, were becoming fewer, while billiard-rooms and drinking-bars or saloons for refreshment and conversation, were increasing in number, in size and handsome style. There is no place in the world with so many billiard-tables in it in proportion to the population, as San Francisco ; and but few places, if any, with more drinking-houses. In such quarters, in 1851, a large proportion of the inhabitants usually spent their evenings. Other crowds nightly filled the large and beautiful theatres that were now erected. Balls, masquerades and concerts, gambling-saloons, visits to frail women,—who always have been very numerous and gay in San Francisco,—and an occasional lecture, filled up the measure of evening amusement. Gayety and personal dissipation were then, as they are now, characteristic features of the city. Nor were these things confined to the upper and richer classes. Labor was paid so highly that all orders of the people had money at command to squander in amusements. During the day, and particularly on Sundays, the "swells" of both the highest and the lowest rank, cantered to the presidio or the mission, or scampered among the sand-hills behind the town, or crossed the bay in the small steamers to Contra Costa, or formed pic-nic excursions to the fort, or the outer telegraph hill, or on the sea-shore, or somewhere among the lonely and picturesque valleys among the hills. San Francisco was certainly a great city ; and its people had great notions ; their deeds of business and amusement were all great in their way.

The large admixture of foreign races, particularly the light-hearted, theatre-loving French, the musical Germans, and the laughter-loving, idle, dancing Hispano-Americans, tended to give a pleasant, gay aspect to the city. The grave national character of United States men was converted into levity and cheerfulness by the example and sympathy of their merry neighbors. It may be said, at the same time, that the foreign population were generally an orderly, obedient and useful class of the community. The Chinese might here perhaps form an exception. They are an exclusive race, and mingle but little save with their own people. They were now beginning to arrive in considerable numbers, bringing with them a number of their women, who are among the filthiest and most abandoned of their sex. They, as well as most of the foreign races, generally dwelt together in particular localities, which gave these quarters a distinctive appearance from the rest of the town. The Chinese and the free negroes, of whom there was now a goodly sprinkling, were "the hewers of wood and the drawers of water" of the place ; and performed washing and women's business, and such menial offices as American white males would scorn to do for any remuneration. The "greasers," too, who are verily "of the earth, earthy," helped the "celestials" and the black fellows, or infernals, in their dirty work.

In various parts of this book, we have dwelt so fully on the state of crime and public morals during 1851, that it is unnecessary to say much more on the subject in this general chapter. The extraordinary action of the Vigilance Committee, proved most salutary to the best interests of the community. After a few hangings, which were signalized by scenes of the most terrible and impressive nature, the social state of the city was much improved ; and people could venture to appear at dark in the streets, or to dwell alone in poorly defended houses, without dread of the assassin, the burglar, or the incendiary. Crime was now principally confined to petty thefts, for which the "chain-gang" was an excellent punishment ; while cases of bloodshed,—and they were frightfully many,—arose chiefly from the rampant, unregulated passions of the people, who thought and called themselves, as they were reckoned by others, respectable men and good citizens.

The financial affairs of the city, which had long been in a very confused and ruinous state, were, towards the close of 1851, much simplified and improved. The general improvidence and corruption of a long series of municipal authorities, from the day when the American flag was first hoisted on the plaza, had squandered or jobbed away many of the most valuable portions of the real estate belonging to the corporation. But the funding of the floating debt, and perhaps the increasing purity, or dread of being found out, on the part of recent officials, with other causes, tended gradually to raise the credit of the city. The next great blow which fell upon the municipal funds was the noted matter of the "Peter Smith" sales, which shall be duly chronicled among the events of 1852.

CHAPTER XIX.

1852.

Dr. Peter Smith.—His contract with the city to take charge of the indigent sick.—The city's indebtedness.—Smith's judgments and executions.—Injunctions of the commissioners of the funded debt.—Sale and sacrifice of the city property under Smith's judgments.

JANUARY.—Some time before this date certain legal proceedings took place which much affected the pecuniary interests of the city. These subsequently involved it in great and expensive litigation, where millions' worth of property were concerned. The whole subject forms one of the most important series of events in the history of the city, and has long excited the close attention of the citizens and the deepest regret in the minds of all honest men that such unfortunate circumstances should have occurred. Charges of official corruption and private jobbery have at different times been made openly, and oftener whispered, against prominent citizens for their connection with the matter, and improper motives have been very freely imputed to them. Lawsuits have been long and vigorously carried on regarding the subject, the final decisions upon some of which have regulated the ownership and titles to a vast amount of property. We have selected the opening of this year for a short general statement of the case, although some of the particular events alluded to occur much later in point of time.

In the course of 1850, Dr. Peter Smith contracted with the city for the care of its indigent sick. For each patient he was allowed a sum of four dollars daily. This may now seem a high allowance, but at that period,—to say nothing of the usual jobbery in the matter,—the cost of house-rent, boarding, medicines and medical attendance, was very great. The city having little money in its exchequer at the time, generally paid Dr. Smith in the shape of *scrip*, which bore a monthly interest of *three per cent.* till redeemed by cash payments. The common council were meanwhile regularly auditing Smith's accounts, at short intervals ; while they continued to give that gentleman the necessary amounts of scrip to satisfy the different balances as they arose. Altogether, the amount of city indebtedness under Smith's contract was $64,431.

The total amount of city scrip granted in 1850 and the beginning of 1851, was exceedingly great, and, as we have already mentioned, an act, after considerable discussion and delay, was finally passed by the Legislature, to fund the floating debt and convert the same into stock, bearing an annual interest of *ten per cent.* General creditors, however, as well as holders of scrip, were neither obliged to await the passage of this act, nor afterwards to accept the terms of conversion. To those who possessed the obligations of the city, or who held it bound as debtor in any actual or implied contract, the ordinary courts of law were open for ascertaining and making effectual the amounts of their claims. Accordingly, some creditors,—and chiefly Dr. Smith,—proceeded to take the necessary legal steps to procure judgments against the city, and to make executions and sales of its property. If all the then holders of scrip or of city indebtedness had acted in this fashion, there would only have resulted "confusion, worse confounded ;" and neither Dr. Peter Smith nor any one of the city creditors would have profited by his hasty and preference-seeking proceedings. As it happened, the party named was almost the sole, as he was the chief creditor, who thought fit thus to secure his strictly *legal* rights.

On the 25th of February, 1851, Smith recovered judgment against the city for $19,239, being a portion of the total amount claimed by him; and on the 8th of July following, the sheriff proceeded to sell so much of the city property as, it was expected, would defray the sum named. At this sale the various wharves belonging to the corporation were sold, as also the old city hall lot, and the city hospital and buildings. By this time the act to fund the municipal floating debt had been passed, and its property conveyed to the commissioners there named. At first sight it appeared improper, and perhaps ridiculous, in the circumstances, for an individual to sue the city to extremities, and seek to gain a preference over the general body of creditors. The commissioners of the funded debt made both public and private statements in the strongest terms, to the effect that any sales which might take place under the Smith judgments would be held as illegal and of not the slightest value. This conduct on their part, as well as a vague general impression among the citizens, that such was, or certainly ought to be the true state of the case, had the effect of discouraging buyers from attending and bidding at the sales in question ; and consequently the property was sold at merely nominal prices, perhaps at not a twentieth, or even a fiftieth part of its real value. The sum realized was therefore insufficient to satisfy Smith's judgment. Accordingly an *alias* execution for the balance was issued on the 7th of August following, upon which the sheriff, on the 17th of September thereafter, sold forty one-hundred-vara lots, fifty-five fifty-vara lots and one water lot. But as the old impression remained that the whole proceedings were illegal, nominal prices were again only obtained for the great amount of property mentioned. On the 2d January, 1852, the sheriff further sold an immense amount of water lot property of the value, at least, of half a million of dollars, also at nominal prices. Still the original judgment was unsatisfied.

Meanwhile a second suit had been raised by Smith against the city, upon which judgment, on the 4th of March, 1851, was duly obtained, for $45,538. Upon this, the sheriff advertised to sell on 14th June following, one hundred and three water lots, twenty-seven blocks on South Beach, and seven one-hundred-vara lots. The commissioners, consequently, in order to save the city's property from the threatened sacrifice, appealed to the proper legal tribunals for injunctions to stay the sheriff's sale ; but for reasons which may not here be named, their appeal was disregarded. Failing to obtain the necessary injunction, and still determined to protect the interests of the people, the commissioners attempted to compromise matters with Dr. Smith, to effect which object, Col. J. W. Geary and Judge P. A. Morse, on behalf of the Board, personally waited upon John McHenry, Esq., counsel for Peter Smith, and guaranteed to secure to Smith from their own private funds the whole amount of his judgment on condition that the sale should be arrested. This generous offer, which had it been accepted, would have saved millions of dollars to the city, from the pockets of a few greedy speculators who were instigating and abetting the proceedings of Smith, was not only rejected, but treated with contempt. The commissioners driven to their last resource, and acting under advice of their attorney, Solomon Heydenfeldt, Esq., who subsequently became and was a judge of the Supreme Court, when the decision against the action of the commissioners and confirming the "Peter Smith Titles" obtained from the sheriff, was given, issued the following address:—

"TO THE PUBLIC.

"A sale of a large number of city lots is advertised to take place this day, by virtue of an execution in the hands of the Sheriff, in favor of Peter Smith against the city of San Francisco. The public are hereby notified, that the city has no legal title to the said lots, nor had any title at the time of the rendition of the judgment. By virtue of an ordinance of Council the city conveyed the said lots in December last to the Commissioners of the Sinking Fund, in trust for the benefit of the creditors of the city; and by virtue of an act of the last Legislature, the Commissioners of the Sinking Fund conveyed said lots to the present Commissioners of the Funded Debt upon the same trusts. Some time since an injunction was obtained in the District Court to prevent this sale. The injunction was dissolved on the ground that the judgment creditor of the city had the right to sell whatever interest the city may have left after the execution of the trust, and that such sale would not interfere with the trust. Every one will readily perceive that a purchase made at the Sheriff's sale will convey no title, because the property of the city is insufficient to pay all of her debts, and under the acts above referred to, it will be the duty of the present Commissioners of the Funded Debt to sell said property in execution of the trusts confided to them, at which sales the purchasers will be enabled to obtain a complete and perfect title. The public are therefore cautioned to disregard the sale to be made by the Sheriff to-day, and the undersigned have given this notice so that no one can complain hereafter that they were purchasers without actual notice of the title held by the undersigned.

P. A. Morse,
D. J. Tallant,
Wm. Hooper,
Jno. W. Geary,
James King, of Wm.
} *Commissioners of Funded Debt.*

Office Commissioner's Funded Debt, June 14, 1851."

This address, which was published in the daily papers, and even read to the people on the day it was issued, failed to produce the effect intended by the commissioners. While, perhaps, they never supposed it would deter the sheriff from proceeding with the sale, which took place according to advertisement; they, at least, and we must believe, honestly supposed that it would prevent citizens from purchasing property which the sheriff, according to their opinion, had no legal right to sell, and of paying money for titles which would never be confirmed, and therefore would be valueless. Their action in the matter, certainly prevented many persons from building or purchasing at the sale, and as before, the lots were disposed of at ridiculously low rates. For this, the commissioners have of late been the objects of much public censure and private calumny. Their conduct has been loudly condemned and their motives impugned. But it should be observed, that they acted by advice of learned counsel; though singularly enough, their adviser subsequently became a judge of the Supreme Court, where he held a seat at the very time the decision was given adverse to his former instructions, and legalizing the sales, by the sheriff, of the city property, under the judgments of Smith.

But it is unnecessary, in this work, which does not profess to be a legal guide to the titles of real estate, to detail minutely the further judgments and sales. It is sufficient to say that Dr. Smith instituted other suits, procured new judgments, and made new executions and sales of the most valuable portions of the property still left to the city. The great sale of the 30th of January, 1852, may only be alluded to, at which about *two thousand acres* of land belonging to the city, and situated within the municipal bounds, were disposed of by the sheriff in the manner above mentioned. As in the beginning, so to the end of these sales, only nominal prices were obtained. The city was losing piece-meal the best part of its real estate, while what between principal, interest and legal costs, the old debt of Smith long remained nearly as great as ever. In the end it was wiped off, but at what an enormous sacrifice!

At first the general public were inclined to treat the whole proceedings as a farce, though a somewhat expensive one to the purchasers at the sheriff's repeated sales. Farther consideration made people begin to think that, after all, the laugh and profit might really be on the side of those supposed foolish persons. The commissioners of the funded debt, in pursuance of their duties, attempted to sell various portions of the city property, but were baffled by repeated injunctions on the part of the holders of what were at this time and have since been commonly called the "Peter Smith Titles." The boards of aldermen next meddled in the fray, and they likewise began to deal in injunctions and other legal annoyances. Matters looked bad, and soon the progress of serious lawsuits made them much worse. Opportunities were still given to cancel or remedy the worst parts of the original objectionable measures. The boards of aldermen and the mayor happened to be opposed in this as in many other matters of consequence, while the funded debt commissioners, were also not on the best terms with the common council, which last body again scarcely possessed the public confidence. Thus there was a general want of union and common action in most municipal matters; while especially in regard to the Smith sales, either nobody knew what to do, or every body pretended nothing could be done. At any rate, nothing effectual was done to save the city's interests.

At the last moment allowed by law for the redemption of property sold under the sheriff's authority, a large sum of money was procured through the liberality and public spirit of a distinguished and worthy firm, Messrs. Theodore Payne & Co., and tender was made of the sums, principal, interest and charges, contained in one of the judgments upon which the sale of the 30th January, 1852, had taken place. This redemption-money was refused by those who had purchased at the sale mentioned; and immediately new lawsuits were raised to try the question whether it had been offered timeously and by the proper parties, or whether indeed there could be any right of redemption whatever in the case. By and by the attorney-general instituted an action against the funded debt commissioners, in which was claimed the twenty-five *per cent.* due to the State of the supposed *real* value of the water lots that had been sold at nominal prices. That action was based on allegations of fraud, or culpable ignorance, or carelessness on the part of the commissioners. The pecuniary value of the whole property involved in these several sales was estimated, in 1852, at about two millions of dollars, although two years later its probable value might be nearer twice, or perhaps thrice that amount.

It was subsequently decided by the Supreme Court, that the sales of the wharves and certain other portions of the city property were legal. This swept away for ever one great portion of the corporation means. The next question was the validity of the redemption above mentioned. It was contended that the mayor and the funded debt commissioners (which parties had made the tender), were not entitled to redeem, especially without instruction from the council boards, that right being only in the city in its corporate capacity. Other legal points of nicety arose, in regard, particularly, to the alleged right of redemption itself. These were long matters of contention, and from the immense pecuniary interests at stake, the action was conducted on both sides with all the talent and chicanery that influence or money could persuade or buy. At length, and while we write (April, 1854), a decision has been given, that the redemption money alluded to was not offered by the parties who alone were entitled to make it, and that therefore the relative sales were legal. This judgment embraced other points of law upon which it was likewise founded, but it is unnecessary here to allude farther to them. These several decisions have had the effect of depriving the city of an enormous amount of property, the possession of which would have much relieved the inhabitants of a great and annually increasing taxation.

There is still, as there has long been, much bitter and angry feeling existing in the city respecting the "Peter Smith Titles." San Francisco has somehow lost its best and most valuable property, and individual citizens have gained immense fortunes by the loss. Little or no money has really been paid by these lucky speculators in "the glorious uncertainty of the law." So far as Smith is concerned, it was his undoubted right to make his claims against the city effectual, if he legally could. The same right was in the power of all its other creditors. That they did not exercise their privileges was not the doctor's fault. At the same time it may just be mentioned as a *fact*, that public indignation was strongly excited against his independent and seek-my-own-good style of action. Still, whatever may be thought of that gentleman's discretion or patriotism in the matter, or of the original nature of his claims, which (perhaps, without that close scrutiny that should have been given), having been sustained by legal judgments, became *settled facts*, he is not lightly to be blamed for the unfortunate events that afterwards occurred. The same may not be said of certain officials and private citizens who joined and acted with them. Every thing was certainly done to cry down the right of Smith to sell, and thereby was lowered the value of the municipal property. If this effect was foreseen and wilfully intended, as many have not scrupled to assert, in order to allow a clique of grand speculators to prey on the city means, their conduct cannot be too strongly condemned. If their proceedings arose simply from an error in judgment, the sad effects can only be deplored. The foregoing relation of facts seem clearly to show that the commissioners acted in good faith. They were men of reputed integrity, and had already "done the State some service." The general public took the same view of the subject as did the commissioners. They believed the sales to be invalid, and that the titles obtained from them would be worthless. Hence the sheriff had only for bidders and buyers those daring speculators, who either knew the law better, or were determined to "chance it;" and who, without competition, had the most valuable lots knocked down to them at the cost of an old song. Then, after all, is *nobody* to be blamed for the unfortunate issue? When millions have been lost in this way to the community, it is hard to convince the citizens that no underhand dealing has taken place; that no corruption, no wilful delay, false statements, gross personal interests and plotting have been at work. It may not be easy to discover and brand the guilty persons, and people may entertain different suspicions as to their names and special concern in the grand game of spoliation. Let every one therefore keep his own thoughts on the business. At this stage of the affair, it is perhaps impossible to get at "the truth—the whole truth—and nothing but the truth." One thing only seems certain—the "manifest destiny" of San Francisco is to be plundered at all hands, and to yield easy and quickly won fortunes to her "most prominent citizens."

CHAPTER XX.

1852.

The Chinese in California.—Act passed to fund the floating debt of the State.—The State Marine Hospital.—Act to convert into a seven *per cent.* stock the floating debt of the County of San Francisco.—Anniversary of fires.—Meetings of the Vigilance Committee.

April.—The immigration of Chinese into California has greatly increased of late. By this month it was supposed that upwards of ten thousand of that people had arrived at San Francisco, while as many more were estimated to be on the way. Considerable public discussion existed at this period on the desirableness of such a vast immigration of the race; and we take occasion to make some general remarks on the subject, as well as upon the present (1854) condition of Chinamen in the city.

The manners and habits of the Chinese are very repugnant to Americans in California. Of different language, blood, religion and character, inferior in most mental and bodily qualities, the Chinaman is looked upon by some as only a little superior to the negro, and by others as somewhat inferior. It is needless to reason upon such a matter. Those who have mingled familiarly with "celestials" have commonly felt before long an uncontrollable sort of loathing against them. "John's" person does not smell very sweetly; his color and the features of his face are unusual; his penuriousness is extreme; his lying, knavery and natural cowardice are proverbial; he dwells apart from white persons, herding only with countrymen, unable to communicate his ideas to such as are not of his nation, or to show the better part of his nature. He is poor and mean, somewhat slavish and crouching, and is despised by the whites, who would only laugh in derision if even a divine were to pretend to place the two races on an equality. In short, there is a strong feeling,—

prejudice it may be,—existing in California against all Chinamen, and they are nicknamed, cuffed about and treated very unceremoniously by every other class. Yet they are generally quiet and industrious members of society, charitable among themselves, not given to intemperance and the rude vices which drink induces, and are reputed to be remarkably attached to their pa-

Chinese Merchants and Coolie.

rents, revering indeed in all persons advanced years, which are supposed to bring wisdom. The Chinese, or certain large tribes of their nation, are of a migratory disposition. They have long since wandered over the many great and rich islands and countries lying around their own land, and have contrived to secure to themselves a large portion of the most valuable trade and commerce of these places. From Canton to Calcutta and Callao, to Melbourne and Manilla, they swarm in all the ports of the Pacific, and more especially in those of the great Malay archipelago. There seems a vast pressure upon the interior multitudes of China, which forces many thousands annually to leave that densely peopled country, for the sake of a bare subsistence, and to save starvation at home. Little food, and that of the coarsest and cheapest kind, suffices to support the life of Chinamen; and to procure that, they will drudge long and patiently at the most painful task. When in a foreign country they have contrived to amass a small sum, which may be considered a fortune by themselves, they generally seek to return to spend it, and enjoy the remainder of their days among kinsmen. This class of people will perhaps form a large portion of the future population of California, especially if any State encouragement should be given them, and a short notice of their character is not out of place in this work. At present they make one of the most striking peculiarities of San Francisco.

From the date of the discovery of gold Chinamen had occasionally appeared in the country; but it was only in 1851 and 1852 that their rapidly increasing numbers began to attract much notice. Considerable apprehension began then to be entertained of the supposed bad effect which their presence would have on the white population. Large bands of Chinese were working at the mines upon conditions which were supposed to be closely allied to a state of slavery. Much misunderstanding arose on the subject. It was believed that the gangs were receiving only subsistence and nominal wages,—some four or five dollars per month for each man,—and that speculators, both yellow and white, were setting them to work on various undertakings which free white laborers conceived should only be executed by themselves. If these vast inroads of Chinese were to continue, the white miner considered that he might as well leave the country at once, since he could not pretend to compete with the poverty-stricken, meek and cheap "coolie," as so John Chinaman was now called by many. It was true that the latter never sought to interfere with the rich claims which the American miner wrought, while he submitted very patiently to be violently driven away from whatever neglected spot he might have occupied, but which the white man suddenly chose to fancy. It was true also that the Chinaman regularly paid, as a foreigner,—and was almost the only foreigner that did so,—his mining license to the State; and was a peaceable and hard-working subject. These things did not matter. Right or wrong, he should be driven from competition with free white men, or his labor should be confined to certain inferior kinds of work, to which the dominant lords of the soil never meant to apply themselves. Angry words, much strife and perhaps some bloodshed, were generated in the mining regions, and the hapless Chinese were driven backwards and forwards, and their lives made miserable.

Governor Bigler, influenced by the American miners' feelings, issued a message in which he stigmatized the Chinese as "coolies," (an appellation which they professed to abhor,) and advised the Legislature to pass a law prohibiting the farther immigration of that people. The terms of this message were considered offensive and uncalled for by most of the intelligent and liberal-minded Americans. The Chinese in San Francisco, who now formed a large class of the community, took the matter much to heart, and, on the 29th April of this year, published a long letter or manifesto in answer to the governor's message. This letter was written temperately, and was an exceedingly able document. Subsequent communications of a like nature passed between the governor and the Chinese. The Legislature meanwhile had appointed a committee to consider and report upon the whole subject, and sundry passionate, and some other amusing speeches were occasionally delivered in the State chambers. In the end, the illiberal action suggested by the governor was not adopted, and soon the matter fell asleep. Farther immigration of this people took place in the course of 1852, and towards the close of that year, there were probably sixteen or twenty thousand of them in the country. Considerable numbers have since left, but as many others have come in their stead, it may be supposed that in 1854 there is still nearly the number mentioned.

In San Francisco, the Chinese were, in 1852, as they have always since continued to be, very numerous—perhaps numbering from three to four thousand. The following description of their present condition is also applicable to the year named. Though individuals of the race reside and carry on business in every quarter of the city, the chief district in which they are located is the upper part of Sacramento street, the whole length of Dupont street, and portions of various other streets adjoining these named. In such places the Chinese are almost the only inhabitants, and the quarter is often called "*Little China.*" There is a considerable number of respectable and wealthy Chinese merchants and shopkeepers in San Francisco, who have extensive business premises in Sacramento street and in various other parts of the city. Their merchandise, as might be expected, is chiefly the goods of their own country. These are of the "upper ten" order, the Corinthian capital of the "celestial" pillar, and would be a credit to any community. They are polite, shrewd, and learned gentlemen ; and are sometimes generous. They can either talk the English language pretty fluently themselves, or by means of an interpreter can conduct any business transaction or private conversation. But the great mass of their countrymen is of a very inferior description. Most of this class, who do really work, engage in the washing and dressing of clothes, for which they receive such wages as must appear to them noble remuneration. The washing and drying are conducted at the different lagoons and wells in the vicinity of the city, while in the smallest, meanest habitation in every street, the Chinaman may be seen diligently ironing and finishing the cleansed garment with his smooth-bottomed chafing-dish of burning coals. They are also employed as porters in warehouses and stores, and in various other kinds of inferior labor.

It appears, however, to most residents in San Francisco, a most curious thing how the great number of that people support themselves. The majority certainly seem to be quite idle, or only busy in gambling, which cannot be a very lucrative pursuit. A portion of the upper end of Sacramento street, and nearly all the eastern side of Dupont street, are occupied with Chinese gambling-houses, which night and day are filled with crowds of that people. The rooms, or "saloons," are generally small, each containing from three to half a dozen tables, or "banks." At the innermost end of some of the principal gambling places, there is an orchestra of five or six native musicians, who produce such extraordinary sounds from their curiously shaped instruments as severely torture the white man to listen to. Occasionally a songster adds his howl or shriek to the excruciating harmony. The wailings of a thousand love-lorn cats, the screams, gobblings, brayings, and barkings of as many peacocks, turkeys, donkeys, and dogs,—the "ear-piercing" noises of hundreds of botching cork-cutters, knife-grinders, file-makers, and the like,—would not make a more discordant and agonizing concert than these Chinese musical performers in their gambling-houses. Heaven has ordered it, no doubt, for wise purposes, that the windy chaos is pleasant to the auricular nerves of the natives. Occasionally a few white men will venture into these places, and gaze with min-

Chinese Gambling-house.

gled contempt and wonder upon the grave, melancholy, strange faces of the gamblers, and their curious mode of playing. There seems to be only one game in vogue. A heap of brass counters is displayed on the plain mat-covered table, and the banker, with a long, slender stick, picks and counts them out one by one, while the stakers gaze with intense interest on the process. The game seems of the simplest nature, though white people scorn to know any thing about it. A few low guttural, gobbling sounds, are occasionally interchanged between the rapt players. A rank smell pervades the place, but that is submitted to for a while by the casual visitor. At last the diabolical music reaches some fortissimo passage of intense meaning, while the wild howls and screams of the singer swell even above the dreadful instrumental din, and then the "outside barbarian" is fain to fly.

While one large portion of the Chinese population of San Francisco seems to be constantly engaged in gambling, another, almost equally large,—the females of the race,—follow prostitution as a trade. In 1851, there were only a few Chinese women in the city, among whom was the notorious Miss or Mrs. Atoy. Every body knew that famous or infamous character, who was alternately the laughing-stock and the plague of the place. Her advices home seem to have encouraged the sex to visit so delightful a spot as San Francisco, and by and by, notwithstanding all the efforts of the male Chinese to keep back their countrywomen, great numbers of the latter flocked to the city. It is perhaps only necessary to say that they are the most indecent and shameless part of the population, without dwelling more particularly upon their manners and customs. Dupont street, and portions of Pacific, and other cross streets, are thickly peopled with these vile creatures.

Notwithstanding all the reputed industry of the Chinese, and which has somehow become a "household word" over the world, it must be confessed that prostitution and gambling seem, in fact, the steady business of the majority of that nation in San Francisco. The truly industrious, well behaved, and worthy part of the people are scattered over the city and its environs, and are seldom seen, while the gamblers, the frail nymphs, and the yellow loafer class are continually loitering about the streets, or in their own proper, open dens, and are every where visible.

In 1852, a regular Chinese dramatic company appeared and performed pieces in their native language. These performances were largely patronized by their countrymen, as well as by many of the white inhabitants, who were curious to witness a real play done by such actors. In 1853, another Chinese theatre was opened. Besides these exhibitions, these people have occasionally other ceremonies and amusements peculiar to themselves. At two periods of the year, in spring and autumn, they form grand processions, and march to Yerba Buena Cemetery with roasted pigs and goats, the smell of which seems grateful to the spirits of their dead lying there. After firing a multitude of crackers.

burning mystic papers, and performing a variety of droll capers, they lift again the dainty meats, and march back in procession to town to feed heartily on them. Huge, gaudy standards, gilded dragons, with long tails, and a national orchestra, astonish and disgust the bystanders, but extravagantly delight the saffron-colored Johns. We have noticed above the nature of their in-

Chinese Females.

strumental and vocal music. Most of their national customs and doings are as little agreeable to white people as those horrible sounds which make the "celestial" harmony.

There seems to be some secret societies among this people, by means of which a few of their number have occasionally been found to grossly oppress their poorer brethren. The police have attempted to interfere and protect the injured, though seldom with much effect. The terror of these, lest vengeance should somehow befall them from their persecutors, have generally prevented full disclosures of the unlawful practices of the secret societies. So proverbial is falsehood among all classes of the Chinese here, that one is quite at a loss to know any thing of their peculiar private associations and customs. One strange idea among them seems to be, that it is a matter of honor for a debtor who cannot pay his obligations to kill himself. Death cancels all debt, and clears scores with hard-hearted creditors. Even Chinese women, at different times, have poisoned themselves here with opium, to satisfy this curious code of honor. Some of the Chinese merchants are reputed to be pretty wealthy. They are now (in 1854) erecting a handsome building as a sort of Merchants' Exchange, specially for their own people. There is a Chinese mission in the city, and some of the race profess themselves Christians.

The Chinese in San Francisco make an extraordinary feature of the city, and appeal very strongly to most organs of the stranger —to his eye, ear, and nose. They are seen in every street quietly passing along. The white immigrant, who may never before have met with specimens of the race, involuntarily stops, and gazes curiously upon this peculiar people, whose features are so remarkable, and whose raiment is so strange, yet unpretending, plain and useful. They are generally peaceable and contented among themselves, and seldom trouble the authorities except in case of mere ignorance of the municipal ordinances. As we have said, there are many most respectable merchants of their race. These are active and keen men in bargaining. They dress in a characteristic and sumptuous manner, and in their own exclusive circles, where no low-caste countryman is allowed to intrude, will no doubt have much refined and intellectual enjoyment. Such flowery grandees as luxuriate in wives are proud to let the white man know that their charmers have the little feet of *ladies*, not the great hoofs of the trolloping damsels who haunt the streets and lie in wait for the foolish stranger. Nearly the whole race, from the "upper ten" to the lower thousands, wear the time-hallowed *tail*; while their every-day garb is the immemorial clothing of Chinamen. Some, indeed, sport one or more articles of the white man's dress—his boots, trousers, coat, or hat; but these are comparatively few. On occasions of public rejoicing, the Chinese muster in numerous bodies, while their banners, cars, and they themselves, in their most superb array, form striking and interesting features in procession, and the like. They are very fond of such shows, and among themselves appear to observe many national, or private holidays, at which an abundance of their famous crackers are discharged. Their dwellings, some of which are brought in frames direct from China, and erected by themselves, are small and incommodious, though extraordinary numbers somehow contrive to creep into them, and live very comfortably. Over the fronts of many of these houses are nightly displayed the common colored paper lanterns of China.

Chinese Merchants.

MAY 1st.—Act passed by the Legislature to fund the floating debt of the State, and to issue stock to the extent of $600,000, bearing interest at the rate of seven *per cent. per annum.* The principal of the debt is declared payable in New York, or at the State Treasury, at the option of the parties receiving the stock bonds, on the 1st day of March, 1870. The interest to be payable either in New York or at the office of the treasurer of the State. Particular provisions are made in regard to a sinking fund, and as to the annual interest.

May 3d.—Of this date acts were passed by the Legislature to amend certain acts which had been passed in the previous session relating to the establishment of a "State Marine Hospital at San Francisco," and providing for its revenue, and also concerning passengers arriving in the ports of California. This hospital received such indigent sick as were objects of State charity, as well as such invalids as were properly chargeable on the city, upon payment of certain fees by the latter. Parties in good health could secure the advantages of the hospital for one year, in the event of sickness, upon payment of the sum of five dollars. Other parties, invalids at the time, might be admitted, after obtaining the certificate of the resident physician, and upon payment of such fees as should from time to time be fixed. The funds and management of the hospital were vested in a board of trustees, to be composed of seven persons, five of whom (residents in San Francisco) were to be chosen annually by the Legislature, and the other two were to be the mayor and president of the chamber of commerce of that city for the time being. Of this board the mayor was declared president. The board was to choose a treasurer and inferior officials, while the Legislature was to appoint one resident and two visiting physicians for the term of two years, to each of whom a salary of five thousand dollars was allowed.

The revenue of the hospital was to be derived from various sources, such as—from a commutation tax upon all immigrants arriving in California by sea, being ten and five dollars upon each cabin and steerage passenger respectively, and which tax was divisible as follows, viz.: three-fifths to the State Marine Hospital at San Francisco, one-fifth to the Sacramento State Hospital (since abolished), and one-fifth to the State Hospital at Stockton; from a tax of one dollar upon each passenger, sailor, or mariner leaving the port of San Francisco,—from the one-half of all sums received by the city of San Francisco on account of licenses to hawkers and peddlers, and on account of auction sales and for licenses for gaming,—from the effects and property of all persons dying in the hospital, which might not be legally claimed by others,—from voluntary donations, and the sums paid by parties to secure the advantages of the institution, &c. An additional one-fourth of the sums received by the city on account of licenses for gaming was also payable by it to the board of trustees, to be applied by the latter, in the first instance, towards payment of the debt of the former "State Marine Hospital;" and after that debt was satisfied, to be set aside as a building fund.

In the following year, the Legislature passed an act materially modifying the arrangements regarding this hospital and its revenues, which will be noticed under its proper date. As the acts particularly above mentioned, and those passed in the session of 1851, form the foundation of the subsequent legislation on the subject, we have thought fit to notice them in this place at some length.

May 4th.—Act passed by the Legislature authorizing the conversion of the floating debt of the County of San Francisco, to an amount not exceeding $400,000, into a seven per cent. stock. The interest of this funded debt is payable half yearly, and the principal is to be redeemed within ten years after the 1st day of July, 1852. Commissioners were appointed under this act to carry out its purposes, who should hold office until the first day of July, 1853, after which date the board of supervisors of the county should enter upon the farther management of the matters in question. Particular provisions are set forth in the act respecting the raising of the annual interest becoming due upon the debt, and for the formation of a sinking fund to redeem the principal.

This day was the anniversary of the second and the fifth great fires. Considerable apprehension was entertained that some attempts would be made to set the city in flames about this time. The different fire companies were therefore on the alert, and took every precaution to provide against the dreaded danger. The men remained in close attendance both day and night, and had all their engines and tackle in instant working order. About ten o'clock at night, on the 4th, the fire-bell was heard loudly booming, and with wonderful speed, "like greyhounds from the slips," the firemen hurried to the quarter announced. This proved a false alarm ; but the circumstance showed the efficiency of the fire-organization. The citizens had now some confidence in it, and a strong feeling of security that no conflagration on the scale of the former great ones would ever again happen.

The Vigilance Committee, which in the early part of this year had held several meetings, both of the executive committee and the general body of members, were again stirring at this time. A common impression existed that there was still an organized band of thieves and incendiaries within the city. So the executive committee recommended the general members to organize themselves into a "night patrol," while they took such other measures as were adequate to meet the emergency. Although this famous association had done many confessedly illegal acts, yet the tendency of these had been so good, and they seemed so justifiable in the terrible circumstances of the time, that the people were led to trust implicitly to their unwearied vigilance and decisive action, and could now lie down to rest at nights without feeling the old constant dread of having their houses robbed or burned before morning.

CHAPTER XXI.

1852.

Clipper Ships.—Enormous Taxation.—Purchase of the Jenny Lind Theatre by the Common Council.—Times and Transcript removes to San Francisco.—Fourth of July celebration.—Great scarcity of printing paper.—Duel between Hon. Edward Gilbert and General Denver.—Custom of Duelling.—Funeral ceremonies on occasion of the death of Henry Clay.

JUNE.—It appears from records kept by the late harbor master, Captain King, that *seventy-four* vessels claiming and entitled to be called "clipper ships," and averaging rather more than 1000 tons burden, had arrived in the port of San Francisco during the last three years. These records commence with the well known brig *Col. Fremont*, in May, 1849, and include the *Aramingo*, which arrived in May, 1852. The average passage was one hundred and twenty-five days. Some of the fleet, however, made much more speedy voyages. The *Flying Cloud*, which arrived in August, 1851, performed the distance from New York in eighty-nine days. The *Sword Fish*, also from New York, arrived in February, 1852, after a passage of ninety days. The *Surprise*, arriving in March, 1851, the *Sea Witch*, in July, 1850, —both from New York,—and the *Flying Fish*, in February, 1852, from Boston, respectively accomplished the voyage in ninety-six, ninety-seven, and ninety-eight days.

The "clipper ship" is virtually the creation of San Francisco. The necessity of bearing merchandise as speedily as possible to so distant a market, one too which was so liable to be suddenly overstocked by goods, early forced merchants and ship-builders interested in the California trade to invent new and superior models of vessels. Hence the modern clipper with her great length, sharp lines of entrance and clearance, and flat bottom. These magnificent vessels now perform the longest regular voyage known in commerce, running along both coasts of the Americas, in about four months ; while the ordinary ships of older models used to take seven and eight months to accomplish the same distance. The contrast is very striking between the short, clumsy vessels, of a few hundred tons burden, which brought the early European navigators to the coast of California, and the large and beautifully lined marine palaces, often of two thousand tons, that

Clipper Ship.

are now continually gliding through the Golden Gate. These are like the white-winged masses of cloud that majestically soar upon the summer breeze. In another part of this work we have given an illustration of the galleon, or sea-going armed merchantman of Drake's day ; here we lay before the reader a representation of one of the finest modern California traders, a clipper ship bound for San Francisco. While these noble vessels have revolutionized, in every maritime country, the model and style of long-voyage ships, they have also introduced a much happier marine nomenclature. The old-fashioned, humdrum *Julias* and *Mary Anns*, the *Trusties* and *Actives* are fast disappearing. The very names of our modern clippers have poetry and music in them, and convey a wonderful sense of swiftness. They confer even dignity on the dry details of the "marine reporter," where the simple words shine like golden particles in the Californian miner's sands.

San Francisco was certainly a wealthy city, yet the amount of taxation laid upon it was enormous. We give here some statistics taken from official documents, showing the amount of cash which had been paid by the citizens during the year previous to this date.

DIRECT TAXES.

Amount collected from City Licenses, from June 1st, 1851, to May 31st, 1852,	$275,873 14
Amount collected from City Taxes, between said dates,	262,665 23
	$538,538 37
Amount collected from State and County Taxes, from May 18th, 1851, to May 18th, 1852,	$231,348 85
Amount of direct taxes paid by the people of San Francisco during the past year,	$769,887 22

INDIRECT TAXES.

Duties collected at the Custom House for six months, ending Dec. 31st, 1851,	$1,012,128 94
Duties collected for three months, ending March 31st, 1852,	450,041 50
" for the fourth quarter (estimated,)	484,056 81
For the year ending June 30th, 1852,	$1,946,227 25
Direct Taxes, as above,	769,887 22
Amount in cash actually contributed by San Francisco for support of City, State, County and National Governments for one year,	$2,716,114 47

These statistics show only the amount actually paid; but there were arrears of direct taxes which would certainly be recovered (since they were secured upon property), and which would swell the amount chargeable on the year to $1,053,773. Adding the last sum to the amount of custom-house duties, it will be seen that about three millions of dollars were drawn, as taxes, from San Francisco in one year. If the population be estimated at 30,000, this would show that the amount of local direct taxation was about $35 per head. In regard to the goods paying custom-house duties, it will be borne in mind that a fair proportion of the necessaries, and at least one-half of the luxuries used in the State were consumed in this city. If we estimate therefore the population of the former at quarter of a million, it may be supposed that the sum of, at least, $300,000 was actually contributed in indirect taxation by the inhabitants of the latter. This is at the rate of $10 per head. Add this to the sum of $35 above mentioned ; and it appears that the total amount of direct and indirect taxation for a single year upon each inhabitant, male or female, infant or adult, of San Francisco, was $45. This is an amount of taxation which few cities or countries can show. But besides these sums, the holders of city real estate were assessed in two-thirds of the expense of grading and planking the streets opposite their properties ; while the general citizens voluntarily incurred a vast amount of additional expense, in the appointment of special police to guard particular localities, in the gratuitous services of firemen, in lighting, watering, cleansing and repairing the public streets, in opening drains and sewers, and in many other ways, the duty of attending to which naturally falls, in the cities of other lands, upon the municipal authorities.

June 4th.—We have already had occasion to mention the unexpected manner in which the common council existing at this time managed to get into office. They never enjoyed the confidence of the people, by whom in reality they were not chosen. Perhaps on that very account, they were the more determined to neglect the public interests and attend solely to their own. Had Mayor Harris not continually been a thorn in their side, much additional mischief would have been perpetrated. Though this gentleman was on their ticket, and came into office in the same doubtful manner with themselves, there existed a marked difference in their public acts. Dr. Harris was a man of undoubted personal integrity, and possessed in a high degree the confidence and esteem of the citizens. By his care and faithfulness, the city was saved from many heavy burdens that would recklessly have been laid upon it by the common council of this year. One noted instance was his refusal to approve of the aldermen's ordinance accepting the terms of the act of the Legislature which relinquished the State claims to the water lots, upon the city recognizing and confirming certain of the old obnoxious "Cotton Grants."

The purchase of the new Jenny Lind Theatre and Parker House for the purposes of a City Hall was another of the common council jobs which excited very much angry discussion at the time, and which afforded interesting and amusing "matter" for the newspapers—(the "Jenny Lind Swindle," or sometimes "Juggle," they facetiously called it),—during half a year. The old City Hall having been destroyed in the fire of 22d June, 1851, the various municipal officials were compelled to get business chambers where they could, for which very high rents had to be paid. As the different public offices were now located in separate parts of the town, much inconvenience was experienced. This arrangement could only be temporary. The rents, which were somewhere about forty thousand dollars per annum, formed a heavy tax upon the public; while ground could be bought and a proper building erected by the city itself for about four or five times that amount. Several desirable sites could be had in the town on moderate terms, and responsible contractors were ready to undertake the construction of the proposed building at fixed rates, which would certainly have reduced the total cost below two hundred thousand dollars. In these circumstances, the common council, for reasons, as the saying is, best known to themselves, and in spite of the indignant cries of the citizens, and the general remonstrances of the press, determined,—in conjunction with the board of supervisors of the county, who were to pay half the cost,—to purchase the Jenny Lind Theatre, and convert it into the proposed City Hall. The purchase-money of the building as it stood was to be $200,000; while to remove all the inside walls, leaving only the outer ones standing, and to build up the interior anew, properly fitted up for municipal purposes, was believed to involve the expenditure of nearly half as much more. At the same time, it was supposed that the building when so altered would be only a miserable structure at the best. An ordinance authorizing the purchase was passed by large majorities in both council boards, and sent to the mayor for approval, which was refused. Notwithstanding, the common council, on the 4th June, re-adopted the obnoxious ordinance, and passed it by a constitutional and almost unanimous vote.

Meanwhile, the public wrath was growing very clamorous, the more so perhaps that it was impotent. On the evening of the 1st of June, one of the usual mass and indignation meetings was held on the plaza, where the proposed purchase was passionately denounced. Mr. William A. Dana presided on the occasion. This was one of the most stormy meetings that had ever been held in the city. Hon. David C. Broderick, who was in favor of the proposed purchase, attempted to make a speech for his cause, but the noise and reproaches of the meeting effectually put him down. Sundry squabbling and wordy sparring took place between Mr. Broderick and Dr. J. H. Gihon, who was on this occasion the people's orator ; and the meeting ended in hubbub, riot and confusion. Little cared the common council for such proceedings—the general ire—the mayor's veto—the denunciations and ridicule of the press. The matter was carried finally into the Supreme Court, at the instance of some public-spirited citizens, and shortly afterwards a judgment was obtained recognizing the right of the city and the board of supervisors to make the purchase. This was forthwith done ; and the contemplated alterations were speedily made on the building, although at a great expense. The whole affair was long a prolific subject for conversation and discussion, for ridicule and the imputation of corrupt motives. It served to glorify the council of this year, as the notorious aldermen's salaries and medal pieces of business had immortalized a previous party of "city *step*-fathers."

After the purchase was made and the alterations were completed, it was found that the new structure answered the purposes intended better than was at first anticipated. The situation is excellent. At the present time, however (1854), it is beginning to be discovered that the building is too small for the increased business of the city. Movements are now making to purchase additional business chambers elsewhere, or to include a portion of the adjoining Union Hotel into the municipal establishment. Doubtless, before many years pass, the whole of either that building, or of the El Dorado gambling-saloon on the other side, if not both, will be required for the necessary extension of the City Hall, unless indeed it be located in some altogether different quarter, and built anew.

JUNE 28th.—The "Placer Times and Transcript," transferred from Sacramento, is first published in San Francisco, under the management of Messrs. Fitch, Pickering & Lawrence.

July 5th.—"Independence-day" falling upon Sunday, was

celebrated the next day. This national festival has always been a grand affair in San Francisco; and on this occasion the citizens exceeded all their former efforts. Prominent in the procession of the day were large bands of foreigners, particularly of the French and the Chinese. The latter displayed numerous fanciful flags and specimens of the finest workmanship of their people. Their gongs, cymbals, wooden bowls or drums, and strange stringed instruments, made the air hideous with diabolical sounds. One wagon was filled with several Chinamen richly and showily dressed, who occupied themselves in continually firing off their national crackers. In the evening there was a brilliant display of fireworks on the plaza, where some fifteen thousand of the inhabitants had assembled to witness the exhibition.

July 11th.—The *Herald* newspaper is printed on coarse brown paper, such as is commonly used for envelopes and for wrapping packages. About this period, and during some months following, all the newspapers of the city were reduced to the same or to even worse descriptions of paper. Day by day, the old broad sheets were becoming narrower and coarser, while they assumed every color of the rainbow. The *Alta* for a long time was published on a small double sheet (which, however, was of a pretty fine quality), where the typographical matter on a page measured only about fourteen inches in length by ten in breadth. The market had suddenly and unexpectedly happened to be without supplies of proper printing paper; and many months elapsed before a sufficient stock could be procured. Of course prices of the material rose enormously.

August 2d.—A duel took place this day between the Hon. Edward Gilbert, senior editor of the Alta California and ex-representative of the State in the Lower House of Congress, and General J. W. Denver, State Senator from Trinity County. Gen. Denver having taken personal offence at certain observations which had appeared in the "Alta California," regarding Governor Bigler's government, published a letter, in which he animadverted strongly on the terms of these observations, and talked of the writer in objectionable language. Mr. Gilbert, the author of the original obnoxious articles, considered the general's letter unjust and offensive to himself, and thereupon challenged that gentleman.

A hostile interview accordingly took place at Oak Grove, near Sacramento. The weapons were rifles, and the distance forty paces. General Denver, it was said, possessed an unerring aim, while Mr. Gilbert scarcely knew how to hold his piece. At the first interchange of shots, the general fired deliberately aside; while Mr. Gilbert missed. The challenger, or his second, insisted on the fight being continued, more especially, perhaps, because the former had been recently in the habit of ridiculing bloodless duels. His antagonist now considered that it was time for him to protect himself; and, at the next shot, sent his ball through Mr. Gilbert's body. The wounded man never spoke again, and in a few minutes expired. This termination of the duel excited great regret in San Francisco, where Mr. Gilbert had been much esteemed. A numerous company of the citizens assembled to pay the last respects to his remains, public institutions passed resolutions to the honor of the deceased, the shipping hung their flags at half mast, many public buildings and private houses were decorated with mourning draperies, and the newspapers appeared with black lines down their columns.

The custom of fighting duels was at the period of which we write, as it at present is, deplorably common among the higher class of people of San Francisco. These encounters are generally conducted in a manner which must appear somewhat strange to the natives of other civilized countries. There is little delicate privacy observed on the occasion. On the contrary, the parties, or their immediate friends, invite all their acquaintances, who invite others to go and witness the proposed engagement. It is sometimes announced the day before in the newspapers—time, place, parties, weapons, and every particular of the ceremony being faithfully given. That no price is mentioned for the sight, seems the only thing that distinguishes the entertainment from a bull or bear fight. If two notable characters be announced to perform a duel, say at the mission, half the city flocks to the place, and, of course, the spectators are much disappointed should nobody be slain. If the bloody entertainment be advertised to "come off," say at Benicia or somewhere in Contra Costa, the steamers of the eventful morning are densely packed with those who prefer the excitement of a gladiatorial show to the dull pursuit of business, or loafing about the streets. The favorite weapons are navy revolvers. The antagonists stand back to back, walk five paces, turn suddenly round, and fire away at their leisure, till one or both are wounded or slain, or the barrels are all discharged. Sometimes rifles are preferred. With these deadly instruments many men can lodge the ball within a hair's breadth of a given mark at forty paces off, which is the usual distance between the parties in a duel of this description.

We intended to have made Mr. Gilbert's death a text, not only for enlarging upon the usual savage and public nature of the numerous duels which take place here, but also for some remarks upon the general carelessness of life among the people, and the frequency of sudden personal quarrels, when revolvers, bowie-knives and "slung shots" are unhesitatingly made use of. But we have at so many other places in this work had occasion to allude to these every-day characteristics of the inhabitants, that little more need be said here on the subject. In the earlier years,—that is, in 1849 and 1850,—fatal affrays were of very frequent occurrence in the streets, and in every place of public amusement. In the gambling saloons, pistols, loaded with ball, would every night be discharged by some hot-headed, revengeful, or drunken fellows. The crowd around were always liable to be wounded, if not killed, but notwithstanding, play at every table went briskly on, as if no danger of the kind existed. A momentary confusion and surprise might take place if anybody happened to be murdered in the room; but soon the excitement died away. Similar events often occurred at the bar, or on the steps of a hotel, in a low dance or drinking-house, or in the open street, and nobody was much surprised, though some of the parties were severely wounded or killed outright. It was their "destiny," or their "luck." Since the years last mentioned, quarrels of this description have become less common, though they are still numerous. There is a sad recklessness of conduct and carelessness of life among the people of California; and nearly all the inhabitants of San Francisco, whatever be their native country, or their original pacific disposition, share in the same hasty, wild character and feeling. The circumstances of the time, the place and people, soon create the necessity in the latest immigrant of thinking and acting like the older residents on this subject. It has always been a practice with a large proportion of the citizens, to carry loaded fire-arms or other deadly weapons concealed about their persons, this being, as it were, a part of their ordinary dress; while occasionally the rest of the inhabitants are compelled also to arm themselves like their neighbors. Of course, these arms are intended for defence against attacks by robbers, as well as to be used, when necessary, against those who would merely assault the person without meaning to steal. Such weapons are not generally produced, except in cases of extremity, or the place would soon be made desolate; while sometimes the fear of provoking their use, may keep the rowdy and the insolent rascal quiet. Yet the unhappy possession of these fatal instruments often gives rise, on occasions of sudden passion, to many lamentable consequences.

August 10th.—Funeral solemnities, on a great scale, took place this day, in commemoration of the death of Henry Clay. On this occasion political parties of all principles, the different associated bodies, native Americans and foreigners of every nation —in short, the whole inhabitants united to pay homage and respect to the memory of the celebrated statesman. The procession was the largest assemblage of respectable people ever seen in the city, and was distinguished as much for the evident heartfelt sorrow in the mourners, as for the pomp and melancholy splendor of the slow-moving train, which extended about a mile in length. The Merchants' Exchange, the Custom House, El Dorado, Bella Union, City Hall, Marshal's Office, and in fact all the public buildings and many private houses were clothed in black draperies, as if the very stones were to bewail the loss of a great man. The whole of Montgomery street was hung in black, the sombre-looking folds of the cloth being relieved at places by wreaths and ornaments of white. Portions of every other main street were decorated in the same elaborate and perhaps over-fanciful manner. The various engine houses were likewise suitably arrayed. While the insensate walls thus wore the aspect of universal gloom, the people themselves were dressed according to the solemnity and grandeur of the occasion—the natives of every land appearing in the recognized national costume that expressed the deepest grief and mourning in the wearer. The tolling of great bells, the measured boom of the bass drum and the swelling wail of wind instruments turned the hearts of the people heavy and sorrowful. A hundred low-hung flags drooped over the city, and numerous bands of music played dead marches. If mechanical means could inspire or strengthen genuine sorrow, it was so on this occasion. The procession moved through the principal streets till it reached the plaza. There, the orator of the day, Judge Hoffman, delivered an appropriate and eloquent address. The dead no longer heard his praises chanted ; but the memory of his deeds, his fiery eloquence, and the numberless benefits conferred on his country and on the world, by the famous orator and statesman, will long gratefully fill the minds of American citizens.

The occasion was worthy of a grand display ; and it was admitted by everybody, that the procession, the ceremonies and general mourning, were of the most novel, imposing, and splendid description that had ever been witnessed in San Francisco.

CHAPTER XXII.

1852.

Australian gold mines.—Restlessness of miners.—Many who emigrated to Australia return to California.—Superior advantages of the latter place.—Second city directory published.—California Telegraph Company.—General election.—Fire in Sacramento city.—Another fire in San Francisco.—Intelligence received of the death of Daniel Webster.—Falling of the waters of Lake La Mercede.—Another city directory.—Firemen's election.—Legal execution of José Forni.—Destructive storm.

SEPTEMBER.—For some time back a large number of vessels had left San Francisco with adventurers to the Australian gold mines, while now other vessels were bringing many of the same parties back again. A short notice on this subject may not be out of place.

Gold is perhaps the most extensively diffused metal in the world, although it is commonly found in very small particles. Every land is historically known to have had its auriferous district. California, however, stood alone in this respect, so far as it yielded large quantities of the precious metal, procured with less labor than any other country. Its gold possessions had already drawn upon it a vast population, who came hither hastily to collect the sparkling treasure, and then leave. The miners generally never contemplated a permanent residence in the country. When they had raised their "pile," they hurried *home*—to the wives and families or the friends they had left in the Atlantic States or in Europe. So long as they remained in California, they were not closely attached to any one gold-bearing district, however rich it might be. More often, they were incessantly moving about and *prospecting*, hoping and looking for new and richer claims. When a particularly valuable district happened to be discovered, then a "rush" to it took place from all the neighboring regions, and even from places hundreds of miles distant.

This restlessness has always been a peculiar feature in the character of the miner, who is naturally speculative. He works hard—harder than an Irish laborer or an English "navvie," for perhaps one month—then he grows weary and discontented with his trifling gains, and wanders about for as long a period prospecting, poking into every odd crevice in likely rocks, sinking pits here and there, and trying the sandy bed of every stream he may see in his rambles, wistfully hoping, though seldom finding, some rich secret deposit that will repay his previous fruitless labor. When his means of living without immediately profitable and earnest work are nearly exhausted, he gets tired of this new occupation, and a supposed good claim may perhaps also be found. Then the digger sets vigorously to work once more, for another month or two, until new ennui and restlessness force him to go on the tramp again, and look about for the fanciful great gains that can alone satisfy his hopes. He chases the rainbow to find its base. The gold miner, like man in the abstract, "never is, but always *to be* blest." His business is closely allied to gambling, with its rare chances of suddenly making a great fortune, or of losing time and labor, which make his capital.

While the miner grew thus restless, and was attracted to new *placers* upon the least rumor of their fancied superiority, and when idle tales arose and were circulated by the weak, indolent or unlucky, that all the best fields had already been gleaned of their rich harvest, he was naturally prepared to go farther, and to seek in other lands the wealth which he had happened somehow to miss in California. It mattered little in what place or country he made his "pile," so that it was found. The discovery of gold in Australia, nearly a year and a half ago, had produced in that country, and subsequently over a great part of the world, a repetition of the troublous scenes which had occurred immediately after the discovery of gold in California. When, therefore, intelligence of the great quantities of the precious metal which were being found in Australia reached San Francisco, and subsequently the mining regions of California, great excitement was produced over all the country. Successive reports confirmed the first astonishing yields. Rich as the Californian placers had been esteemed, the Australian diggings appeared much to exceed them in that respect. A good story by travelling loses nothing of the marvellous. The first wonderful tidings of the Sydney diggings —including the notable hundred-weight of pure gold, were almost forgotten, when later intelligence came of the newer gold fields of Victoria—of the famous Mount Alexander region, and its districts ; Forest Creek, Friar's Creek and the rest, and also of the

Scene in the gold mines.

renowned Ballarat and Bendigo. Large numbers of the migratory and discontented miners in California now hurried to San Francisco, to depart for the newer and perhaps true Dorado, just discovered in Australia. Many adventurers from the city joined these emigrants, and set sail for Sidney and Melbourne. At the same time, great numbers of Australians, who had come to California after 1848, now took the opportunity of returning to their original homes. Some of these had wrought patiently at the mines, or lived as good citizens in various parts of the country, while others had long been the disgrace and terror of the community. The "Vigilance Committee" of San Francisco, and similar associated bodies that had been formed in other towns of California, had already driven the worst of the last class of Australians away. The news of the gold discoveries in their own country, speedily carried off the rest. The migration from California at this period was therefore not an unmingled evil, although its own mines wanted every hand that could dig a hole or feed a long-tom.

After a time, most of the Californians in Australia grew sick of their new country. They had perhaps found the auriferous earth in general rather richer than what it was in California; but not so rich as their brilliant hopes had pictured it. At the same time, since the gold happened in general to be buried much deeper in the ground, the labor of extracting it was greater, while the water for washing purposes was often lamentably deficient. Then there was the moral contamination of working beside the convicts of Van Dieman's Land and New South Wales, the unhealthiness of the mining country, the scarcity of proper water to drink, the privations from want of food and severity of the weather, and excessively severe labor. The Californians were farther disgusted by the imposition of a tax of seven and a half dollars per month, laid by the government upon all miners for license to work, as well as by the occasional outbreaks of national jealousy, and disputes between themselves and British subjects. On the whole, therefore, the Americans were glad to leave the country to its first inhabitants and their coming brethren from England; and so soon as the former contrived to gather the pecuniary means, and had the opportunity, they hastened back to their old quarters in California, now doubly endeared to them by their luckless absence. The reports brought by these returned emigrants before long satisfied the wavering and adventurous, that no special benefit was to be obtained by any American in leaving the rich mines of his own country for those, however promising they might appear, of another. On the contrary, all he could look for were many additional hardships, physical and moral, and severe labor ill-requited. Of late, accordingly, comparatively few adventurers have sailed from San Francisco for the Australian gold fields. This is well for California. It may just also, while on this subject, be said in passing, that *other* labor in

Australia—from that of the rudest workman to that of the highest skilled mechanic—is only paid about one-half the rates which it commands, has always received, and probably for many years to come, will continue to receive in California. Let interested people say what they will, there is no land so well fitted for the comfortable residence of the poor and industrious man as California. Soil, climate, wages, and political, religious and domestic institutions here make his position more ennobling and agreeable than he can expect or possibly find in any other country.

This month the *second* (wrongfully said in the preface to be the first,) San Francisco "City Directory" was published by A. W. Morgan & Co. It was a well printed, thin octavo, of one hundred and twenty-five pages. The names were not more in number than what C. P. Kimball's Directory of 1850 contained These, however, in Morgan's book were stated both alphabetically and classified into trades and professions. Some useful general information was also given in an appendix.

OCTOBER 22d.—A city ordinance was passed and approved of, granting a right of way to the "California Telegraph Company." Some time elapsed before the company could erect posts and extend the wires through the State ; and it was only late in the following year that they got into working order. By means of this telegraph, San Francisco was brought into instant communication with San José, Stockton, Sacramento, Marysville, and other towns in the interior.

NOVEMBER 2d.—Election of State, county and city officials, as well as others for the United States. The county and city returns were as follows :—

Senate.—John N. Baird, John S. Hager.

Assembly.—Samuel Flower, John Sime, Frederick A. Snyder, George H. Blake, James M. Taylor, Isaac N. Cordoza, Elcan Heydenfeldt.

County Surveyor.—W. P. Humphreys.

Public Administrator.—David T. Bagley.

District Judge.—Delos Lake.

Mayor.—C. J. Brenham.

City Marsnal.—R. G. Crozier. *Recorder.*—George W. Baker.

Comptroller.—R. Matheson. *Street Commissioner.*—Wm. Divier.

Tax Collector.—Lewis Teal. *Treasurer.*—Hamilton Bowie.

Harbor Master.—W. T. Thompson. *City Attorney.*—John K. Hackett.

City Assessors.—M. D. Eyre, J. L. Anderson, J. O'Callahan.

Aldermen.

J. P. Flint,	W. A. Dana,	T. H. Selby,	Geo. K. Gluyas,
J. P. Haven,	C. L. Case,	A. J. Bowie,	E. J. Moore.

Assistant Aldermen.

H. N. Squier,	H. R. Haste,	James De Long,	J. B. Piper,
W. H. Bovee,	G. W. Bryant,	Edward Byrne,	Thomas Hayes.

NOVEMBER 2d and 3d.—Great fire at the city of Sacramento, by which nearly two thousand buildings were destroyed. The conflagration extended over fifty-five blocks, and deprived seven thousand people of their usual homes. The value of the buildings and goods destroyed was differently estimated at from five to ten millions of dollars. Much distress was suffered by the inhabitants on this lamentable occasion. The people of San Francisco, bearing in mind their own great fires, and the loss and misery these had caused, held public meetings, at this time, to express sympathy and to devise measures for relieving their suffering brethren. A sum of sixteen thousand dollars was immediately collected and remitted to Sacramento for the general relief of those who had been burned out. Other subscriptions swelled the amount to thirty thousand dollars. Many medical gentlemen offered their gratuitous professional services, while the steamers bore supplies thither free of freight. Signora Biscaccianti, who had recently been performing in San Francisco, generously offered to give a concert for the benefit of the sufferers. This was largely attended, and realized the sum of seven hundred dollars, which was paid into the relief fund. Other public performers gave benefits for the sufferers at Sacramento.

NOVEMBER 9th.—While the people of San Francisco were thus nobly sympathizing with the losses of others, fire again broke out among themselves. The flames were first noticed about half-past eight o'clock on the evening of this day, in a wooden building at the corner of Merchant and Kearny streets. The fire companies speedily turned out, and succeeded after working vigorously, though under difficult circumstances, for about an hour and a half, in subduing the conflagration; although not before thirty-two buildings, all of which, excepting one or two, were of wood, had been consumed in Merchant and

Clay streets. Among these was the Union Hotel. The loss was estimated at about $100,000. The new supposed fire-proof walls were severely tested on this occasion. The substantial masses of the City Hall on one side, the California Exchange on another, and on the east the brick building that faced Montgomery street, effectually prevented the flames from spreading beyond them.

This month was a disastrous one to many places in the State. Not only had Sacramento been nearly altogether destroyed, while San Francisco had sustained much loss, but Marysville, San Diego, and other towns and agricultural districts had been severely scourged by fire. It was estimated that the total losses which had fallen on the State from fire alone during the previous three years amounted to sixty-six millions of dollars.

NOVEMBER 21st.—Intelligence received of the death of Daniel Webster. The flags of the shipping, and others on shore, were hung at half mast, minute guns were fired during the day, and the city generally presented the appearance of sincere mourning for the loss of a "leader in Israel." The common council passed resolutions of honor to the deceased statesman; and it was afterwards proposed by the boards of aldermen that funeral solemnities on a great scale should be performed by the city, as had recently been done in the case of the death of Henry Clay. This proposal, however, through motives of economy, and partly perhaps on account of the rainy season having commenced, was ultimately negatived. It mattered naught to the illustrious dead. His fame here will live for ever, as on the Atlantic shore.

NOVEMBER 23d.—The waters of Lake La Mercede, in the vicinity of the city, and which cover several hundred acres, sank about thirty feet. Shortly before midnight of this day, a shock like that of an earthquake was felt by parties residing near the place; and the following morning it was discovered that a great channel between the lake and the sea had been opened, through a broad and high sand bank, during the night, by which the waters had found a way and been discharged. It was supposed by some, either that the bed of the lake had been suddenly uplifted, by volcanic agency, whereby the raised waters scooped through the yielding bank the channel just mentioned, and that afterwards the bed of the lake had fallen to its former level, or else that a great sinking of the bank itself had taken place (supposed to have been produced by subterranean causes), owing to which depression, the water had been drawn off to the extent mentioned. The most probable conjecture is, that the excessive rains of the season had simply forced open a passage through the broad and loose sand-bank from the lake to the ocean. Formerly the lake had no visible outlet whatever; and its waters had insensibly been kept about the same level by means of evaporation, or by concealed underground communications with the sea.

December.—"City Directories" seem to be lucrative properties. We have already noticed that of A. W. Morgan & Co., which appeared in September of this year. Another was published this month by James A. Parker. This was a much superior publication to either Kimball's or Morgan's. It was an octavo volume of one hundred and forty-six pages, and was well printed. The names were about nine thousand in number, being considerably more than double those contained in either of its forerunners. There was prefixed a creditable sketch of the rise and progress of the city, and the volume contained an appendix of miscellaneous useful information. Such publications in every place become curious and interesting after the lapse of a few years. Especially this will be the case in a rapidly increasing community like San Francisco. To the patient student of the social and personal, as well as the material history of our city, and to the future antiquarian, these little works will be inestimable.

December 6th.—The election for chief and assistant engineers to the firemen is yearly becoming of more importance. That spirited body of men, who, without fee or reward, save the gratitude of the people, are ever ready to peril life and limb to save the persons and properties of the citizens, had become a numerous and influential association. Their annual election of officers took place this day, when George H. Hossefros was chosen chief engineer, and Charles P. Duane, A. R. Simons, and Edward A. Ebbets, assistant engineers.

December 10th.—José Forni—or Forner, as he described himself in his first confession—a Spaniard, was hanged upon Russian Hill, for the murder of José Rodriguez, a Mexican, in

Happy Valley. This was the only *legal* execution that had taken place in San Francisco, where so many crimes deserving the punishment of death had been committed. The prisoner confessed having killed the deceased, but to the last maintained that the act was done only in self-defence. This, however, was not established by evidence. The gallows had been originally erected upon the summit of the hill; but just before the execution, it was removed about one hundred yards towards the west, so that it was not visible from the principal portions of the city. A very large crowd,—variously estimated at from six to ten thousand people,—gathered round the place of execution, at least one-fourth of whom seemed to be youths, women and children.

DECEMBER 17th.—A furious gale from the S. S. E., accompanied by excessive rains. Considerable damage was sustained by some of the more slimly constructed houses, while the shipping suffered severely. The losses of both were estimated at $200,000. Early in the previous month, a severe "Norther" had threatened much damage to the shipping, and carried away the outer portion of one of the smaller wharves. The want of docks, or of breakwaters, upon the north and south sides of the harbor, is felt more and more as the old sheltered cove gets gradually covered with streets and houses by the extension of the water front of the town.

The storm, first above noticed, seriously affected the rivers of the interior, which rose to an unusual height, and inundated most of the towns on their banks. The levee at Sacramento was burst through by the pressure of the flood, and nearly the whole of that unfortunate city, which so recently had been half destroyed by fire, was submerged to a depth of from five to ten feet. Marysville and Stockton were equally flooded. Many substantially built houses were undermined at all these places by the waters, and fell; whereby much valuable property was destroyed. All communication was cut off from the mining quarters, and great distress was suffered there by the enormous prices of provisions, particularly of flour, and the difficulty, or impossibility of keeping open a connection with the towns for supplies.

CHAPTER XXIII.

1852.

Increase of population.—Mixed character of the immigrants.—Chinese, Peruvians, Chilenos, and other foreigners, notoriously vicious.—Sufferings of the overland immigrants.—Greater attention paid to agricultural pursuits.—City improvements still progressing.—Great fires no longer possible.—Fire insurance agencies established.—Manufactories.—New gold discoveries.—Emigration to Australia.—Merchandise and provisions commanding high prices.—The clipper ships.—Filthy condition of the streets.—Great abundance of rats.—The city extension, bay, and shipping.—The strong winds preventive of disease.—Peculations of officials.—San Francisco only suitable for the industrious.—The city growing in importance.—Change of inhabitants.—Fascinations of San Francisco life.—Reflections concerning the moral condition of the city.

THE population of both the State and city was largely increased in 1852. The departures by sea from San Francisco were only 23,196, while there were 66,988 arrivals. This immigration was about double the amount that had taken place in 1851. The immigrants from the Atlantic States generally crossed the Isthmus, while the greater number of European foreigners came round Cape Horn. The Germans, a most valuable and industrious class of men, and the French, perhaps by nature not quite so steady and hard-working a race, though still a useful body of citizens, were year by year arriving in large numbers, and were readily remarked among the motley population. The most untutored eye could distinguish and contrast the natural phlegm and common-sense philosophy of the fat Teuton, and the "lean and hungry look" and restless gestures of the Celt. Both races were generally "bearded like the pard," though in this respect they were only like the commonalty of San Francisco, who pride themselves much upon hair. The people named cherished many of their old nationalities, and generally frequented their own particular boarding and eating houses and places of recreation. The English, Scotch and Irish immigrants, were also numerous, but their characteristics, although something different, were less distinguishable from those of native Americans than were the manners and customs of other foreigners. Besides these, there were always arriving numerous specimens of most other European nations,—Spaniards, Portuguese, Italians, Swiss, Greeks, Hungarians, Poles, Russians, Prussians, Dutch, Swedes, Danes, Turks, too—all visited California. Many of them went to the mines, although a considerable proportion never left San Francisco. The country and city were wide enough to hold them all, and rich enough to give them all a moderate independence in the course of a few years. A considerable number of German and French women were constantly arriving, as also many more of the sex from the Atlantic States. The female part of the population, though still numerically very far below the male portion, was increasing, perhaps faster in proportion to their previous numbers.

Upwards of twenty thousand Chinese are included in the general number of arrivals above given. Such people were becoming very numerous in San Francisco, from whence the recent immigrants from their country scattered themselves over the various mining regions of California. At one period of 1852 there were supposed to be about 27,000 Chinese in the State. A considerable number of people of "color" (*par excellence*) also arrived. These were probably afraid to proceed to the mines to labor beside the domineering white races, and therefore they remained to drudge, and to make much money and spend it in San Francisco, like almost every body else. Mexicans from Sonora and other provinces of Mexico, and many Chilians, and a few Peruvians from South America, were likewise continually coming and going between San Francisco and the ports of their own countries. The Chinese immigrants had their mandarins, their merchants, rich, educated and respectable men, in San Francisco; but all the Mexicans and Chilians, like the people of negro descent, were only of the commonest description. The women of all these various races were nearly all of the vilest character, and openly practised the most shameful commerce. The lewdness of fallen white females is shocking enough to witness, but it is far exceeded by the disgusting practices of these tawny visaged creatures.

The land immigration into the State was also exceedingly great this year, numbering probably about thirty thousand persons of all ages and both sexes. Among these was a large predominance of youths just entering upon the early prime of manhood. Much suffering was experienced by those who crossed the great desert, and supplies of provisions and other help were forwarded to them by the State Government of California. The steadily increasing production of gold had held out strong hopes to the adventurous of the Eastern States, and of many other portions of the world, that, after all, as great chances existed of still making a moderate, if not a large fortune, in a short period at the mines, as in the memorable years of 1848, '49 and '50.

Owing to the high prices of all kinds of provisions towards the fall of 1852, many of the older residents in the country, and a few of the later immigrants, began to turn their attention to agricultural pursuits, which promised to yield even larger profits, while they offered a pleasanter, healthier and surer occupation than gold-digging. The choicer districts of the country were thus getting gradually settled by "squatters" and pre-emptors, and some legal purchasers of land; and a beginning was made towards rendering California independent of foreign countries for supplies of food. A fair proportion of the recent immigrants remained in San Francisco, while many who had been laboring in the mines for the previous year or two with indifferent success, or who had become wearied of that kind of life, now visited the city with the view of permanently residing and entering upon some kind of business there. From the census taken this year, by authority of the Legislature, the total population of the State appeared to be 264,435, while that of the County and City of San Francisco was 36,151. These numbers were generally allowed to be too small, arising from perhaps unavoidable errors in taking the census. More particularly, the population of San Francisco was supposed to be considerably underrated, the inhabitants of some districts having been imperfectly enumerated. The census was taken towards the close of 1852, and by the end of December of that year, we think the true population of the city alone may be reasonably estimated at 42,000 persons.

The material improvements begun in 1851 were briskly continued during the following year. California, Sansome, and Battery streets were lined by a great many additional brick and stone buildings. Front and Davis streets were formed, and closely built upon with houses of frame. The various wharves continued to stretch eastward, as if it were intended that they should soon connect Yerba Buena Island with the mainland. The sand-hills behind supplied ample material for filling up the bay, and giving solid foundations for the increasing number of substantial stores. Every where in the business portion of the city new and handsome fire-proof edifices were rising. The lower story of these was often constructed of Chinese granite, and the upper ones of brick. The piling across the bay and the filling in were constantly going on. No sooner was a water lot piled and capped than up sprang a frame building upon it; no sooner was the hollow beneath filled than the house of wood was destroyed, and replaced by some elegant brick or granite structure.

At another part of the city, Stockton street was being ornamented with many handsome brick tenements, which were intended for the private residences of some of the wealthier citizens; while over all the western and northern limits additional and much finer frame buildings, and occasionally brick ones, were being erected. Telegraph Hill continued to be seriously encroached upon by the excavating and blasting operations going on at Clark's Point. Even more rapid progress was making towards the extreme south. Happy Valley now contained a large number of commodious and handsome habitations, chiefly of frame. Over all the city the process of grading and planking new streets was going on, so that communication between the principal districts was becoming easy. In the centre, the spirit of improvement was busily at work. The plaza indeed remained a disgrace to the authorities; but Montgomery street, and Commercial, Clay, Merchant, Washington and other cross streets, which touched it, were being rapidly covered with substantial and beautiful fire-proof buildings. At the north-west corner of Montgomery and California streets a large and imposing edifice of granite was erected. This was occupied by Adams & Co., express agents, and Page, Bacon & Co., bankers, and was the first of the superior class of private edifices which are now so numerous in many parts of the city, and particularly on Montgomery street. The stone for this building was prepared in China and put up in San Francisco by Chinese workmen. It was erected, and is owned by Mr. John Parrott. More to the south, great changes were taking place for the better. The faithful "paddy" or steam-excavator never tired. Market street was cut through from Battery to Kearny street; while the sand-hills at the adjoining

Parrott's Granite Block.

ends of First and Second streets were rapidly disappearing. Bush street, that recently had been only a huge mound of sand, was levelled. California, Sacramento and other streets leading to the west, were cutting through or climbing over the obstructing eminences. Higher grades were being adopted for the streets in most of the lower quarters of the city, to which the houses were being gradually conformed.

On the whole, a vast improvement had taken place in the aspect of the town, and in the elegance and substantial comfort of the newer buildings. No longer could conflagrations, like the great fires of '50 and '51, destroy the centre and most valuable parts of the city. The fire department was organized on the most efficient scale, and included among its members many of the most respectable inhabitants. The different companies were supplied with an excellent stock of engines and other apparatus. The *men* were enthusiastic, bold fellows, capable of enduring the severest fatigues, and ever ready to hazard life and limb upon the least alarm of fire, when their services could be made useful. An unlimited supply of water could not be depended upon; but generally there was enough in the many artificial reservoirs formed at the intersection of the chief streets, to extinguish any ordinary conflagration. Confidence was now felt in the stability of the city and its comparative immunity from fire. Two fire insurance agencies, one for a New York and the other for a London company, were established, so that the cautious could insure their properties at reasonable rates. This was a striking sign of the improved times. Lenders upon stored goods and on real estate could now secure their advances against all hazard from fire; while the speculative owners of property were encouraged to undertake permanent and most expensive improvements.

In the vicinity of the city numerous brick fields had long been established. The new style of fire-proof buildings occasioned a constant demand for this material. California-made bricks are certainly much inferior to well-burned English or United States bricks, yet they are considerably cheaper, and when painted or in some way protected from the weather serve their purpose very well. Besides these extensive manufactories of brick, there were other manufactories and workshops which were being constantly formed. In the district of Happy Valley particularly,—which had been early selected for the site of such establishments,—there existed numerous flour mills and timber saw-mills, iron-foundries, marine and land steam-engine works, and steamer and other boat-building yards. In addition to these larger and more imposing establishments, there were many workshops, in various parts of the city, of upholsterers, saddle and harness makers, boot and shoe makers, carpenters, blacksmiths, painters, jewellers and other craftsmen. *All* manufactured articles were no longer imported direct from the distant maker; but some of the more necessary were beginning to be made on the spot from the raw material. The letter-press printers, as might have been anticipated from the character of the American people, were a numerous body; and on the many newspapers and in extensive job work found ample employment at lucrative rates.

The shops were daily assuming a more splendid appearance, while on their well loaded shelves and the neatly laid out window fronts and counters were displayed a brilliant assortment of the particular goods they dealt in. Stylishly dressed, and often lovely women were constantly seen, in fine weather, promenading the principal streets, and idling their time (which they knew not how otherwise to "kill,") and spending somebody's money in foolish shopping, just as is the custom with the most virtuous dames in the great cities on both sides of the Atlantic. Omnibuses and superb public carriages plied through the streets, and beautiful private equipages glittered and glided smoothly along. While the ladies dressed extravagantly, perhaps to please the other sex, perhaps only to please themselves or annoy some meaner souled or less rich sister, the gentlemen were scarcely behind them in this respect. The days of the blouse, the colored shirt and the "shocking bad hat" had fled, never, like time, to return.

The incessant immigration gave liveliness to the streets, and caused much profitable business to be done. At the same time there was a vast emigration. Not only were the usual number of departures to the Eastern States taking place; but, as we have seen, the discovery of gold in Australia was attracting many Californians to that country. The whole world seemed to be restless and morbidly excited by the cry of gold. Where it was all to end who could tell? Originally the Americas had been peopled by the same intense desire for the precious metals. Now, the portions of the New World that had been overlooked, and Australia,—a continent in itself,—were being filled by gold hunters, who would assuredly in the course of time play an important part in the history of mankind. San Francisco itself possessed a share of the precious metal. Gold was found in pieces of quartz quarried from Telegraph Hill, in earth excavated in Broadway, in the sand taken from a great depth in sinking wells in Stockton street, and at various other parts of the city, in 1850. Indeed, we have seen hundreds of persons occupied in gathering it in small particles from the surface of the plaza itself, after a long continued rain. But all these deposits in the centre of the city, there is reason to believe, were scattered through the careless or mischievous behavior of parties who were either unable or too indifferent to take care of the precious metal brought by themselves or others from the well known mining regions, and some of whom doubtless felt repaid for the cost in the wonderment they excited.

Over all California, however, gold was continually being discovered in new places. It was the mineral wealth of the country that had created San Francisco, and which was the source of its continued prosperity. If this should suddenly fail, or the cry increase of other and richer gold countries, easily accessible like Australia, the city would undoubtedly receive a great shock. Thousands were already moving away, and it was only the unusually great immigration of the year that prevented their loss from being seriously felt by the city and the country at large. In the end it was found that the Australia mines were not better places for making a speedy fortune than were those of California, while the former were less salubrious and agreeable to the American personally. The emigration therefore to Australia began sensibly to slacken towards the close of this year; while gradually many of those who had gone thither early began now to return.

In our review of 1851, we had occasion to remark the general fall in the prices of merchandise, and the serious losses sustained by shippers of goods to the San Francisco market during all that year. The "good time" that had been long looked for by merchants came at last; and during the close, and generally over the greater part of this year, not only remunerating but extravagantly high prices were obtained for most goods, particularly for all kinds of provisions. Flour, that had been only eight dollars a barrel in March, by November had risen to upwards of forty dollars, with a firm market. Rice, that was usually worth only a few cents a pound, advanced, in the course of the year, to forty-five and fifty cents. The Chinese, who preferred rice to every other kind of food, suffered severely from these high prices. Butter ranged from fifty-five to seventy cents a pound, over the early and greater part of the year. Other provisions and indeed most kinds of merchandise rose in proportion. The usual reaction, though long delayed, had taken place—the scarcity followed the glut; and the fortunate holders of goods realized large profits, that compensated those who had continued in trade for the losses of the previous seasons. Late in the year, when markets, in particular articles, were at the highest, it was known that a large fleet of clipper ships was on the passage with supplies, many of which vessels were overdue; but as the stock actually on hand was very limited, and day by day was lessening in amount, which might be totally exhausted before the expected arrivals happened, consumers had to submit to necessity and pay the rates demanded. Time was every thing in such a market as San Francisco, where prices of merchandise usually fluctuated as do "fancy stocks" on the 'Change of New York, London or Paris. A week lost or gained in the arrival of a well selected cargo might just be a fortune lost or gained to the shipper. The clipper ships, as we have already remarked, were peculiarly the consequence of such a trade and the natural creation of the needs and commerce of our city. These clippers after being hastily unloaded, were dispatched to India or China, where they either competed successfully with English ships for return cargoes to the Atlantic, or were profitably employed in bringing from the latter country many thousands of Chinese emigrants to California. Year by year, the clipper character of ship was being more adopted, until it became, commercially speaking, foolish and dangerous to freight any other kind of vessel to San Francisco.

Cholera again visited the city in the fall of this year; though its ravages were slight. However much may be said for the general healthiness of the place, little praise can be given for the very dirty state in which the greater part was allowed to remain —and nearly the same may just be said of its condition in 1854. The streets were thickly covered with black rotten mud. These were the proper dunghills of the town, and were made a general depot for all kinds of rubbish and household sweepings, offals and filth. Sometimes the rains came and scattered the abominable stuffs, carrying part of them into the bay; at other times, the heats gradually dried them up. Rats—huge, fat, lazy things, prowled about at pleasure, and fed on the dainty garbage. The pedestrian at night, stumbling along the uneven pavements, and through streets that were only a series of quagmires, would occa-

A Street-scene on a rainy night.

sionally tread on the loathsome, bloated, squeaking creatures, and start back in disgust and horror, muttering a curse or two at such a villainously unclean town. These animals abounded in such great numbers that entire sacks and barrels of flour and bread have been destroyed by them on a single night in a storehouse. They were of several varieties, each differing in color. Besides the common grey rat, there were others white, blue and black. These latter descriptions have materially decreased in numbers of late; the gray fellows, being the stronger, having, it is said, either driven away or destroyed them. Sickening stenches pervaded every quarter. Owing to the raising of the streets in the lower part of the city when establishing the grades, many of the building blocks became great hollow spaces, surrounded on the four sides by high banks of earth. In these places also, which had no drainage, every foul thing and unsightly rubbish were carelessly thrown, and soon deep pools of stagnant water collected in the midst. Beneath the houses and streets which had been formed over the bay, and which had been only partially filled up, there was accumulating a vast mass of putrid substances, from whence proceeded the most unwholesome and offensive smells. In any other place as near the tropic these things would undoubtedly have generated a pestilence; but here the cool winds from the ocean which prevail during the summer season, and which at times are so unpleasant to the shivering inhabitant, had the beneficial effect of neutralizing many of the bad effects which must otherwise have arisen from the want of cleanliness over all the city. From the dead level preserved in that part of the city which was built across the bay, it would seem impossible that a thorough drainage can ever now be had in the lower and most valuable district. This is one of the inconveniences which the indefinite extension of the town eastward has produced. Perhaps it would have been better, if instead of streets and houses, there had been constructed substantial quays and wet docks sufficient to contain all the shipping that had ever visited the harbor. Ships then would have lain in safety from the "South-easters" and the "North-easters," which now so terribly plague and damage them when lying exposed at anchor in the tidal channel.

Crime, during 1852, was perhaps not sensibly diminished; but in the increasing importance of other matters of public discussion, lower-class criminals were tolerated, or less pursued. Legalized robberies, in the shape of "Peter Smith" purchases, more occupied the attention of the citizens. It would be unjust to individuals and to human nature, to challenge *every* public officer in San Francisco with gross peculation and corruption in office; yet it was confessed on all sides that almost every citizen, who had a *chance* of preying upon the corporation means, unhesitatingly and shamefully took advantage of his position. His brother harpies kept him in countenance. This gave rise to a general opinion that the city never could possibly obtain a pure and good government until the bone of contention among rival candidates for office,—its property, to wit,—was all exhausted, squandered, stolen or gifted away. When that perhaps happy day came,—as its advent seemed close at hand,—the "fathers" and salaried servants of the city might possibly work only for the common good, and not chiefly for their own. Had matters been prudently and patriotically managed, San Francisco might, at this day, have been the richest city, of its size, in the world. As the case stands, it is one of the poorest, as certainly its inhabitants are perhaps the most heavily taxed of any community for a feeble and inefficient government. This is chiefly to be attributed to the people themselves. Incapable, weak and corrupt officials are blamable, but the people who choose them, and of whom they are part, are perhaps much more in fault. Where the mass think, and talk, and act, without any particular regard to high moral principle, it can scarcely be expected that their chosen representatives should differ materially from them. When even a man of severe probity and high talent is elected to an office of trust, he finds often insuperable difficulties in his way, from the want of co-operation, and the carelessness or corruption of his own constituents. The most righteous judge can do little good on the bench when interested witnesses disguise the truth, and juries will return verdicts in defiance of it.

However, in spite of local jobbery and mismanagement, enormous municipal expenses, and iniquity every where, the city grew in size, beauty and importance. Its admirable maritime position, and chiefly the determined energy and perseverance of its people, who *believed* in its glorious future, and found their own interest in the work, were raising it year by year to still more remarkable grandeur. Many of the citizens were opulent, while none needed to be in poverty. Intemperance and dissipation alone could squander the enormous wages of the most inferior laborers and the large profits of capital in every kind of business. Then, as now, no healthy man of ordinary strength need want lucrative and honest employment of some kind or other. As for the sick and weak, San Francisco is indeed not a place for them, although hospitals and occasional private charities may serve to alleviate for a time their hapless situation. San Francisco is a place for work—real, useful, *hard* work. If any man can give *that*—it may sometimes be with the head, but oftener with the hand, he is sure, not merely of subsistence, but of a competence, and indeed a fortune in the long run. If lazy, or incapable of such work, the sooner the useless thing takes his departure, the better for himself and the place.

No important change had occurred in the social or moral condition of San Francisco during 1852. The characteristics of the people which were noticed in our review of the previous year, still existed. The old dizzy round of business and pleasure continued. There were now only more people, greater wealth, finer houses, more shops and stores, more work, trade and profits, more places of dissipation and amusement, more tippling and swearing, more drunkenness and personal outrages, nearly as much public gambling and more private play. There were also a few more modest women, and many more of another class ; more benevolent institutions and orphans' asylums ; more fire companies, military companies, and masonic lodges. Likewise there were more newspapers, that discoursed eloquently, ever railing "in good set terms" against corruption in high places, but which not being supported by the sincere feeling of a pure and honest people, made no such irresistible body of public opinion as they sometimes do in other countries. Then there were more churches, more moral teachers and religious publications, more Sabbath and day schools ; and, too, more of every thing that was beautiful and bad, more vice, debauchery and folly, and perhaps also a little more real religion, and sometimes a deal of outward decency. The moral sepulchre was occasionally receiving a fresh coat of paint. It should not be forgotten, at the same time, that with the increase of population, there was also an increase of occasional charities and high-minded liberal deeds. These things are done in secret, or they lose their noble character. The public generally know not of them. However much the sordid pursuit of wealth may cloud the true friendships and generous actions of many of the San Franciscans, the native worth of heroic and pure souls will at times shine through all. As kings reigned before Agamemnon, so there are here great and worthy, honest and true men, as well as there have been elsewhere. Their exact number cannot be counted, but the student of human nature, according to his temperament and means of information, may hazard an estimate on the subject.

Residents of a few years' standing—the landmarks, by turns, of the ancient village, town and city, began now to disappear. These perhaps had made a fortune, and sown their "wild oats" in the place. They now retired to the Atlantic States or Europe, —to *home*, in short,—to enjoy their gains at ease, astonish quiet neighbors with their wondrous tales, speculate on the future of San Francisco, and become disgusted and ennuied with the slowness, tameness, decorum and insipidity of the conventional mode of existence they were leading. New faces and new names were rising into importance, in place of the earliest pioneers and the "forty-niners." The majority, however, of the first settlers had faith in the place; they relished its excitements as well of business as of pleasure; they had no family or fond ties elsewhere, or these had been long rudely broken; and so they adhered to San Francisco. Many of these persons had waxed very rich, in spite of themselves, by the sudden rise in the value of real estate, or by some unexpected circumstance, while others, after expending a world of ingenuity, wickedness and hard work, remained almost as poor as when, hopeful and daring, they landed in the ship's boat at Clark's Point, or when the tide was high, at the first rude wharf that ran a short distance out from the beach at Montgomery street. There is a fascination in even the loose, unsettled kind of life at San Francisco. Of many who have left the city, after a residence of years, and when they have accumulated a handsome fortune, a considerable number have gladly returned. For many months, perhaps for even a year or two, the immigrant thinks he can never worthily or rationally enjoy existence in such a place; so he determines to make a fortune as soon as possible, and decamp for ever. But fortunes are now made more slowly, and the old citizen—a few years here make one old in sensation, thought and experience—changes his sentiments, and he begins to like the town and people for their own sake. The vices and follies, the general mode of living, that frightened and shocked him at first, seem natural to the climate, and, after all, are by no means so very disagreeable. If he returned to settle in ultra or pseudo-civilized and quiet States, he would surely feel himself but a "used-up" man; so he continues where he made his money, still to feel, speculate and enjoy, to work and contend with real men, in their keenest and strongest characters.

It may be thought by some that we have said many over-harsh things in this and other chapters of this work, regarding our fellow citizens. We cannot help that, for the occasions seem to justify the language used. If unmingled praise, or hesitating censure were adopted when talking of San Francisco, people elsewhere would not believe the tale, while those here would only laugh in their sleeve at the decent hypocrisy and cant of the writer. Better proclaim the worst at once; and then let who will find explanations, excuses and palliations. These will be readily advanced by the wiser portion of mankind, who know the temptations that beset poor human nature, and how often it falls when fatal opportunity offers. Let it be always understood that we describe the place as at particular periods, and not what we think will be its grand coming destiny. San Francisco was, at the times of which we have discoursed, and it still is, in a state of moral ferment. When the ebullition ceases, though years may elapse before that happens, the natural qualities of its adventurous and clever people will be more clearly and generously developed. The scum and froth of its strange mixture of peoples, of its many scoundrels, rowdies and great men, loose women, sharpers and few honest folk, are still nearly all that is visible. The current of its daily life is muddied and defiled by the wild effervescence of these unruly spirits. It may be said that nearly all came to the city only as devout worshippers of mammon; scarcely one, to find a home, which might unjustly have been denied him elsewhere. In order to accumulate the greatest heap of gold in the shortest possible time, schemes and actions had often to be resorted to, which nice honor could not justify nor strict honesty adopt. In the scramble for wealth, few had consciences much purer than their neighbors; few hands were much cleaner. Some were found out and victimized; others were wise and provoked not discussion. The few lamented, and the wise and good hoped and foresaw better things. Time, and a sounder public opinion, will cure most of the evils we have alluded to, leaving the undoubted talent, shrewdness, capacity for hard, practical work, and the original honesty, honor and high liberal spirit of the people free to show themselves. Cities, like men, have their birth, growth and maturer years. Some are born Titans, and from the beginning promise to be mighty in their deeds, however wilful and destructive. Few spring into being full armed, wise and sedate as Minerva. San Francisco, while it can show so many enduring marvels for its few years, has also wasted much of its means in "riotous living;" but its young hot blood will cool by and by. Then ripened years and wisdom will subdue its foolish levities and more disgraceful vices. Meanwhile, let us treat the noble city kindly, just as we deal with the beautiful woman that offends us—look upon her face and forget her follies. We pardon the careless, extravagant, yet high spirited youth, who lavishes his substance in wild pleasure, when he stops short and vows repentance; nay, even though he break out again and again, we cannot seriously feel offended with the charming gallant, so only that he hurts nobody but himself. Let us view San Francisco in something of the same gentle and forgiving, if not sympathizing spirit.

CHAPTER XXIV.

1853.

Commerce.—Mercantile Library Association.—The Limantour claim.—Election of delegates to revise the City Charter.—Third annual celebration of the organization of the Fire Department.—Steamships lost.—Extension of the city water front.—United States Marine Hospital.

JANUARY.—We have taken occasion to notice in various parts of this work the progress of commerce in San Francisco. Year by year, the number of vessels visiting the harbor was increasing. We present here some statements on the subject, compiled from a table of statistics by Colonel Cost, of the naval office.

ARRIVALS AND CLEARANCES IN THE PORT OF SAN FRANCISCO DURING THE YEAR 1852.

Arrivals.			*Clearances.*		
Nations.	Vessels.	Tons.	Nations.	Vessels.	Tons.
American	346	188,575	American	405	216,642
British	225	74,931	British	196	76,270
French	29	11,286	French	33	12,949
Chilian	37	9,393	Chilian	25	6,444
Mexican	41	5,279	Mexican	34	4,567
Danish	12	2,215	Danish	10	1,959
Bremen	11	3,132	Bremen	11	2,977
Norwegian	4	1,100	Norwegian	2	576
Hamburg	20	4,628	Hamburg	20	4,185
Dutch	15	6,965	Dutch	5	1,523
Hawaiian	28	3,562	Hawaiian	25	3,190
Peruvian	14	2,024	Peruvian	8	1,599
Prussian	2	960	Prussian	2	540
Swedish	4	1,156	Swedish	5	1,700
Portuguese	3	675	Portuguese	2	450
Brazilian	1	738	Brazilian	1	728
Sardinian	3	1,038	Sardinian	7	1,383
Austrian	1	521	Austrian	1	300
Am. Coasters	351	196,282	Am. Coasters	833	115,462
Total	1147	514,460	Total	1625	453,444
In 1851, the arrivals were	847	245,678	In 1851 the clearances were	1315	422,043
Increase	300	268,782	Increase	310	31,401

The shipments of gold dust during 1852 from San Francisco, as appears from the custom-house record of clearances, amounted in all to $46,599,044. Of this amount the value of $45,251,724 was cleared for Panama; $511,376, for San Juan; $482,596, for Hong Kong; and the remainder principally for various ports on the Pacific. Sums carried away by individuals are not included in the amounts mentioned.

JANUARY 25th.—Election of officers of the Mercantile Library Association. It had long been evident that such an association was much needed in San Francisco. In the absence of any thing like a home or domestic comfort, all classes seemed to be alike forced to frequent places of public recreation, and were exposed to the many degrading influences which drink, gambling, and still worse vices have upon the personal character. To withdraw youths in particular from the haunts of dissipation, and to give to persons of every age and occupation the means of mental improvement, and a suitable place for passing their leisure hours, were the great objects of the Mercantile Library Association. Public meetings were held, at which the purposes and advantages of the proposed institution were strongly urged by its benevolent projectors and patrons; and committees were formed to collect contributions of books and subscriptions from the general public. By these means a considerable deal of interest was excited on the subject, and liberal donations and subscriptions were procured. The following gentlemen were unanimously elected as the first officers:—

President.—David S. Turner.
Vice-President.—J. P. Haven. *Treasurer.*—C. E. Bowers, jr.
Recording Sec'y.—R. H. Stephen. *Corresponding Sec'y.*—Dr. H. Gibbons.
Directors.—E. E. Dunbar, J. B. Crockett, D. H. Haskell and E. P. Flint.

The rooms of the association, which were on the second floor of the California Exchange,—a central and most convenient locality,—were first opened on the evening of the 1st of March of this year. The largest apartment was elegantly fitted up as a reading and lecture room, and was abundantly supplied with local newspapers, and with some of the leading journals of the Eastern States, as well as with a choice selection of magazines and reviews. The library contained fifteen hundred volumes by the best authors, and was being constantly increased by donations and purchases. Only one year later, it numbered about three thousand volumes, comprising many of the best standard works in the English language, besides many valuable works in French, Spanish, German, &c.

This institution is of the most excellent character, and deserves the active support and well wishes of every liberal-minded citizen. It is the best substitute for a portion of the comforts of a home that can be provided in the present condition of San Francisco. Occasional lectures on interesting topics, literary and dramatic essays and readings, and frequent public debates on political and other subjects of the day, give variety and excitement to the ordinary business of the association. The pleasures and advantages of this institution have not hitherto been sufficiently understood, or sought by the people for whom they were intended; but it may be presumed that the intrinsic and growing merits of the association will in future excite more fruitful notice from all classes of the community. The terms of membership are very moderate, being an entrance fee of ten dollars (since reduced to five dollars, "for clerks and others in employ"), and a monthly payment of one dollar. A subscription of twenty-five dollars, and a monthly payment of one dollar, entitle the party to one share in the *stock* of the institution, and to the profits arising on the same. The library and reading rooms are open every day, from 9 o'clock A. M. to 10 o'clock P. M. For two hours after noon they are only open to ladies, and gentlemen accompanying ladies. The chambers of the association are now in the Court Block, Merchant street.

FEBRUARY 5th.—The claim of José Yves Limantour presented to the Board of Land Commissioners. San Francisco, which had survived the Leavenworth and Colton grants, the Peter Smith sales, and other legalized robberies and "squatters" without number, though it suffered terribly in the struggle, was now threatened by a claim, which if held valid, would turn over to a single individual one-half of its real estate, owned partly by the city itself, and partly by thousands of onerous and bona fide holders, who fancied their possessions were their own by the strongest legal titles. Limantour, who was a Frenchman by birth, and had been a trader along the coast, stated, that he had advanced, in the year 1843, to Manuel Micheltorrena, who was then Mexican Governor and Commandante-General of the Californias, considerable sums of money for the use of the departmental government of that country, at a period when it was impoverished. In return for this service, or as it is expressed in the deed itself, "in consideration of loans in merchandise and ready money which he has made to this government at different times" (somewhere about $4000), Limantour said that he had received a complete grant of certain large tracts of land in the neighborhood of Yerba Buena. The deed of conveyance and several relative papers have been produced to the Board of Commissioners, and appear at first sight regular and legal documents. The first seems to have been given at Los Angeles, the 27th day of February, 1843, and is signed by Micheltorrena. It conveys "the land contained from the line of the *pueblo de la Yerba Buena*, distant four hundred varas from the settlement house (*casa fundadora*) of Don William Richardson to the south-east, beginning on the beach at the north-east, and following it along its whole edge (*margen*), turning round the point of Rincon to the south-east, and following the bay as far as the mouth of the estuary of the mission, including the deposits of salt water, and following the valley (*cañada*) to the south-west, where the fresh water runs, passing to the north-west side, about two hundred varas from the mission to where it completes two leagues north-east and south-west to the Rincon, as represented by the plat (*diseño*) No. 1, which accompanies the *Expediente*.

"Second: Two leagues of land, more or less, beginning on the beach of the '*Estacada*' at the ancient anchorage of the port of San Francisco, below the castle (*castillo*) following to the south-east, passing the "*presidio*" (military post)—following the road of the mission, and the line to the south-west as far as the beach which runs to the south from the port, taking the said beach to the north-west, turning round the Point Lobos, and following to the north-east, along the whole beach of the castle (*castillo*) two hundred varas, and following the beach as far as the '*Estacada*,' where begins the plat (*diseño*) No. 2."

The tracts of land contained within the boundaries mentioned (which are vague and very unsatisfactorily given), comprise four square leagues, and include a great part of the most valuable portion of the city. It may also be mentioned here, that, in addition to these four square leagues, Señor Limantour likewise claimed the Islands of Alcantraz and Yerba Buena in the bay, and the whole group of the Farallones, which lie twenty or thirty miles off the Heads, and a tract of land, one square league in extent, situated opposite the Island of Los Angeles, at the westward of Racoon Straits. Besides these islands and square leagues, Limantour has also claimed before the Board of Land Commissioners still more extensive properties in various parts of the State, amounting in all to considerably more than a hundred square leagues of land. All other claims are a bagatelle to this.

These great claims seemed so ridiculous and untenable at first sight, that the press and individuals pecuniarily interested were generally disposed to think very lightly of them. That Limantour should have been so long silent as to his alleged rights was a very odd circumstance that generated suspicion all was not told. He had looked on during years when the property included in his grants was being transferred over and over again to new buyers, always rising in value at every sale, and had tacitly appeared to assent to the existing state of things. When the ground was worth many millions of dollars, and hundreds, if not thousands of individuals were pecuniarily interested in it, then Limantour first declared his pretensions. His claim seemed monstrous—to one half of the great City of San Francisco, with all its houses and improvements and future prosperity!—a claim that had been mysteriously concealed for eight or ten years! Pshaw! it could not be an honest, valid one. So folks said to themselves. As while we write the matter remains under judicial consideration,—though some years may pass before a judgment can be obtained,—we are prevented from examining minutely the nature both of the claim and the objections to it. We may only state generally that many believe the former is "false, fraudulent, or simulated;" while Gen. James Wilson, Limantour's attorney, says—"With a perfect knowledge of all the papers and documents in the case; a careful consideration of all the testimony taken, I am constrained to say, and I do most conscientiously say, that there is not, and in my firm belief there cannot possibly be, the slightest indicia of fraud in it, or in any way connected with it. 'Fraud is to be proved, not inferred.'" In the pamphlet from which these quotations are made, and which was printed and published by order of Limantour, Gen. Wilson discusses Micheltorrena's alleged grant, and finds it abundantly proved. He thus settles his client's cause with a thunder-clap sentence, which must frighten the very souls of Limantour's "nimble adversaries:"—"Say *that deed* of grant is not valid! *Never*—NEVER! It cannot be so said without rushing roughshod and blindfold over all the facts in the case, and all the law and equity in Christendom." If proof and the Land Commissioners sanction Limantour's claim, there will be a day of reckoning and lament to many of our citizens, who have fondly imagined themselves the true proprietors of much valuable real estate. Then will be tried the truth and worth of the maxim—*Justitia fiat, ruat Cœlum.*

FEBRUARY 16th.—Election of delegates from the different wards to a convention to revise the city charter. The following parties were elected:—

First Ward.—Henry Meigs, Edward McGowan, William Carr.
Second Ward.—F. L. Jones, James Gallagher, E. W. Graham.
Third Ward.—D. A. Magehan, Eugene Casserly, W. H. Martin.
Fourth Ward.—S. W. Holliday, C. S. Biden, J. R. Dunglisson.
Fifth Ward.—Louis R. Lull, T. D. Greene, F. O. Wakeman.
Sixth Ward.—James Grant, Henry Richardson, David Jobson.
Seventh Ward.—A. C. Wakeman, James Hagan, Henry Sharpe.
Eighth Ward.—Thomas Hayes, I. D. White, William Green.

These parties met on the 7th of March at the council chambers in the City Hall, and proceeded to discuss the provisions of the existing charter and the proposed alterations upon it. The charter, as revised, was afterwards submitted to the people at the annual election of municipal officers. Little interest seemed to be manifested on the subject, except by the inhabitants of the eighth ward, whose personal interests were particularly affected by the contemplated measure. Though rejected by six wards, it was, on the whole, approved of by a majority of votes. Subsequently it was laid before the Legislature, to be formally passed by it as a new charter of the city. At the date of writing this notice, that event has not taken place. It differs materially from the former charter, and the propriety of some of its declarations, particularly what may be called the "squatter" provisions, has been much disputed. In many other respects, it is a decided improvement upon the present charter.

FEBRUARY 22d.—The anniversary of the birth-day of Washington had been adopted on previous occasions as a fit time to celebrate the organization of the fire companies of the city. On this day, the third annual celebration took place. It was distinguished by the large attendance of the firemen, the splendor of the procession, the fineness of the weather, and the great number of citizens, who as sympathetic spectators participated in the festivities of the occasion. The firemen were dressed in the uniform of the different companies, and their engines and various apparatus were burnished as brightly and decorated as beautifully as hands could manage. Several bands of music formed part of the procession, while banners and devices of various kinds gave increased animation to the scene. The chief interest, however, of the exhibition lay in the appearance of the *men* themselves. These were of every class in the community, and were a fine athletic set of fellows. Their voluntary occupation was a good and grand one, and required much skill and courage, while it was pursued under circumstances involving great personal danger, and often much inconvenience and pecuniary loss to individuals, who, at the call of duty, cheerfully forsook their own private business to save the community from a terrible calamity. At the awful peal of the alarm-bell, no matter at what hour or place, or how occupied, the fireman rushed to his post, to drag and work his pet engine where most needed. At busy noon, he threw aside his cash-book and ledger; in the evening, he abruptly left the theatre, or other place of amusement; at midnight, he started from sleep, and only half-dressed, leaped and ran to his appointed quarters. A few minutes later, and the whole city might be in a blaze! This thought gave speed to his heels and strength to his arms. Scarcely had the first heavy strokes of the alarm-bell ceased to vibrate on the panic-stricken

28

ear, when were heard the lighter, cheerful peals of the bells of the engines, as they were wheeled from their houses and hurried rapidly through the streets.

Fires in San Francisco used to be dreadful affairs, and no pen can adequately describe the terror, confusion and despair that spread far and wide when the wild cry was heard. The danger and horror of conflagration are now much lessened, partly by the increase of fire-proof brick buildings, and partly by the continually growing efficiency of the fire companies. Still the alarm of fire can never be listened to without many sad misgivings as to the possible result. The centre and business part of the city may now seem to be beyond the reach of total destruction or even of a serious loss ; yet large districts lying around the fire-proof nucleus may any day be altogether consumed, if it were not for the unflagging and desperate efforts of the unpaid, volunteer firemen. From the peculiar risk and circumstances attending conflagrations in San Francisco, these noble men have always had a difficult and dangerous task to perform. Their boldness, their alertness, energy, and unwearied perseverance in their praiseworthy calling, have been long celebrated in America ; and, to this day, it is a high term of honor over the civilized world to belong to their body. Many foreigners are members of the different companies. Later in this year, some of the French inhabitants of the city formed themselves into a company by themselves, called the "Lafayette."

On the occasion of the anniversary of the Fire Department of this year, the procession alluded to moved through the principal streets, attended, admired, and cheered by a large concourse of people. Indeed the whole city seemed to have turned out *en masse.* The firemen then proceeded to the American Theatre, where an occasional address was delivered by Frank M. Pixley. The house was filled to overflowing, and presented a fine show. There was a large attendance of ladies in the boxes.

March 6th.—The Pacific mail steamship *Tennessee* went ashore this morning at Tagus Beach, in Bolinas Bay, about three or four miles north of the Heads, at the entrance to the Bay of San Francisco. Dense fogs, which had misled the captain as to the ship's position, were the cause of the vessel striking the shore. These fogs are very prevalent along the coast, and have often been the cause of serious shipwrecks. The Tennessee had about six hundred passengers on board, one hundred of whom were women and children. By happy chance, the ship went upon a small, sandy beach, on both sides of which at a short distance were enormous cliffs, on which if the vessel had struck she

Wreck of the Tennessee.

would have gone immediately to pieces, and probably most of those on board would have perished. As it was, and the sea being smooth, the passengers were all safely landed, as well as the mail-bags and express matter. It was expected that the Tennessee would afterwards have been safely towed off. The Goliah and the Thomas Hunt, steam-tugs, were sent to perform that operation ; but after some trials, it was found to be impracticable. After removing therefore a considerable quantity of cargo, stores, &c., the vessel was abandoned, and shortly afterwards went to pieces.

The loss of the Tennessee was the first known of a series of calamities at sea, which happened about this time, and in which

San Francisco was deeply interested. The most terrible and disastrous of these was the loss of the steamship *Independence*, of Vanderbilt's Independent Line, from San Juan to San Francisco. Upon the morning of the 16th of February, about daybreak, and when the atmosphere was perfectly clear, the ship struck upon a sunken reef, about a mile from the shore of Margarita Island, off the coast of Lower California. The sea was quite smooth at the time. The engine was backed, and the ship hove off the reef. As she was making water rapidly, it was thought best to beach her. She was accordingly run ashore in a small cove on the south-west side of the island, about five miles distant from the place where she had first struck. At this time it was discovered that the vessel was on fire. The people, who had hitherto been quiet and self-possessed, now lost all control of themselves; and many in a frantic state leaped overboard. All order seemed to be lost, and everybody thought only how best to save himself. The scene is said to have been horrible in the extreme. The crew and passengers amounted to four hundred and fourteen persons; and of this number nearly two hundred perished, among whom were seventeen children and fifteen females. When intelligence of the sad occurrence reached San Francisco, it caused much excitement and general sorrow. Many had to mourn the loss of a relative or friend, whose coming had been fondly expected. Liberal contributions were made by the citizens to alleviate the sufferings of the surviving passengers of the Independence, and to carry them to a place of safety from the desolate and dangerous island upon which they were thrown, naked, and without food or shelter.

On the morning of the 9th April following, the steamship *S. S. Lewis*, of the Nicaragua line, went ashore at a place six miles north of Bolinas Bay, and about fifteen miles north of the Heads. Dense fogs were the cause of this loss, as they had been the cause of the loss of the Tennessee. There were three hundred and eighty-five persons on board when the ship struck, all of whom were saved, as well as the greatest part of their personal baggage. The sea was running high at the time, and soon afterwards the vessel went to pieces.

Thus were three of the large ocean steamers connected with San Francisco lost within little more than a month, two of which had gone ashore within the distance of a few miles from the city. It was remarked that there seemed to be a kind of fatality attending the passenger steamers connected with our port. Eleven vessels of that description, some of which were of a magnificent character, had been lost within the previous two years. The list is as follows :—

Commodore Preble.—May 3d, 1851, on Humboldt Bar.

Union.—July 5th, 1851, at San Quentin.

Chesapeake.—Rudder lost at sea, put into Port Oxford for repairs, October 10th, 1851; proceeded to Humboldt, and was condemned and sold.

Sea Gull.—Jan. 26th, 1852, on Humboldt Bar.

General Warren.—Jan. 31st, 1852, Clatsop Spit.

North America.—Feb. 27th, 1852, forty miles south of Acapulco.

Pioneer.—Aug. 17th, 1852, San Simeon's Bay.

City of Pittsburg.—Oct. 24th, 1852, burned in the Bay of Valparaiso, on her way to California.

Independence.—Feb. 16th, 1853, burned at Margarita Island.

Tennessee.—March 6th, 1853, entrance to San Francisco Bay.

Lewis.—April 9th, 1853, three miles north of Bolinas Bay.

April.—For some months back the citizens have been much excited by the introduction and progress through the legislative chambers, of a bill to extend the water front of the city six hundred feet beyond the existing boundary line. It appears that the annual expenditure of the State was year by year greatly exceeding its income, and financial difficulties were the natural consequence. To procure some relief from these, Governor Bigler, in a message to the Senate and House of Assembly, recommended that the limits of San Francisco should be extended towards the water, and that such extension should be sold or leased for the benefit of the State. This counsel appeared most unjust, and caused much alarm to the inhabitants of the city. The mayor and the boards of aldermen and assistant aldermen severally issued messages and reports against the passage of the contemplated measure. The board of aldermen, on the 31st January, unanimously adopted a memorial to the Legislature, in which they represented that any measure of the nature suggested by the governor would be productive of incalculable hurt to the prosperity of San Francisco.

"Your memorialists," the document said, "have spared no labor to procure a full and frank expression of opinion by the most competent to decide upon the merits of the proposed extension, and have received the concurrent testimony of every captain and merchant in the city, that the sanction of your honorable body to such a proceeding would place in jeopardy the entire shipping of the port, by depriving it of the protection and shelter of the headlands which it at present enjoys.

"Your memorialists feel warranted in asserting, from their own observation, as well as from the assurance of the present distinguished officer in command of the Hydrographical Party of the United States Coast Survey, that the extent to which the present filling up of the City Front has been pushed, has worked material injury to the safe anchorage of vessels already, by shoaling the waters of the harbor, and compelling ships of heavy draft to anchor further out, exposed to the full force of the tide and the fury of the strong gales from the south-east that prevail during the rainy season."

These opinions were fully shared in by the inhabitants generally. Not only would San Francisco, the commercial metropolis of the State, be materially damaged as a port, but much grievous wrong would be committed against the owners of property upon the line of the existing water front. By the Act of 26th March, 1851, which leased the State's interest in the water lots for ninety-nine years, and which specifically defined the boundary lines, it was declared that the same "shall be and remain a *permanent* water front" of the city. In the knowledge and faith of this constitutional and binding declaration, the water lots had been sold and improvements made upon them. The present owners had every reason to believe that the water front could not legally, and would not illegally and inequitably, be further extended. The doing so would be most prejudicial to their rights, while at the same time it would be a most serious injury to the general interests and privileges of the city.

Notwithstanding these and other objections, the obnoxious bill passed the House of Assembly by a majority of four, in which majority were two of the representatives from San Francisco. The other five representatives, who had voted against the measure, and some of whom had spoken often and forcibly upon its manifest injustice, now resigned their seats, and appealed to their constituents for an approval of their conduct, by standing as candidates for re-election. On the 14th of April, a new election took place. The course taken by the old representatives was chiefly opposed by a certain small section of the community, which was supposed to be personally interested in the passing of the bill complained of. On the 2d of January, in the preceding year, at one of the noted Peter Smith's sales, already mentioned, a great belt of land "covered with water," and extending six hundred feet beyond the existing and recognized water front, and embracing many thousand distinct lots, had been sold by the sheriff for something less than $7000, in order to satisfy a judgment against the city. The particular nature of the right of the city to this ground "covered with water," and the rights of the party holding the judgment, and of the sheriff to sell it, were matters imperfectly understood. Therefore the exact rights acquired by the purchasers nobody could distinctly estimate. As things stood, the buyers, who had speculated on a fortune of twice as many millions as they had paid thousands, could do nothing. But by enlisting the State on their side, and exciting the cupidity of the government, the Peter Smith jobbers might hope to derive incalculable benefits from their desperate bargains, by making a "compromise" with the commissioners proposed to be appointed under the contemplated bill. By the express terms of this bill, they would, most probably, have secured two-thirds of their purchases. To raise a fund for carrying on their scheme, and to interest parties personally in its success, certain of the new water lots were disposed of at low or nominal prices.

It was these original and subsequent buyers then, and their immediate friends and those whom they could in any way influence, that opposed the re-election of the representatives to the House of Assembly. The people generally felt that this matter was one of the utmost consequence to the welfare of the community. On the day of election many of the leading citizens closed their places of business, and devoted themselves to watching over the polls. The question at issue was one of principle, and not the mere personal choice of favorite candidates. The anti-extensionists, as they were called, were completely successful. Five votes to one of those polled were in favor of the old representatives; while, if it had been necessary, a still larger majority would have been obtained. At the close of the poll, the following parties were elected, viz.:—Samuel Flower, John Sime, John H. Saunders, James M. Taylor, and Elcan Heydenfelt.

Meanwhile, the bill had been carried into the Senate, and

the parties for and against it seemed nearly balanced. Repeated public meetings were held at San Francisco on the subject, at which resolutions were passed strongly condemnatory of the bill and its known supporters. All classes of the community, except the reckless speculators who hoped to profit by the iniquitous Act, were bitterly opposed to the measure. If adopted, it would certainly have the effect of injuring the harbor and city to an incalculable, an irreparable extent; while, by throwing back the existing water front, and altering the grades of the streets, an immense deal of damage would be done upon private property. And all for what? Principally to enrich a few water-lot gamesters, and perhaps put a little money in the exhausted exchequer of the State. The pecuniary advantage of the transaction to the State was exceedingly doubtful at the best; while it was abundantly evident that interminable litigation and grievous loss to private parties and to the port itself were sure to arise. A large number of the members of the Legislature seem to have been at all times opposed to the prosperity of San Francisco; and would fain lay upon it what has often been considered,—by the citizens themselves, at all events,—more than a proportionate share of the burdens of the State. In the case in question, if even the government had the legal right to carry out the measure proposed by the obnoxious bill, which right was disputed by able and disinterested lawyers, the advantage to be derived by the State was very paltry in comparison with the vast amount of damage that would be occasioned to the city and individual citizens. This consideration plead for mercy from the spoiler, but it had little effect. The Senate, like the House of Assembly, seemed determined to kill the bird that laid the golden egg—for such were the taxes that San Francisco, in its prosperity, paid into the coffers of the State.

To show further the injustice and impropriety of the steps contemplated by the Extension Bill, we give an extract from a Report made by a portion of the committee appointed by the Senate on the subject:

"The harbor known in 1849 as the harbor of San Francisco, flanked north and south by the headlands of North and Rincon Points, and stretching inwards somewhat in the form of a crescent as far as Montgomery street, is now almost entirely filled up and occupied as the business part of the city. The boundary line of this, the eastern front, as fixed and declared permanent by the 4th section of an act of the Legislature, passed March 26th, 1851, extends even a little farther out into the bay than the headlands, and when the same shall be fully built up to and improved, the city will have a water front of sufficient extent and adequate depth of water to supply all the wants of her commerce and trade. The farther extension of said front six hundred feet into the bay would not materially increase the extent on the eastern front, while a greater depth of water than the present front now enjoys, would not be necessary to enable vessels of the largest class to lie at the wharves.

"So far, therefore, as the eastern front of the city is concerned, we can discover no public necessity or conveniency which demands any action on the part of the Legislature, conflicting either in letter or spirit with the guarantee, or at least the declaration, that 'the said boundary line shall be and remain a permanent water front of said city,' contained in the act above referred to.

"The testimony taken by the committee conclusively shows that the shipping of the harbor would be materially injured by the further extension. Protection to the headlands, which is still to some extent enjoyed, would be destroyed, and the roadstead between the city and Goat Island, with a rapid current, and subject to strong south-easterly and north-westerly gales, would be materially contracted. This acknowledged injury, it has been suggested, can be counteracted by the erection of breakwaters off either or both North and Rincon Points. In a bay with such a variety of powerful currents, it would be difficult to predict the effect should such a plan be carried into execution. It might prove a greater injury to the water front than any yet inflicted upon it. But were the erection of breakwaters clearly demonstrated to be of great service, the practicability of accomplishing such a task by the State in so deep and turbulent a bay, by any expenditure within her means, is extremely doubtful. Any appropriation adequate even to the commencement of such a work, would, under Art. 8 of the Constitution, have to be submitted to the people for their approval.

"No necessity now exists for such a hazardous project, and it would be truly impolitic to create a necessity for it by making the proposed extension.

"But should the Legislature determine in any manner to extend the city front, we are decidedly of opinion that the necessity or use of erecting breakwaters would follow; and that if profit to the treasury should be a motive in making such extension, the connection of any breakwater scheme with it would entail upon the treasury losses infinitely greater than any imaginary or hoped-for profits could liquidate. The cost of breakwaters can only be reckoned by millions, and if the State embarks in the project with the hope that the proceeds of the sales of water lots will raise an adequate fund for that purpose, she will surely be disappointed.

"The right of the State to sell lots in the place indicated would be questioned perhaps by men most anxious for the sale to proceed; the title of the State could not escape being clouded in the minds of purchasers, when it is considered that a variety of interests adverse to the State would no doubt be in active operation. With these interests the public are familiar, and from one of them has proceeded the only proposition before the Legislature for an extension, and that proposition is based upon the assumption of a title adverse to and independent of the State, coupled with the proffer of a partnership interest of an entangling and intricate nature, as a consideration for the influence and authority of the State in carrying into effect a plan which your committee believe destructive to commerce, injurious to the property of a large class of citizens, and inconsistent in legislation.

"Respectful and temperate language cannot be employed in giving complete expression to the sentiments entertained of this proposition, and therefore your committee refrain from further allusion to it."

The Report, from which the above extract is taken, then discusses at length the nature of the various rights claimable by Congress, by the State, and by the city, to the land "covered with water," in question; and concludes thus: "Even if the water front right, being a vested right, could be successfully questioned, *bad faith* to the citizens of San Francisco would be truly chargeable against the government, were an act passed by which said water front privileges and advantages would be destroyed."

The united people of San Francisco, excepting always the small clique of speculators already mentioned, considered that all law, justice, and expediency, were opposed to the projected extension; the supporters of the bill in the Legislature could only talk of the absolute and wilful *right* of the State to do what it chose with its own pretended property, without regard to those who might be ruined by its so doing. After several debates, the bill came to a final vote in the Senate upon the 26th of April, when thirteen members voted for, and the like number against it. Happily, the president of the chamber, Lieutenant-Governor Purdy, who in cases of parity possesses a casting vote, gave his against the bill. Thus, by the narrowest chance, San Francisco escaped this severe stroke. Perhaps the Peter Smith speculators in extension water lots may at some future time renew their attempt to carry out their views, and may persuade even a majority of the Legislature—at all times jealous of the greatness and independence of San Francisco—to further their iniquitous schemes. The citizens, therefore, will require to be ever watchful on this subject, until a constitutional and legal declaration be obtained, and which will be beyond all cavil or question, that the existing boundary line shall be really and truly the *permanent* water front of the city.

April 7th.—The corner-stone laid of the United States Marine Hospital, when the usual interesting ceremonies observed on similar occasions, were performed. On the 10th of December, 1852, the mayor approved of an ordinance, which the common council had passed, by which he was directed to convey to the Government of the United States six fifty-vara lots, situated at

United States Marine Hospital.

Rincon Point. These were intended for the site of the magnificent structure, the corner-stone of which was laid to-day. The building was erected in the course of this year (completed December 12th), and is now a striking ornament to the city. It is built of brick, and is four stories high. It is 182 feet long by 96 feet wide. At one time five hundred patients can be comfortably lodged, while, in cases of necessity, so many as seven hundred can be accommodated. The total cost has been about a quarter of a million of dollars. This hospital has been built and will be supported by the United States, from the fees paid into the treasury by the sailors of every American vessel entering our ports. The sum of twenty cents a month is deducted from their wages, and paid by the master of every vessel to the custom-house. In return, every sick and disabled seaman reaching San Francisco is entitled to a certificate from the collector for admission to the hospital. As sailors under foreign flags pay no fees, they are of course not entitled to the privileges of the institution. This hospital and the State Marine Hospital sufficiently provide at present for the wants of the sick in San Francisco. There are several other hospitals of a semi-public or private nature, which take care of such sick persons as may not be entitled to admission into either of the two mentioned, or who may prefer the accommodations of less public institutions.

APRIL 11th.—The *Jenny Lind* steamer, when on her passage from Alviso to San Francisco, with about one hundred and twenty-five passengers on board, met with a dreadful accident. At half-past twelve o'clock, when nearly opposite the Pulgas Ranch, and when the company on board were about sitting down to dinner in the after cabin, a portion of the connecting steam-pipe was blown asunder, and instantly the destructive vapor burst open the bulkhead of the cabin, and swept into the crowded apartment. Many were dangerously scalded, and a large number instantly struck dead, by inhaling the intensely heated atmosphere. Thirty-one persons were either killed on the spot, or soon afterwards died, from the effects of injuries received from the explosion. This catastrophe occurring immediately after the losses of so many fine steamships at sea, already noticed, excited much sorrowful interest in the city.

CHAPTER XXV.

1853.

Russ's garden.—The German population.—May-day celebration by school-children.—Burning of the Rassette House.—Mountain Lake Water Company.—General State Hospital.—Drinking houses.—Clipper ships and short passages.—Military parade and celebration of 4th of July.—Dedication of the First Congregational Church.—St. Mary's (Catholic) Church.—Unitarian Church.—Seamen's Bethel.—Squatter difficulties.—Store-ships burned.—Strikes by mechanics and laborers for higher wages.—Anniversary of the German Turnverein.—City and county election.—Lafayette Hook and Ladder Company organized.—The French inhabitants.—Sweeney & Baugh's electric telegraph.

MAY 1st.—May-day was celebrated by a large number of our German citizens in the cheerful and imposing style observed in Fatherland. The *Turner Gesang Verein* (Gymnastic Musical Union) took the most active part in the festivities. Dressed in loose brown linen coats and pantaloons, proper for their exercises, they marched, with banners flying, and musical instruments sounding, to the gardens of Mr. Russ, near the Mission road. There somewhere about eighteen hundred persons of German blood participated in the different enjoyments of the day. They leaped, balanced and twirled, danced, sang, drank, smoked and made merry, as only such an enthusiastic race of mortals could. The weather happened to be very fine, and the grounds seemed beautiful beyond all expression of praise from the full heart that could only enjoy, while it knew not and cared not why. *Das Deutsche Vaterland* was chanted in the most rapturous manner, and for the moment the different performers seemed to forget all their native local distinctions and the very land that now gave them shelter, to become in heart and spirit only members of the one common brotherhood of Germans. Prizes to the best performers in the various athletic and other games were distributed, and several appropriate addresses were afterwards delivered.

The German population in San Francisco has always been

very large, and may now (1854) be estimated at between five and six thousand. They are an orderly and intelligent people, and show fewer criminals than a proportionate number of any other class of citizens. They learn the English language very readily, and many of them are naturalized citizens. Very different from the French population in this respect, they appear to have little wish to return to their native country. When Germans do leave California, it is generally for the Atlantic States, from whence most of them directly came. In San Francisco, they take considerable interest in local affairs, and easily enter into the spirit of the place. The different fire companies show many Germans on their rolls. This people have a daily newspaper in their own language, and at one time had two. They also possess a school, and at different times have supported a national theatre, while they often have both vocal and instrumental concerts. The professional musicians in San Francisco are chiefly Germans. Various other occupations are extensively and almost exclusively followed by them. The cigar and beer-shops are chiefly kept by them. A large number of the Jews in San Francisco are of German blood, many of whom are from Prussian Poland.

Though comparatively few Germans intend to return to Fatherland, they all bear a strong feeling towards it, and when opportunity serves are always ready to celebrate their nationality and praise the old country customs. Some of these are of an interesting and most pleasing character, in which music generally bears a leading part. Though usually somewhat phlegmatic both in person and mind, and not so brilliantly gay as the French, or so carelessly wanton in their mirth as the Hispano-Americans, the Germans are perhaps the most thoroughly *cheerful* of all the national races in San Francisco. Though many of them possess considerable property, they are not as a class distinguished for wealth; and they are generally of a saving, and sometimes a penurious character. Touch their nationality, or their pecuniary interests, and they may spend money lavishly; but in most other matters they are totally opposed, in feeling and behavior, to the princely extravagance of native Americans. The Germans pursue all professions, while they monopolize a certain few, and number some rich and many highly educated individuals among their people. Some of these have formed themselves into the *Deutsches Club*. The Germans have a society for the protection of immigrants, and various other benevolent and social institutions. Many of their naturalized citizens manifest

Lager Bier Politicians.

a lively interest in the politics of our country, which they discuss with much warmth in their favorite beer-house .

May 2d.—May-day happening upon Sunday, a procession of school-children, to celebrate the occasion, took place the next day. This was a new and pleasant sight in San Francisco, and the event is worthy of being recorded. There were about a thousand children of both sexes in the train. They appeared all in holiday costume, the girls being dressed in white. Each one carried a bouquet of fresh and beautiful flowers. There was the usual " Queen of May," with her " Maids of Honor," and various other characters, all represented by the juvenile players. The children of seven schools bore distinctive banners. A fine band of music accompanied the happy procession. After proceeding through the principal thoroughfares, the children moved to the school-house in Broadway. Here some pleasant ceremonies, songs, and occasional addresses took place, in which the children themselves were the chief actors. A repast of such delicate eatables as suited youthful palates was next enjoyed, after which the glad multitude dispersed.

About eleven o'clock on the evening of this day, the *Rassette House*, at the corner of Bush and Sansome streets, and some of the adjoining buildings, were destroyed by fire. The Rassette House was a first-class hotel, well known in the city. It was a frame building, of five stories in height, including the basement. The fire began in a room above the kitchen, and in a few minutes spread over the enormous structure of dry timber. The hotel happened to be well filled with lodgers at the time, nearly all of whom were in bed when the flames broke out. There were four hundred and sixteen boarders at the house, the most of whom also lodged there. The horror and danger of their situation, in the midst of such a combustible mass, may be imagined, but can scarcely be described. A north-east wind was blowing fresh at the time, and strong fears were entertained lest the conflagration should spread over that district of the city which had escaped all the great fires of 1850 and '51. The firemen were early in attendance, and did all that men could do in the circumstances. Though they could not save the blazing pile of lumber, nor some of the neighboring houses, they prevented the conflagration spreading beyond a limited, short distance. The loss of property was estimated at nearly $100,000, without including the valuable property belonging to the many lodgers in the Rassette House. Several of the inmates of the latter building were severely burned, and it was supposed for a considerable time that some had perished. A new hotel has since been built on the same site. It is one of the most magnificent, as it is the largest private edifice, devoted to a single business, in the city.

In the week previous to that in which the fire just noticed occurred, several very extensive conflagrations had taken place in various districts of the city. However, the numerous fire-proof brick tenements, and the rapid movements and unwearied exertions of the firemen, prevented these fires from spreading far. The daring and persevering labors of the Fire Department were constant themes of praise and public gratitude.

New Rassette House.

May 14th.—The origin and privileges of the Mountain Lake Water Company have been already noticed. The commencement of their works was this day celebrated by some imposing ceremonies at the foot of the hill near the presidio. The completion of this important undertaking has been considerably delayed, and while we write the works are at a stand. Want of funds is presumed to be the reason. The cost has far exceeded the first calculations of the projectors. Doubtless the necessary moneys will be raised before long, and the original project carried fully out. No single measure is of so much vital importance to the city as this, and all good citizens must wish well to the success of the enterprise. Hitherto San Francisco has been chiefly provided with fresh water from a considerable number of artesian wells sunk in various parts of the city, and from supplies brought in tanks by small steamers from Saucelito, on the opposite side of the entrance to the bay. The water from all these sources is deficient at the best, and its cost forms a considerable item in the expenses of housekeepers. It is expected that the Mountain Lake Water Company will be enabled, with a handsome profit to itself, to supply millions of gallons daily of the softest and purest fresh water at greatly lower rates than what are now being paid for much smaller supplies. In a place like San Francisco, so much exposed from position and circumstances to conflagration, the unlimited supply of water for extinguishing fires is particularly requisite; and that will surely be obtained when this company has completed its works. Its name is taken from the Mountain Lake, which is but a small sheet of water, and of itself could not yield the expected supplies. This lake has no visible outlet. A few hundred yards from its northern margin, there gushes through the ground a full stream of water, which is believed to be amply sufficient for all the purposes of a city thrice the size of San Francisco. It is matter of doubt whether this great spring, or rather subterranean river, is the vent of the small Mountain Lake, or whether it is not the open end of a natural siphon, which discharges the rains and dews that fall among the mountains on the opposite shores of the bay.

May 19th.—We have already noticed various acts of the Legislature establishing a State Marine Hospital at San Francisco. Of this date, an act was passed which considerably altered the constitution of the existing establishment, and which was henceforward intended to be the sole general State Hospital in California. The administration of the hospital was declared to be under the control of a board of five trustees, to be annually elected by the Legislature, in joint convention. The trustees should themselves choose by ballot a president and vice-president from their own number. A treasurer, with a salary of $2,000 should also be chosen by them. The Legislature should elect every two years two resident and two visiting physicians, the former to receive annually the sum of $4,000, and the latter the same sum, each, in both cases payable quarterly. Particular provisions are made in the act as to the respective duties of the trustees, the treasurer and physicians. All invalid persons desirous of being received into the hospital should apply to the resident physicians or either of them, and on their certificate should be admitted. Indigent sick persons, not residents of any county in the State might likewise be admitted to the hospital, as State patients ; as also the indigent sick of the city, upon such terms as the municipal authorities and the board of trustees might determine. All the State patients in the Sacramento and Stockton State Hospitals at the time when these should be abolished by law should be admitted as patients into the State Marine Hospital at San Francisco. There should be set apart by the State Treasurer, as a hospital fund, the net amounts accruing to the State Treasury, as follows, viz. :—Three-fifths of the amount derived as a commutation or tax on passengers arriving at the ports of the State, and the fines and penalties collected by reason of a violation of the laws regulating the same ; and all sums paid into the State Treasury for license for auction, gaming, billiards, ten-pin or bowling alleys, hawkers and peddlers, or collected as fines or penalties for a violation of the same. Of the amounts derived from these several sources, the one-half should be appropriated to the support and maintenance of the State Marine Hospital at San Francisco, and the other half should be distributed to each organized county in the State, proportionably to the population of said counties, as a special fund, to be appropriated exclusively to the support and maintenance of the indigent sick of such counties respectively. It was, however, provided that such allowance to the hospital at San Francisco should not exceed the sum of $100,000, and that if it did not amount to that sum then the State Comptroller should draw his warrant for the deficiency, if the necessities of the hospital should require it.

The State Marine Hospital at San Francisco is, while we write, located in Stockton street, in a large and commodious building (formerly at various periods, the American Hotel, the Marine Hospital, the Kremlin, and the Clarendon Hotel), and which is rented at a large sum. It has been much enlarged, and was expressly fitted up for the purposes of a hospital. The situation is pleasant and healthy, although the inhabitants of the adjacent houses have grumbled, with some reason, that such an establishment should have been located in a thickly peopled and fashionable part of the town. This hospital is efficiently conducted, and as might naturally have been expected, has been productive of much benefit to both foreigners and Americans. The average number of patients is about two hundred and fifty. The only other State Hospital is one solely for insane persons at Stockton.

JUNE.—For some things San Francisco has been always particularly notorious. Among these may be mentioned its gambling saloons and drinking bars. Many keepers of these places have made large fortunes. A great proportion of the community still gamble—the lower classes in public, and the upper, or richer classes in private. Very many also continue the habit of occasionally taking a daily "drink," or two; while most of the inhabitants take many more "drinks" than they would perhaps care to confess to a rigidly sober acquaintance. In the *Christian Advocate* (a San Francisco weekly newspaper), about this date, there appeared some information which exhibits the intemperance and dissipation of San Francisco in a very alarming light. Religious journals are not always trustworthy, especially in facts and figures, when commenting on the vices of the age; but in this case there is ample room for all possible exaggeration in the statements, and still there would be statistics enough left to grieve the philanthropist. We copy the following from the *Herald*:

"The *Christian Advocate* has found, *by actual count*, the whole number of places where liquor is sold in this city to be five hundred and thirty-seven. Of these, eighty-three are purely liquor, in retail line, and fifty-two wholesale; making one hundred and twenty-five places which do not keep an onion to modify the traffic. Of the four hundred and twelve places where it is sold in connection with other business, one hundred and forty-four are tavern restaurants; one hundred and fifty-four groceries; forty-six gambling-houses; and forty-eight supposed to be kept by bawds. Some of these appear genteel, others are dance-houses and such like, where Chinese, Mexican, Chilian and other foreign women are assembled. There were five hundred and fifty-six bar-tenders present in the various places at the time when the memoranda were taken. We think we may safely add one-quarter, if not one-third, as reserve corps, making, including women, seven hundred and forty-three bar-tenders in our city."

These statements, in all conscience, make matters black and and bad enough. Opposed to such an array—" seven hundred and forty-three bar-tenders!"—all the "Sons of Temperance," the clergymen, churches, religious publications, Mercantile Library Associations and the like, can hope to do little good for strict sobriety. It happens to be the custom in San Francisco to take a "drink" occasionally, while the great mass of the people either have not, or will not avail themselves of any places of recreation or of retirement at the close of daily labor and business other than those where liquor is sold. The usual active and speculative mode of life at San Francisco encourages, if it does not necessarily lead to much indulgence in intoxicating liquors. Yet though so many are tasting again and again, in the course of the day, there is not so much gross drunkenness visible as one might expect. Many of the thirsty, better class San Franciscans are more tipplers than downright drunkards. Among the lowest and the rowdy classes, however, there is much brutal and degrading drunkenness, the effects of which are seen at all hours of day and night upon our streets. It is in the mixed dance and drinking-houses above noticed, that so many noisy brawls and desperate assaults, often ending in murders, chiefly take place, that make San Francisco so infamous for its crimes. It is impossible at present completely to close such places without bringing perhaps worse evils upon society. Only time, a naturally better set of citizens, the example and benefits of good men and good institutions, homes and domestic society, and an improved public opinion, will gradually reduce the number of the haunts of vice, close the drinking and gambling-saloons, and purify the general moral condition of the city.

We have already described the character of the "clipper ships" which the trade and necessities of San Francisco created, and have mentioned several of the shortest passages that had been performed by these vessels between the Atlantic ports and our city. These passages were the quickest that had ever been made. The voyage from San Francisco to the Atlantic ports is generally accomplished in a considerably shorter period, which arises chiefly from the prevalence of westerly winds in the region of Cape Horn, by reason of which homeward-bound ships are speedily wafted round that dreaded place, where usually so much delay is caused to outward-bound vessels. The *Northern Light* sailed from San Francisco, on the 13th of March this year, and arrived at Boston on the 29th May thereafter, thus accomplishing the voyage in the wonderfully short space of seventy-six days. This is the fastest passage that has ever been made between the places by any ship, not a steamer.

First Congregational Church.

July 4th.—Independence-day this year was chiefly remarkable in San Francisco for the first battalion parade of the military companies. These, numbering seven in all, inclusive of the "Sutter Rifles," from Sacramento City, which were here on a visit, formed into line and passed in review before Major General John A. Sutter and a brilliant staff. The benevolent and true hearted old pioneer was rapturously welcomed wherever he appeared. The battalion afterwards marched to the gardens of Mr. Russ, about a mile and a half from the plaza, where Mrs. C. N. Sinclair presented it with a set of colors.

Independence-day being the great annual festival of the American people, was otherwise celebrated in the usual manner. The Irish population turned out in large numbers, and marched in procession through the city, preceded by a band of music. In the evening there was a discharge of fireworks on the plaza, at the city's expense.

July 10th.—Dedication of the new First Congregational Church, at the south-w. corner of Dupont and California streets. This is a very elegant brick building, and forms one of the striking ornaments of the city. It is sixty feet in front, by one hundred feet deep, and is seated for about twelve hundred persons. According to the plan there is to be a steeple one hundred and sixty feet in height, but this has been as yet only raised to the top of the tower, leaving the spire to be constructed at some future date. The cost of the building was $40,000. The pastor of the congregation, the Rev. T. Dwight Hunt, was the first regular clergyman in San Francisco.

July 17th.—The various religious bodies of the city are gradually improving the style of their churches. The old, small wooden buildings that served the purposes of religious meeting-houses well enough a few years back are being discarded, and magnificent brick structures are rising in their stead. This day the corner-stone of a new Roman Catholic church was laid, at the north-east corner of Dupont and California streets, with the many imposing ceremonies performed on similar occasions by that body of Christians. A long train of priests and dignitaries officiated on the occasion. The building, St. Mary's, is still in course of erection.

The same day the dedication of the First Unitarian Church took place. The exterior of this church is not yet finished; the interior is very fine. It is situated on Stockton street, near Sacramento street. The services at the dedication were conducted by the pastor of the church, the Rev. F. T. Gray.

These are among the most imposing and substantial edifices

for public religious worship that have yet been erected in the city. The most of the other churches are still of wood. Among them may be noticed that eminently useful place the Seaman's Chapel, or Bethel. This structure has been formed upon the hull of an old forsaken ship, and exhibits a remarkably chaste and beautiful interior. As congregations get larger and wealthier,

Unitarian Church.

the many churches constructed of frame which are now existing will gradually be supplanted by handsome edifices of brick or stone, in conformity with the improved character of other buildings throughout the city.

JULY 20th.—The under-sheriff, John A. Freaner, was shot on Mission street by one Redmond McCarthy, a "squatter," when the former, in the performance of his duty, was endeavoring to execute a writ of ejectment against the latter. Revolvers were produced and fired by both parties, and both were severely wounded. The circumstance is particularly mentioned as illustrative of the "times" in San Francisco. About this period the "squatters" on city lands became suddenly more numerous and daring than ever. These were not like the legitimate "settlers," who took possession of vacant unclaimed lands, under the ordinary pre-emption laws of the United States. On the contrary, many of the squatters seized upon lands known to be claimed by others, and who held them by the strongest legal titles known. As these titles, however, happened in almost all cases to have some nice legal doubt affecting them, "squatters" settled the matter in their own way, and at once forcibly seized upon every piece of ground that had no permanent improvements made upon it. They "squatted" every where; not only on choice lots along the line of public streets, and among the distant sand hills, but on the public and private burying grounds and on the open squares of the city. If they had the least colorable title adverse to the party in constructive possession, good and well; but generally there was no other right pretended than that of force. The intruder displayed only his six-shooter and with a scowl and a sullen curse would mutter to the offended owner—*My title is as good as yours; I have now the ground, and I will keep it, ay, until death. Out of the way!* Of course those who considered themselves the proper owners were not inclined tamely to submit to this violation of their rights. Sometimes they took counsel and aid from the law, but nearly as often they met the invader with his own weapons, the axe to destroy fences and buildings, and the revolver to frighten or kill his antagonist. Hired persons on both sides sometimes helped to carry on the war. Occasionally one "squatter" would envy, and seek to steal the already stolen possession of another; and then both would have a bloody fight about the matter. "*To the victors belonged the spoils.*"

Many lives were lost in these savage contests, and bitter enmity engendered among rival claimants. The law was almost powerless to redress wrong and punish guilt in such cases. It said that the owner of ground was entitled by every means in his power, to prevent unlawful and hostile intrusion upon it; and thus men had not the slightest scruple to use fire-arms upon all occasions. In the confusion and conflict of adverse titles, it could not be instantly determined who were the true owners, and judges therefore could not punish the trespassers and murderers. If even the title of one slain in such a struggle were clear, juries could not be found who would bring in the slayer guilty of murder. His plea, however false and ridiculous, of supposed title to the ground which was the cause of the fatal dispute, was always held sufficient to save him from any verdict that would justify the extreme penalty of the law. Probably one or more of the jurors themselves had committed similar outrages, and would not condemn in the prisoner their own principles of action, and weaken the titles to their own properties. It was supposed that many of these "squatters" were secretly instigated in their reckless proceedings by people of wealth and influence, who engaged to see their pupils out of any legal difficulty into which they might fall. Such wealthy speculators shared, of course, in the spoils of the proceedings. To this day, many of the most valuable districts in and around San Francisco are held by "squatter's titles," which had been won perhaps at the cost of bloodshed, and in defiance of other titles, that, if not the best in law, had at least a colorable show, and should have been always strong enough to resist the strong-hand claim of the mere robber. In this way the city itself, the great victim of real estate speculators, "squatters" and plunderers, has lost, for a time at least, much of its remaining property. The new charter, if passed by the Legislature, will make many of these temporary losses, final and irretrievable ones. If it were desirable to enlarge on this painful subject, as showing the independent and lawless state of society in California, a history might be given of the great gang of squatters who have stolen the broad rich acres of the native Peraltas on the opposite side of the bay, in Contra Costa. However, it is sufficient merely to mention the subject, in illustration of the like practices that had been long carried on, and at this time seemed to be at their height in San Francisco and its environs.

July 24th.—Fire broke out in the store-ship *Manco*, which lay in close proximity to the wharves, near the corner of Mission and Stewart streets. The store-ship *Canonicus*—an old "forty-niner,"—which was moored alongside, next caught fire. The firemen turned out, as usual, but from the want of proper resting-places found much difficulty in working their engines with effect. There happened to be a large quantity of gunpowder on board the Manco at the time, the knowledge of which fact, when circulated, speedily sent to a respectful distance the curious crowd that had gathered on the neighboring ships, and wherever they could procure a view of what was going on. The firemen, however, gallantly stuck to their posts, and poured vast quantities of water into the hold of the burning ship. By these means the powder was so damped that only partial explosions of small quantities took place. At last, the ship was scuttled, and she sank in shallow water. The flames continued, and were only extinguished a considerable time afterwards. The losses sustained by both the Manco and Canonicus were estimated at about $50,000.

JULY—AUGUST.—There was a succession of "strikes" during these months, among most classes of mechanics and laborers, when wages were generally raised from fifteen to twenty per cent. The following may be quoted, as being the average rate of daily wages payable at this time to journeymen :—Bricklayers, $10 ; stone-cutters, $10 ; ship carpenters and caulkers, $10 ; plasterers, $9 ; house carpenters, $8 ; blacksmiths, $8 ; watchmakers and jewellers, $8 ; tinners, $7 ; hatters (but few employed), $7 ; painters and glaziers, $6 ; tenders, $5 ; 'longshoremen, $6 ; tailors, $4 ; shoemakers, $100 per month, without boarding ; teamsters, $100 to $120 per month, finding themselves ; firemen on steamers, $100 per month ; coal-passers, $75 per month ; farm hands, $50 per month, and found. These wages are at least five times higher than what are paid similar workers in the Atlantic States ; while they are about double the highest rates of wages that are now (1854) given mechanics and laborers in the gold-producing country of Australia. Most trades and occupations other than those above named were paid equally well. The printers, who have been always a highly remunerated class, could earn, according to skill and employment, from $10 to $15 a day. Perhaps the former sum may be taken as a low average. As we have elsewhere said, there is no place in the world where so high remuneration is given for labor—useful, wanted labor, as in San Francisco. The rates above mentioned do not vary much in the course of the year; and may, in 1854, be still quoted as nearly correct. At the same time it should be mentioned that it is not always the case that the applicant can find constant employment at his particular trade. However, if necessity should compel him to work for a time at an inferior occupation, and provided only he have bodily strength, he may always fairly calculate in finding employment as a laborer in coarse work, or in doing odd jobs, at from $3.50 to $5 a day. The immigrant, however, must work at *something*, unless he means to starve outright. The expenses of living are very much greater in San Francisco than in the dearest of the Atlantic cities, while there is very little charity or sympathy bestowed on idle, healthy men. People who would honestly succeed in this country must be prepared to turn their hand and attention to any kind of labor that promises to *pay*, no matter how disagreeable, or how little used to it may be the hesitating beginner. That has been the case with many of the most respectable and wealthy citizens, who at earlier times in San Francisco have been without a dime in their pocket or a friend to give them a gratuitous meal. They had to strip to the shirt, and earn the beginning of their present fortunes by "the sweat of their brow." If all employment should by possibility fail in the city, the robust immigrant has still the gold mines to fall back upon for sustenance and wealth, as well as the rich unclaimed lands of the United States, that seek only a tiller to produce marvellous crops, or he may always secure a situation as an agricultural laborer for others. Again, then, we say, there is no country in the world to be compared for wages and profits to California. It is emphatically the poor working-man's paradise on earth.

August 14th.—The second anniversary of the German *Turnverein* (the gymnasts already noticed) was observed to-day, in the park of Dr. Wedekind, in the southern quarter of the city. This affair was a very grand one with the whole German race here; and nearly three thousand persons participated in the festivities of the occasion. Besides Dr. Wedekind's grounds, the gardens of Mr. Russ adjoining were thrown open to the people, where athletic games and many amusing sports, music, dancing and singing, and the indispensable smoking and drinking were kept up till a late hour at night. The amusements were resumed on the following day.

SEPTEMBER 7th.—The annual election of city and county officers. The following parties were chosen :—

Senate.

E. J. Moore, Samuel Brannan, *and subsequently on his resignation*, David Mahoney.
W. M. Lent (*for short term*),

Assembly.

J. C. Hubbard,	A. A. Green,	N. Hubert,
E. P. Purdy,	W. J. Swasey,	Elijah Nichols,
F. W. Koll,	J. W. Bagley,	James A. Gilbert.

Sheriff.—William R. Gorham.

County Judge.—T. W. Freelon (J. D. Creigh, *to fill vacancy.*)

District Attorney.—Henry H. Byrne. *County Clerk.*—Thos. Hayes.

County Recorder.—James Grant. *County Treasurer.*—G. W. Green.

County Surveyor.—James J. Gardner. *Coroner.*—J. W. Whaling.

Public Administrator.—S. A. Sheppard. *County Assessor.*—J. W. Stillman.

Mayor.—C. K. Garrison.

Recorder.—Geo. W. Baker. *Tax Collector.*—W. A. Matthews.

Comptroller.—Stephen R. Harris. *City Attorney.*—S. A. Sharp.

Treasurer.—Hamilton Bowie. *Street Commissioner.*—John Addis.

Marshal.—B. Seguine. *Harbor Master.*—Robert Haley.

Clerk of the Supreme Court.—Henry Haskell.

Assessors.—Robert Kerrison, Jas. H. Keller, Richard Parr.

Aldermen.

H. Meiggs,	Richard M. Jessup,	John D. Brower,	John Nightingale,
Chas. O. West,	Joseph F. Atwill,	D. H. Haskell,	Jas. Van Ness.

Assistant Aldermen.

Chas. H. Corser,	Geo. O. Ecker,	Wm. H. Talmage,	Saml. Gardner,
C. D. Carter,	J. R. West,	Frank Turk,	J. G. W. Schulte.

On this occasion the proposed new charter of the city, framed by the delegates already mentioned, was submitted to the people for their approval or rejection. There were given for it 747 votes, and against it 620 ; showing a majority of 127 votes in its favor. In all the wards, except the 2d and 8th, there were considerable majorities against it. In the 2d ward, the numbers were nearly equal ; and in the 8th almost the whole votes were for it. The people, except perhaps in the last-named ward, seemed to take little interest in the proposed measure.

SEPTEMBER 19th.—The French inhabitants of the city organized among themselves the "Lafayette Hook and Ladder Company." The uniform they adopted was that common to firemen in France. We have at different places alluded to the public spirit of this class of citizens, and their appearance in large bodies on occasions of public ceremonial. They are nearly as numerous as the Germans in San Francisco, and may now (1854)

French Shoeblacks.

number about 5000 persons of both sexes. They preserve many of their national characteristics, and do not seem capable of thoroughly adopting American thoughts and fashions. But a small proportion seek to become naturalized citizens, and they do not readily acquire our language. California, and America itself, are but places where money may be made to enable them to return to their own land in Europe. In San Francisco they have monopolized many professions of a semi-artistic character. They are the chief shoeblacks and hairdressers, cooks, wine importers and professional gamblers. In the first-named capacity, they form one of the street features of the place. They are posted at many of the prominent corners, with seats for their customers, whose boots they are ever ready to polish at the charge of twenty-five cents; and some of them have at this singular business gathered money enough to open shops, neatly furnished, for the same purposes. It is not uncommon to see a dozen of these shoeblacks in a row upon the edge of the side-walks, scouring and scrubbing away at the muddy or dusty boots of their patrons. But besides these occupations, this people pursue all other callings here, and many of them are among the most distinguished, wealthy and respectable inhabitants of the city. They are partial to public amusements, and have often a theatre open, when plays, vaudevilles and operas in their own language are performed. They have a society for the relief of poor immigrants, besides several other benevolent associations. Two tri-weekly newspapers are published in their language, a portion of one of which is written in Spanish.

The presence of the French has had a marked influence upon society in San Francisco. Skilled workmen of their race have decorated the finer shops and buildings, while their national taste and judicious criticism have virtually directed the more chaste architectural ornaments, both on the exterior and in the interior of our houses. Their polite manners have also given an ease to the ordinary intercourse of society which the unbending American character does not naturally possess. The expensive and fashionable style of dressing among the French ladies has greatly encouraged the splendid character of the shops of jewellers, silk merchants, milliners and others whom women chiefly patronize, while it has perhaps increased the general extravagance among the whole female population of the city.

There are in San Francisco many natives of Switzerland and Alsace, those debatable lands between the French and German people. The Alsatians are claimed, and sometimes rejected by both. There does not seem much sympathy between the rival races, less a great deal than is between either of them and the Americans. The French complain that they are not treated so kindly by the last as are the Germans. The reason seems obvious. It is because they do not take the same pains to learn the

American language and character. The naturalized Germans are professed and acknowledged brethren ; the French—foreign in manner and physical appearance, in thoughts and hopes—can never be considered as such. The occasional devotion of Germans to old Fatherland does not so fill their hearts that they become insensible to the numberless political and social blessings which

Outer Telegraph Station.

they receive in their adopted country. But the wild glorification of Frenchmen to every thing connected with their beautiful France, is often a neglectful insult to the land that shelters them, and which they would ignore, even although they seek not to become its permanent citizens. Both races have played a prominent part in the industrial history of San Francisco, and in that of California generally. Their numbers are very large in the various mining districts ; while, as we have seen, they form a considerable proportion of the population of the city. They are not the dominant spirits of the place—for these are of the true American type that ever cry *go ahead !*—but they help to execute what the national lords of the soil, the restless and perhaps unhappy people of progress contrive. The character of a man may at least partially be inferred from his " drinks." The true Germans dote on *lager-bier*—and they are a heavy, phlegmatic, unambitious race ; the French love light wines—and they are as sparkling, yet without strength or force of character ; the genuine Yankee must have a burning *spirit* in his multitudinous draughts—and he is a giant when he begins to work, tearing and trampling over the *impossibilities* of other races, and binding them to his absolute, insolent will.

Inner Telegraph Station.

SEPTEMBER 22d.—Opening of the first electric telegraph in California celebrated. This extended eight miles, between San Francisco and Point Lobos, and was erected by Messrs. Sweeny & Baugh, to give early information of shipping arrivals. Early in 1849 this enterprising firm had erected a station-house on Telegraph Hill, which commanded a view of the entrance to the Golden Gate and the ocean in that immediate vicinity ; and having adopted a variety of appropriate signals, well understood by merchants and others in the city, were enabled to give early intimation of the approach and peculiar character of all vessels coming into the harbor. This proved of immense value to newspaper publishers and other business men, from whom the enterprise received a liberal patronage, it being principally supported by voluntary contributions. Thus encouraged, Messrs. Sweeny & Baugh afterwards established another station at Point Lobos, overlooking the ocean, from which, on a clear day, vessels may be distinguished many miles distant. This station is in full view of that on Telegraph Hill, which, receiving early signals from it, communicated them at once to the citizens, who were thus apprised of the arrival many hours before the vessel entered the harbor. The electric telegraph is still another improvement, and increases materially the facilities previously afforded by the method of signalling. Occasionally heavy fogs prevented the signals from being intelligible, or even seen, which difficulty is measurably obviated by the electric telegraph. The proprietors have also established in Sacramento street, near Montgomery, a Merchants' Exchange, supported by subscription, in the spacious rooms of which are always to be found the latest papers from all parts of the world. These enterprises have proved exceedingly lucrative to their projectors.

CHAPTER XXVI.

1853.

Important legal decision of the Supreme Court confirming Alcaldes' grants.—Burning of the St. Francis Hotel.—Opening of the telegraph communication to Marysville.—Lone Mountain Cemetery.—Anniversary of the day of St. Francis.—The Mission Dolores.—The Spanish races in California.—The Custom House Block.—The steamship Winfield Scott wrecked.—Election of officers of the Fire Department.—The Sonorian Filibusters.—Opening of the Metropolitan Theatre.—Great sales of water lots.—Montgomery block.

October 13th.—The most important decision ever given by the Supreme Court of California was pronounced to-day in the case of *Cohas* vs. *Rosin and Legris.* Previous decisions both of this and the lower legal tribunals had established principles which unsettled the city titles to nearly every lot of ground within the municipal boundaries, and mightily encouraged squatterism. By these decisions, one title had just seemed as good or as bad as another ; *possession* being better than any. The alarming consequences of these doctrines forced both bench and bar into further inquiries and minute researches into the laws, usages and customs of Spanish or Mexican provinces and towns. The new information thus acquired was brought to bear upon the suit above named, where principles were evolved and a precedent formed of the utmost consequence to the community, and which have nearly settled, though not quite, the "squatter" questions. The decision was pronounced by Judge Heydenfeldt, and was concurred in by Chief Justice Murray (although upon somewhat different grounds) and Judge Wells. Without entering upon the merits of the particular case in question we give the "conclusions" come to :

"*Firstly,* That by the laws of Mexico, towns were invested with the ownership of lands.

"*Secondly,* That by the law, usage and custom in Mexico, alcaldes were the heads of the Ayuntamientos, or Town Councils, were the executive officers of the towns, and rightfully exercised the power of granting lots within the towns, which were the property of the towns.

"*Thirdly*, That before the military occupation of California by the army of the United States, San Francisco was a Mexican pueblo, or municipal corporation, and entitled to the lands within her boundaries.

"*Fourthly*, That a grant of a lot in San Francisco, made by an alcalde, whether a Mexican or of any other nation, raises the presumption that the alcalde was a properly qualified officer, that he had authority to make the grant, and that the land was within the boundaries of the pueblo."

St. Francis Hotel immediately after the fire.

These conclusions sustain all alcaldes' grants in the city, no matter though the alcalde himself had been illegally appointed and had made a dishonest use of his power. By this decision—all opposing precedents having been expressly set aside by the court–many notoriously fraudulent alcalde grants have been legalized ; but that seems a small price to pay for the full assurance of title now given to the proprietors of the most valuable part of the ground within the municipal bounds.

OCTOBER 22d.—Destruction by fire of the St. Francis Hotel, at the corner of Dupont and Clay streets. This was a famous house in the history of San Francisco. It was built in the fall of 1849, and in the basement story the polls were held of the first State election. It was afterwards converted into a first-class hotel. The structure was composed of the slightest and most inflammable materials; and it had long been matter of surprise that it had escaped the many conflagrations which had so repeatedly destroyed great portions of the city. When, at last, it was consumed, people were not only no whit surprised, but many were absolutely glad that it was so, since the danger of its long anticipated burning spreading to the neighboring tenements was thereby put an end to. The strenuous exertions of the firemen confined the fire to the building in which it originated. The damage was estimated at $17,000. One lodger was burned to death; and several firemen were very severely injured by the flames. The masterly efforts of the Fire Department on this occasion were much praised.

OCTOBER 24th.—First telegraphic communication between San Francisco and Marysville. This was the completion of the line of the State Telegraph Company, already noticed. The whole length of the wire is two hundred and six miles; and it was erected in seventy-five days. The rates charged were, and are now as follows: From San Francisco to Stockton, Sacramento or Marysville, two dollars for the first ten words; and for each additional five words, seventy-five cents. From San Francisco to San José, for the first ten words, one dollar, and for each additional five words forty cents.

NOVEMBER.—The "Lone Mountain Cemetery" projected. A tract of land three hundred and twenty acres in extent, lying between the presidio and the mission, is to be laid out in a proper manner as a new resting-place for the dead, the cemetery of Yerba Buena being considered, by the planners of the new grounds, too near the city for a permanent burial-place. The new cemetery is located near the well-known "Lone Mountain," situated three or four miles west of the plaza. From the summit of this beautifully shaped hill may be obtained one of the finest and most extensive views of land and water. At the date of writing, very material and expensive improvements are being made upon the grounds, to adapt them for the purposes of a cemetery.

NOVEMBER 9th.—The day of St. Francis, the anniversary of the foundation of the Mission Dolores, in 1776. In the preceding pages, occasional allusions have been made to the former grandeur and subsequent decline of this mission. At present, the chief thing worthy of notice about the place is the old church. This is constructed of *adobes*, and is a spacious building. The exterior is partially whitewashed and is very plain in appearance, although the front pretends to some old-fashioned architectural

Interior of a Mission Church.

decorations, and shows several handsome bells. The capacious interior is dark, cold and comfortless. The walls and roof are roughly painted, and upon the former are several common paintings of saints and sacred subjects. The ornaments upon and around the great altar are of the tinsel character usually adopted in ordinary Roman Catholic churches. It is presumed they are of no great pecuniary value. Public worship is still regularly celebrated in this huge and gloomy temple. The usual audiences are a few women, whose features and dress proclaim their Spanish origin. If any of the fast-thinking, doing and living people of San Francisco could be induced to "pause and moralize a while," there is no spot so fitted to encourage the unwonted mood, as the dismal, silent and deserted interior of the Mission Church.

There is an awe and apparent holiness about the place which the casual heretical visitor cares not to disturb, as he perhaps humbly kneels on the damp, earthen floor, and worships in secret his own God. A walk round the small graveyard attached to the church will only deepen his meditation as he gazes on the tombs of departed pioneers and gold-hunters, and reflects upon the glory of the ancient patriarchal times of tame Indians and their ghostly keepers.

The mission has always been a favorite place of amusement to the citizens of San Francisco. Here, in the early days of the city, exhibitions of bull and bear fights frequently took place, which attracted great crowds; and here, also, were numerous duels fought, which drew nearly as many idlers to view them. At present, there are two race-courses in the neighborhood, and a large number of drinking-houses. Two plank-roads lead thither from the city, upon both of which omnibuses run every half hour. The mission lies within the municipal bounds, and probably will soon be united with the city by a connected line of buildings. The highway to San José and the farther south, runs through the village, while around it are fine green hills and fertile fields, and hotels and places of public recreation. These things all make the old home of the "fathers" a place of considerable importance to our health and pleasure seekers. On fine days, especially on Sundays, the roads to the mission show a continual succession, passing to and fro, of all manner of equestrians and pedestrians, and elegant open carriages filled with ladies and holiday folk.

Since we have given elsewhere short separate notices of some of the leading races, not American, that people San Francisco, we may here say a few words upon that one which first settled in the country—the Spanish. Over the whole of California, there may be probably about 20,000 persons of Spanish extraction; and in San Francisco alone, some 3,000. It is of the last only that we would speak. Few of them are native Californians. Perhaps one-half of the number are Mexicans, and one-third Chilians. The remaining sixth consists of Peruvians and natives of Old Spain, and of parts of Spanish America other than Mexico, Chili and Peru. The Hispano-Americans, as a class, rank far beneath the French and Germans. They are ignorant and lazy, and are consequently poor. A few of their number may have a high social standing in the city, while some more bear a respectable position. For these there is one page of a French tri-weekly newspaper written in the Spanish language. It is not of them, nor of the few native Californians, who are gentlemen by nature, that we speak, but of the great mass of the race. Many of the Chilians are able both to read and write; few of the Mexicans can. Both peoples, when roused by jealousy or revenge, as they often are, will readily commit the most horrid crimes. In proportion to their numbers, they show more criminals in the courts of law than any other class. The Mexicans seem the most inferior of the race. They have had no great reason to love the American character, and, when safe opportunity offers, are not slow to show detestation of their conquerors. The sullen, spiteful look of the common Mexicans in California is very observable. The Chilians in the time of the "Hounds" were an oppressed and despised people. Since that period the class has perhaps improved. The Hispano-Americans fill many low and servile employments, and in general engage only in such occupations as do not very severely tax either mind or body. They show no ambition to rise beyond the station where destiny, dirt, ignorance and sloth have placed them. They seem to have no wish to become naturalized citizens of the Union, and are morally incapable of comprehending the spirit and tendencies of our institutions. The most inferior class of all, the proper "greaser," is on a par with the common Chinese and the African; while many negroes far excel the first-named in all moral, intellectual and physical respects.

The Hispano-Americans dwell chiefly about Dupont, Kearny and Pacific streets—long the blackguard quarters of the city. In these streets, and generally in the northern parts of the city, are many dens of gross vice, which are patronized largely by Mexicans and Chilians. Their dance, drink and gambling houses are also the haunts of negroes and the vilest order of white men. In the quarrels which are constantly arising in such places many treacherous, thieving and murderous deeds are committed. A large proportion of the common Mexican and Chilian women are still what they were in the days of the "Hounds," abandoned to lewd practices, and shameless.

The large and elegant building called "Custom-House Block," at the south-east corner of Sansome and Sacramento streets, was completed and partially occupied during this month. It was constructed at a cost, exclusive of the land, of $140,000; and is a substantial structure, three stories high, besides a basement, fronting eighty feet on Sansome and one hundred and eighty-five

Custom-House Block.

feet on Sacramento street. The various offices connected with the custom-house and naval department, besides a billiard room, and sundry other offices and stores, are in the second and third stories.

December 2d.—The mail steamship *Winfield Scott*, on her way from San Francisco to Panama, was wrecked on the rocky and desolate Island of Anacapa, near the Island of Santa Cruz, off Santa Barbara. The passengers and most of the mail bags were saved, but the ship was a total loss. The accident was caused by dense fogs and ignorance of the exact position of the ship.

December 5th.—Annual election of the Fire Department, when the following officers were chosen: *Chief Engineer.*—

Charles P. Duane. *Assistant Engineers.*—E. A. Ebbetts, Joseph Caprise and Charles F. Simpson.

DECEMBER 13th.—The Barque *Anita* sailed with about two hundred and forty volunteers to join a small band of adventurers that had lately left San Francisco on a filibustering expedition against Lower California and Sonora. The circumstances attending this expedition show in a remarkable manner the wild and restless spirit that influences so many of the people of California. Not content with their own large territory, much of which is still unexplored, and nearly all of which that is known is characterized by extraordinary richness in minerals, fertility of soil, beauty of scenery, and mildness and salubrity of climate—by everything, in short, that could tempt an energetic immigrant to develope its unusual advantages—many of our restless people sighed for new countries, if not like Alexander for new worlds, to see and conquer. The Mexican province of Sonora had long been reputed to be among the richest mineral regions in the world. Its mines, however, had never been properly developed. The Mexican character is not a very enterprising one. At the same time, the ravages of the numerous tribes of warlike Indians that inhabit many parts of Sonora and its frontier, had farther checked all efforts to work the known gold and silver mines there. The country otherwise was a fine agricultural and pastoral one ; and, if slaves could only be introduced to cultivate and reap the teeming fields, the owners would draw immense revenues from them. To conquer, or steal this rich country, was therefore a very desirable thing. That it belonged in sovereignty to a friendly and peaceable power, and that some seventy thousand white people inhabited and possessed the land, appeared matters of no great con sequence. The government of Mexico was a worthless one, surely, and the citizens of Sonora were, or should be, dissatisfied with it, and had a right to rebel, and call upon foreigners to aid them in their rebellion. If they did not, why, their culpable negligence was certainly no fault of the filibusters. The Sonorians *ought* to rise, proclaim their independence, and cry for help from all and sundry. That was enough. The filibusters needed no particular invitation. They were determined to succor the poor Sonorians, and themselves ; and so they gathered together with arms and ammunition for the purpose. Walker was another Lopez; Sonora, another Cuba.

About a twelvemonth before this date the grand scheme was first projected, and during the following summer was matured. Scrip was largely printed and circulated at fair prices among speculative jobbers. This paper was to be redeemed by the first proceeds of the new government. The nominal and perhaps real leader of the movement was a gentleman, William Walker to wit, who has already figured in these pages, as the champion of the press and popular rights against the alleged corrupt judiciary of former times. Walker is said to be personally a brave, highly educated and able man, whatever may be thought of his discretion and true motives of conduct in the expedition. He seems to have taken a high moral and political position in the affair, though his professions were peculiar and their propriety not readily admitted by downright sticklers for equity and natural justice. A few of his coadjutors were perhaps also men of a keen sense of honor, who forgot, or heeded not, in the excitement of the adventure, the opinions of mere honest men upon the subject. But the vast majority of Walker's followers can only be viewed as desperate actors in a true filibustering or robbing speculation. The good of the wretched and Apache-oppressed Sonorians was not in their thoughts. If they succeeded, they might lay the sure foundations of fortunes; if they failed, it was only time and perhaps life lost. In either event, there was a grand excitement in the game.

What Americans generally are to other nations, so are the mixed people of California to Eastern Americans themselves. All the impulsive characteristics of the natives of the Atlantic States are on the Pacific carried out to excess. Americans, and particularly those in California, are not altogether devoted to money; they oftentimes love change and excitement better. The golden gains to be sometimes won here by strange speculations early engendered a most restless disposition in society. The adventurous character of the succeeding immigrants readily received the impress and spirit of the place. What, our people seem to think, is the worth of life, wanting emotion, wanting action? At whatever hazard, most persons here must have occasional excitement—new speculations, leading to personal adventure, change of scene and variety of life. Danger to life and limb and loss of property will not stand in the way. They will overlook the fairest prospect close at hand, with its dull routine of duty and labor, to seek for an inferior one at a distance. They are almost invariably dissatisfied with their present condition, whatever that may be. The world moves not fast enough for their boundless desires. Thus a new land, where hope and fancy see all things, is to them a charmed land. They will seek and know its qualities, or perish in the attempt. *Discontent* and *restlessness* make the true spirit of "progress" that is ever unsatisfied with the dull present, the practical and real. These are the characteristics of all great men and great races, and are the strongest signs of their superior intellect.

The spirit of progress is probably a most unhappy one to individuals, although it tends to raise a nation to the height of wealth and glory. Knowledge is power, the attribute of a god; yet as the satirist says, increase of knowledge is only increase of sorrow. Knowledge—power—"progress," is the Anglo-Saxon disposition, which has been developed on a large scale in the American character. Brother Jonathan, like the Israelite of old, seems doomed everlastingly to wander over the earth. His journey fairly began nearly a century since. On, on he must go. *Excelsior!* is his cry. The morality of the various steps in the fated pilgrimage—as morals, social and political, are commonly understood among old-fashioned people—may be dubious; yet the weary work must proceed. It is the fate of America ever to "go ahead." She is like the rod of Aaron that became a serpent and swallowed up the other rods. So will America conquer or annex all lands. That is her "manifest destiny." Only give her time for the process. To swallow up every few years a province as large as most European kingdoms is her present rate of progress. Sometimes she purchases the mighty morsel, sometimes she forms it out of waste territory by the natural increase of her own people, sometimes she "annexes," and sometimes she conquers it. Her "progress" is still steadily onward. Pioneers clear the way. These are political agents with money bags, or settlers in neglected parts of the continent, or peaceable American citizens who happen to reside in the desired countries, and who wish to dwell under the old "Stars and Stripes," or they may be only proper filibusters, who steal and fight gratuitously for their own fast-following Uncle Sam. When they fail in their schemes, they are certainly scoundrels, and are commonly so termed; when they succeed, though they be dubbed heroes, they are still the old rogues. Meanwhile AMERICA (that is the true title of our country) secures the spoils won to her hand, however dishonestly they may have come. That is only her destiny, and perhaps she is not so blamable as a nation in bearing it willingly. One may profit by the treason, yet hate the traitor. Let the distant monarchs of the lands beyond the great lakes and the tawny people of the far south look to it. America must round her territories by the sea. Like Russia, she is steadily creeping over the world, but different from that empire, her presence bestows freedom and good upon the invaded nations, and not despotism, ignorance, and unmanly, brutal desires.

The pioneers into Sonora were Walker and his people. They never reached their destination. Lower California was in the way, and they thought it best to begin on the small scale, and secure it first. On the 30th of September of this year, the brig *Arrow*, which was about to be employed to convey the filibusters to the land of promise, was seized by order of General Hitchcock, commanding the United States forces on the Pacific, and acting under orders or a sense of his duty to protect a neighboring friendly power from being wrongfully attacked by Americans. This measure involved General Hitchcock in unpleasant litigation, and seems to have disgusted him with attempting to interfere farther in the filibusters' movements. For want of sufficient legal evidence to show the destination of the *Arrow* and the character of the preparations making by those connected with the affair, or rather, perhaps, through disinclination of the prosecutors to go on with the proceedings, the case was abandoned and the vessel released. Meanwhile, the other officials here of the United States Government, whose duty it was to prevent all piratical and filibustering expeditions from leaving the port, gave little attention to the subject, and appeared wilfully to neglect their most urgent duties. As for the State and city authorities, it seemed to be considered none of their business to move in the matter. The newspaper press was neutral, or at all events did not (with one or two exceptions) loudly condemn the course intended to be pursued by the known filibusters. Encouraged by these circumstances, the adventurers soon procured another vessel, the barque *Caroline*, and shortly afterwards (16th October), forty-six of their number sailed in her from San Francisco for the lower coast. Early in November, they reached the town of La Paz, situated within the Gulf of California, and in the southern division of the peninsula. There they landed, scattered the surprised inhabitants, secured the governor, proclaimed the independence of Lower California, declared the civil code of Louisiana the law of the land, hauled down the Mexican flag and hoisted their own—all within half an hour. A slight engagement afterwards took place between the Mexicans and the invaders, in which the latter were successful, after killing a few of the enemy. This was the *battle* of La Paz. Mr. Walker then was nominated "President of the Republic of Lower California," and chose, or had chosen for him his various Secretaries of State, War and Navy, and other grand functionaries of the new government. As there were fewer than fifty men to select from, a pretty fair proportion of the party became suddenly dignitaries in the Republic. The President, his staff and whole forces soon forsook La Paz, the particular reason for attacking which town at this juncture of events is not plain, though perhaps it was only to create a "sensation." There was not even the pretence made that the inhabitants of the place, or any of the natives of Lower California, had invited the presence of the spoilers of their property. Walker and his party now retreated altogether from the gulf; and carrying with them the archives of the government, sailed for Ensenada, a place about a hundred miles below San Diego, on the Pacific side of the peninsula. Here, in a thinly peopled and unattractive country, and at a long distance from any Mexican troops, they were safe for a time; and here they established their "Head Quarters," until reinforcements should reach them from San Francisco. It was understood that the seizure of Lower California was only the first step in the proposed conquest of Sonora, which was all along the grand object of the expedition.

When news of this short campaign reached San Francisco, there was a mighty ado with the friends and sympathizers of the expedition. Among the few initiated in the supposed secret causes of the adventure, there were brilliant hopes of the indefinite extension of one of the peculiar "domestic institutions" of the South, and among all were glorious dreams of conquest and plunder. The national flag of the new Republic was run up at the corner of Kearny and Sacramento streets, and an office was opened for the purpose of enlisting recruits. The excitement was great in the city. At the corners of the streets and in bar-rooms, groups of intending buccaneers and their friends collected, and discussed the position of affairs. More volunteers appeared than there were means of conveying to the scene of action. News next reached the city of the *battle* of La Grulla, near Santo Tomas, where the filibusters, when said to be in the act of helping themselves to the cattle and provisions of the natives, were severely handled, and a few of them slain. This, however, only fired the recruits the more to help their oppressed brethren. Why could not the Lower Californians, poor, ignorant brutes, have been contented with the beautiful scrip of the new Republic for their paltry provisions? The rage for war—freedom to the Mexicans, death to the Apaches, and plunder to the Americans—spread over all California, and numbers hastened from the mining regions to San Francisco, to depart southward in time and share in the spoil of the conquered land. The authorities meanwhile, looked calmly on, and took no steps to prevent the departure of the filibusters. The newspapers recorded their various movements at length, and in general either indirectly praised, or did not strongly condemn them. People in private circles laughed, and talked over the business coolly. They generally thought, and said, it was all right—at all events, it was a fine specimen of the go-aheadism of Young America. Moneyed men even advanced considerable sums for the use of the expeditionists, and the scrip of the new Republic was almost saleable on 'Change, at a dime for a dollar.

We have mentioned this affair at some length, more to show the general wild and reckless character of the people, and the state of public opinion upon filibustering, in San Francisco, and in California at large, than to chronicle the particular doings of the adventurers. Our people are mostly in the prime of life, their passions are of the strongest, they have an acute intellect, absolute will and physical strength, but they are not distinguished by high moral and political principle. They are sanguine in whatever things they undertake, and are more inclined to desperate deeds, than to the peaceful business of ordinary life. Had Walker's party succeeded in reaching Sonora and been able to stand their own for a time or perhaps signally to defeat the Mexicans in a pitched battle, ten thousand of our mixed Californians would have hastened to their triple-striped two-star standard. Against such a force not all the power of Mexico would have been sufficient to dislodge the invaders from Sonora. Other tens of thousands would have flocked into the country, and perforce it would have been thoroughly Americanized. Undoubtedly this will happen some day. Is it not "manifest destiny?" People here certainly look upon it as such, and hence very little fault has been found, in general, with the proceedings of the filibusters. The principles of action now existing in California, in so far at least as regards neighboring countries, are something like those of Wordsworth's hero, who acted upon

> "The good old rule, the simple plan—
> That they should take who have the power,
> And they should keep who can."

Rob Roy was a great man in his day; and in our own times the Californians are the greatest of a great people. That is a fact.

To finish the story of Walker's exploits. The *Anita* safely bore her contingent to "Head Quarters" at Ensenada, and by other opportunities a considerable number of volunteers went thither. They were generally well armed with revolvers, rifles and knives. On their departure, the recorder's court at San Francisco had much less daily business, and the city was happily purged of many of the old squad of rowdies and loafers. Strengthened by such an accession to his forces, opposed to which no body of Mexicans in that part of Lower California could appear in the field, Walker now, with a stroke of his pen, for he is said to be even abler as a writer than as a warrior, abolished the

Republic of "Lower California," and proclaimed in its stead that of "Sonora," which comprised the province of that name and the peninsula itself. Most of the great prizes in the lottery had already been distributed. However, Col. H. P. Watkins, of the *Anita* contingent, had the honor of being appointed the "Vice-President." This gentleman and some of his fellow-dignitaries subsequently underwent a trial at San Francisco for their filibustering practices, the result of which will be noticed under the proper date. In Lower California, various "decrees," proclamations and addresses to the natives and to his own soldiers were made by the "President." They dwelt upon the "holiness" of the invaders' cause, and were very grandiloquent. The march was being formed for Sonora, straight.

Meanwhile, dissensions were breaking out among the men. The rank and file, the tag, rag and bobtail of the expedition, had considerable difficulty in digesting the stolen or scrip-bought beef, always beef, and Indian corn, always corn, that formed their rations. They fancied that their officers "fared sumptuously every day," which very likely was not the case. Any thing will serve as an excuse for behavior that has been predetermined. So these epicures and haters of beef and corn, to the number of fifty or sixty, gave up, without a sigh, Walker, Sonora and their frugal meals. Other desertions subsequently took place, and the staunch filibusters were gradually reduced to a very few. To improve the moral tone of his army, Walker caused two of his people to be shot and other two to be flogged and expelled, partly for pilfering and partly for desertion. The San Franciscan journals had now little mercy on the expedition and all connected with it. It was a farce, they said; and its end was just what they had expected. For a while there remained a remnant of the filibusters loafing about Ensenada, or Santo Tomas—or God knows where—looking, like the immortal Micawber, for "something to turn up." Subsequently, however, as will hereafter be seen, they surrendered themselves as prisoners to the United States authorities.

DECEMBER 24th.—Opening of the "Metropolitan Theatre." Theatricals, and especially that class of them in which music bears a considerable share, have always been largely patronized by the San Franciscans. It was thought proper to have a more magnificent temple for dramatic and operatic entertainments than any hitherto erected in the city, and the "Metropolitan" accordingly was built and opened. This is one of the finest theatres in America, and is distinguished by the beautiful and chaste appearance of the interior. The house is built of brick. The management of the theatre was under the care of Mrs. Catherine N. Sinclair. She opened the splendid structure with an excellent stock company, among whom there immediately began to appear "stars" of the first magnitude, which have since continued in rapid succession. The prices of admission were—for the orchestra and private boxes, $3, for the dress circle and parquette, $2, and for the second and third circles, $1. The *School for Scandal*, in which Mr. James E. Murdock played the part of "Charles Surface," and Mrs. Sinclair, the manageress, that of "Lady Teazle," and the farce of *Little Toddlekins*, were the performances of the evening.

December 26th.—Great sale of one hundred and twenty water lots belonging to the city, when the gross sum realized was $1,193,550. These lots formed in all four small sized blocks of land, covered with water, lying upon each side of Commercial street wharf. They extended between Sacramento and Clay streets, and from Davis street eastward two blocks. Most of the lots measured twenty-five feet in front to a street, and fifty-nine feet nine inches in depth. These brought on an average between $8,000 and $9,000 a lot. The corner lots, which faced two streets, brought from $15,000 to $16,000. A few larger lots brought from $20,000 to $27,000. There was an average depth of about eight feet of water, at low tide, upon these blocks of land; and to make them fit to receive buildings would require the expenditure of large sums of money. The enormous prices obtained for such small lots of ground, "covered with water," show the confidence which capitalists had in the future prosperity of the city. The sale was only for ninety-nine years, after March, 1851, being the period for which the State had conveyed the property to the city. In terms of the original grant, the city was obliged to pay over to the State twenty-five *per cent.* of the proceeds of the sale. The sum of $185,000 was likewise appropriated to satisfy any claims which several of the wharf companies adjoining the lots disposed of had pretended to the slips, now sold. After these deductions were made, a very handsome sum was left to replenish the municipal exchequer, and relieve it from many pressing obligations which had been gradually accumulating.

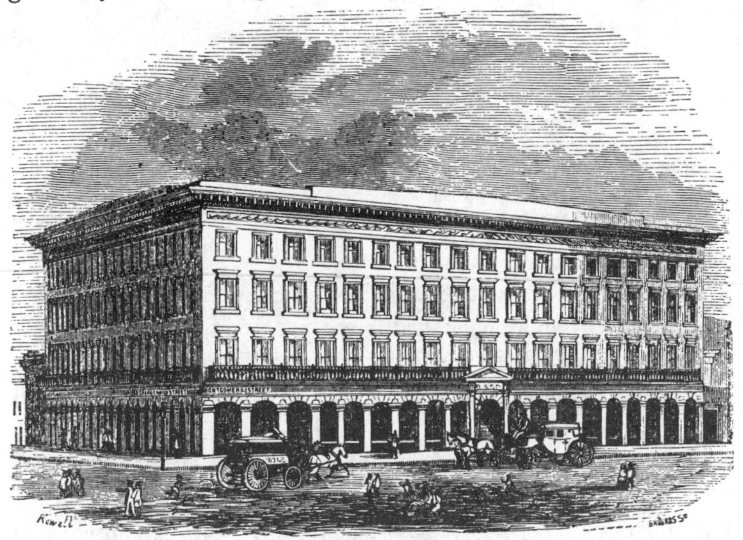

Montgomery Block.

DECEMBER 28th.—Great sale of the State's interest in water property, when lots to the value of $350,000 were sold. This property was situated between Broadway and Pacific streets. It was partly covered with water, and partly dry land, although covered with water in 1849, and is a portion of the property called the "Government Reserve" on the ordinary maps of the city.

The magnificent structure known as "Montgomery Block" was completed toward the close of this year. This is the largest, most elegant, and imposing edifice in California, and would attract especial attention in any city, though it occupies a site that was partially covered by the waters of the bay as late as 1849. It has a front of 122 feet on the west side of Montgomery street, from Washington to Merchant street, along which streets it extends 138 feet, presenting an unbroken façade on these three streets of nearly 400 feet. It is owned by the law firm of Halleck, Peachy, Billings & Parke.

CHAPTER XXVII.

1853.

Numbers and description of the population of the State.—Amount of gold produced from California mines.—San Francisco as related to California.—Population of San Francisco.—City improvements.—Commercial statistics

THE year 1853 was not remarkable for any great increase in the permanent population of California. A vast immigration certainly took place, but the emigration was also very great. Before noticing the estimated increase in the number of inhabitants in San Francisco, we take this opportunity of making a few remarks on the progress of population in the country at large.

The Government census, taken at the close of 1852, returned the population of California at 264,435; but this number was considered by those best able to judge to be considerably understated. In his message communicating the census returns to the Legislature, the governor of the State, commenting upon them, expressed his belief that the population of the country, at the close of 1852, might properly be estimated at 308,000 persons of both sexes, and of all races and ages. In 1853, it was supposed that the immigration by land from the United States and Mexico amounted to about 15,000 persons, while the number of those leaving California by land was too inconsiderable to affect materially any calculations on the subject. The number of immigrants by sea, who landed at San Francisco, was about 34,000, while the departures were about 31,000. There were, therefore, probably about 18,000 persons, on the whole, added to the population of the country. If this number be added to the *estimated* number at the close of 1852, it will appear that at the close of the following year the total population of California was

326,000 persons. As while we write, in the spring of 1854, the ordinary immigration of the year has not fairly commenced, which, however, promises to be very large, the last-mentioned number may be taken as a fair approximation to the present number of inhabitants. Estimates have been made, at different times, of the various *races* forming the total number, but none of these can be confidently relied upon. The French and German peoples generally claim a greater number of their countrymen in California than the Americans are willing to allow. The following may be taken as a rough calculation on this subject. Under the term "Americans" are included the natives of Great Britain and Ireland, who are less easily distinguishable from native Americans than are other foreigners. Many, however, of the British-born, are American by adoption and naturalization. Since the common language of the Americans and British is English, and their customs and habits of thought are generally the same, there seems no impropriety in calling them all in California simply Americans. At the same time, it may be observed that the vast majority of those so called are really natives of the United States :—

Americans, 204,000 ; Germans, 30,000 ; French, 28,000 ; Hispano-Americans, 20,000 ; all other foreigners of white extraction, 5,000 ; Chinese, 17,000 ; Indians (estimated by the census agents at 33,000, which number is considered much too high), 20,000 ; Negroes, 2,000 ; total, 326,000.

Of this number, about 100,000 are believed to be working miners, the remainder forming the population of the different towns and the pastoral and agricultural districts of the country. It is estimated that there are about 65,000 women in the country and perhaps 30,000 children. In the mining regions the females are much fewer relatively to the local population than in the towns. As among the Indians and the native Californians the sexes may be supposed to be nearly equal, it will be seen that among the other races, the number of females must be very small in proportion to the number of male inhabitants. The class of small farmers and generally the agricultural population increased considerably during 1853. They produced a large portion of the provisions which supplied the wants of the people ; and it is probable that in a few years the State will be altogether independent of foreign supplies in the great staples which support life.

The quantity of gold produced from the Californian mines cannot be correctly ascertained, though reasonable approximations on the subject may be made. The custom-house returns at San Francisco do not show the great amount of gold carried off by private parties, and not manifested, nor the quantity retained in the country, where the circulation of local gold pieces is very large. Perhaps the quantity of gold dust deposited and coined at the different mints of the United States, with a fair allowance for what may be shipped directly or transhipped to foreign countries, and used in manufactures throughout the Union, and as coin in California itself, and what may be still in the hands of miners and others, may make a sufficiently exact statement on the subject. This allowance, after a careful consideration of many circumstances, we would put, for the last five or six years, at $44,000,000, which we think moderate. The total production of the different years may therefore be estimated, and given as follows:

	Deposits at the various mints of Californian gold.	Total estimated produce.
1848	$45,301	$3,000,000
1849	6,151,360	25,000,000
1850	36,273,097	40,000,000
1851	55,938,232	60,000,000
1852	53,452,567	63,000,000
1853	55,113,487	65,000,000
Add, the manifested shipments of gold dust from San Francisco in the month of December, 1853, but which would not be deposited at the mints until January following	4,846,743	
	$211,820,787	$256,000,000

As manifested in the custom-house, the export of gold from San Francisco, during 1853, was $54,906,956 74. Of this amount, the sum of $47,914,448 was for New York; $4,795,662 for London; $926,134 for China; $445,778 for Valparaiso; $390,781 for New Orleans; $191,000 for the Sandwich Islands,—and the remainder for New South Wales and various ports on the Pacific.

It will be observed that between six and seven millions were shipped, during the last year, directly to foreign countries, and would not therefore appear in the returns of the United States mints.

It seems unnecessary, in the "Annals of San Francisco," to enter more largely into the mere statistics of gold. The yearly production has steadily continued to increase, and the manifested semi-monthly shipments of specie regularly range from two to three millions. These shipments, as we have explained, do not show the total production, since large quantities of dust are carried off by private parties, which do not appear in the custom-house records. In the beginning of 1854 the mines are unusually productive ; and so far as can be estimated, the total production of the year named may be expected to show a considerable increase on the production of 1853.

It is admitted by all who bestow a moment's attention upon the subject, that hitherto it has been gold, almost alone, which has given such an impetus to the progress of California at large, and particularly to San Francisco. The latter is the one great port through which the enormous foreign supplies of provisions and all other kinds of goods pass to the interior, and from whence the payments in gold dust are shipped abroad. Most of the miners reach California by way of San Francisco, and all who leave the country depart from the same city. Many years hence the fertile and genial California will be a rich and populous country, irrespective entirely of her mineral wealth ; and as farming, and, by and by, manufacturing immigrants pour in, that time will be hastened. San Francisco will then, as now, be the great port of the State, and the emporium of a vast commerce. The Atlantic and Pacific Railway, which has been discussed for so many years, and which must soon be really set agoing, will increase to an incalculable extent the population and prosperity both of California and San Francisco. By whatever route the proposed railroad communication is made, our city must be the chief terminus on the Pacific. Meanwhile, she is closely dependent for prosperity upon the success of the miners and the increasing production of gold. If these grow fewer, or the production be seriously reduced, San Francisco must suffer most severely for a time. From the figures given above, it appears that the annual production of gold has been steadily increasing; while, from what is known of the character of the mining regions, there seems no reason to fear a serious falling off in the amount for many years to come. Scientific apparatus and superior methods of working are every year being applied to the auriferous earth and rocks, which readily yield richer returns than ever. Long before the mining districts can be worked out, for profitable labor, San Francisco will have the millions of California for supporters of her commerce and patrons of her magnificence. Hitherto she has been, and from her unequalled maritime position, her wealth, population and enterprise, must always be, the financial and political, the vital centre of the State.

During 1853, the population of San Francisco was considerably increased. At the close of the year, the city was estimated to contain nearly fifty thousand inhabitants, or more than a seventh part of the whole population of California. It is true that many of these were only temporary residents, but as they gradually left the city, their places were supplied by an equally large number of occasional visitors or fresh immigrants. The population, permanent and fluctuating, was composed of all kindreds and peoples, and may be divided thus:

Americans (including British and Irish born—who probably amounted to one-sixth of the number), 32,000; Germans, 5,500; French, 5,000; Hispano-Americans, 3,000; other races of white extraction, and negroes, 1,500; Chinese, 3,000; total 50,000.

About 8,000 of this population are females, and 3,000 children; while the great majority of the remainder are men between the ages of twenty and forty years. The greatest number of votes given at any one election have, however, been only 11,000. This is partly explained by the fact that a large portion of the adult males are neither native nor naturalized citizens.

San Francisco, during 1853, was particularly improved by the erection of a large number of elegant and substantial fireproof brick and stone buildings. Some of these would be remarkable in any country for their great size, strength and beauty. The principal portion of them are situated on the east side of the plaza, in Montgomery, Battery, Sansome and Front streets, and in those parts of the cross thoroughfares, from Jackson to California streets, inclusive, that touch or lie between those first named. There are also many fine brick buildings in Stockton street. "Montgomery Block" has upwards of one hundred and fifty rooms, and the "New Rassette House," nearly two hundred and fifty. Such great structures, the piles called the "Armory Hall," the "Express building," the "Custom-House Block," and many others of nearly as grand a character, have cost enormous sums of money to build. At North Beach, Mission Bay and Pleasant and Happy Valleys, many elegant private dwellings and manufacturing establishments have been reared, and on Rincon Point towers the splendid United States Marine Hospital, surrounded on the land sides by numerous elegant structures. Some of the more finely finished edifices have either the whole front or the lower story formed of polished Chinese granite; while the fronts of nearly all the larger buildings, constructed of brick, are covered with a fine gray-colored mastic which gives them all the appearance of being made of stone. The distant reader can scarcely have any proper conception of the magnificence of some of these edifices, so different from the character of buildings which were constructed in the early years of the great cities on the Atlantic border. It was the repeated recurrence in former days of conflagrations, which occasionally destroyed half the city, and the perpetual liability, from local position, to similar disasters, that induced capitalists to endeavor to make the best and most valuable portion of the city thoroughly fire-proof. To accomplish that, a peculiarly massive and imposing style of architecture has been adopted, the character of which has been more particularly noticed in a previous page. The later fire-proof buildings, like the earlier ones, are all provided with exterior window-shutters and doors of thick wrought-iron. This circumstance gives the best street architecture of San Francisco an appearance which is peculiar to itself. Engraved illustrations can scarcely represent the general *effect*, arising from the cause, and which the actual spectator feels.

While in the centre of the city these great buildings were rapidly rising, in the districts beyond and in the outskirts, other material improvements, in levelling the unequal ground and erecting additional houses, generally of frame, and in the formation of gardens, were being daily carried on. A second and a third time, new and supposed better street grades were being everywhere established. To carry out these, enormous and costly excavations had to be made at particular localities, while at others immense mounds of earth had to be thrown over deep valleys. Generally the streets in the lower part of the city were raised several feet above the former height, while on the high grounds towards the north and west, the lines of streets had to be lowered from ten to fifty feet. Although the city generally may in the end be much improved by the adoption of these grades, the necessity thereby created of excavating, or of filling up the building lots along the artificial street line, and of raising or of lowering substantial buildings already erected, to suit the new level, has caused incalculable injury and loss to individual citizens. Perhaps, under the existing plan of San Francisco, which, as we have elsewhere explained, is on the principle of strait lines of street crossing each other at right angles, without regard to the natural inequalities of the ground, something like the existing grades of the streets was unavoidable, if a prudent regard was to be had to the future appearance of the city and convenient access to the remotest parts of it. But on viewing the sad destruction of property caused to particular persons by these new grades, we are only the more imbittered against the original designers of the town for their absurd mathematical notions. If the great thoroughfares had been adapted to the natural configuration of the tract of country upon which the city stands, there might have been some apparent irregularity in the plan, and some, perhaps some little ground available for building purposes lost, yet many millions of dollars would have been saved to the community at large, which, as matters stand, have already been unprofitably expended, while millions more must still be spent in overcoming the obstacles wilfully placed in the way by the originally defective plans.

But leaving such unprofitable discussion, we may only remark that owing to the adoption of these new grades, an immense deal of labor was performed during the year, both in forming the streets themselves and in altering the buildings along the sides of them. Many new streets were planked for the first time, and some of the old ones replanked. Planking has served well in the infancy of the city, but it is probable that so perishable a material will soon give place to cobble-stones or Macadamized paving, or even square dressed blocks of granite or whinstone. San Francisco, like Rome, cannot be built in a day. Already, portions of Montgomery and Washington streets are finely laid down with cobble-stones. Meanwhile, the streets in general have gradually been getting into clean and regular order, and have a pleasant appearance. They and the buildings lining them are in many respects equal, and in some respects superior to the streets and buildings of long established and populous cities in the Atlantic States. The San Franciscans are proud of their noble city that sits enthroned beside calm waters, and as Queen of the Pacific receives homage and tribute from all seas and oceans. Richly freighted ships from every land visit her harbor. Her buildings are becoming palaces, and her merchants, princes. Wealth, gayety and luxury characterize her people. She is fast approaching that peculiar and regal character which in days of old was borne by the great maritime cities of the Mediterranean, in more recent times by Venice and Genoa, and perhaps at this date by Amsterdam and St. Petersburgh. Like the great mercantile cities of the past, San Francisco may fall in her pride; but centuries shall first pass. She is very young yet, and has a long age of growing grandeur before her. The commerce of the Pacific is only beginning, and with its certain increase will San Francisco certainly wax greater and more marvellous. Her spirit is GO AHEAD! We have seen her, but a few years since, only a barren waste of sand-hills—a paltry village—a thriving little town—a budding city of canvas, then of wood, and next a great metropolis of brick. In a few years more, if she be not changed into marble, like Augustan Rome, she may be turned into as beautiful and enduring substance, into Chinese or rather Californian granite. After the wonders we have already seen, and part of which we have described, nothing seems impossible in the progress of San Francisco. Her future will be far more glorious than even the present. As the lover expatiates rapturously upon his mistress, whose perfections, though nature may have been bountiful, he chiefly himself creates, so do the San Franciscans speak of their beloved city, whose magnificence is principally the work of their own hands. Some glorification is natural and allowable on the subject.

To give a general notion of the condition in some respects of the city at the close of 1853, we here present a variety of miscellaneous statistical facts. These have been drawn from the columns of various newspapers of the day, from the city directory, custom house and other records, and from personal observation.

San Francisco, at the close of 1853, is divided into 8 wards for municipal purposes, and has nearly 250 public streets and alleys open, many of which are graded and substantially planked. It has 2 public squares formed and already surrounded by buildings. Besides an immense number of handsome and commodious edifices of frame, there are 626 brick or stone buildings, already erected or in course of erection, within the limits of Broadway and Bush street, Stockton street and the water front. Of these 350 are two stories in height; 154, three stories; 83, one story; 34, four stories; 3, five stories; and 1, six stories. Many of the houses are very large, and a few rival in size and grandeur the finest buildings in the United States. Nearly one half of the whole number were built during 1853, and about two thirds have been constructed in the most substantial manner, and made secure against the hottest fires. The real estate of the city was valued, on the 1st of July, at $28,880,200. As, since that period, this kind of property has risen twenty-five per cent. in marketable value, while extensive improvements were making in the interval, the valuation will justify an increase of $10,000,000 on the estimate made in the summer. There are 160 hotels and public houses with a descriptive name, 66 restaurants and coffee saloons, 63 bakeries, 5 public markets and 43 private ones, 20 bathing establishments, 15 flour and saw mills, 13 foundries and iron works, and 18 public stables.

There are 19 banking firms, of which more than one-half are extensive establishments of the highest credit; and the operations of a single one, including its agencies, have been $80,000,000 in one year. There are 9 fire, life and marine insurance companies. There are 10 public schools, with 21 teachers, and 1250 scholars, besides several private educational establishments. There are 18 churches, and about 8000 church members. There are 6 military companies (one of them, however, being chiefly for target practice), with 350 members in all, of which number about 260 are on active duty. The companies have a common armory and drill room. There are 14 fire companies, numbering about 840 members, with 12 engines, and 3 hook and ladder trucks. There are 38 large public cisterns for the use of the fire companies. There are 2 government hospitals, 1 hospital in the course of erection by a benevolent society, and an alms-house, all having together about 600 patients, besides private establishments of the same nature. There are 8 lodges of secret benevolent associations, and 4 public benevolent societies, connected with different races. There is a fine law library, and, be it said, about 200 attorneys. There are all the usual public buildings which are required in a city of the size, a handsome city hall, a jail, post-office, custom-house, and city, county and state court rooms of various denominations. There is also a mint erecting. There are a great number of societies for mercantile, professional, literary, social and religious purposes, among which are the Chamber of Commerce, a gas and water company, a plank road and various wharf companies, the Mercantile Library Association, the Christian Library Association, Bible and tract societies, several asylums for orphans, the California Pioneers, the Philharmonic Society, the Medical Society, the New England Society, the *Turnverein* (Gymnastic Society), the *Saengerbund* (Singer's band), the San Francisco *Verein*, and the German Club. There are resident consuls for 27 foreign governments. There are 12 daily newspapers, of which 8 are morning papers, 3 evening papers, and 1 a German morning paper. There are 2 tri-weeklies, both of them French; and 6 weeklies, of which 3 are religious, 1 commercial, 1 French, and 1 a Sunday paper. There are 2 monthly publications, of which 1 is an agricultural journal, and the other literary. Among places of public amusement, there are 5 American theatres (generally three or four of which are at all times open), a French theatre, a musical hall for concerts, balls, lectures, exhibitions, &c., a gymnasium and two race courses. During the year, there were open, besides the American and French theatres, a German theatre, a Spanish theatre, and a Chinese theatre. The billiard rooms, and the public and private places at which gambling is carried on, can scarcely be counted; and the same may be said of the places where vast quantities of intoxicating liquors are daily consumed.

There are 18 ocean steamers, of which 8 run to Panama, 4 to San Juan del Sud, 2 to Oregon, and 4 to points on the coast of California; and there are 23 river steamers, which ply to different parts on the bay and its tributaries. There is one line of daily stages to San José, another to the Red Woods, and one thrice a week to Monterey. There are regular lines of omnibuses on the plank roads, which run to the mission every half hour. There is a magnetic telegraph eight miles in length, from Point Lobos, for reporting vessels; and another, extending altogether upwards of three hundred miles, to Marysville, through San José, Stockton and Sacramento. There are 2 great, and some smaller express companies, which convey letters and packages to all parts of the Union, and to many foreign countries. The great Atlantic mails leave twice a month, *via* Panama; and there are daily mails to all places of importance around the bay or on the Sacramento and San Joaquin Rivers. For nearly two months, in the summer of 1853, a weekly mail left for the Eastern States, but this, not being sufficiently supported by government, came abruptly to an end. About 1,000,000 of letters were sent during the year to foreign and Atlantic ports.

The settled portion of the city covers about three square miles. The principal part of the business is carried on in houses erected on piles, or built on earth filled in where the waves of the bay rolled three years ago. There are 2 plank roads to the mission, and one across the hills on Pacific street, on the way to the presidio. There are 12 large wharves projecting directly into the stream, besides nearly as many small cross ones. About 2½ miles of streets and wharves are made on piles over the water.

During 1853, there were, in round numbers, imported into San Francisco, 100,000,000 pounds of flour and meal, worth $5,000,000; 20,000,000 pounds of butter, worth $4,000,000; 25,000,000 pounds of barley, worth $500,000; nearly 80,000,000 feet of lumber, worth $4,000,000; 29,500 casks, and 12,000 packages, of hams; 8,400 tierces, hogsheads and casks, 700 barrels and 9,400 boxes, of bacon; 51,000 barrels of pork; 16,000 barrels of beef; about 40,000 barrels of refined, and 160,000 bags, 3,000 barrels and 4,000 boxes, of raw sugars; 100,000 boxes of soap; 170,000 cases of candles; 1,100,000 pounds of tea; 115,000 bags of coffee, (not including some 13,000 boxes of the article ground); 2,300 tierces, and 14,000 barrels of Carolina rice, and over 400,000 bags of foreign rice; and, of unspecified provisions, 50 tons and 55,000 packages. There were also imported, among a variety of other articles, 67,600 cases of boots and shoes; 31,000 bales, 20,000 cases and boxes, and 6,000 packages, of dry goods; 80,000 tons of coal, and 550,000 packages of unspecified merchandise. Likewise, whiskey equal to 20,000 barrels, and 400 barrels of rum; 9,000 casks, hogsheads and pipes, 13,000 barrels, 2,600 kegs and 6,000 cases, of brandy; 34,000 baskets of champagne; and, of other wines, 9,150 hogsheads and casks, 2,500 barrels, 1,800 kegs and 156,000 cases. To complete the long list of "drinks," there were also imported, of beer, 24,000 casks and hogsheads, 13,000 barrels, and 23,000 cases and boxes; and of "unspecified liquors," 5,000 pipes and casks, 6,000 barrels, 5,000 kegs, 8,000 cases and 1,600 packages. These importations were to supply the wants of fewer than four hundred thousand persons, resident in California and Oregon, and some of them in the Sandwich Islands. The total imports of the year were about 745,000 tons of goods, and were valued at upwards of $35,000,000; or, on an average, two tons, and about $100 for every person in the State of California and Territory of Oregon. The freights to vessels coming into San Francisco during the year were $11,752,084; and the duties collected at the custom house were $2,581,975. The only exports worthy of notice were about $65,000,000 of gold dust (part only of which was manifested), and 18,800 flasks of quicksilver, valued at $683,189.

The arrivals of the year were 1028 vessels, of 558,755 tons (though carrying about one-third more), and the departures were 1653 vessels, of 640,072 tons. Of the entrances, 634 vessels, of 428,914 tons, were American, and 394 vessels, of 126,880 tons, were foreign. The difference between the statements of the entrances and departures arises chiefly from the circumstance that the many vessels engaged in the Californian coasting trade were cleared, but not entered in the custom house. The quickest passages of the year were made by the *Flying Fish* and the *John Gilpin*, both "clipper ships." These were from New York, and arrived on the 31st January, and 2d February, in 92 and 97 days respectively. At the close of the year, there were 72 square rigged sailing vessels in the port, consisting of 21 ships, 36 barques, and 15 brigs. A few weeks, and sometimes a few days only, were now sufficient to discharge the largest vessels, and fit them ready to depart again for sea. Besides the vessels mentioned as being in port, there was also there a proportion of the large ocean steamers and those that plied along the coast, and in the bay and tributaries. Many old "forty-niners" and other vessels that had arrived in various late years, served as storeships, or lay dismantled and neglected in various parts of the harbor.

CHAPTER XXVIII.

1853.

Prosperity of San Francisco.—Business activity.—Fortunes rapidly made.—Disputes concerning titles to real estate.—Real property commanding extravagantly high prices.—Social, moral and intellectual characteristics.—Gambling.—Vice less concealed in San Francisco than in other cities.—The female population.—Expenses of house-keeping.—Foreign population.—The marvellous progress of the city during the past few years.

MANY of the observations regarding San Francisco and its citizens made in the reviews of the several years since 1849, and in the chronological order of the proper "Annals," may be fitly applied in describing the place and people at the present time. Cities change neither their moral nor physical nature in a twelvemonth. The same broad characteristics that marked the first great increase in the number of inhabitants are still visible. At the beginning of 1854, the citizens are as remarkable, as in 1849 they were, for energy for good and evil, and the power of overcoming physical obstacles, and creating mighty material changes. Every where in the city is the workman busy at his trade. Laborers of various kinds are still hewing down the rocky hills, excavating the streets, grading and planking them; they are levelling building lots, and rearing mammoth hotels, hospitals, stores, and other edifices; they are piling and capping water lots, and raising a new town upon the deep; gas and water works are forming; sand hills are being continually shifted, and cast, piecemeal, into the bay. The wharves are constantly lined with clipper and other ships, the discharge of whose cargoes gives employment to an army of sailors and boatmen, stevedores and 'longshoremen. The streets are crowded with wagons and vehicles of every description, bearing goods to and from the huge stores and warehouses. The merchant and his clerk are busily buying and selling, bartering and delivering; and fleets of steamers in the bay and rivers are conveying the greater part of the goods disposed of to the interior towns and mining districts. The ocean is covered with a multitude of ships that bear all manner of luxuries and necessaries to San Francisco. *Seven hundred and forty-five thousand tons of the most valuable goods were brought into port in one year.* All the inhabitants of the city are in some measure engaged in commerce, or in those manufactures and trades that directly enable it to be profitably carried on, or in supplying the wants, the necessities and extravagances of the proper commercial community. The gold of the mines pays for every thing, and it all passes through San Francisco. Elsewhere we have talked of the high ordinary prices of labor, and the assurance of employment to the earnest workman, who is not above turning his hand to any kind of work, however severe and irksome it may be.

Numerous fortunes were rapidly made in the early days of San Francisco, when the golden gains were shared among a few long-headed speculators, who fattened on the public means, or who took advantage of peculiar circumstances, or who had fortune absolutely thrust upon them by lucky accident. The ordinary rates of profit in all kinds of business were very great, and unless the recipients squandered their gains in gambling, debauchery, and extravagance, they were certain in a very short time to grow rich. Capital, when lent, gave at all times a return of from thirty to sixty *per cent. per annum*, with the best real security that the country and the times could afford. In two years' space, the financier doubled his capital, without risk or trouble to himself; and the accumulation went on in geometrical progression. But chiefly it was the holders of real estate that made the greatest fortunes. The possession of a small piece of building ground in or about the centre of business was a fortune in itself. Those lucky people who held lots from the times before the discovery of gold, or who shortly afterwards managed to secure them, were suddenly enriched, beyond their first most sanguine hopes. The enormous rents paid for the use of ground and temporary buildings in 1849 made all men covetous of real estate. By far the greater part had originally belonged to the city, formerly the so-called pueblo, or village of Yerba Buena; but the guardians of its interests, from the conquest downwards, liberally helped themselves and their friends to all the choice lots. In later years, the unappropriated lots were more remote from the centre of business, although the gradual increase of population was constantly adding to their value. Numerous attempts were then made to filch from the city its more distant tracts of land, and these were often successful. Meanwhile, the legal title of the city itself to all its original estate was disputed, and hosts of rival claimants started up. Conflicting decisions on the subject were given in the courts of law, and all was uncertainty and confusion, violence, ending sometimes in death to the parties, and interminable litigation. The great value of the coveted grounds led to reckless squatterism, and titles by opposite claimants, three or four deep, were pretended to almost every single lot within the municipal bounds. Those who had really made permanent improvements, or who held actual and lucrative possession, might defy the squatter; but the multitude of unimproved land and water lots, and the large tracts around the business part of the city, upon which as yet there was not even a fence, were fair spoils to the resolute invader. No matter what previous title was alleged; all titles were doubtful—except possession perhaps, which was the best. We have, under different dates, noticed at length the speculations of the city guardians in real estate, the Colton grants, Peter Smith sales, and squatter outrages.

The temptation to perpetrate any trick, crime, or violence, to acquire real estate, seemed to be irresistible, when the great returns drawn from it were considered. The reader in the Atlantic States, who may think of the usual cheapness of land in new towns, can scarcely realize the enormous prices chargeable in San Francisco for the most paltry accommodation. We have seen the excessive rents paid in 1849. Four years later, they were nearly as high. The commonest shops, or counting-rooms, in ordinary situations, would rent at from $200 to $400 per month, while larger ones would readily bring $500 and $600. Capacious and handsome stores, auctioneers' halls, and the like, in desirable localities, would often be held at $1000 per month, or more.

The rents of the larger hotels, of the restaurants, coffee saloons, gambling and billiard rooms, and of the finer stores and warehouses, would appear almost incredible to the distant reader. Ordinary stores, offices, and dwelling-houses were rented at equally extravagant sums. One paid away a moderate fortune as a year's rent for but a sorry possession. The profits of general business were so great that large rents, before they became quite so enormous, were readily given. Capitalists built more and handsomer houses, which were tenanted as soon as ready for occupation. In a couple of years, the building speculator in real estate had all his outlay (which, since labor and materials were so very high, was exceedingly great) returned to him in the shape of rents. Henceforward his property was a very mine of wealth. As rents rose, so did the prices of such property. The richest men in San Francisco have made the best portion of their wealth by the possession of real estate.

For several years, rents and the marketable value of real estate had been slowly, though steadily rising. Towards the close of 1853, they were at the highest. At that period, and generally over a great part of the year named, trade and commerce in San Francisco were unprofitable, and in many cases conducted at a serious loss. An excessive importation of goods, far exceeding the wants of California, and which arose doubtless from the large profits obtained by shippers during the previous year, led to a general fall in prices, and occasionally to a complete stagnation in trade. Then it was found that the whole business of the city seemed to be carried on merely to pay rents. A serious fall in these, and in the price of real estate, more especially of unimproved land, followed this discovery, some notice of which will be given in a subsequent chapter.

As we have said, during 1853, most of the moral, intellectual, and social characteristics of the inhabitants of San Francisco were nearly as already described in the reviews of previous years. There was still the old reckless energy, the old love of pleasure, the fast making and fast spending of money, the old hard labor and wild delights, jobberies and official and political corruption, thefts, robberies and violent assaults, murders, duels and suicides, gambling, drinking, and general extravagance and dissipation. The material city was immensely improved in magnificence, and its people generally had an unswerving faith in its glorious future. Most of them were removed from social trammels, and all from the salutary checks of a high moral public opinion. They had wealth at command, and all the passions of youth were burning within them. They often, therefore, outraged public decency ; yet somehow the oldest residenters and the very family men loved the place, with all its brave wickedness and splendid folly.

Interior of the El Dorado.

In previous chapters we have dwelt so fully upon the general practice of gambling in San Francisco, that it seems unnecessary to do more than merely allude to it in this portion of the "Annals." The city has been long made notorious abroad for this vice. Though not now practised to the large extent of former years, gambling is still very prevalent among many classes of the inhabitants. The large public saloons, so numerous in 1849, and immediately succeeding years, have become few in number at the date of writing (April, 1854). The chief of them are the "El Dorado," on the plaza, and the "Arcade" and "Polka," in Commercial street. These places still exhibit the old lascivious pictures on the walls, while orchestral music, excellently performed, continues to allure the idle, the homeless and familyless, as to a place of enjoyment, where their earnings are foolishly spent. The cards are often still dealt out and the wheels turned, or dice thrown, by beautiful women, well skilled in the arts calculated to allure, betray and ruin the unfortunate men who become their too willing victims. About the wharves, and in various inferior streets, there are other public gaming tables, of a lower description, where the miner particularly is duly fleeced of his bags of dust. There are also some half a dozen noted houses, of a semi-public character, where play is largely carried on by the higher order of citizens. In these places, sumptuous refreshments are provided gratuitously for visitors. The keepers are wealthy men, and move in the better social circles of the town. At their "banks," single stakes are quite frequently made as high as a thousand dollars, and even five thousand dollars are often deposited upon one hazard. The "bankers," however, are not too proud to accept a single dollar stake. The game played is faro. At such places, very large sums are lost and won; and many fine fellows have been ruined there, as well in mind as in pocket. In strictly private circles, there is likewise a great deal of play carried on, involving large sums. The good old game of "long whist" is ridiculously slow and scientific for the financial operations of the true gambler, and the seducing "poker" is what is generally preferred. All these things unhappily harmonize but too well with the general speculative spirit that marks the people of San Francisco.

Though there be much vice in San Francisco, one virtue—though perhaps a negative one, the citizens at least have. They are not hypocrites, who pretend to high qualities which they do not possess. In great cities of the old world, or it may be even in those of the pseudo-righteous New England States, there may be quite as much crime and vice committed as in San Francisco, only the customs of the former places throw a decent shade over the grosser, viler aspects. The criminal, the fool, and the voluptuary are not allowed to boast, directly or indirectly, of their bad, base, or foolish deeds, as is so often done in California. Yet these deeds are none the less blamable on that account, nor perhaps are our citizens to be more blamed because they often seek not to disguise their faults. Many things that are considered morally and socially wrong by others at a distance, are not so viewed by San Franciscans when done among themselves. It is the hurt done to a man's own conscience that often constitutes the chief harm of an improper action; and if San Franciscans conscientiously think that, after all, their wild and pleasant life is not so very, very wrong, neither is it so really and truly wrong as the puritanic and affectedly virtuous people of Maine-liquor-prohibition, and of foreign lands would fain believe.

There was a small, though steady increase, during the year in the number of female immigrants. New domestic circles were formed, and the happy homes of old countries were growing more numerous. Yet while there are very many beautiful, modest, and virtuous women in San Francisco, fit friends and companions to honest men, it may be said that numbers of the sex have fallen very readily into the evil ways of the place. Perhaps the more "lovely" they were, the more readily they "stooped to folly." It is difficult for any woman, however pure, to preserve an unblemished reputation in a community like San Francisco, where there is so great a majority of men, and where so many are unprincipled in mind and debauchees by inclination. Not all women are unchaste whom voluptuaries and scandal-mongers may wish to think such. The wives and daughters of respectable citizens must be held pure and worthy. Their presence here confers inestimable blessings upon society. There are known mistresses and common prostitutes enough left to bring disgrace upon the place. By the laws of California divorces are readily obtainable by both husband and wife, one of whom may think him or herself injured by the unfaithful or cruel conduct of the other, and who, perhaps, disliking his or her mate, or loving another, may wish to break the bonds of wedlock. Divorces are accordingly growing very numerous here, and have helped to raise a general calumny against the sex. Some of the newspapers now regularly give, without comment, these "matrimonial

San Francisco Beauties—the Celestial, the Señora, and Madame.

jars" as pieces of news in their columns, facetiously placing "divorces" between the ordinary lists of "marriages" and "deaths." Like the male inhabitants, the females of San Francisco are among the finest specimens, physically, of the sex, that can anywhere be seen.

The subject of females naturally introduces that of housekeeping; and we accordingly take occasion here to mention a few items regarding the expenses of a family in San Francisco at the beginning of 1854. The wages of female servants are from fifty to seventy-five dollars per month. Wood costs fifteen dollars per cord; coal, per hundred-pound sack, three dollars; and the same, per ton, delivered, fifty dollars. At market, the best cuts of beef, pork, and mutton, are thirty-seven and a half cents per pound; venison is thirty-one cents; salmon, twenty-five cents;

best fresh butter, one dollar; second quality of the same, seventy-five cents; Goshen butter, fifty cents; fresh eggs, one dollar and twenty-five cents per dozen; Boston eggs, seventy-five cents per dozen; turkeys, six to ten dollars each; wild geese, or ducks, one dollar each; chickens, two dollars and fifty cents to three dollars each; quails, six dollars per dozen; potatoes, two to three cents per pound; cabbages, twenty-five cents a head; cauliflowers, thirty-seven to fifty cents each; turnips, parsnips, and beets, one dollar per dozen; milk, twenty-five cents per quart. Rents of dwelling-houses vary from fifteen or twenty dollars per month, for a single small apartment, up to five hundred dollars per month, or what more one will, if a stylish mansion must be had.

The multitude of foreign races in San Francisco, French, Germans, and Hispano-Americans, with all their different complexions, tongues, modes of dressing, amusements, manner of living, and occupations, so different from those of the Americans, and the numerous half-helot tribes of Chinese, Lascars, and negroes, who are still more unlike our people in their natural and acquired characteristics,—all make the city the most curious Babel of a place imaginable. There are many less, though still considerable shades of difference existing among Americans themselves, who are drawn from all corners of the Union, and between them and the various distinctive natives of the British Isles. Again, there are numerous individuals from European countries, not yet named, such as Italians, Spaniards, Greeks, Dutch, Danes, Swedes, and others. All these peoples, differing in language, blood, and religion, in color and other physical marks, in dress and personal manners, mental habits, hopes, joys, fears, and pursuits, and in a multitude of nice particulars, stamp upon San Francisco a peculiarly striking and motley character. The traveller and the student of mankind will meet here with specimens of nearly every race upon earth, whether they be red, yellow, black, or white. Many of them are still seen in their national state, or at least with the broadest traces of their native qualities. In some respects, however, perhaps most of them have been deeply impressed by the genius of the place. Such show the peculiar mark of Young America on the Pacific—the Californian, and especially the San Franciscan "go-ahead" disposition. Let the immigrant be from what country and of what personal temperament and character he may, a short residence here will make him a shrewder and more energetic man, who works harder, lives faster, and enjoys more of both intellectual and sensuous existence than he would be

Colored population—Greaser, Chinaman, and Negro.

able to do in any other land. On any occasion of public excitement, such as a fire, a fight, an indignation or filibustering meeting, or the like, there is gathered together a multitude, which cannot be paralleled in any other place, of stalwart, bearded men, most of whom are in the early prime of life, fine, healthy, handsome fellows. The variety and confusion of tongues and personal characteristics, the evident physical strength, reckless bravery, and intelligence of the crowd, make a *tout ensemble* that is very awful to contemplate. Turn these men into an angry mob, armed, as at all times most of them secretly are, with revolvers and bowie-knives, and a legion of drilled soldiers could scarcely stand before them. These youthful giants are the working spirits of San Francisco, that have given it a world-wide fame for good and evil.

When the early California pioneer wandered through the city, and contrasted the lofty structures which he saw on all sides; the broad, level, and bustling streets, the chief of them formed where once rolled the long swell of the sea; the great fire-proof warehouses and stores, filled with the most valuable products of all lands; the wharves, crowded with the largest and finest vessels in the world; the banks, hotels, theatres, gambling saloons, billiard-rooms and ball-rooms, churches, hospitals and schools, gin palaces and brick palaces; the imposing shops, within whose plate-glass windows were displayed the richest assortment of articles of refined taste and luxury; the vast amount of coined money incessantly circulating from hand to hand; the lively and brilliant array of horse and carriage riders; the trains of lovely women, and the crowds of well-dressed, eager men, natives of every country on the globe, most of whom were in the flower of life, and many were very models of manly or of feminine beauty—for the cripple, the hunchback, the maimed and deformed find not their way hither—when the veteran immigrant contrasted these things with what had been only a few years before, he could scarcely persuade himself that all the wonders he saw and heard were aught but a dream. The humble adobes, and paltry wooden sheds; the bleak sand hills, thinly dotted with miserable shrubs; the careless, unlettered, ignorant, yet somewhat gallant Californians; the few ragged Indians and fewer free white men; the trifling trade and gentle stir of the recently founded settlement of Yerba Buena, where coin was a curiosity; the great mud flat of the cove with its half dozen smacks or fishing boats, canted half over at low tide, and perhaps a mile farther out, a solitary square-rigged ship, the peaceful aspect of the *village* of the olden time—all flashed across the gazer's memory. Before one hair had turned gray, ere almost the sucking babe had learned his letters, the magic change had been accomplished. Plutus rattled his money bags, and straightway the world ran to gather the falling pieces. The meanest yet most powerful of gods waved his golden wand, and lo! the desert became a great city. This is an age of marvels; and we have seen and mingled in them. Let the pioneer rub his eyes: it is no *mirage*, no Aladdin's palace that he sees—but real, substantial tenements—real men and women—an enduring, magnificent city.

When the later pioneer took *his* sentimental stroll, memory only recalled the frantic scenes of the memorable '49—a period that never can be forgotton by those who saw and shared in its glorious confusion. The lottery of life that then existed; the wild business and wilder amusements; the boundless hopes; the ingenious, desperate speculations; the fortunes made in a day and lost or squandered nearly as quickly; the insatiable spirit of play; the midnight orgies; the reckless daring of all things; the miserable shanties and tents; the half-savage, crime and poverty-stained, joyous multitudes, who had hastened from the remotest parts of the earth, to run a terrible career, to win a new name, fortune and happiness, or perish in the struggle; the commingling of races, of all ranks and conditions of society; the incessant rains and deep sloughs in the streets, with their layers, fourteen feet deep, of hams, hardware, and boxes of tobacco, where among clamorous and reckless crowds people *achieved* the dangerous passage; the physical discomforts; the sickness, desertion, despair and death of old, heart-broken shipmates and boyhood companions, whom remorse could not bring again to life, nor soothe the penitent for his cruel neglect; the rotting, abandoned fleets in the bay; the crime, violence, vice, folly, brutal desires and ruinous habits; the general *hell* (not to talk profanely) of the place and people—these things, and many of a like saddening or triumphant nature, filled the mind of the moralizing "forty-niner."

If these pioneers—and like them every later adventurer to California may think and feel, for all have contributed something to the work—lent themselves to the enthusiasm and fancy of the moment, they might be tempted with the Eastern king to proudly exclaim, and as truly: *Is not this great Babylon that I have built, for the house of the kingdom, by the might of my power, and for the honor of my majesty?* Many obstacles, both

LITH. OF SARONY & Co. N. York

SAN FRANCISCO IN 1854.

FROM THE HEAD OF SACRAMENTO ST.

of a physical and moral nature, have been encountered and gradually overcome before the grand result was obtained. Hills were removed and the deep sea filled up. Town after town was built, only to be consumed. Great fires destroyed in one hour the labor of months and years. Commercial crises and stagnation in trade came to crush individuals. The vagabonds and scoundrels of foreign lands, and those too of the federal Union, were loosed upon the city. Robbers, incendiaries and murderers, political plunderers, faithless "fathers" and officials, lawless squatters, daring and organized criminals of every description, all the worst moral elements of other societies, were concentrated here, to retard, and if possible finally destroy the prosperity of the place. All were successively mastered. Yet the excesses of the "Hounds," the scenes of the great fires, the action of the "Vigilance Committee," and the crimes that created it, the multitude of indignation meetings and times of popular strife, the squatter riots, and the daily occurrence of every kind of violent outrage—whatever was most terrible in the history of the city, will ever be remembered by the early citizens. Some of the worst of these things will never again occur ; and others are being yearly modified, and deprived of much of their old frightful character. For the honest, industrious and peaceable man, San Francisco is now as safe a residence as he can find in any other large city. For the rowdy and "shoulder-striker," the drunkard, the insolent, foul-mouthed speaker, the quarrelsome, desperate politician and calumnious writer, the gambler, the daring speculator in strange ways of business, it is a dangerous place to dwell in. There are many of such characters here, and it is principally their excesses and quarrels that make our sad daily record of murders, duels, and suicides.

CHAPTER XXIX.

1854.

Meeting of citizens regarding the State Revenue Act.—Run on Adams & Co.—Banking and banking-houses.—The Express Building.—Weather unusually cold.—Effects of the weather upon the interests of the country.—Le Count & Strong's Directory for 1854.—Loss of the clipper ship San Francisco.—The city lighted with gas.—Riot at the Mercantile Hotel.

JANUARY 9th.—Large public meeting held, of parties chiefly interested, at the Merchants' Exchange, to consider the effect of certain late decisions by the Supreme Court, which had established the constitutionality of the State Revenue Act of 15th May, 1853. Many of the provisions in this Act, such as the heavy license duties laid upon auctioneers and others; the duty of one *per cent.* chargeable on goods and real estate exposed to auction; that of "ten cents upon each one hundred dollars of business estimated to be transacted" by bankers, and dealers in exchanges, stocks, gold dust, and similar occupations; and particularly the tax of sixty cents *per* one hundred dollars laid upon "consigned goods," were considered to be unequal, oppressive and unconstitutional in their operation. The following were declared to be "consigned goods" within the meaning and intent of the Act: "All goods, wares, merchandise, provisions, or any other property whatsoever, brought or received within this State (California) from any other State, or from any foreign country, to be sold in this State, owned by any person or persons not domiciled in this State." It was estimated, that if the tax upon "consigned goods" were enforced, an annual burden of $300,000 would be laid upon shippers to the port. In like manner, the tax upon the sales of personal property, to say nothing of those of real estate, would form a burden of $125,000 annually; while the duties leviable upon the banking class would be so monstrous that their business could not be carried on. The parties against whom these duties were leviable, refused to pay them; and accordingly actions had been raised by the proper officials on the part of the State to try their legality. The Supreme Court of California had just established that point in favor of the State, but those who were affected by the obnoxious provisions of the Revenue Act still refused to acknowledge their validity.

At the meeting above mentioned (Alfred Dewitt, *chairman*), resolutions were unanimously passed—condemning the objectionable parts of the Revenue Act as "flagrantly oppressive and unjust"—declaring that they never would be submitted to, until "all lawful and proper methods of redress should be exhausted"—instructing counsel to move for a rehearing of the case before the Supreme Court, and to prosecute all appeals that could be made to the Supreme Court of the United States—that a memorial should be prepared and laid before the Legislature praying for a repeal of the Act complained of—and that various committees should be appointed to collect subscriptions from the citizens and carry out the views expressed in the resolutions. Such committees were accordingly chosen, and the meeting separated.

While we write, the matters complained of remain in an unsatisfactory and unsettled state. The law has not been enforced and there is considerable doubt whether it ever can or will be. The subject is one of great importance to the prosperity of San Francisco, and has added strength and bitterness to the charges often made against the Legislature, that it consults in its proceedings more the interests of the mining and agricultural than of the commercial portion of the State.

January 18th.—Run upon Adams & Co., bankers. This commenced on the evening of the 17th, and continued all next day. It arose from the circumstance that the name of Adams & Co. did not appear among the published list of those who had exported gold by the semi-monthly steamers. The firm named had actually shipped their usual quantity of specie, but this fact was not known to the public. Upwards of a thousand of the smaller depositors took the alarm, and hastened to withdraw their money. The house, whose solvency was undoubted by large capitalists, was well able to meet the unexpected demand, and, by the close of business on the 18th, had paid out $416,000. In a short time afterwards, their old customers gladly re-deposited the sums so hastily drawn. We take this opportunity to make a few remarks upon banking in San Francisco.

There are no chartered banks in California. By the Constitution, no corporation for banking purposes can exist in the State, nor is any species of paper circulation admitted. The first regular banking house in San Francisco was established on the 9th day of January, 1849, under the firm of Naglee & Sinton. Their "Exchange and Deposit Office" was on Kearny street, fronting the plaza, in the building known as the Parker House, and on the site of the present City Hall. Mr. Sinton soon retired from the firm. The business was then continued by Mr. Naglee until the run already noticed, on the bank, in September 1850, when he closed. Prior to the opening of this office, deposits were made with the different mercantile houses having safes, such as Ward & Co.; W. H. Davis; Mellus, Howard & Co.; Dewitt & Harrison; Cross & Co.; Macondray & Co., and others. This was not only the case at San Francisco, but at places in the interior. At Sutter's Fort, and afterwards at Sacramento City, the principal houses of deposit were S. Brannan & Co.; Hensley, Reading & Co.; and Priest, Lee & Co.

As the population increased, the work of receiving and paying out deposits became so great, that the necessity of houses devoted especially to the business began to be felt; and these accordingly were soon established. At the close of 1849, the following houses were in operation:

Henry M. Naglee..................	established	January 9th,	1849.
Burgoyne & Co....................	do	June 5th	"
B. Davidson......................	do	about September	"
Thomas G. Wells (afterwards Wells & Co).	do	do October	"
James King of William............	do	December 5th,	"

Previous to the discovery of gold and the consequent rapid influx of population, there was but very little coin in the country, and that little mostly in the towns of Monterey, San Francisco, San Diego and Los Angeles. Payments throughout the country were frequently made in cattle, hides, &c. The gentleman,—an eminent banker in San Francisco,—from whom we have obtained these and the following facts upon banking, has seen an account, credited, "*by two cows in full*," for a physician's bill of $20. This was in 1847, and near Los Angeles. After the discovery of gold, that substance in its natural state became the currency, and passed in all business operations at $16 per ounce. The scarcity of coin was so great about and for some time after that period, and the demand for it to pay custom-house duties so urgent, that gold dust was frequently offered at $8 and $10 per ounce. This was particularly the case in the months of November and December, 1848. During the same months in 1849, the bankers' rates were as follows: for grain dust, $15.50 to $15.75 per ounce; and for quicksilver dust, $14.50 to $14.75 per ounce. This was when coin was paid out for the dust. When the bankers received it in deposit, they valued it at $16 per ounce and repaid it at the same rate.

D. J. Tallant (now Tallant & Wilde), opened his banking house in February, 1850; and Page, Bacon & Co., and F. Argenti & Co., theirs in June of the same year. Subsequently several others were established. At this date (April, 1854), the following houses are in operation:—Burgoyne & Co., established June 5th, 1849; B. Davidson, September, 1849; James King of Wm., December 5th, 1849; Tallant & Wilde, February, 1850; Page, Bacon & Co., June, 1850; Adams & Co. (first as express agents, now express and banking house); Palmer, Cook & Co.; Drexel, Sather & Church; Robinson & Co. (savings bank); Sanders & Brenham; Carothers, Anderson & Co.; Lucas, Turner & Co.

January 20th.—The "Express Building," north-east corner of Montgomery and California streets, completed, the foundations having been laid in September, 1853. This is another of Mr. Samuel Brannan's magnificent street improvements. The building is seventy-five feet high, having four stories and a basement, and has a front on Montgomery street of sixty-eight feet, and on California street, of sixty-two and a half feet, and cost, exclusive of the land, $180,000. The lot is valued at $100,000. Wells, Fargo & Co., bankers and express agents, and Pollard & Co., real estate and money brokers, occupy the lower floor. In the fourth story the society of California Pioneers have their hall and secretary's office. The remainder of the building is used for a variety of business purposes.

Express Building.

An unusual degree of cold was experienced in San Francisco for several days about this time, exceeding any thing that "the oldest inhabitant" recollected. To-day, ice, in some places an inch thick, was formed in the streets. Within doors, the water in pitchers was generally frozen. At two o'clock P. M., icicles a foot in length hung from the roofs of houses on which the sun had been shining all day. The small lagoons around the city were frozen over, and excellent skating was had on ponds near the mission. The hills in Contra Costa and near the mission had their summits covered with snow.

There is a whimsical notion among native Californians, that the coming of "these Yankee devils" has completely changed the character of the seasons here, the winter months especially being, it is believed, now wetter and colder than before the American advent. The excessive rains of the winters of 1849-50, and 1852-53, lent some fanciful support to the Californian faith. The frosts and snows of January, 1854, seemed to corroborate it. The winter of 1850-51 on the other hand, was warm, dry and agreeable, to a degree seldom experienced even in the usually mild climate of California.

We have alluded here particularly to these facts, from the circumstance that San Francisco is peculiarly dependent on the weather, inasmuch as the character of the latter materially affects the production of gold in the mining regions. Too much water or too little, at particular seasons of the year, will equally prevent mining from being very successful. In summer, the miners are generally engaged at what are called the "wet diggings," in or beside the beds of rivers, when these are low. There, unexpected rains and consequent floods would ruin all their prospects. At other periods of the year, when the rivers are full, the miners work upon the "dry diggings," upon plains, uplands, and in ravines, which are often at a considerable distance from any stream. As, however, large quantities of water are required for the purpose of washing the auriferous earth, rains then become necessary. In many districts at certain seasons, rich "dry diggings" have been prematurely deserted for want of sufficient supplies of water. To rectify this want, large rivers have been turned, at great labor and expense, from their course, and their waters led by artificial channels to whatever places they may be in demand, those persons using the water paying certain rates for the privilege. The water companies, many of which possess large capitals, form peculiar features of the mining districts. They, however, can assist but a small portion of the whole number of "dry diggings," and copious rains are indispensable for the rest. The rains in the early part of the winter of 1853-54 had been very slight; and great inconvenience was experienced at the mines for want of the usual supplies of water. The rivers were too full for "wet diggings," and the plains and hill sides too dry for "dry diggings." The production of gold was therefore materially lessened, and this fact, joined with a glut of imported goods, and heavy charges upon business, particularly the enormous rents, had produced much commercial distress about this period in San Francisco. In the spring of 1854, abundant rains fell, which set the miners all busy at profitable work, and it was expected by many that commerce would consequently revive. Other circumstances, however, prevented that desirable event, which shall be noticed in the next chapter.

FEBRUARY.—Publication of the San Francisco Directory for 1854. This is only noticed from the circumstance of its being much the fullest and most reliable directory that had appeared here. It contained the names and addresses of about twelve thousand persons; and, in an Appendix, a very great deal of useful and curious information about the city. The canvasser and compiler was Frank Rivers. It was published by LeCount & Strong.

FEBRUARY 8th.—Loss of the clipper ship *San Francisco*, from New York to this port. This was a fine new ship of large tonnage, whose cargo was valued at $400,000. In beating through the entrance to the bay, she missed stays and struck the rocks on the north side, opposite Fort Point. This was nearly at the spot where the English outward-bound ship *Jenny Lind*, from the same cause, was wrecked a few months before. The "Golden Gate" is narrow, but the channel is deep and perfectly safe, if only its peculiarities be known and attended to. The loss of the ships named was supposed to be more attributable to the ignorance or neglect of their pilots than to any natural dangers in the place at the time. If it were obligatory on masters of sailing vessels, not small coasters, to employ steam-tugs to bring their ships from outside the Heads into the harbor, such accidents as these could not occur. It appears that twenty-three large vessels have either been wrecked, stranded, or seriously injured in San Francisco Bay since 1850. This number is exclusive of any accidents occurring to vessels at anchor in the roadsteads, or lying at the wharves. The total losses in the harbor, since 1850, are estimated to have exceeded a million and a half dollars.

The wreck of the San Francisco was attended by circumstances very discreditable to some of the people in and around the city. So soon as the occurrence was known, a multitude of plunderers hastened to the wreck, and proceeded to help themselves from the ship's hold. It was in vain that the owners or their agents attempted to drive them away. Some two hundred dare-devil Americans, nearly all armed with the usual weapons, five or six-shooters and bowie knives, were not to be frightened by big words. They stood their ground, and continued to take and rob as they pleased, plundering from each other as well as from the ship. It was said that even some of the soldiers from the presidio crossed the strait, and became wreckers themselves. Then a storm came, and scattered and capsized the deep-laden boats that were bearing the spoil away. Some were carried out to sea, and were lost ; others were swamped close beside the wreck and a few of their passengers were drowned. The number of lives lost could not be exactly ascertained, although it was supposed that, at least, a dozen persons must have perished in the midst of their unhallowed occupation. There were no lives lost of those connected with the *San Francisco*. She was sold after the wreck, as she lay, her contents included, for $12,000. A short time afterwards, and when some of the lighter parts of the cargo had been removed, the ship went to pieces, as had been the case with the *Jenny Lind*, before her.

February 11th.—The city was first lighted with coal gas on the evening of this day. The occasion was celebrated by several hundred citizens at a banquet given by the trustees of the "San Francisco Gas Company," in the Oriental Hotel. Already about three miles of pipes were laid in the streets, to be increased as the public accommodation required. At first, only a few of the principal streets and some of the leading hotels and large mercantile establishments were lighted with gas ; but every day the number is increasing. The "Metropolitan" theatre, a few weeks after this date, adopted the new light. It will, of course, soon become general, and prove a great benefit to the city. When in addition to gas, the leading street-grades are completed, the streets themselves properly paved with stone, and fresh water introduced by the "Mountain Lake Water Company," San Francisco will present an appearance equally agreeable and striking to those who recollect the dangers and troubles of traversing its old swampy paths on dark nights. The price charged by the company for the gas was $15 per thousand feet. In regard to this rate, J. M. Moss, the president of the company, remarked at the entertainment above alluded to, that, considering that in San Francisco the price of coal was $36 to $40 *per* ton—money, 36 *per cent. per annum*—labor, $6 to $7 *per* day—gas was furnished here 50 *per cent.* lower than in New Orleans, and about 20 *per cent.* lower than in New York. The San Francisco Gas Company was incorporated with a capital of $450,000, and their works were commenced in November, 1852. These are situated on Front street, one hundred and thirty-seven and a half feet, extending from Howard to Fremont street, along which streets they have a depth of two hundred and seventy-five feet. The company was organized with the following officers :—*President*—Beverley C. Sanders ; *Vice-President*—J. Mora Moss ; *Secretary*—John Crane ; *Trustees*—B. C. Sanders, J. M. Moss, James Donahue, John H. Saunders, John Crane.

The first street lamps in San Francisco were erected in Merchant street, by Mr. James B. M. Crooks, in October, 1850. They were lighted with oil, and to be paid for by private subscription. The same gentleman had also completed the erection of ninety lamps, on the 20th of February, 1852, on Montgomery, Clay, Washington and Commercial streets, to be paid for in a similar manner. These, with the exception of four posts, were all destroyed by the fire of the 4th of May following. In the autumn of 1852, the common council contracted with Mr. Crooks to light the city within the limits of Battery, Kearny, Jackson and California streets. This contract was carried out until the introduction of gas as above related, by a contract made with Mr. James Donahue for the "San Francisco Gas Company."

FEBRUARY 17th.—A serious riot took place this afternoon at the Mercantile Hotel, when the policemen in their endeavors to perform their duty by apprehending the rioters, were maltreated by them, and severely injured.

CHAPTER XXX.

1854.

Commercial depression.—Decrease in the value of real estate and merchandise.—Combination of the steamboat owners.—Rates of freight and passage on river steamers.—Duels and duelling.—Sale of "government reserve" town lots.—Celebration of St. Patrick's day.—Conviction of filibusters —Opening of the San Francisco branch mint.—The Pacific railroad.—Falling of the U. S. bonded-warehouse.—Explosion of the boiler of the steamboat "Secretary."—Arrival of Chinese immigrants.—Quick passage of the clipper ship "Flying Cloud."—Wreck of the "Golden Fleece."

MARCH.—San Francisco is passing through a time of much mercantile distress. For many months before this period, commercial business had been unprofitable to those conducting it. We have already alluded to the circumstance that an excessive quantity of goods had arrived during the latter part of 1853. In the spring of 1854, importations continued very large. The market was completely glutted, and prices of the great staples of commerce fell day by day. Several bankruptcies ensued, and the whole commercial community were suffering severe losses. The clipper ship *Bald Eagle*, and some other vessels, were fully freighted to New York and other eastern ports with goods similar to those they had recently brought from thence. Besides the general lack of business and low prices of merchandise, one great cause of commercial losses here was the high rents charged for stores and general business premises. During 1853, an unusually large number of expensive fire-proof buildings had been erected, which at first were in great demand at much increased rates. When sales and prices of goods fell off, dealers could no longer afford to pay the raised rents. It was found, at the same time, that builders had been largely anticipating the natural demand for business accommodation, and had erected far more houses than could be profitably occupied. Soon the large number of empty stores forced owners of house property to reduce rents from twenty to thirty *per cent.*; at which reduction not many more tenements were occupied than before.

All this while, as building was briskly going on and rents were rising, the marketable value of all kinds of real estate was greatly enhanced. Unimproved lots, within a wide circle round the settled portions of the city, became suddenly in demand, at many times their recent price. Speculation in real estate was rife, and holders who had the prudence timeously to sell out, realized large sums. Many people thought that surely the advance could not last, but it did; and prices still continued to rise. Had trade been good, it is hard to say how high and how long the increased prices,—great part of which was certainly without just cause,—would have gone on; although doubtless the reaction would have come by and by. The bad condition of commercial affairs, and the reduction in store rents, hastened the downfall. About the close of December, 1853, at the time of the great sales of water lots, prices of real estate were about the highest. Two months later, unimproved town lots were almost unsalable at any price, while house property suffered a fall corresponding to the reduction in rents. This led to the failure of a few speculators in real estate. Looking, disinterestedly, at the great extent of ground around the city still unbuilt upon, the number of empty stores, the acknowledged overdoing of commercial business, and, above all, the comparatively slow rate at which, of late, the population of the State and city is increasing, it appears to us highly probable that many years will pass before the recent high prices be again witnessed. Most likely, the present reduced prices for all kinds of real estate, but more particularly for unimproved lots, will continue, for some months, to fall lower. When the population of the State, and by consequence that of its great port, are materially increased, prices of real estate in San Francisco may be expected to rise far above the present or even the recent high rates.

While there seemed not much hope for any rise in the value of real estate for a long period, prices of merchandise in the latter part of this month began slightly to improve. The prospects of a general European war, and the expected diminution of shipments from other ports to San Francisco, as well as the increasing production of gold at the mines, led to the belief that before long the commercial market would, at last, become again profitable to merchants. All mercantile communities are subject to occasional depression, but these in the end work their own cure. In the instance before us, the chief loss would fall, not upon the general inhabitants of San Francisco,—who only got their merchandise cheaper,—nor even on its many commission merchants; but on the foreign shippers who wilfully and recklessly continued to flood our market with goods that were not wanted at the time.

About this time, a combination was formed among the owners of the various steamboats plying on the bay and interior waters. The capital of this great joint-stock association, called the "California Steam Navigation Company," was declared to be $2,500,000; divided into shares of $1000. It was provided that the partnership should exist for *fifty years* after the 22d day of February, 1854,—that being the date of incorporation. Merchants and others, both in San Francisco and the large interior towns, considered that their interests would be prejudicially affected by this combination, which would, for a time at least, effectually hinder all competition. Very soon, the people of Marysville and Sacramento began to call public meetings, and agitate the question of no monopoly. Preliminary arrangements, while we write, are being undertaken to form companies to start opposition boats.

The rates of freight and passage established by the old combined companies are as follows:—From San Francisco to Sacramento; passage, $10 cabin, and $7 deck; freight, $8 *per* ton. From San Francisco to Marysville; passage, $12 cabin, and $10 deck; freight, $15 *per* ton, and $12 measurement. From San Francisco to Stockton; passage, $10 cabin, and $7 deck; freight, $6 *per* ton.

March 9th.—Much excitement was caused by a duel which took place this day between Mr. Philip W. Thomas, district attorney for Placer County, and Dr. James P. Dickson, of the State Marine Hospital at San Francisco. Mr. Thomas had been challenged by another party for certain derogatory remarks he had made upon the character of the challenger, but had refused to fight a duel with the latter, on some such ground as that he was "no gentleman." Dr. Dickson, a friend of the challenger, thereupon took the quarrel on himself, and in his own name challenged Mr. Thomas. The parties met at Oak Grove, near Sacramento, close by the spot where the fatal duel between Gilbert and Denver had taken place, in August, 1852. On this occasion, the weapons were duelling pistols, and the distance fifteen paces. At the first fire, Dr. Dickson fell mortally wounded. He was shot through the body, and died the same evening. His death was much regretted by a numerous body of friends.

The practice of duelling seemed to be on the increase about this time, and much attention was drawn to the subject. It was admitted to be a barbarous custom, and many suggestions were made as to how it could best be put down. Perhaps a Cervantes or a Butler may hereafter arise to laugh it out of fashion. "Courts of honor," if only patronized by the leading politicians, who are usually here compelled to be great "fire-eaters," might have much influence in banishing the vice from among us. Newspaper editors in California have long been particularly exposed not merely to the literary raking fire of antagonists but to their literal fire. Their professional motto should surely be *tam Marte quam Minerva*—by pen and rifle to do business. Shortly after the Dickson duel, rival editors of the *Alta California* and *Times and Transcript*, of San Francisco, thought fit to afford each other a long shot. Rifles, and forty paces, were of course the weapons and distance. At the third fire, one of the combatants had a good hat spoiled by a ball which passed through it, within an inch of the head that was in it. At the *fifth* fire, the same party received a bullet in his body, and was "satisfied." Only about a hundred persons were witnesses of the occurrence. Usually there is a much larger number of spectators on such occasions. Of course, the duellists and their friends were not molested by the civil authorities. Why should they have been? No legal evidence could be obtained on the subject; and, if it could, no jury would convict. Several other duels were fought during this month; and some others that were feared, or hoped for, were happily nipped in the bud. The excitement, which ran high for a time on the general subject of duelling, and led to many admirable appeals by journalists on the surpassing folly of such encounters, speedily died away.

Elsewhere we have noticed the facts, that the constitution declares all those who have been directly or indirectly concerned in duelling to be incapable of filling any office in the State, and that, notwithstanding, many of the highest officials are notorious for having fought duels. The provision in the constitution is quite inoperative. A general opinion was expressed about this time that the law of Louisiana on this subject should be adopted, which obliges parties, before entering upon any State office to which they may have been elected, to take an oath to the effect that they had not been engaged in any manner of way, as principal or second, in any duelling affair. By striking thus directly at a man's pecuniary interest, Louisiana, formerly noted for duels, has ceased to be so. It is believed by many that such a compulsory oath would materially help to put down duelling in California. Most citizens hope in time to fill some lucrative post in the government, and some of them would pause awhile before they allowed a momentary gratification of passion to spoil all their political prospects. The scheme may be worth trying, although its effect,—where so many in California are neither native nor naturalized citizens, and whom therefore the proposed law would not affect,—might not lead to the universal good anticipated. Still, many who are urged to duelling and who do fight, through mere force of a supposed public opinion or senseless clamor that hounds them on, would be very glad to have the excuse of such a law as is proposed, for their refusal to accept a challenge.

March 9th.—Sales took place this and the next day of the interest which the State had in certain portions of the town lots called the "Government Reserve," when the sum of $241,100 was realized. The prices obtained were considerably lower than what had been freely given at the great sale rather more than two months before.

March 17th.—St. Patrick's day. The Irish population in San Francisco celebrated this occasion in a very grand manner. Two of their associations—the "Hibernian Society of San Francisco," and the "Sons of the Emerald Isle," united in performing the ceremonies. There was a large procession of the members formed, which paraded through the city, and then proceeded to the mission. In the old church there the Rev. Father O'Connell addressed the people in a suitable oration. Previously, they had been entertained by a substantial collation served on the green at the residence of Mr. Wallace, at the mission. The procession

Wilson's Exchange, Sansome Street.

next returned to the city, and made sundry evolutions in the plaza, and marched through some of the principal streets. There were nearly a thousand persons engaged at the ceremony, some hundreds of whom were on horseback. All were dressed in holiday garb, and many wore characteristic green sashes. A fine band of music, and a beautifully painted flag, showing the wolf-dog and harp of Erin, headed the procession. There was much excitement among the Irish citizens, and *Erin go bragh!* was the order of the day. In the evening the festivities were wound up by a grand dinner at Wilson's Exchange (Henry Toomy in the chair), and a splendid ball at the Musical Hall.

March 24th.—Col. H. P. Watkins was this day convicted, in the United States District Court, of setting on foot a military expedition against the Republic of Mexico—in other words, of "filibusterism." This gentleman had been "Vice-President" of the new Republics of Lower California and Sonora. Though he was found guilty by a jury of the alleged offence, it is not to be supposed that the general opinions of the inhabitants of California on the subject of filibustering expeditions were different from those which have been previously mentioned. If the very judge in his charge to the jury on this occasion could openly declare his sympathy with the prisoner, it may naturally be supposed that the people in general felt and expressed a similar sentiment. Judge Hoffman, who presided at the trial, is reported to have thus spoken: "From my heart I sympathize with the accused, but I am sworn to the execution of the law, and must discharge my duty, whatever my sympathies may be. To the law and to the evidence then we must turn our exclusive attention. I may admire the spirited men who have gone forth on these expeditions, to upbuild, as they claim, the broken altars, and rekindle the extinguished fires of liberty in Mexico or Lower California. It may be that they are not adventurers, gone forth to build up for themselves a cheap fortune in another land. But even were my opinion of their purposes such, and their objects as glowing and as honorable as depicted by counsel, still, sitting as a judge, I should regard only the single question, has the law been violated?"

The evidence was clear, and decidedly against the accused, and the jury had no help but to convict him. On the 7th of April following, he was sentenced to pay a fine of $1500. On the 10th of the same month, Major Frederick Emory, another of the filibusters, and Secretary of State for the new Republic, entered a plea of "guilty" to a similar charge to that of which Col. Watkins had been convicted. Maj. Emory also was fined $1500. The parties afterwards professed their inability to pay these fines. While we write, it appears to be a doubtful question in law, or in fact, whether they can be compelled either to pay them or to be imprisoned till they do so, and it is probable that neither Col. Watkins nor Maj. Emory will be much troubled about the business. Thus are matters managed in California.

April 3d.—Opening, for business purposes, of the Mint. The bill by the United States Government for the establishment of this much-needed, long looked-for institution, dates so far back as 3d July, 1852; but it was only towards the end of 1853 that active steps were taken to construct the edifice, and provide the necessary machinery. The building is situated in Commercial street, between Montgomery and Kearny streets. It is sixty feet square, and three stories high; it is built of brick, covered

San Francisco United States Branch Mint.

with a fine cement, and is thoroughly fire-proof. The machinery is of the newest, finest and strongest kind used in such establishments. This Mint can coin, in gold, about thirty millions of dollars yearly, in different kinds of pieces, or nearly $100,000 daily. The silver coinage produced by it will be comparatively small.

For some years, many private coining establishments existed here, though, at this date, there is only one in operation. It was, however, the firm of Moffat & Co., long the United States Assay Contractors, which chiefly supplied the large gold coinage that was required by the increasing population and commercial tranactions of the country.

April 10th.—Lecture given by Gov. Isaac J. Stevens, of Washington Territory, in Musical Hall, to a large and respectable audience, on the subject of the great Inter-oceanic Railway. It is evident that the agricultural and other resources of California can never be fairly developed, until some cheaper, more expeditious, and less hazardous and painful mode of reaching the country be provided, than the present overland way across the great plains, or the Isthmus, or round by Cape Horn. What California wants is population; an industrious, active, intelligent population. If the long talked of Atlantic and Pacific Railroad were once formed, the western terminus being in the State, this want would soon be remedied. Three general routes have at different times been proposed for this great undertaking. These are: first, the southern route, which proceeds from Texas through the Mesilla Valley, in the northern part of the Mexican territories, and enters California at the southern extremity of the State; second, the middle route, which proceeds from the State of Missouri across the plains to Utah, and from thence across the Sierra Nevada to some point on the Sacramento River; and third, the northern route, which would connect the basin of the St. Lawrence with Puget Sound, passing along the lines of the Upper Missouri and the Colombia Rivers. This last route lies considerably to the north of California. Gov. Stevens, in his lecture, dwelt much on the advantages which the extreme northern route possessed over all other proposed routes—on its comparatively low levels, its freedom from deep snows, the fertile country in its course, &c. In the present thinly peopled condition of the immense regions which lie between the Eastern States and the Pacific coast, it is probable that no more than one through railway will be made for a great length of time. It is therefore of the utmost consequence to San Francisco, and to California, that that railway should terminate within the bounds of the State, and if possible at its chief city. It should never be forgotten, that Puget Sound offers commercial advantages nearly as many and as great as the Bay of San Francisco presents, for the establishment of a great maritime city upon its shores. If the western terminus of the Inter-oceanic Railway be made at the former great inlet of the sea, immigration will be prematurely diverted from California, and turned directly, and chiefly, to the advantage of a far northern territory. The people of San Francisco and of California, if they study their own interest, will take care that a rival State and city do not suddenly arise to overshadow their own greatness. The best way to maintain the supremacy of the former is to make sure, by all and whatever means, that the *first* great Inter-oceanic Railroad terminate at San Francisco. Later through lines may terminate where they will; only let our city have the first one.

City of Oakland, Contra Costa.

April 10th.—Oakland, on the eastern side of the bay directly opposite San Francisco, is to the latter, something like what Brooklyn is to New York. Between the two former places there are frequent daily opportunities of communication by steamers. Many people who carry on business during the day in San Francisco, have their dwellings and families at Oakland. The latter is one of the sweetest and most beautiful places on the bay. It is a great excursion quarter for holiday folk from San Francisco. As its name implies, Oakland is celebrated for its trees, of the live-oak kind, which give at all times a peculiarly cheerful and refreshing character to the place. Recently a small village, then a thriving town, it has now assumed the name, if not all the pretensions of a city, although the inhabitants number only two or three thousand. Of this date, the first election under the city charter took place, when Mr. Horace W. Carpentier was chosen mayor.

April 12th.—A portion of the U. S. Bonded Warehouse, at the corner of Battery and Union streets, fell. This was only one of several accidents of a like nature which happened about this time. Public attention on this occasion was strongly drawn to the generally inferior character of building materials used in San Francisco, and to the supposed frail condition of many of the most elegant and apparently substantial structures in the city. Not only is the greater part of the materials—such as brick, lime and timber, employed in building, of an inferior quality, but the sites on which the houses have been erected are of a shifting and treacherous nature. Nearly all the edifices situated below the line of Montgomery street have been built on what was only a few years ago the bed of the sea. The mud bottom of Yerba Buena Cove, on which dry sand has been loosely heaped, to form the foundations of these edifices, could scarcely be expected to be very secure. Accordingly, by the unequal sinking of the walls, many fine houses have been, or will soon be, totally ruined. The tides are also continually washing out particles of the loose sand, and thus still more danger is threatened to the stability of many buildings. It seems absolutely necessary for the protection of the lower part of the city, that a great sea wall, on the outer front of the harbor, be soon constructed. Until, however, the various schemes which are being continually hatched, for extending the water front are for ever settled, one way or another, and the really *permanent* water front fixed, nothing can be done regarding a sea wall. If, in addition to such a breastwork against the waves on one side and the rolling sands on the other, the foundations of the larger and more important buildings, to be erected on the "beach and water lots," were deeply and closely piled, much farther security would be obtained for the structures.

April 15th.—Explosion of the boiler of the steamer *Secretary*, while midway between San Francisco and Petaluma. Out of between fifty and sixty persons on board at the time of the accident, upwards of one-half were killed, and nearly all the rest were more or less severely wounded.

April 19th.—The *Lord Warriston* arrived from China with 780 Chinese passengers, 200 of whom were females. About this time, there was a very large immigration of Chinese, and it was understood that many thousand more of these people were only waiting for ships to embark in from the ports of their country for San Francisco. The State and city press discussed at much length the propriety of excluding the race altogether from California, or at all events of only admitting it to labor under certain specified restrictions, particularly reserving the gold mines to the white population. It was admitted on all sides, that the Chinese were naturally an inferior race, both mentally and corporeally, while their personal habits and manner of living were peculiarly repulsive to Americans. It would be out of place in a work of this nature to discuss the general Chinese question, which promises to give much debatable ground for philosophers, statesmen, politicians, and mere laborers in California, for many years to come.

April 20th.—The clipper ship *Flying Cloud* arrived at San Francisco from New York, having accomplished the voyage in eighty-nine days, eight hours. This is the quickest passage recorded as having been made by a sailing vessel between the ports named. On a former occasion, the *Flying Cloud* made the same voyage in eighty-nine days, twenty-one hours.

April 22d.—The *Golden Fleece* was wrecked at Fort Point, on leaving the harbor.

CHAPTER XXXI.

1854.

Trial of the Mexican consul.—Arrest of the French consul.—Chinese newspaper established.—German May-feast at Russ's Garden.—The Hoadley street grades.—Indictment by the Grand Jury of Sonora filibusters.—Dedication of the Lone Mountain Cemetery.—Extensive Conflagration.—Report of the funded debt commissioners.—Squatter difficulties.—Sale of public property.—Captain Adams arrived with the Japan treaty.—Alderman elected.

April 28th.—Conclusion in the U. S. District Court of the trial of the Mexican consul at San Francisco, Don Luis del Valle, for a breach of the neutrality laws. This was only one of a series of important events, connected with the subject, which took place about this time. It appeared that the Mexican consul, some two months before this date, had received instructions from his government, to enlist, or select, a body of emigrants, chiefly of French or German origin, who were to proceed (at the cost of the Mexican Government,) to the province of Sonora. There, after a year's service, they were each to receive a grant of a certain portion of land. The particular service which these emigrants were to render was not exactly known, either by the emigrants themselves or by the federal authorities in San Francisco of the United States, although the latter presumed it was service of a military description. The attention of the federal authorities had been recently attracted to the filibustering movements of Col. Walker and his associates upon Lower California and Sonora. It was understood that the governmental instructions of Gen. John E. Wool, the chief military officer on the Pacific coast, bore particular reference to the necessity of putting down all filibustering schemes whatever. In furtherance of his duty, Gen. Wool took occasion to narrowly watch the proceedings of the Mexican consul in regard to the expedition which he was fitting out for Sonora. The British ship *Challenge*, on board of which five or six hundred of the expeditionists were embarked, was seized, on 29th March, for a violation of the revenue laws; and, under various unusual pretences, was prevented from sailing, until the federal authorities could make up their mind what next to do. On 1st April, the *Challenge* was formally allowed to leave, and on the morning of the following day she sailed. Gen. Wool, just before this time, was of opinion, it was said, that the men in the vessel named, who were bound for Sonora, were proceeding thither only as "colonists." But before the *Challenge* actually sailed, it seemed that the general found reason to change his ideas as to the supposed object of the expedition. Without troubling himself farther with the expeditionists,—the true filibusters, if there had been any filibusterism in the matter,—Gen. Wool immediately caused the necessary steps to be taken to arrest the Mexican consul. The arrest was made on 31st March. The charge against the consul was, his having violated the second section of the law of 1848, which forbids the enlistment, within the territories of the United States, of soldiers to serve under a foreign power.

During the trial, the United States (the prosecutors) found it necessary for their case to procure the testimony of Mons. Patrice Dillon, the French consul in San Francisco. By a consular convention, recently entered into between France and America, it appeared, that consuls of either nation could not be compelled to appear in courts of justice to give evidence, but that they could only be "invited" to do so. Two "invitations," in terms of the convention, were forthwith transmitted to M. Dillon by the court, at the desire of the district attorney. Both of these M. Dillon politely declined. Judge Hoffman, of the U. S. District Court, now held, that he could not, under the circumstances, compel the attendance of the French consul, as a witness for the prosecution.

Señor Del Valle, the defendant in the cause, on the broad constitutional principle, that a party accused is entitled to be confronted with witnesses to prove his innocence, next applied to the court for compulsory process to bring forward M. Dillon. It was not, however, generally supposed that the Mexican consul really wished the presence of his brother consul in court as a witness either for or against him. It was only imagined that the former, or his counsel, believed that they would fail to enforce the attendance of the French consul; and that being the case, and having appeared to consider M. Dillon as a witness most material to the defence, it was expected, that either the district attorney would abandon the process against the Mexican consul, or that the court would dismiss it, or that the jury would return a verdict in his favor, on the ground that he had sustained a constitutional wrong by being deprived of the testimony of a witness said to be essential to the defence. M. Dillon was accordingly cited, in the usual manner, as a witness in the cause for the defendant; but, as had been anticipated, he made no appearance. Judge Hoffman, therefore, issued a writ of *subpœna*, and M. Dillon was forcibly brought into court in custody of the United States marshal. It was now found that some irregularity had taken place in the technical order of proceedings, and the issuing of the warrant was held to be premature. By consent of parties, the pleadings proceeded on the assumption that the warrant of apprehension had not yet been issued. After elaborate pleadings on both sides, where the great question seemed at first to be whether, as the consular convention and the constitution seemed to conflict, the one or the other should yield, Judge Hoffman decided, that they did not conflict, but that virtually, under the consular convention, the French consul must be held to be in this country only in his consular capacity—his true domicile, in the eyes of the law, being France; and that, therefore, he could not legally be compelled to appear in court as a witness. French consuls were thus declared to have some of the most sacred privileges of ambassadors. The decision implied that the defendant, Sr. Del Valle, in the particular case, by not being able to procure the testimony of M. Dillon, suffered no more constitutional wrong, than he would have suffered by not being able to procure the evidence of any witness, alleged to be material to his cause, who might be residing in a foreign country, and therefore not naturally amenable to the jurisdiction of the U. S. District Court. In consequence of this decision, all the rights and privileges which the French consul had claimed at the commencement of the proceedings against him were allowed. Much evil, however, had been done, by the premature and unlawful step of his actual apprehension. M. Dillon had chosen to take high ground in the matter; had presented long protests denying the jurisdiction of the court, and had struck his national flag, considering that the French nation had been insulted in his person, by the proceedings above alluded to. Considerable excitement existed among the French inhabitants of San Francisco on the subject.

In the mean time, the trial of the Mexican consul proceeded, and he was, in the end, found guilty of the offence charged in the indictment. The jury recommended him "to the kind consideration and mercy of the court." The evidence having showed that the French consul had been closely mixed up with the unlawful transactions, M. Dillon was accordingly next arrested, and charged with having "aided and abetted" Sr. Del Valle in the commission of a breach of the neutrality laws. In defence, the French consul, like his Mexican brother, pleaded, *inter alia*, that instead of the expedition by the *Challenge* having been a filibustering one, it was an expedition of the very reverse character. It had been chiefly, if not solely, projected to break up true filibusterism, particularly the schemes of Count Raousset de Boulbon, who had been long notorious for his hostile designs on Sonora. The passengers on board the *Challenge* were chiefly people who had been previously connected with and were attached to Count Boulbon; and who, by the bribe of a free passage to Sonora and the offer of a grant of land there, had been persuaded to desert their former leader and to serve under, and for the Mexican Government, in place of serving against it. In opposition to this argument, it was contended by the prosecution, that, even admitting that the expedition was really of the nature alleged, still it was unlawful under the express terms of the statute. But further, in the case of the French consul, the prosecution maintained, that M. Dillon had only been using Sr. Del Valle as an unconscious tool; and that, while the former pretended only to be aiding the latter in putting down the filibustering projects of Count Boulbon, he, M. Dillon, for purposes of his own or his government, was secretly working in concert with and for the benefit of the count, and with the intention of counteracting the plans of him whom he was professedly assisting but really thwarting—the blind and simple Sr. Del Valle.

After nearly the same evidence had been adduced in the case of the French consul that had been led in the case of the Mexican consul, the jury in the case of the former could not agree, and were discharged. They had been six hours in deliberation, and, at midnight, on 25th May, when they were discharged, it was understood that ten stood for conviction and two for acquittal. In such circumstances, on 29th May, the district attorney entered a *nolle prosequi* in the case of M. Dillon; and in the case of Sr. Del Valle (who had not yet been sentenced, though long before convicted), he moved the court to suspend further proceedings. The effect of this motion was simply to discharge the defendant, and free him from further molestation in the suit.

The various proceedings briefly above narrated lasted during many weeks, and occasioned much local excitement. The revelations made in these trials and in the trial of Col. H. P. Watkins (one of Walker's party), the *ex*-vice-president of the short-lived "Republic of Sonora," showed unmistakably the general loose feeling of society in San Francisco and California on the subject of filibusterism. The imputed motives of certain federal authorities in pushing the former prosecution to a conviction, as well as the supposed guilt or innocence of the accused, with all the mixed character of the expedition and the suspected and attributed opposite reasons of the Mexican and French consuls for being connected with it, were much discussed in private circles and by the public press. Many offensive personal charges were made on both sides. Hearing altogether different statements from opposite counsel, neither of which seemed to be fully established by evidence, an impartial observer could scarcely know what to think of the subject. The consequences of the trials, being of a purely political nature, will fall to be adjusted by the governments of the respective countries involved.

April 29th.—The first number of a Chinese newspaper, called "The Gold Hills' News," appeared to-day. It was a small sheet of four pages, wholly printed in Chinese characters. "Gold Hills" is the Chinese name for San Francisco. There were now English, French, German, Spanish, and Chinese journals published in San Francisco.

May 7th.—The German inhabitants observed in grand style their annual May-feast during this and the following day, at the gardens of Mr. Christian Russ, on the Mission road. Between two and three thousand persons shared in the entertainment.

Celebration at Russ's Garden.

The conductors of the arrangements were the members of the German Turn-verein, or Gymnast Union. These performed a variety of gymnastical feats and much vocal and instrumental music. As we have previously mentioned at some length the annual May festivities of the Germans in San Francisco, we think it unnecessary to do more than merely allude to them on this occasion.

On the 29th of April of this year, the children attending the various public schools of the city held their annual May festival in Musical Hall.

May 12th.—The subject of the street grades had long been a vexatious one. We have already alluded to the grievous loss and injury occasioned to many private citizens by the adoption of the "official," or, as they were commonly called, the "Hoadley grades." As these grades were being carried out, and it was seen that they involved an enormous amount of excavations and the partial destruction of Telegraph Hill, and the other hills to the west of the city, public dissatisfaction was much increased on the subject. In the end, the common council referred the whole matter to the consideration of a committee of three scientific gentlemen, who had no personal interest in the question. Of the above date, these gentlemen presented a long and interesting report to the common council, in which they strongly recommended the abandonment of the "official" or "Hoadley" system of grades. This report was printed for circulation among property holders. Afterwards, an answer by Mr. Miles Hoadley, the city surveyor, was likewise printed and circulated. The boards of aldermen and assistant aldermen then met in joint convention to discuss the subject. On the 26th of May, they referred the report and answer, the remonstrances and petitions of citizens, both for and against the existing and the proposed systems of grades, and generally the whole question, back to the committee already alluded to, for further consideration. While we write, no further action has been taken on the subject. It is probable, however, that material modifications will be made upon the existing "official grades."

MAY 24th.—Of this date, the grand jury found true bills of indictment against William Walker, Howard A. Snow, and John M. Jarnigan. These were severally the president, the secretary of naval affairs, and the secretary of war, of the "Republic of Sonora." The formal conclusion, therefore, of Col. Walker's filibustering expedition against Lower California and Sonora is close at hand. For some months back, the expeditionists had suffered much distress in the lower country. Without sufficient arms or ammunition, or supplies of any kind, and with the Mexican natives bitterly enraged against them, the few filibusters left, who were through necessity, or choice, faithful to each other, only sought safely to leave the country they had invaded, to fly to some neutral soil. As this, however, seemed scarcely practicable, Col. Walker and his party crossed the boundary line, below San Diego, which separated Mexico from the United States, and surrendered themselves prisoners to the federal troops, who were in waiting to receive them. On arriving at San Francisco, on May 15th, the greater number of the prisoners were discharged upon their simple parole. The chief parties were then indicted, as Col. Watkins and Maj. Emory had recently been. The trials of the former have not been set down for hearing at the time of writing this notice. Col. Walker was

Lone Mountain Cemetery.

cited as a witness for the prosecution in the case of the United States *vs.* M. Dillon, referred to above; but he declined to give evidence, on the ground that his doing so might implicate himself.

May 30th.—The "Lone Mountain Cemetery" was solemnly dedicated to-day, when many interesting ceremonies were performed on the ground before a large assemblage of ladies and gentlemen. Col. E. D. Baker delivered an occasional address, Mr. F. B. Austin an ode, Mr. Frank Soulé a poem, Bishop Kip the dedication address, and the Rev. F. T. Gray the closing address. Appropriate hymns and prayers hallowed the new "city of the dead." Herr Mengis, and the singers of the German Turn-verein, performed the musical pieces.

When noticing the projection of this cemetery, under date *November*, 1853, we said, that the tract of land to be used for burial purposes was three hundred and twenty acres in extent, and included the hill, or "mountain," from which it took its name. That was the original intention of the projectors. Subsequently, it was found that one hundred and sixty would form a sufficiently large cemetery, and to that extent the limits of the ground have meanwhile been reduced. The "Lone Mountain" is not situated within the restricted boundaries, but adjoins them on the south. The present mode of access to the cemetery is by a circuitous route, nearly four miles in length, by way of Pacific street and the presidio. When the western extension of Bush street is graded and planked, which is proposed to be done during the summer of 1854, the distance from the plaza to the magnificent gateway of the cemetery, about to be erected at the termination of that extension, will be about two miles.

May 31st.—Fire broke out this morning between two and three o'clock in a grocery, on the east side of Dupont street, between Broadway and Vallejo street. Notwithstanding the efforts of the fire companies, the conflagration raged for two hours, and consumed more than one-half of the entire buildings on the block. Property was destroyed to the estimated value of $50,000. The buildings were all of frame, and some of them were little better than mere shanties. They were tenanted chiefly by Mexicans, French and Germans. The wind was blowing fresh at the time from the south-west. Had it been a little stronger, and its direction from the north-west, from whence it usually blows at this season, a great part of the city might have been laid in ashes. Notwithstanding the great and daily increase of fire-proof buildings in the city, there still exists an immense number of wooden edifices, which may supply fuel for some terrible conflagration to come. About this period of the year, those high winds fairly set in, which fan flames to their height and suddenly communicate them to new materials across wide empty spaces and streets, notwithstanding all the unwearied exertions of perhaps the bravest and most skilful set of firemen in the world. During this month large portions of two important towns in the State were destroyed by fire, when the dreadful summer winds mightily increased the loss and danger. Marysville sustained loss to the amount of $200,000, and Yreka to the amount of $150,000, by the fires alluded to.

May 31st.—The Board of Commissioners of the Funded Debt (now consisting of Messrs. P. A. Morse, D. J. Tallant, Wm. Hooper and Smyth Clark,) present their yearly report. The total amount of bonds issued by the Board, for debts of the city contracted prior to May 1st, 1854, was $1,635,600, of which $126,100 have been redeemed, leaving as the balance of outstanding debt of San Francisco, $1,509,500 ; which, bearing ten *per cent.* interest, requires annually $150,950 to meet that sum. The high price which this stock bears in the Atlantic cities and in Europe, renders it improbable that any more will be offered for redemption, and hence this item of interest may be considered an annual requisition on the city treasury, until the Sinking Fund, under the management of the Board, shall have accumulated sufficient to meet the final payment of the bonds.

June 5th.—The occurrences of the last few weeks have shown the futility of the hope that the recent decisions of the Supreme Court would be sufficient to settle the numerous disputes concerning land titles. Squatters, in the face of law and the decisions of the land commissioners and judges, are endeavoring to maintain their assumptions by force. Much distress has been the result of these proceedings, since every member of the community is liable to become a victim of the robberies of these outlaws—the poor man who owns a single lot, as well as the wealthy proprietor of acres of land. Capt. Joseph L. Folsom, one of the most extensive landholders in the city, has been the principal sufferer by the squatting rascality, but many owners of single spots of ground have been no less unjustly treated ; and one aggravated case particularly has just occurred, in which a poor woman, who owned a solitary house on a small lot, had her house burned down, the land fenced in and herself turned into the street to starve, without even the means to live, and of course unable to resort to a twelvemonth lawsuit in such a place of problematic uncertainties as San Francisco. The evil was unchecked by the authorities; riot followed on riot; the squatters armed themselves and threatened to kill whoever should attempt to dispossess them; and finally executed their threat by murdering Mr. George Dillon Smith, one of Capt. Folsom's party, who were attempting to dislodge a set of squatters on his property in Howard street. Undismayed, squatters on some of Folsom's neighboring lots, fortified their tenements and prepared for resistance. A few days after this affair, a terrible fight on Green street resulted in the fatal wounding of a Mrs. Murphy by a party of squatters, who had attacked her husband's house.

Property-holders at last became seriously alarmed at the progress of these dissensions, and held a meeting, this evening, at the office of Theo. Payne & Co. (Dr. Samuel Merritt, *chairman*), at which Messrs. S. W. Park, Theodore Payne, Dr. Samuel Merritt, T. K. Stevens, Wm. Sharron, Louis McLane, jr., F. A. Woodworth, Jas. C. Ward and Thos. O. Larkin were appointed a committee to draft a plan of organization of a *special police* for the protection of their own property, and to issue a call for a general meeting of citizens to act upon such a plan. On Tuesday (6th inst.), this meeting was held at the Musical Hall, and the report of the committee unanimously adopted by a large body of citizens, who formed themselves into an *Association for the Protection of Property and the Maintenance of Order*, adopting a series of appropriate rules for their government. On the next day the meeting reassembled at the Merchants' Exchange, and completed the organization by electing the following officers:

President.—Col. David S. Turner.
Vice-Presidents.—Benjamin Haywood, G. B. Post, Henry M. Naglee.
Secretary.—Chas. R. Bond.
Treasurer.—Dr. Samuel Merritt.
Executive Committee.—G. B. Post, John Sime, E. J. Hassler, Wilson Flint, F. A. Woodworth, J. P. Manrow, Jas. George, Edward Vischer, Louis Cohen, John C. Maynard, Chas. L. Case, James F. Curtis, Henry M. Naglee, John Perry, jr.

After a general expression of views and intentions the association adjourned, subject to the call of the president. About *one thousand* citizens had enrolled themselves as its members, who were ready at all hazard to defend one another in their rightful possessions. It was not designed, however, like the Vigilance Committee of old, to oppose in any way the legal authorities, although the police had more than once sided rather obviously with the squatters. It was rather hoped that the moral effect of the decided and united action of so many reputable citizens would be sufficient to check any further disturbances, and incite the authorities to something like action. They had had ample premonition that some such rencontres would occur, and were repeatedly told that owners of land would not suffer themselves to be tamely plundered of their property. Promptness and energy on their part could have prevented every outbreak. As we close, inquests are being held over the murdered bodies, and various rioters are detained for trial in the hospitals and prison.

June 6th.—Interest of the State in twenty-two lots in the square bounded by Pacific street and Broadway, Davis and Front streets, sold for over $100,000.

June 8th.—Capt. Adams, U. S. N., arrived *en route* for Washington with the treaty concluded between Com. Perry and the Empire of Japan.

June 12th.—Dr. J. W. Van Zandt was elected Alderman of the Third Ward, to fill the vacancy occasioned by the resignation of R. M. Jessup, Esq.

CHAPTER XXXII.

1854.

Commercial depression.—Reduction of prices of merchandise and real estate.—Fall in rents.—Improved character of the buildings.—The plaza being improved.—Government fortifications of the harbor commenced.—Immigration and emigration.—The population.—Yield of the gold mines.—Labor profitable in California.—The quicksilver mines.—Agricultural resources.—Fisheries.—Telegraphs and railroads.—Ship-building.—Foreign relations.—Ice and coal trade.—Mail steamers between San Francisco and Shanghae.—The international railway.—San Francisco water front extension.—The proposed new city charter.—Claim of the city to pueblo lands.—Increase of sources of domestic comfort.—Immoralities continue to prevail.—Duels and duelling.—Theatrical entertainments.—Daily newspapers.—Means of moral and educational improvement.

July.—It is not very necessary to say much more upon the general physical and moral aspect of San Francisco, than has already been said in reviewing its appearance and characteristics at the close of the year 1853. During the six months immediately preceding the date of the present notice, the city passed through a period of great commercial depression. At this time, the extreme mercantile distress is beginning slowly to disappear ; and the best judges hope that soon again prosperity will visit commerce and all connected with it in San Francisco.

The prices of real estate may, in some few instances, have rallied, but generally they continue much below those readily obtainable at the close of 1853. Many years must pass, and our population be much increased, before those high rates can again be witnessed. While prices of real estate have fallen from twenty to fifty *per cent.*, and in some cases still lower, rents, particularly in the lower or business part of the city, have likewise been considerably reduced. Rents may, perhaps, continue to fall for some time, and yet a fair profit will be left to the owners of house property. The wages of such classes as are employed in building, and the cost of building materials, have both been materially reduced ; so that houses can now be erected at much less expense than formerly.

Arising no doubt partly from this circumstance, and notwithstanding the continued and steady fall in rents and the prices of real estate, a great deal of fire-proof and costly building has been carried on since the beginning of the current year. In Stockton, Montgomery, California, Battery and many other principal streets, the old buildings of frame are being gradually pulled down, and magnificent granite and brick structures are rapidly rising in their stead. Vacant lots in the line of streets over all the business part of the city are being covered with substantial buildings. The new Merchants' Exchange and new U. S. Custom House will be massive and beautiful public edifices. These material improvements are particularly observable upon the northern extremity of Montgomery and Battery streets, at the base of Telegraph Hill. The great depth of water at the wharves in the neighborhood of Clark's Point, which depth, from the character of the shore and tides, will probably long, if not always, exist, will necessarily make that quarter a peculiarly shipping and mercantile part of the city. Accordingly huge hotels and stores, of the most beautiful and substantial character, are rising up in all parts of the district.

At the same time the spirit of improvement is visible over all the other parts of the city. Many new and elegant buildings of brick and stone, within the fire-limits, and chiefly of frame beyond them, are continually being constructed. New streets are being graded and planked, and new public cisterns formed for the use of the fire department. Even the plaza, the long-neglected, miserable plaza, the standing reproach and mockery to the boasted "progress" of our world-renowned city, is being at last, after many years of public agitation, just a little "improved" by its unkind guardians, the city fathers. While we write, it is being graded, and is about to have an iron fence erected around it. The wondrous fabrics of iron and glass, which were to have turned it, as assuredly they would, if properly designed, into a Crystal Palace, or rather into a veritable "Palais Royal," the centre of Californian taste, luxury, fashion and folly, have been all left to the next generation, or perhaps only to the still hopeful projectors and the speculative common council of the next year.

The long-desired fortification of the harbor of San Francisco has been at last commenced by the government. The system proposed consists of two lines of batteries inside the entrance to

The Plaza, or Portsmouth Square, June, 1854.

the harbor. Works are already in process of construction on Fort Point and Alcatraz Island. Point San José and Angel Island will, probably, be selected to complete the line of defence. The fortress at Fort Point, which will be the strongest position, will present one hundred and fifteen guns of eight and ten inch calibre, in four tiers. Directly opposite, on Lime Rock Point, a battery of one hundred guns will complete the outer line. The second point of fortification on the inner line is on Alcatraz Island. The shipping battery here will consist of about fifty guns, with batteries on other points yet to be selected. Majors Barnard and Turner, Capt. Whiting and Lieut. Prince are directing the works, which are estimated to cost not less than two millions of dollars. Much doubt is expressed by officers of high rank as to the sufficiency of water defence—many believing that an invading army could readily land any where between San Francisco and Monterey.

The arrivals for the last six months from the Isthmus, exceeded the departures by several thousands. The immigration of Chinese from their own country during the same period, amounted perhaps to five thousand persons of both sexes, while their emigration was slight. The incomers generally departed, after a short sojourn in San Francisco, to the mines ; so that the general population of the city may still be estimated at the supposed number inhabiting it at the close of 1853, viz., something over *fifty thousand* of both sexes and of all ages and nations. The bulk of the great overland immigration does not appear till the fall of the year. The immigration by land for the approaching season is expected to be very great.

The gold mines, the prime source of prosperity and wealth to California, have not for many years yielded better returns to the labor applied to them, than they have done during 1854, so far as the year has elapsed. Every day new and rich auriferous fields are being discovered, while it is found that the old ones, by the application of more careful and scientific methods of extracting the precious metal, continue to supply an ample reward to the miners. But it is not gold alone that has filled up the replete coffers of the State. The quicksilver mines of Alameda County are the largest yielding and most profitable in the world. The only ones that at all compare with them, are those of Almaden in Spain, and Idria in Austria—tho latter, one of the old monuments of Roman revenue.

But if the success of the miner has been great, how shall we term the unexampled prosperity of the less romantic tiller of the soil. Crops, throughout the State, have been immense, and have had the effect to reduce the prices of articles of food to a very low figure—far lower than they at present are on the Atlantic. The splendid agricultural resources of the country are only beginning to be understood. A new and equally profitable source of employment has been found in the fisheries on the Sacramento and its tributaries. Salmon, sturgeon, pike, perch, dake, chub, suckers, hard-heads, narrow-tails, &c., are being caught in large quantities. The salmon fisheries are the most important—the fish being far over the average size in the East and ranging from twenty to fifty pounds weight. This business must ere long be one of the most considerable items of the commercial resources of California. Who can tell the limit of the capabilities of this State? All it has accomplished is but preparatory to new exhibitions of power and wealth. Its career lies yet before it. The telegraph has already furnished nerves to the land, by which the impulses of its distant parts are communicated to its great *sensorium commune*—its brain at San Francisco. Railroads, too, those great arteries by which vivifying nourishment is carried to and from the remotest members of its body, soon will be completed. The Sacramento Valley Railroad from Sacramento to Mormon Island, now projected, will be the pioneer of this improvement. All these facts, together with the extensive shipbuilding carried on at Happy Valley and the Rincon, are preparing the State, and San Francisco particularly, for the great part she has yet to play. Into the past six years, have been crowded the most remarkable and important events that have occurred to our country since its revolutionary birth; and the great pole to which they have all tended is San Francisco. California henceforth will no longer direct her energies on herself. She has attained her majority and donned her freedom-suit, ready to start upon the field of adventure. Foreign relations are engaging the thoughts of citizens and government; hence the ease with which such expeditions as those of the Count de Boulbon and President Walker are fitted up, and the apparent official countenance bestowed on them. Vessels are already departing for Japan, and numerous companies are being formed for foreign traffic. Two of these are in the full tide of success,—one for the importation of ice from Russian America, and the other for the mining of coal in Bellingham Bay, Puget Sound, Washington Territory. The establishment by Congress of the line of mail steamers between San Francisco and Shanghae, and the great treaty with Japan, come fortuitously to meet and give a field for this new and longing spirit. The Pacific between this country and Asia has at last been bridged over: California, the Sandwich Islands, Japan and China are the great piers—white sails, and great steamers in continuous lines, will span the intervals. Let the Interoceanic

Railway now be built, and San Francisco will then be the great *entrepôt* of America,—the Tyre of the Pacific,—and California, the most populous, enlightened, and civilized country in the world.

The project of extending the water-front of the city (already noticed at length), was revived in the Legislature this year. However, political disputes among its supposed patrons, and the parties pecuniarily interested in the scheme, as well as clamant remonstrances of all San Francisco—collectively, in boards, associations and committees; and individually, by public-meetings and signed petitions—had the effect of causing this unnecessary, unjust, and perhaps "infamous" project, to be abandoned. The new city charter was likewise lost in the Legislature. On the expediency of passing this charter as a whole, public opinion was divided, although many of its provisions were generally admitted to be improvements on the existing charter. Many other bills, introduced in the legislative chambers, and which were peculiarly obnoxious to large classes of the citizens, were likewise lost. While we write, the claim of San Francisco is being pleaded before the Board of Land Commissioners, established by the United States, to settle disputed titles in California to four square leagues of land around the city, in virtue of its being, as alleged, a Mexican "*pueblo.*" Whatever be the result of the claim, many private titles to lots within the municipal bounds will be deeply affected by the decision, and for a time "confusion, worse confounded," will reign among property-holders. Pending the discussion, many parties are busy over all the four square leagues in question, selecting convenient and desirable "claims;" and outrages of a daring description are continually taking place between the old settlers and the new squatters, in consequence of these lawless proceedings.

San Franciscans can now ask for nothing more on the score of domestic comforts. Their streets and houses are well lighted by a beautiful gas-light; they dwell in elegant and handsomely-furnished houses; their tables are largely supplied with fish, flesh, and fowl from the mountains, rivers and valleys of their teeming land; they have pure and limpid water for drink and cleanliness, in no stinted measures; and, finally, they have discovered, near at home, a boundless supply of excellent stone-coal, sufficient to satisfy all their demands for fuel, in cooking their meals, melting their gold, driving their steam-engines and drying their houses in their wet seasons. Bellingham Bay now furnishes the great demand of the city. Hitherto, all the coal used was brought, at great expense, partly from Vancouver's

Charcoal-vender.

Island and Chili, but chiefly from such immense distances as Philadelphia, Liverpool, and other foreign parts. In 1849 and 1850, the townspeople were furnished with fuel by men, chiefly of the lower class of Hispano-Americans, who cut it from the little gnarled oaks and thick brushwood grown on the low sand-hills bordering the town—not a stump of which is now to be seen. Wood and charcoal were brought into the city either on the backs of these men, or in panniers carried by asses, and two dollars were paid for as much as a man could carry in his arms. The charcoal men are yet features of the place. They announce their coming by the ringing of a small bell, and may be seen in every street offering their little bundles for sale.

The old round of business, pleasure, folly, vice and crime, still went merrily on. Cases of *divorce* were nearly as common as cases of drunkenness. Cases of political corruption, of party jobbery, of personal scandal, of ruin by debauchery and gambling, by duelling and suicide, of squatter violence, of robbery and burglary, of assault and murder—why, these were, as before, nearly "as plentiful as blackberries." It is unnecessary to single out particular cases for remark and reproach. Every day produced a new crop of moral weeds. Still San Francisco contrived to flourish, and its people, in their fashion, to enjoy life. To enforce some measure of outward decency, the common council passed a stringent ordinance regarding houses of ill-fame, making the keeping of them highly penal. This ordinance had the effect, for a time, of closing a few of the most notorious Mexican and Chinese brothels. But it was sought to be enforced against fashionable white Cyprians, who had money enough to employ able counsel to show the intrinsically illegal and tyrannous character of its particular provisions; and then it was found to be utterly impracticable in operation. It seemed all at once to be discovered, that the impurity which was hid by walls, could not be put down by mere legislation.

Duels appeared to be getting more numerous. In the months of May and June several fatal "affairs of honor" took place, and the performance with swords by a couple of Frenchmen varied the monotony of pistols and rifles, and introduced a new fashion for the benefit of future gladiators. Occasionally the death of some well-known citizen would rouse the press and the pulpit to a spasmodic burst of indignation and high-toned sentiment against the foolish and criminal practice of settling personal quarrels by mortal combat. The public looked wise, savage, and virtuous, and talked and drank; then it looked wiser, and so on, and talked and drank again. Still nothing was done, or perhaps could be done, in the matter. Grand juries occasionally offered a proper presentment on the subject, but their words fell dead. Men in California, who generally want the peaceful, endearing joys of home and family, which best make life worth living for, set little value on existence, and in their hot rage will hazard it for the veriest trifle.

California Exchange, corner of Clay and Kearny streets, June, 1854.

Theatrical entertainments have never been so well patronized in San Francisco as during the past half year. A rapid succession of musical and dramatic "stars" attracted continual crowds to the various "houses." English, French and Italian versions of the most noted modern operas were excellently performed in the Metropolitan and Union Theatres, where four ladies, who each claimed the rank of *prima donna*, successively appeared. At the theatres named, though particularly at the Metropolitan and American, some of the most celebrated American actors and actresses made their regular nightly appearance. These, it is said, have reaped a large harvest from their professional visit to the land and the city of gold. The San Franciscans, truly, are no niggards with their wealth.

A few of the immense number of daily newspapers, existing at the beginning of 1854, have silently disappeared. In their stead have risen the "Pioneer," a monthly magazine of great typographical beauty and considerable literary merit ; a Chinese journal, and one or two weekly newspapers of fair pretension. The "Mercantile Library Association" has largely increased its stock of books and its members. Churches, schools, and charitable, and other good and laudable associations, flourished contemporaneously with the spread of ignorance, folly and vice, which they have been designed to counteract. A larger female population, and a few more years, and San Francisco may yet be as distinguished for its public and private morals, as it has long unhappily been for the reverse.

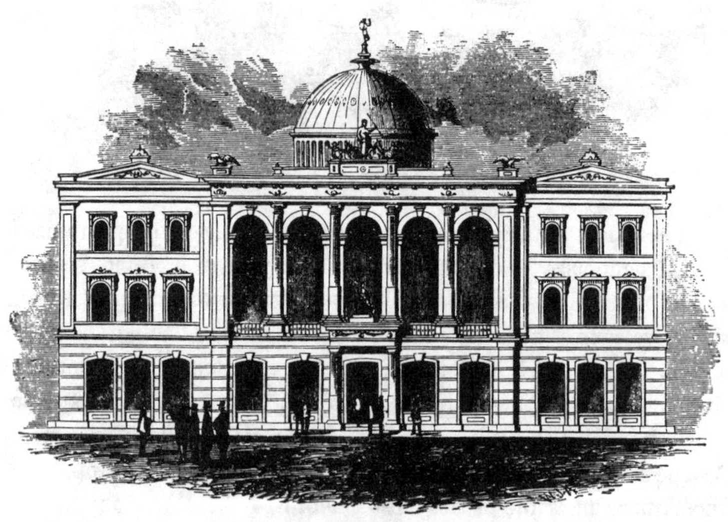

Merchants' Exchange, Battery street.

The Hounds.

PART THIRD.

THE HOUNDS.

In the spring and early summer months of 1849, San Francisco was afflicted with the presence and excesses of a parcel of the veriest rogues and ruffians that ever haunted a community. The first intelligence of the discovery of gold in California naturally sent thither the most daring and clever adventurers of blemished reputation from their own countries, who saw in this modern *Dorado* a fit theatre for the profitable repetition of those tricks and outrages, the exercise of which had rendered their native homes no longer lucrative or safe places to reside in.

Long before any great number of the general public had emigrated from the Atlantic States or from Europe, San Francisco was overrun with such men from the various countries and ports on the Pacific, and particularly from the west coast of the Americas. A little later came stray vagabonds from Australia, where had been collected the choice of the convicted felons of Great Britain. The regiment of New York volunteers, which some time before had been disbanded, and from which so much good had been expected in ultimately peopling the land with first-class settlers, had greatly disappointed the hopes of its projectors and friends. Many of the most noted blackguards of the country turned out to have been formerly soldiers in that corps; and perhaps these very men formed the nucleus and strength of the "hounds" themselves. The very earliest arrivals also from the eastern ports were largely composed of the rowdy and knavish class. They indeed had required no long time to make preparations for the voyage. Their baggage was on their backs, and their purse in every honest man's pocket. They stepped on board the first ship—and hey for California! These vagabonds never intended to follow a reputable calling there, but as sharpers, gamblers, and cheating adventurers in every variety of scheme, were prepared only to prey upon the community at large. Every thing in San Francisco encouraged them to think it was what their fellows would call a safe speculation. The municipal and State organizations were both still unformed, and the few local authorities were quite inadequate to cope with such a body of villainy as was shortly developed.

The "hounds" were the natural consequence of such a state of things. A party, calling themselves by that name, was first faintly heard of towards the close of 1848; but it was only in the spring of the following year that their depredations excited much notice. In the desire to make fortunes easily and in a hurry, the overtoiled people of San Francisco paid little attention to any thing but what immediately concerned themselves individually, and much crime was allowed to be committed with impunity, because nobody cared, or had time to think about it, or to interfere in the matter. Thus the "hounds" had perpetrated many outrages before public indignation was fully aroused.

These were directed chiefly against foreigners—Chilians, Peruvians and Mexicans, as being supposed less able to defend themselves, and who were likewise imagined to possess fewer sympathies from the community in their behalf. This class of the foreign population was generally of the lowest and most degraded character. Their habits were unclean and their manners base. The men seemed deceivers by nature, while the women (for there had been extensive speculators in their own country, who brought many females to San Francisco,) were immodest and impure to a shocking degree. These were washerwomen by day; by night—and, if a dollar could be earned, also by day,—they were only prostitutes. Both sexes lived almost promiscuously in large tents, scattered irregularly upon the hill sides. Their dwellings were dens of infamy, where drunkenness and whoredom, gambling, swindling, cursing and brawling, were constantly going on. Such were the common victims of the "hounds." It may at first sight seem hard to tell which were the worst members of the community.

We have seen that among the first immigrants to the mines were a multitude of foreigners of Spanish extraction, from the various republics and provinces on the Pacific shores of America. The presence of these people—many of whom seemed little better than slaves—in the pay and under the command of their own wealthier countrymen, was considered by the American miners to be unfair towards themselves, as natural lords of the soil, purchased by their own blood and treasure, and as tending to lower both the dignity and profits of gold digging. Many disputes, occasionally attended with bloodshed, had taken place in the mines between the people of the United States and these foreigners, the latter of whom were slowly but surely driven away from the mining districts they had selected, partly by violence, though principally by threats.

This state of matters in the mining districts, which was often not discountenanced, but was even openly approved of by many respectable citizens, as well as the low character of the class alluded to in San Francisco itself, mightily encouraged and lent a flimsy pretext to the criminal attacks by desperadoes in that city against the foreign population. The "hounds," who were a numerous body of youths and men in the prime of life, professed themselves only an association for "mutual defence," but in reality were but a band of self-licensed robbers, who thought every Chileno was fair game for their plundering propensities. They organized themselves so far that they had a place of regular meeting, or *Head Quarters*, which they called *Tammany Hall*, in a large tent, near the City Hotel. Leaders were appointed to conduct operations, and afterwards apportion the spoil. To such a daring extent were matters carried that the body, proud of their strength and numbers, attempted a sort of military display, and on Sundays, armed with bludgeons and loaded revolvers, paraded the streets, in open daylight, with drum and fife playing, and banners flying. It was in the dead of night, however, when their outrages were done. There were then neither lights in the unformed streets, nor a police force to watch over the safety of the town. The well-disposed citizens, fearful of brawls, retired early to their dwellings, and the more noise and rioting they might hear at a distance the closer they crept into bed, or prepared their weapons for the defence alone of their own proper domiciles. At such times the "hounds" would march to the tents of known Chilenos, and tearing them down, rob and spoil the contents of value, and shamefully maltreat and even murder the inmates. At other times they would content themselves with extorting by threats large sums of money and gifts of jewels and articles of value from all classes of foreigners, and sometimes from Americans themselves, though it was seldom they meddled with the latter. A favorite sport was to intrude themselves, even in open day, in a numerous gang, upon taverns and hotels, and demand high priced drinks and food, which on receiving,—for people were too much afraid of their lives and property to refuse,—they would recklessly destroy the furniture nearest at hand, and forthwith decamp as boldly as they had entered, without troubling their heads as to who should pay for the damage or the articles consumed.

This state of things had continued for some months, when in one of their destructive expeditions upon the tents and chattels of the Chilenos, a young man by the name of Beatty, not properly one of themselves, but who happened to be among or near the band at the time, received a fatal shot from one of the attacked foreigners. This roused the "hounds" to vengeance against the whole population of Spanish origin, and they became fiercer and more destructive in their excesses than ever. People now could not avoid taking notice of these lawless abuses; but public indignation was not yet full. About this time the "hounds" changed their name to "regulators," and had the impudence to profess themselves guardians of the community against the encroachments of Spanish foreigners. At the sound of the "assembly beat" on the drum, they would collect in great numbers at "Tammany Hall," ready to commit whatever violence their leaders might direct.

On the afternoon of Sunday, the 15th of July, a large band of the "hounds" or "regulators," returning from a marauding excursion to Contra Costa, determined to signalize the occasion by some new exploits. Armed with firearms and heavy sticks, and under the command of one dressed in regimentals, whom they called *Lieutenant*, they paraded through the town in their usual ridiculous fashion, and towards evening proceeded to attack various Chilian tents. These they violently tore down, plundering them of money and valuables, which they carried away, and totally destroying on the spot such articles as they did not think it worth while to seize. Without provocation, and in cold blood, they barbarously beat with sticks and stones, and cuffed and kicked the unoffending foreigners. Not content with that, they repeatedly and wantonly fired among the injured people, and amid the shrieks of terrified women and groans of wounded men, recklessly continued their terrible course in different quarters, wherever in fact malice or thirst for plunder led them. This was in broad daylight; but there were no individuals brave or foolhardy enough to resist the progress of such a savage mob, whose exact force was unknown, but who were believed to be both numerous and desperate.

On the following day, Monday, the 16th July, when the news of these last outrages were circulated among the citizens, the whole town rose in the greatest state of excitement. Alcalde Leavenworth, who was himself powerless to quell the disturbance, was waited upon by Captain Bezer Simmons and Mr.

Samuel Brannan, and urged by these gentlemen instantly to take some steps to organize the community to protect itself, and put down decidedly these disturbers of the public peace. Thus forced to some definite action, the alcalde the same day issued a proclamation, calling on the public instantly to assemble in Portsmouth Square. At three o'clock of that day, the whole honest part of the community seemed to turn out at the place appointed. Mr. W. D. M. Howard was chosen president of the meeting, and Dr. Victor J. Fourgeaud, secretary. Mr. Samuel Brannan then addressed the meeting, and denounced in forcible terms, the depredations and many crimes of the "hounds." Upon his motion, a subscription list was opened for relief of the sufferers by the riots of the previous evening. It was next suggested that the citizens should organize themselves into a police force to apprehend the criminals and drag them to justice. This was immediately done; and two hundred and thirty people of those present at the meeting enrolled themselves as special constables. The general command of the body was given to Mr. W. E. Spofford, while Messrs. Stevenson, Wadleigh, Simmons, Smith, Turk, Gillespie, Hughes, Priest, Webb and Stevens were appointed captains. They were armed with muskets, sixty of which were furnished gratuitously by Mr. Hiram Webb, now of the firm of Webb & Harris. This volunteer force exerted themselves so diligently, that, in spite of several attempts at open resistance by the "hounds," nearly twenty of the rioters were the same afternoon apprehended, examined and put in prison on board the United States ship "Warren," there being then no safe place on shore in which to keep them in custody. The leader, "Sam" Roberts, was also arrested on his way to Stockton. Mr. A. J. Ellis, who had been chosen to act as sheriff, took an effective part in making these arrests.

The same day another meeting of the citizens was held on Portsmouth Square, at which Dr. Wm. M. Gwin and James C. Ward were unanimously elected associate judges, to relieve from excessive responsibility the alcalde, and to aid him in trying the prisoners. Mr. Horace Hawes was then appointed district attorney, and Mr. Hall McAllister his associate counsel. The next day, Tuesday, a grand jury of twenty-four citizens met, and, upon evidence, found a true bill against Samuel Roberts and other supposed members of the "hounds," to the number of nineteen, on the different charges of conspiracy, riot, robbery, and assault with intent to kill.

The following day, Wednesday, the trials began. All the usual judicial forms were observed, and there was no apparent desire to press harshly on the prisoners. Probably if they had been caught in their very acts of violence on the preceding Sunday, the enraged people would at once have executed popular justice on them; but now public indignation was somewhat calmed, and the trials proceeded with the greatest decorum and impartiality. Francis J. Lippitt, Horace Hawes, Hall McAllister, and Frank Turk appeared as counsel for the people; while P. Barry and Myron Norton were deputed to act for the accused. The judges were the alcalde, T. M. Leavenworth, and Messrs. Gwin and Ward. Counsel for the defence having waived all exceptions to the form of the indictment, a jury was impanelled, consisting of the following named gentlemen:—Thomas B. Winston, J. R. Curtis, J. V. Plume, A. De Witt, Clarence Livingston, Benjamin Reynolds, Z. Cheney, John Sime, William Hood, John W. Thompson, Francis Mellus and Frederick Teschemacker.

Witnesses were next called, on the part of the prosecution, who proved the existence of the association called the "hounds," its organization under leaders, its professed and imputed objects, and general violent proceedings. Other witnesses, among whom were one of the wounded Chilenos, then presumed to be in a dying state, and who subsequently died in consequence of his wounds, established the facts of the riots, assaults and robberies of the Sunday night preceding, and identified some of the prisoners as having been actors in the scene. After some observations by counsel for the defence, evidence was led by them, the drift of which seemed to be to confound the persons of the panels at the bar with those described by the witnesses for the prosecution as having been engaged in the occurrences of Sunday, and in some faint degree also to establish an *alibi*. After an impartial charge by the alcalde, the jury found Roberts, the leader of the gang, guilty of all the counts, and eight others guilty of one or more of them. Roberts and Saunders (another of the more active "hounds,") were then sentenced to ten years imprisonment, with hard labor, in whatever penitentiary the governor of California might direct, and the remainder to imprisonment with hard labor for shorter periods, as well as most of them to considerable fines, some of them also being required to grant bonds for large sums to keep the peace for twelve months. From various circumstances these penalties were never inflicted; but the prisoners, some of whom were sent out of the country, were shortly afterwards set at liberty.

Thus ended the affair of the "hounds," which had alarmed the community so much, and which had compelled them, in the absence of a firm and regular judicature, to take the law into their own hands, and administer justice in a prompt and decisive manner. The early success and safety of the "hounds," for a long period afterwards led to still more daring and criminal excesses on the part of the desperadoes with whom the town continued to be haunted, and who were checked for only a little while in their crimes by the examples made of Roberts and his mates. On the other hand, the ease with which a number of respectable and determined men could thus put down a disorderly gang, afterwards encouraged the formation of the famous "Vigilance Committee" of the year 1851, when, what between theft and burglary, assault, murder and arson on the great scale, it became almost a life and death struggle for the honest citizen to preserve his property and inhabit the town in peace and personal safety. Some of the "hounds," who had escaped the due punishment of their crimes at this time, met it shortly afterwards at the mines, where several of them were unceremoniously hanged, at an hour's notice, by the enraged miners, upon whom they had attempted to try the tricks they had so long played with impunity in San Francisco.

Notwithstanding all that we have said, there is yet another phase of the "hounds" business, which may be just noticed. At that period, there happened to be influential parties in San Francisco, who were determined to make "political capital" for themselves, and who considered that a gentle course of public disturbance, while it might not conduce to any materially evil results, could be employed, or at least its instruments, to facilitate the objects they had in view, and further their own personal interests. These persons were suspected at the time, and long afterwards were known, to have had secret intimacies and mysterious dealings with certain leaders of the "hounds," who undertook to promote the purposes of the former while at the same time they served their own. But the monster, which if not born, was, at least, nursed into strength by these very respectable aspirants, soon outgrew the power of its protectors to keep it within bounds, and became at last their disgrace and terror. Fearful of committing themselves by owning a former connection, however slight, with such a vile association, some of the richest and most influential people in the town calmly heard of all the abuses committed by their *protégés*, but took no steps to quell them. It would be imprudent at this time to mention names, but the fact is so nevertheless. The truly liberal, honest and brave portion of the community had therefore a doubly difficult task to accomplish; for not only had they to put down the "hounds" themselves, who were emboldened to resist by the knowledge that they had "friends at court," but they had also to overcome the unconcealed reluctance of many of their fellow-citizens to move at all in the matter, and to set aside the various obstacles which these factiously were enabled to throw in the way.

Hanging of Whittaker and McKenzie.

THE VIGILANCE COMMITTEE.

THERE is probably no portion of the history of San Francisco which has more excited the attention, the mingled wonder and applause, scorn and indignation of the civilized world, than the proceedings of the famous "Vigilance Committee." To law-loving, peaceable, worthy people in the Atlantic States and Europe, it did certainly seem surprising, that a city really of thirty thousand inhabitants,—though since the population was chiefly composed of male adults, of virtually the pretension, the riches, business and character of a city of twice that number,—should patiently submit to the improvised law and arbitrary will of a secret society among themselves, however numerous, honest and respectable the members might be reputed. Few people, abroad, who had been trained from infancy to revere "the majesty of the law," and who had never seen any crime but what their own strong legal institutions and efficient police could detect and punish, could possibly conceive such a state of things as would justify the formation and independent action of an association which set itself above all formal law, and which openly administered summary justice, or what they called justice, in armed opposition and defiance to the regularly constituted tribunals of the country. Therefore, in other lands, it happened that the Vigilance Committee became often a term of reproach, and people pointed to it as a sign that society in California was utterly and perhaps irredeemably impure and disorganized. In San Francisco itself, while some citizens, it must be confessed, did condemn the proceedings of that body, by far the greater number cordially approved of them. The public press was almost unanimous in its support of the association. The officers of the law were often obliged to take cognizance of the existence and actions of the committee, and thought it a matter of public duty to denounce them; but many of even these parties, in private conversation, and still more in heart, applauded the course which had been adopted by their fellow-citizens.

We have already had occasion to mention the affair of the "hounds" in 1849. The summary measures taken at that period by the people had the effect, for a while, of keeping the blackguards who had been long infesting the city within some moderate bounds. But the great immigration in the fall of that year, and the confusion in San Francisco which followed, naturally encouraged new depredations, which in the bustle of the time and place were unnoticed and unfelt by any but the actual victims. Over all California it was the same. The inroad of nearly a hundred thousand *strangers*, who were likewise strangers to each other, scattered among a dozen newly established towns, and over the various mining districts, and who themselves knew not the laws of the land, and perhaps expected, as they could find, no protection from them, but trusted only to their own watchfulness and revolvers, produced a state of things which greatly favored the increase of crime. In 1850, a similar vast immigration took place. The legal institutions and executive, that just before had served the needs of a population of twenty or thirty thousand, now failed to secure safety to a quarter of a million, in which number were some of the most daring and clever rascals in the world. Among the immigrants were many of the same stamp with the older criminals of the country, and who readily aided in the lawless exploits of the latter. When the towns, or any particular localities, became too hot to hold them, the mining regions, over a length of seven hundred miles, were ready to receive and shelter the fugitives. After a few months, under a new garb and name, the rascals would boldly return to their former haunts, and with impunity commit new crimes. Society was every where continually changing; while disguised in every imaginable way, by dress and an *alias*, and not least by the growth and trimming of the beard, it was almost impossible that the old offenders could be recognized. The natural migration of honest diggers from mine to mine, often far distant from each other, and to the greater towns to spend their gains or recruit their health, was so great, that no notice could be taken, by the really few permanent residents in any place, of the arrival and departure of strangers, or of those traits in their behavior which might have seemed strange and suspicious, if witnessed by idle, inquisitive people of long settled lands. While this constant immigration favored the freedom of criminals from arrest, it also helped to extend their acquaintance among kindred rogues. Wherever they went, they knew there were one, two, or half a dozen noted haunts for fellows like themselves, upon whose aid they could always rely, to execute new outrages, to swear an *alibi*, or give any kind of false testimony that might be wished; to fee counsel or offer straw-bail, or to plan an escape from pursuit or prison of themselves, or some hotly pressed associate in crime. Thus there was gradually formed a secret combination among the chief thieves, burglars and murderers of the country, minute ramifications of which extended down to the pettiest pilferers. To occasionally cut off a single member of this class would do little good, so long as the grand gang was at large and in full operation. Nothing less than the complete extirpation of the whole body of miscreants, with their numerous supporters and sympathizers, aids and abettors, would relieve society from the fearful incubus that now oppressed it.

America no doubt supplied a number of these plunderers, while the different countries of Europe likewise contributed a proportion. But the most daring, and probably the most numerous class had come from Van Dieman's Land and New South Wales, whither England had sent shiploads of her convicted felons. The voyage from Sydney to San Francisco was neither a very tedious nor an expensive one; and great numbers of "ticket-of-leave" men and old convicts who had "served their time," early contrived to sail for California. There the field seemed so rich and safe for a resumption of their quondam pranks, that they yielded to the temptation, and forthwith began to execute villanies that in magnitude and violent character far exceeded those for which they had been originally convicted. Callous in conscience, they feared nothing save the gallows. But that they had little reason to dread in merciful, gentle, careless California, where prosecutors and witnesses were few, or too busy to attend to the calls of justice; where jurors, not knowing the law and eager to be at money-making again, were apt to take hasty charges from the bench as their sole rule of conduct; where judges, chosen by popular election, were either grossly ignorant of law, or too timid or careless, corrupt or incapable, to measure out the full punishment of crime; and where the laws themselves had not yet been methodically laid down, and the forms and procedure of legal tribunals digested into a plain, unerring system. These "Sydney coves" therefore were comparatively safe in their attacks on society. They lost not the opportunity; and, unchecked, during the fall of 1849, the whole of 1850, and the early part of 1851, reaped a large harvest.

There was a district of San Francisco that was noted as being the rendezvous of the numerous rascals we have been describing; and from which perhaps at this time emanated as much villainy as at any period the "Seven Dials" or the "Five Points" produced. This quarter lay around Clark's Point, in Broadway, Pacific street, and the immediate vicinity. It was the notorious Sydney-town of San Francisco. Low drinking and dancing houses, lodging and gambling houses of the same mean class, the constant scenes of lewdness, drunkenness and strife, abounded in the quarter mentioned. The daily and nightly occupants of these vile abodes had every one, more or less, been addicted to crime; and many of them were at all times ready, for the most trifling consideration, to kill a man or fire a town. During the early hours of night, when the Alsatia was in revel, it was dangerous in the highest degree for a single person to venture within its bounds. Even the police hardly dared to enter there; and if they attempted to apprehend some known individuals, it was always in a numerous, strongly-armed company. Seldom, however, were arrests made. The lawless inhabitants of the place united to save their luckless brothers, and generally managed to drive the assailants away. When the different fires took place in San Francisco, bands of plunderers issued from this great haunt of dissipation, to help themselves to whatever money or valuables lay in their way, or which they could possibly secure. With these they retreated to their dens, and defied detection or apprehension. Many of these fires were believed to have been raised by incendiaries, solely for the opportunity which they afforded for plundering. Persons were repeatedly seen in the act of kindling loose inflammable materials in out-houses and secret places; while the subsequent confessions of convicted criminals left no doubt of the fact, that not only had frequent attempts been made to fire the city, but that some of these had unfortunately been successful. Fire, however, was only one means of attaining their ends. The most daring burglaries were committed, and houses and persons rifled of their valuables. Where resistance was made, the bowie-knife or the revolver settled matters, and left the robber unmolested. Midnight assaults, ending in murder, were common. And not only were these deeds perpetrated under the shade of night; but even in daylight, in the highways and byways of the country, in the streets of the town, in crowded bars, gambling saloons and lodging houses, crimes of an equally glaring character were of constant occurrence. People at that period generally carried during all hours, and wherever they happened to be, loaded firearms about their persons; but these weapons availed nothing against the sudden stroke of the "slung shot," the plunge and rip of the knife, or the secret aiming of the pistol. No decent man was in safety to walk the streets after dark; while at all hours, both of night and day, his property was jeopardized by incendiarism and burglary.

All this while, the law, whose supposed "majesty" is so awful in other countries, was here only a matter for ridicule. The police were few in number, and poorly as well as irregularly paid. Some of them were in league with the criminals themselves, and assisted these at all times to elude justice. Subsequent confessions of criminals on the eve of execution, implicated a considerable number of people in various high and low departments of the executive. Bail was readily accepted in the most serious cases, where the security tendered was absolutely worthless; and where, whenever necessary, both principal and cautioner quietly disappeared. The prisons likewise were small and insecure; and though filled to overflowing, could no longer contain the crowds of apprehended offenders. When these were ultimately brought to trial, seldom could a conviction be obtained. From technical errors on the part of the prosecutors, laws ill understood and worse applied, false swearing of the witnesses for the prisoners, absence often of the chief evidence for the prosecution, dishonesty of jurors, incapacity, weakness, or venality of the judge, and from many other causes, the cases generally broke down and the prisoners were freed. *Not one criminal had yet been executed.* Yet it was notorious, that, at this period, at least one hundred murders had been committed within the space of a few months; while innumerable were the instances of arson, and of theft, robbery, burglary, and assault with intent to kill. It was evident that the offenders defied and laughed at all the puny efforts of the authorities to control them. The tedious processes of legal tribunals had no terrors for them. As yet every thing had been pleasant and safe, and they saw no reason why it should not always be so. San Francisco had been just destroyed, a fifth time, by conflagration. The cities of Stockton and Nevada had likewise shared the same fate. That part of it was the doing of incendiaries no one doubted; and too, no one doubted but that this terrible state of things would continue, and grow worse, until a new and very different executive from the legally-constituted one should rise up in vengeance against those pests that worried and preyed upon the vitals of society. It was at this fearful time that the Vigilance Committee was organized. They knew they had no ordinary duty to perform. They foresaw not merely much time, labor, expense, and actual danger occasioned to themselves—these were trifles—but also grievous responsibility, and perhaps much misconception and undeserved personal obloquy thrown upon their motives and conduct. They were prepared for all; for what will not a man suffer to save life, limb, and property? They knew they might possibly open a gate to insubordination and general anarchy, thereby periling all future law, peace and happiness; but they did not think that a probable case, and at any rate the risk must be run. The chances were all calculated beforehand; and the result showed only a clear winning game.

The law of nature, which is the foundation of, and is superior to, all civil law, justifies every means for self-preservation. An individual or a community attacked has a right to defend itself; and where that attack cannot be otherwise resisted, then is extermination of the offender proper. Where the constituted tribunals of a country fail to accomplish the ends for which they were created, society becomes resolved into its first elements, and some new method must be adopted to preserve its very existence. Opinions may differ as to the particular instant of time when formal law and legal courts become inoperative, and sanction a community in resorting to new and extraordinary measures for its own safety; but in regard to the general principle, all history, and what is better, common sense and moral feeling, abundantly establish it. The people of San Francisco,—and they of all the world could alone know their own troubles,—believed that the unhappy point of time had been reached; and they accordingly seized the occasion to make some terrible experiments, by which to check the growth of those crimes that were so rapidly surrounding them.

In the case of Stuart *alias* Burdue, in February, 1851, the want of organization and previous arrangements on the part of the people, had been severely felt. As the popular demonstration of that period had failed to strike criminals with terror or lessen crime, a number of the leading citizens organized themselves into the Vigilance Committee. This was in June, 1851. The constitution of the association was as follows:—

"WHEREAS, it has become apparent to the citizens of San Francisco, that there is no security for life and property, either under the regulations of society as it at present exists, or under the law as now administered; *Therefore*, the citizens, whose names are hereunto attached, do unite themselves into an association for the maintenance of the peace and good order of society, and the preservation of the lives and property of the citizens of San Francisco, and do bind ourselves, each unto the other, to do and perform every lawful act for the maintenance of law and order, and to sustain the laws when faithfully and properly administered; but we are determined that no thief, burglar, incendiary or assassin, shall escape punishment, either by the quibbles of the law, the insecurity of prisons, the carelessness or corruption of the police, or a laxity of those who pretend to administer justice. And to secure the objects of this association we do hereby agree:

"1. That the name and style of the association shall be the COMMITTEE OF VIGILANCE, for the protection of the lives and property of the citizens and residents of the city of San Francisco.

"2. That there shall be a room selected for the meeting and deliberation of the committee, at which there shall be one or more members of the committee, appointed for that purpose, in constant attendance, at all hours of the day and night, to receive the report of any member of the association, or of any other person or persons whatsoever, of any act of violence done to the person or property of any citizen of San Francisco; and if in the judgment of the member or members of the committee present, it be such an act as justifies the interference of the committee, either in aiding in the execution of the laws, or the prompt and summary punishment of the offender, the committee shall be at once assembled for the purpose of taking such action as a majority of the committee when assembled shall determine upon.

"3. That it shall be the duty of any member or members of the committee on duty at the committee room, whenever a general assemblage of the committee is deemed necessary, to cause a call to be made by two strokes upon a bell, which shall be repeated with a pause of one minute between each alarm. The alarm to be struck until ordered to be stopped.

"4. That when the committee have assembled for action, the decision of a majority present shall be binding upon the whole committee, and that those members of the committee whose names are hereunto attached, do pledge their honor, and hereby bind themselves to defend and sustain each other in carrying out the determined action of this committee at the hazard of their lives and their fortunes.

"5. That there shall be chosen monthly a president, secretary and treasurer, and it shall be the duty of the secretary to detail the members required to be in daily attendance at the committee room. A sergeant-at-arms shall be appointed, whose duty it shall be to notify such members of their details for duty. The sergeant-at-arms shall reside at and be in constant attendance at the committee room. There shall be a standing committee of finance, and qualification, consisting of five each, and no person shall be admitted a member of this association unless he be a respectable citizen, and approved of by the committee on qualification before admission."

An occasion soon happened to test the character and uses of this most extraordinary association. On the evening of the 10th of June, 1851, a person of the name of John Jenkins feloniously entered a store on Long Wharf, and stole a safe. He was subsequently seen with a large burden slung across his back, and, an alarm being raised, was pursued. He then got into a boat, and sculled out into the bay, followed by a dozen other boats in keen pursuit. The fugitive was soon overtaken; but before his captors reached him he was seen to throw the burden into the water. This was soon drawn up, and proved to be the stolen safe. The prisoner was next taken to the rooms of the Vigilance Committee, in Battery street, near the corner of Pine street. About ten o'clock of the same night, a signal was given on the bell of the Monumental Engine Company; and shortly afterwards about eighty members of the committee hurried to the appointed place, and on giving the secret password were admitted. Meanwhile, knots of people, some of whom knew and all suspected what was going on, gathered about the premises, and impatiently awaited the farther progress of events. For two long hours, the committee were closely occupied in examining evidence; and soon they had no reason to doubt the prisoner's guilt—though this he denied to the last. At midnight, the bell of the California Engine House was tolled, as sentence of death by hanging was passed upon the wretched man. The solemn sounds at that unusual hour filled the anxious crowds with awe. The condemned at this time was asked if he had any thing to say for himself, when he answered: "No, I have nothing to say, only I wish to have a cigar." This was handed to him, and afterwards, at his request, a little brandy and water. He was perfectly cool, and seemingly careless, confidently expecting, it was believed, a rescue, up to the last moment.

A little before one o'clock, Mr. S. Brannan came out of the committee rooms, and ascending a mound of sand to the east of the Rassette House, addressed the people. He had been deputed he said, by the committee, to inform them that the prisoner's case had been fairly tried, that he had been proved guilty, and was condemned to be hanged; and that the sentence would be executed within one hour upon the plaza. He then asked the people if they approved of the action of the committee, when great shouts of *Ay! Ay!* burst forth, mingled with a few cries of *No!* In the interval a clergyman had been sent for, who administered the last consolations of religion to the condemned.

Shortly before two o'clock, the committee issued from the building, bearing the prisoner (who had his arms tightly pinioned) along with them. The committee were all armed, and closely clustered around the culprit to prevent any possible chance of rescue. A procession was formed; and the whole party, followed by the crowd, proceeded to the plaza, through Sansome, California, Montgomery and Clay streets. Arrived at the flagstaff, some thoughtlessly suggested that it might serve to hang the condemned upon, but the proposal was indignantly overruled, as desecrating the liberty pole. Those in charge of the execution then proceeded to the south end of the adobe building, which then stood on the north-west corner of the plaza. The opposite end of the rope which was already about the neck of the victim was hastily thrown over a projecting beam. Some of the authorities attempted at this stage of affairs to interfere, but their efforts were unavailing. They were civilly desired to stand back, and not delay what was still to be done. The crowd, which numbered upwards of a thousand, were perfectly quiescent, or only applauded by look, gesture, and subdued voice the action of the committee. Before the prisoner had reached the building, a score of persons seized the loose end of the rope and ran backwards, dragging the wretch along the ground and raising him to the beam. Thus they held him till he was dead. Nor did they let the body go until some hours afterwards, new volunteers relieving those who were tired holding the rope. Little noise or confusion took place. Muttered whispers among the spectators guided their movements or betrayed their feelings. The prisoner had not spoken a word, either upon the march or during the rapid preparations for his execution. At the end he was perhaps strung up almost before he was aware of what was so immediately coming. He was a strong-built, healthy man, and his struggles, when hanging, were very violent for a few minutes.

This Jenkins was one of the notorious "Sydney coves," and was believed to be a man of desperate and crime-stained character. The committee who tried him were generally people of respectability in San Francisco. Stern necessity had led them to make this first terrible example, and their conduct was almost unanimously applauded by the citizens. The public press, with one exception, likewise gave a hearty approval of their proceedings. That the execution was conducted during the dead of night, was simply owing to the fact that the criminal had been apprehended only late in the preceding evening. The crime, apprehension, trial, sentence and execution, all took place within a few consecutive hours. The latter steps were managed as swiftly as convenient to the ends of justice. If the crime had been committed in the morning, the result would have been the same, and the condemned would then only have been hanged in open day. That the trial took place in secret was owing to the constitution of the committee, which was devised to prevent the excesses and turbulence of a mere mob sitting in judgment upon offenders.

A coroner's inquest was held, the 11th of June, upon the body of the hanged man. To illustrate further the constitution, real objects, and spirit of the Vigilance Committee, we give a portion of the testimony of Mr. Brannan before the jury on this occasion. After declining to answer some questions on the ground that his statements might implicate himself, the witness said :

"I believe the man had a fair and impartial trial. He was tried before from sixty to eighty men. I believe the verdict of guilty was unanimous, and they came to the conclusion unanimously to hang him. I don't know how the jury was empanelled; think they empanelled themselves. The jury consisted of the Committee of Vigilance; they were all citizens of the town. I don't know that the committee has by-laws. The declared object of the committee was to consider themselves constantly on duty, to protect the lives and property of their fellow-citizens; to see that they are not troubled by burglars, and incendiaries, and murderers; and to arrest and punish promptly parties caught in the act. The man was executed in accordance with the finding of the committee. I understood a record was kept of the evidence adduced on the trial; six or eight witnesses were examined. The prisoner had the privilege of bringing in evidence in his behalf. He said he had but one witness, who came and testified that he did not know him. There was no counsel assigned him. I don't know whether the man's witness saw him. He said he did not know any such man before he reached the house. Don't know that the witnesses were put under oath. I did not make any motion that the man should have a new trial. Don't know whether any other persons than those of the committee were in the room. A man is admitted to the committee on a motion by a friend who vouches for his character, and that he will devote a portion of his time to watching for burglars and other scoundrels. I don't know of any other secrecy than that of an honest man. There is no oath used. The object is to assist the law and administer justice. I do not believe the prisoner would have been hanged if the committee had not found him guilty. The committee are good citizens, and of good standing in society. I saw the prisoner's witness out of doors; heard him say he did not know any such man as Jenkins; don't know whether he went inside; did not see him; could not give the names of any of the witnesses. I object to give the names of any of the committee. I have understood that threats have been made against their property and lives; have heard threats made; have heard it said that my own house would be burned; threats have come to me from the prisoners in the county prison that I should not live ninety days. I know of nothing done by the Vigilance Committee that they would conceal from the officers of the law under proper circumstances. The avowed object of the committee is to protect the city, and punish crime. I know of no other purpose for which they are organized. I believe it was through the instrumentality of the committee that the man was hanged."

Upon the above and much other evidence of a like nature, the jury on the 12th June, returned the following verdict :—

"We, the Jurors of a Jury of Inquest, empanelled by the Coroner of the County of San Francisco, to inquire into the death of one John Jenkins, *alias* Simpton, do find upon our oaths that the said Jenkins, *alias* Simpton, came to his death on the morning of the 11th of June, between the hours of two and three o'clock, by violent means, by strangulation, caused by being suspended by the neck, with a rope attached to the end of the adobe building on the plaza, at the hands of, and in pursuance of a preconcerted action on the part of an association of citizens, styling themselves a Committee of Vigilance, of whom the following members are implicated by direct testimony, to wit: Captain Edgar Wakeman, William H. Jones, James C. Ward, Edward A. King, T. K. Battelle, Benjamin Reynolds, John S. Eagan, J. C. Derby and Samuel Brannan; and the following members by their voluntary avowal of participation in the act." [Here followed a list of the members of the Vigilance Committee.]

In consequence of this verdict (which, it may be just said in passing, was never attempted to be followed up by the authorities), the Vigilance Committee held a meeting on the 13th June, when a unanimous resolution to the following effect was passed, and ordered to be published. As the names appended to this resolution make a pretty complete roll of the original, or more prominent members of the Vigilance Committee, many of whom still reside in San Francisco and move among the most respectable circles, we give them at length. The curious and scandal-loving may spell over the list at their leisure, and discover some of the chief bankers, merchants and real estate proprietors now flourishing in this city. There is, however, a better reason for the present republication of these names, albeit some feebler-minded folk may fervently wish that their "unco guid" friends *at a distance* may never hear of their graceless connection with the Vigilance Committee. Since common fairness compelled the disclosure in 1851, to give moral support to the parties singled out by the verdict of the coroner's jury; therefore, so long as these gentlemen continue well known, and while they must be specially designated in any history pretending to be full and accurate of the proceedings, the same spirit of fairness enforces the publication now. It would be doing gross injustice to a dozen worthy men, if the full list were omitted in the "Annals of San Francisco." At the same time, there is no reason why any one of the whole number should be ashamed of his appearance in the list.

"*Resolved*, That we, members of the *Vigilance Committee*, remark with surprise the invidious verdict rendered by the coroner's jury, after their inquest upon the body of Jenkins, *alias* Simpton, after we have all notified to the said jury and the public that we were all participators in the trial and execution of said Jenkins. We desire that the public will understand that Capt. E. Wakeman, W. H. Jones, James C. Ward, Edward A. King, T. K. Battelle, Benjamin Reynolds, J. S. Eagan, J. C. Derby and Samuel Brannan, have been unnecessarily picked from our numbers, as the coroner's jury have had full evidence of the fact, that all the undersigned have been equally implicated, and are equally responsible with their above-named associates."

S. E. Woodworth,
Fred. A. Woodworth,
Francis E. Webster,
Wm. N. Thompson,
Clinton Winton,
James B. Huie,
B. Frank Hillard,
S. W. Haight,
George H. Howard,
Caleb Hyatt,
Samuel R. Curwen,
James F. Curtis,
L. Hulsemann,
A. G. Randall,
S. Brannan,
George J. Oakes,
R. D. W. Davis,
Wm. H. Jones,
Edward A. King,
Jesse Southam,
T. H. Robinson,
George R. Ward,
C. L. Wilson,
W. H. Taber,
Isaac Bluxome, jr.,
Lathrop L. Bullock,
John W. Rider,
Theodore Kuhlman,
Joseph E. Dale,
Julius D. Shultz,
J. P. Stevens,
Thomas McCahill,
Wm. Peake,
Jonas Minturn,
Lloyd Minturn,
F. O. Wakeman,
Wm. Forst,
John W. Jackson,
James Shinaler,
J. W. Rickman,
W. S. Bromley,
A. Ottenheimer,
B. H. Davis,
P. Frothingham,
E. E. Schenck,
Geo. Austinworn,
E Botcher,
Samuel Marx,
Daniel J. Thomas, jr.,
J. E. Farwell,
Jacob P. Leese,
Edgar Wakeman,
A. Markwell,
Samuel A. Sloane,
W. B. Lucas,
Henry M. Naglee,
J. Thompson Huie,
A. Wheelwright,
C. F. Fourgeaud,
A. Jackson McDuffie,
P. D. Headley,
S. B. Marshall,
H. Hazeltine,
W. Iken,
George D. Lambert,
John P. Half,
Joseph T. Harmer,
J. Seligman,
H. F. Von Lenyerk,
J. E. Derby,
T. J. West,
Wm. T. Coleman,
J. S. Clark,
C. H. Clark,
Herman R. Haste,
H. F. Teschemacker,

William A. Howard,
Henry Dreshchfeldt,
James Ryan,
Wm. Browne,
Robert Wells,
H. D. Evans,
John J. Bryant,
E. Kirtus,
Thos. N. Deblois,
E. Gorham,
Frank S. Mahoney,
James C. Ward,
R. S. Watson,
George Mellus,
J. D. Stevenson,
Chas. R. Bond,
B. B. Arrowsmith,
S. E. Teschemacker,
C. H. Brinley,
J. W. Salmon,
Benjamin Reynolds,
A. W. Macpherson,
John S. Eagan,
J. C. L. Wadsworth,
William Hart,
George M. Garwood,
R. S. Lanot,
A. C. Tubbs,
J. R. Curtis,
A. H. Hill,
Wm. H. Graham,
B. E. Babcock,
J. A. Fisher,
Hartford Joy,
Joshua Hilton,
John F. Osgood,
James Pratt,
E. Kemp,
Wm. G. Badger,
J. Mead Huxley
S. J. Stabler,
Geo. Clifford,
Charles Soulé, jr.,
Robert H. Belden,
N. Smith,
Randolph M. Cooley,
Chas. H. Hill,
J. Neal, jr.,
F. A. Atkinson,
Charles Miller,
John O. Earle,
N. T. Thompson,
N. Reynolds Davis,
Gabriel Winter,
Otis P. Sawyer,
Wm. Meyer,
W. N. Hostin,
John G. McKaraher,
Eugene Hart,
John Raynes,
J. C. Treadwell,
John H. Watson,
Wm. Burling,
F. Quincey Coale,
Thomas N. Cazneau,
Geo. W. Douglass,
Wm. C. Graham,
Chas. H. Vail,
Charles Minturn,
Howard Cunningham,
Charles L. Case,
Charles Moore,
James R. Duff,
E. M. Earle,
J. L. Van Bokkelen,
George N. Blake,
Dewitt Brown,
Edward F. Baker,
F. Argenti,
Stephen Payran,
C. Spring,
Wm. J. Sherwood,
W. L. Hobson,
E. W. Travers,
W. H. Tillinghast,
Wm. Langerman,
J. F. Hutton,
Thos. K. Battelle,
Horace Morrison,
Augustus Belknap,
F. L. Dana,
Horatio S. Gates,
O. P. Sutton,
Jer. Spalding,
A. J. Ellis,
John M. Coughlin,
Samuel Moss, jr.,
C. O. Brewster,
Charles L. Wood,
William Tell,
James Dow,
E. W. Crowell,
A. H. Gildemeester,
Samuel S. Philipps,
Chas. Del Vecchio,
Joseph Post,
Jas. King of William.

These were signatures of some of the richest, most influential, orderly and respectable citizens of San Francisco. They show, however, only a small portion of the people who subsequently joined the Vigilance Committee, since every day was increasing its numbers by the accession of the best inhabitants of the place. At the time when the above resolution was formed and published the committee likewise put forth the following by-laws, as an address to the people :—

"Whereas, The citizens of San Francisco, convinced that there exists within its limits a band of robbers and incendiaries, who have, several times, burned and attempted to burn their city, who nightly attack their persons and break into their buildings, destroy their quiet, jeopardize their lives and property, and generally disturb the natural order of society; And Whereas many of those taken by the police have succeeded in escaping from their prisons by carelessness, by connivance, or from want of proper means or force to secure their confinement, *therefore* be it

"Resolved, That the citizens of this place be made aware that the *Committee of Vigilance* will be ever ready to receive information as to the whereabouts of any disorderly or suspicious person or persons, as well as the persons themselves when suspected of crime.

"That as it is the conviction of a large portion of our citizens, that there exists in this city a nucleus of convicts and disorderly persons, around which cluster those who have seriously disturbed the peace and affected the best interests of our city—such as are known to the police of the city, or to the members of the Committee of Vigilance, as felons by conduct or association, be notified to leave this port within five days from this date; and at the expiration of which time they shall be compelled to depart, if they have not done so voluntarily within the time specified.

"Resolved, That a safety committee of thirty persons be appointed, whose sacred duty it shall be to visit every vessel arriving with notorious or suspicious characters on board, and unless they can present to said committee evidences of good character and honesty, they shall be re-shipped to the places from whence they came, and not be permitted to pollute our soil.

"Resolved, That all good citizens be invited to join and assist the Committee of Vigilance in carrying out the above measures so necessary for the perfect restoration of the peace, safety, and good order of our community."

These sweeping resolutions were not suffered to lie dormant; but were instantly and effectively acted upon. The terrible example made of Jenkins, and the announcement of farther steps by the committee, had already succeeded in frightening many of the more fearful rogues away. The steamers to Sacramento and Stockton were crowded with the flying rascals. But such a partial exodus was not enough. The more desperate characters were left, and unless the work was thoroughly done, the city would be in as bad a state as before. An old Mexican law really forbade the immigration into California of such persons as had been convicted of crime in other countries; but this law, in the confusion of the vast immigration of 1849 and succeeding years had been disregarded. The committee, however, now proceeded to render it of use, and give a somewhat wider scope to its operation. So notices were forthwith served on all such persons as were known or reputed to be vicious characters, upon the different "Sydney Coves," and upon all who harbored or kept close companionship with them, that they instantly leave the city, on pain of being forcibly expelled, and shipped to the place from whence they had last come. These notices were served always in presence of three members of the committee, and after due inquiry, although a secret one, had been made on the subject. If the party warned considered himself an innocent or ill-used person, he was at liberty to appeal to the committee, and have his cause reheard. He could produce all evidence within his power in regard to general character or to rebut specific charges; and upon that, or its absence, the committee altered or confirmed their former judgment. Repeated cases of rehearing took place; and where the parties appealing were "white-washed," or turned out really "good citizens," generally no malice was manifested by them against the committee; because they, like their judges, considered that the whole proceedings had been conducted in good faith and for the public benefit. A few actions of damages for false imprisonment and defamation of character were about this time and subsequently raised against members of the Vigilance Committee, by parties who considered themselves aggrieved by their proceedings. In the end, however, these actions were either quashed, nominal damages only awarded by the jury, or the plaintiffs indemnified. Meanwhile, the committee pursued "the even tenor of their way," nowise daunted by the reproaches and threats of offended individuals, nor by the continual opposing action of mortified officials. When some of the warned were contumacious, and refused to depart, they were seized by force, in spite of their appeals to the courts of law, and imprisoned on board a safe ship in the bay until arrangements could be made for their transportation abroad. The legal authorities, with numerous practising lawyers in their train, meanwhile "fretted and fumed" at thus losing their own proper business; and denounced in angry language the sweeping action of the committee. Those personages did not deny the good result of this action, nor did they disguise the alarming increase of crime and the inability of the regular tribunals to cope with it; but still they harped upon the illegality,—the illegality of the whole proceedings. *Illegality* truly! People were abused, robbed and murdered on all sides, their houses set in flames, and their goods consumed or stolen, and yet they were to be forbidden the only remedy in their power, because *form* was to be observed, while the criminals escaped! The reproaches of mere lawyers were disregarded, and the work of purification went on.

Some individuals having chosen to throw obstacles in the way of the Vigilance Committee's action, that body issued the following notice to the public. It is here given to show the spirit of their proceedings, and the ceaseless watchfulness with which they were conducted. Not a word need be said as to their *illegality*; that is confessed by all.

"VIGILANCE COMMITTEE ROOM:—It having become necessary to the peace and quiet of this community that all criminals and abettors in crime should be driven from among us, no good citizen, having the welfare of San Francisco at heart, will deny the Committee of Vigilance such information as will enable them to carry out the above object. Nor will they interfere with said committee when they may deem it best to search any premises for suspicious characters or stolen property. *Therefore*,

"RESOLVED, That we the Vigilance Committee do CLAIM to ourselves the right to enter any person or persons' premises where we have good reason to believe that we shall find evidence to substantiate and carry out the object of this body; And further, deeming ourselves engaged in a good and just cause—WE INTEND TO MAINTAIN IT.

"By order of
"THE COMMITTEE OF VIGILANCE,
No. 67, *Secretary*."

"*San Francisco, July* 5, 1851."

The next striking occasion when the Vigilance Committee exercised its power was on the 11th of July following. A person of the name of James Stuart—the real party of that name, and for whom Burdue had been mistaken in the affair of the 19th of February preceding, had been for some days in the hands of the committee upon various charges. He had been regularly and fairly tried, found guilty, and was sentenced to be hanged. Subsequently he made a full confession of his crimes, and acknowledged the justice of his punishment. He was an Englishman, and had many years before been transported from Great Britain to Australia for forgery. At that time he was only sixteen years of age. His whole life afterwards was one continued tissue of the most daring crimes. After wandering about various parts of the Pacific, he lighted at last upon California, and during his short residence there was supposed to have perpetrated more murders, burglaries, and other crimes of every dark and desperate description, than any other villain in California. His confession revealed an extraordinary state of social impurity, and showed, clearly and minutely, the alarming mass of villany which existed among the community, and the support it received from the lax and culpable behavior of the executive. This confession was immediately published, and the people warned against the many persons whom it named and implicated in the crimes acknowledged.

About nine o'clock on the morning of the 11th, the customary taps on the bell of the Monumental Engine House, which showed that a matter of life and death was under consideration, summoned together the Vigilance Committee. Immediately a numerous assemblage of members convened at their rooms, and proceeded to try the prisoner. Evidence was duly led and considered, and Stuart's guilt being fully established, he was sentenced by a unanimous voice, to immediate death by hanging. Before the execution, Col. J. D. Stevenson went forth to the crowd of people waiting outside, and addressing them, stated the facts of the case briefly, as established by evidence, the subsequent confession of the prisoner himself, and the proposed judgment of the committee. He then inquired whether the people approved of their proceedings, and would confirm the sentence. A loud shout in the affirmative from a great crowd answered his inquiry, against which there were only several voices in the negative. During this time the committee were in consultation as to their further proceedings, while the prisoner remained manacled in an adjoining room. He appeared quite reckless of his fate, and only at times said that the business was "d——d tiresome." He begged a piece of tobacco from one of the members, which he continued to chew until he heard his doom. When sentence was delivered, he was permitted to have a delay of two hours, to frame his mind to the solemnity of the occasion; and to that end the assistance of a clergyman was given, although the prisoner seemed very indifferent about religious duties. This clergyman, the Rev. Mr. Mines, was closeted with the condemned during the time granted. In the interval, the members present of the committee —some four hundred in number, sat grimly on their seats, silent and determined. They felt the responsibility and unpleasant nature of the task before them; but they did not hesitate. It was for the good of the community and their own safety that they had been laboring, and while conscience approved of their proceedings, they did not so much court, as they hoped and expected the confidence and applause of their fellow-citizens. The silence in that chamber of judgment was profound; a pin could have been heard to fall on the floor.

After the two hours' grace, the condemned was led forth, still manacled, and closely surrounded by those who had the direct charge of watching over him. The rest of the committee formed in a line behind. They were all well armed, and prepared to resist any attempted rescue, either by the prisoner's friends, or the authorities themselves. In this order they marched, two by two, as in funeral procession, after Stuart and his guards, along Battery street to Market street wharf, down which they proceeded to its extremity. A great crowd of citizens followed.

Hanging of James Stuart.

Hitherto the prisoner had preserved much coolness, but towards the close, fear was beginning to overcome him, and he was at last obliged to be supported by two of his guards. At the end of the wharf every thing had been hastily arranged for the execution. So soon as the procession reached the spot, the fatal rope was fastened, and the condemned quickly hoisted up with a jerk upon a derrick. He did not struggle much. After hanging a few seconds his hat fell off, and a slight breeze stirred and gently waved his hair. This was a sorry spectacle—a human being dying like a dog, while thousands of erring mortals, whose wickedness only had not yet been found out, looked on and applauded! But necessity, which dared not trust itself to feelings of compassion, commanded the deed, and unprofitable sentiment sunk abashed. Reason loudly declared—*So perish every villain who would hurt his neighbor!* and all the people said *Amen!*

About twenty-five minutes afterwards, when life was supposed to have fled, the body was lowered, and possession allowed to be taken on the part of the authorities. These had, previous to the execution, made some attempts to recover the person of the deceased; but were resolutely opposed, though no overt act of violence took place. The verdict of the coroner's jury was as follows:—"We, the jury, find that the deceased came to his death by strangulation by hanging, at the hands of a body of men styling themselves the Vigilance Committee of San Francisco." It is, perhaps, unnecessary to say that the authorities took no legal action on this verdict. The grand jury empanelled for the special July term by the court of sessions, towards the close of a long report on the state of crime in San Francisco, and in which they had made allusion to the Vigilance Committee, took occasion to say:—

"When we recall the delays and the inefficient, and we believe that with truth it may be said, the corrupt administration of the law, the incapacity and indifference of those who are its sworn guardians and ministers, the frequent and unnecessary postponement of important trials in the District Court, the disregard of duty and impatience while attending to perform it manifested by *some* of our judges, having criminal jurisdiction, the many notorious villains who have gone unwhipped of justice, lead us to believe, that the members of that association have been governed by a feeling of opposition to the manner in which the law has been administered and those who have administered it, rather than a determination to disregard the law itself.

"Under institutions so eminently popular as those under which we live, the power of correcting all these abuses is with the people themselves. If our officers are unfit for the stations they occupy, if the laws are not faithfully executed, if an arraigned criminal procures his own friends to be placed on the jury that tries him, where is the fault, and where the remedy? If those of our citizens who are most interested in having good and wholesome laws, and in seeing them well and purely administered, will not give sufficient attention to our elections to secure proper and sober legislators, judicial and other officers, and neglect to obey the mandates of our courts when summoned as jurors and witnesses, as has been too often the case, can they expect to see justice prevail or crime punished? And is it not in the neglect of their duties in these important particulars, that they may find the true fountains from whence have sprung many of the evils we have suffered? The Grand Jurors, believing, whilst they deplore their acts, that the association styling themselves the 'Vigilance Committee,' at a great personal sacrifice to themselves, have been influenced in their actions by no personal or private malice, but for the best interest of the whole, and at a time too when all other means of preventing crime and bringing criminals to direct punishment had failed, here dismiss the matter, as among those peculiar results of circumstances that sometimes startle communities, which they can neither justify, or by a presentment effect any benefit to individuals or the country; and with the assurance that there is a determination on the part of all well-disposed citizens to correct the abuses referred to by selecting proper officers to take the place of those who have violated their trusts, and by performing each his part in the administration of the laws. When this is done, the axe will have been laid at the root of the tree—the proper remedy applied for the correction of the grievous evils our city and country have so long suffered, and there will be no necessity for the further action of that committee. To them we are indebted for much valuable information and many important witnesses."

The above testimony to the purity of motives and prudence of conduct in the Vigilance Committee is highly important; and shows the estimation in which they were held by some of the most enlightened members of the community, who themselves had a *legal* duty to perform respecting crime in the district. The public press, excepting as before, continued to give cordial and effective aid, and even from the pulpit was heard a sound of applause. As for the commonalty, it was almost unanimously in favor of the committee. In consequence of the examples made of Jenkins and Stuart, crime was now fast diminishing in San Francisco, and the number of notorious criminals was much reduced.

The next great occasion on which the committee figured was in August following. They had had in their custody for some time back, two persons of the names of Samuel Whittaker and Robert McKenzie, who were charged with the various crimes of burglary, robbery and arson. These persons had been fairly tried, had confessed their guilt, and were sentenced to be hanged. The particular time for the execution had not yet been fixed, although a rumor spread abroad, on the evening of the 20th August, that it would take place next day.

Meanwhile the governor of the State, the Hon. John McDougal, issued (on the 20th August,) a proclamation to the people in the County of San Francisco, directed against the Vigilance Committee by name, and which called upon "all good citizens of said county to unite for the purpose of sustaining public law and tranquillity, to aid the public officers in the discharge of their duty, and by all lawful means to discountenance any and every attempt which may be made to substitute the despotic control of a self-constituted association, unknown and acting in defiance of the laws, in the place of the regularly organized government of the country." To this proclamation the following strange certificate was published in answer :—

"*San Francisco, August 20th*, 1851.

"We, the undersigned, do hereby aver, that the present governor, McDougal, asked to be introduced to the Executive Committee of the Committee of Vigilance, which was allowed, and an hour fixed. The governor, upon being introduced, stated that he approved the acts of the committee, and that much good had taken place. He hoped that they would go on, and endeavor to act in concert with the authorities, and in case any judge was guilty of mal-administration, to hang him, and he would appoint others," &c.

Comment upon the above document is unnecessary. It shows that although the governor, in prosecuting the duties of his office, felt bound to oppose the proceedings of the Vigilance Committee on the ground of their illegality, as an individual, he was willing to acknowledge their beneficial effects. Indeed, the *private* opinion and well-wishes of the "good citizens" upon whom he called for aid against the actions of the committee, were nearly unanimous in their favor.

On the morning of the 21st, before dawn, the sheriff, Col. John C. Hayes, holding a warrant of *habeas corpus*, procured upon the affidavit of Governor McDougal himself, went with one of his deputies to the rooms of the committee, which he entered without experiencing any resistance. A party of policemen followed behind, to be ready in case of need. There were a sufficient number of the committee at hand to have forcibly and successfully resisted the authorities; but, taken by surprise, and unwilling to proceed to actual blows and bloodshed, they suffered the prisoners to be removed. Some of the committee, however, hastening from the apartment, immediately began to ring the bell of the California Engine House. This soon aroused the numerous members of the committee from slumber, and sent them quickly to the scene of action. By the time they arrived the sheriff had left with the prisoners. There was something strange and unexpected in the whole affair, and treachery on the part of some of the prisoners' guards was suspected. The authorities had known for weeks that Whittaker and McKenzie had been in the hands of the committee, and during that time they had made no effort to procure their release. It was generally believed indeed that the authorities, knowing the good the committee had done in diminishing crime, took ready advantage of their situation in protesting that feebleness alone kept them quiet. Yet now they were perilling all the benefits that had already resulted from the action of the committee. The latter deeply deplored the hasty conduct of the officials, but resolved to be cool and proceed cautiously in their farther steps. Villany meanwhile looked stealthily on, and began to breathe more freely. The old tribunals, and old delays—perjury—quibbles and technical errors—corrupt and bribed prosecutors—ignorance and corruption among the jury—misunderstood and misapplied laws—ay, life itself, and freedom again to run a long course of rapine and murder, all were suddenly opened, by this *legal* stroke of the executive, to the astonished and delighted criminal! As for the authorities themselves, they were wonderstruck at, and almost afraid of their own boldness and success; and many could scarcely believe that they had managed, at last, to circumvent the formidable Vigilance Committee. So they made preparations to resist any attempt that might be tried to rescue the prisoners; while fear and trembling, arising from many different causes, filled the hearts of all "good citizens."

About half-past two o'clock, on the afternoon of Sunday, the 24th of August, an armed party, consisting of thirty-six members of the Vigilance Committee, forcibly broke into the jail, at a time when the Rev. Mr. Williams happened to be engaged at devotional exercises with the prisoners, among whom were Whittaker and McKenzie. The slight defence of the jailers and guards was of no avail. The persons named were seized, and hurried to and placed within a coach, that had been kept in readiness a few steps from the prison. The carriage instantly was driven off at full speed, and nearly at the same moment the ominous bell of the Monumental Engine Company rapidly and loudly tolled for the immediate assemblage of the committee and the knell itself of the doomed. The whole population leaped with excitement at the sound; and immense crowds from the remotest quarter hurried to Battery street. There blocks, with the necessary tackle, had been hastily fastened to two beams which projected over the windows of the great hall of the committee. Within seventeen minutes after the arrival of the prisoners, they were both dangling by the neck from these beams. The loose extremities of the halters being taken within the building itself and forcibly held by members of the committee. Full six thousand people were present, who kept an awful silence during the short time these preparations lasted. But so soon as the wretches were swung off, one tremendous shout of satisfaction burst from the excited multitude; and then there was silence again.

After the bodies had hung about half an hour, the people were addressed by Mr. Brannan, Dr. Robinson and Mr. Peyran; and shortly afterwards they slowly dispersed. In the course of an hour later, the bodies were delivered over to the authorities, and the same evening a coroner's jury returned the following verdict:—"In accordance with the foregoing testimony, the jury, after deliberate consideration, have come to the conclusion, and accordingly render their verdict, that Samuel Whittaker and Robert McKenzie came to their death by being hanged by the neck, thereby producing strangulation, by the act of a body of citizens styling themselves the 'Vigilance Committee of San Francisco,' on the afternoon of Sunday, August 24th, instant, at about three o'clock, in front of the Vigilance Committee Rooms, on Battery street, near California street, from the second story thereof." As heretofore, no steps were taken by the authorities to implement the verdict of the jury.

This was the last time the committee took or found occasion to exercise their functions. Henceforward the administration of justice might be safely left in the hands of the usual officials. The city now was pretty well cleansed of crime. The fate of Jenkins, Stuart, Whittaker and McKenzie showed that rogues and roguery, of whatever kind, could no longer expect to find a safe lurking-place in San Francisco. Many of the suspected, and such as were warned off by the committee, had departed, and gone, some to other lands, and some into the mining regions and towns of the interior. Those, however, who still clung to California, found no refuge any where in the State. Previously, different cases of Lynch Law had occurred in the gold districts, but these were solitary instances which had been caused by the atrocity of particular crimes. When, however, the Vigilance Committee of San Francisco had started up, fully organized, and began their great work, Sacramento, Stockton, San José, as well as other towns and the more thickly peopled mining quarters, likewise formed their committees of vigilance and safety, and pounced upon all the rascals within their bounds. These associations interchanged information with each other as to the movements of the suspected; and all, with the hundred eyes of an Argus and the hundred arms of a Briareus, watched, pursued, harassed, and finally caught the worst desperadoes of the country. Like Cain, a murderer and wanderer, as most of them were, they bore a mark on the brow, by which they were known. Some were hanged at various places, some were lashed and branded, but the greater number were simply ordered to leave the country, within a limited time, under penalty of immediate death if found after a stated period within its limits. Justice was no longer blind or leaden-heeled. With the perseverance and speed of a bloodhound, she tracked criminals to their lair, and smote them where they lay.

Thus by almost a universal—a national effort, was our beautiful country, which had so long contained and been defiled by the sweepings from the prisons and the thieves'-alleys of other lands, once more made pure, sweet and safe. Hercules did no greater labor when he cleansed the Augean stable by turning a river through it. The people of California, and more particularly the people of San Francisco, had turned the great stream of justice, from its former slow, devious and uncertain course, and sent its waters headlong to overwhelm criminals and wash society clean from the stains that crime had left. For a long time afterwards, the whole of California remained comparatively free from outrages against person and property.

From all the evidence that can be obtained, it is not supposed that a single instance occurred in which a really innocent man suffered the extreme penalty of death. Those who were executed generally confessed their guilt, and admitted the punishment to have been merited. We have seen that it was so in the case of three of those hanged at San Francisco.

The Vigilance Committee has long ceased to act, but the association has never been formally dissolved. The original members are doubtless ready, if ever sad occasion should require, again to assert the right of self-preservation, and the supremacy of natural law over defective civil rules, tedious if not corrupt tribunals, mastery of scoundrels and the quirks of professional tricksters, if thereby the substantial ends of justice can be best or alone obtained, and society relieved from the horrors of unchecked and triumphant villany. Let rogues then beware! It is, however, to be sincerely hoped, that never again shall there need to be revived those terrible times of 1851. California is perhaps not yet quite so subject to the influence and strength of LAW as most of the Atlantic States or the more civilized countries in Europe; but she is fast being gently and securely broken in to its majestic and salutary sway. Her career has been unlike that of any other modern nation, and the many anomalies in her history must be peculiarly and leniently judged. GOD SAVE CALIFORNIA!

INDEX